Oracle SQL
High-Performance Tuning

Second Edition

ISBN 0-13-012381-1

90000

9 780130 123817

ORACLE8™ AND UNIX® PERFORMANCE TUNING
  Alomari
ORACLE8*i*™ AND UNIX® PERFORMANCE TUNING
  Alomari
SOFTWARE ENGINEERING WITH ORACLE: BEST PRACTICES FOR MISSION-CRITICAL SYSTEMS
  Bonazzi
ORACLE8*i*™ AND JAVA™: FROM CLIENT/SERVER TO E-COMMERCE
  Bonazzi/Stokol
ORACLE8™ DATABASE ADMINISTRATION FOR WINDOWS NT®
  Brown
ORACLE DESK REFERENCE
  Harrison
ORACLE SQL HIGHPERFORMANCE TUNING, SECOND EDITION
  Harrison
ORACLE DESIGNER: A TEMPLATE FOR DEVELOPING AN ENTERPRISE STANDARDS DOCUMENT
  Kramm/Graziano
ORACLE DEVELOPER/2000 FORMS
  Lulushi
ORACLE FORMS DEVELOPER'S HANDBOOK
  Lulushi
ORACLE SQL® INTERACTIVE WORKBOOK
  Morrison/Rischert
ORACLE FORMS INTERACTIVE WORKBOOK
  Motivala
ORACLE PL/SQL™ INTERACTIVE WORKBOOK
  Rosenzweig/Silverstrova
ORACLE DBA INTERACTIVE WORKBOOK
  Scherer/Caffrey
ORACLE DEVELOPER 2000 HANDBOOK, SECOND EDITION
  Stowe
DATA WAREHOUSING WITH ORACLE
  Yazdani/Wong
ORACLE CERTIFIED DBA EXAM: QUESTION AND ANSWER BOOK
  Yazdani/Wong/Tong

Oracle SQL High-Performance Tuning

Second Edition

Guy Harrison

PH
PTR

Prentice Hall PTR
Upper Saddle River, NJ 07458
www.phptr.com

Library of Congress Cataloging-in-Publication Data

Harrison, Guy
  Oracle SQL High-Performance Tuning 2ed. / Guy Harrison
    p. cm.
  ISBN 0-13-012381-1
    1. Oracle (Computer file) 2. SQL tuning I. Title.

QA76.9.D3 A5519 2000
005.75'85--dc21   00-056795

Editorial/Production Supervisor: *Rose Kernan*
Acquisitions Editor: *Tim Moore*
Marketing Manager: *Debby vanDijk*
Manufacturing Buyer: *Maura Zaldivar*
Manufacturing Manager: *Alexis Heydt*
Cover Design Director: *Jerry Votta*
Cover Designer: *Nina Scuderi*
Interior Formatting: *Pine Tree Composition, Inc.*

ISBN 0-13-012381-1

Prentice-Hall International (UK) Limited, *London*
Prentice-Hall of Australia Pty. Limited, *Sydney*
Prentice-Hall Canada Inc., *Toronto*
Prentice-Hall Hispanoamericana, S.A., *Mexico*
Prentice-Hall of India Private Limited, *New Delhi*
Prentice-Hall of Japan, Inc., *Tokyo*
Pearson Education Asia Pte. Ltd.
Editora Prentice-Hall do Brasil, Ltda., *Rio de Janeiro*

CONTENTS

PART II SQL TUNING THEORY

PART III   SQL TUNING IN PRACTICE

Contents

PART IV   BEYOND SQL TUNING

PREFACE

INTRODUCTION

This book is about tuning Oracle databases and applications with an emphasis on the tuning of SQL statements. Tuning SQL is not the only way to tune an application: The design of an application will often dictate its performance limits, and tuning the physical layout of an Oracle database can be critical to reaching those limits. However, tuning SQL is usually the most cost-effective way of improving the performance of an existing application, while other measures—such as changing database parameters or altering disk layouts—will usually be ineffective unless the application's SQL is properly tuned.

It is common for the performance of an Oracle application to appear to be acceptable during development only to degrade abruptly when the application encounters production data volumes or transaction rates. While this may result from a number of causes, inefficient SQL that fails to maintain good performance as data volumes increase is a major factor.

Poorly performing SQL arises in applications for a number of reasons. Although SQL is a relatively easy language to learn, its nonprocedural nature tends to obscure performance-related issues. As a result, its much harder to write efficient SQL than it is to write functionally correct SQL. Additionally, there seems to be insufficient awareness of the need to monitor carefully and tune SQL performance, and the tools and techniques needed to tune SQL are not sufficiently well known.

Another factor that has increased the significance of well-tuned SQL is the emergence of data warehouses or On-Line Analytical Processing (OLAP) systems. These databases are often extremely large and are subject to a great deal of ad hoc query activity. If the SQL that supports these queries is inefficient, then queries may take hours or even days to complete or may fail to complete at all.

When Oracle applications start to underperform, it's typical for performance experts to be called in to perform benchmark tests or tune the Oracle database engine. For the most part, they will tune the operating system, change Oracle configuration parameters, reconfigure input/output (I/O), disks and so on. At the end of the process, you can (if you are lucky) expect a 10 to 20 % improvement in performance.

During these tuning exercises it is usually that apparent the SQL contained within the application is the most important factor in determining performance. If the SQL can be tuned, then performance increases of 100 percent or more are not uncommon. But there is a dilemma: By the time performance problems are recognized, it is often difficult to make changes to the production SQL. Furthermore, performance experts usually don't have the application knowledge required to understand and tune the SQL, while the developers don't have the necessary understanding of SQL performance tuning.

It follows that the best way to improve substantially the performance of most Oracle applications is to improve the efficiency of the application SQL. To make this happen, developers needed to acquire SQL tuning skills together with a commitment to tuning.

The objective of this book is to provide SQL programmers with the theory and practice of SQL tuning together with hints and guidelines for optimizing specific SQL statement types. We'll see how to diagnose and correct problems with existing SQL and briefly explore performance issues beyond SQL tuning, such as application design and server tuning. By following the guidelines in this book, SQL programmers should be able to write SQL that will perform well both in development and in production and will be able to detect and correct inefficiencies in existing SQL. The result will be SQL that performs to its peak potential.

THE NEED FOR THIS BOOK

With the Oracle server documentation set consisting of more than a dozen manuals—including a tuning guide—and a number of independent Oracle tuning texts on the market, is there really a need for this book?

There is a need, and the basis for this need lies in two fundamental imperfections in all alternative tuning guides: They are aimed almost exclusively at database administrators (DBAs), and they gloss over the processes of tuning SQL statements. There is a need for a book that is aimed not at the administrators of the Oracle databases, but at those writing the access routines (that is, the SQL) for the database, such as application developers, users of data warehouses, and others whose work involves writing high-performance SQL.

Additionally, while tuning the database engine can help poorly performing applications, nothing can match improving the efficiency of SQL for getting massive performance improvements. Unfortunately, most tuning texts spend most of their time focusing on database and I/O subsystem tuning.

WHO SHOULD USE THIS BOOK

This is not a book for Oracle DBAs, although DBAs should find many things of interest here. Rather, this is a book for anyone who needs to write SQL that has a performance requirement.

People who need to write high-performance SQL are as follows:

❑ Developers of Oracle-based applications. These developers will typically need to embed SQL statements within the code of the development tool (such as C++, Java, or Visual Basic). Alternately, the SQL may be contained within stored procedures that they will call from their client tool. These SQL statements will need to be efficient; otherwise the applications concerned will fail to meet reasonable performance requirements.

❑ Those querying data warehouses or decision-support databases. These databases are typically very large and hence these queries must run efficiently; otherwise they may take an unreasonable time to complete (or not complete at all).

❑ Anyone who writes Oracle SQL statements and cares about their response time or throughput.

HOW TO USE THIS BOOK

Few people read a book of this type from beginning to end. Depending on your background, you may wish to skip sections that review database theory and jump right into the details of SQL tuning.

However, apart from the "Review of SQL" and the "Beyond SQL Tuning" sections, most readers should attempt to read or at least review the majority of this book.

The book has the following major sections:

PART I: INTRODUCTION TO SQL TUNING

This section contains a review of the importance of SQL tuning, an overview of the tuning process and a review of SQL. The chapters in Part I are as follows:

- ❑ Chapter 1: Introduction to SQL Tuning
- ❑ Chapter 2: SQL Tuning Quick Start
- ❑ Chapter 3: Review of SQL

PART II: SQL TUNING THEORY

Chapters in Part II introduce a number of important topics, such as the role of the query optimizers, indexing and hashing concepts, SQL parsing, basic data retrieval strategies, and tools for explaining and tuning SQL execution. Although Part II is heavy on theory, its difficult to tune SQL successfully without at least a broad understanding of these topics. All readers are therefore encouraged to read this section.

The chapters in Part II are as follows:

- ❑ Chapter 4: SQL Processing Internals
- ❑ Chapter 5: The Optimizer
- ❑ Chapter 6: Indexing and Clustering
- ❑ Chapter 7: Tracing and Explaining SQL

PART III: SQL TUNING IN PRACTICE

Chapters in Part III contain tuning guidelines for specific SQL statement types and circumstances. While it will be useful to read Part III from start to finish, it may also be used as a reference. You may wish to consult the relevant portions of this section as appropriate tuning requirements arise. Chapters in Part III are as follows:

- ❑ Chapter 8: Tuning Table Access
- ❑ Chapter 9: Tuning Joins and Subqueries
- ❑ Chapter 10: Sorts, Aggregates, and SET Operations
- ❑ Chapter 11: Parallel SQL
- ❑ Chapter 12: Optimizing DML
- ❑ Chapter 13: VLDB and Warehousing
- ❑ Chapter 14: Using and Tuning PL/SQL
- ❑ Chapter 15: Using and Tuning Oracle Java
- ❑ Chapter 16: Oracle Object Types
- ❑ Chapter 17: Miscellaneous Topics

PART IV: BEYOND SQL TUNING

At the beginning of the application life cycle, effective database and application design can define the constraints that will ultimately determine the limits on your SQL's performance. For a well-designed application with tuned SQL, the configuration of your database—disk layouts, SGA configuration, etc.—may be the key to getting further gains in performance. Chapters in Part IV discuss these "beyond SQL" issues:

- ❑ Chapter 18: Application Design Issues
- ❑ Chapter 19: Oracle Server Design
- ❑ Chapter 20: Oracle Server Tuning

APPENDICES

The appendices contain details of configuring client programs and the Oracle server for specific circumstances, a reference guide, and a guide to further reading and other resources.

THE SAMPLE DATABASE

Whenever possible, any SQL tuning principle in this book will be illustrated with an example SQL statement. Usually, these SQL statements will be based on the sample database shown in Figure P-1. This database is not intended to illustrate good or bad data modeling principles but to be a basis for illustrating a wide range of SQL statements. You can find an export of one of the variations of this database at the book's website.[1,2]

The sample database implements a simple and familiar business schema containing Customers, Employees, Products, and Sales. In addition, the database contains the results from an imaginary marketing survey in the Subjects and Scores table.

Figure P-1 shows a logical representation of the sample database. Many different physical implementations of this logical schema were implemented during the development of the book. For instance, the Sales table was subjected to a variety of partitioning schemes, the Customer table was represented in one example

---

[1]Because implementation details of the sample database were changed many times during the development of this book to test or demonstrate certain features, the copy of the sample database on the book's website might not match the structure of the sample database used in each example.

[2]Throughout the book, the term "website" refers to the following ftp site: ftp://fpt. prenhall.com/pub/ptr/database.w-050/oraclesql2

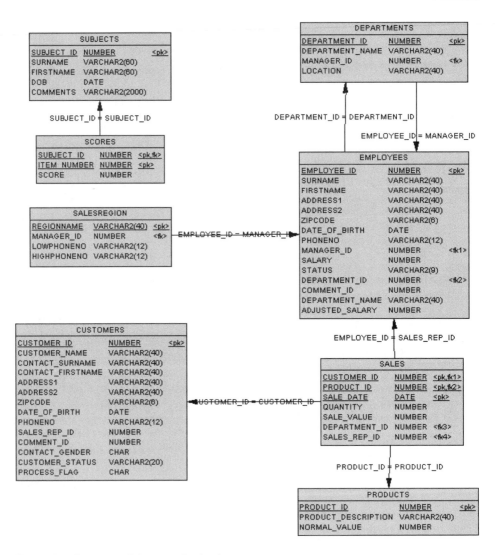

Figure P-1 Structure of the sample database.

as an Index-Organized table, while Subject and Score data were represented in a variety of ways including nested tables, VARRAYS, and object tables.

Many of the examples contained in this book are accompanied with a graphical illustration of the performance gains that can be achieved by various optimizations. These performance measurements were collected on a range of computer hardware, ranging from a high-end UNIX host to a Pentium laptop. Performance measurements are shown in either elapsed times or logical database

I/Os ("block reads"), whichever was most appropriate to the optimization being performed.

ABOUT QUEST SOFTWARE

Since writing the first edition of this book, I have had the pleasure to work with Quest Software in the development of software that assists in the tuning of SQL and Oracle databases. In particular, the *SQLab Xpert* SQL tuning tool implements many of the tuning principles outlined in this book. I have also been heavily involved in the development of Quest's *Spotlight on Oracle* product, which implements the database tuning philosophies outlined in the final chapters of this book. Because I'm so familiar with Quest products and believe that they make substantial contributions to SQL tuning, I often refer to them in the text of the book. However, be warned that I'm a Quest employee and hardly unbiased when it comes to Quest products.

ACKNOWLEDGMENTS

Families of authors often carry the heaviest burden during the authoring process, and this has certainly been the case with my family. My wife, Jenni, and our children, Christopher, Katherine, Michael, and William, have supported me through two editions of this book and through the first edition of the Oracle desk reference. I love you all and dedicate this book to you.

I'd also like to acknowledge my sister Gabrielle, who has been a close friend and important influence for as long as I can remember.

Tim Moore at Prentice Hall was always supportive and helpful. Rose Kernan contributed as Production Editor and many others at Prentice Hall also contributed to make this book a reality. Vadim Loevski and Gerrard "the pedant" Hocks from Quest provided technical review of the second edition and built on the firm foundation of technical advice and review provided by Steve Adams, Mike Farrar, and Nick Goldsmith in the first edition.

As in the first edition, I have to thank those in the Oracle community who selflessly share their time and expertise to help increase the understanding of Oracle performance management, development, and tuning. You'll find references to sites run by some of these people in Appendix E.

Working at Quest Software has given me the opportunity to expand my knowledge and skills and implement practical software solutions for database and SQL tuning. There are too many to thank at Quest, but in particular I'd like to thank John Symington for establishing such a brilliant working environment in the Melbourne office.

Part I: Introduction To SQL Tuning

INTRODUCTION TO SQL TUNING

INTRODUCTION

This book is about improving the performance of Oracle-based applications and databases, with a particular emphasis on the process of tuning Oracle SQL statements. As argued in the Preface, improving SQL performance is usually the most effective way of improving the performance of Oracle applications. Additionally, it is an approach that is available to a wide range of developers and users of Oracle databases and that can improve performance at all stages of the application development life cycle.

In this chapter, we examine in some detail the incentive to tune SQL, the effects of poorly tuned SQL, and the performance benefits that can be obtained from SQL tuning. We'll also examine some of the common objections to SQL tuning.

We will then move to a discussion of the SQL tuning process, including the following:

❑ The place of SQL tuning in overall performance management
❑ The establishment of an effective tuning environment
❑ Skills and tools required for a successful SQL tuning effort
❑ An overview of the steps involved in SQL tuning

WHY TUNE SQL?

To many, the objectives and importance of SQL tuning are so self-evident that there seems little need to articulate them. However, before we undertake any exercise as time-consuming and potentially difficult as SQL tuning, we need to understand what we are trying to achieve and the costs and benefits we can expect.

INCENTIVES FOR TUNING

Tuning SQL is not always easy. As often as not, the effort of tuning a piece of SQL takes more time than writing and testing the SQL in the first place. So why bother?

There are a number of reasons why we undertake the sometimes difficult process of SQL tuning:

❑ **To improve the interactive response time of an Oracle-based application.** A major component of the response time of these applications is the amount of time taken to retrieve or update data in the database. By tuning the SQL underlying these applications, response times can be reduced from excessive to acceptable—or even sensational!

❑ **To improve batch throughput**. Batch systems may be required to process thousands or millions of rows of data within some rigidly defined "batch window" (the period of time allocated for batch jobs). Improving the SQL that drives these batch jobs will allow more rows to be processed within a given time period and allow these jobs to complete within their allotted time. Often problems within batch reports are not noticed until a steadily degrading batch job suddenly exceeds its time limit—for instance, when the daily report takes longer than 24 hours to run.

❑ **To ensure scalability in our application**. As we increase the load on our system (as measured by the number of users connected to our system or the data volumes in our database), we hope that our performance (as measured by response time or throughput) degrades gradually. The sad truth is that many applications degrade anything but gracefully as load increases. Figure 1.1 illustrates some of the ways application performance degrades under increasing load.

❑ **To reduce system load**. Even if performance is, strictly speaking, within acceptable bounds, tuning the application can free system resources for other purposes.

❑ **To avoid hardware upgrades**. This reason is a powerful incentive for those who actually have to pay for computer hardware. It's not uncommon for hardware upgrades to be recommended as a solution for poorly performing applications. This solution, while having the advantage of avoiding tuning,

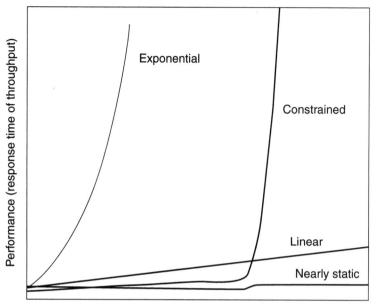

FIGURE 1.1 Patterns of application scalability.

is often ultimately futile since a nonscalable application may require an escalating series of hardware upgrades that rapidly reach the limits of what is available or affordable.

Patterns of scalability A well-tuned application will continue to deliver acceptable performance as the user population or data volumes increase. For instance, indexed retrieval of a single row from a table should perform well no matter how big the table gets, although there will be some minor degradation when the height of the index increases.[1]

However, it's common to see performance degrade more dramatically. The degradation can follow one of the following patterns:

❑ **Steady decrease in performance (linear degradation).** This is the least serious case because the degradation tends to be predictable and responsive to hardware upgrades. For example, the time taken to perform a full-table scan of a table is directly proportional to the number of rows in the table. As the number of rows increases, we would see a linear degradation in scan performance.

---

[1]The "height" of an index is discussed in depth in Chapter 6.

❑ **Increasing at an increasing rate (exponential).** This is more serious because the exponential increase is not always recognized and tends to "creep up." Hardware upgrades are likely to be ineffective ultimately. A SQL statement that performs "nested" table scans will exhibit exponential degradation as the number of rows in the tables increases.

❑ **Abruptly encountered (bottleneck).** In this case, an abrupt degradation ("we hit a brick wall") is encountered. Frequently, there is no advance warning and no hardware upgrade solution. This might occur because of internal contention for Oracle resources (certain latches, for instance) or because operating system resources—most typically memory—have become exhausted.

OBJECTIONS TO TUNING

Because producing high-performance SQL is much more difficult than producing functional SQL, it's possible to encounter resistance to the tuning process. In this section we'll discuss some of the more common objections to SQL tuning.

The optimizer will do it for me   We discuss the optimizer in detail in Chapter 3. The optimizer is that part of the Oracle server that tries to determine the most efficient way to execute your SQL statements. While the optimizer gets smarter with every release of the Oracle software and can often make very good decisions, it lacks critical information that the SQL programmer is likely to possess regarding the distribution and nature of data in your application. Also, you might be able to spend hours or days determining the best approach, while the optimizer must make a decision in a split second. In short, the optimizer can help but usually cannot do as good a job as the experienced SQL programmer/tuner.

I'm not an SQL programmer, I'm a [insert your specialty here]   In many development environments SQL coding is often the responsibility of those whose primary expertise is in a software development tool (for instance, Java, C, Microsoft Visual Basic, or other similar tools). These programmers might regard SQL programming as a side line and feel that SQL tuning is not their responsibility. This is a dangerous attitude since poorly tuned SQL is likely to have an impact on overall application performance far more severe than anything contained in the front-end code. In general, if you write the SQL, you need to take responsibility for it—and that includes performance.

I'll write the SQL—someone else can tune it   It's often believed that it's the responsibility of some other team member—possibly the DBA—to tune the application SQL. Regardless of whether or not this other person has the time, mandate, or skills necessary to tune the SQL, it's usually the person who writes the SQL who has the critical knowledge required for tuning.

For instance, when trying to tune someone else's SQL, DBAs will have to expend a fair amount of effort in determining what the SQL is trying to do. They will need to understand the underlying data at least as well as the author of the SQL and may be concerned that in tuning the SQL, they might inadvertently change the semantics (the meaning) of the SQL.

Generally, only the author of the SQL has all of the knowledge required to tune the SQL. All that might be missing is the necessary SQL tuning principles—and that's the purpose of this book.

I'll tune it later The problem with this attitude is the same as the problem with procrastination in general, and specifically with delaying quality control in software development. It has become well understood that the cost of fixing a software defect increases throughout the software development life cycle. For instance, it may take 1 hour to fix a software defect if it is picked up in development, 10 hours to fix if picked up in system testing, and 20 hours if picked up in production.

The same principle holds true for SQL tuning. Usually, the longer you wait, the more difficult it is to tune. For instance, the data model may be finalized—preventing denormalization—or the code may now be in production and can't be fixed without an extensive quality assurance and change control process.

Don't put it off—tune your SQL as you write it.

We can't afford to tune it In reality, you probably can't afford not to tune. Failure to implement efficient SQL may lead to unnecessary hardware upgrades, to lost productivity by system users, to end-user dissatisfaction, and often to the cancellation of software projects.

Failure to tune early in the development life cycle usually leads to a more substantial tuning effort later. Almost always, untuned systems are running on hardware much more expensive than would be required for a tuned system. It's possible for millions of dollars to be spent on hardware upgrades that could have been avoided by a couple of weeks of application tuning.

SQL tuning is always cost-effective.

> SQL tuning is almost always a cost-effective exercise. It helps avoid costly hardware upgrades and improves the scalability and performance of applications.

THE PLACE OF SQL TUNING IN THE OVERALL TUNING PROCESS

SQL tuning is only one of a number of aspects of the total tuning process. One view of this total process is given in Figure 1.2. Some of the other tuning components are as follows:

❑ **Performance requirements specification.** During the initial requirements specification phase, the performance requirements of the application should

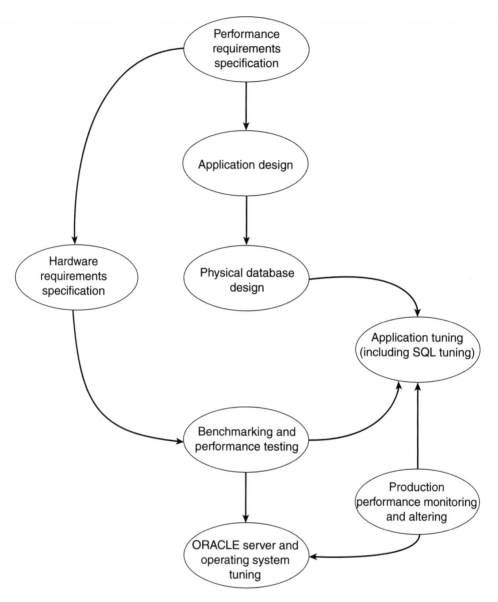

FIGURE 1.2   A view of the overall performance management process.

have been identified. These requirements can be specified in terms of transactions per second, response times, or some other measure. These requirements set the performance objectives that will be used to determine the success of subsequent tuning efforts.

❏ **Application design**. During this stage, the functionality and architecture of the application are determined. The functionality determines the deliverables of the application, and the architecture determines how the application will provide these deliverables. Decisions made at this stage can determine both the performance requirements and possibilities of the system. This stage also incorporates the development of a logical database design.

❏ **Physical database design**. While the logical model defines the data that will be held within the database, the physical model describes how this data is stored in the real-world database of tables, indexes, etc. The physical design usually determines the ultimate limits on the performance of your application. Usually, it is difficult to change the data model substantially once the model is beyond the design stage because of the impact on existing programs. For instance, you may be able to add an index to the physical database, but you probably won't be able to merge two tables without recoding substantial portions of the application.

Application and database design changes often offer the most significant performance improvements. Unfortunately, changing the application or database design after implementation is often impractical at worst or costly at best. It's therefore important to attempt to optimize the design before implementation. Chapter 18 discusses aspects of application/database design.

❏ **The hardware requirements specification** will usually be developed before the application is ready for benchmark and performance testing. The capacity of the hardware platform will have a significant effect on the system performance. Chapter 19 discusses issues involved in sizing a hardware platform.

❏ **Application tuning (excluding SQL)**. This usually involves changing the application's algorithms to improve performance. For instance, you might change the application so that it reads some file into memory and caches it there rather than rereading the file every time it is required.

❏ **Application tuning (SQL)**. For database-centric applications, the most significant improvements in performance are often realized by the tuning of application SQL. Improving SQL performance is the major focus of this book.

❏ **Benchmark and performance testing** often occur prior to system implementation to ensure that the performance requirements specifications can be met. In some cases, benchmark testing might occur prior to finalization of the hardware requirements specification.

❏ **Oracle server tuning** is the process of improving database performance without changing the application SQL or data model. This might require changing configuration parameters or spreading database files across multiple disks.

❏ **Operating system tuning**. This is similar to tuning the Oracle server. We might change configuration settings or reorganize the machine's resources. Additionally, we may acquire more resources if deemed necessary.

Tuning Oracle and/or your operating system can lead to significant improvements in performance, although not usually as substantial as those realized by tuning your SQL. Tuning the Oracle server or the operating system is particularly effective when contention for a resource or a bottleneck in processing exists. In Chapter 20, we introduce ways of identifying and addressing such bottlenecks.

❏ **Hardware upgrades** can result in substantial improvements to performance but are often a costly solution. Additionally, upgrading hardware can be futile ultimately if your application scalability is poor. For instance, you may have to quadruple your hardware resources in order to get a twofold improvement in performance.

Figure 1.3 shows the potential improvement you might expect from each of these measures. We can see from the figure that SQL tuning can offer substantial improvements in performance, without the cost of hardware upgrades and without the difficulty of changing the design of a production application.

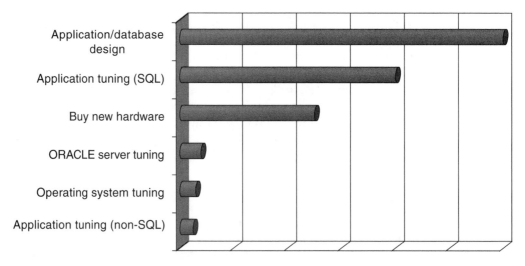

FIGURE 1.3   Potential performance improvements from various components of the total tuning process.

WHEN SHOULD SQL BE TUNED?

Ideally, SQL should be tuned as it is written. As we progress through the normal system development life cycle (design-development-test-implementation), it becomes increasingly costly to tune SQL, and the performance improvements we can expect to achieve diminish. There are a number of reasons for this:

❑ Certain aspects of the application become impossible to change without reimplementing large portions of the design. For instance, the design of the database can form the basis for all application programs. We can change it quite easily in the design stage, but changing it at a later stage might require that we recode every program to adjust to the new data model.

❑ If we tune the SQL when it is first written, then we only have to test the SQL once. However, if we have to tune the SQL following its first round of testing, then those tests will have to be repeated once the SQL is tuned. Furthermore, when the SQL is first being constructed, the functional requirements, underlying table designs, and other critical information will already be at hand. Returning to tune an SQL statement at some later date will require a review of the purpose and logic of the SQL.

❑ Once SQL enters a production system, there are often restrictions on the tuning measures that can be put in place. For instance, building or altering an index on a large table may require substantial time, during which the application might be unavailable. For applications that are required to be available around the clock, creating such a new index might be a major problem.

Figure 1.4 illustrates the costs and benefits of tuning during various stages of the application life cycle.

Tuning should be introduced into the development process as early as possible, and to do so is more effective and economical than waiting until the implementation stage.

Performance issues are often ignored until an application is deployed or, at best, subjected to a stress test shortly before implementation. Although this makes the job of tuning SQL more difficult, tuning SQL is the best hope for improving application performance.

As with most tuning and quality assurance processes, SQL tuning is less expensive and can result in greater improvements the earlier it is addressed within the application development life cycle. However, SQL tuning is an effective measure at any stage and can often be the only useful tuning measure available for production systems.

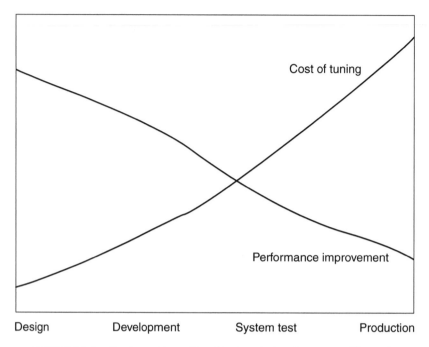

FIGURE 1.4   Costs and benefits of tuning during the system life cycle.

THE TUNING PROCESS

Although this book contains numerous SQL tuning techniques, guidelines, and examples, it cannot provide a rule or an example for every circumstance. What it can do is present an effective approach to tuning that will result in well-tuned SQL statements and offer some suggestions for common situations.

There is a substantial element of trial and error in SQL tuning. However, this trial and error is characteristic of a scientific process rather than a random process—the expert SQL tuner is formulating and evaluating theories and iteratively establishing the best SQL. Like the scientist, the SQL tuner collects data, formulates theories, tests those theories, and repeats the process until the best SQL statement is found.

Figure 1.5 illustrates the SQL tuning process. It is important to keep in mind the following:

1. SQL tuning is an iterative process. That is, we repeat the process until we reach a satisfactory outcome.
2. The concept of measuring SQL performance is critical. Without measurement, we have no way of knowing the effect of our tuning efforts. We

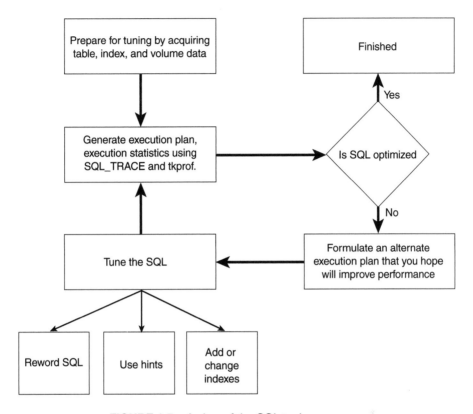

FIGURE 1.5 A view of the SQL tuning process.

therefore have to be familiar with the tools that are available for measuring performance.

3. Tuning the SQL can involve a range of methods, such as altering the text of the SQL statement, and creating or altering indexes. To do this effectively, you need to understand how Oracle processes SQL and you need to have some familiarity with the options for improving performance. Therefore, this book contains details of Oracle SQL processing and examples of improving specific types of SQL statements.

Although experience and good techniques can hasten the SQL tuning process, SQL tuning remains an iterative process in which several improvements may need to be tested before the optimal SQL is found. Effective measurement is essential to ensure that each change can be evaluated accurately.

CONSTRUCTING A TUNING ENVIRONMENT

Before you can start to tune, you need to establish an environment that promotes an efficient and accurate measurement of SQL. You also need to have on hand details of your database structure and volumes.

There are many projects in which tables that have millions of rows in production contain only a few tens of rows in development, and developers have no idea what indexes exist and don't know about the tools for tuning SQL. In such an environment, tuning SQL is impossible.

The ideal tuning environment is one in which

❏ Data volumes are realistic.
❏ Data model documentation is available and is easy to understand.
❏ System performance requirements are explicit.
❏ Validation of performance requirements is built in to the quality assurance process.

REALISTIC DATA VOLUMES

Plenty of systems seem to be performing well in development but suffer drastic and dramatic performance problems in production. Generally, these systems were developed in an environment in which the amount of data in the database was unrealistic. In fact, it's not uncommon to find that developers are writing SQL statements against empty tables—tables that will contain millions of rows in production.

Using realistic data volumes has at least two desirable effects:

❏ Any problems with the performance of SQL are noticed before they hit production.
❏ Tuning efforts that work in development will also work in production.

What are realistic data volumes? In an ideal tuning environment, the data volumes and distribution would be exactly the same as that in the target or production environment. Unfortunately, processing and resource restrictions often make it difficult to realize this ambition.

If you can't populate your tuning environment with the same volumes as your target environment, you may be able to use your target environment for some of your tuning. If your SQL is query only (e.g., does not change any of the data in the target environment) and you have an off-peak or noncritical window in your target system, then testing your SQL against the target environment can be an option.

However, in many cases there is no window of opportunity for running ad hoc SQL against the production environment, or production control procedures prohibit such activities.

The following principles may help when establishing data volumes in the development or tuning environment:

❏ Small tables, such as code and reference tables, should be the same size in the tuning environment as in the target environment.

❏ Larger tables should be larger than the small tables just mentioned. They should also be large enough so that reading every row of the table takes at least 10 to 100 times longer than reading a single row from an index.

❏ These larger tables should be scaled down by approximately the same degree. That is, if one of the tables is 5% of its size in the target environment, then all of these larger tables should be 5% of their target size. This preserves the relative sizes of the tables.

For example, in the sample database outlined earlier, you might set up a tuning environment as shown in Table 1.1.

COPYING OPTIMIZER STATS

Oracle8i provides a technique for moving optimizer statistics from one environment to another. If you copy the optimizer statistics from production to development, then the optimizer in development will "think" that the data volumes are the same as in production. This technique—explained in more detail in Chapter 5—helps you tune more effectively because the execution plans—explained in Chapter 7—will be the same in development as in production.

TABLE 1.1 Possible tuning environment data volumes for the sample database

TABLE NAME	SIZE IN TARGET ENVIRONMENT (PRODUCTION DATABASE)	SIZE IN TUNING DATABASE (DEVELOPMENT DATABASE)	COMMENT
Departments	100	100	Reference table: Maintain same volumes
Products	100	100	Reference table: Maintain same volumes
Employees	5,000	1,000	20% sample
Products	30	30	Reference table: Maintain same volumes
Sales	1,000,000	200,000	20% sample
Customers	20,000	4,000	20% sample
Sales Region	500	500	Reference table: Maintain same volumes
Comments	250,000	50,000	20% sample

DOCUMENTATION

When tuning an SQL statement, you need ready access to your database structure—table definitions, index definitions, table sizes, relationships between tables, etc. If you don't have this information at hand, you will find yourself working in the dark. If a CASE tool was used to generate your database, then the same tool can generate this information. Otherwise, you can obtain the necessary information by writing queries against the data dictionary.

KNOW YOUR SYSTEM REQUIREMENTS

It's always a good idea to define the performance requirements for the database system. In other words, how fast is fast enough? For instance, for an on-line system, how quickly should a query return the data? In 5 seconds, 1 second, less than 1 second? This information will allow you to determine when your tuning efforts have succeeded.

MEASURING SQL PERFORMANCE

Oracle provides tools that reveal the way in which Oracle is processing your SQL and the resources (CPU, I/O, etc.) expended. These tools are as follows:

❏ The EXPLAIN PLAN statement, which can be used to show Oracle's strategy for retrieving the data requested by your SQL statement
❏ The SQL_TRACE facility, which generates a trace of your SQL statements' execution
❏ The tkprof utility, which transforms this trace file into useful output

These tools are powerful but unfortunately not always easy to use. Guidelines for using these tools are contained in Chapter 7.

TUNING SQL

Improving the performance of your SQL can be achieved using a number of techniques:

❏ Rewording your SQL
❏ Giving Oracle explicit instructions (called hints) that direct Oracle to use particular approaches to retrieving and processing data
❏ Creating or changing indexes or clusters
❏ Changing the table structure

Determining which combination of approaches is likely to result in performance improvements requires the following:

- ❏ An understanding of how Oracle processes SQL
- ❏ An understanding of table volumes and relationships
- ❏ An understanding of how you can influence Oracle's processing
- ❏ An understanding of how to make the most of indexes and clustering
- ❏ An awareness of the possible alternative approaches to various types of SQL statements

Some additional skills will help you ensure that your SQL is getting every opportunity to work effectively:

- ❏ Effective application and database design is an essential ingredient for a high-performance application. Tuning SQL may be futile if the underlying design is flawed.
- ❏ Knowledge of Oracle server performance monitoring and tuning can be invaluable. It may be that although your SQL is optimally tuned, bottlenecks in the Oracle server are preventing it from reaching its full potential.

We will elaborate on the techniques for tuning SQL throughout the rest of this book.

Try to establish a productive environment in which to tune your SQL. Obtain realistic or representative data volumes for your key tables. Ensure that application and database design information is at hand and that tuning tools are available.

SUMMARY

As the database size, user populations, and performance expectations of Oracle databases have increased, so has the interest in improving the performance of Oracle applications. Much of this interest has focused on tuning the configuration of the database server, while the tuning of application SQL has been somewhat neglected.

Tuning SQL can improve the response time, throughput, and scalability of an application and can help to avoid costly hardware upgrades. Tuning SQL is a cost-effective way of improving system performance because it can yield substantial improvements at any stage of a system's life cycle, although addressing SQL tuning during early stages will result in the greatest performance gain.

Tuning SQL involves measuring the performance and characteristics of the SQL to be tuned. The performance of SQL can be improved in a number of ways:

❏ Adding or changing Oracle indexes
❏ Rewording the SQL statement
❏ Using Oracle hints
❏ Changing the database structure

Best tuning results will be obtained if you establish an effective tuning environment with representative data volumes, clearly defined performance objectives, and comprehensive database documentation.

To tune SQL effectively, you will need the following:

❏ An understanding of how Oracle processes SQL
❏ An understanding of Oracle indexing facilities
❏ An ability to use Oracle SQL tuning tools, such as tkprof, EXPLAIN PLAN, and hints
❏ Methods for improving the performance of specific categories of SQL
❏ An elementary understanding of database and application design principles
❏ Some familiarity with Oracle server architecture and how bottlenecks in that architecture might affect the performance of your SQL

SQL TUNING QUICK START

INTRODUCTION

This chapter provides a quick start to SQL tuning. It's intended both to fore-shadow the tuning material to come and to provide a place to start for those who are pressed for time. The chapter starts with a quick review of the most useful SQL tuning tips and techniques. It follows with a listing of tips for specific circumstances. These tips appear as boxed text throughout the book.

TOP TIPS AND HINTS FOR SQL TUNING

HINT: DESIGN AND DEVELOP WITH PERFORMANCE IN MIND

Too often, SQL tuning is performed on an application designed and developed with virtually no consideration given to performance requirements. SQL tuning is often the best option for tuning such applications, but it is both more efficient and effective to design an application with performance in mind.

Producing good performance by design requires that the following activities occur within the development life cycle:

❑ Explicit specification of the performance characteristics of the system at an early stage of development.

❏ Focus on critical transactions and queries during logical and physical modeling. Simulation of these SQL statements on prototype designs can often reveal key performance weaknesses.

❏ Effective simulation of the target environment. This can include simulating concurrent user loads and/or acquiring representative data volumes.

❏ Continual measurement of critical transaction performance. If possible, this should be integrated with other quality assurance measures.

Chapter 18 contains a more fully developed discussion of this topic and other design issues.

HINT: ESTABLISH A TUNING ENVIRONMENT

It's not uncommon for SQL that seemed to be working well in the development environment to exhibit poor performance once it is released to a production system. A primary cause of these unpleasant surprises is an inadequate development or volume testing environment. In particular, environments without realistic or representative data volumes are bound to lead to unrealistic SQL performance.

The ideal tuning or development environment is one in which

❏ Data volumes are realistic or at least proportional. With today's increasingly large production databases, it's often impossible to duplicate production data volumes exactly. However, it should always be possible to construct a reasonable subset of the data. For instance, a 20% sample of a 1-GB database may be adequate for performance tuning. At all costs, avoid the situation in which SQL developers are constructing and testing code against empty or almost empty tables—even the proverbial "SQL query from hell" will appear efficient in these environments.

❏ Tuning facilities are available. Supply your volume and development environments with as many tuning tools as you have available. This could involve third-party SQL tuning tools but will at least involve enabling the default Oracle tools. Make sure developers know how to use EXPLAIN PLAN, SQL trace, and tkprof. Make sure that relevant database options are set to enable their effective use (see Chapter 7).

❏ Documentation is available. This documentation should include the database design, index details, performance requirements, and volume metrics. The SQL programmer needs all this information to produce efficient SQL.

HINT: USE SQL TUNING TOOLS

An execution plan is a representation of the steps that Oracle will undertake in order to execute a SQL statement. For instance, the execution plan will reveal whether an index will be used, the order in which tables will be joined, and so on.

You will be working in the dark unless you determine the execution plan and collect other statistics relevant to SQL statement execution.

Explain Plan   The EXPLAIN PLAN command is available to generate the execution plan for an SQL statement.

To use EXPLAIN PLAN you do the following:

❏ Create the PLAN_TABLE using the script in $ORACLE_HOME/rdbms/ admin/utlxplan.sql (on UNIX) or %ORACLE_HOME%\rdbms\admin\ utlxplan.sql (on Windows).

❏ Issue the "EXPLAIN PLAN for *sql_statement*" command.

❏ Display the execution plan for the statement using a query such as this:

```
SELECT RTRIM (LPAD (' ', 2 * LEVEL) ||
        RTRIM (operation) || ' ' ||
        RTRIM (options) || ' ' || object_name) query_plan
   FROM plan_table
 CONNECT BY PRIOR id = parent_id
 START WITH id = 0;
```

❏ Delete the contents of the PLAN_TABLE.

SQL trace/tkprof   A more powerful cousin of the EXPLAIN PLAN command is the SQL trace facility. To use SQL trace you do the following:

❏ Execute the command *ALTER SESSION SET SQL_TRACE TRUE* from within an Oracle session.

❏ Locate the trace file that has been generated in the destination specified by the init.ora parameter user_dump_dest.

❏ Use the tkprof program to format the trace file. For instance,

```
tkprof input_trace_file output_report_file
sort='(prsela,exeela,fchela)'
explain=username/password
```

The output file will contain execution plans (with some additional information not normally available from an execution plan) and execution statistics for every SQL statement executed following the initiation of SQL trace.

AUTOTRACE   You can also get limited statistics and explain plans from within SQL*PLUS by using the "SET AUTOTRACE ON" command. This produces an execution plan and some execution statistics, though not as sophisticated as those produced by tkprof. Interpretation of tkprof output and execution plans is provided in Chapter 7.

HINT: INDEX WISELY

Indexes exist primarily to improve the performance of SQL statements. In many cases, establishing the best indexes is the easiest path to high performance.

Use concatenated indexes   Try not to use two indexes when one would do. If searching for SURNAME and FIRSTNAME, don't necessarily create separate indexes for each column. Instead create a concatenated index on both SURNAME and FIRSTNAME. You can use the "leading" portions of a concatenated index on their own, so if you sometimes query on the SURNAME column without supplying the FIRSTNAME then SURNAME should come first in the index.

Overindex to avoid a table lookup   You can sometimes improve SQL execution by overindexing. Overindexing involves concatenating columns that appear in the SELECT clause, but not in the WHERE clause to the index. For instance, imagine that we are searching on SURNAME and FIRSTNAME in order to find EMPLOYEE_ID. Our concatenated index on SURNAME and FIRSTNAME will allow us quickly to locate the row containing the appropriate EMPLOYEE_ID, but we will need to access both the index and the table. If there is an index on SURNAME, FIRSTNAME, and EMPLOYEE_ID, then the query can be satisfied using the index alone. This technique can be particularly useful when optimizing joins, since intermediate tables in a join are sometimes queried merely to obtain the join key for the next table.

Consider advanced indexing options   Oracle default B*-tree indexes are flexible and efficient and are suitable for the majority of situations. However, Oracle offers a number of alternative indexing schemes that can improve performance in specific situations.

❑ **Index clusters** allow rows from one or more tables to be located in cluster key order. Clustering tables can result in a substantial improvement to join performance. However, table scans of an individual table in the cluster can be severely degraded. Index clusters are usually only recommended for tables that are always accessed together. Even then, alternatives such as denormalization should be considered.

❑ In **hash clusters**, the key values are translated mathematically to a hash value. Rows are stored in the hash cluster based on this hash value. Locating a row when the hash key is known may require only a single I/O, rather than the two or three I/Os required by an index lookup. However, range scans of the hash key cannot be performed. Furthermore, if the cluster is poorly configured, or if the size of the cluster changes, then overflows on the hash keys can occur, or the cluster can become sparsely populated. In the first case, hash key retrieval can degrade and, in the second case, table scans will be less efficient.

❑ **Bit-mapped indexes** suit queries on multiple columns made against multiple columns that each have relatively few distinct values. They are more compact than a corresponding concatenated index and, unlike the concatenated index, they can support queries in which the columns appear in any combination. However, bit-mapped indexes are not suitable for tables with high modification rates, since locking of bit-mapped indexes occurs at the block rather than row level.

❑ In an **index-organized table**, all table data is stored within a B*-tree index structure. This can improve access to data via the primary key and reduces the redundancy of storing key values both in the index and in the table. Index-organized tables can be configured with infrequently accessed columns located in an overflow segment. This keeps the index structure relatively small and efficient.

Make sure your query uses the best index   Novice SQL programmers are often satisfied if the execution plan for their SQL statement uses any index. However, there will sometimes be a choice of indexed retrievals, and the Oracle optimizer—especially the older rule-based optimizer—will not always choose the best index. Make sure that the indexes being selected by Oracle are the most appropriate and use hints to change the index if necessary.

HINT: REDUCE PARSING

Parsing an SQL statement is the process of validating the SQL and determining the optimal execution plan. For SQL that has low I/O requirements but is frequently executed (for example, the SQL generated by OLTP-type applications), reducing the overhead of SQL parsing is very important.

When an Oracle session needs to parse an SQL statement, it first looks for an identical SQL statement in the Oracle *shared pool*. If a matching statement cannot be found, then Oracle will determine the optimal execution plan for the statement and store the parsed representation in the shared pool.

The process of parsing SQL is CPU intensive. When I/O is well tuned, the overhead of parsing the SQL can be a significant portion of the total overhead of executing the SQL. There are a number of ways of reducing the overhead of SQL statement parsing:

❑ **Use bind variables**. Bind variables allow the variable part of a query to be represented by pointers to program variables. If you use bind variables, the text of the SQL statement will not change from execution to execution and Oracle will usually find a match in the shared pool, dramatically reducing parse overhead.

❑ **Reuse cursors.** Cursors (or context areas) are areas of memory that store the parsed representation of SQL statements. If you reexecute the same SQL statement more than once, then you can reopen an existing cursor and avoid issuing a parse call. The mechanism of reusing cursors varies across development tools and programming languages. Appendix C contains some guidelines for specific tools.

❏ **Use a cursor cache.** If your development tool makes it hard or impossible to reuse cursors, you can instruct Oracle to create a cursor cache for each session using the SESSION_CACHED_CURSORS init.ora parameter. If SESSION_CACHED_CURSORS is greater than 0, then Oracle will store that number of recently reexecuted cursors in a cache. If an SQL statement is reexecuted, it may be found in the cache and a parse call avoided.

HINT: TAKE ADVANTAGE OF THE COST-BASED OPTIMIZER

The component of the Oracle software that determines the execution plan for an SQL statement is known as the *optimizer*. Oracle supports two approaches to query optimization:

❏ The *rule-based optimizer* determines the execution plan based on a set of rules that rank various access paths. For instance, an index-based retrieval has a lower rank than a full-table scan and so the rule-based optimizer will use indexes wherever possible.

❏ The *cost-based optimizer* determines the execution plan based on an estimate of the computer resources (the cost) required to satisfy various access methods. The cost-based optimizer uses statistics, including the number of rows in a table and the number of distinct values in indexes, to determine this optimum plan.

Early experiences with the cost-based optimizer in Oracle7 were often disappointing and gave the cost-based optimizer a poor reputation in some quarters. However, the cost-based optimizer has been improving in each release while the rule-based optimizer is virtually unchanged since Oracle 7.0. Many advanced SQL access methods, such as star and hash joins, are only available when you use the cost-based optimizer.

The cost-based optimizer is the best choice for almost all new projects, and converting from rule- to cost-based optimization will be worthwhile for many existing projects. Consider the following guidelines for getting the most from the cost-based optimizer:

❏ **Optimizer_mode.** The default mode of the cost-based optimizer (optimizer_mode=CHOOSE) will attempt to optimize the throughput time taken to retrieve all rows of SQL statements and will often favor full-table scans over index lookups. When converting to cost-based optimization, many users are disappointed to find that previously well-tuned index lookups change to long-running table scans. To avoid this, set OPTMIZER_MODE=FIRST_ROWS in init.ora or ALTER SESSION SET OPTIMIZER_GOAL=FIRST_ROWS in your code. This instructs the cost-based optimizer to minimize the time taken to retrieve the first row in your result set and encourages the use of indexes.

❏ **Hints**. No matter how sophisticated the cost-based optimizer becomes, there will still be occasions when you need to modify its execution plan. SQL hints are usually the best way of doing this. Using hints, you can instruct the optimizer to pursue your preferred access paths (such as a preferred index), use the parallel query option, select a join order, and so on. Hints are entered as comments following the first word in an SQL statement. The plus sign "+" in the comment lets Oracle know that the comment contains a hint. Hints are fully documented in Appendix A. In the following example, a hint is instructing the optimizer to use the CUST_I2 index:

```
SELECT /*+ INDEX(CUSTOMERS CUST_I2) */ *
   FROM CUSTOMERS
  WHERE NAME=:cust_name
```

❏ **Analyze your tables**. The cost-based optimizer's execution plans are calculated using table statistics collected by the analyze command. Make sure you analyze your tables regularly, that you analyze all your tables, and that you analyze them at peak volumes (for instance, don't analyze a table just before it is about to be loaded by a batch job). For small to medium tables, use ANALYZE TABLE *table_name* COMPUTE STATISTICS; for larger tables take a sample such as ANALYZE TABLE *table_name* ESTIMATE STATISTICS SAMPLE 20 PERCENT.

❏ **Use histograms**. Prior to Oracle 7.3, the cost-based optimizer would have available the number of distinct values in a column but not the distribution of data within the column. This meant that it might decline to use an index on a column with only a few values even if the particular value in question was rare and would benefit from an index lookup. Histograms, introduced in Oracle 7.3, allow column distribution data to be collected and will allow the cost-based optimizer to make better decisions. You create histograms with the FOR COLUMNS clause of the analyze command (for instance, ANALYZE TABLE *table_name* COMPUTE STATISTICS FOR ALL INDEXED COLUMNS). Note that you can't take advantage of histograms if you are using bind variables (which we discussed earlier).

HINT: AVOID ACCIDENTAL TABLE SCANS

One of the most fundamental SQL tuning problems is the accidental table scan. Accidental table scans usually occur when the SQL programmer tries to perform a search on an indexed column that can't be supported by an index. This can occur when

❑ **Using != (not equal to)**. Even if the not equals condition satisfies only a small number of rows, Oracle will not use an index to satisfy such a condition. Often, you can recode these queries using > or IN conditions, which can be supported by index lookups.

❑ **Searching for NULLS**. Oracle won't use an index to find null values, since null values are not usually stored in an index (the exception is a concatenated index entry where only some of the values are NULL). If you're planning to search for values that are logically missing, consider changing the column to NOT NULL with a DEFAULT clause. For instance, you could set a default value of "UNKNOWN" and use the index to find these values.

❑ **Using functions on indexed columns**. Any function or operation on an indexed column will prevent Oracle from using an index on that column. For instance, Oracle can't use an index to find SUBSTR(SURNAME,1,4)='SMIT'. Instead of manipulating the column, try to manipulate the search condition. In the previous example, a better formulation would be SURNAME LIKE 'SMIT%'. In Oracle8i you can create *functional indexes*, which are indexes created on functions, provided that the function always returns the same result when given the same inputs. This allows you, for instance, to create an index on UPPER(surname).

HINT: OPTIMIZE NECESSARY TABLE SCANS

In many cases, avoiding a full-table scan by using the best of all possible indexes is your aim. However, it's often the case that a full-table scan cannot be avoided. In these situations, you could consider some of the following techniques to improve table scan performance.

Use the Parallel Query Option   Oracle's Parallel Query Option is the most effective—although most resource intensive—way of improving the performance of full-table scans. Parallel Query allocates multiple processes to an SQL statement that is based at least partially on a full-table scan. The table is partitioned into distinct sets of blocks, and each process works on a different set of data. Further processes may be allocated—or the original processes recycled—to perform joins, sorts, and other operations.

The approach of allocating multiple processes to the table scan can reduce execution time dramatically if the hardware and database layout is suitable. In particular, the host computer should have multiple CPUs and/or the database should be spread across more than one disk device.

You can enable the Parallel Query option with a PARALLEL hint or make it the default for a table with the PARALLEL table clause.

Reduce the size of the table   The performance of a full-table scan will generally be proportional to the size of the table to be scanned. There are ways of reducing the size of the table quite substantially and thereby improving full-table scan performance.

❏ **Reduce PCTFREE**. The PCTFREE table setting reserves a certain percentage of space in each block to allow for updates that increase the length of a row. By default, PCTFREE is set to 10%. If your table is rarely updated, or if the updates rarely increase the length of the row, you can reduce PCTFREE and hence reduce the overall size of the table.

❏ **Increase PCTUSED**. The PCTUSED table setting determines at what point blocks that have previously hit PCTFREE will again become eligible for inserts. The default value is 40%, which means that after hitting PCTFREE, the block will only become eligible for new rows when deletes reduce the amount of used space to 40%. If you increase PCTUSED, rows will be inserted into the table at an earlier time, blocks will be fuller on average, and the table will be smaller. There may be a negative effect on INSERT performance—you'll have to assess the trade-off between scan and insert performance.

❏ **Relocate long or infrequently used columns**. If you have LONG (or big VARCHAR2) columns in the table that are not frequently accessed and never accessed via a full-table scan (perhaps a bitmap image or embedded document), you should consider relocating these to a separate table. By relocating these columns you can substantially reduce the table's size and hence improve full-table scan performance. Note that Oracle8 LOB types will almost always be stored outside of the core table data.

The CACHE hint   Normally, rows retrieved by most full-table scans are flushed almost immediately from Oracle's cache. This is sensible since otherwise full-table scans could completely saturate the cache and push out rows retrieved from index retrievals. However, this does mean that subsequent table scans of the same table are unlikely to find a match in the cache and will therefore incur a high physical I/O rate.

You can encourage Oracle to keep these rows within the cache by using the CACHE hint or the CACHE table setting. Oracle will then place the rows retrieved at the least recently used end of the LRU chain and they will persist in the cache for a much longer period of time.

Use partitioning   If the number of rows you want to retrieve from a table is greater than an index lookup could effectively retrieve, but still only a fraction of the table itself (say between 10 and 40% of total), you could consider partitioning the table.

For instance, suppose that a SALES table contains all sales records for the past 4 years and you frequently need to scan all sales records for the current financial year in order to calculate year-to-date totals. The proportion of rows scanned is far greater than an index lookup would comfortably support but is still only a fraction of the total table. If you partition the table by financial year you can restrict processing to only those records that match the appropriate financial year. This could reduce scan time by 75% or more.

Partitioning is discussed in detail in Chapter 13.

Consider fast full index scan.   If a query needs to access all or most of the rows in a table, but only a subset of the columns, you can consider using a fast full index scan to retrieve the rows. To do this, you need to create an index that contains all the columns included in the select and where clauses of the query. If these columns comprise only a small subset of the entire table, then the index will be substantially smaller and Oracle will be able to scan the index more quickly than it could scan the table. There will, of course, be an overhead involved in maintaining the index that will affect the performance of INSERT, UPDATE, and DELETE statements.

HINT: OPTIMIZE JOINS

Determining the optimal join order and method is a critical consideration when optimizing the performance of SQL that involves multitable joins.

Join Method   Oracle supports three join methods:

❏ In a nested loops join, Oracle performs a search of the inner table for each row found in the outer table. This type of access is most often seen when there is an index on the inner table, since otherwise, multiple nested table scans may result.

❏ When performing a sort-merge join, Oracle must sort each table (or result set) by the value of the join columns. Once sorted, the two sets of data are merged, much as you might merge two sorted piles of numbered pages.

❏ When performing a hash join, Oracle builds a hash table for the smaller of the two tables. This hash table is then used to find matching rows in a somewhat similar fashion to the way an index is used in a nested loops join.

The nested loops method suits SQL that joins together subsets of table data and where there is an index to support the join. When larger amounts of data must be joined and/or there is no index, use the sort-merge or hash-join method. Hash join usually outperforms sort merge, but will only be used if cost-based optimization is in effect or if a hint is used.

Join Order   Determining the best join order can be a hit-and-miss affair. The cost-based optimizer will usually pick a good join order, but if it doesn't, you can use the ORDERED clause to force the tables to be joined in the exact order in which they appear in the FROM clause.

In general, it is better to eliminate rows earlier rather than later in the join process, so if a table has a restrictive WHERE clause condition you should favor it earlier in the join process.

Special Joins   Oracle provides a number of optimizations for special join types. Some of these optimizations will be performed automatically if you are using the cost-based optimizer, but all can be invoked in either optimizer by use of hints:

❑ The Star join algorithm optimizes the join of a single massive fact table to multiple, smaller dimension tables. The optimization can be invoked with the STAR hint. A further optimization rewrites the SQL to take advantage of bitmap indexes that might exist in the fact table. This optimization can be invoked by the STAR_TRANSFORMATION hint.

❑ The antijoin is usually expressed as a subquery using the NOT IN clause. Queries of this type can perform badly under the rule-based optimizer but can run efficiently if the init.ora parameter ALWAYS_ANTI_JOIN is set to HASH or if a HASH_AJ hint is added to the subquery.

❑ The semijoin is usually expressed as a subquery using the EXISTS clause. This query may perform poorly if there is no index supporting the subquery, but can be run efficiently if the init.ora parameter ALWAYS_SEMI_JOIN is set to HASH or if a HASH_SJ hint is added to the subquery.

❑ Hierarchical queries using the CONNECT BY operator will degrade rapidly as table volumes increase unless there is an index to support the CONNECT BY join condition.

HINT: USE ARRAY PROCESSING

Array processing refers to Oracle's ability to insert or select more than one row in a single operation. For SQL that deals with multiple rows of data, array processing usually results in reductions of 50% or more in execution time (more if you're working across the network). In some application environments, array processing is implemented automatically and you won't have to do anything to enable this feature. In other environments, array processing may be the responsibility of the programmer. Appendix C outlines how array processing can be activated in some popular development tools.

On the principle that "if some is good, more must be better," many programmers implement huge arrays. This can be overkill and may even reduce performance by increasing memory requirements for the program. Most of the gains of array processing are gained by increasing the array size from 1 to about 20. Further increases result in diminishing gains, and you won't normally see much improvement when increasing the array size over 100.

HINT: AVOID LOCK CONTENTION

Applications that contend for locks can exhibit unpredictable and disappointing performance. Oracle's row-level locking strategy and the absence of read locks allow you to reduce lock contention to a minimum. Follow these guidelines to minimize locking overhead:

Adopt an appropriate locking strategy The two most common approaches to locking are known as the *pessimistic locking strategy* and the *optimistic locking strategy*. In the pessimistic locking strategy, a row is locked when it is first retrieved (using the FOR UPDATE clause of the SELECT statement). This lock is held until the transaction completes. In the optimistic locking strategy, the row is not locked when first selected. If the row subsequently needs to be updated, it is first checked to make sure that it has not been updated. If it has been updated, then an error is generated and the transaction must be retried.

The optimistic locking strategy reduces the duration of table locks and in an interactive application prevents locks from being held while a user "goes to lunch." On the other hand, the optimistic strategy can result in frustration if a user must retry a transaction or there are delays in the throughput of batch jobs that frequently need to retry transactions. However, the optimistic strategy is often the best strategy, especially for interactive applications.

Use sequences   Oracle sequence generators exist to supply applications with unique sequence numbers in an efficient and nonblocking manner. The alternative approach of keeping next key values in a control table leads to a high degree of lock contention for that table. Sequence generators do have some small drawbacks—in particular it is possible to "lose" sequence numbers when a transaction rolls back. However, unless you have a truly compelling reason to do otherwise, use sequence generators—and not a control table—to generate key values.

Use FOR UPDATE wisely   The FOR UPDATE clause of the SELECT statement allows rows to be locked as they are selected. This is a powerful and useful clause but can lead to performance problems if it is not used wisely. In particular, SELECT statements that use FOR UPDATE may lead to response time problems because all rows must be locked before the first row can be returned. Also, every row that matches the where clause is locked even if only a few are fetched, and this might result in too many rows being locked and consequent lock contention.

Beware of unindexed foreign keys   Oracle's row-level locking facility removes many of the locking conflicts that occur in RDBMSs with page- or block-level locking. However, there are a few circumstances in which row-level locking can break down. The most common circumstance is the case of the unindexed foreign key constraint.

Oracle may lock the entire parent table during an update to the child table if a foreign key index does not exist. Therefore, you should index foreign key constraints if you know that the child table will be updated frequently and if table locks on the parent table are likely to cause problems.

HINT: USE PARTITIONING FOR LARGE TABLES

Partitioning allows a single table or index to be implemented as multiple database segments. This approach has a number of advantages:

❑   Parallel UPDATE and DELETE can only be performed on partitioned objects.
❑   Many maintenance operations can be performed on individual partitions, reducing or eliminating downtime.

- ❏ Partitioning can allow you to remove old rows simply by dropping the nominated partition. Deleting the same number of rows might be impractical.
- ❏ It is possible to restrict certain queries to a subset of partitions, thus reducing the overhead of what would otherwise have been a scan of the entire table. This is called partition elimination.
- ❏ Joining two similarly partitioned tables can be performed efficiently in parallel.

Oracle provides three partitioning schemes:

- ❏ Range partitioning allocates rows to partitions based on the values of a column. This is typically used, for instance, to partition on sales date so that each quarter's sales are located in a separate partition. However, such partitions may vary substantially in size, which diminishes the advantages of parallel operations.
- ❏ Hash partitioning allocates rows to partitions based on a hash computation of a column value. This usually results in an even distribution of rows in each partition but does not provide some of the advantages of range partitioning, such as partition elimination and rapid purging of old data.
- ❏ Composite partitioning partitions data first by range and then into subpartitions by hash. If done carefully, this can deliver the benefits of both range and hash partitioning schemes.

HINT: CONSIDER PL/SQL FOR TRICKY SQL

SQL is a nonprocedural language that is admirably suited for most data retrieval and manipulation tasks. However, there are many circumstances in which a procedural approach will yield better results. In these circumstances, the PL/SQL language (or possibly Java) can be used in place of standard SQL.

Although it's not possible to categorize exhaustively all the situations in which PL/SQL can be used in place of standard SQL, it's possible that PL/SQL is a valid alternative when

- ❏ There is little or no requirement to return large quantities of data (for instance, UPDATE transactions or when retrieving only a single value or row).
- ❏ Standard SQL requires more resources than seems logically required and no combination of hints seem to work. This is particularly likely if there are some implicit characteristics of the data that the optimizer cannot "understand" or where the SQL is particularly complex.
- ❏ You have a clear idea of how the data should be retrieved and processed but can't implement your algorithm using standard SQL.

Some of the specific circumstances in which PL/SQL was found to improve performance within this book are as follows:

❏ Determining second highest values
❏ Performing range lookups for tables that have a LOW_VALUE and HIGH_VALUE column
❏ Performing correlated updates where the same table is referenced within the WHERE and SET clauses of an UPDATE statement with a subquery within the SET clause

PL/SQL triggers can also be invaluable when implementing denormalization.

SQL TUNING QUICK TIPS

This section lists the boxed hints that appear throughout the book. These hints emphasize critical recommendations leading from the more detailed discussion included within the main text. Although these hints may be of some use on their own, I urge you to read the corresponding section of the book before implementing the advice.

CHAPTER 1: INTRODUCTION TO SQL TUNING

❏ SQL tuning is almost always a cost-effective exercise. It helps avoid costly hardware upgrades and improves the scalability and performance of applications.
❏ As with most tuning and quality assurance processes, SQL tuning is less expensive and can result in greater improvements the earlier it is addressed within the application development life cycle. However, SQL tuning is still an effective measure at any stage and can often be the only useful tuning measure available for production systems.
❏ Although experience and good techniques can hasten the SQL tuning process, SQL tuning remains an iterative process in which several improvements may need to be tested before the optimal SQL is found. Effective measurement is essential to ensure that each change can be evaluated accurately.
❏ Try to establish a productive environment in which to tune your SQL. Obtain realistic or representative data volumes for your key tables. Ensure that application and database design information is at hand and that tuning tools are available.

CHAPTER 4: SQL PROCESSING INTERNALS

❏ Parsing is expensive, and excessive parsing defeats scalability. Minimize parse overhead by reusing cursors and by implementing bind variables in your applications.

CHAPTER 5: THE OPTIMIZER

❏ The cost-based optimizer includes many sophisticated algorithms designed to improve the performance of your SQL and is vastly superior to the rule-based optimizer. All new applications should be developed against the cost-based optimizer. Existing applications that are still using rule-based optimization should consider a migration to the cost-based optimizer.

❏ When using the cost-based optimizer, collect optimizer statistics regularly or when table volumes are known to have changed.

❏ The DBMS_STATS offers more powerful methods for collecting table statistics than the ANALYZE command. In particular, it allows statistics to be gathered in parallel.

❏ You can use stored outlines to ensure that an ideal execution plan for a statement does not change. However, EXPLAIN PLAN might not reflect this stored execution plan.

❏ You can use hints or optimizer tricks to change the execution plan for an SQL statement. However, hints are more powerful and are self-documenting and should be used as a first preference.

CHAPTER 8: TUNING TABLE ACCESS

Table scan versus indexed access

❏ There is no "one-size fits all" break-even point for indexed versus table scan access. If only a few rows are being accessed, then the index will be preferred. If almost all the rows are being accessed, then the full-table scan will be preferred. In between these two extremes your "mileage" will vary.

❏ Help the cost-based optimizer choose between indexes and table scans by keeping your tables analyzed, specifying the correct optimizer goal, using histograms where appropriate, and using hints.

❏ Create column histograms on indexed columns where there are only a few distinct values but where some values are very infrequent. Remember that histograms cannot be used to search for a value supplied to the query via a bind variable.

❏ Histograms can improve the optimization of range scans or lookups on unevenly distributed data. However, bind variables should usually be used to reduce parsing in transaction processing environments, and histograms can't be used in conjunction with bind variables.

Effective use of indexes

❑ Oracle will not use an index if the query condition is "not equals" (!=). If you think the query could benefit from an indexed approach, reword the query using IN, OR, or ">". You may still need to use hints or a column histogram to encourage Oracle to use the appropriate index.

❑ Avoid searching for NULL values in an indexed column. Instead, define the column as NOT NULL with a default value.

❑ You can use an index to find values that are NOT NULL. If most values are NULL, the index will be very small and efficient because NULL values are not indexed.

❑ Use hints or column histograms to avoid full-table scans when searching for a rare value in an otherwise nonselective index.

❑ Avoid applying functions or operations to indexed columns in the WHERE clause. Instead, apply functions to the values against which the indexed column is being compared.

❑ When you can't avoid applying functions to indexed columns in the WHERE clause, consider using functional indexes based on the same functions.

❑ Bitmap indexes can still perform well when a column has many thousand distinct values. However, storage required for the bitmap index will rise rapidly.

❑ Index organized tables can offer advantages for tables where all or most queries are resolved by an index scan on the primary key and/or where you want to split the data into frequently and infrequently accessed columns.

❑ Where possible, optimize a query by including all of the columns contained in the WHERE clause within a concatenated index.

❑ Carefully determine the best order of columns in a concatenated index. Columns that are subject to being queried make good candidates for the first column in the index. If the index is created with the COMPRESS flag, placing low cardinality columns first will improve the compression and improve scan performance.

❑ If you can't construct concatenated indexes to suit all your queries, you may be able to use index merges. However, be aware that indexes with few values cannot be merged efficiently if they are B*-tree indexes.

❑ For range scans (greater than, less than) on a selective index, the use of bind variables will promote an index. If this is inappropriate, you should change it using hints. If you provide literals, the optimizer will perform a more well-informed decision (but the parse overhead will increase). Column histograms will also help if the data is not evenly distributed between maximum and minimum values.

❏ Range lookups—a matching range in a table that contains "high" and "low" values—may fail to optimize successfully with standard SQL. In these cases, a PL/SQL or other procedural approach may be necessary.

❏ Oracle can use indexes to resolve queries involving the LIKE operator only if there is not a leading wildcard (%,_) in the search string.

❏ Queries involving OR conditions can be difficult for the cost-based optimizer to resolve efficiently. Sometimes (but not always) a histogram can help. Otherwise, FULL or USE_CONCAT and INDEX hints can be used to select the best execution plan.

❏ Use the row count column of tkprof output to highlight indexes that are inefficient. A higher than expected value in the row count column may indicate that not all columns in a concatenated index are being used.

❏ Take advantage of the index fast full scan for queries that can be resolved by reading all the rows in an index. Counting the number of rows in the table is a perfect example.

Optimizing bit map indexes

❏ The performance of bitmap indexes can sometimes be improved by increasing BITMAP_MERGE_AREA_SIZE or by applying the MINIMIZE RECORDS_ PER_BLOCK clause to the underlying table.

Optimizing hash clusters

❏ Ensure that you only use hash clusters for static tables, or be prepared to rebuild the hash cluster periodically. When deciding on a hash cluster, ensure that the SIZE and HASHKEYS parameters are correctly configured.

Optimizing index organized tables

❏ Think carefully about how to split your index organized table. Data in the index segment will be quicker to access, while data in the overflow segment may take much longer to access. However, if you place too much data in the index segment you risk adding another level to the B*-tree and losing the advantages of index organized tables.

Optimizing table scans

❏ Tables that contain substantially fewer rows than they did in the past may require a rebuild in order to reset the high-water mark. This will reduce the number of blocks required for a full-table scan.

❏ If a table is subject to frequent table scans, ensure that PCTFREE is no higher than necessary, especially if the table is not updated. Also consider increasing PCTUSED, especially if there are not high rates of concurrent inserts.

❏ For tables in which full-table scan performance is critical, consider locating long, infrequently accessed columns in a separate table. For LOBs and CLOBs, consider the DISABLE STORAGE IN ROW clause.

❏ Table scans do not usually experience good hit rates in Oracle's buffer cache. If you need better hit rates for table scans you may be able to improve the hit rate by using the CACHE clause, the CACHE hint, or by exploiting multiple buffer caches.

❏ The SAMPLE clause can be used to get approximate answers to aggregate queries that would normally require a full-table scan.

❏ Use array fetches to retrieve batches of rows from the database in a single call. This will reduce both database and network overhead. In general, array fetch can provide an about order of magnitude (10 times), an improvement in bulk queries.

❏ When you need to optimize for response time rather than throughput, be cautious of the FOR UPDATE and ORDER BY clauses—these can make optimization for the first row difficult or impossible.

CHAPTER 9: TUNING JOINS AND SUBQUERIES

Choosing the best join method

❏ The nested loops join method suits joins involving subsets of table data where there is a supporting index.

❏ The hash-join algorithm almost always outperforms the sort-merge algorithm. However, the cost-based optimizer often favors the sort-merge join, so you may need to use the USE_HASH to take advantage of the faster hash join.

❏ The cost-based optimizer will favor sort-merge joins when your optimizer goal is set to CHOOSE or ALL_ROWS. If you are primarily concerned with response time, set your optimizer goal to FIRST_ROWS. The cost-based optimizer will then favor the nested loop join.

Choosing the best join order

❏ The most important consideration in determining the join order is to eliminate unwanted rows as early as possible. Beyond this, both hash join and nested loops work best when joining a larger table to a smaller table. The sort-merge join is not affected by the order in which a larger and smaller table are joined.

Optimizing hash joins

❏ Increases in the value of HASH_AREA_SIZE will improve the performance of hash joins up to the point at which the hash table fits into memory. Improving HASH_IO_MULTIBLOCK_IO_COUNT may improve the performance I/O-bound hash joins up to an operating-system-dependent limit, although very large hash joins may perform better with a medium value.

Clustering tables to improve join performance

❏ Clustering tables can improve performance when the tables are joined but can degrade the performance of many other operations on the tables. Only consider clustering tables if they are almost always accessed together. Even then, consider alternatives such as denormalization.

Special joins: outer, star, and hierarchical

❏ The outer join operation limits the join orders that the optimizer can consider. Don't perform outer joins needlessly.

❏ Consider using Oracle's STAR query optimization when joining a very large fact table to smaller, unrelated dimension tables. You will need a concatenated index on the fact table and may need to specify the STAR hint.

❏ When performing a hierarchical query using the CONNECT BY operator, ensure that both the START WITH and CONNECT BY clauses can be resolved using an index.

❏ If selecting only part of a hierarchy, eliminate rows using the START WITH clause rather than the WHERE clause. The WHERE clause will be processed only after the entire hierarchy has been built.

Subqueries

❏ For a correlated subquery, ensure that the subquery is completely optimized. If possible, allow the subquery to be resolved by a direct index lookup without a table access.

❏ Correlated subqueries can often be more efficiently executed using a procedural approach—perhaps by using PL/SQL.

❏ When using EXISTS, either ensure that the subquery can be executed efficiently or use a semijoin optimization. Ideally, the subquery should be able to be satisfied using an index lookup only.

Semijoins and Antijoins

❏ If you have an EXISTS subquery without a supporting index, use the HASH_SJ or MERGE_SJ hints to resolve the query as a semijoin. You can also use the ALWAYS_SEMI_JOIN configuration parameter, but this could have a slight negative effect for some indexed EXISTS subqueries.

❏ If using rule-based optimization, avoid using NOT IN to perform an antijoin. Use NOT EXISTS instead.

❏ The MINUS operator can be used to perform an antijoin efficiently. However, there are restrictions on the columns that can be returned in the query.

❏ When wanting to retrieve all rows in a table except those not found in another table (an antijoin), try to take advantage of Oracle's antijoin hints. Otherwise (if using rule-based optimization or prior to Oracle 7.3), use NOT EXISTS subqueries in preference to NOT IN subqueries.

CHAPTER 10: SORTS, AGGREGATES, AND SET OPERATIONS

Sorting

❏ Increasing SORT_AREA_SIZE can reduce the chances that a disk sort will occur and—within certain ranges of values—can improve the performance of memory sorts.

❏ Setting a lower SORT_AREA_RETAINED_SIZE parameter does not cause sort memory to be released to the operating system. Make sure your setting for SORT_AREA_SIZE does not exceed the memory capacity of your system.

❏ If disk sorts are occurring, the configuration of the temporary tablespace and the database can be critical to ensure that contention for disk sort areas does not occur.

❏ The cost-based optimizer will try to avoid sorting if the optimizer_ mode=FIRST_ROWS.

❏ Don't use the DISTINCT operator unless you are sure that you need it. DISTINCT will usually perform a sort. Use UNION ALL in preference to UNION unless you really need to eliminate duplicates.

❏ Using an index to avoid a sort will generally lead to better response time (time to retrieve the first row) when retrieving rows in order. But such a plan will usually lead to much worse throughput (time to retrieve all rows).

❏ When performing a sort based on a full-table scan, consider using the parallel query option to improve scan and sort performance, but watch for increased system overhead.

Aggregate functions

❏ The fastest way to get the maximum or minimum value for a column is to have a B*-tree index on that column.

❏ Oracle 8.1.6 analytic functions can help avoid procedural or expensive self-join solutions to many common business and analytic queries.

❏ If using an index to optimize a GROUP BY, a fast full-index scan solution will probably result in better throughput, while an index full scan solution will probably result in better response time.

❏ Where possible, use the WHERE clause in place of the HAVING clause to eliminate rows before they are grouped. Use the HAVING clause with group functions only.

Set operations

❏ If you don't need to eliminate duplicate rows in a UNION operation, use UNION ALL instead of UNION. This will avoid a potentially expensive sort.

❏ When performing an intersect, consider recoding the statement to a join, using either a nested loops or hash-join method.

❏ When performing a MINUS operation, consider recoding the statement into an ANTI-JOIN using the HASH_AJ hint.

CHAPTER 11: PARALLEL SQL

❏ Parallel processing can only help when your machine configuration is suitable. Increasing parallelism beyond the capabilities of your hardware can actually harm performance.

❏ Use the OTHER_TAG column of the PLAN_TABLE to determine the parallelism of each step in your SQL. Explain your SQL using a tool that makes good use of this column. Beware of the PARALLEL_FROM_SERIAL tag, which may point to a serial bottleneck.

❏ You can query the V$PQ_TQSTAT table to determine the actual degree of parallelism used in your last parallel query and to ensure that there was a good load balance across parallel query slaves.

❏ Configure your database for parallel query. Ensure that your data is spread across multiple disk devices, there are sufficient CPUs and memory, and parallel configuration parameters are set appropriately.

❏ Don't use parallel query if your host computer is not suitably configured or if you are liable to severely degrade the performance of other users.

❏ Set a degree of parallelism for your query that will maximize your throughput without having an unacceptable impact on other users.

❏ Use the ANALYZE command regularly on tables involved in parallel query.

❏ In complex queries, try to parallelize all query execution steps. Use the OTHER_TAG column of the plan table to highlight execution steps that are processed serially. Watch out for tables that are set to NOPARALLEL but are joined to tables that are parallel by default.

❏ INTERSECT and MINUS operations do not parallelize—use equivalent join and antijoin alternatives if you wish to parallelize these operations.

CHAPTER 12: OPTIMIZING DML

❏ If a DML statement contains a WHERE clause or a subquery, ensure that the subquery or WHERE clause is optimized using the standard query optimization principles.

❏ Indexes always add to the overhead of INSERT and DELETE statements and may add to the overhead of UPDATE statements. Avoid overindexing, especially on columns that are frequently updated.

❏ Bitmap indexes usually have more maintenance overhead than B*-tree indexes, especially if there are a lot of distinct values for the column. Bitmap indexes also add a much greater lock overhead when there is concurrent DML activity.

❏ When removing all rows from a table, use TRUNCATE in preference to DELETE.

❏ If deleting stale rows from large tables is a significant overhead, consider creating a table that is range partitioned on a date column that is used to identify rows to be purged. You can then remove these rows by dropping the partition in question.

❏ Use referential integrity constraints to maintain self-consistency in your data, but be aware of the performance impact for DML statements. Ensure that you have an index on the foreign key columns to avoid costly full-table locks.

❏ Use the array INSERT facility whenever possible to improve bulk insert performance.

❏ Consider direct mode insert—using the APPEND hint—when there is contention for blocks in the buffer cache or when you want to insert into an unpartitioned table in parallel.

❏ You can use UNLOGGED to reduce the redo log overhead for INSERT operations. But you will need to make a special effort to ensure that the objects involved can be recovered in the event that the database needs recovery.

❏ Use the FREELISTS clause of the CREATE TABLE statement to create multiple freelists for tables that experience heavy concurrent insert activity.

❏ Discrete transactions can improve the performance of certain small transactions in very specific circumstances. However, they can prevent successful execution of long-running queries.

❏ Since committing a transaction involves an I/O overhead, COMMIT infrequently during bulk updates.

❏ Ensure that you minimize your locking contention by COMMITING transactions appropriately, avoiding user interaction while locks are held, and carefully considering your locking strategy.

CHAPTER 13: VLDB AND WAREHOUSING

Partitioning

❏ Partition views can be useful if the percentage of rows that you are retrieving is too high to allow an index to be helpful, but you are retrieving substantially less than the entire table. However, partition views can be difficult to administer. Oracle8 partitioned tables are usually a superior solution.

❏ In general, local (partitioned) indexes help release the maximum benefits of partitioning. Avoid global indexes on partitioned tables.

❏ Consider a range partitioning when you want to take advantage of partition elimination for range queries or purge historical data by quickly dropping a partition.

❑ Consider hash partitioning when balance of rows between partitions is more important than the benefits of partition elimination or purging data by dropping a partition. Remember to make the number of partitions a power of 2.

❑ If you need range partitioning but need good balance in the sizes of each partition, consider subpartitioning by hash (composite partitioning). You will probably need to adjust the number of subpartitions to achieve a good balance.

Snapshots and materialized views

❑ Consider using snapshots to facilitate complex queries on large tables where the results do not have to be entirely current.

❑ Use snapshot logs and the fast refresh mechanism when a minority of rows in the source table are changed. If a majority of rows are changed, avoid the overhead of the snapshot log and use complete refreshes, which will be faster than "fast" refreshes anyway.

❑ Query rewrite will occur only if the QUERY_REWRITE_ENABLED parameter is TRUE and if the user has the QUERY REWRITE privilege.

❑ Because of the overhead of materialized views and the risk of incorrect results if the ON COMMIT clause is not used, materialized views with query rewrite are really only suitable to relatively static environments such as data warehouses.

CHAPTER 14: USING AND TUNING PL/SQL

Uses of PL/SQL

❑ Consider using PL/SQL triggers to denormalize your tables. PL/SQL triggers can automate and improve the efficiency of denormalization.

❑ PL/SQL can offer substantial improvements to UPDATE and DELETE transactions, particularly in the case of a correlated UPDATE or an UPDATE based on a join query.

PL/SQL code tuning

❑ When possible, reduce the number of iterations of a PL/SQL loop. Each loop consumes CPU, so EXIT the loop if there is no need to continue. Also reduce processing within the loop by moving "loop invariant" statements outside of the loop if possible.

❑ If an IF statement is to be executed repeatedly, placing the most commonly satisfied condition earlier in the IF structure may optimize performance.

❑ Avoid recursive programming. Iterative solutions will almost always outperform recursive solutions.

Efficient database access with PL/SQL

❏ When processing or querying a large number of rows, take advantage of Oracle8i array processing using the FORALL and BULK COLLECT clauses.

❏ It is sometimes possible to achieve parallel execution of PL/SQL functions by embedding them in a parallel SQL statement.

❏ Use the WHERE CURRENT OF clause, or store and use the ROWID, when you want to modify a row you have just retrieved within a cursor.

❏ Use the RETURNING INTO clause when you need to report on rows processed by a DML statement.

❏ Always consider the NOCOPY clause when passing large PL/SQL tables as arguments to functions or procedures.

❏ Take advantage of PL/SQL packages to reduce dynamic recompilation of sorted subprograms. Consider pinning large or performance critical packages in the shared pool.

Triggers

❏ Make use of the OF COLUMNS and WHEN clauses of the CREATE TRIGGER statement to ensure that your trigger only fires when necessary.

❏ Don't use FOR EACH ROW triggers unnecessarily. If using FOR EACH ROW triggers, use AFTER triggers in preference to BEFORE triggers.

General improvements

❏ Use explicit cursors in preference to implicit cursors created by SELECT statements embedded in PL/SQL, especially if the query might involve a full-table scan.

❏ Using PL/SQL tables to cache frequently accessed values can improve performance markedly.

❏ Take advantage of temporary tables when your PL/SQL program needs to store data that doesn't need to persist beyond the session or the transaction.

Dynamic SQL with PL/SQL

❏ If you go to the effort of using DBMS_SQL, make sure you exploit bind variables and array processing.

❏ Where possible, make sure you implement bind variables with the USING clause in EXECUTE IMMEDIATE.

❏ Although it is more complex to implement, dynamic SQL using DBMS_SQL can often outperform dynamic SQL implemented using EXECUTE IMMEDIATE. This is particularly true when array processing or parse overhead is important.

❏ Take advantage of the DBMS_PROFILER package to identify "hot spots" in your PL/SQL code.

CHAPTER 15: USING AND TUNING ORACLE JAVA

PL/SQL versus Java

❏ Use Java stored procedures in preference to PL/SQL stored procedures for computationally expensive tasks, particularly those involving floating point arithmetic.

❏ PL/SQL stored procedures will typically outperform JDBC stored procedures for database-intensive routines.

❏ If performance is the only consideration, use Java stored procedures for computationally intensive routines and PL/SQL for database-intensive routines.

Optimizing JDBC

❏ Always use PreparedStatements with bind variables for statements that are executed repeatedly.

❏ If you know you are going to reexecute a PreparedStatement many times, declare it as a public object and don't issue the close() method until after the last execution.

❏ For JDBC programs that are running outside of a stored procedure, disable the autocommit behavior with the setAutoCommit method.

❏ Always use the Oracle array extensions setDefaultRowPrefetch and set ExecteBatch when fetching or modifying multiple rows.

❏ Using the Oracle JDBC extensions—including Oracle datatype classes and the defineColumnType methods—can result in small but significant performance improvements.

Optimizng SQLJ

❏ Make sure you size the SQLJ statement cache to a value that is appropriate for your application.

❏ Make sure you use SQLJ batching to improve the performance of bulk inserts or other DML. This facility is only available in 8.1.6.

CHAPTER 16: ORACLE OBJECT TYPES

VARRAYs, Nested Tables and Object types

❏ In-line VARRAYs significantly increase row length and degrade full scans. If full scan performance is critical, then store the VARRAY out of line. Other object solutions (nested tables, object tables) also slightly increase row length and degrade scan performance.

❏ When using nested tables of nontrivial size, strongly consider creating an index on (at least) the NESTED_TABLE_ID column of the nested table segment.

❏ Nested tables make accessing the "nested" data across parent rows very inefficient. VARRAYs have a similar drawback when trying to access individual elements across multiple rows.

❏ If you require efficient navigation from REF columns to the referenced object row, consider using the WITH ROWID clause to store the column's ROWID in the REF column.

❏ In Oracle 8i, it is almost always best to create a nested table in an index-organized table segment. This improves both performance and storage.

❏ EXPLAIN PLAN is the most fundamental tool for tuning SQL statements. However, be aware that it can provide incomplete information about object and nested table accesses.

LOBs and LONGS

❏ Because LOBs can be stored in a separate segment, they will have little or no effect on full-table scan performance.

❏ Using the CACHE setting improves LOB retrieval time, although possibly at the expense of other data stored in the cache.

❏ LOB types (CLOB, BLOB, BFILE) allow efficient random access to any part of the data, whereas for LONG datatype, the entire structure must always be read.

CHAPTER 17: MISCELLANEOUS TOPICS

Views

❏ Embed hints in views to influence SQL generated by third-party query or development tools that generate SQL over which you have no control.

Distributed SQL

❏ Creating a view of a table join at a remote node can cause the join to be executed at the remote node rather than at the driving site. This may improve performance if conditions are suitable.

❏ Choose the driving site for your distributed SQL carefully. The ideal driving site is the site with the most powerful processing capabilities, the most local data, and the most recent version of Oracle.

Sequences

❏ When creating sequences, specify a cache value that reflects the frequency with which the sequence will be accessed. Do not specify the ORDER option unless you are in a parallel server environment.

❏ Use sequence generators in preference to sequence tables unless there is a definite requirement that no unique key values be skipped. When using a sequence generator, ensure that the CACHE value is appropriate and consider fetching sequence numbers in batches in busy transaction processing environments.

DECODE

❏ Consider using DECODE to compile aggregate statistics for expressions that are too complex for a GROUP BY clause. You can aggregate ranges by using the SIGN function.

Optimizing DML

❏ Consider using the NOLOGGING option when creating temporary tables or indexes. Be aware that objects created with the NOLOGGING option will not be restorable until they are included in a backup.

❏ Using parallel and unlogged options in conjunction is the fastest way to create tables from subqueries and indexes.

Optimizing V$ queries

❏ Indexes on the V$ tables can only be used for exact lookups and will be disabled if a function is applied to either side of the equality condition.

❏ Because there are no statistics on V$ tables, the optimizer is unable to determine a proper join order or method. You need to use hints to force an optimal join order.

CHAPTER 18: APPLICATION DESIGN ISSUES

❏ Build performance tuning into your data modeling and application design process. Define performance requirements in the system requirements specification and measure performance during the build phase, or even earlier, by using prototype transactions.

Logical to physical modeling

❏ Don't create a physical model that is a one-to-one representation of the logical model. Take the time to build a physical model that allows your application to reach its full performance potential. Remember that time spent during physical modeling is likely to be repaid many times during production tuning.

❏ When implementing tables derived from subtypes, avoid implementing both supertype and subtype tables. Instead, implement a single table for all subtypes, or multiple subtables without a supertype table.

❏ Where possible, use numeric artificial keys, populated by sequences, in preference to natural keys comprising concatenated or nonnumeric columns.

❏ Use VARCHAR2s in preference to CHARs in order to reduce the row length and optimize table scans unless the risk of row chaining is excessive.

❏ Don't use LONG or LOB datatypes in your design unless you have fully considered the benefits and limitations and have considered alternative storage options. LOBs should generally be used in preference to LONG data.

❏ Don't define a column as nullable if it is expected that queries will be constructed that will search for the NULL values. Instead, define the column as NOT NULL with a default.

Denormalization

❏ Consider replicating columns to avoid excessive joins in critical queries. This can be very effective when the denormalized data is stored on static lookup tables.

❏ Queries that perform aggregate operations can be very resource intensive. Consider maintaining denormalized aggregate information, possibly by using materialized views.

❏ Maintain redundant columns with derived data if you are required to perform indexed searches on derived values. In Oracle8i, ensure that a functional index is not a more efficient approach.

❏ If a large table is expected to be subject to frequent table scans, consider moving long, infrequently accessed columns to a separate subtable to reduce row length and improve table scan performance.

❏ Use database triggers to maintain denormalized data in preference to application code. Database triggers reduce the risk of inconsistent denormalized data, simplify application code, and will often perform more efficiently.

Application design

❏ Build the ability to enable SQL_TRACE into your application. Tag the trace files by issuing a dummy SQL statement.

❏ Build into your application the ability to report on critical performance indicators. Consider the use of profiling tools to determine the time spent in various subroutines.

❏ Choose a locking strategy that is right for your application. When possible, implement the optimistic locking strategy, which tends to reduce the duration of locks.

❏ Caching frequently accessed data from small- or medium-sized static tables can be very effective in improving program performance. However, beware of memory utilization and program complexity issues.

❏ Carefully consider the break-up of application processing between client-based processing and server-based PL/SQL stored programs. Keep in mind the level of user interaction and database processing required by each transaction and the relative power of client and server hardware.

❏ Ensure that long-running batch jobs can make use of available processing power by running in parallel.

CHAPTER 19: ORACLE SERVER DESIGN

Disk Requirements

❏ The number of disk devices available to your database determines the maximum I/O rate that can be achieved. Try to calculate the likely I/O rates and use these rates to estimate the number of disk devices required by your application. Redo logs should be on a dedicated device if there is significant update activity.

❏ If considering a RAID 5–based solution, give preference to RAID arrays that are configured with a nonvolatile cache. Such a cache can reduce the write I/O overhead associated with RAID 5.

Multiple CPUs

❏ Because of the scalability deficiencies of multi-CPU systems, it is better to have a smaller number of more powerful CPUs than to have a large number of less powerful CPUs. Don't assume that doubling the number of CPUs will double the processing capacity.

Physical database layout

❏ Ensure that your database block size is at least as large as your operating system block size.

❏ Reduce your disk read overhead by adequately sizing your buffer cache.

❏ To maximize transaction processing performance, locate redo logs on a fast dedicated disk device.

❏ If running in archivelog mode and in a high-update environment, allocate an additional dedicated device (for a total of two) for the redo logs and another dedicated device (or devices) for the archive destination.

❏ Use some form of striping for your database files, but avoid RAID 5 unless your write activity is very low or the disk array has a nonvolatile cache. Oracle striping can be used if operating striping is not available.

❏ Under the UNIX or Windows operating systems, consider the use of raw devices for databases with very high I/O requirements.

❏ Optimize database writer performance by striping database files across multiple devices and enabling some form of parallel database write capability. Asynchronous or list I/O is preferred. If these facilities are not available, create multiple database writers with the DBWR_IO_SLAVES parameter.

❏ Make sure that the tablespace that holds temporary segments is created with the TEMPORARY clause of the CREATE TABLESPACE.

CHAPTER 20: ORACLE SERVER TUNING

Operating system bottlenecks

❏ If you observe a shortage of free memory, swapping, or excessive paging, you probably have a memory bottleneck. Acquire more memory or take action to reduce memory requirements.

❏ Ensure that no disk devices are forming a bottleneck for your system. Spread data files across multiple devices and ensure that the redo logs are on fast dedicated devices.

❏ If your application is CPU bound, consider reducing CPU load by tuning SQL or eliminating unnecessary parsing. If adding CPU, remember that the benefit of additional CPUs diminishes as the number of CPUs added increases.

Critical performance ratios

❏ To improve the buffer cache hit ratio, increase the number of buffer cache blocks with the DB_BLOCK_BUFFERS configuration parameter.

❏ To increase the get hit rate in the library cache, ensure that bind variables rather than literals are used in your SQL statements. Beware of disabling column histograms.

❏ Low hit rates for the library cache pin hit ratio (<99%) or for the dictionary cache hit ratio (<95%) probably indicate that the shared pool is too small. Increase the size of the shared pool with the SHARED_POOL configuration parameter.

❏ A high value for the chained fetch ratio (>0.1%) suggests a need to rebuild tables with a higher value for PCTFREE.

❏ If both the parse/execute ratio and the CPU parse overhead are high, then you have a strong incentive to reduce the parse overhead of your application. Use bind variables, reuse SQL cursors, or try enabling a session cursor cache.

❏ Consider increasing the value of SORT_AREA_SIZE if you have a high disk sort ratio.

Analyzing wait events

❏ Log buffer space waits suggest that either the log buffer is too small or the redo log file layout is suboptimal.

❏ Log file switch waits for checkpoint, archiving, or completion can indicate that your redo log and archive log configuration needs improvement.

❏ Buffer busy waits usually indicate that heavily inserted tables should be re-created with multiple free lists or that there are insufficient rollback segments.

❏ Free buffer and write complete waits often indicate inefficiencies in the database writer process or untuned disk I/O.

❏ Enqueue waits occur when a process is waiting to obtain a lock. This may mean contention for specific rows in the database, table locks resulting from unindexed foreign keys, or contention for Oracle internal locks.

Latches

❏ Contention for the cache buffer lru chain and cache buffer chain latches can occur if a database sustains very high physical or logical I/O rates. Reduce I/O rates by tuning SQL or increasing the size of the buffer cache. Increasing the values of DB_BLOCK_LRU_LATCHES may help.

❏ Contention for library cache and library cache pin latches can occur when there are heavy parsing or SQL execution rates. Misses on the library cache latch are usually a sign of excessive reparsing of nonsharable SQL.

❏ High miss rates on the redo copy latch are normal and do not usually indicate serious latch contention.

❏ If you encounter latch contention and have spare CPU capacity, consider increasing the value of SPIN_COUNT. If CPU resources are at full capacity, consider decreasing the value of SPIN_COUNT.

Other

❏ If sessions are waiting to make entries in the rollback segments, increase the number or size of rollback segments. Set the OPTIMAL size of the rollback segment so that dynamic extension and contraction occurs only rarely.

❏ Ensure that the number of dispatchers, parallel servers, and shared servers is properly configured. Too few servers can degrade the performance of sessions connecting via MTS or parallel servers. Too many servers may overload CPU, disk, or memory resources.

Chapter 3

REVIEW OF SQL

INTRODUCTION

In this chapter, we briefly review the SQL language. This chapter is intended for readers who are relatively new to the SQL language or for those who need to refresh their knowledge of SQL functionality. This chapter is not a comprehensive guide to the facilities of either ANSI standard or Oracle SQL. The topics covered include the following:

- ❑ The history of SQL and the relational data model
- ❑ ANSI standard SQL and Oracle SQL
- ❑ Categories of SQL statements, such as queries, data manipulation and data definition language statements
- ❑ The use of NULL values
- ❑ Grouping of SQL statements into indivisible transactions
- ❑ Types of SQL query operations, including joins, subqueries, set, and aggregate operations
- ❑ The performance impact of the nonprocedural nature of SQL

THE HISTORY OF SQL

PRE-SQL DATABASES

Prior to the development of SQL and the relational model, the predominant models for database systems were the network model and the hierarchical model. The hierarchical model is best represented by a number of successful mainframe-based database packages (IMS is a good example), and the network model is often associated with the CODASYL database standard and such databases as Cullinet.

The hierarchical model represented data as a tree of parent and child records (Figure 3.1). A special language, DL/I, was used to navigate this tree and retrieve records. Since not all data structures can be represented easily by a hierarchy, the special work-arounds had to be developed for some applications.

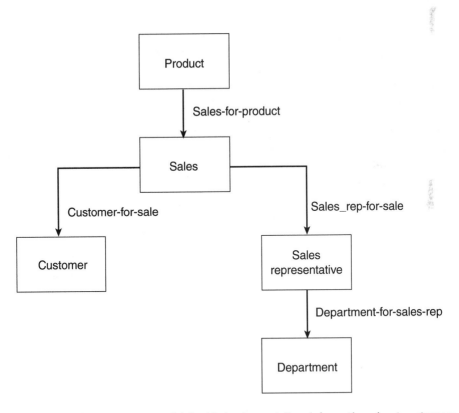

FIGURE 3.1 A hierarchical data model. In this implementation, information about customers, sales representatives, and departments would need to be repeated for each sale.

The network model was capable of more flexibly representing data structures. In the network model, records are linked via pointers (Figure 3.2). For instance, there could be a pointer in a child record to the parent record. This pointer facility made the network model fairly efficient but meant that data could not easily be accessed in ways that had not been anticipated.

Both models presented substantial obstacles to the storage and retrieval of data. In general, only professional programmers could write the programs needed to extract the data. Consequently, long backlogs of report requests built up in MIS departments. Furthermore, the implementation of these databases was very complicated. The data model design essentially determined the queries that could be executed. If a need arose to combine data in an unexpected way, this typically could not be done easily or efficiently.

THE RELATIONAL MODEL

In June 1970, Dr. E. F. Codd presented a paper called "A Relational Model of Data for Large Shared Data Banks." In this paper, Dr. Codd described a model for storing data in computer systems that was based on mathematical set theory.

Although the mathematical underpinning of the relational model is moderately complex, the implementation typically appears fairly simple to the end user—data is represented as a set of two-dimensional tables (or relations). Rows in the table correspond to records in a traditional dataset and columns in the table correspond to fields. One or more of the columns is defined as a primary key, and this column or combination of columns will uniquely define the row.

In a relational database implementation, tables are related by the shared column values and not by pointers or other artificial structures.

Operations in a relational database are not processed record-at-a-time as in other implementations, but instead groups of data are processed in single operations. The output of relational operations is itself a table (or a relation or result set) that can be processed by further relational operations.

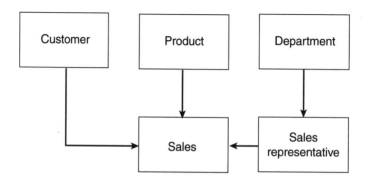

FIGURE 3.2 Network data model.

In the relational model, the logical representation of data is unaffected by its physical representation. That is, users of a relational model can manipulate the data without needing to know the details of its actual location or storage method.

The first relational database system was a prototype called System R, developed by IBM between 1974 and 1978. This system used a language called Structured English QUEry Language, or SEQUEL. In subsequent implementations, the name was shortened to SQL.

The first commercial relational database was Oracle version 2 (version 1 was a prototype) in 1979. IBM released SQL/DS in 1981, followed by the successful mainframe relational database DB/2 in 1983.

Despite misgivings about poor performance, the relational model quickly gained ground over hierarchical, network, and other database models. By 1985, it seemed that a database system could not survive unless it at least claimed to be relational. Many commercial databases of this time that claimed to be relational were, in fact, variations on the network model.

However, as the relational database concepts became more widely understood, most "pretend" relational databases gave way to "nearly" relational databases (few databases can claim to implement all the features of the relational model). Most popular nonrelational databases withered and died fairly rapidly, and the relational model became the dominant paradigm for database systems in the late 1980s and 1990s. Object-oriented database systems appeared to gain some momentum in the mid-1990s, but at the time of this writing (late 2000), the relational database is still by far the dominant database system architecture.

SQL AND THE RELATIONAL MODEL

A relational database is required to support a "data sublanguage" that implements relational operations. In general, this will require that the language

❏ Supports operations on sets or groups of data (i.e., the opposite of record-at-a-time processing).

❏ Is able to refer to data independent of physical storage. For instance, there should be no requirement to specify the name of the file in which a table is stored—the table name alone is sufficient.

❏ Should be nonprocedural. That is, it does not instruct the DBMS how the data is to be retrieved. It only needs to describe unambiguously the data to be retrieved.

SQL is the implementation of such a sublanguage in almost all relational databases, including Oracle.

Prior to the relational model, the language used to access database languages was procedural. That is, the request would include the instructions required to access the data as well as the data to be retrieved. For instance, the following instructions might be required to total all the sales for a customer:

```
MOVE '9999' TO CUSTOMER-NO IN CUSTOMER
OBTAIN CALC CUSTOMER
LOOP:
    OBTAIN NEXT SALES WITHIN CUSTOMER-SALES
    ADD SALE-AMOUNT IN SALES TO SALES-TOTAL
    ... Do something with the data ...
GOTO LOOP
```

The preceding example illustrates two common features of nonrelational databases:

❏ The DBMS is told exactly how to obtain the required data.
❏ Data is processed one row at a time.

By contrast, a relational model must support a nonprocedural language for retrieving information. This means that the language will specify the data to be retrieved but will not specify how the data is to be obtained:

```
SELECT SUM (sale_value)
  FROM sales
 WHERE customer_id = 9999
```

In the first example, the order and exact method of retrieving the rows is specified. In the second example, the order in which the tables is to be accessed is undefined, and the use of indexes or other access methods is left to the discretion of the database management system.

SQL (Structured Query Language) was developed by IBM for the SQL/DS system and is an example of such a nonprocedural data access language. Although *SQL* and *relational database* seem somewhat synonymous today, SQL itself is not part of the relational model, and hence a database may implement a non-SQL access language and still be truly relational.

Although a number of non-SQL access languages were developed (the most notable being QUEL in early versions of INGRES), SQL rapidly gained acceptance as the de facto standard for database access languages.

THE ANSI STANDARD

The ANSI SQL Standards Committee was formed in 1982 and the first standard was released in 1986. This standard is commonly known as SQL. It was amended in 1989 (hence SQL-89). A major revision to the standard, SQL-92, was released in 1992.

The SQL-89 standard provided the basis for most SQL dialects in common use today, including Oracle's. SQL-89 provided definitions of the common SQL operations—queries and data manipulation—but omitted facilities to alter database schema, control security, and implement data integrity. SQL-92 implements many of these features, together with some substantial changes to SQL grammar and capabilities.

TYPES OF SQL STATEMENTS

QUERIES

The most common SQL operation is the query or select statement. This statement implements the standard relational operations such as SELECTION, PROJECTION, and JOIN.

This is the simplified syntax for an Oracle select statement:

```
SELECT (column_list)
  FROM table_list
[WHERE join conditions and query conditions]
[GROUP BY (column_list)]
[HAVING (condition)]
```

The SELECT statement forms the basis for many other SQL operations. SELECT statements are used when creating views, in subqueries, or when creating a table defined as the result of a query.

DATA MANIPULATION LANGUAGE (DML)

DML statements allow data in the database to be added, amended, or deleted. This functionality is provided by the INSERT, UPDATE, and DELETE statements.

INSERT   The INSERT statement adds new rows to a single table. Its simplest syntax is

```
INSERT INTO (table_name)
       (column_list)
VALUES (value_list)
```

Often a query is used to populate rows:

```
INSERT INTO (table_name)
   query_statement
```

For instance,

```
INSERT into customers
        (customer_id,Customer_name , Contact_Surname,
         Contact_Firstname , Address1 ,Address2 ,
         ZipCode,Date_of_birth, PhoneNo,
         Sales_rep_id)
SELECT customer_id,Customer_name , Contact_Surname,
         Contact_Firstname , Address1 ,Address2 ,
         ZipCode,Date_of_birth, PhoneNo, Sales_rep_id
  FROM customer_upload
```

UPDATE   The UPDATE statement allows rows in a single table to be updated. Its simplified syntax is

```
UPDATE (table_name)
   SET (column_list)=(value list)
  WHERE query_condition
```

The value list can be a subquery (see "Subqueries," discussed later). For example,

```
UPDATE customers c
   SET sales_rep_id=
      (SELECT manager_id
         FROM employees
        WHERE surname=c.contact_surname
          AND firstname=c.contact_firstname
          AND date_of_birth=c.date_of_birth)
  WHERE    (contact_surname, contact_firstname,
           date_of_birth) IN
         (SELECT surname,firstname,date_of_birth
           FROM employees)
```

DELETE   The DELETE statement allows one or more rows in a table to be deleted. The syntax is

```
DELETE FROM (table_name)
  WHERE query_condition
```

DATA DEFINITION LANGUAGE (DDL)

The Data Definition Language allows database objects to be created or altered. You should refer to the Oracle Server SQL reference manual for detailed definitions. Some of the Oracle DDL statements are as follows:

- ❏ CREATE TABLE
- ❏ DROP TABLE
- ❏ ALTER TABLE
- ❏ CREATE INDEX
- ❏ DROP INDEX
- ❏ ALTER INDEX
- ❏ CREATE SEQUENCE
- ❏ DROP SEQUENCE
- ❏ CREATE SCHEMA
- ❏ DROP SCHEMA
- ❏ ALTER SCHEMA

Of particular note (from the point of view of SQL tuning) are the DDL statements that are based on queries. In particular, the CREATE TABLE statement and CREATE VIEW statement can be defined in terms of a query. For example,

```
CREATE TABLE customer_sales_totals
    AS
SELECT  customer_name,sum(sale_value) sale_total
  FROM sales s,customers c
 WHERE s.customer_id=c.customer_id
 GROUP by c.customer_name
```

Another DDL statement that is of particular importance to SQL tuning is the CREATE INDEX statement, which is used to index selected rows to improve retrieval performance or to enforce uniqueness.

QUERY OPERATIONS: THE SELECT STATEMENT

SUBQUERIES

A subquery is a SELECT statement that occurs within another SQL statement. Such a nested SELECT statement can be used in a wide variety of SQL contexts, including SELECT, DELETE, UPDATE, and INSERT statements.

The following statement uses a subquery to count the number of employees who share the minimum salary:

```
SELECT count(*)
  FROM employees
 WHERE salary=(SELECT MIN(salary)
                FROM employees)
```

Subqueries may also be used in the FROM clause wherever a table or view definition could appear:

```
SELECT count(*)
  FROM (SELECT * FROM employees
             WHERE department_id=12)
```

CORRELATED SUBQUERY

A correlated subquery is one in which the subquery refers to values in the parent query. A correlated subquery can return the same results as a join but can be used where a join cannot, such as in UPDATE, INSERT, and DELETE statements. For instance, the following statement assigns the sales representative for a customer who is also an employee to the employee's manager. Note the reference in the subquery to the CUSTOMERS table—this is the correlated part of the subquery.

```
UPDATE customers
   SET sales_rep_id=
       (SELECT manager_id
          FROM employees
         WHERE surname=customers.contact_surname
           AND firstname=customers.contact_firstname
           AND date_of_birth=customers.date_of_birth)
  WHERE (contact_surname,contact_firstname,date_of_birth)
        IN
           (SELECT surname,firstname,date_of_birth
              FROM employees)
```

TABLE SPECIFICATIONS IN THE FROM CLAUSE

Table specifications in the FROM clause may take a number of forms.

Simple table specification   This form of the table specification refers to an existing table, view, or snapshot. It has the following form:

[schema.]table_or_view_name[@dblink] [alias]

Schema specifies the name of the schema that contains the object, table_or_view_ name names an existing table or view, dblink specifies a database link to the database that contains the object, and alias specifies a table alias that can be used to qualify column references elsewhere in the SELECT statement.

Subquery   A subquery may be used in place of a table or view name. These subqueries are sometimes referred to as in-line views. For instance,

```
SELECT COUNT(*)
  FROM (SELECT *
          FROM sales
         WHERE department_id=2)
```

Partition specification   The FROM clause may nominate a specific partition. In Oracle 8.0, the PARTITION keyword specifies the partition concerned. In Oracle 8i, the SUBPARTITION clause may also restrict the operation to a subpartition. For instance, the following query counts the number of rows in the partition Q1_98 within the partitioned table SALES_PART:

```
SELECT COUNT(*)
  FROM sales_part PARTITION(q1_98)
```

Collection specification   In Oracle 8.0 or later, a FROM clause may include a collection specification. This will generally be used to expand a nested table or VARRAY into a relational table representation.

In Oracle 8.0 the THE keyword is used to identify the collection expression. For instance, in the following example the SUBJECTS_NT_SCORES table contains a nested table column TEST_SCORE. The query expands the nested table column for a particular SUBJECT_ID and then selects the appropriate ITEM_NUMBER:

```
SELECT s.score
  FROM THE (SELECT test_score
              FROM subjects_nt_scores
             WHERE subject_id=10) s
 WHERE s.item_number=1;
```

In Oracle 8i the TABLE keyword provides a similar functionality:

```
SELECT s.score
  FROM TABLE (SELECT test_score
                FROM subjects_nt_scores
               WHERE subject_id=10) s
 WHERE s.item_number=1
```

Sampling   Oracle 8i allows a random sample of rows to be selected. The sample clause has the following form:

```
FROM table [SAMPLE [BLOCK] percent]
```

SAMPLE returns a random selection of rows amounting to a percent of the table's row count. The BLOCK keyword causes the sampling to be based on a random sample of blocks rather than a random sample of rows.

JOINS

The join operation allows the results from two or more tables to be merged based on some common column values.

Inner join   The inner join is the most common type of join operation. In this join, rows from one table are joined to rows from another table based on some common ("key") values. Rows that have no match in both tables are not included in the results. For instance, the following query links employee and department details:

```
SELECT department_name,surname,salary
  FROM employees e,
       departments d
 WHERE e.department_id=d.department_id
```

Note that a department without employees would not be returned in the result set.

Equijoin and theta join   An equijoin is one in which the equals operator is used to relate two values. This is commonly used to look up a unique key or to join master and detail tables, such as in our previous inner join example. A join that uses an operator other than the equals operator (such as >, BETWEEN, or !=) is called a theta join. The previous query is an example of an equijoin. The following query is an example of a theta join:

```
SELECT customer_id,regionname
  FROM customers c,
       Salesregion s
 WHERE c.phoneno BETWEEN s.lowphoneno AND s.highphoneno
```

Outer join   The outer join allows rows to be included even if they have no match in the other table. Rows that are not found in the outer join table are represented by NULL values. In Oracle, the outer join operator is "(+)". The following query illustrates an outer join—it will return department names even if the department has no employees:

```
SELECT department_name,surname
  FROM departments d,
       employees   e
 WHERE d.department_id=e.department_id(+);
```

Although there can be more than one outer join in a query, each table may be outer joined to only one other table (although this outer join table may itself be outer joined to a third table).

Antijoin It is often required to select all rows from a table that do not have a matching row in some other result set. This is typically implemented using a subquery and the IN or EXISTS clause. The following examples illustrate the anti-join using the EXISTS and IN operators. Each example selects employees who are not also customers.

```
SELECT surname,firstname,date_of_birth
  FROM employees
 WHERE (surname,firstname,date_of_birth) NOT IN
       (SELECT contact_surname,contact_firstname,
               date_of_birth
          FROM customers)


SELECT surname,firstname,date_of_birth
  FROM employees
 WHERE NOT EXISTS
       (SELECT *
          FROM customers
         WHERE contact_surname=employees.surname
           AND contact_firstname=employees.firstname
           AND date_of_birth=employees.date_of_birth)
```

Self-join In a self-join, a table is joined to itself. This is performed in exactly the same manner as any other join. The following example shows the employees table in a self-join to link employees with their manager:

```
SELECT m.surname manager ,e.surname employee
  FROM employees m,
       employees e
 WHERE e.manager_id=m.employee_id
```

Set operations SQL implements a number of operations that deal directly with result sets. These operations, collectively referred to as set operations, allow result sets to be concatenated, subtracted, or overlaid.

The most common of these operations is the UNION operator, which returns the sum of two result sets. By default, duplicates in each result set are eliminated. By contrast, the UNION ALL operation will return the sum of the two result sets, including any duplicates. The following example returns a list of customers and employees. Employees who are also customers will only be listed once:

```
SELECT contact_surname,contact_firstname,date_of_birth
  FROM customers
 UNION
SELECT surname,firstname,date_of_birth
  FROM employees
```

MINUS returns all rows in the first result set that do not appear in the second result set. The following example returns all customers who are not also employees:

```
SELECT contact_surname,contact_firstname,date_of_birth
  FROM customers
 MINUS
SELECT surname,firstname,date_of_birth
  FROM employees
```

INTERSECT returns only the rows that appear in both result sets. The following example returns customers who are also employees:

```
SELECT contact_surname,contact_firstname,date_of_birth
  FROM customers
INTERSECT
SELECT surname,firstname,date_of_birth
  FROM employees
```

All set operations require that the component queries return the same number of columns and that those columns are of a compatible datatype.

Group operations   Aggregate operations allow for summary information to be generated, typically upon groupings of rows. Rows can be grouped using the GROUP BY operator. If this is done, the select list must consist only of columns contained within the GROUP BY clause and aggregate functions. Some of the aggregate functions are as follows:

AVG:	Calculate the average value for the group.
COUNT:	Return the number of rows in the group.
MAX:	Return the maximum value in the group.
MIN:	Return the minimum value in the group.
STDDEV:	Return the standard deviation for the group.
SUM:	Return the total of all values for the group.

The following example generates summary salary information for each department:

```
SELECT department_id, SUM(salary)
  FROM employees
 GROUP BY department_id
```

Hierarchical queries   A hierarchical query is one in which parent and child rows exist in the same table. This is sometimes referred to as the "explosion of parts" query. In a simple self-join, a child row is joined to a parent row. In a hierarchical query, the child is joined to the parent row, the parent row is joined to its parent row, and so on, until the entire hierarchy is exposed. For instance, in the EMPLOYEES table, the column MANAGER_ID points to the EMPLOYEE_ID of the employees' manager. We can easily display the manager for each employee by issuing a self-join:

```
SELECT e.surname employee ,m.surname manager
  FROM employees e,
       employees m
 WHERE e.manager_id=m.employee_id;


EMPLOYEE          MANAGER
---------------   ---------------
RAMPTON           EVANS
STOKES            MILLS
NUTTALL           LEE
LEE               MCDOWELL
......
```

If we want to display the employees in the organizational hierarchy, we can use the hierarchical operators CONNECT BY and START WITH (the RPAD function indents each level of the hierarchy).

```
SELECT   RPAD(' ',LEVEL*3)||surname employee
  FROM   employees
 START   WITH manager_id=0
CONNECT BY PRIOR employee_id=manager_id;
EMPLOYEE
------------------------------
   REID
      GOSLEY
      POOLE
      KEYWORTH
         WALKER
         FRYER
         MILLS
            STOKES
            BURNS
.........
```

This query shows that REID is the senior employee in the hierarchy. WALKER reports to KEYWORTH, who reports to REID, and so on.

LOCKING

The FOR UPDATE clause allows rows retrieved to be locked and thereby to prevent the specified rows from being modified until the transaction is terminated by a COMMIT or ROLLBACK statement. If the NOWAIT modifier is used, then an error will be returned if the rows cannot be locked immediately.

DATA MANIPULATION AND TRANSACTION CONTROL

THE INSERT STATEMENT

The INSERT statement allows rows to be added to a table. Its basic form is as follows:

```
INSERT INTO table_expression
    [(column_list)]
    {VALUES(value_list)
```

Table_expression specifies the table, partition, view, subquery, or table collection into which rows will be inserted. *Column_list* provides an optional list of columns into which data is to be inserted. *Column_list* is only optional if the values clause or subquery contains data for all columns in the same order in which they appear in the table definition. Omitting the column list is generally bad practice.

The VALUES clause contains a list of literals or variables containing the data to be inserted. The variables may be array bind variables, in which case multiple rows may be inserted in a single operation. If the VALUES clause is not specified, then a subquery must be specified that returns the data to be inserted. The subquery may return multiple rows.

THE UPDATE STATEMENT

The UPDATE statement modifies existing data within a database table. It has the following basic form:

```
UPDATE table_expression
        SET [(]column_expression=value_expression
                [,column_expression=value_expression...]
[)]
WHERE where_condition
```

Table_expression specifies the table, partition, view, subquery, or table collection that is to have its rows updated into which rows will be inserted. *Column_* *expression* may be a single column name or a list of columns enclosed in parentheses. Using a column list is convenient when setting multiple columns to the values returned by a subquery. For instance,

```
UPDATE employees c
   SET (manager_id,department_id)
         =(SELECT manager_id,department_id
             FROM departments

             WHERE department_name='BOSTON')
WHERE employee_id=1234
```

The *where_condition* is a standard WHERE clause as described earlier. It may include subqueries.

Correlated updates   A correlated update is one that includes a subquery that contains references to columns in the table being updated. The query is evaluated for each row that is eligible for update. The correlated update is very similar to the correlated subquery described earlier. The following statement executes a correlated update: the subquery within the SELECT statement is executed once for each row in CUSTOMERS that satisfies the WHERE clause:

```
UPDATE customers c
   SET sales_rep_id=
       (SELECT manager_id
          FROM employees
         WHERE surname=c.contact_surname
           AND firstname=c.contact_firstname
           AND date_of_birth=c.date_of_birth)
  WHERE (contact_surname,contact_firstname,date_of_birth)
     IN (SELECT surname,firstname,date_of_birth
          FROM employees)
```

The DELETE statement   The delete statement removes rows from a database table. It has the following form:

```
DELETE [FROM] table_expression
  [WHERE where_condition]
```

Table_expression specifies the table, partition, view, subquery, or table collection from which rows will be deleted. The *where_condition* is a standard WHERE clause as described earlier in this chapter. It may include subqueries.

TRANSACTIONS

Transactions are indivisible units of work that must either be applied to the database in their entirety or not at all. A transaction implicitly commences when a DML statement or transaction control statement (such as SET TRANSACTION) is issued to the database. The following events terminate a transaction:

❑ A COMMIT or ROLLBACK statement.
❑ Program termination. Normal termination generates an implicit COMMIT. Abnormal termination generates an implicit ROLLBACK.
❑ Data Definition Language statements (such as CREATE TABLE) generate an implicit COMMIT. This restricts the use of Data Definition Language statements within transactional entities such as triggers.

Savepoints   Savepoints are named rollback points that allow a transaction to be partially undone. Savepoints are created with the SAVEPOINT command and can be specified within the ROLLBACK command.

Locks   Locks are applied during a transaction implicitly when a row is modified or explicitly by the LOCK TABLE statement or the FOR UPDATE clause. Locks are released when the transaction terminates.

Autonomous Transactions   In Oracle 8i, a PL/SQL program unit may execute within an autonomous transaction. Autonomous transactions operate outside the scope of any transaction that may be current. A COMMIT or ROLLBACK within the autonomous transaction has no effect on the status of the parent transaction.

Triggers   Triggers are stored PL/SQL programs that are initiated when specified DML activities occur (and in Oracle8i, on specified DDL or database events). Triggers can affect DML operations in the following ways:

❑ Triggers can cause valid DML to fail. For instance, a trigger might implement a business rule that prevents updating salaries outside of guidelines.
❑ Triggers can themselves issue DML statements.
❑ INSTEAD OF triggers can be defined on views. These triggers will fire instead of the DML statement on the view. See the following section, "DML Statements on Views."

VIEWS

Views can be thought of as stored queries or virtual tables. A view appears logically to the user as a table but is defined in terms of a query. A view can be based on more than one table, and a view can be updated if logically possible. An alternative to creating the CUSTOMER_SALES_TOTALS table in the previous example would be to create a view:

```
CREATE VIEW customer_sales_totals_v
AS
    SELECT customer_name, SUM (sale_value) sale_total
      FROM sales s, customers c
    WHERE s.customer_id = c.customer_id
    GROUP BY c.customer_name
```

DML statements on views DML statements can be performed on views, but there are some fairly strict restrictions:

❑ The view must not use set operations such as UNION, MINUS, and DIS-TINCT.

❑ The view should not include a group by clause, use group functions, or use the distinct keyword.

❑ The view should not include a collection expression in the SELECT list.

❑ If the WITH CHECK OPTION is specified, the DML statement cannot create or modify rows such that the rows concerned would no longer appear in the view.

❑ The view must not have been created with the WITH READ ONLY option.

❑ If the view contains a join, only columns belonging to a table whose primary key can uniquely identify every row returned by the query can be updated. If there is only one such table in the view, then a delete can succeed against the view.

Oracle8i allows "INSTEAD OF" triggers to be defined against views. These triggers will fire instead of the specified DML statement. Oracle developed "INSTEAD OF triggers primarily to allow application developers to define complex logic that would control how multitable views would be updated.

NULLS AND THREE-VALUED LOGIC

NULL values are used to indicate that a data item is missing or undefined. The use of NULL values in relational databases is a hotly debated topic because of the misleading or unexpected results that sometimes occur. For instance, the following query does not include all rows in the table because it will not include rows where JOB is NULL:

```
SELECT count(*)
    FROM PEOPLE
  WHERE JOB='ACCOUNTANT'
    OR JOB!='ACCOUNTANT'
```

The concept of NULL or missing values extends the traditional and intuitive two-valued logic (TRUE/FALSE) to a new, three-valued logic (TRUE/FALSE/ UNKNOWN). Using this three-valued logic, if a job is UNKNOWN, it is also unknown whether JOB!='ACCOUNTANT.' While this fairly trivial example seems somewhat reasonable (after all, if a job is unknown, then it might be 'ACCOUNTANT'), many people argue that three-valued logic leads to wrong answers and should be abandoned.

We can't pursue this debate here, but later we will see that NULL values are important in SQL tuning because they are not included in indexes. Operations that search for NULL values therefore pose particular tuning challenges and run the risk of unexpected results.

SOME COMMENTS ON THE NONPROCEDURAL APPROACH OF SQL

The movement from procedural, record-at-a-time processing used in prerelational databases to the nonprocedural, set-oriented processing used in SQL has had a major effect on the ease and efficiency of data access.

Early critics of relational databases frequently claimed that the relational model could not deliver acceptable performance. This criticism was largely based on the relational model's reliance on indexes rather than pointers for data navigation. The perceived performance problems impeded takeup of relational databases for some time, but eventually were overcome by the theoretical and practical benefits being delivered by the relational model, together with improvements in the performance of relational databases and computer hardware.

Today, the average size of relational databases is probably 10 to 100 times greater than that of the early 1980s. User requirements for throughput and response time are higher than ever. Relational database vendors constantly release competing benchmark results to support the proposition that their implementation is the fastest. Clearly the user community is still concerned with the performance of relational databases.

While relational databases can provide adequate performance for almost any application type, many relational databases are performing several levels below their potential. A major reason for this failure to perform may be the nonprocedural nature of SQL. SQL encourages the user to specify the data to be retrieved without giving any thought to the way the data will be retrieved. Since the retrieval path is absolutely central to the performance of the query, SQL actively discourages users from thinking about, or optimizing, performance.

It may be that eventually, relational database engines will be so advanced that no SQL tuning effort will be needed. However, this is not the case at present. Whatever happens in the future, the simple fact now is that to implement high-performance relational systems, substantial investment in SQL tuning must be made. The philosophy of "state what you want, not how to get it" should be rejected if optimal performance is the target.

SUMMARY

A relational database presents data to the user as a series of tables. Tables are linked by common data values. Users can issue commands against a relational database without needing to know the physical implementation details for the database. Relational databases have become the dominant model for database management because they offer flexible access to data. SQL is a language designed for the retrieval and manipulation of data in relational databases.

SQL is defined by ANSI standards. Oracle SQL conforms to the entry-level ANSI 92 standard for SQL. Extensions to Oracle SQL include a facility for hierarchical queries and a facility to perform outer joins.

The major categories of SQL are as follows:

❏ Queries, which are represented by the SELECT statement
❏ Data Manipulation Language (DML) to UPDATE, DELETE, and INSERT data
❏ Data Definition Language (DDL) to create tables, indexes, and other database objects

Issuing queries is one of the primary operations of the relational database. Some typical query operations are as follows:

❏ Joins, which allow rows from two or more tables to be combined based on common key values
❏ Subqueries, which are select statements that may appear within other SQL statements
❏ The ORDER BY clause, which allows results to be returned in sorted order
❏ The GROUP BY operator, which allows aggregate information for groups of rows to be calculated

A NULL value is one that is missing or unknown. The use of NULLs results in three-valued logic—TRUE, FALSE, or UNKNOWN—rather than the two-valued logic typical of many computing environments.

Groups of SQL statements can be combined into a transaction. Statements in a transaction will succeed or fail as a unit. The COMMIT statement causes statements in a transaction to be made permanent, and the rollback statement causes the changes to be aborted.

Part II: SQL Tuning Theory

SQL Processing Internals

This chapter explains the operations that Oracle performs when processing your SQL statements.

It's possible to tune an SQL statement without having a full understanding of how Oracle processes SQL, but having such an understanding usually saves a lot of wasted effort. As we discussed in Chapter 1, tuning SQL can be an iterative process involving a fair deal of trial and error. With an understanding of Oracle's processing techniques, you should be able to reduce the number of errors and move more directly to the best result.

The major aspects of SQL processing that we will discuss in this chapter are as follows:

❏ The overall procedure that Oracle undertakes from the receipt of your SQL statement to its successful execution

❏ The process of SQL parsing, in which Oracle checks your SQL for errors, checks for existing identical SQL statements, and prepares the SQL for execution

❏ A brief overview of Oracle's data retrieval mechanisms, such as table scans, index fetches, and sorts

❏ An overview of multitable operations, such as joins and set operations

❏ An overview of Oracle transaction processing

OVERVIEW OF SQL PROCESSING

Figure 4.1 shows a simplified overview of Oracle SQL processing. We'll be discussing each of these stages in detail in this chapter. Here is a brief overview of each step:

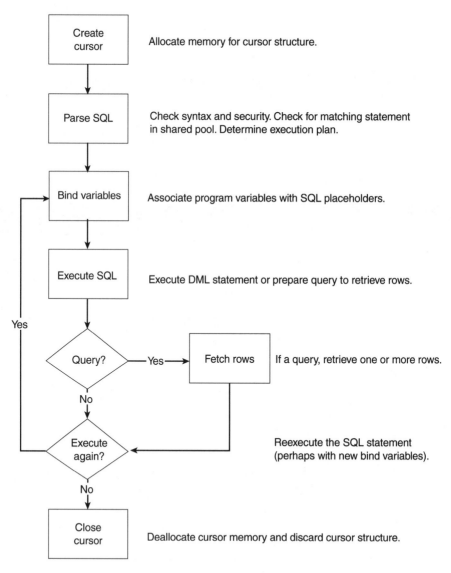

FIGURE 4.1   Overview of SQL processing.

❏ **Create cursor.** The cursor is the area in memory that holds the definition of a currently open SQL statement.

❏ **Parse SQL.** Parsing SQL involves checking the SQL for syntax and object references. A check for a matching statement that is already in the shared pool is performed. If none is found, then an entry in the shared pool is created and an execution plan for the SQL determined.

❏ **Bind variables.** Before the SQL statement can be executed, the values of any bind variables—placeholders that represent values to be supplied by the calling program—must be associated with the SQL.

❏ **Execute SQL.** If the SQL statement is not a query, then execute involves processing the DML or DDL statement in its entirety. If the SQL statement is a query, then execute prepares the statement for fetch operations

❏ **Fetch rows**. For queries, fetching involves retrieving one or more rows from the result set.

❏ **Close cursor.** This involves releasing all the memory and resources associated with the cursor (although a shared representation of the cursor may be retained in Oracle shared memory).

CREATING AND PARSING CURSORS

CURSORS

A cursor, or context area, is an area in memory in which Oracle stores your SQL statement and associated information. This includes the parsed and unparsed representation of your SQL statement, the execution plan, and a pointer to the current row. When SQL statement execution is complete, the memory associated with the cursor can be freed for other purposes or can be saved for reexecution.

In most tools, the allocation of cursors is performed by the client tools and is transparent to the programmer. In the programmatic interfaces (for instance, PRO*C or Oracle Call Interface [OCI]) and in some other tools, the programmer may create and destroy cursors explicitly. In Java JDBC, a cursor is equivalent to a Statement or PreparedStatement object.

PARSING

Parsing is the process of preparing your SQL statement for execution. This process is analogous to the process a language compiler or interpreter must undertake in order to translate high-level statements into machine code. The parse process will

❏ Check that the SQL statement is syntactically valid, that the SQL conforms to the rules of the SQL language, and that all keywords and operators are valid and correctly used.

❑   Check that the SQL is semantically valid. This means that all references to database objects (i.e., tables, columns) are valid.

❑   Check security: that the user has permission to perform the specified SQL operations on the objects involved.

❑   Determine an execution plan for the SQL statement. The execution plan describes the series of steps that Oracle will perform in order to access and/or update the data involved. This done by the Oracle optimizer which is discussed in detail in Chapter 5.

Parsing can be an expensive operation, although often its overhead is masked by the greater overhead of high I/O requirements. However, eliminating unnecessary parsing is always desirable, and we will discuss how to do this shortly.

SHARED SQL

In order to avoid unnecessary parsing, Oracle maintains a cache of recently executed SQL statements together with their execution plans. Technically speaking, this cache is maintained in the SQL area of the shared pool (see Chapter 18 for more details on the shared pool). Whenever a request to execute an SQL statement is issued, Oracle looks for a matching statement in this cache. If a matching statement is found, Oracle uses the execution plan stored in the cache and so avoids most of the overhead involved in parsing.

Oracle uses a hashing algorithm in order to locate a matching statement in the shared pool. This means that it uses a mathematical process to translate the SQL text into a number and uses that number to find that SQL in the shared pool. It therefore stands to reason that for a match to be found, the SQL must be exactly identical—including spaces, upper/lower casing, use of aliases, etc.

You may see a recommendation—based on the implications of this hashing algorithm—to code SQL identically throughout your application. This allows SQL with the same functionality (but contained within separate programs) to share the same slot in the shared pool. However, you'll rarely see much advantage from such an approach—the SQL cache is big, and there is room enough for a few nearly identical SQL statements coming from different modules.

A more common reason why SQL cannot be found in the shared pool is because it contains hard-coded literals instead of bind variables.

BIND VARIABLES

An SQL statement may contain variables that change from execution to execution. These variables are typically parameters to the SQL statement that define the rows to be processed or new values to be inserted or updated. We can specify these variables either as literals or as bind variables. For instance, using literals, we could retrieve details for employee 1234 with the following SQL statement:

```
SQL> SELECT firstname,surname
2      FROM employees
3      WHERE employee_id=1234
```

The next time we wished to select an employee, we would change the "1234" literal to the new value and reexecute. This will work, but remember that the SQL statement must be absolutely identical if a match is to be found in the shared pool. Since the employee_id is likely to be different for every execution, we will almost never find a matching statement in the shared pool, and consequently the statement will have to be reparsed every time.

An alternative approach is to specify these variable portions with bind variables. Bind variables (sometimes called host variables) are fixed references to variables contained elsewhere in the programming language or development tool. Within most languages or tools, bind variables are recognizable because they are prefixed by a colon. For instance, in the following statement, the value of employee_id is stored in a bind variable (the SQL*PLUS VARIABLE command allows us to define a bind variable):

```
SQL> VARIABLE employee_number_ws NUMBER
SQL> BEGIN
2    :employee_number_ws:=1;
3  END;
4  .
SQL> /
PL/SQL procedure successfully completed.
SQL> SELECT firstname,surname
2    FROM employees
3    WHERE employee_id=:employee_number_ws
4  /
FIRSTNAME            SURNAME
------------------   -----------------------------
CLIFFORD             MCLENNAN
```

There are two compelling reasons for using bind variables:

❑ If the value of the bind variable changes, you don't need to create a new cursor or reparse the SQL statement when reexecuting the SQL.
❑ If another session executes the same SQL statement, it will find a match in the shared pool, since the name of the bind variable does not change from execution to execution.

Conversely, if you use literals instead of bind variables, you'll suffer from the following problems:

❏ Every time you change the value of a literal, you (or your software tool) will have to request that the SQL be reparsed.

❏ When you do request the parse, the chance of finding a match in the shared pool will be negligible.

❏ The SQL cache will fill up with "one-off" SQL and may need to be bigger than it otherwise would be.

❏ When an Oracle session wants to place a new SQL statement in the shared pool, it has to acquire an Oracle internal lock (a latch). Under extreme circumstances, contention for these latches can result in a performance bottleneck at best or dramatic performance problems at worst.

Figure 4.2 illustrates the flow of activities that occur when Oracle is required to parse an SQL statement. Note the amount of processing that is avoided if we can avoid reparsing the SQL statement or if a matching SQL statement is found in the shared pool.

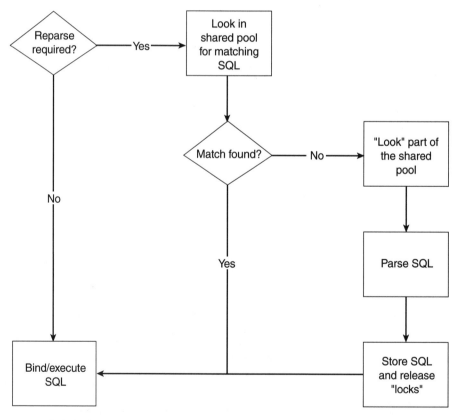

FIGURE 4.2   Flow of processing during parsing of an SQL statement.

THE CURSOR_SHARING OPTION IN ORACLE 8.1.6

Oracle release 8.1.6 introduced a new parameter, CURSOR_SHARING. If CURSOR_SHARING is set to FORCE, then statements that use literal values will be transparently rewritten by Oracle so that they use bind variables. For instance, the following statement specifies a literal value for the employee_name:

```
SELECT *
  FROM customers
 WHERE customer_name = 'CLARK AND SONS'
```

If we set CURSOR_SHARING to FORCE, such as with an ALTER SESSION statement,

```
ALTER session set cursor_sharing=FORCE
```

Oracle will transparently rewrite the statement to use bind variables and will set the value of the bind variable to 'CLARK AND SONS':

```
SELECT *
  FROM customers
 WHERE customer_name = :SYS_B_0
```

Setting CURSOR_SHARING to FORCE is useful when it is difficult or impossible to change an application to use bind variables. However, there are a couple of situations in which it can cause the execution plan to change for the worse. In particular, statements whose execution plans are based on stored outlines or histograms might end up with changed execution plans, and these new plans might be less desirable than the original plan.

RECURSIVE SQL

Recursive SQL is SQL that Oracle generates on your behalf in order to parse or execute your SQL. For instance, in order to determine that all table and column names in your SQL are valid, Oracle must check a number of tables known collectively as the data dictionary. Usually this information can be found in memory (in the dictionary cache or row cache). However, if the information cannot be found in memory, then Oracle will issue a recursive SQL statement to retrieve it.

Since recursive SQL is frequently generated during parsing operations, reducing parsing will reduce recursive SQL.

REDUCING PARSE OVERHEAD

Parsing is an expensive operation. Sometimes the relative cost of parsing can seem inconsequential next to the relatively higher overhead of I/O, but in extreme cases excessive parsing can completely bottleneck an application system. It's also very difficult to scale an application that performs excessive parsing.

When implementing SQL within a programming language, you should ensure the following:

❑ Always use bind variables in preference to literals for SQL statements that will be reexecuted.

❑ Don't needlessly discard cursors that may be reexecuted later in your program.

Depending on your development tool, reducing parse overhead may be automatic or may require careful coding. Guidelines on reusing cursors and using bind variables within some popular development tools can be found in Appendix C.

Sometimes you may be required to improve the performance of applications without being able to change the source code. In this case, Oracle provides two parameters that can help you reduce parse overhead for poorly designed applications:

❑ The SESSION_CACHED_CURSORS parameter can be used to create a cache of recently executed cursors in the server process. If the application requests a reparse of a cursor that is identical to one in the cache, Oracle will intercept the parse request and return the information in the cache. This negates the need to search the shared pool for a matching SQL statement.

❑ Oracle 8.1.6 CURSOR_SHARING=FORCE will instruct Oracle to transparently rewrite SQL statements that use literals and use bind variables instead.

Parsing is expensive, and excessive parsing defeats scalability. Minimize parse overhead by reusing cursors and by implementing bind variables in your applications.

EXECUTING SQL

EXECUTING AND FETCHING

Once the SQL statement is parsed and all variables are bound, Oracle is ready to execute the statement. In the case of DML (INSERT, UPDATE, DELETE), executing the statement results in the SQL being actioned immediately (although the changes do not become permanent until a COMMIT is issued).

In the case of a SELECT statement, the execute call readies the cursor for fetch operations. In the case of certain queries (for instance, where the rows must be sorted or locked), opening the cursor makes Oracle retrieve all the rows to be returned. In other cases, opening the cursor simply locates the record pointer at the first row.

Regardless of whether the open call must access all rows to be returned, it is the fetch call that returns data to the client environment. The fetch call retrieves one or more rows from the database and stores the results in host variables that can be manipulated by the program.

ARRAY FETCH

Each fetch request can return more than one row. When a fetch returns a batch of rows in this manner, it is known as an array fetch. Array fetches are much more efficient than fetching a row at a time. Often your client tool (for instance, SQL*PLUS) will automatically perform array fetches. Other tools might require that you explicitly perform an array fetch (for instance, PRO*C or PRO*COBOL). See Appendix C for guidelines on configuring array fetch in various development tools. We will look in detail at the performance of array processing in Chapters 8 and 12.

RESULT SETS

The output from an SQL query is referred to as a result set. A result set consists of rows and columns and may be thought of as a temporary table containing the queries results. Result sets are also created during intermediate operations. For instance, in a join of tables A, B, and C, first table A is joined to B, creating an intermediate result set. This result set is then joined to table C to create the final result set that is returned to your program.

TYPES OF TABLE ACCESSES

Oracle can retrieve your data in a number of ways. The most common techniques for retrieving table data are to

- ❏ Read the entire table using a full-table scan.
- ❏ Access a specific row using its ROWID.
- ❏ Use an index to locate the rows.
- ❏ Use a hash key lookup.

We will briefly examine each access mechanism. Detailed guidelines for optimizing table accesses are contained in Chapter 8.

TABLE SCAN

The full-table scan is the simplest way for Oracle to get your data. In a full-table scan, every row of data in the table is read into memory. This access mechanism is always available to Oracle.

To perform a full-table scan, Oracle reads all blocks (the basic unit of data storage) allocated to the table, starting with the first block and continuing until it reaches the high-water mark. The high-water mark is the "highest" block in the table that has ever held data. For instance, immediately after creating a table, the high-water mark will be set at five blocks. As rows are inserted into the table, the high-water mark will move up. However, even if all rows in a table are deleted, the high-water mark never moves down. The only way to reset it is to truncate or recreate the table.

ROWID ACCESS

The ROWID is a pseudocolumn, which means that although you can SELECT it, it isn't really part of the table data. The ROWID represents the physical location of a row. Accessing a row by its ROWID is usually the quickest way to get the row, since the ROWID tells Oracle exactly where the row is in the database.

ROWID accesses typically happen for one of the following reasons:

❏ The ROWID was obtained from an index that was used to locate the rows.
❏ The ROWID was obtained from a currently open cursor (using the WHERE CURRENT OF CURSOR clause).

INDEX LOOKUP

An index allows rows matching values stored in the index to be retrieved quickly. Oracle will search the index for matching key values. The index links these key values to the ROWIDs of matching rows. The ROWIDs can be used to retrieve quickly the matching rows from the table.

Oracle supports two types of indexes: B*-tree and bitmap indexes. Details of these indexes are contained in Chapter 6.

HASH KEY ACCESS

A hash function is a mathematical function that can be applied to a column value to obtain a hash value. A hash cluster is a table in which data is physically stored according to the hash value of a key column. To find rows corresponding to some key value, Oracle can apply the hash function to some key value and then access the rows corresponding to the resulting hash value. Hash clusters are discussed in detail in Chapter 6.

JOINS

Joins allow rows from two or more tables to be merged, usually based on common key values. Most nontrivial SQL statements involve joins. The different types of join operations supported by the relational model are described in Chapter 3. Here, we discuss the variety of techniques that Oracle can employ to perform your join efficiently. Optimization of joins is discussed in detail in Chapter 9.

Oracle supports three join techniques:

- ❑ The sort-merge join
- ❑ The nested loops join
- ❑ The hash join

SORT MERGE

The sort-merge join is a join method that does not require indexes. When applying the sort-merge algorithm, Oracle sorts each table (or the result set from a previous operation) on the column values used to join the two tables. Oracle then merges the two sorted result sets into one.

You can conceptualize this process by imagining that you have two piles of numbered pages (perhaps odd numbers in one pile and even in the other) in some random order. To get these two piles into a single pile in correct order, you would arrange each pile in sorted order and then interleave the odd and even pages.

NESTED LOOPS

The nested loops join is a join algorithm that usually involves an index (or hash cluster) on at least one of the tables. In a nested loops join, a full-table scan is done on one of the tables or result sets (probably either the smaller table or the table that does not have an index on the join column). For every row found in this result set, a lookup—usually involving an index—is performed on the second table and the matching row is retrieved.

You can imagine doing such a join yourself if you had two piles of paper, one sorted, one not, and you wanted to find matching numbers in each pile and you didn't care about the order of the final pile. You could do this by going through the unsorted pile sheet by sheet. For each sheet, you could quickly find the matching sheet in the other pile (since that pile is sorted). When you had finished going through the unsorted pile, you would have matched sheets in both piles. However, the resulting pile would not be in any particular order.

HASH JOIN

In a hash join, a hash table (a sort of on-the-fly index) is constructed for the larger of the two tables. The smaller table is then scanned, and the hash table is used to find matching rows in the larger table. This can work very well, especially if the hash table can fit in memory (otherwise, temporary tables have to be allocated). It performs particularly well if the two tables are of different sizes. Hash joins also work well for antijoins and with parallel SQL.

SORTING AND GROUPING

Following the accessing and joining of raw table data, the SQL statement may require that the data be

- ❑ Returned in sorted order (due to ORDER BY)
- ❑ Aggregated (due to GROUP BY, DISTINCT, MAX or other statistical operators)
- ❑ Compared with some other result set (UNION, INTERSECTION, MINUS)

These operations all need to sort the final or intermediary result set. To do this, Oracle allocates an area of memory (defined by the configuration parameter SORT_AREA_SIZE) that it will use to perform the sort. If the memory allocation is insufficient to perform the sort, a temporary segment is allocated and the sort becomes a disk sort. Optimizing operations that involve sorting and aggregation is the topic of Chapter 10.

MODIFYING DATA

Data manipulation language (DML) statements allow data to be inserted, deleted, or updated. Optimization of DML statements, and of DML statements grouped in transactions, is discussed in Chapter 9.

Typically, most of the overhead involved when you UPDATE or DELETE data is in locating the data to be processed. Once the rows to be altered are retrieved and loaded into Oracle shared memory, they may be altered or deleted with only a small overhead. However, if a column to be updated is heavily indexed, or a row is deleted from a heavily indexed table, finding and modifying index entries may be expensive.

INSERTs AND FREE LISTS

When an INSERT statement is executed, Oracle must find a block that has sufficient free space to accommodate the new row. To do this, Oracle maintains one or more lists of free blocks for each table, called a free list. If there are multiple concurrent inserts into a table, there can be contention for these free lists and it may be necessary to create multiple lists. Chapter 12 contains a more detailed discussion of this topic.

ARRAY INSERTs

The array INSERT is similar to the concept of the array fetch and allows Oracle to insert rows in batches. Array INSERTs are much more efficient than inserting a row at a time. See Appendix C for guidelines on implementing array processing in various client tools and Chapters 13 and 14 for details on implementing array insert in PL/SQL and Java.

You can also implement array UPDATEs and DELETEs, in which arrays of bind variables are passed to the WHERE clause of the query, but these typically do not result in the same level of performance improvement as the array INSERT.

LOCKING

Like all RDBMSs, Oracle implements a locking scheme to prevent concurrent updates to table rows. Oracle's locking scheme has the following features:

- ❏ Only the rows that are updated or deleted are locked. In the case of a table with a unique index, an INSERT locks the index row with that unique value.
- ❏ Locks do not prevent the row from being selected. However, the row values seen by other processes will be the row values before the update occurred (provided that it is not yet committed).
- ❏ All locks are released when a COMMIT or ROLLBACK is issued.
- ❏ Entire tables can be locked explicitly using the LOCK TABLE command.
- ❏ Rows may be locked without being altered with the FOR UPDATE clause of the SELECT statement.
- ❏ Implementing bitmapped indexes may cause locks to be applied to many rows when the bitmap index is updated.
- ❏ Implementing referential integrity can cause table locks to be applied.

TRANSACTIONS

A transaction is an indivisible unit of work that must succeed or fail as a unit. A transaction is implicitly created by any DML statement or explicitly with the SET TRANSACTION statement. Transactions end with a COMMIT or ROLLBACK statement, when a DDL statement is issued (implicit COMMIT), or when the program ends (COMMIT if successful termination, ROLLBACK otherwise).

To allow for a ROLLBACK statement to succeed, Oracle stores "before images" of modified data in structures called *rollback segments*. If a ROLLBACK statement is issued, then Oracle must retrieve the original copies of the changed rows from the rollback segment and use these to undo any changes.

When a COMMIT occurs, Oracle need only mark the transaction entry in the rollback segment as COMMITed and (eventually) mark transaction entries in the database blocks.

One implication of this approach is that the ROLLBACK command can involve a significant overhead—equal to or greater than the overhead of the transaction itself.

READ CONSISTENCY

Queries are guaranteed to see a read-consistent view of their result set. This means that they will see only data that was already committed when the query commenced.

To implement this read-consistent view of the result set, Oracle may have to refer to the rollback segments if some of the data has been changed since the query commenced. It does this by comparing the value that a global sequence number—the System Change Number—had when the query commenced with the value written into each database block when it is changed. If the value in the database block is higher than when the query commenced, then the block has to be reconstructed from rollback segment entries.

This process of reconstructing the data blocks can involve significant overhead, especially for long-running queries on tables subject to concurrent update.

COMMITTING

Changes made during your transaction are not being made directly to the database files on disk. Instead, they are being made to copies of the disk blocks contained in Oracle's buffer cache within the System Global Area (SGA). This means that changes are initially made in memory only.

A COMMIT causes all changes made in the transaction to become permanent. In order for Oracle to guarantee that no committed data will be lost, the transaction details must be written to disk. When you issue a COMMIT, Oracle writes the transaction details to a transaction log known as the redo log. You have to wait for this disk write to occur before continuing. Therefore, when inserting or updating large quantities of data, it can be advantageous not to COMMIT too often, since every COMMIT requires some disk I/O.

SUMMARY

This chapter discussed how Oracle processes SQL statements.

A cursor is an area in memory that contains the essential information about your SQL statement that Oracle needs in order to process the SQL statement efficiently.

Parsing is the process of validating an SQL statement and determining its execution plan. You should reduce parse overhead as much as possible. The best way to do this is to ensure that you make intelligent use of bind variables, although the CURSOR_SHARING option introduced in Oracle 8.1.6 can be used where bind variables are not an option.

Oracle can retrieve (fetch) or insert data in arrays or batches. Making use of this array interface can result in impressive performance improvements, especially when large quantities of data are being processed.

Oracle can access data in a table using one of the following methods:

❑ Scanning every row in the table (full-table scan)
❑ Accessing a specific row through the physical address of the row—the ROWID
❑ Accessing specific rows by obtaining the relevant ROWIDs from an index
❑ Determining the physical location of a row within a hash cluster by performing a hash key lookup

Oracle can join data from two or more tables using one of the following methods:

❑ Sorting and merging rows from each table—the sort-merge algorithm
❑ Performing a lookup (usually index) on the second table for every row in the first table—the nested loops method
❑ Creating a hash table—a sort of on-the-fly index—on one table and using that to find matches for rows in the other table

Oracle often needs to create temporary or intermediate result sets during processing. Many operations (GROUP BY, ORDER BY) require that result sets be sorted.

Chapter 5

THE OPTIMIZER

INTRODUCTION

This chapter provides an overview of the Oracle query optimizer. This is the part of the Oracle program that determines how an SQL statement will be processed.

SQL is a nonprocedural language: You define the data you want, not how to get it. Although the nonprocedural nature of SQL represents a big breakthrough in programmer productivity, the RDBMS must support a set of very sophisticated algorithms to determine the optimal method of retrieving the results or processing the modification. In Oracle, these algorithms are collectively referred to as the optimizer.

The optimizer is critical to high-performance SQL, and an understanding of it critical to SQL performance tuning. In this chapter we'll examine the optimizer in detail, including the following:

- ❏ An overview of the optimization process
- ❏ The rule-based optimizer
- ❏ The cost-based optimizer
- ❏ Collecting and managing statistics for the cost-based optimizer
- ❏ Using the plan stability feature in Oracle8i
- ❏ Using hints and other methods to modify optimizer decisions

OVERVIEW OF OPTIMIZATION

For almost all SQL statements, there will be more than one way for Oracle to retrieve the rows required. When Oracle parses an SQL statement, it must decide which approach will be fastest. The process of determining this optimal path to the data is referred to as query optimization.

Query optimization is applied to all queries and to any other statement (for instance, UPDATE, INSERT, DELETE, CREATE TABLE AS queries) that contains a query or that contains a WHERE clause. The part of the Oracle software that performs query optimization is referred to as the optimizer.

Oracle supports two approaches to query optimization:

❑ The rule-based optimizer is the older of the two optimizers and has its roots in the origins of the Oracle RDBMS. This optimizer makes its decisions based on a set of rules and on the rankings of various access paths. The rule-based optimizer is not aware of—and cannot take into account—data volumes. For instance, the rule-based optimizer will always prefer an index lookup to a full-table scan. However, the rule-based optimizer cannot distinguish between a full-table scan of a table with two rows and that of a table with 2 million rows.

❑ The cost-based optimizer was introduced in Oracle 7. It incorporates may features of the rule-based optimizer but has the advantage of being able to take into account statistical information relating to the volume and distribution of data within tables and indexes. This optimizer therefore can distinguish between a two-row table and a 2-million-row table and will usually generate different execution plans for each table.

THE OPTIMIZATION PROCESS

The aim of both optimizers is to establish an effective execution plan. Because SQL is a nonprocedural language, the SQL itself does not include instructions for retrieving the data. It is up to Oracle to devise a means of retrieving the data, and the resulting scheme is referred to as the execution plan.

For instance, consider the following SQL:

```
SELECT DISTINCT customer_name
  FROM customers c, sales s, employees e
 WHERE s.sale_date > SYSDATE - 7
   AND e.surname = 'Flintstone'
   AND e.firstname = 'Fred'
   AND c.sales_rep_id = e.employee_id
   AND s.customer_id = c.customer_id
```

In English, this query might be stated as "give me the names of all customers who bought something from Sales Representative Flintstone in the past week." The optimizer has to decide which is the best way to get the data. Some possible approaches are as follows:

❏ Get all sales for the past week. Then get the names of all the customers matching those sales. Then filter out any customers who aren't handled by Mr. Flintstone.

❏ Get Flintstone's employee_id. Using that id, get all customers handled by Flintstone. Then filter out any customers who haven't bought anything in the last week.

❏ Get all customers. Then filter out those who aren't represented by Flintstone. Then filter out those who haven't made any sales.

It is apparent that the decision on which approach to take will affect significantly the amount of time taken to retrieve the results. It may also be obvious that the last approach is likely to be the worst, since all customer records would have to be read—so we hope the optimizer won't pick that path.

CHOOSING THE OPTIMIZATION APPROACH

Although the cost-based optimizer has been around for some years, many systems are still using a rule-based approach. There are a number of reasons for this:

❏ Early versions of the cost-based optimizer contained significant deficiencies, and better performance could often be achieved by using the rule-based optimizer.

❏ Converting existing systems to the cost-based optimizer can be a substantial task, since existing SQL will be tuned for the rule-based optimizer and may need to be retuned to take advantage of cost-based optimization.

❏ Developers and DBAs were used to the rule-based optimizer. Using the cost-based optimizer required training and familiarization.

❏ Execution plans from the cost-based optimizer could change when the data changed. This made the cost-based optimizer less predictable. It also meant that queries developed in small to medium development environments could behave differently in the larger production environments.

Although these drawbacks made cost-based optimization a risk in early releases of Oracle7, many of these drawbacks no longer exist in Oracle8i. Consider the following advantages of cost-based optimization and work-arounds for the drawbacks noted previously:

❏ Cost-based optimization is improved with each release of Oracle; rule-based optimization is virtually unchanged since the final releases of Oracle6.

❏ Cost-based optimization is necessary if you want to take advantage of advanced optimization plans involving hash joins, bitmap indexes, and other new features.

❏ Oracle8i *stored outlines* (discussed in detail later in this chapter), can be used to implement plan stability. This allows you to ensure that an execution plan will not change when changes occur to table statistics.

❏ Stored outlines can also be used to aid in the migration from rule-based optimizer by allowing SQL statements to be migrated to the cost-based optimizer on a case-by-case basis.

❏ The Oracle8i DBMS_STATS package allows statistics to be copied between databases. This allows you to simulate the plans that would be generated in a large production system on a database with different data distributions.

❏ Cost-based optimization can be particularly good for untunable SQL. Untunable SQL is SQL over which you have no control, such as the SQL generated by a third-party tool (such as Microsoft Access) or ad hoc SQL entered by casual users. These sorts of SQL are common in decision support or data warehousing environments, and here the cost-based optimizer can be particularly helpful.

Despite the advantages of cost-based optimization, you should not conclude that using the cost-based optimizer will relieve you of the need to tune SQL. The cost-based optimizer can make the tuning process easier, since it will usually pick the best (most selective) of all available indexes and choose a good driving table. However, the cost-based optimizer can't rewrite badly formulated SQL, and it certainly can't create an index if a useful one is missing. Whichever optimization approach you choose, it is still up to you (or the author of the SQL) to ensure that it is properly tuned.

The cost-based optimizer includes many sophisticated algorithms designed to improve the performance of your SQL and is vastly superior to the rule-based optimizer. All new applications should be developed against the cost-based optimizer. Existing applications that are still using rule-based optimization should consider a migration to the cost-based optimizer.

DETAILS COMMON TO BOTH OPTIMIZERS

While the two flavors of optimization use totally different techniques to determine the optimal execution plan, there are a number of initial steps and restrictions that they share.

Statement transformation   Certain SQL statements are transformed into logically equivalent statements.

A statement that incorporates a subquery involving the IN clause can often be represented as a join. For instance, the following statement selects all employees who work for departments in the Melbourne location.

```
SELECT employee_id, surname, firstname
  FROM employees
 WHERE department_id IN (SELECT department_id
                          FROM departments
                         WHERE location = 'Melbourne')
```

The same query can be expressed as a join:

```
SELECT e.employee_id, e.surname, e.firstname
  FROM employees e, departments d
 WHERE d.location = 'Melbourne'
   AND d.department_id = e.department_id
```

Using join logic to resolve statements of this type is usually more efficient than using IN logic, so Oracle automatically transforms statements with correlated subqueries using an IN into a join where possible.

Another example of automatic transformation is the transformation of statements containing OR conditions. A statement involving an OR condition may be expressed as a UNION ALL. For instance, the following query retrieves the names of all departments in Melbourne and London:

```
SELECT department_name
  FROM departments
 WHERE location = 'Melbourne'
    OR location = 'London'
```

Rather than use an OR clause, the same query can be expressed using a UNION, as follows:

```
SELECT department_name
  FROM departments
 WHERE location = 'Melbourne'
UNION ALL
```

```
SELECT department_name
  FROM departments
 WHERE location = 'London'
```

The UNION approach promotes the use of indexes, and so Oracle may translate statements using OR into UNIONS.

If a statement references a view, the definition of the view can be "pushed into" the SQL statement. For instance, if we had a view defined as follows:

```
CREATE OR REPLACE VIEW managers_view
AS
   SELECT *
     FROM employees
    WHERE manager_id IS NULL;
```

and a query on that view like this:

```
SELECT firstname, surname
  FROM managers_view
 WHERE salary > 100000
```

the optimizer might insert the view definition in the SQL so that it looks like this:

```
SELECT firstname, surname
  FROM employees
 WHERE manager_id IS NULL
   AND salary > 100000
```

Other similarities in approach Both optimizers must compare a number of possible access paths and join orders. The questions the optimizers will consider are as follows:

❑ For each table, what options do I have for retrieving the data?
❑ With which table should I start? In what order should the tables be joined?

Depending on the complexity of the SQL, there may be hundreds of possible combinations of access paths and join orders.

Regardless of the optimizer selected, the following rules always apply:

❑ If a join would result in a single row only (perhaps both tables had a primary or unique key lookup specified in the where clause), then that join will be given preference.
❑ If there is an outer join, the outer join table (the table that may not have matching rows) will only be joined after the other (inner) table.

SETTING THE OPTIMIZER GOAL

The optimizer goal determines the overall approach that the optimizer takes in determining an execution plan. There are four possible settings for the optimizer goal:

❑ **RULE:** Specifies that the optimizer is to take the rule-based approach to optimization.

❑ **CHOOSE:** Specifies that the optimizer is to use the cost-based approach if any of the tables in the SQL statement have been analyzed. If no tables have been analyzed, then the rule-based approach will be used.

❑ **ALL_ROWS:** Use the cost-based optimizer (regardless of the presence of statistics) and choose an execution plan that will minimize the cost of processing all rows specified. This is the default behavior for the cost-based optimizer. It is suitable for batch processing and reporting queries.

❑ **FIRST_ROWS:** Use the cost-based optimizer and choose an execution plan that will minimize the cost of retrieving the first row. This setting can be useful for interactive applications because the critical performance measure may be the time taken to display the first row or page of information.

There are three ways to set the optimizer goal:

❑ You can specify a default for the entire database in the database configuration file (the init.ora file). For instance, the following line sets the default goal to be a cost-based optimization of response time:

```
OPTIMIZER_MODE=FIRST_ROWS
```

If no setting is specified in the init.ora file, then the default setting is CHOOSE.

❑ You can change the default setting for your session by using the ALTER SESSION statement. For instance, after issuing the following statement, the optimization mode will be set to RULE for all subsequent statements (unless another ALTER SESSION command changes this):

```
ALTER SESSION SET OPTIMIZER_GOAL=RULE
```

❑ You can change the optimization goal for an individual statement by using a hint. (We'll discuss hints in detail later in this chapter). For instance, the following statement will be optimized for throughput using cost-based optimization:

```
SELECT /*+ ALL_ROWS*/
  FROM EMPLOYEES
WHERE MANAGER_ID=(SELECT EMPLOYEE_ID
```

```
     FROM EMPLOYEES
WHERE SURNAME='Flintstone'
  AND FIRSTNAME='Fred')
```

RULE-BASED OPTIMIZATION

The rule-based optimizer takes the following approach when determining an execution plan:

1. For each table in the where clause, every possible access path is considered and ranked.
2. The access path with the lowest rank is selected.
3. For each remaining table, every possible path for joining the table to the previous result set is considered and ranked.
4. The access path with the lowest rank is selected.
5. This procedure is repeated until no more tables remain

The rankings for each operation are shown in Table 5.1. These access path rankings can be hard to remember, so you may wish to remember just a few basic principles:

❑ Single-row lookups are preferred to multiple-row lookups.
❑ Indexes are preferred to table scans or sort merges.
❑ Equality lookups are preferred to range lookups.

Table 5.1 Rankings of the rule-based optimizer

RANK	OPERATION
1	Single row by ROWID
2	Single row by cluster join
3	Single row by hash cluster key with unique or primary key
4	Single row by unique or primary key
5	Cluster join
6	Hash cluster key
7	Indexed cluster key
8	Composite key (but only if all keys are used)
9	Single column indexes
10	Bounded range search on indexed columns
11	Unbounded range search on indexed columns
12	Sort-merge join
13	MAX or MIN of indexed column
14	ORDER BY on indexed columns
15	Full-table scan

❏ Bounded ranges (for instance, BETWEEN) are preferred to unbounded ranges (e.g., GREATER THAN).

❏ Using every column of an index is preferred to using only some columns of a concatenated index.

The rules for determining join order can be complex, but it boils down to the following principles:

❏ The rule-based optimizer will tend to choose the join order with the least number of unoptimized joins. Unoptimized joins are generally those that don't use indexes.

❏ The rule-based optimizer will choose as the "driving" table (first table in the join order) the table with the lowest ranking access path.

COST-BASED OPTIMIZATION

The cost-based optimizer also compares between many possible access paths. The cost-based optimizer then constructs a list of possible execution plans and tries to estimate the cost that would be required to satisfy each execution plan. The execution plan with the lowest cost is selected.

The calculation of cost is based on a number of factors, including

❏ Estimated number of database reads required

❏ Requirements for sorting

❏ Availability of the parallel query option

The cost-based optimizer may not consider all possible plans, as this may result in an excessive overhead. The higher the cost of the SQL statement, the more plans the cost-based optimizer will consider.

This cost-based approach is somewhat less predictable than the rule-based optimizer, since the execution plan selected will depend on the statistics collected for a table, which are subject to change, and on its costing algorithms, which are unpublished and also subject to change. However, as we shall see, it is possible to stabilize execution plans using stored outlines.

COLLECTING OPTIMIZER STATISTICS

THE ANALYZE COMMAND

Analyze is a DDL command that causes table and index statistics to be collected. Prior to Oracle8i, the ANALYZE command was the only way to collect optimizer statistics. In Oracle8i, the DBMS_STATS package, described later, offers some more powerful options for collecting statistics.

The ANALYZE command has the following (simplified) syntax:

```
ANALYZE {TABLE|INDEX|CLUSTER} segment_specification
     [{COMPUTE STATISTICS |
        ESTIMATE STATISTICS
           SAMPLE sample_size [ROWS|PERCENT] }
           [FOR {    TABLE |
                   ALL [INDEXED] COLUMNS
                        [SIZE histogram_size] |
                   column_list [SIZE histogram_size]  |
                        ALL [LOCAL] INDEXES ] } ... ]
                ]
```

The ANALYZE command collects information from the nominated tables and its indexes and stores them in data dictionary tables, which can be accessed by the cost-based optimizer to calculate SQL statement costs. The following statistics are always collected:

❏ For a table, number of rows, number of blocks used and empty, average row length, and average amount of used space within each block
❏ For indexes, number of distinct keys, number of leaf blocks, and depth of the B*-tree (see Chapter 4 for a detailed explanation of these terms).

The ANALYZE command allows you to read all table and index blocks to generate exact statistics (the COMPUTE STATISTICS option) or to sample a certain percentage or certain number of rows (ESTIMATE STATISTICS). For instance, the following command estimates statistics for the EMPLOYEES table using a 10% sample:

```
ANALYZE TABLE employees
        ESTIMATE STATISTICS SAMPLE 10 percent
```

Examining every row using the CALCULATE STATISTICS option is usually impractical for very large tables—it will either take too long, or fail completely due to insufficient temporary segment space. In these cases, ESTIMATE STATISTICS, using a sample size of between 10 and 25% (perhaps even smaller for huge tables) will generate statistics that are sufficiently accurate.

When using the cost-based optimizer, collect optimizer statistics regularly or when table volumes are known to have changed.

COLLECTING COLUMN HISTOGRAM DATA

If we used the ANALYZE TABLE example in the previous section, Oracle will collect information about the number of unique keys in an index but will not collect any information about the distribution of the key values. This can cause the optimizer to disregard an index that has a small number of key values, even if some of those values are very infrequent and therefore good candidates for index lookup.

For instance, consider a database that contains details of handedness (e.g., right-handed, left-handed, ambidextrous). An index on this column will only contain three values and, as a result, will not normally be used by the cost-based optimizer. This decision would be sensible if the query involved searching for right-handers, since over 90% of the database would be selected and an index would not be appropriate. However, if searching for ambidextrous individuals, the index would be useful since less than 1% of rows would be selected.

The creation of column histograms allows Oracle to recognize selective values within otherwise unselective columns. The histogram stores information about the frequency of various column values that Oracle can use to decide whether or not to use the index.

To create a histogram, you use the following syntax in the analyze command:

```
ANALYZE TABLE table_name [ESTIMATE...|CALCULATE...]
    {FOR COLUMNS column_list|
    FOR ALL COLUMNS|
    FOR ALL INDEXED COLUMNS }
    SIZE n
```

You can choose to generate histograms for all columns in the table, for all indexed columns, or for nominated columns only. Normally, you would choose to create histograms only for columns where the data were not evenly distributed (e.g., the data are skewed).

HISTOGRAMS AND BIND VARIABLES

Oracle cannot use a histogram if the values to be selected are contained in bind variables. As we saw in the previous chapter, bind variables are an alternative to presenting the query parameters as literals and are beneficial because they reduce the overhead of parsing the SQL statement.

However, if Oracle is to make use of histograms that may have been created on a column, then it will be necessary to explicitly include the value in the SQL statements. This is because Oracle determines the access path for a statement without examining the values in bind variables. For instance, the following statement cannot make use of a histogram:

```
max_salary:=100000;
SELECT COUNT(*)
  INTO :output_bind
  FROM employees
 WHERE salary > :max_salary
```

However, the following statement would be able to make use of a histogram on salary:

```
SELECT count(*)
  INTO :output_bind
  FROM employees
 WHERE salary > 100000
```

Therefore, you may decide not to use bind variables if you believe that the SQL statement will benefit significantly from the use of histograms. The trade-off between histograms and bind variables is discussed in more detail in Chapter 8.

USING DBMS_STATS

Oracle8i introduces the DBMS_STATS package, which provides a number of useful procedures for managing optimizer statistics. These packages allow you to

❏ Collect optimizer statistics in parallel.
❏ Copy statistics between schemas.
❏ Arbitrarily modify statistics.

COLLECTING STATISTICS WITH DBMS_STATS

DBMS_STATS offers a number of routines to collect statistics:

❏ GATHER_DATABASE_STATS:	To collect statistics for an entire instance
❏ GATHER_INDEX_STATS:	To collect statistics for a nominated index
❏ GATHER_TABLE_STATS:	To collect statistics for a nominated table
❏ GATHER_SCHEMA_STATS:	To collect statistics for an entire schema

Syntax for these and other DBMS_STATS routines can be found in Appendix A.
Here's a simple example of collecting statistics for the EMPLOYEES table with a 10% sample:

```
BEGIN
    dbms_stats.gather_table_stats(
        ownname=>USER,
```

```
        tabname=>'EMPLOYEES',
        estimate_percent=>10);
END;
```

In this more complex example, we also create column histograms, collect statistics for all indexes on the table, and perform the sampling in parallel:

```
BEGIN
    dbms_stats.gather_table_stats(
        ownname=>USER,
        tabname=>'EMPLOYEES',
        estimate_percent=>10,
        method_opt=>'FOR ALL INDEXED COLUMNS',
        degree=>4,
        cascade=>TRUE          );
END;
```

The ability to perform statistic gatherings in parallel is obviously one of the key advantages of DBMS_STATS over the ANALYZE command.

DBMS_STATS offers more powerful methods for collecting table statistics than the ANALYZE command. In particular, it allows statistics to be gathered in parallel.

COPYING STATISTICS TO ANOTHER SCHEMA

The DBMS_STATS package allows you to save your statistics into a statistics table and to load these statistics into the data dictionary. This allows for a couple of possibilities:

❑ Save the current statistics to the statistics table before gathering new statistics. You might do this so that you can restore the old statistics in the event that performance degrades.

❑ Copy statistics from one instance to another. You might do this if you wanted to work on execution plans in a small test environment yet still see the execution plans that would occur in the bigger production database.

Let's look at copying statistics from a production environment into a smaller test environment. In the production environment, we create a statistics table and copy statistics for the SALES table into our statistics table:

```
BEGIN
    dbms_stats.create_stat_table(
```

```
        ownname=>USER,
        stattab=>'PRODUCTION_STATISTICS');
    dbms_stats.export_table_stats(
        ownname=>USER,
        tabname=>'SALES',
        stattab=>'PRODUCTION_STATISTICS');
END;
```

Now, we copy the statistics table from the product instance to the development instance. This could be done using export and import, but here we use the SQL*PLUS COPY command:

```
SQL> COPY FROM username/password@production
     CREATE production_statistics USING
     SELECT * FROM production_statistics;
```

Finally, we import the statistics from the statistics table into the data dictionary in the development instance:

```
BEGIN
    dbms_stats.import_table_stats(
        ownname=>USER,
        tabname=>'SALES',
        stattab=>'PRODUCTION_STATISTICS');
END;
```

The statistics for the table SALES in the development instance will now be the same as those in the production instance.

STRATEGIES FOR OPTIMIZING STATISTIC COLLECTIONS

The overhead involved in gathering statistics from large tables can be high, and in high-availability, performance-critical installations, it may be unacceptable to simply analyze tables at frequent intervals.

One option for reducing the overhead of statistics collection is to collect statistics only when tables have been subjected to significant modification. This can be done in Oracle8i by using the MONITORING clause of CREATE or ALTER TABLE together with the DBMS_STATS package.

The monitoring clause causes Oracle to keep track of the number of updates, inserts, and deletes applied to a table. These are periodically recorded to the view USER_TAB_MODIFICATIONS. So to start monitoring the SALES table, we simply execute the following command:

```
ALTER TABLE sales MONITORING
```

From this point on, Oracle will track the number of modifications to the table and periodically update the view USER_TAB_MODIFICATIONS with this data. There is very little overhead to this monitoring, because the count of modifications is maintained in Oracle shared memory and written out to the data dictionary only every few hours.

Routines in DBMS_STATS such as GATHER_SCHEMA_STATS can use this data to either list or gather statistics for objects whose statistics are stale.[1] In the following example, tables with stale statistics are listed, and then statistics for those tables are gathered:

```
DECLARE
    t_stale_objects                         dbms_stats.objecttab;
BEGIN

    - List the stale objects
    dbms_stats.gather_schema_stats (
        ownname => USER,
        options => 'LIST STALE',
        objlist => t_stale_objects);
    FOR i IN 1 .. t_stale_objects.COUNT
    LOOP
        dbms_output.put_line
          (t_stale_objects (i).objname);
    END LOOP;

    - Gather statistics for the stale objects
    dbms_stats.gather_schema_stats (
        ownname => USER,
        options => 'GATHER STALE',
        estimate_percent => 10);
END;
```

SCHEDULING REGULAR STATISTICAL COLLECTIONS

It is generally wise to schedule automatic collection of statistics. The addition of new tables and indexes and the general change in data distribution over time can lead statistics to become out of date and perhaps to cause the optimizer to use suboptimal plans. For instance, statistics may be collected on a table soon after its creation when it has only a few hundred rows. Unless statistics are gathered as the table grows, it's possible that the optimizer will ignore indexes on the table because it believes that the full-table scan is the optimal path for such a small table.

---

[1]The statistics become stale when the inserts, deletes, and updates reach 10% of the number of rows in the table.

Automated gathering of statistics can be implemented using a variety of means, including operating system facilities such as UNIX "cron" or Windows "at" services. You can also use Oracle's inbuilt DBMS_JOB scheduler. For instance, the following command instructs Oracle to gather statistics for the SQL-TUNE schema each week:

```
DECLARE
    l_jobno NUMBER;
BEGIN
    dbms_job.submit(
        job=>l_jobno,
        next_date=>TO_DATE('23:30','HH24:MI'),
        interval=>'SYSDATE+1',
        what=>'BEGIN dbms_stats.gather_schema_stats
                    (ownname=>''SQLTUNE'',
                     estimate_percent=>10,
                     method_opt=>''FOR ALL INDEXED
COLUMNS'');END;'
        );
END;
```

USING PLAN STABILITY

When using the rule-based optimizer, the execution plan for a given statement will rarely change. If you add or remove an index, the execution plan might change, but you will not change the plan through adding or removing data.

However, when using the cost-based optimizer, execution plans can change if the statistics upon the tables concerned change. So if you collect statistics for a table that has recently undergone a lot of DML, the optimizer might change the execution plan for statements that use that table.

Usually, these execution plan changes will be for the best. However, if you have determined that a specific plan is the one you want, you might want to be sure that the optimizer will not "change its mind" in the future. This is where plan stability using stored outlines comes in.

A stored outline is a way of recording the execution plan for a specific SQL statement at a specific point in time. You can then activate the stored outline to ensure that the specific execution plan is used.

CREATING AN OUTLINE WITH *CREATE OUTLINE*

The simplest way to create a stored outline is to use the CREATE OUTLINE command:

```
CREATE OR REPLACE OUTLINE my_outline
      FOR CATEGORY active_outlines on
select * from sales
 where product_id=:prod_id
   and customer_id=:dept_id
```

We can look at the outline in the USER_OUTLINES view:

```
SQL> select name,category,sql_text
      from user_outlines where name='MY_OUTLINE';

NAME          CATEGORY            SQL_TEXT
----------    ----------------    -------------------------
MY_OUTLINE ACTIVE_OUTLINES  SELECT * FROM sales
                            WHERE product_id=:prod_id
                               AND customer_id=:dept_id
```

Stored outlines work by recording a set of hints that can be used to obtain the execution plan that was current when the outline was created. We can see the hints used by looking at the USER_OUTLINE_HINTS view:

```
SQL> select hint from user_outline_hints
      where name='MY_OUTLINE' order by stage;

HINT
-------------------------------------------
NOREWRITE
NOREWRITE
NO_EXPAND
ORDERED
NO_FACT(SALES)
INDEX(SALES SALES_CUST_I)
```

CREATING OUTLINES FOR ALL SQL STATEMENTS

As well as creating outlines by using the CREATE OUTLINE command, you can instruct Oracle to create outlines for all SQL statements by setting the CREATE_STORED_OUTLINES parameter to true. For example, the following statements will implicitly create stored outlines for all statements executed in the session. Note that the optimizer mode has been set to RULE.

```
SQL> ALTER SESSION SET optimizer_mode=rule;
SQL> ALTER SESSION SET create_stored_outlines=true;
```

```
Session altered.

SQL> select * from customers where
customer_status='INVALID';

Rem Other SQL statements.........
```

ACTIVATING THE OUTLINE

By default, the outline is not activated. The easiest way to manage outlines is to move the outlines you want activated to a certain category and then activate that category.

In the case of the previous example, we would first need to identify the name of the outlines concerned, since implicitly generated outlines are given system-generated names. We can do this through the USER_OUTLINES view:

```
SQL> select name,sql_text from user_outlines
  2  /

NAME        SQL_TEXT
----------  -----------------------------
SYS_OUTLIN  select * from customers where
E_00041320  customer_status='INVALID'
44450000

SYS_OUTLIN  DELETE FROM PLAN_TABLE WHERE S
E_00041320  TATEMENT_ID=:1
44450002
```

Having identified the name of the relevant outline, we can move it to an active outline category and, if necessary, activate the outline:

```
SQL> ALTER OUTLINE SYS_OUTLINE_0004132044450000
         CHANGE CATEGORY TO active_outlines;

SQL> ALTER SESSION SET use_stored_outlines=active_outlines;
```

Although we can use ALTER SESSION to set the USE_STORED_OUTLINES parameter to the desired outline category, it is more common to set this parameter in the server configuration file ("init.ora").

STORED OUTLINES AND EXPLAIN PLAN

In the preceding example we stored and activated an outline for an SQL statement while in rule-based optimizer mode. Now, we should be confident that the execution plan will not change when we switch to the cost-based optimizer.

Under the rule-based optimizer, we noted the following execution plan for the SQL statement:

```
Execution Plan
------------------------------------------------------------
   0      SELECT STATEMENT Optimizer=RULE
   1    0    TABLE ACCESS (BY INDEX ROWID) OF 'CUSTOMERS'
   2    1      INDEX (RANGE SCAN) OF 'CUSTOMERS_I4'
```

When we switch to the cost-based optimizer, and with the stored outline enabled, we get the following plan:

```
Execution Plan
------------------------------------------------------------
   0      SELECT STATEMENT Optimizer=CHOOSE
   1    0    TABLE ACCESS (FULL) OF 'CUSTOMERS'
```

What happened? We expected to retain the stored execution plan, but instead our execution plan changed to a full scan. In fact, we've hit an irritating characteristic of stored outlines: Even if the stored execution plan is executed, explain plan still returns the plan that would occur if the outline were disabled. We can prove that the stored plan was followed by looking at the raw SQL_TRACE file (SQL trace is discussed in detail in Chapter 7):

```
PARSING IN CURSOR #2 len=56 dep=0 uid=37 oct=3 lid=37 tim=0
hv=551874162 ad='37faacc'
select * from customers where customer_status='INVALID'
END OF STMT
PARSE #2:c=0,e=0,p=0,cr=0,cu=0,mis=0,r=0,dep=0,og=4,tim=0
EXEC #2:c=0,e=0,p=0,cr=0,cu=0,mis=0,r=0,dep=0,og=4,tim=0
FETCH #2:c=0,e=0,p=13,cr=13,cu=0,mis=0,r=8,dep=0,og=4,tim=0
*** 2000-04-14 21:06:45.111
STAT #2 id=1 cnt=8 pid=0 pos=0 obj=21982 op='TABLE ACCESS
BY INDEX ROWID CUSTOMERS '
STAT #2 id=2 cnt=9 pid=1 pos=1 obj=21985 op='INDEX RANGE
SCAN '
```

This output is hard to interpret but does indicate that the SQL statement was executed by an index range scan.

You can use stored outlines to ensure that an ideal execution plan for a statement does not change. However, EXPLAIN PLAN might not reflect this stored execution plan.

THINGS TO REMEMBER WITH STORED OUTLINES

❏ You must use the ALTER SESSION or ALTER SYSTEM command with the USE_STORED_OUTLINES to activate the stored outline.

❏ The SQL in the outline must match *exactly* the SQL being executed. This means that you must use bind variables if the parameters of the SQL change.

❏ When stored outlines are in effect, the EXPLAIN PLAN command might return inaccurate results.

❏ Your execution plan can still change if you drop or rename an index.

USING HINTS

Hints are instructions that you can include in your SQL statement to instruct or guide the optimizer. Using hints, you can specify join orders, type of access paths, indexes to be used, the optimization goal, and other instructions.

An optimizer hint appears as a comment following the first word of the SQL statement (e.g., SELECT, INSERT, DELETE or UPDATE). A hint is differentiated from other comments by the presence of the plus sign ("+") following the opening comment delimiter ("/*"). For instance, the following statement will be processed using the rule-based optimizer:

```
SELECT /*+ RULE */ *
  FROM employee
 WHERE salary > 1000000
```

Table 5.2 lists some of the more commonly used hints. A more complete list can be found in Appendix A.

Multiple hints can appear in the same comment, separated by a space. For instance, the following hint requests a full-table scan on both DEPARTMENT and EMPLOYEES:

```
SELECT /*+ FULL(E) FULL(D) */
       e.employee_id, e.surname, e.firstname
  FROM employees e,
```

```
               departments d
    WHERE  d.location='Melbourne'
        AND  d.department_id=e.department_id
```

TABLE 5.2   SOME OPTIMIZER HINTS

HINT	USE
CHOOSE	Use the CHOOSE optimizer goal.
RULE	Use the RULE optimizer goal.
FIRST_ROWS	Use the FIRST_ROWS optimizer goal.
ALL_ROWS	Use the ALL_ROWS optimizer goal.
FULL(*table_name*)	Use a full-table scan to access the nominated table, even if there is an appropriate index path to the data.
INDEX(*table_name index_name*)	Use the specified index on the specified table.
HASH(*table_name*)	Use hash cluster based retrieval on the specified table (this will obviously only work if the table is in a hash cluster).
INDEX_DESC(*table_name index_name*)	Use the specified index on the specified table, but scan the index from high values to low values. Normally, if an index is used to scan a range, the scan occurs from low value to high value.
AND_EQUALS(*table_name index_name index_name index_name ....*)	This hint instructs the optimizer to merge the specified indexes when retrieving rows for the specified table.
USE_NL(*table_name*)	This hint specifies that when this table is first joined, the nested loops approach should be used.
USE_MERGE(*table_name*)	This hint specifies that when the table is first joined, the sort-merge approach should be used.
USE_HASH(*table_name*)	Use the hash-join technique when joining this table.
MERGE_AJ(*table_name*)	This hint is placed in a subquery that is referred to by NOT IN in the main query. The hint specifies that an antijoin is to be performed using the sort-merge method.
HASH_AJ(*table_name*)	This is used in the same context as HASH_AJ and specifies that the antijoin should be performed using the hash-join method.
PARALLEL(*table_name degree_ of_parallelism*)	This hint directs that the table should be accessed via parallel table scan. The parallelism parameter determines how many query processes shall be used. See Chapter 11 for more information.
NOPARALLEL(*table_name*)	Don't use parallel query, even if table or database default would normally result in parallel processing.
CACHE(*table_name*)	When performing a full-table scan, encourage the caching of the table within Oracle shared memory. NOCACHE has the opposite effect.
ORDERED	Use the order of tables in the FROM clause as the join order. This overrides normal preference for an alternative join order based on cost calculations.

USING HINTS TO CHANGE THE ACCESS PATH

One of the most frequent uses of hints is to force a particular access path to be selected, and typically this means forcing the use of a particular index.

The simplest hint for forcing an index is the rather appropriately named INDEX hint. Typically, the INDEX hint is used to force the use of a particular index in this manner:

```
SELECT /*+ index(e,employee_mgr_idx) */ surname
  FROM employees e
 WHERE department_id=:1
   AND manager_id=:2
```

However, you can also instruct the optimizer to choose between a subset of indexes by specifying multiple index names:

```
SELECT /*+ index(e,employee_sal_idx,employee_mgr_idx) */
       surname
  FROM employees e
 WHERE department_id=:1
   AND manager_id=:2
```

You can simply specify that you want an index to be used but leave it up to the optimizer to choose the appropriate index:

```
SELECT /*+ index(e) */ surname
  FROM employees e
 WHERE department_id=:1
   AND manager_id=:2
```

You can also specify that you would like multiple indexes to be merged using the AND_EQUAL hint (although most of the time, merging indexes suggests you are missing an appropriate concatenated index):

```
SELECT
   /*+ AND_EQUAL(e,employee_dept_idx,employee_mgr_idx)*/
       surname
  FROM employees e
 WHERE department_id=:1
   AND manager_id=:2
```

By default, Oracle scans indexes in ascending order. You can, however, specify that you wish the index to be scanned in descending order. For instance,

```
SELECT /*+ index_desc(e,employee_sal_idx) */ surname
  FROM employees e
 WHERE salary < :1
```

If you don't want to use an index, you can use the FULL hint. You might want to do this if

❑ You're using rule-based optimization and the optimizer is selecting a very unselective index.

❑ You're using cost-based optimization and the optimizer is using an index that appears to be selective (e.g., has a large number of distinct values) but you happen to know that the particular value being searched is not selective (for instance, you have a query that is using an index to get all people under 100 years of age).

Here is an example of using the FULL hint:

```
SELECT /*+ FULL(e) */ surname
  FROM employees e
 WHERE department_id=:1
   AND manager_id=:2
```

USING HINTS TO CHANGE THE JOIN ORDER

The other common reason for using hints is to change the join order, or to change the type of joins performed.

The ORDERED hint instructs the optimizer to join tables in the order in which they appear in the FROM clause. If all other factors are equal (perhaps both tables are the same size and both have equivalent indexes), then the optimizer will join tables in this order anyway—so it's a good idea always to specify tables in the order you want them joined. However, the cost-based optimizer will usually be able to pick a specific join order based on the statistics collected for the table. By using ORDERED, you can force the join order to be the same order as in the FROM clause.

```
SELECT /*+ORDERED*/ d.department_name,e.surname
  FROM employees e,
       departments d
 WHERE d.department_id=e.department_id
   AND d.department_name=:1
```

We can select the join method (nested loops, sort merge, or hash) by using the USE_NL or USE_MERGE hints. This example forces a nested loops join:

```
SELECT /*+ORDERED USE_NL(d)*/
           d.department_name,e.surname
   FROM employees e,
        departments d
  WHERE d.department_id=e.department_id
    AND d.department_name=:1
```

ERRORS IN HINT SPECIFICATIONS

If you make an error in a hint specification (for instance, forgetting the plus sign or specifying an invalid hint), Oracle will ignore the hint without generating an error or warning. Therefore, it is important that you validate that your hint worked (using the explain plan or tkprof utilities documented in Chapter 7).

It's particularly easy to make mistakes when specifying table names. If the table name is given an alias in the FROM clause, you must specify this alias in the hint. However, you must not specify an owner (or "schema") name, even if it appears in the FROM clause. For instance, assume this is the query:

```
SELECT surname,firstname
  FROM employees e
 WHERE salary=0
```

The following are some valid and invalid hints:

/*+ INDEX(e salary_idx) */	Correct usage. Then index salary_idx will be used.
/* INDEX(e salary_idx) */	Invalid, because the "+" is missing after the opening comment marker.
/*+ INDEX(employees salary_idx) */	Invalid, because employees is given a table alias in the FROM clause but not in the hint.
/*+ INDEX(e, salary_idx */	Invalid, because the ending bracket is missing.
/*+ INDEX(e, salary_idx) */	Valid, although the comma following the table alias is not necessary.
/*+ INDEEX(e salary_idx) */	Invalid, because the hint is misspelled.

USING OPTIMIZER TRICKS

Before the introduction of the cost-based optimizer and the advent of hints, SQL programmers were still able to influence the query optimizer. They did this by disabling certain access paths and by changing the order of tables in the FROM clause. These methods still work, although hints are more powerful and self-documenting.

DISABLING ACCESS PATHS

If a column in the WHERE clause is modified by a function or other operation, an index using that column cannot be used. By disabling certain indexes, you can prevent the optimizer using certain access paths. By disabling the access paths you do not want the optimizer to use, you hope that the optimizer will eventually use the access path of your choice. For example, in the following query, Oracle could choose to use the index on either the surname columns or on the salary column:

```
SELECT *
  FROM employees e
 WHERE e.salary > 100000
   AND e.surname like 'S%'
```

By modifying the surname column (concatenating a blank), we prevent any index on surname being used, hence forcing the salary index access path:

```
SELECT *
  FROM employees e
 WHERE e.salary > 100000
   AND e.surname||'' like 'S%'
```

In the case of numeric or date columns, you can get the same effect by adding 0 to the column. For instance,

```
SELECT *
  FROM employees e
 WHERE e.salary+0 > 100000
   AND e.surname like 'S%'
```

CHANGING THE JOIN ORDER

Sometimes you can change the join order by suppressing various access paths using the trick discussed in the preceding section. If this doesn't work, the order of tables in the FROM clause does influence the rule-based optimizer. If access path rankings are equal, then the table specified last in the FROM clause will be the first table in the join order. Note that this is exactly the opposite behavior of the cost-based optimizer. For instance, Oracle resolves the following SQL statement by performing a full-table scan of SALESREGION and then using an index to find matching records in DEPARTMENTS:

```
SELECT /*+RULE*/ department_name,regionname
  FROM departments d,
       salesregion s
 WHERE d.manager_id=s.manager_id
```

However, if we change the order of the tables in the FROM clause, the opposite join order results: A full-table scan of departments is used.

```
SELECT /*+RULE*/ department_name,regionname
  FROM salesregion s,
       departments d
 where d.manager_id=s.manager_id
```

You can use hints or optimizer tricks to change the execution plan for a SQL statement. However, hints are more powerful and are self-documenting and should be used as a first preference.

SUMMARY

The process of determining the most efficient way to get or change the data requested by the SQL statement is called query optimization. There are two query optimizers: the rule-based optimizer (which uses the characteristics of tables and indexes to determine the best path) and the cost-based optimizer (which also takes into account the size of tables and the number of keys in an index). The cost-based optimizer is the best choice in most circumstances.

Whichever optimizer is chosen, it's up to the SQL programmer to ensure that the best execution plan has been chosen. The SQL programmer knows more about the application and data characteristics than the optimizer and has the benefit of possessing both more time to decide on the optimum path and a superior query optimizer (i.e., the human brain). Both the rule-based optimizer and the cost-based optimizer will sometimes make poor decisions for which the SQL programmer is ultimately responsible.

The optimizers must determine the way in which table data are to be accessed (the access path) and the order in which tables will be joined (join order).

The major factors influencing both join order and access paths are the presence or absence of indexes (both optimizers) and the size and distribution of table and index data (cost-based optimizer only).

When using the cost-based optimizer, make sure you analyze your tables regularly or when they have realistic data volumes. The DBMS_STATS package, introduced in Oracle8i, allows for more efficient collection of statistics and also allows statistics to be modified or copied between environments.

If you want to make sure that an SQL execution plan will not change in the future (due to changes in table statistics, for instance), then you can use stored outlines to fix the execution plan.

You can influence either optimizer by using hints, which are comments embedded in the SQL statement that contain instructions to the optimizer. Mastery of hints is one of the key skills required for SQL performance tuning.

INDEXING AND CLUSTERING

INTRODUCTION

In this chapter, we examine the indexing and clustering facilities provided by Oracle.

Indexes and clusters are Oracle schema objects that exist primarily to enhance performance. Understanding and using indexes or hash clusters effectively is therefore of paramount importance when optimizing SQL. Effective indexing can result in huge improvements to SQL performance.

The advantages of indexes do not come without a cost. Creating the index can be a very time-consuming process and often can't be done on line. In addition, indexes must be updated during inserts, deletes, and updates, and this can slow down these operations. Finally, indexes take up storage space; it's not uncommon for indexes to take as much disk space as the tables to which they refer.

Indexing and clustering decisions are important and can be complex. Simply indexing everything is not usually a good idea since updates will be degraded. On the other hand, almost any database of a significant size is going to require indexes in order to perform effectively. The solution, of course, is to index or hash selectively, creating indexes or hash clusters only when you get a benefit from it.

In this chapter, we examine the implementation of Oracle indexes and clusters:

❑ The structure of the B*-tree index, Oracle's default index structure
❑ Multicolumn (concatenated) indexes
❑ Implicit indexes created by referential integrity constraints
❑ Clustering one or more tables on common key values (an index cluster)
❑ Clustering a table using hash key values (a hash cluster)
❑ Bitmapped indexes
❑ Index-only tables

B*-TREE INDEXES

The B*-tree ("balanced tree") index is Oracle's default index structure. Figure 6.1 shows a high-level overview of B*-tree index structure.

The B*-tree index has a hierarchical tree structure. At the top of the tree is the header block. This block contains pointers to the appropriate branch block for any given range of key values. The branch block will usually point to the appropriate leaf block for a more specific range or, for a particularly big index, point to another branch block. The leaf block contains a list of key values and pointers (ROWIDS) to the appropriate rows in the table.

Examining the diagram in Figure 6.1, let's imagine how Oracle would traverse this index. Should we need to access the record for "BAKER," we would first consult the header block. The header block would tell us that key values starting with A through K are stored in the leftmost branch block. Accessing this branch block, we find that key values starting with A through D are stored in the leftmost leaf block. Consulting this leaf block, we find the value "BAKER" and its associated ROWID, which we would then use to get to the table row concerned.

Leaf blocks contain links to both the previous and the next leaf block. This allows us to scan the index in either ascending or descending order and allows range queries using the ">", "<", or "BETWEEN" operators to be processed using the index.

Each leaf block is at the same depth. This means that from the header block, you always consult the same number of branch blocks before locating the leaf block.

B*-tree indexes have the following advantages over traditional indexing strategies (for instance, indexed sequential access method [ISAM]):

❑ Because each leaf node is at the same depth, performance is predictable. In theory, no row in the table will be more than three or four I/Os away.

❑ B*-trees offer good performance for large tables, again because the depth is at most four (one header block, two levels of branch blocks, and one level of leaf block). Again, no row in even the biggest table would take more than four I/Os to locate. In fact, because the header block will almost always be

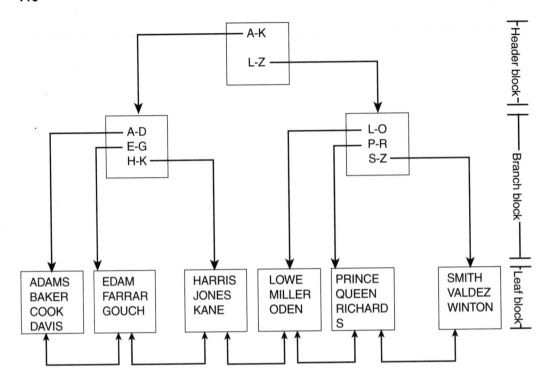

Figure 6.1   B*-tree index structure.

already loaded in memory, and branch blocks, are usually loaded in memory, the actual number of physical disk reads is usually only one or two.

❑   The B*-tree index supports range queries as well as exact lookups. This is possible because of the links to the previous and next leaf blocks.

The B*-tree index provides flexible and efficient query performance. However, maintaining the B*-tree when changing data can be expensive. For instance, consider inserting a row with the key value "NIVEN" into the table index diagrammed in Figure 6.1. To insert the row, we must add a new entry into the "L-O" block. If there is free space within this block, then the cost is substantial but perhaps not excessive. But what happens if there is no free space in the block?

If there is no free space within a leaf block for a new entry, then an index split is required. A new block must be allocated and half of the entries in the existing block moved into the new block. In addition, there is a requirement to add a new entry to the branch block (in order to point to the newly created leaf block). If there is no free space in the branch block, then the branch block must also be split.

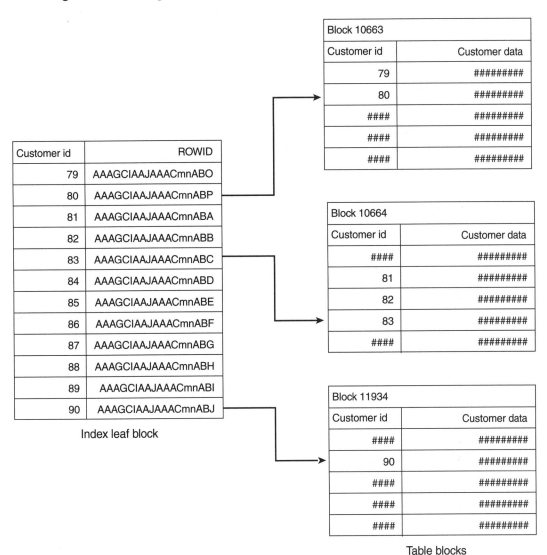

Figure 6.2 Leaf blocks contain ROWIDs that point to the physical location of table blocks.

Index splits are an expensive operation: New blocks must be allocated and index entries moved from one block to another. Index splits can be avoided if key values are inserted in ascending sequence. This is one of the advantages of using an artificial key (artificial keys are discussed in Chapter 18). You can also reduce index splits by increasing the amount of free space kept within the index for new entries. This is defined by the PCTFREE clause of the CREATE INDEX statement.

INDEX SELECTIVITY

The selectivity of a column or group of columns is a common measure of the usefulness of an index on those columns. Columns or indexes are selective if they have a large number of unique values or few duplicate values. For instance, the DATE_OF_BIRTH column will be very selective while the GENDER column will not be selective.

Selective indexes are more efficient than nonselective indexes because they point more directly to specific values. The cost-based optimizer will determine the selectivity of the various indexes available to it and will try and use the most selective index. We will revisit the issue of selectivity in Chapter 8.

UNIQUE INDEXES

A unique index is one that prevents any duplicate values for the columns that make up the index. If you try to create a unique index on a table that contains such duplicate values, you will receive an error. Similarly, you will also receive an error if you try and insert a row that contains duplicate unique index key values.

A unique index is typically created in order to prevent duplicate values rather than to improve performance. However, unique index columns are often efficient—they point to exactly one row and are therefore very selective. Both the rule-based and cost-based optimizers will tend to prefer unique indexes to nonunique indexes.

IMPLICIT INDEXES

Implicit indexes are created automatically by Oracle in order to implement either a primary key or unique constraint. Implicit indexes may also be created when implementing Oracle object type tables and in other circumstances.

You may recall from our earlier discussion of relational database principles that every row in a table should have a unique identifier and that this unique identifier is known as the primary key. In addition to the primary key, there may be a number of candidate keys that are also unique. Oracle allows you to define these keys (and also foreign keys) when you create a table. In order to implement either a primary or unique constraint, Oracle creates a unique index. In addition to enforcing uniqueness, these indexes are available to enhance the performance of queries.

For tables that are defined as being of an Oracle object type, an implicit index is created against the object identifier (OID) of each row.

CONCATENATED INDEXES

A concatenated index is simply an index comprising more than one column. The advantage of a concatenated key is that it is often more selective than a single key index. The combination of columns will point to a smaller number of rows than indexes composed of the individual columns. A concatenated index that contains all of the columns referred to in an SQL statement's WHERE clause will usually be very effective.

If you frequently query on more that one column within a table, then creating a concatenated index for these columns is an excellent idea. For instance, we may often query the EMPLOYEE table by SURNAME and FIRSTNAME. In that case, we would probably want to create an index on both SURNAME and FIRSTNAME. For instance,

```
CREATE INDEX employee_name_idx ON employee
        (surname, firstname)
```

Using such an index, we could rapidly find all employees matching a given surname/firstname combination. Such an index will be far more effective than an index on surname alone or separate indexes on surname and firstname.

Choosing the Best Column Order   If a concatenated index could only be used when all of its keys appeared in the WHERE clause, then concatenated indexes would probably be of limited use. Luckily, a concatenated index can be used provided that any of the initial or leading columns are used. Leading columns are those that are specified earliest in the index definition. For instance, with the concatenated index we created on the employee table (on SURNAME, FIRSTNAME), we could use the index to retrieve employees matching a surname, but not employees matching on firstnames (a full-table scan would be required). To extend this example, imagine a concatenated index on SURNAME, FIRSTNAME, and DATE_OF_BIRTH. Table 6.1 shows how this index can be used. Only the leading, or leftmost, parts of the index can be used.

Guidelines for Concatenated Indexes   The following guidelines will help in deciding when to use concatenated indexes and which columns should be included and in which order.

TABLE 6–1   Using an index on SURNAME, FIRSTNAME, DATE_OF_BIRTH.

COLUMNS SPECIFIED IN THE WHERE CLAUSE	COLUMNS IN THE INDEX THAT CAN BE USED
SURNAME, FIRSTNAME, DATE_OF_BIRTH	SURNAME, FIRSTNAME, DATE_OF_BIRTH: All columns in the concatenated index are specified.
SURNAME, FIRSTNAME	SURNAME, FIRSTNAME: The two columns are leading columns, so both can be used.
SURNAME, DATE_OF_BIRTH	SURNAME only. DATE_OF_BIRTH cannot be used, because it comes after FIRSTNAME, which is not specified.
FIRSTNAME	None! The index cannot be used unless the first column is specified.

❑ Create a concatenated index for columns from a table that appear together in the WHERE clause.

❑ If columns sometimes appear on their own in a WHERE clause, place them at the start of the index.

❑ The more selective a column is, the more useful it will be at the leading end of the index.

We'll discuss the optimization of concatenated indexes in greater detail in Chapter 8.

INDEX MERGES

If more than one column from a table appears in the WHERE clause and there is no concatenated index on the columns concerned but there are indexes on the individual columns, then Oracle may decide to perform an index merge.

In order to perform an index merge, Oracle retrieves all rows from each index with matching values and then merges these two lists or result sets and returns only those that appear in both lists. For instance, consider the case in which there is an index on EMPLOYEE.SURNAME and another index on EMPLOYEE.FIRSTNAME. If we issued a query for "Ian Smith", we would first retrieve all employees with the surname of "Smith" and then retrieve all employees with the first name of "Ian." The two lists would be merged, and only employees in both lists would be returned.

Performing index merges is almost always less efficient than the equivalent concatenated index. If you see an index merge (shown in execution plans with the AND EQUALS operator), consider creating an appropriate concatenated index.

NULL VALUES

When an indexed column is NULL, or when all columns in a concatenated index are NULL, then the row concerned will not have entry in the index. In other words, NULLs are not indexed. This is a fundamental and important concept since it is not possible to use an index to find NULL values, although it is possible to find a value NOT NULL. If you find yourself coding an IS NULL condition in the WHERE clause, be sure to consider the potential performance impact of the resulting full-table scan.

REVERSE KEY INDEXES

Oracle8 and Oracle8i provide a REVERSE keyword that will cause the actual key value stored in the index to be reversed. So, for instance, a REVERSE index would store "Smith" as "htimS". If you are inserting entries into the table in ascending order (perhaps using a sequence), the leading or rightmost block will always be very active. Furthermore, space might be wasted if you periodically purge most—but not all—older entries. The old entries that are not purged will remain in blocks that are sparsely populated. If you use the REVERSE keyword, new index entries will be spread more evenly across existing index blocks and the blocks will be more tightly packed than might otherwise be the case. However, it would no longer be possible to perform range scans using the index. This facility was introduced mainly to counter contention for hot index blocks in an Oracle Parallel Server environment and would not often be useful in single-instance Oracle configurations.

INDEX COMPRESSION

Oracle8i allows index leaf block entries to be compressed. The compression approach used involves removing leading columns of the index key that do not change and storing them in a prefix entry. This leading part of the index entry then can be omitted from the leaf block.

Index compression works best on concatenated indexes where leading parts of the index are repeated. For instance, an index on SURNAME, FIRSTNAME, GIVEN_NAME would be an excellent candidate for compression because we would expect surnames to be repeated.

For an index on SALES(PRODUCT_ID,CUSTOMER_ID,DEPARTMENT_ID), using the COMPRESS flag reduced the number of leaf blocks from 4042 to 2451.

Using compression on suitable indexes has the following beneficial effects:

❑ The storage requirements for the index are reduced.
❑ Because more rows can be stored in each leaf block, range scans will require fewer I/O operations.
❑ Because more rows can be stored in each leaf block, the height of the B*-tree might be reduced.

You cannot compress partitioned or bitmap indexes. You also cannot compress a single-column unique index.

The COMPRESS keyword can take the number of prefix columns to use as an argument. This will default to the number of indexed columns for a nonunique index or less than the number of indexed columns for unique indexes. You may wish to reduce the default if you know that an indexed column will not repeat. For instance, consider an index on SURNAME, TIME_OF_BIRTH, where TIME_OR_BIRTH is the exact minute, hour, and day of birth. It's possible, but very unlikely, that two people of the same surname would have been born on the exact same minute. Therefore, compression on both columns would not be efficient and you would probably create the index with a "COMPRESS 1" clause.

FUNCTIONAL INDEXES

Functional indexes—available from Oracle8i onward—allow you to create an index on a function or an expression. The function or expression must be deterministic, which means that if given the same inputs it must always return the same outputs regardless of changes in the environment or the date and time. For instance, the following is a legal index definition in Oracle8i:

```
CREATE INDEX emp_upper_surname
    ON employees( UPPER(surname))
```

However, the following is invalid because the value of the AGE function will change over time:

```
CREATE OR REPLACE FUNCTION AGE(p_dob DATE) RETURN NUMBER IS
BEGIN
    RETURN(SYSDATE-p_dob);
END;

CREATE INDEX emp_age on employees( age(date_of_birth) );
```

The DETERMINISTIC keyword can be used when creating the function to indicate that it will always return the same values. We could apply the DETERMINISTIC keyword to the preceding age function and the index would be created. However, the index that was created would become invalid over time because index entries would continue to reflect the age of the employee when the index entry was created, while the age function would report their current age.

FOREIGN KEYS AND LOCKING

You can declare referential integrity constraints to prevent rows being inserted into detail (or child) tables that do not have a matching row in a master (or parent) table. This facility preserves the integrity of your data and is implemented automatically by most CASE tools. For instance, the following statement creates a foreign key constraint between EMPLOYEES and DEPARTMENTS:

```
ALTER TABLE employees
ADD CONSTRAINT fk1_employees
    FOREIGN KEY (department_id)
    REFERENCES departments (department_id);
```

Once the constraint is enabled, attempting to create an EMPLOYEE row with an invalid DEPARTMENT_ID, or to delete a DEPARTMENT row that has matching employees, will generate an error. However, in order to prevent inconsistencies during the operation, Oracle applies table-level locks (rather than the usual row-level locks) to the child table when the parent table is modified.

These table locks are not required if there is an index on the foreign key in the child table (for instance, an index on EMPLOYEES.DEPARTMENT_ID). Often, you will create such an index anyway in order to optimize joins and queries. However, if you omit such a foreign key index and if the parent table is subject to update, you may see heavy lock contention. If in doubt, it's safer to create indexes on all foreign keys, despite the possible overhead of maintaining unneeded indexes.

CLUSTERING

Indexing involves creating a separate structure that allows you to locate specified data rapidly. Indexes are entirely analogous to the index at the back of this book.

Clustering, on the other hand, involves physically locating the data in some convenient location. Oracle provides two techniques for clustering data:

❏ An index cluster stores rows with the same key values in close physical proximity. These rows might be thought as having been prejoined.
❏ A hash cluster stores specific rows in a location that can be deduced from mathematical manipulation of the row's key value.

INDEX CLUSTERS

Index clusters are a mechanism for storing related rows from one or more tables in the same segment. Rows that have common cluster key values are stored together. In theory, this will speed up joins because the rows to be joined are stored in the same block. In practice, multitable index clusters are of severely limited value and should only be used when the tables are always referenced together. Here are some of the disadvantages of index clusters:

❏ Full-table scans against only one of the tables in the cluster will be slower, since blocks for other tables in the cluster will also have to be scanned.
❏ Inserts can be slower because of the additional effort required to maintain the cluster.
❏ The performance benefit for joins may be minimal.

Figure 6.3 shows how an index cluster would be implemented for the PRODUCTS and SALES tables. We'll examine the effect of index clusters on join and scan performance in greater detail in Chapter 7.

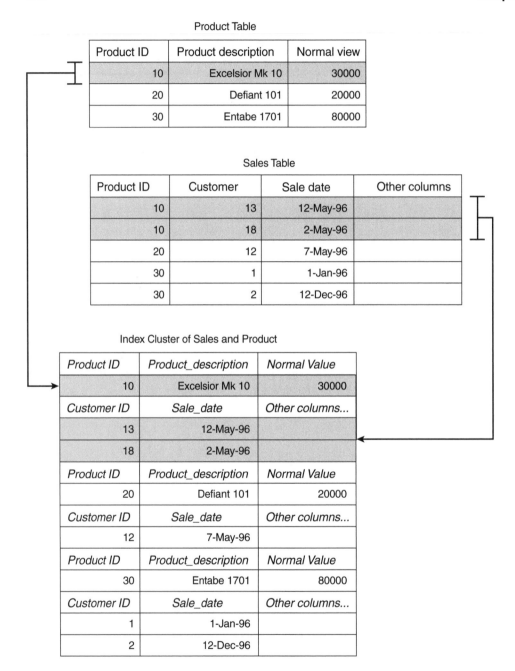

Figure 6.3   A multitable index cluster.

HASH CLUSTERS

The term *hashing* refers to the process of using a mathematical transformation that translates a key value into a storage address. In Oracle hash clusters, key values are translated into hash keys, and rows with the same hash key are stored together. The hash key tells Oracle where these blocks are located. In this way, Oracle can go directly to the blocks required without expending any I/O on an index lookup.

Hash clusters minimize the number of block reads required to locate a row using the hash key. With a hash cluster, retrieving the row in question may require only one block access—the access of the block containing the row. In comparison, a B*-tree index will require at least four block reads (index header block, index branch block, index leaf block, and table block).

Requirements for Hash Clusters The cluster key should have a high cardinality (large number of unique values). In fact, unique or primary keys are usually good candidates for the hash key. The hash key should normally be selected by an exact match rather than by a range or "like" condition. For example, if we created a hash cluster based on the employee table, we could not use the hash cluster to enhance the search to scan for all employee_ids between one and ten.

Structure of Hash Clusters When a hash cluster is created, it is necessary to specify the number of hash key values that are expected; this is done using the HASHKEYS clause of the CREATE CLUSTER statement. The SIZE clause of the CREATE CLUSTER statement determines the number of hash key values stored in each block. The overall initial size of the hash cluster will therefore be dependent on the setting of these two values.

The setting for SIZE and HASHKEYS is critical to the performance of the hash cluster. If HASHKEYS is set too high, then the hash cluster will become sparsely populated and full-table scan performance will degrade. On the other hand, if HASHKEYS is set too low, then multiple cluster keys will be allocated the same hash key. These collisions can result in the block allocated for the hash cluster overflowing and additional blocks being chained. Once chaining occurs, cluster key lookups can require more than one I/O to resolve and the benefit of the hash cluster is reduced or eliminated.

By default, Oracle uses an internal algorithm to convert the cluster key into a hash value. This algorithm works well for most circumstances. However, you can also use the cluster key (if it is uniformly distributed) or you can specify your own function (written in PL/SQL).

Figure 6.4 shows an example of a hash cluster. The diagram illustrates some important principles:

❑ The hash key serves as a relative offset into the hash cluster. That is, once Oracle calculates the hash key, it can move directly to the relevant block in the hash cluster.

Employee Table (unclustered)

Employee_id	Surname	Firstname	Date of Birth
10	Potter	Jean Luc	21/04/23
11	Smith	Ben	23/05/78
12	Thomas	Dianna	5/08/47
15	Jones	Katherine	11/11/34
89	Smith	Montgomery	19/02/20
34	Cane	Beverly	9/09/38
54	Main	Leonard	7/05/30
69	Ryder	William	3/06/40

Cluster key	Hash key
10	0
11	1
12	2
15	0
89	4
34	4
54	4
69	4

Table of conversion from cluster key to hash key

Hash Key	Employee_id	Surname	Firstname	Date of Birth
0	10	Potter	Jean Luc	21/04/23
	15	Jones	Katherine	11/11/34
1	11	Smith	Ben	23/05/78
2	12	Thomas	Dianna	5/08/47
3				
4	89	Smith	Montgomery	19/02/20
	34	Cane	Beverly	9/09/38
	54	Main	Leonard	7/05/30

Hash Cluster of the Employee Table

4	69	Ryder	William	3/06/40

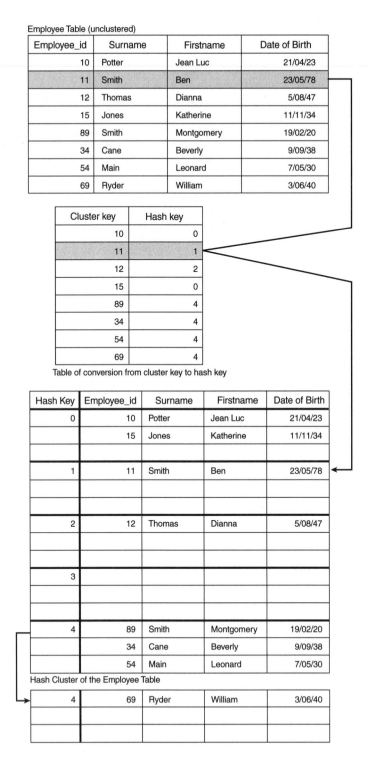

Figure 6.4   Structure of a hash cluster.

❏ The same amount of space is allocated for each hash value. If the space allocated is too high, then space will be wasted and the cluster will be sparsely populated—and this will degrade full-table scan performance (for instance, the space allocated for hash key 2 is completely unused).

❏ If the amount of space allocated for a hash value is too high, then additional blocks will have to be chained. This degrades lookup performance, since Oracle must perform additional I/Os to get to the rows stored in these chained blocks. For instance, in Figure 6.4 the data for employee 69 is stored in a chained block. Retrieving the details will require an additional I/O.

When to Use Hash Clusters You could consider using hash clusters in the following circumstances:

❏ Data in the table are accessed primarily by an EQUALS TO condition on the cluster key.

❏ Range scans on the cluster key are rarely, if ever, performed.

❏ Full-table scans are rarely, if ever, performed.

❏ The table is either static in size, or you are prepared to rebuild the cluster periodically when the size changes.

We'll discuss the optimization of hash clusters in detail in Chapter 8.

BITMAP INDEXES

In a bitmap index, Oracle creates a bitmap for each unique value of the column in question. Each bitmap contains a single bit (0 or 1) for every row in the table. A "1" indicates that the row has the value specified by the bitmap and a "0" indicates that it does not. Oracle can rapidly scan these bitmaps to find rows matching specified criteria. Oracle can also rapidly compare multiple bitmaps to find all rows matching multiple bitmapped criteria. Bitmaps suit columns with a limited number of distinct values that are often queried in combination.

Figure 6.5 shows an example of bitmapped indexes on an imaginary table called SURVEY. Bitmapped indexes exist on GENDER, MARITAL STATUS, and OWN_HOME (the person owns his or her own home). To find all single males who own their own home, Oracle extracts each bitmap and finds rows who have a "1" in each bitmap.

FEATURES OF BITMAP INDEXES

❏ Bitmap indexes offer fast retrieval for columns that have only a few distinct values and that are often queried together. However, full-table scans will usually be more efficient if the columns are queried individually.

Partial contents of the SURVEY table

Gender	Marital Status	Children_yn	Income	Own_home
M	Married	N	$20,000	N
M	Single	N	$30,000	Y
F	Divorced	Y	$12,000	N
F	Married	Y	$70,000	Y
F	Married	Y	$20,000	Y
M	Single	Y	$10,000	N
F	Married	N	$13,000	N

Male	Female
1	0
1	0
0	1
0	1
0	1
1	0
0	1

Bitmap index on gender

Married	Single	Divorced
1	0	0
0	1	0
0	0	1
1	0	0
1	0	0
0	1	0
1	0	0

Bitmap index on Marital Status

Male	Female
1	0
1	0
0	1
0	1
0	1
1	0
0	1

Bitmap index on own_home

Select "from survey where sex" 'Male' and marital_status 'Single' and own_home 'Yes'

Male		Single		Yes		
1		0		0		0
1		1		1		1	← This row satisfies the query
0		0		0		0
0	AND	0	AND	1	EQUALS	0
0		0		1		0
1		1		0		0
0		0		0		0

Figure 6.5   Example of bitmap index retrieval.

❏ Bitmapped indexes are especially suitable for large tables and for aggregate (e.g., "how many") queries.

❏ Bitmapped indexes can be used in any order and in any combination, so they are more flexible than a corresponding concatenated index, which requires that you use at least the first column in the index.

❏ If used appropriately, bitmapped indexes are very compact—much more compact than the equivalent concatenated index (provided that the number of distinct values is not too high).

❏ Contrary to early recommendations from Oracle, bitmap indexes can be efficient even when there is a large number of distinct values. However, they are not suitable for columns where values are rarely repeated or for unique columns.

❏ Merging multiple bitmaps is an operation that can be performed efficiently by the computer (bit operations are fast).

DRAWBACKS OF BITMAP INDEXES

❏ Oracle is unable to lock a single bit and, consequently, updating a bitmap may result in locks being applied to a large number of rows. This makes bitmap indexes inappropriate for applications with even moderately high transaction rates.

❏ Bitmap indexes cannot be used to optimize range queries. Use B*-tree indexes, if necessary, for columns subject to these sorts of operations.

INDEX ORGANIZED TABLES

Earlier in this chapter we considered the importance of including all required columns in a concatenated index in order to optimize query performance. It is also a significant optimization to include all columns that appear in the select list in the concatenated index so that we can satisfy the query using the index alone without a table access.

Imagine a table for which every column was included in such a concatenated index and for which all queries were satisfied using that index. In this circumstance the table itself has become superfluous—it is the index alone that stores the data required and that is used to satisfy queries. However, the table still exists and consumes valuable disk storage and incurs an overhead when rows are added, removed, or modified. We might wish we could dispense with the table and keep just the index.

Oracle8 allows us to create index organized tables. These may be used in the same way as other tables but are stored internally in a B*-tree index format. By storing a table in a B*-tree index format, we avoid the duplicating data in both the table and the index and ensure that queries that access the table by its primary key are very fast, since only an index lookup—without the normal corresponding table access—will be required. We create an index-only table using the ORGANIZATION keyword of the CREATE TABLE statement. For instance,

```
CREATE TABLE customers_iot
(
    customer_id         NUMBER NOT NULL ,
    customer_name       VARCHAR2(40) NOT NULL ,
    contact_surname     VARCHAR2(40) NOT NULL ,
    contact_firstname   VARCHAR2(40) NOT NULL ,
    phoneno             VARCHAR2(12) NOT NULL ,
    address1                VARCHAR2(40) NOT NULL ,
    address2                VARCHAR2(40) NOT NULL ,
    zipcode             VARCHAR2(6) NOT NULL ,
    date_of_birth       DATE NOT NULL ,
    sales_rep_id        NUMBER NOT NULL ,
    comment_id          NUMBER,
    contact_gender          CHAR(1),
    process_flag        CHAR(1),
    pgp_sig             VARCHAR2(4000),
    PRIMARY KEY (customer_id) )
ORGANIZATION INDEX
INCLUDING zipcode OVERFLOW —Overflow storage here
```

Index-only tables are organized as a B*-tree index constructed against their primary key. The primary key plus the additional columns are stored in the leaf blocks of the B*-tree. Storing all the columns in the leaf block might cause the index structure to degrade because as the number of entries per leaf block declines, the overhead of index scans increases as does the chance that the B*-tree height will increase. For this reason, you can nominate the columns that will be stored in the leaf block with the INCLUDING clause. Columns that come after the INCLUDING column will be stored in an overflow segment, which can be defined in the CREATE TABLE statement. Figure 6.6 compares the layout of a B*-tree index and table with that of an index organized table.

The ability to relocate longer columns away from the B*-tree structure allows Oracle to keep the B*-tree relatively small and efficient while keeping small, frequently accessed columns in the B*-tree. When creating an index-only table, define frequently accessed, small columns early in the column list and large, infrequently accessed columns later in the list. Specify the INCLUDING clause so that only the frequently accessed columns are retained in the B*-tree. The primary key should include all columns that might appear in the WHERE clause.

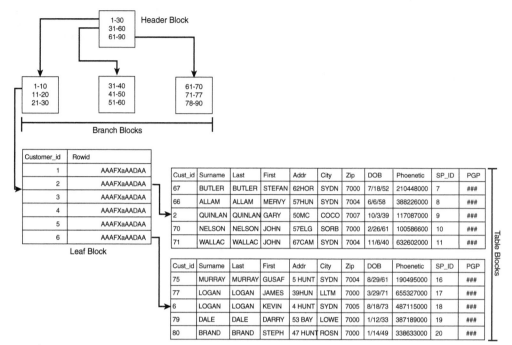

A. B* tree index and associated table blocks

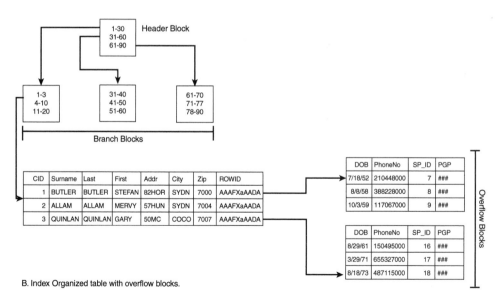

B. Index Organized table with overflow blocks.

Figure 6.6   Index organized table compared with B*-tree index and table.

SUMMARY

Effective indexing or hashing is essential if your SQL is to perform at peak efficiency. Oracle supports five indexing/hashing schemes:

❏ B*-tree indexes, which offer flexible and fast retrieval for range or equality lookups for tables of all sizes

❏ Index clusters, which may be useful to physically colocate two or more tables that are often joined together

❏ Hash clusters, which can optimize lookups of single values for static tables

❏ Bitmapped indexes, which may be useful if you need fast resolution of aggregate queries incorporating multiple columns with few unique values for large tables

❏ Index-organized tables, in which the table data is organized as a B*-tree index

B*-tree indexes are suitable for the vast majority of applications. Use the following guidelines when creating B*-tree indexes:

❏ Create indexes for columns that have a large number of distinct values.

❏ Consider indexes for columns that are used in the where clause to select rows or to join tables.

❏ There is an extra overhead in maintaining an index on columns that are frequently updated, so avoid indexing these columns.

❏ Consider creating multicolumn (concatenated) indexes when columns are queried together in the where clause. Put the most frequently queried columns at the leading edge of the index (first in the list of columns).

❏ Consider indexing foreign key columns if you implement referential integrity.

Use the following guidelines when contemplating clustering or bitmapped indexing:

❏ Be wary of implementing index clusters. The small potential benefit in join performance is often not worth the cost in table scan performance.

❏ Consider using hash clusters for tables where you need to optimize the lookup of a key value using an EQUALS TO condition and where full-table scans are not required. If you implement a hash cluster, make sure you carefully configure its storage—see Chapter 8 for details on doing this.

❏ Consider bitmap indexes for large tables with low update rates, for which you wish to query on multiple, low- to medium-cardinality columns. Decision support systems and data warehouses may find bitmapped indexes useful.

Index organized tables can be advantageous when all or most of a table's columns would be stored in an index anyway. Index organized tables also offer a convenient mechanism for storing infrequently accessed columns outside of the main table segment.

TRACING AND EXPLAINING SQL

In this chapter, we explore the tools provided by Oracle that allow you to examine how your SQL statement is or will be executed. Without these tools, you will have only a vague understanding of how your SQL is being processed. You might know if it's running fast or running slow, but you will not know why, and you will be in a poor position to predict how it might behave if data volumes change.

Using the tools covered in this chapter, you'll be able to determine exactly how Oracle processes your SQL and you'll also be able to measure exactly the resources required to execute it. Effective measurements of SQL statement execution and a determination of the execution plan used by Oracle to execute the SQL are essential prerequisites for efficient SQL statement tuning.

The tools we discuss are as follows:

❏ EXPLAIN PLAN, which can reveals how Oracle will obtain your data (the execution plan)
❏ SQL_TRACE, which generates a trace file containing SQL statements executed by your session and their resource requirements
❏ tkprof, which formats the output of SQL_TRACE
❏ The SQL*PLUS AUTOTRACE command, which allows execution plans and statistics to be displayed from within an SQL*PLUS session

There are many third-party tools available that can assist in tuning SQL. You'll find links to some of these at this book's website. These tools can be useful but are not always available. The tools discussed in this chapter are part of the default Oracle distribution and hence are always available. Although they may not be as easy to use as some of the graphical third-party tools, they are capable of providing all the information you need to tune SQL effectively.

EXPLAIN PLAN

The EXPLAIN PLAN command allows you to determine the execution plan Oracle will apply to a particular SQL statement. The execution plan is inserted into a plan table, which you can query to extract the execution plan.

EXECUTING EXPLAIN PLAN

The EXPLAIN PLAN command has the following syntax:

```
EXPLAIN PLAN
  [SET STATEMENT_ID = 'statement_id'}
 [INTO table_name ]
   FOR sql_statement
```

The options for EXPLAIN PLAN are as follows:

STATEMENT_ID	Some unique identifier for your SQL statement. By using a statement identifier, you can store multiple SQL statements in one table.
TABLE_NAME	The name of the plan table you want to use to store the execution plan. This table must already exist and must conform to the standard structure of a plan table (see the following section). If you don't specify a plan table, EXPLAIN PLAN will attempt to use the name "PLAN_TABLE."
SQL_STATEMENT	The SQL for which you wish to determine the execution plan. The SQL must be valid and you must have sufficient privileges to run the SQL. The SQL may contain bind variables.

THE PLAN TABLE

Oracle distributes an SQL script to create the plan table with the Oracle server software. The script is called utlxplan.sql and is usually found in the rdbms/admin subdirectory of the software distribution. You can copy and edit this script to change the name of the plan table (if you use the "INTO *table_name*" option of the EXPLAIN PLAN command) or you can use the script as is to create a plan table called PLAN_TABLE.

The EXPLAIN PLAN command will insert a row into the plan table for every step of the execution plan. Table 7.1 shows the columns in the PLAN table for Oracle8 (not all columns are present in Oracle 7 and earlier).

FORMATTING PLAN TABLE OUTPUT

The most common way of making sense of the plan_table data is to execute a hierarchical query against the table. The PARENT_ID and ID columns allow for a self-join, which can be implemented using the CONNECT BY clause of the SELECT statement. A common representation of such a query is

```
SELECT RTRIM (LPAD (' ', 2 * LEVEL) ||
       RTRIM (operation) || ' ' ||
       RTRIM (options) || ' ' ||
             object_name) query_plan,
       cost,
       cardinality rows
  FROM plan_table
 CONNECT BY PRIOR id = parent_id
 START WITH id = 0
```

This produces the typical nested representation of an explain plan. For instance, if we EXPLAIN the following statement,

```
EXPLAIN PLAN for
SELECT e.surname, e.firstname, e.date_of_birth
  FROM employees e, customers c
 WHERE e.surname = c.contact_surname
   AND e.firstname = c.contact_firstname
   AND e.date_of_birth = c.date_of_birth
 ORDER BY e.surname, e.firstname
```

the execution plan query will produce the following output:

Query Plan	Cost	Rows
SELECT STATEMENT	312	1
SORT ORDER BY	312	1
HASH JOIN	310	1
TABLE ACCESS FULL EMPLOYEES	2	800
TABLE ACCESS FULL CUSTOMERS	130	99999

Table 7.1   Structure of the PLAN table

COLUMN NAME	DESCRIPTION
STATEMENT_ID	The statement identifier provided by the SET STATEMENT_ID clause.
TIMESTAMP	The date and time the explain plan statement was executed.
REMARKS	Not populated by the EXPLAIN PLAN command, but you can insert your own comments here.
ID	A unique identifier for the step.
PARENT_ID	The parent of this step. The parent step is the step that is processed after the current step. In other words, the output of a step is fed into its parent step.
POSITION	If two steps have the same parent, the step with the lowest position will be executed first.
OPERATION	The type of operation being performed (for instance, TABLE ACCESS or SORT).
OPTIONS	Additional information about the operation. For instance, in the case of TABLE SCAN, the option might be FULL or BY ROWID.
OBJECT_NODE	If this is a distributed query, this column indicates the database link used to reference the object. For a parallel query, it may nominate a temporary result set.
OBJECT_OWNER	Owner of the object.
OBJECT_NAME	Name of the object.
OBJECT_INSTANCE	Location of the object in the SQL statement.
OBJECT_TYPE	Type of object (TABLE, INDEX, etc.).
OPTIMIZER	Optimizer goal in effect when the statement was explained.
SEARCH_COLUMNS	Unused.
OTHER	For a distributed query, this might contain the text of the SQL sent to the remote database. For a parallel query, it will indicate the SQL statement executed by the parallel slave processes.
OTHER_TAG	Indicates the type of value in the OTHER column. This can denote whether the step is being executed remotely in a distributed SQL statement or the nature of parallel execution.
COST	The relative cost of the operation as estimated by the cost-based optimizer.
CARDINALITY	The number of rows that the cost-based optimizer expects will be returned by the step.
BYTES	The number of bytes expected to be returned by the step.
PARTITION_START	If partition elimination is to be performed, this column indicates the start of the range of partitions which will be accessed. It may also contain the keyword "KEY" or "ROW LOCATION", which indicates that the partitions to be accessed will be determined at run time.
PARTITION_END	Indicates the end of the range of partitions to be accessed.
PARTITION_ID	The column lists the execution plan ID (as indicated in the ID column) for the execution plan step that performed the partition operation outlined by PARTITION_START and PARTITION_END.
DISTRIBUTION	This column describes how rows from one set of parallel query slaves— the "producers" are allocated the subsequent "consumer" slaves. Possible values are "PARTITION (ROWID)", "PARTITION (KEY)", "HASH", "RANGE", "ROUND-ROBIN", "BROADCAST", "QC (ORDER)" and "QC (RANDOM)".

You may want to modify the SELECT statement to retrieve additional columns depending on your specific circumstances. For instance, if explaining a parallel query—as outlined in Chapter 11—you might want to see the OTHER_ TAG columns; if explaining a query against a partitioned table, you might want to see the PARTITON_START and PARTITION_STOP columns.

Oracle distributes two scripts in the rdbms/admin directory that can display formatted execution plans:

❑ Utlxpls.sql shows the execution plan with partition information but without any parallel query information.
❑ Utlxplp.sql shows the execution plan, including information that is useful when explaining parallel query execution.

INTERPRETING THE EXECUTION PLAN

Interpreting a formatted execution plan such as that shown in the previous section requires practice and often some degree of judgment. However, the following fundamental principles guide the interpretation:

❑ The more heavily indented an access path is, the earlier it is executed.
❑ If two steps are indented at the same level, the uppermost statement is executed first.
❑ An access path may be comprised of a number of steps in the execution plan. For instance, an index access is shown as an INDEX SCAN together with a TABLE SCAN BY ROWID. In this case, the indentation level of the outermost access determines the precedence of the execution. For instance, in the preceding explain plan the most heavily indented operation is the index range scan of an EMPLOYEES index. However, this operation is combined with the ROWID access of the EMPLOYEES table. It's therefore the CUSTOMERS access that is the first step executed.

With these principles in mind, let's interpret the following execution plan:

```
Query_plan
-------------------------------------------------------
SELECT STATEMENT
    SORT ORDER BY
       NESTED LOOPS
          TABLE ACCESS FULL CUSTOMERS
          TABLE ACCESS BY ROWID EMPLOYEES
             INDEX RANGE SCAN EMPLOYEE_BOTHNAMES_IDX
```

Here's how this plan would be interpreted:

❏ The most heavily indented statement is the index scan of index, EM-PLOYEE_BOTHNAMES_IDX. However, this is an index scan associated with a table lookup. As we said earlier, an index lookup coupled with a table lookup is effectively a single step, and so the index lookup is not the first step in the execution plan.

❏ The uppermost and most heavily indented step is therefore the full-table scan of the CUSTOMERS table. This step is therefore the driving access path and CUSTOMERS is the driving table.

❏ The index lookup of EMPLOYEES is at the same level of indentation as the scan of EMPLOYEES. This indicates that the steps have a common parent. We therefore need to examine the parent step to establish the relationship. The parent step is nested loops, which means that the two tables are joined using the nested loops method described in Chapter 3.

❏ The next step is the SORT ORDER BY step. This step simply supports the ORDER BY clause in the SELECT statement.

Table 7.2 Lists the operations and options that can be returned by EXPLAIN PLAN.

EXECUTION PLAN STEPS

Table 7.2   Operations and options returned by EXPLAIN PLAN

CATEGORY	OPERATION	OPTION	DESCRIPTION
Table Access Paths	TABLE ACCESS	FULL	The well-known full-table scan. This involves reading every row in the table (strictly speaking, every block up to the table's high-water mark).
		CLUSTER	Access of data via an index cluster key.
		HASH	A hash key is issued to access one or more rows in a table with a matching hash value.
		BY ROWID	Access a single row in a table by specifying its ROWID. ROWID access is the fastest way to access a single row. Often, the ROWID will have been obtained by an associated index lookup.
		BY USER ROWID	Access via a ROWID provided by a bind variable, literal, or WHERE CURRENT OF CURSOR clause.
		BY INDEX ROWID	Access via a ROWID obtained through an index lookup.
		BY GLOBAL INDEX ROWID	Access via a ROWID obtained from a globally partitioned index.

(continued)

Table 7.2   *(Continued)*

CATEGORY	OPERATION	OPTION	DESCRIPTION
		BY LOCAL INDEX ROWID	Access via a ROWID obtained from a locally partitioned index.
		SAMPLE	A subset of rows are returned as a result of the use of the SAMPLE clause.
Index Operations	AND-EQUAL		The results from one or more index scans are combined.
	INDEX	UNIQUE SCAN	An index lookup that will return the address (ROWID) of only one row.
		RANGE SCAN	An index lookup that will return the ROWID of more than one row. This can be because the index is nonunique or because a range operator (e.g., ">") was used.
		FULL SCAN	Scan every entry in the index in key order.
		FULL SCAN (MAX/MIN)	Find the highest or lowest index entry.
		FAST FULL SCAN	Scan every entry in the index in block order, possibly using multi-block read.
	DOMAIN INDEX		Lookup of a domain index (user defined index type).
Bitmap Operations	BITMAP	CONVERSION	Convert ROWID to Bitmaps or bitmaps to ROWID.
		INDEX	Retrieve a value or range of values from the bitmap.
		MERGE	Merge multiple bitmaps.
		MINUS	Subtract one bitmap from another
		OR	Create a bitwise OR of two bitmaps.
Join Operations	CONNECT BY		A hierarchical self-join is performed on the output of the preceding steps.
		MERGE JOIN	A merge join performed on the output of the preceding steps.
		NESTED LOOPS	A nested loops join is performed on the preceding steps. For each row in the upper result set, the lower result set is scanned to find a matching row.

Table 7.2 *(Continued)*

CATEGORY	OPERATION	OPTION	DESCRIPTION
	HASH JOIN		A hash join is performed of two row sources.
	Any join operation	OUTER	The join is an outer join.
	Any join operation	ANTI	The join is an antijoin.
	Any join operation	SEMI	The join is a semijoin.
	Any join operation	CARTESIAN	Every row in one result set is joined to every row in the other result set.
Set operations	CONCATENATION		Multiple result sets are merged in the same way as in an explicit UNION statement. This typically occurs when an OR statement is used with indexed columns.
	INTERSECTION		Two result sets are compared and only rows common to both are returned. This operation usually only takes place as a result of an explicit use of the INTERSECT clause.
	MINUS		All result sets in the first result set are returned, except those appearing in the second result set. This occurs as a result of the MINUS set operator.
	UNION-ALL		Two result sets are combined and rows from both are returned.
	UNION		Two result sets are combined and rows from both are returned. Duplicate rows are not returned.
	VIEW		Either a view definition has been accessed or a temporary table has been created to store a result set.
Miscellaneous	FOR UPDATE		The rows returned are locked as a result of the FOR UPDATE clause.
	FILTER		Rows from a result set not matching a selection criteria are eliminated.
	REMOTE		An external database is accessed through a database link.
	FIRST ROW		Retrieve the first row of a query.
	SEQUENCE		An Oracle sequence generator is accessed to obtain a unique sequence number.

(continued)

Table 7.2   *(Continued)*

CATEGORY	OPERATION	OPTION	DESCRIPTION
	INLIST ITERATOR		Perform the next operation once for each value in an IN list.
	LOAD AS SELECT		Denotes a direct path INSERT insert based on a SELECT statement.
	FIXED TABLE		Access a "fixed" (X$) table.
	FIXED INDEX		Access an "index" on "fixed" (X$) table.
Partition operations	PARTITION	SINGLE	Access a single partition.
		ITERATOR	Access multiple partitions.
		ALL	Access all partitions.
		INLIST	Access multiple partitions based on the values contained in an IN list.
Aggregation	COUNT		Count the rows in the result set in order to satisfy the COUNT() function.
	COUNT	STOPKEY	Count the number of rows returned by a result set and stop processing when a certain number of rows are reached. This is usually the result of a WHERE clause, which specifies a maximum ROWNUM (for instance, WHERE ROWNUM <= 10).
	SORT	ORDER BY	A result set is sorted in order to satisfy an ORDER BY clause.
		AGGREGATE	This occurs when a group function is used on data that are already grouped.
		JOIN	Sort the rows in preparation for a merge join.
		UNIQUE	A sort to eliminate duplicate rows. This typically occurs as a result of using the distinct clause.
		GROUP BY	A sort of a result set in order to group them for the GROUP BY clause.
		GROUP BY NOSORT	A group by based that does not require a sort operation.
		GROUP BY ROLLUP	A group by that includes the ROLLUP option.
		GROUP BY CUBE	A group by that includes the CUBE option.

USING EXPLAIN PLAN

There are a couple of things you need to keep in mind when using EXPLAIN PLAN:

❑ The plan generated by the EXPLAIN PLAN command depends on the optimizer goal in force (RULE, COST, FIRST_ROWS, LAST_ROWS) and the statistics present for the tables in question. Be cautious if you are using explain plan in one environment (for instance, development or test) and trying to apply the results to a different environment (such as production). Differences in table statistics will likely lead to different execution plans in the two environments.

❑ Take care not to insert duplicate rows into your plan table. Either use a unique statement_id for each EXPLAIN PLAN statement or ensure that you clear the plan table before use.

The process of executing EXPLAIN PLAN and issuing the appropriate SQL to query the plan table can be fairly tedious, especially when you have to execute additional statements to clear the plan table. It's much easier to use a product

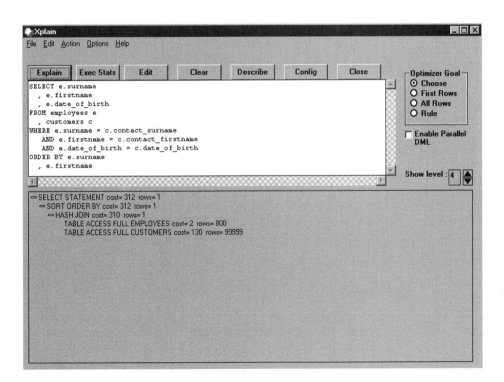

FIGURE 7.1 The freeware Xplain plan tool.

which contains integrated explain plan support. There are a number of freeware and commercial products that can make running explain plan much easier:

❏ The SQL*PLUS AUTOTRACE facility, described later in this chapter, can generate explain plans from within SQL*PLUS.

❏ The Xplain utility, available from this book's web-site, is a freeware utility that generates explain plans in a GUI environment. Figure 7.1 shows the Xplain plan main screen.

❏ Quest Software's SQLab product, shown in Figure 7.2, provides possibly the most advanced EXPLAIN PLAN functionality of any product. SQLab can display EXPLAIN plan data in an advanced annotated tree format, as a flowchart diagram or as an English description. It can also show details about the tables and indexes involved in the statement, allow you to test the execution characteristics of your statement, and integrates with the SQL Trace facility described in the next section. If you buy the Xpert edition, it can even make recommendations for tuning your SQL. (However, be aware that I work at Quest Software and have been heavily involved in the construction of the explain plan display and the expert advice, so I'm hardly an uninterested party!)

❏ Other commercial tools are available; for instance, the Oracle Enterprise Manager tuning pack and Computer Associates Plan analyzer both allow you to work with Explain plans in a graphical environment.

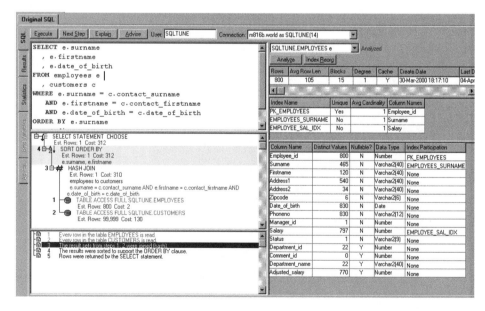

FIGURE 7.2   Quest Software's SQLab SQL tuning window.

SQL TRACE

The EXPLAIN PLAN statement is extremely useful but is not a complete SQL tuning tool. For instance, EXPLAIN PLAN cannot tell you which of two execution plans is the more efficient—it provides no information about the resources required to execute a particular SQL statement.

Luckily, Oracle does provide a facility for tracing SQL statement execution that can provide all of the information provided by EXPLAIN PLAN together with details of CPU and I/O requirements and even the number of rows processed by each step in the execution plan. This facility essentially consists of two components:

❑ The ALTER SESSION SET SQL_TRACE TRUE SQL statement allows SQL tracing to be initiated.

❑ The tkprof command allows the trace files generated to be formatted in a meaningful way.

The SQL tracing facility and tkprof utility are a powerful tuning combination, but they are somewhat awkward to use and the output is sometimes difficult to interpret. Consequently, these tools are not used as widely as they should be. However, the SQL tracing facility is one of the most powerful and widely available tools for tuning SQL statements.

OVERVIEW OF THE SQL TRACING PROCESS

The usual tuning cycle when using SQL_TRACE/tkprof is as follows:

1. Enable SQL_TRACE for the instance or sessions in question.
2. Locate the trace files(s) of interest.
3. Use tkprof to generate trace output.
4. Interpret the formatted trace file.
5. Tune SQL and repeat.

This process is essentially the one outlined in Chapter 1. We'll cover each of these steps in detail.

PREPARING TO USE SQL TRACE

You may find that you have difficulty using SQL_TRACE unless your database is set up appropriately. Guidelines for setting up Oracle for SQL_TRACE can be found in Appendix D. In particular, you should ensure that the TIMED_STATISTICS option is set to "true."

ENABLING SQL TRACE WITHIN A SESSION

From within a session, SQL_TRACE is activated with the following statement:

```
ALTER SESSION SET SQL_TRACE TRUE;
```

Because not all versions of PL/SQL can issue the alter session statement directly, a special function call can be used to switch on SQL_TRACE in PL/SQL blocks:

```
dbms_session.set_sql_trace(TRUE)
```

ENABLING SQL TRACE FROM ANOTHER SESSION

Sometimes you can't easily turn on SQL_TRACE for the session in which you are interested (for instance, if you don't have the source code). To overcome this difficulty, Oracle provides a facility to invoke SQL tracing from a different session. The DBMS_SYSTEM.SET_TRACE_IN_SESSION package provides this functionality. The syntax is

```
dbms_system.set_sql_trace_in_session
     sid,serial#,TRUE|FALSE)
```

where *sid* and *serial* are the session identifier and serial number for the session you wish to trace. You can get these values from the V$SESSION pseudotable. For instance, the following PL/SQL block enables tracing for all sessions matching a given username:

```
BEGIN
   FOR sess_rec IN ( SELECT sid, serial#
                        FROM v$session
                        WHERE username
                        LIKE UPPER ('&user_mask'))
   LOOP
      sys.dbms_system.set_sql_trace_in_session
         (sess_rec.sid, sess_rec.serial#, TRUE);
   END LOOP;
END;
```

To use this facility, you or your DBA must ensure the DBMS_SYSTEM package is installed and grant execute on this package to users who require access to it.

FINDING THE TRACE FILE

Having enabled SQL_TRACE, your next challenge is often to find the trace file that has been generated. The trace file is written to the location defined by the Oracle configuration parameter USER_DUMP_DEST. The name of the trace file is port specific, but in UNIX and many other operating systems it will be

```
header_pid.trc
```

where *header* is usually "ora" but sometimes "oracle_sid_ora," and *pid* is the process identifier for the Oracle server process.

You can determine your USER_DUMP_DEST with the following query (provided that you have access to the V$PARAMETER pseudotable—see your DBA if you don't):

```
SELECT VALUE
  FROM v$parameter
 WHERE name = 'user_dump_dest'
```

However, there might be numerous trace files in the USER_DUMP_DEST directory, and typically they will all be owned by the Oracle account. You can determine which trace is yours as follows:

❑ Examine timestamps of the files.
❑ Search for a particular SQL statement. A handy way of "tagging" your trace file is by issuing a statement such as "select `'Catherines trace file'` `from dual`;"—then you can search among trace files for the string "Catherines trace file."
❑ Have your program tell you where the trace will be written. For instance, the following function enables SQL_TRACE and returns the location of the trace file. The calling program could display the trace file name and location in a log file or on the screen[1]:

```
CREATE FUNCTION set_trace RETURN varchar2 IS
   CURSOR udd_csr
   IS
      SELECT VALUE
        FROM sys.v_$parameter
       WHERE name = 'user_dump_dest';
```

---

[1]Because the format of the trace file differs across operating systems, this function might need minor changes on Windows and some UNIX platforms.

```
CURSOR my_pid_csr
IS
    SELECT spid
      FROM sys.v_$process
     WHERE addr = (SELECT paddr
                     FROM sys.v_$session
                    WHERE audsid =
                    USERENV ('sessionid'));

l_user_dump_dest                VARCHAR2(256);
l_pid                           VARCHAR2(20);
l_trace_file_name               VARCHAR2(2000);
BEGIN
    — set trace on
    dbms_session.set_sql_trace (TRUE);
    — Get user_dump_dest
    OPEN udd_csr;
    FETCH udd_csr INTO l_user_dump_dest;
    CLOSE udd_csr;
    — Get process id for the shadow
    OPEN my_pid_csr;
    FETCH my_pid_csr INTO l_pid;
    CLOSE my_pid_csr;
    — Return the name of the trace file
    RETURN(l_user_dump_dest || '/ora_' || l_pid
          || '.trc');
END;
```

USING TKPROF

Once the trace file is found, the tkprof utility is used to render it into a usable form. The basic syntax for tkprof is

```
tkprof trace_file output_file
       explain=username/password sort=(sort options)
```

where

       `trace_file`   is the raw trace file generated by the SQL_ TRACE facility.

`output_file`	is the file to which formatted trace information will be written.
`explain=username/ password`	specifies the connection that will be used to generate SQL execution plans. If you don't specify the explain keyword, no execution plans will be generated.
`sort=(sort keys)`	displays the SQL statements in descending values of the sort keys. The sort keys "(prsela,exeela,fchela)" sort the SQL statements in descending order of elapsed time and are a common choice.

A typical tkprof invocation would be

```
tkprof ora_12345.trc trace1.prf explain=/
     sort='( prsela,exeela,fchela)'
```

which processes the raw trace file ora_12345.trc and writes the output file trace1.prf, generating execution plans using your default ("OPS$") account and sorting SQL statements by elapsed time. Note that because this example was under the UNIX operating system, the parentheses were enclosed in quotes.

TKPROF SORT OPTIONS

Tkprof sort keys consist of two parts: The first part indicates the type of calls that are to be sorted, and the second part indicates the values to be sorted. So "exedsk" indicates that statements are to be sorted on disk reads during execute calls. Adding options together causes statements to be sorted by the sum of the options specified, so "prsdsk,exedsk,fchdisk" causes statements to be sorted by overall physical disk reads. A few combinations are not valid:

❑ "mis" can only be applied to "prs".
❑ "row" can only apply to "exe" or "fch".

Table 7.3 outlines the components of the sort options.

OTHER TKPROF OPTIONS

The tkprof options used in the previous examples will give you output that contains all the information needed to tune your SQL. Table 7.4 details the other tkprof options that may be useful in specific circumstances.

Table 7.3   Tkprof sort options

FIRST PART		SECOND PART	
prs	Sort on values during parse calls	cnt	Sort on number of calls.
exe	Sort on values during execute calls (equivalent to open cursor for a query)	cpu	Sort on CPU consumption.
fch	Sort on values during fetch calls (queries only)	ela	Sort on elapsed time.
		dsk	Sort on disk reads.
		qry	Sort on consistent reads.
		cu	Sort on current reads.
		mis	Sort on library cache misses.
		row	Sort on rows processed.

Table 7.4   More Tkprof Options

OPTION	COMMENTS
table=owner.tablename	By default, tkprof creates a plan_table in your account to generate the execution plans. If you don't have privileges to create the table or your site likes to use a central plan table, you can specify it with this option.
print=number_of_statements	Restricts the number of SQL statements printed.
aggregate=yes/no	If set to "yes" (the default), SQL statements in the trace file that are identical will be reported only once and execution statistics will be summed. If set to "no," each time an SQL statement is parsed, a separate entry will be written to the tkprof output, even if the statements are identical to one encountered previously. This option doesn't appear to be active in recent releases.
sys=no	If set to "no," statements executed as the SYS user will not be included in the trace output. These statements are usually recursive SQL that are often not of interest.
record=filename	Generates a file containing all the SQL statements (aside from recursive SQL) in the trace file.
insert=filename	Generates a file that can be run under SQL*PLUS to keep a record of the SQL statements in the trace file and their execution statistics. This facility was introduced to allow you to set and compare SQL statement execution over time, perhaps to establish the effect of increasing data volumes or user load.
verbose=yes	In early versions of Oracle 7, the verbose flag could generate an analysis of wait information contained in the trace file. In current releases, its only effect seems to be to cause a summary of recursive SQL execution statistics to be generated.

TROUBLESHOOTING SQL_TRACE AND TKPROF

You may encounter one of the following problems when trying to format your trace file:

❑ "I can't read my trace file." Oracle usually generates trace files as read-only to the Oracle user or DBAs in case they contain sensitive information (such as passwords for roles or hardcoded data values such as account numbers). If you can't read the trace file and are confident that there are no security implications, have your DBA set the undocumented initialization parameter _TRACE_FILES_PUBLIC=TRUE. This should result in trace files being created with public read permission.

❑ "My SQL_TRACE is spread across multiple files." This can happen if you are connected to multithreaded servers. Since a different server might execute each SQL statement, the trace information ends up spread across files associated with each server. The work-around is to use a dedicated server connection.[2]

INTERPRETING TKPROF OUTPUT

When you first encounter tkprof output, there appears to be a lot of information and very little guidance on how to interpret it. Figure 7.3 shows some sample tkprof output. Some highlighted superscripts have been added, which are mentioned in the commentary.

TKPROF EXECUTION STATISTICS

In this section we examine closely each item in the tkprof output. First, let's look at the top half of the output. Numbers and letters in parenthesis refer to superscripts in Figure 7.3:

1. The SQL text is displayed (1).
2. Next is a table containing the execution statistics. Working across the top of the table,
   ❑ The number of times each category of call was issued (2).
   ❑ The CPU time required in centiseconds (3). One centisecond is one-hundredth of a second.
   ❑ The elapsed time required in centiseconds (4).
   ❑ Number of disk reads required (5).
   ❑ Number of buffers read in query (consistent) (6) or current (7) mode. Blocks read in query mode are usually for consistent read queries.

---

[2]For instance, in your *tnsnames.ora* file, insert the keyword (SERVER=DEDICATED) in the CONNECT_DATA section.

```
******************************************************************
SELECT contact_surname,contact_firstname,date_of_birth¹
  FROM customers c
WHERE EXISTS
      (SELECT 1 from employees e
        WHERE e.surname=c.contact_surname
          AND e.firstname=c.contact_firstname
          AND e.date_of_birth=c.date_of_birth)
```

call	count[2]	cpu[3]	elapsed[4]	disk[5]	query[6]	current[7]	rows[8]
Parse[a]	1[d]	0.02	0.01	0	0	0	0
Execute[b]	1[e]	0.00	0.00	0	0	0	0
Fetch[c]	20[j]	141.10	141.65	1237	1450011	386332	99[i]
total	22	141.12	141.66	1237[k]	1450011[f]	386332[g]	99[h]

```
Misses in library cache during parse: 0ⁿ
Optimizer goal: CHOOSE
Parsing user id: 33   (SQLTUNE)
```

Rows	Row Source Operation[o]
99	FILTER
96681	TABLE ACCESS FULL CUSTOMERS
96582	TABLE ACCESS FULL EMPLOYEES

Rows[l]	Execution Plan[m]
0	SELECT STATEMENT GOAL: CHOOSE
99	FILTER
96681	TABLE ACCESS GOAL: ANALYZED (FULL) OF 'CUSTOMERS'
96582	TABLE ACCESS GOAL: ANALYZED (FULL) OF 'EMPLOYEES'

```
******************************************************************
```

Figure 7.3 Sample tkprof output, before optimization.

Blocks read in current mode are often for modifications to existing blocks. I don't believe the distinction is particularly important when tuning SQL, so I usually add them together and call them "logical reads."

❑ The number of rows processed (8).

3. Working down the table, we see that each measurement is broken down by the category of Oracle call. The three categories are as follows:

❏ Parse (a), in which the SQL statement is checked for syntax, valid objects, and security, and in which an execution plan is determined by the optimizer.

❏ Execute (b), in which an SQL statement is executed or, in the case of a query, prepared for first fetch. Some queries, such as those that use FOR UPDATE or perform a sort, will actually retrieve every row at this point.

❏ Fetch (c), in which rows are returned from a query.

We can tell a great deal about the efficiency of the SQL statement by deriving some ratios from this output. Some of the important ratios are as follows:

❏ Blocks read (f + g) to rows processed (h). This is a rough indication of the relative expense of the query. The more blocks that have to be accessed relative to the number of rows returned, the more "expensive" each row is. A similar ratio is blocks read (f + g) to executions (e). In our example, the blocks-to-rows ratio is about 18,548, which means that each row "cost" almost 18,548 logical I/Os. Ratios above 10 to 20 (or lower for simple index lookups) may indicate room for improvement for simple queries. However, this rule of thumb has little applicability for complex statements. For instance, a COUNT(*) will always return only one row no matter how may rows must be accessed to produce the result.

❏ Parse count (d) over execute count (e). Ideally, the parse count should be close to one. If it is high in relation to execute count, then the statement has been needlessly reparsed. We discussed the problems and causes of excessive parsing—lack of bind variables or poor cursor reuse—in Chapter 5. Guidelines for minimizing parsing in client tools are contained in Appendix C.

❏ Rows fetched (i) to fetches (j). This indicates the level to which the array fetch facility has been exercised (see Chapters 8 and 12 for a discussion of array processing). In our example the ratio was about 5, which indicates that rows were fetched five at a time. A ratio close to one indicates no array processing—which may indicate a significant opportunity for optimization.

❏ Disk reads (k) to logical reads (f + g). This is a measurement of the "miss rate" within the data buffer cache. We usually aim to get this ratio less than about 10%. In our case, we had only 1237 disk reads and over 1 million logical reads, representing a miss rate of less than 1%.

TKPROF EXECUTION PLANS

If the "explain=" command line option has been used, the SQL statement's execution plan is displayed in the familiar nested display format. A significant enhancement to the tkprof execution plan is the presence of both the step (m) and also the number of rows processed by each step (l). The row count (l) can indicate which step did the most work and hence might be most effectively tuned.

These execution step row counts provided by SQL_TRACE/tkprof cannot be obtained by any other method and are an invaluable aid to SQL tuning. All other things being equal, the more rows processed, the more computer resources required. Therefore, the step with the highest execution count is usually the step that is most in need of optimization.

In some versions of tkprof (8.1.5 for instance), the execution plan may be displayed twice. The first execution plan, marked in our example as (o), is based on information stored in the trace file when the statement is first parsed. This execution plan is not constructed using the output of the EXPLAIN PLAN statement and represents the "real" plan that was used at execution time. If present, this additional plan is potentially more accurate than that generated by EXPLAIN PLAN because

❏ The execution plan may have been affected by session options such as OPTIMIZER_GOAL, PARALLEL DML ENABLED, or SORT_AREA_SIZE, which were set in the session when the SQL was executed. Tkprof cannot take these settings into account when executing EXPLAIN PLAN.

❏ If you wait too long before executing tkprof, table statistics might change sufficiently to alter the execution plan.

TUNING SQL WITH TKPROF OUTPUT

When looking at tkprof output, you should consider the following:

❏ How efficient is the statement as indicated by block gets per row returned?
❏ How were the data retrieved? In other words, what does the execution plan mean?
❏ Which steps in the execution plan processed the most rows? How can I improve or avoid these steps?

Applying these questions to the output in Figure 7.3, you could conclude the following:

❏ The ratio of blocks read to rows returned is very high (18,548). The statement is very inefficient by this criterion and you might suspect that substantial improvement is possible.
❏ The execution plan shows that full scans were performed against both CUSTOMERS and EMPLOYEES. One solution might be to encourage an index-based retrieval of at least one of those tables.
❏ We can see from the row counts against each execution plan step that 96,482 EMPLOYEE rows were processed, but there are only 800 employees! This is

an example of how the row counts can highlight inefficiencies. Since we are processing more rows than exist in the EMPLOYEE table, it is obvious that we are scanning the EMPLOYEE table more than once. In fact, the FILTER step in the execution plan indicates that the scan of the EMPLOYEE table occurs once for each row in CUSTOMERS.

The SQL statement in the tkprot output is an example of a semijoin. We discuss semi-joins in Chapter 9. There are a number of possible optimizations:

❏ If we created an index on EMPLOYEE(SURNAME, FIRSTNAME, DATE_OF_BIRTH), then each lookup could scan the index rather than having to scan the whole EMPLOYEES table.
❏ We could reword the SQL to use a join or an IN subquery, which would allow the optimizer to use a more efficient join-based solution.
❏ The semijoin hints (HASH_SJ and MERGE_SJ) could be used to encourage the more efficient semijoin algorithm (Oracle8+ only).

Let's try the simplest of these solutions and add a HASH_SJ hint to the SQL statement. Our tkprof output now looks that shown in Figure 7.4.

We are now doing only one table scan of each table. Our blocks-to-row ratio has dropped to 13.5 and the overall logical I/O requirement for the query is now only 0.07% of the original requirement—a considerable improvement.

TKPROF RULES, OK?

We've just seen an example of how tkprof can be used to tune SQL. In the example, we reduced logical I/O requirements by 99.93%—an impressive improvement. It's true that this SQL statement was written with the intention of demonstrating poor performance characteristics. However, it's not uncommon to see impressive improvements to SQL statement performance as shown in the preceding example.

It would, of course, be possible to get such an improvement without tkprof. But think of how much harder it would be. Tkprof told us exactly how I/O requirements changed as we tuned the SQL. Also, tkprof led us directly to the execution step responsible for the poor performance. Virtually no other tool can do this,[3] and that is why you should master tkprof and use it as your primary tool in your pursuit of high-performance SQL.

---

[3]The only tool I am aware of that can provide this sort of information is the SQLab product from Quest Software. SQLab can initiate a SQL trace when you execute your SQL statement. It can fetch the raw trace file from the remote host and extract the row counts, which could otherwise only be displayed by tkprof.

```
*****************************************************************
SELECT contact_surname,contact_firstname,date_of_birth
  FROM customers c
 WHERE EXISTS
        (SELECT /*+ hash_sj*/ 1 from employees e
           WHERE e.surname=c.contact_surname
             AND e.firstname=c.contact_firstname
             AND e.date_of_birth=c.date_of_birth)
```

call	count	cpu	elapsed	disk	query	current	rows
Parse	1	0.03	0.03	0	0	0	0
Execute	2	0.00	0.00	0	0	0	0
Fetch	20	1.27	9.30	1689	1291	31	99
total	23	1.30	9.33	1689	1291	31	99

```
Misses in library cache during parse: 0
Optimizer goal: CHOOSE
Parsing user id: 33   (SQLTUNE)
```

Rows	Row Source Operation
99	HASH JOIN SEMI
96680	TABLE ACCESS FULL CUSTOMERS
800	TABLE ACCESS FULL EMPLOYEES

Rows	Execution Plan
0	SELECT STATEMENT GOAL: CHOOSE
99	HASH JOIN (SEMI)
96680	TABLE ACCESS GOAL: ANALYZED (FULL) OF 'CUSTOMERS'
800	TABLE ACCESS GOAL: ANALYZED (FULL) OF 'EMPLOYEES'

FIGURE 7.4   tkprof output, after optimization.

THE SQL*PLUS AUTOTRACE OPTION

As we've seen, SQL_TRACE and tkprof are powerful tools, but they are not always easy to use. Each time you use SQL_TRACE, you have to find the trace file (which, in a client/server environment, will often be on a different machine) and then format and interpret the tkprof output. Finding and interpreting the trace files can be time-consuming, and you might wish that you could get tkprof-like feedback immediately after executing a new SQL statement.

There are a number of commercial tools that allow you to edit and execute SQL statements and generate execution plans and execution statistics.[4] However, if you don't have any of these tools, the SQL*Plus "autotrace" facility provides at least some of this functionality. This facility is enabled with the SET AUTO-TRACE command within SQL*PLUS. AUTOTRACE can generate execution plans and execution statistics for SQL statements executed from SQL*PLUS. However, it doesn't provide all the facilities of tkprof—in particular, it doesn't show rows processed for each step in the execution plan.

REQUIREMENTS FOR USING AUTOTRACE

Your DBA should grant the PLUSTRACE role to users who are required to use the AUTOTRACE utility. You must have a plan table called PLAN_TABLE in your account. You can create this table using the script rdbms/admin/utlxplan.sql, which is found in the Oracle distribution.

INITIATING AUTOTRACE

The AUTOTRACE command has the following options:

OFF	Normal behavior, generate no trace output.
ON EXPLAIN	Following each SQL statement execution, display the execution plan in the normal nested format.
ON STATISTICS	Following each SQL statement execution, print a report detailing I/O, CPU, and other resource utilization.
ON	After SQL statement execution, display both the execution plan and the execution statistics.
TRACEONLY	Same as the "ON" setting, but suppresses the display of data from an SQL statement so that only the execution plan and statistics are shown.

For instance, to have the execution plan displayed after each SQL statement, use the statement

```
SET AUTOTRACE ON EXPLAIN
```

---

[4]For instance, Quest SQL*Navigator, Quest SQLab, CA-Platinum SQL Station, Quest TOAD.

To show both the execution plan and the execution statistics but to suppress the display of rows returned by queries, use the following statement:

```
SET AUTOTRACE TRACEONLY
```

AUTOTRACE OUTPUT

Figure 7.5 shows some output from a sample autotrace session.

```
SQL> set autotrace traceonly explain statistics
SQL> SELECT   /*+ ORDERED USE_HASH(C) */c.contact_surname,
c.contact_firstname,
c.date_of_birth
  2    FROM employees e, customers c
  3   WHERE e.surname = c.contact_surname
  4     AND e.firstname = c.contact_firstname
  5     AND e.date_of_birth = c.date_of_birth
  6  /
99 rows selected.

Execution Plan
----------------------------------------------------------
    0       SELECT STATEMENT Optimizer=CHOOSE
            (Cost=911 Card=1 Bytes=136)
    1    0  HASH JOIN (Cost=911 Card=1 Bytes=136)
    2    1    TABLE ACCESS (FULL) OF 'EMPLOYEES'
                (Cost=1 Card=800 Bytes=42400)
    3    1    TABLE ACCESS (FULL) OF 'CUSTOMERS'
                (Cost=78 Card=96670 Bytes=8023610)

Statistics
----------------------------------------------------------
        0  recursive calls
        8  db block gets
     1298  consistent gets
     1293  physical reads
        0  redo size
     4337  bytes sent via SQL*Net to client
     1090  bytes received via SQL*Net from client
        8  SQL*Net roundtrips to/from client
        0  sorts (memory)
        0  sorts (disk)
       99  rows processed
```

FIGURE 7.5 Autotrace output.

AUTOTRACE COMPARED TO TKPROF

The AUTOTRACE facility can be extremely useful, but it has the following deficiencies when compared with SQL_TRACE and tkprof:

❏ Row counts are not assigned to individual execution steps. We have seen that the SQL_TRACE/tkprof facility can show the number of rows processed by each stage of execution. This capability is one of tkprof's greatest strengths because it allows you quickly to focus on a particular stage of the execution plan. This often shows up an inappropriate index or other weakness. The AUTOTRACE facility cannot produce this information and is accordingly less powerful.

❏ SQL_TRACE can be turned on from within any Oracle session, but AUTO-TRACE only works from within SQL*PLUS.

❏ AUTOTRACE statistics do not include CPU or elapsed times and do not break execution down by parse, execute, and fetch.

So tkprof output is definitely more useful than AUTOTRACE output, but you shouldn't discount AUTOTRACE's usefullness. You can use AUTOTRACE under the following circumstances:

❏ AUTOTRACE is easy to use, and you get the results more quickly than if you have to find and format a trace file. Therefore, you may wish to use AUTOTRACE to compare multiple approaches to an SQL statement (e.g., changing hints, wordings, perhaps even indexes). When the SQL statement seems to be close to optimal, you may use SQL_TRACE and tkprof to confirm this.

❏ Some client/server developers may not have access to the server platform. Therefore, they won't have access to the trace files produced by SQL_TRACE. In this case, the AUTOTRACE facility may be the best option for tuning available.

SUMMARY

In this chapter, we've looked at the tools provided by Oracle for tuning SQL statements. These tools allow you to determine the steps that Oracle will undertake to execute your SQL statement and can measure the resources required.

The EXPLAIN PLAN command can be used to determine the execution plan for an SQL statement. To use EXPLAIN PLAN, you must first create a plan table. The EXPLAIN PLAN command will insert the details of your SQL statement's execution plan into this table. You can then use SQL queries to retrieve and format the execution plan.

Because the procedure for retrieving execution plans using EXPLAIN PLAN is cumbersome, most SQL programmers use scripts to simplify the process. There are also commercial and shareware products available to simplify the process. Some of these tools can be found on this book's web site.

The SQL_TRACE facility provides a more powerful way of generating tuning information for SQL statements. SQL_TRACE generates a trace file containing details of the SQL statements executed and the resources required. The tkprof program can be used to format these trace files and can also generate execution plans for each statement included.

SQL_TRACE is usually enabled by issuing the ALTER SESSION SET SQL_TRACE TRUE statement. The location of the trace file is dependent on the operating system and database configuration and is defined by the configuration parameter USER_DUMP_DEST.

Tkprof includes a number of command line options. A common usage, which sorts SQL statements by elapsed time and which shows the execution plan for each statement, is

```
tkprof trace_file output_file
       sort='(prsela,exeela,fchela)'
       explain=username/password
```

Tkprof generates details of I/O and CPU requirements for each stage (parse, execute, fetch) of SQL statement execution. It also shows the number of rows processed by each stage of the execution plan. Tkprof output can be complex, but the following guidelines for interpretation are always useful:

❑ The ratio of query and current to rows gives a measure of the cost (number of I/Os) required to fetch each row.

❑ The execution steps with the highest row counts are often the best candidates for tuning.

❑ Low ratios of parse to execute for statements that are frequently executed may indicate unnecessary parsing of SQL statements.

❑ The ratio of rows to fetch indicates the use of the array fetch facility. Values close to one indicate that array processing was not enabled.

The SET AUTOTRACE option can be used to generate execution plans and statistics directly from SQL*PLUS. This facility is easier to use than SQL_TRACE and tkprof but provides less detailed output.

Part III: SQL Tuning In Practice

TUNING TABLE ACCESS

INTRODUCTION

In this chapter, we look at ways of improving the performance of SQL statements that access a single table. The single-table query is the building block of more complex SQL queries, so understanding how to optimize the single-table access is a prerequisite for improving the performance of more elaborate queries.

There are usually a number of possible access methods for any given query. A full-table scan is always an option and, depending on the indexes that have been created on the table, there may be a number of index retrieval options. Storing your data in a hash cluster or index organized table provides another option for optimizing data access.

The optimizer will not always choose the best access path, and you need to be able to evaluate the optimizer's choice and sometimes encourage the use of a different access path. Furthermore, you need to make the best possible access paths available to the optimizer by creating appropriate indexes or clusters.

The topics covered in this chapter are as follows:

❏ Comparing full-table scans with other access paths
❏ Using column histograms to improve optimization
❏ Avoiding "accidental" full-table scans
❏ Choosing the best indexing strategy (such as B*-tree, bitmap, or index organized table)

- ❑ Creating and optimizing indexes
- ❑ Optimizing range scans
- ❑ Optimizing queries that include "OR"
- ❑ Optimizing the configuration of hash clusters
- ❑ Optimizing the configuration of bitmap indexes
- ❑ Optimizing the configuration of index organized tables
- ❑ Configuring tables to maximize scan performance

WHEN TO USE A FULL-TABLE SCAN

The two most commonly used methods to retrieve rows from a table are as follows:

- ❑ Full-table scan, in which all rows from the table are read and compared against the selection criteria
- ❑ Index lookup, in which an index is used to determine the rows to be processed

SQL programmers are usually initially taught to avoid the full-table scan. However, table scans will sometimes consume fewer resources than the equivalent index lookup: This will always be true when the selection criteria reference a large proportion of the table data.

Indexed retrieval requires reading both the index blocks and (usually) table blocks. Furthermore, during an index scan Oracle may have to alternate between index blocks and table blocks and may read an individual index block many times. If a large portion of the table is being accessed, the overhead of using the index may be greater than the overhead of scanning the entire table.

At what point does an index retrieval outperform the table access? You will often be given rules of thumb to help you decide whether to use a full-table scan or an index lookup. Here are some of the suggestions that you may encounter:

- ❑ Use a full-table scan if accessing more than 25% of the table data.
- ❑ Use a full-table scan if accessing more than 8 or 16 (or some other number) of data blocks.
- ❑ Use a full-table scan if accessing more than 5% (or 2%) of the table data.
- ❑ Use a full-table scan if it is faster than an index lookup.

These rules of thumb vary so much because it is not possible to generalize across all types of SQL statements, hardware platforms, and data distributions.

Some of the factors that affect the break-even point for indexed retrieval are as follows:

❏ Hit rate in the buffer cache. Index retrievals tend to get very good hit rates in Oracle's buffer cache, while full-table scans generally get a much poorer hit rate. This can help improve index performance.

❏ Row size. Each index access will cost about the same in terms of I/O regardless of the size of the row. However, the longer the row, the greater the number of blocks that must be read by a full-table scan.

❏ Data distribution. If rows in the table are in approximately the order of the indexed column (which can happen if rows are inserted in primary key order), then the index may have less blocks to visit and experience a much higher hit rate.

Figure 8.1 shows the elapsed time for indexed and full-table scan accesses under various conditions. Changing parameter DB_FILE_MULTIBLOCK_ READ_COUNT (discussed later in this chapter and shown as "dfmr" in the chart legend) from 8 to 32 reduced full-table scan time from almost 8 seconds to about 4.5 seconds. Changing the buffer cache size radically changed the index retrieval time, as did loading the data into the table in index key order or in random order.

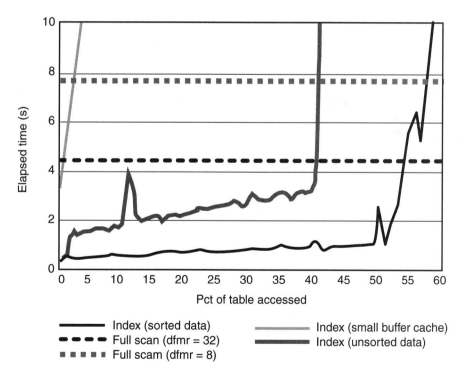

FIGURE 8.1 Comparison of index and full-table scan retrieval times under various environmental conditions.

Making these changes varied the break-even point for indexed retrieval from about 2% of the table to up to 60%, and that's without comparing different index key combinations or changing the table row size. Clearly, there is no single break-even point that can be applied across the board.

Although it's not really possible to provide a "one-size fits all" cutoff point for index retrieval, the following statements are indisputable:

❏ If all rows or a large proportion of rows in the table need to be accessed, then a full-table scan will be the quickest way to do this.

❏ If a single row is to be retrieved from a large table, then an index based on that column will offer the quicker retrieval path.

❏ Between these two extremes, it may be difficult to predict which access path will be quicker.

In many cases, you are either selecting a small number of rows from a table to satisfy a transaction processing (OLTP) type of query or selecting a large number of rows to satisfy a decision support (OLAP) type of query. In these circumstances, your decision will be an easy one: Use the index or hash for the OLTP query and use a full-table scan for the OLAP query.

There is no "one-size fits all" break-even point for indexed versus table scan access. If only a few rows are being accessed, then the index will be preferred. If almost all the rows are being accessed, then the full-table scan will be preferred. In between these two extremes your "mileage" will vary.

HOW THE OPTIMIZER CHOOSES BETWEEN INDEXES AND FULL-TABLE SCAN

The rule-based optimizer will almost always favor an access path involving an index to one involving a full-table scan. This is because in the absence of any information about the sizes of tables, the index-based access path is the safer choice. A full-table scan might be faster than an index lookup in some circumstances—say 50% faster. However, a full-table scan could be 10,000% slower depending on the size of the table. So the rule-based optimizer plays it safe and favors the index-based path.

The cost-based optimizer knows more—or thinks it knows more—about the distribution of data in the tables. As a result, it will often choose a full-table scan even where an index is available if it calculates that the full-table scan will be less expensive. Factors influencing the cost-based optimizer's decisions include the following:

❏ Number of blocks allocated to the table that have ever contained data (that is, the blocks below the high-water mark)

❏ Size of data blocks

❏ Number of blocks that can be read in a single I/O operation (partially determined by the configuration setting DB_FILE_MULTIBLOCK_READ_COUNT)

❏ Selectivity of the index—the number of rows returned for each index key

❏ Depth of the index—number of I/O operations required to resolve a single index key

The decisions that the cost-based optimizer arrives at can be misguided if

❏ A candidate index has only a few distinct values, but the value being queried is quite selective. Unless you have created a histogram on the column and explicitly coded the value being selected into the SQL, the cost-based optimizer will probably ignore the index. Creating column histograms is discussed later in this section.

❏ The optimizer goal is set to ALL_ROWS or CHOOSE, but the requirement is really for response time. A full-table scan might result in the best response time to retrieve all the rows, but an index will usually be quicker when retrieving just the first row.

❏ If you haven't kept your optimizer statistics up to date (by using the ANALYZE command or DBMS_STATS package), the cost-based optimizer may think that the table is smaller than it really is. This might lead it to choose incorrectly the full-table scan.

❏ The cost-based optimizer is heavily biased toward reducing I/O. CPU overheads, such as those involved in sorting rows for a merge join, are not always accurately estimated. On some systems these overheads can be substantial.

To encourage the cost-based optimizer to use suitable indexes, you should therefore do the following:

❏ Create histograms on indexed columns where there are only a few distinct values but where most of the values are very rare. Hardcode these values in the SQL statement (e.g., don't use bind variables) to allow the histogram information to be used.

❏ Specify the FIRST_ROWS optimizer goal if interactive response time is your aim. This can be specified as a hint, in an ALTER SESSION statement, or in the database configuration.

❏ Use hints to direct the optimizer toward specific indexes.

Help the cost-based optimizer choose between indexes and table scans by keeping your tables analyzed, specifying the correct optimizer goal, using histograms where appropriate, and using hints.

COLUMN HISTOGRAMS

Column histograms, introduced in Chapter 3, provide the cost-based optimizer with details of the distribution of data within a column. By creating a histogram, you provide the cost-based optimizer with more information about column data and help it to make a more informed choice. In particular, the presence of a histogram can help the optimizer decide between an index retrieval and a full-table scan. This is especially true when the access involved is on a column with a small number of values and some of the values are particularly selective (because they appear relatively rarely). Histograms also help the cost-based optimizer make the right decision during range scans. For example, without a histogram the cost-based optimizer might resolve the following query with a full-table scan, since it would not know the proportion of persons over 90:

```
select *
  from people
 where age>90
```

Creating a histogram on the age column would allow the optimizer to determine that only a small proportion of people are over 90 and that an index-based execution plan was therefore preferred.

We create a histogram for a column by specifying the column name in the ANALYZE command. For instance, the following command creates histograms for DATE_OF_BIRTH, CONTACT_SURNAME, and CUSTOMER_STATUS:

```
ANALYZE TABLE customers
    ESTIMATE STATISTICS SAMPLE 20 PERCENT FOR COLUMNS
        date_of_birth       SIZE 50,
        contact_surname     SIZE 200,
        customer_status     SIZE 3
```

The size parameter specifies the number of "buckets" in the histogram. Each bucket specifies a range of values. Where there are only a few distinct values in a column, a small size can be specified. For columns with a larger number of values, a higher size will increase the accuracy of the histogram. We can also use DBMS_STATS to create histograms—and potentially utilize parallel processing—as in the following example:

```
BEGIN
    dbms_stats.gather_table_stats (
        ownname => 'SQLTUNE',
        tabname => 'CUSTOMERS',
        estimate_percent => 20,
        method_opt => 'for columns
                    date_of_birth          size 50,
                    contact_surname        size 200,
                    customer_status        size 3',
        degree => 4
    );
END;
```

We'll see examples of histograms applied to various types of queries in subsequent sections.

Create column histograms on indexed columns where there are only a few distinct values but where some values are very infrequent. Remember that histograms cannot be used to search for a value supplied to the query via a bind variable.

Histograms and Bind Variables Histograms can dramatically improve the quality of the cost based optimizer's decisions for certain queries. Unfortunately, there is a catch. The cost-based optimizer cannot take advantage of a histogram if the column values are specified with bind variables. You may recall from Chapter 3 that bind variables are a way of hiding the actual value of a variable from the optimizer until after the statement has been parsed. This allows SQL statements that have different search criteria to be recognized as the same statement and allows Oracle to avoid reparsing the statement.

Because the value of the bind variable is evaluated after the statement has been parsed, the cost-based optimizer cannot take the value of a bind variable into account and therefore cannot take advantage of a column histogram. This leads us to a dilemma: Bind variables reduce parsing, and histograms improve cost-based optimizer decisions, but you can't have both!

You need to weigh a number of factors when deciding upon bind variables versus histograms. Table 8.1 shows some of these considerations.

The conditions in which histograms are favored are typical of decision support or data warehousing applications, while the conditions in which bind variables are favored are typical of transaction processing applications.

Histograms can improve the optimization of range scans or lookups on unevenly distributed data. However, bind variables should usually be used to reduce parsing in transaction processing environments, and histograms can't be used in conjunction with bind variables.

TABLE 8.1 Choosing Between Histograms and Bind Variables

SITUATION	USE BIND VARIABLES?	USE HISTOGRAMS?
The value of the search variable never changes.	No need, since the value doesn't change, the SQL statement will always match.	Maybe, if other criteria suggest it.
The SQL statement is performing a range scan.	Not unless strongly indicated by other factors.	Yes, if the range scan varies in the amount of rows picked up (so that sometimes a scan will be preferred, sometimes an index).
The SQL statement is performing an exact lookup, but some of the values are common and some are rare.	Not unless strongly indicated by other factors	Yes, since the histogram will help the cost-based optimizer decide between a full-table scan and an index lookup.
The SQL statement is executed very frequently and is expected to complete quickly.	Yes. For an inexpensive statement executed very frequently, the cost of parsing can be significant.	No. Bind variables are indicated here. Use a hint if the optimizer makes the wrong decision.
The SQL statement is executed infrequently and takes a long time to run.	Probably not. Parse overhead will be a small component of overall requirements, so using bind variables will probably not help much.	If indicated by other factors.
The SQL is ad hoc and user driven. It alternates between the specific and the general or uses range conditions.	Probably not. End users are unlikely to use bind variables, and the statement probably wouldn't find a match in the shared pool anyway.	Yes. Allow the optimizer to make the most informed choice.
The SQL is being generated by some third-party product (perhaps a query tool).	You probably don't get a choice.	Since you can't control the SQL, you're probably dependent on the cost-based optimizer, so give it all the information you can.

> Histograms can improve the optimization of range scans or lookups on unevenly distributed data. However, bind variables should usually be used to reduce parsing in transaction processing environments, and histograms can't be used in conjunction with bind variables.

AVOIDING "ACCIDENTAL" TABLE SCANS

Even if there is an appropriate index or hash retrieval available, the optimizer may not be able to take advantage of the access because of the wording of the SQL statement. Some of the query types that prevent indexes from being used are as follows:

- ❑ Queries involving a NOT EQUALS (<>) condition
- ❑ Searching for NULL values
- ❑ Accidentally disabling an index with a function

NOT EQUALS CONDITIONS

Oracle will not employ an index if the NOT EQUALS operator (<>) is employed. This is generally sensible, because when retrieving all rows except for those matching a single value, a full-table scan will usually be the fastest way of retrieving the data. However, if the value in question accounts for the majority of the rows in the database, then an index-based retrieval of the minority of rows (which don't match the value) might be preferable.

For example, let's say that CUSTOMER_STATUS has two values, '1' and '2', and that 99% of rows are in status '1'. A histogram on CUSTOMER_STATUS allows Oracle to determine that an index is the best option when retrieving all customers who have a status of '2':

```
SQL> SELECT * FROM customers WHERE customer_status='2'

Execution Plan
-------------------------------------------------------
0        SELECT STATEMENT Optimizer=CHOOSE
1     0    TABLE ACCESS (BY INDEX ROWID) OF 'CUSTOMERS'
2     1      INDEX (RANGE SCAN) OF 'CUSTOMERS_I4'
                  (NON-UNIQUE)
```

However, if we look for all customers who have any status but '1', we see that Oracle declines to use the index:

```
SQL> SELECT * FROM customers WHERE customer_status<>'1'
Execution Plan
-------------------------------------------------------
0        SELECT STATEMENT Optimizer=CHOOSE
1     0    TABLE ACCESS (FULL) OF 'CUSTOMERS'
```

If you have an SQL statement involving a not equals condition that you believe should be using an index, you should recode the query so that it uses IN, "=", or OR (see later in this chapter for guidance on optimizing these kinds of operations).

You might be tempted to use an INDEX hint to force a table access, and a brief glance at the execution plan may convince you that this approach has worked. For instance, we add an INDEX hint to the previous statement:

```
SQL> SELECT /*+ index(c) */ *
        FROM customers c WHERE customer_status<>'1'

Execution Plan
----------------------------------------------------------
0      SELECT STATEMENT Optimizer=CHOOSE
1    0    TABLE ACCESS (BY INDEX ROWID) OF 'CUSTOMERS'
2    1      INDEX (FULL SCAN) OF 'CUSTOMERS_I4'
                  (NON-UNIQUE)
```

At first glance the hint seems to work—an index lookup is occurring. However, if you look carefully you'll note that the hint is causing a FULL SCAN of the index rather than a RANGE SCAN as before. This means that every single index entry was read rather than only those that matched our criteria. Figure 8.2 shows the relative execution time of each approach.

Of course, if the data were different, it may be that the full-table scan was the more appropriate approach. But you still need to be aware that by using not equals you are effectively ruling out an indexed retrieval approach.

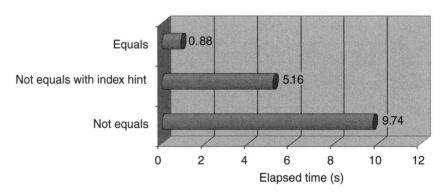

FIGURE 8.2   Performance of a not equals query and its equivalent equals query.

> Oracle will not use an index if the query condition is "not equals" (!=). If you think the query could benefit from an indexed approach, reword the query using IN, OR, or ">". You may still need to use hints or a column histogram to encourage Oracle to use the appropriate index.

SEARCHING FOR NULLS

As we discovered in Chapter 6, index entries are not created when all the columns in the index have the NULL value. As a result, you can't use an index on a column to search for a NULL value. For instance, let's suppose the CUSTOMERS.CUSTOMER_STATUS column may contain NULL values (perhaps prior to the customer being fully registered). We might have a query to find these customers, as follows:

```
SELECT customer_name
  FROM customers
 WHERE customer_status IS NULL

Execution Plan
-----------------------------------------------------
0      SELECT STATEMENT Optimizer=CHOOSE
1    0    TABLE ACCESS (FULL) OF 'CUSTOMERS'
```

To find customers with the NULL status, we must perform a full-table scan. We redefine the column so that it is not NULL and has a default value of unknown:

```
ALTER table customers modify customer_status
default 'UNKNOWN';

UPDATE customers
   SET customer_status = 'UNKNOWN'
 WHERE customer_status IS NULL;
```

Now we can then use the index to find these NULL values:

```
SELECT /*+ INDEX(c) */ customer_name
  FROM customers c
 WHERE customer_status = 'UNKNOWN'
```

In this example, using the index reduced elapsed time by about 75%. See Figure 8.3. For bigger tables, the improvement can be even more pronounced although it

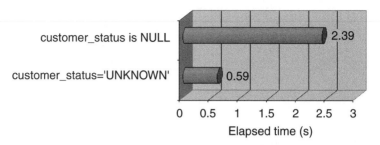

FIGURE 8.3   Searching for NULL values compared with searching for a default value.

clearly depends on what proportion of rows contain the NULL value. Note that, as in the not equals example, it may be necessary to use a hint or define a histogram if the number of unique values is low.

Avoid searching for NULL values in an indexed column. Instead, define the column as NOT NULL with a default value and then search for that default.

SEARCHING FOR VALUES THAT ARE NOT NULL

Although Oracle cannot use an index to search for NULL values, it can use the index to find those values that are NOT NULL. The cost-based optimizer will choose to do this only if it calculates that the combined cost of accessing the table and the relevant index will be less than the cost of performing a full-table scan.

In most circumstances, the cost-based optimizer will determine that the full-table scan is the cheaper cost and will perform a full-table scan. For instance, in the following example only 5% of the rows have a NULL value for PROCESS_FLAG, and consequently the cost-based optimizer chooses the full scan option:

```
SQL> select * from customers where process_flag is not null;

Execution Plan
-------------------------------------------
   0      SELECT STATEMENT Optimizer=CHOOSE
   1    0    TABLE ACCESS (FULL) OF 'CUSTOMERS'
```

The cost-based optimizer may favor a full index scan to identify the NOT NULL rows if most of the rows are NULL and if the query can be resolved by the use of the index alone. For instance, in the following example, 95% of the rows have a PROCESS FLAG of NULL (and an ANALYZE has been performed to ensure that the optimizer knows this):

```
SQL> select count(*) from customers
       where process_flag is not null;

Execution Plan
----------------------------------------------------
0       SELECT STATEMENT Optimizer=CHOOSE
1    0    SORT (AGGREGATE)
2    1      INDEX (FAST FULL SCAN) OF
               'CUSTOMER_PROCESS_FLAG_I'
                 (NON-UNIQUE)
```

Note that Oracle scans the entire index. Since NULL values are not indexed, this is equivalent to looking up only those values that are NOT NULL.

You can use an index to find values that are NOT NULL. If most values are NULL, the index will be very small and efficient because NULL values are not indexed.

CREATING INDEXES ON NULLABLE COLUMNS

It's usually wise to define the columns referenced in the where clause as NOT NULL so that indexing these columns can be effective. However, it can be worthwhile to use NULL values in an indexed column if the following conditions apply:

❑   The column is almost always NULL.
❑   We never want to find rows where the column is NULL.
❑   We do want to search for rows where the column is NOT NULL.
❑   We want to minimize the space required by the index.

Since NULLs are not stored in an index, an index created when the preceding conditions are true will be compact and can be used to locate rows quickly where the column contains a value. Ensure that the cost-based optimizer makes use of the appropriate index and uses a hint, if necessary.

SEARCHING FOR A SELECTIVE VALUE IN AN UNSELECTIVE COLUMN

If the column is of marginal selectivity, it may be difficult for Oracle to determine whether the full-table scan or the index retrieval is preferable. If the column has only a few values but you know that the values concerned are rare, then you could force an index lookup using a hint.

For instance, only a handful of customers have the status of "INVALID." Nevertheless, the cost-based optimizer will decline to use an index on status for the following statement, since there are only three values for CUSTOMER_STATUS and—at the time—no histogram existed on the CUSTOMER_STATUS column:

```
SQL>  select count(distinct customer_name)
         from customers where customer_status = 'INVALID'

Execution Plan
----------------------------------------------------------
0       SELECT STATEMENT Optimizer=CHOOSE
1     0    SORT (GROUP BY)
2     1       TABLE ACCESS (FULL) OF 'CUSTOMERS'
```

The INDEX hint can be used to encourage the cost-based optimizer to perform the more efficient index scan:

```
SQL> select /*+ INDEX(C,CUSTOMERS_I4) */
  2          count(distinct customer_name)
  3       from customers c
  4*  where customer_status = 'INVALID'

Execution Plan
--------------------------------------------------
0       SELECT STATEMENT Optimizer=CHOOSE
1     0    SORT (GROUP BY)
2     1       TABLE ACCESS (BY INDEX ROWID) OF 'CUSTOMERS'
3     2          INDEX (RANGE SCAN) OF 'CUSTOMERS_I4'
                     (NON-UNIQUE)
```

If you don't know in advance whether the value to be selected will be INVALID (< 1% of rows) or "VALID" (>90% of rows), it may be a mistake to force the use of an index in all cases. A column histogram might be a better solution. Provided that bind variables are not being used, you could use a column histogram to promote the use of the index for searches on "INVALID" while retaining full-table scans when searching for "VALID" rows.

Use hints or column histograms to avoid full-table scans when searching for a rare value in an otherwise nonselective index.

UNINTENTIONALLY DISABLING AN INDEX WITH A FUNCTION

We saw in Chapter 5 how we can influence the rule-based optimizer by disabling certain indexes. The trick is to apply an operator or a function to the column in question. If a column is subjected to any modification, then an index on that column cannot be used. In the past, this was a useful way to influence the rule-based optimizer. Nowadays, hints provide a much more powerful and self-documenting method.

Obviously, if index paths can be intentionally disabled, they can also be unintentionally disabled. For instance, consider this query, which seeks customers who are over 100 years old (usually a minority):

```
SQL> SELECT *
  2    FROM customers
  3   WHERE date_of_birth < SYSDATE--(100 * 365.25);

Execution Plan
----------------------------------------------------
0      SELECT STATEMENT Optimizer=CHOOSE
1    0    TABLE ACCESS (BY INDEX ROWID) OF 'CUSTOMERS'
2    1      INDEX (RANGE SCAN) OF 'CUSTOMER_DOB_I'
                  (NON-UNIQUE)
```

This query can make use of an index on DATE_OF_BIRTH and executes very rapidly. However, consider the following query, which is identical in intent:

```
SQL> SELECT *
  2    FROM customers
  3   WHERE (SYSDATE--date_of_birth) / 365.25 > 100
  4  /

Execution Plan
----------------------------------------------------
0      SELECT STATEMENT Optimizer=CHOOSE
1    0    TABLE ACCESS (FULL) OF 'CUSTOMERS'
```

Because this query manipulated the DATE_OF_BIRTH column, the index could not be used and subsequently this form of the query took much longer to manipulate.

Avoid applying functions or operations to indexed columns in the WHERE clause. Instead, apply functions to the values against which the indexed column is being compared.

FUNCTIONAL INDEXES

Sometimes it's simply not possible to avoid applying a function to an indexed column. For instance, consider the following query to get customer details:

```
SELECT customer_id, customer_name
  FROM customers
 WHERE contact_surname = :1
   AND contact_firstname = :2
```

We can use an index on surname and firstname to satisfy this query with only a couple of I/Os. However, let's suppose that the query is issued from an on-line inquiry screen. It might be decided to make the search ignore distinctions between upper- and lowercase by rewording the query as follows:

```
SELECT customer_id, customer_name
  FROM customers
 WHERE UPPER (contact_surname) = UPPER (:1)
   AND UPPER (contact_firstname) = UPPER (:2)
```

Of course, by placing a function around the indexed columns we prevent the column from being used. However, performing a case-insensitive search is a reasonable business requirement, and users will expect reasonable response time, so we need a solution.

Prior to Oracle8i, we would have recommended creating two new columns (UPPERCASE_SURNAME, UPPERCASE_FIRSTNAME) and maintaining them by using a trigger (see Chapter 13). However, in Oracle 8i we have a much more elegant solution: the *functional index*.

Functional indexes are simply indexes that may include functions within their definition, as in the following example:

```
CREATE INDEX customers_upcase_idx ON customers
    (UPPER(contact_surname), UPPER(contact_firstname))
```

Once the index is created, queries that use the same functions that are used in the index definition may be used in the WHERE clause and the functional index will be used to retrieve the results:

```
SELECT *
  FROM customers
 WHERE UPPER(contact_surname)='ANDERSON'
   AND UPPER(contact_firstname)='ANDREW'
```

```
Rows      Execution Plan
-------   -----------------------------------------
     0    SELECT STATEMENT    GOAL: CHOOSE
     1     TABLE ACCESS (BY INDEX ROWID)OF 'CUSTOMERS'
     2      INDEX (RANGE SCAN) OF 'CUSTOMERS_UPCASE_IDX'
```

The functions that are included in the index may be user-defined functions or built-in functions. If user-defined functions are used, they must be created with the DETERMINISTIC keyword. This declaration requires that the function to return the same outputs whenever it is supplied with the same inputs. This is necessary because entries made when the functional index is created cannot change.

For instance, a functional index on UPPER(surname) will work because UPPER("Harris") will always be equal to "HARRIS". However, consider a function AGE(p_birthday DATE). As I write this, AGE('21-DEC-60') will return 39. However, by the time you read this the function may well return 40 or more. If we created a functional index based on the AGE function, it would become invalid as time passed because the function would return different values but the entries in the index would not be updated.

When you can't avoid applying functions to indexed columns in the WHERE clause, consider using functional indexes based on the same functions.

CHOOSING THE BEST INDEXING STRATEGY

We looked at Oracle indexing and clustering strategies in detail in Chapter 6. To review briefly the three most commonly used indexing options,

- ❏ Oracle's default index type—the B*-tree index—is suitable for improving access for a wide range of queries. B*-tree indexes can optimize exact lookups and range queries and can sometimes be used to resolve queries in their own right and without reference to the underlying table.
- ❏ The hash cluster allows you to store table data in a location that is derived from a mathematical manipulation of a key value. Hash clusters can improve access for exact key lookups but cannot enhance range queries and require careful sizing to prevent degradation of the hash cluster.
- ❏ Bitmap indexes are useful to optimize queries in which multiple columns of low cardinality (few distinct values) are queried in combination. Unlike

B*-tree indexes, bitmap indexes can work for any combination of columns but increase locking contention.

Table 8.2 compares the three options to a range of scenarios.

If you are in doubt about the most appropriate indexing strategy, you will usually be safe using Oracle's default B*-tree index. The B*-tree index can be

TABLE 8.2 Comparison of B*-tree indexes, hash clusters and bitmap indexes

SITUATION	B*-TREE INDEXES	HASH CLUSTER	BITMAP INDEXES
Exact key lookup on a column with lots of values.	Yes	Yes	Probably not. Bitmap index retrieval performance diminishes as the number of column values increase
Exact key lookups on multiple columns.	Yes	Yes	Maybe, depending on the cardinality (number of values) in the column.
Queries on multiple columns in various combinations.	You will probably need multiple concatenated indexes to support the various combinations.	No. The hash cluster can only support a single order of values.	Yes. Bitmap indexes can support any combination of columns provided that all have a bitmap index.
Queries on ranges of values (>, <, . BETWEEN).	Yes	No. Hash clusters do not support range queries.	Possibly not. It is possible to perform range scans on bitmap indexes, but because doing so involves accessing multiple bitmaps, it might be less efficient than a B*-tree index.
Table is subject to high rates on update, insert, or delete.	Yes	Yes	Probably not. Locking on tables with bitmap indexes is very restrictive.
You want to enforce UNIQUEness.	Yes	No	No
Table changes in size over time.	Yes	Only if you can either afford to rebuild the table periodically (to avoid overflows) or can afford to allocate space up front for future growth (degrading table scans).	Yes

useful in most circumstances and requires less administration and care than other indexing methods.

HOW MANY DISTINCT VALUES ARE TOO MANY FOR A BITMAP INDEX?

It's clear that we don't want to use bitmap indexes in a transaction processing environment due to the overhead of locking the bitmaps (this was discussed in more depth in Chapter 6). But if all other conditions suit bitmap indexes, at what point should we decide that the column has too many unique values to be suitable for a bitmap?

Most examples of bitmap indexes (including those shown in Chapter 6) show multiple columns of *very* low cardinality, such as sex, marital status, and so on. When we look at those examples we'd be forgiven for thinking that bitmap indexes are not suitable when there are more than a handful of key values.

In truth, bitmap indexes are capable of performing well even when there are many thousands of unique values. Figure 8.4 shows the relative performance of bitmap and B*-tree-based queries on a million row table for columns with between 5 and 10,000 distinct values. As we can see, bitmap indexes are still quite effective even when the number of distinct values is very large. For this example,

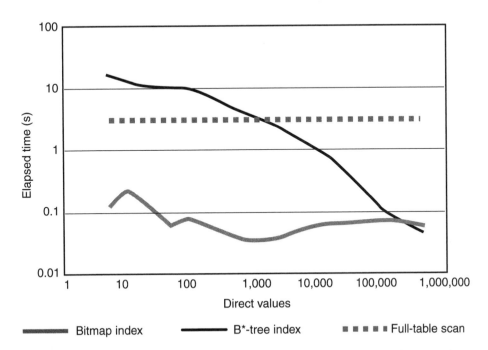

FIGURE 8.4 Relative performance of bitmap versus B*-tree index depends on number of distinct values in indexed column.

the query requested the number of rows matching a specific column value—a query that the bitmap index could resolve without having to access table rows. When the query can be resolved by an index alone, bitmap indexes give very good performance even when the number of distinct values is high. As the number of distinct values increases the storage savings offered by bitmap indexes decreases. For five unique values, a very compact bitmap index can be created (only five bitmaps). For 10,000 distinct values, 10,000 bitmap indexes will be created. Each has to have a bit for every row in the table, so the amount of storage required rises rapidly. (Figure 8.5)

> Bitmap indexes can still perform well when a column has many thousand distinct values. However, storage required for the bitmap index will rise rapidly.

DECIDING TO USE AN INDEX ORGANIZED TABLE

An index organized table is a table that is structured as a B*-tree index. We examined the structure of a B*-tree index in Chapter 6. There are a number of circumstances in which you might find the index organized table advantageous:

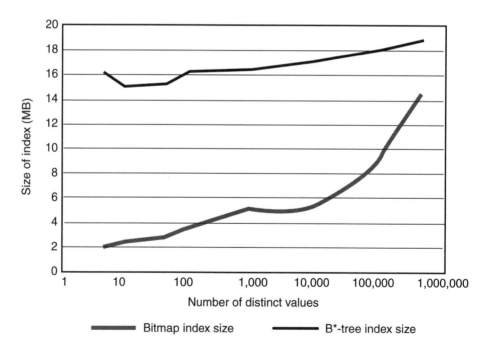

FIGURE 8.5 Relationship between number of distinct values and index size for B*-tree and bitmap index.

❏ All your queries can be resolved through a primary key index. If you find that this is the case, then creating an indexed organized table effectively removes the storage and I/O overhead associated with the table.

❏ Access to the certain rows in the table via the primary key is critical. Because table rows in the index organized table are stored in the leaf block of the index, you can save a single I/O when accessing via the primary key because you don't have to jump to the table row.

❏ You want to split a table into frequently accessed and infrequently accessed segments. This can be done easily through the INCLUDING clause. Columns up to and including that specified in the INCLUDING clause are stored in the leaf blocks and can be accessed quickly. However, those after the INCLUDING clause are stored in an overflow segment that will require an additional I/O to access.

Against these advantages, consider the following potential disadvantages:

❏ Indexes tend to waste more space when rows are deleted than do tables (because an index entry often can't be reused until a new row with the same or similar key sequence occurs). This might mean that your index organized table actually takes longer to scan than the equivalent traditional table. You will probably want to reorganize an index organized table more frequently than a traditional table.

❏ If you store a lot of data in the leaf block, then the number of rows per leaf block will be much less than the equivalent B*-tree index on a traditional table. This may mean that an additional level in the B*-tree will be required to store the index entries, and accessing the index organized table will be just as expensive as accessing a traditional table by B*-tree index.

❏ Prior to Oracle8i, you could not create any secondary (that is, nonprimary) key indexes on an index organized table.

The benefits of index organized tables can be relatively minor and sometimes hard to achieve. Therefore, you should ensure that the benefits of the index organized table outweigh the drawbacks for your specific circumstances.

Index organized tables can offer advantages for tables where all or most queries are resolved by an index scan on the primary key and/or where you want to split the data into frequently and infrequently accessed columns.

We will look at some specific hints for optimizing index organized tables later in this chapter.

OPTIMIZING B*-TREE INDEX LOOKUPS

The inexperienced SQL programmer will often use EXPLAIN PLAN to determine that a full-table scan has been avoided. If there is no full-table scan, then the programmer may conclude that the plan is a good one. In fact, usually a wide variety of index-based retrievals are possible, and merely ensuring that one of these indexes is used does not mean that the SQL statement is optimized. Selecting the best of all actual and potential indexes, and ensuring that the indexes are being used to their full potential, is at least as important as avoiding a full-table scan.

TYPES OF INDEX RETRIEVALS

Some of the types of index retrievals that can occur are as follows:

❑   Finding a single row by lookup of a unique index
❑   Finding multiple rows matching a single value in a nonunique index
❑   Finding rows matching all the values in a concatenated index
❑   Finding rows matching some of the values in a concatenated index
❑   Finding rows matching a range of values in a concatenated index
❑   Using multiple indexes to find matching values

For all but the first type of index retrieval, some sort of optimization is possible. For instance,

❑   If the index is not unique, are all the columns used in the selection criteria used in the index? If not, perhaps adding the missing columns to a concatenated index will improve the index's efficiency.
❑   If multiple indexes are being merged, you can be almost certain that the use of a concatenated index would improve performance (although index merges have become much more efficient in Oracle8).
❑   If you are only using some of the columns in the concatenated index, are the additional columns in the index used by other queries?
❑   Even if the columns in the concatenated index match the columns in the WHERE clause, is the order of the columns in the index optimal?
❑   If searching on a range, have we restricted the range correctly? Is Oracle performing the range scan efficiently?

The primary techniques for improving index lookups are as follows:

❑   Create new indexes.
❑   Add or remove columns from a concatenated index.

❏ Use alternative techniques, such as hash clustering or bitmap indexing.
❏ Create column histograms.
❏ Use hints.

USING CONCATENATED INDEXES

If we are querying against multiple column values in a table, then a concatenated index on all of those values will usually offer the most efficient retrieval.
A concatenated index is optimized if

❏ It contains all columns referenced for that table in the WHERE clause.
❏ The order of columns in the concatenated index supports the widest range of queries.
❏ The most selective columns come first in the column list.
❏ If possible, the concatenated index contains the columns in the SELECT list as well as the columns in the WHERE clause. This may improve query performance by allowing the query to be satisfied from the index lookup alone.

Selecting the Columns for the Concatenated Index   Usually, the more columns specified in the concatenated index, the more selective the index will be and the better your query performance will be. Figure 8.6 provides an example of typical improvements gained by adding columns to the concatenated index for the following query:

```
SELECT contact_surname, contact_firstname,
       date_of_birth, phoneno
  FROM customers c
 WHERE contact_surname = 'BROWN'
   AND contact_firstname = 'COLIN'
   AND date_of_birth =
         to_date('5-JUN-1950','DD-MON-YYYY');
```

> Where possible, optimize a query by including all of the columns contained in the WHERE clause within a concatenated index.

Optimizing the Order of Columns in an Index   Changing the column order can have the least significant improvement and can have the biggest negative effect on other queries. For instance, it might make good sense to create a concatenated index on the CUSTOMERS table on the following columns:

```
CONTACT_SURNAME, CONTACT_FIRSTNAME, DATE_OF_BIRTH
```

This allows us to search on contact_surname alone, contact_surname+contact_firstname, or all three columns combined. Putting the surname first in the index seems a sensible choice, since there might be other queries that specify only the surname—and these can use the index if the surname is the first column. However, if we ignore the effect on other queries, what is this optimal order when all three columns are specified?

It is often stated that the most efficient order is that which places the most selective column first in the index. However, by doing this, you might reduce the efficiency of index compression, which was described in Chapter 6. If your index is created with the COMPRESS option, putting the least selective columns first will improve the efficiency of the compression and might, in turn, improve index scan performance.

Carefully determine the best order of columns in a concatenated index. Columns that are subject to being queried individually and columns with high selectivity make good candidates for the first column in the index. If the index is created with the COMPRESS flag, placing low-cardinality columns first will improve the compression and improve scan performance.

Overindexing   Sometimes we only want to select a small number of columns from a table. For instance, in the following example, we know surname, firstname, and date of birth, but we want to retrieve the phone number:

```
SELECT contact_surname, contact_firstname,
       date_of_birth, phoneno
  FROM customers c
 WHERE contact_surname = 'BROWN'
   AND contact_firstname = 'COLIN'
   AND date_of_birth
       = to_date('5-JUN-1950','DD-MON-YYYY');
```

With our index on the surname, firstname, and date of birth, we can satisfy this query effectively. Oracle will access the head index block, one or two branch index blocks, and the appropriate index leaf block. This leaf block will contain the ROWID for the row in question, which will then be retrieved from the table block. A total of four or five block I/Os will be required.

If we still want to speed up this query, we can add the phone number to the index. If we do this, we can resolve the query without having to access the table at all, since all the data required are contained in the index. This usually saves a single I/O—not very noticeable for a single lookup, but a 20 to 25% savings that could be a significant improvement if the query is being executed frequently

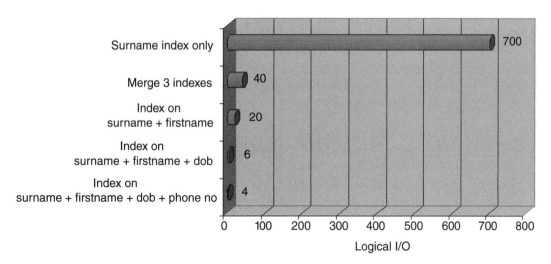

FIGURE 8.6 Improvements gained by adding columns to a concatenated index.

(perhaps in an OLTP environment). Figure 8.6 illustrates the reduction in I/O when we fine-tune a concatenated index.

INDEX MERGES

It's possible for Oracle to resolve a query against multiple columns by using multiple indexes. For instance, our preceding example statement queries on CONTACT_SURNAME, CONTACT_FIRSTNAME, and DATE_OF_BIRTH:

```
WHERE contact_surname = 'BROWN'
   AND contact_firstname = 'COLIN'
   AND date_of_birth =
       to_date('5-JUN-1950','DD-MON-YYYY');
```

If we had separate indexes on each of the columns concerned, Oracle could perform an index merge to obtain the results. To do this, Oracle retrieves from the indexes all the rows that meet each of the criteria and then selects from each list only those rows that are common to all. So in our preceding example, Oracle would retrieve all the "Browns", all the "Colins", and all those born on 5 June, 1950.

In Oracle7 these index merges were usually horrendously inefficient and generally to be avoided. However, index merge performance has improved in recent releases. Our tests in Figure 7.6 show that although the index merge required more I/O than any of our concatenated indexes, it still outperformed a single-column index.

You can force an index merge with the AND_EQUAL hint. The AND-EQUAL execution step indicates that the index merge was executed:

```
SELECT  /*+AND_EQUAL(c,CUSTOMER_SURNAME_I,
        CUSTOMER_FIRSTNAME_I,CUSTOMER_DOB_I) */
        contact_surname, contact_firstname,
        date_of_birth, phoneno
   FROM customers c
  WHERE contact_surname = 'BROWN'
    AND contact_firstname = 'COLIN'
    AND date_of_birth = '5-JUN-1950'


Rows      Execution Plan
-------   ------------------------------------------
      0   SELECT STATEMENT
      2    TABLE ACCESS (BY INDEX ROWID) OF 'CUSTOMERS'
      3     AND-EQUAL
     10      INDEX (RANGE SCAN) OF 'CUSTOMER_DOB_I'
      8      INDEX (RANGE SCAN) OF 'CUSTOMER_FIRSTNAME_I'
      8      INDEX (RANGE SCAN) OF 'CUSTOMER_SURNAME_I'
```

Index merges for multiple low-cardinality columns (columns with few distinct values) may still cause problems. For these queries you should either use a concatenated index or consider bitmap indexes.

If you can't construct concatenated indexes to suit all your queries, you may be able to use index merges. However, be aware that indexes with few values cannot be merged efficiently with B*-tree indexes.

SEARCHING FOR RANGES

Using indexes to select rows matching a range of data is a common operation. We can identify the following types of range scans:

- ❑ Unbounded range scan. This involves getting all rows with a column value greater or less than a particular value.
- ❑ Bounded range scan. This involves getting all rows with column values between two values.
- ❑ Range lookup. Find a row in a table where one column is less than the specified value and the other column is greater. In other words, the table has a high value column and a low value column.

From the optimizer's point of view, range scans present particular problems:

❑ Unless a column histogram is present, the cost-based optimizer cannot calculate the cost of the range lookup since it does not know the extent of the range.

❑ Regardless of the optimizer mode (e.g., RULE, FIRST_ROWS, ALL_ROWS), Oracle will almost always perform an index range scan to resolve a query containing a bounded range condition (if an appropriate index exists).

❑ The rule-based optimizer and cost-based optimizer in "FIRST_ROWS" mode will use an index to resolve a bounded range scan. The cost-based optimizer in "ALL_ROWS" mode will usually perform a full-table scan to resolve an unbounded range query.

❑ Both optimizers prefer exact value lookups to range lookups. If an alternative path involving an equality condition exists, then it will probably be used in preference to a range condition.

❑ Range lookups tend to be fairly inefficient by default since Oracle doesn't know that the high value is always higher than the low value and cannot assume that there are no overlaps.

Unbounded Range Scan Consider a query based on the date of birth of our customers:

```
SELECT contact_surname,customer_status
  FROM customers
 WHERE date_of_birth > to_date(:dob,'DD-MON-YYYY')
```

The optimizer doesn't know what value will be provided to ":dob" and therefore cannot accurately determine how many rows will be retrieved. In Oracle8i, it will take into account the number of unique values and in this case assumes that 5% of the rows will be retrieved and will use an index. Note the "Card" entries in the following execution plan; the optimizer guessed that 5000 from a total of 100,000 rows would be retrieved:

```
Execution Plan
-------------------------------------------------------
0       SELECT STATEMENT (Cost=326 Card=5000 Bytes=
           215000)
1    0     TABLE ACCESS (BY INDEX ROWID) OF 'CUSTOMERS'
                  (Cost=326 Card=5000)
2    1       INDEX (RANGE SCAN) OF 'CUSTOMER_DOB_I'
                  (Cost=13 Card=5000)
```

Of course, this 5% value is nothing but a guess on the optimizer's part. If we feed 01-JAN-1990 into the bind variable, all the rows will be retrieved and the index plan will be a disaster.

If we use literals instead of bind variables, the optimizer can compare the value provided with the maximum and minimum columns values calculated by the ANALYZE command or DBMS_STATS and make a more accurate estimate of the number of rows retrieved. For instance, in this case the optimizer wisely decides not to use an index (note the "Card" tag on the execution plan: The optimizer estimates that 100,000 rows will be retrieved):

```
SQL> SELECT  contact_surname,customer_status
  2    FROM customers
  3*  WHERE date_of_birth >
          to_date('01-JAN-1880','DD-MON-YYYY')

Execution Plan
------------------------------------------------
SELECT STATEMENT (Cost=326 Card=100000 )
  TABLE ACCESS (FULL) OF 'CUSTOMERS'
      (Cost=326 Card=100000)
```

In this case the optimizer wisely decides to use the index (note the "Card" tag on the execution plan: The optimizer estimates that 195 rows will be retrieved):

```
SQL> SELECT  contact_surname,customer_status
  2    FROM customers
  3   WHERE date_of_birth >
          to_date('01-JUN-1976','DD-MON-YYYY');

Execution Plan
-----------------------------------------------------
SELECT STATEMENT (Cost=200 Card=195)
  TABLE ACCESS (BY INDEX ROWID) OF 'CUSTOMERS'
    INDEX (RANGE SCAN) OF 'CUSTOMER_DOB_I' (NON-UNIQUE)
```

> For range scans (greater than, less than) on a selective index, the use of bind variables will promote an index. If this is inappropriate, you should change it using hints. If you provide literals, the optimizer will perform a more well-informed decision (but the parse overhead will increase). Column histograms will also help if the data is not evenly distributed between maximum and minimum values.

Bounded Range Scans A bounded range scan is one in which we provide a maximum and a minimum, as in the following example:

```
SELECT  contact_surname,customer_status
  FROM customers
 WHERE date_of_birth > to_date(:dob1,'DD-MON-YYYY')
   AND date_of_birth < to_date(:dob2,'DD-MON-YYYY')
```

As we might expect, the same principles apply as to unbounded range scans. The optimizer uses its 5% guess as in our previous example, but because there are now two range scans it estimates that only 0.25% of rows will be returned (5% of 5%):

```
Execution Plan
----------------------------------------------------
SELECT STATEMENT (Cost=326 Card=251)
1    0    TABLE ACCESS (BY INDEX ROWID) OF 'CUSTOMERS'
2    1      INDEX (RANGE SCAN) OF 'CUSTOMER_DOB_I'
```

As with bounded range scans, the use of literals and histograms can help the optimizer make a better choice.

Range Lookups In a range lookup, we are trying to find a particular value in a table that is keyed on a low value–high value pair of columns. For instance, in the sample database, the SALESREGION defines each region in terms of a range of phone numbers that exist in that region. To find the region for any given phone number, you might enter a query like this:

```
select /*+FIRST_ROWS */ * from salesregion
where '500000015' between lowphoneno and highphoneno
```

```
Rows    Execution Plan
-------  ----------------------------------------------------
     0   SELECT STATEMENT    HINT: FIRST_ROWS
     1    TABLE ACCESS OF 'SALESREGION'
 40002     INDEX (RANGE SCAN) OF 'SALESREGION_HINUMBER'
               (NON-UNIQUE)
```

Instead of using the index to go directly to the matching row, we see that Oracle scans a very large number of index rows. What's going on?

To understand why Oracle's retrieval plan seems so poor, we have to recognize the hidden assumptions we make when formulating our mental execution plan. For instance, Oracle does not know that LOWPHONENO is always higher than HIGHPHONENO, whereas we know this intuitively from the names of the columns. Furthermore, we assume that there are no overlaps between rows (i.e., that any given phone number only matches a single SALESREGION)—Oracle cannot assume this.

Without knowing what we know about the data, the optimizer must perform the following steps:

1. Search the index to find a row where the lowphoneno is less than the phone number specified. This will be the first (i.e., lowest) matching entry in the index.
2. Check to see if the highphoneno is greater than the number specified.
3. If it is not, check the next index entry.
4. Continue performing a range scan of this nature until it finds an entry where lowphoneno is higher than the phone number provided. The entry just prior to this entry will be the correct entry.

So, in essence, the optimizer must perform a range scan from the lowest range in the index until the row after the range for which we're looking. Therefore, on average, half of the index will be scanned.

How can we improve this query? If we know that a match will be found, we can specify a "rownum=1" condition to prevent Oracle from continuing the scan once a match has been found:

```
SELECT *
  FROM salesregion
 WHERE '500000015' BETWEEN lowphoneno AND highphoneno
   AND ROWNUM = 1
```

This works, but only when there is a valid matching row. If there is no matching row, then Oracle will still continue the scan until the end of the table.

A better solution can be achieved by employing PL/SQL (or another procedural language). By using an index on the high value (highphoneno, in this case), we can position ourselves at the first row in the lookup table that has a high value greater than our search value. If the low value is less than our lookup value, then we have found a match. The following PL/SQL block illustrates the technique:

```
DECLARE
   CURSOR salesregion_csr (cp_phone_no VARCHAR2)
   IS
      SELECT *
        FROM salesregion
       WHERE cp_phone_no < highphoneno
       ORDER BY highphoneno;
```

```
    salesregion_row     salesregion_csr%ROWTYPE;
BEGIN
    OPEN salesregion_csr ('500000015');
    FETCH salesregion_csr INTO salesregion_row;

    IF salesregion_csr%NOTFOUND THEN
        -- No match found;
        NULL;
    ELSIF salesregion_row.lowphoneno > '500000015' THEN
        -- Still no match
        NULL;
    ELSE
        -- The row in salesregion_row is the matching row
        dbms_output.put_line (salesregion_row.lowphoneno
                    || ' ' || salesregion_row.highphoneno);
    END IF;

    CLOSE salesregion_csr;
END;
```

Range lookups—finding a matching range in a table that contains high and low values—may fail to optimize successfully with standard SQL. In these cases, a PL/SQL or other procedural approach may be necessary.

USING THE LIKE OPERATOR

You can use the LIKE operator to search for rows columns that match a wildcard condition. For instance, the following query selects all customers with a surname that starts with "HARD":

```
SELECT COUNT (*)
  FROM customers
 WHERE contact_surname LIKE 'HARD%'
```

This query makes good use of our index on surname and requires only a few I/Os to satisfy. However, if we use a wildcard to match the starting portion of a column, we cannot use the index directly. For instance, we can search for all surnames ending in "RDY" using the following query:

```
SELECT COUNT (*)
  FROM customers
 WHERE contact_surname LIKE '%RDY'
```

The optimizer will resolve this query using a full-table scan. This is because it cannot find an appropriate index entry unless the first characters of the entry are known.

Oracle can use indexes to resolve queries involving the LIKE operator only if there is not a leading wildcard (%,_) in the search string.

QUERIES INVOLVING OR

When a query on a single table contains an OR clause on a single column (or the equivalent IN clause), it can be processed in one of the following ways:

❑ Perform a full-table scan and check each row against the selection criteria (which shows up as a filter in the execution plan).
❑ Perform multiple index-based lookups of the table.
❑ Perform a UNION of all the results obtained (which show up as a CONCATENATION in the execution plan). This is roughly equivalent to issuing a separate query for each of the OR conditions.

The cost-based optimizer tries to estimate when the cost of performing multiple index lookups will be higher than the cost of a full-table scan. If the column values are not evenly distributed, the cost-based optimizer's calculations will be improved by the presence of a histogram on the relevant column. For instance, consider the following query:

```
SQL> SELECT customer_id
  2      FROM customers
  3    WHERE contact_surname = 'ZIRBEL'
  4        OR contact_surname = 'ZIRBELL'
  5        OR contact_surname = 'ZIRRBEL'
  6        OR contact_surname = 'ZIRRBELL'

Execution Plan
--------------------------------------------------
  0      SELECT STATEMENT (Cost=326 Card=516)
  1    0    TABLE ACCESS (FULL) OF 'CUSTOMERS'
```

Because four OR conditions were specified, the cost-based optimizer calculated that the effort of performing four index lookups will outweigh the effort of performing a full-table scan and so concludes that the full-table scan is the best path.

Looking at the preceding query, we see that the optimizer expected to retrieve 516 rows. However, we can see that the query is really looking for a few variations in spelling on a fairly uncommon name. If we decide that we'd like to try an index-based retrieval plan, then we can provide a hint as follows:

```
SQL> SELECT /*+ USE_CONCAT
              INDEX(CUSTOMERS CUSTOMERS_SURNAME_IDX) */
              customer_id
  2     FROM customers
  3    WHERE contact_surname = 'ZIRBEL'
  4       OR contact_surname = 'ZIRBELL'
  5       OR contact_surname = 'ZIRRBEL'
  6       OR contact_surname = 'ZIRRBELL'


Execution Plan
-------------------------------------------------------
0        SELECT STATEMENT (Cost=520 Card=520)
1     0    CONCATENATION
2     1      TABLE ACCESS (BY INDEX ROWID) OF 'CUSTOMERS'
3     2        INDEX (RANGE SCAN) OF 'CUSTOMER_SURNAME_I'
4     1      TABLE ACCESS (BY INDEX ROWID) OF 'CUSTOMERS'
5     4        INDEX (RANGE SCAN) OF 'CUSTOMER_SURNAME_I'
6     1      TABLE ACCESS (BY INDEX ROWID) OF 'CUSTOMERS'
7     6        INDEX (RANGE SCAN) OF 'CUSTOMER_SURNAME_I'
8     1      TABLE ACCESS (BY INDEX ROWID) OF 'CUSTOMERS'
9     8        INDEX (RANGE SCAN) OF 'CUSTOMER_SURNAME_I'
```

The USE_CONCAT hint works in both Oracle7 and Oracle8. Note, however, that the "Inlist iterations" execution plan may deliver superior performance in Oracle8 (we look at the "inlist iterator" in the next section).

The concatenation execution step just shown is typical of index retrievals of OR queries. The concatenation step indicates that the subsequent steps were executed independently and the result sets concatenated in much the same manner as for the UNION operator. To influence the optimizer to perform such a retrieval, it's usually not sufficient to use the INDEX hint on its own. You must also specify the USE_CONCAT hint.

We can understand that Oracle doesn't correctly determine that an index lookup is the best plan since without a histogram it doesn't know that "ZIRBEL" is a rare surname. So perhaps a histogram would improve its decision. Unfortunately not: After creating a histogram on CONTACT_SURNAME the optimizer still declined to use the index unless the optimization mode was FIRST_ROWS.

Histograms don't actually contain the number of rows matching every distinct value, so the cost-based optimizer still has to do some guesswork when choosing between the index-based retrieval and a full-table scan. It's up to you to monitor its decisions and amend them when it seems warranted.

Queries involving OR conditions can be difficult for the cost-based optimizer to resolve efficiently. Sometimes (but not always) a histogram can help. Otherwise, FULL or USE_CONCAT and INDEX hints can be used to select the best execution plan.

IN LISTS (INLIST ITERATOR)

Prior to Oracle8, queries that involved lists of values within an IN clause could be resolved either by a full-table scan or by performing a concatenation of multiple queries in exactly the same way as is done for queries involving OR.

Using a concatenation approach for queries that have a large number of elements in the IN list can be time-consuming, because the cost-based optimizer is required to calculate costs for each of the concatenated subqueries. In Oracle8 and higher, a new path called "INLIST ITERATOR" cycles more efficiently through the elements in an IN list. So in the following example, the INLIST ITERATOR step indicates that each subsequent step was executed once for each value in an IN list:

```
SQL> l
  1  select * from customers c
  2* where customer_id in
(1,2,3,4,5,6,10,23,890,345,23,8990,223,134)

Execution Plan
----------------------------------------------------------
   0       SELECT STATEMENT (Cost=4 Card=)
   1    0    INLIST ITERATOR
   2    1      TABLE ACCESS (BY INDEX ROWID)
                   OF 'CUSTOMERS'
   3    2        INDEX (RANGE SCAN)
                     OF 'PK_CUSTOMERS' (UNIQUE)
```

By contrast, the concatenation operation that will be invoked if you use the USE_CONCAT hint is both harder to read and slightly harder for the cost-based optimizer to process:

```
Execution Plan
----------------------------------------------------------
   0       SELECT STATEMENT Optimizer=CHOOSE
   1    0    CONCATENATION
```

```
 2    1      TABLE ACCESS (BY INDEX ROWID) OF 'CUSTOMERS'
 3    2        INDEX (UNIQUE SCAN) OF 'PK_CUSTOMERS'
 4    1      TABLE ACCESS (BY INDEX ROWID) OF 'CUSTOMERS'
 5    4        INDEX (UNIQUE SCAN) OF 'PK_CUSTOMERS'
 6    1      TABLE ACCESS (BY INDEX ROWID) OF 'CUSTOMERS'
 7    6        INDEX (UNIQUE SCAN) OF 'PK_CUSTOMERS'
 8    1      TABLE ACCESS (BY INDEX ROWID) OF 'CUSTOMERS'
 9    8        INDEX (UNIQUE SCAN) OF 'PK_CUSTOMERS'
10    1      TABLE ACCESS (BY INDEX ROWID) OF 'CUSTOMERS'
11   10        INDEX (UNIQUE SCAN) OF 'PK_CUSTOMERS'
12    1     TABLE ACCESS (BY INDEX ROWID) OF 'CUSTOMERS'
13   12       INDEX (UNIQUE SCAN) OF 'PK_CUSTOMERS'
14    1      TABLE ACCESS (BY INDEX ROWID) OF 'CUSTOMERS'
15   14        INDEX (UNIQUE SCAN) OF 'PK_CUSTOMERS'
16    1      TABLE ACCESS (BY INDEX ROWID) OF 'CUSTOMERS'
17   16        INDEX (UNIQUE SCAN) OF 'PK_CUSTOMERS'
18    1      TABLE ACCESS (BY INDEX ROWID) OF 'CUSTOMERS'
19   18        INDEX (UNIQUE SCAN) OF 'PK_CUSTOMERS'
20    1      TABLE ACCESS (BY INDEX ROWID) OF 'CUSTOMERS'
21   20        INDEX (UNIQUE SCAN) OF 'PK_CUSTOMERS'
22    1      TABLE ACCESS (BY INDEX ROWID) OF 'CUSTOMERS'
23   22        INDEX (UNIQUE SCAN) OF 'PK_CUSTOMERS'
24    1      TABLE ACCESS (BY INDEX ROWID) OF 'CUSTOMERS'
25   24        INDEX (UNIQUE SCAN) OF 'PK_CUSTOMERS'
26    1      TABLE ACCESS (BY INDEX ROWID) OF 'CUSTOMERS'
27   26        INDEX (UNIQUE SCAN) OF 'PK_CUSTOMERS'
```

Unfortunately, there doesn't seem to be a way forcing the INLIST ITERATOR path with a hint. This means that if you have a IN list that the cost-based optimizer insists on resolving by a full-table scan, you may be forced to use the USE_CONCAT path instead.

DETECTING INEFFICIENT INDEXES WITH TKPROF

One of the useful features of tkprof output is that it highlights the number of rows processed by each step of the execution plan. In the case of an index, these row counts indicate how many rows were picked up by the index. If there's a big discrepancy between these counts and the number of rows processed by the query or in subsequent steps, then the index probably isn't as efficient as it could be.

For instance, consider the following tkprof output:

```
select contact_surname,contact_firstname
  from customers c
```

```
where contact_surname='SMITH'
  and contact_firstname='STEPHEN'
order by contact_surname,contact_firstname
```

call	count	cpu	elapsed	disk	query	current	rows
Parse	1	0.00	0.06	0	0	0	0
Execute	1	0.00	0.00	0	0	0	0
Fetch	1	0.00	0.03	0	88	0	3
total	3	0.00	0.09	0	88	0	**3**

```
Rows    Execution Plan
-------  --------------------------------------------------
     0  SELECT STATEMENT   HINT: CHOOSE
    43    TABLE ACCESS   HINT: ANALYZED (BY ROWID) OF 'CUSTOMERS'
    44      INDEX (RANGE SCAN) OF 'CUSTOMER_FOO_INDEX' (NON-UNIQUE)
```

Although only three rows are returned from the query, the index is processing 44 rows. Perhaps the index could be improved. Sure enough, the index was on SUR-NAME only. Replacing this index with one on SURNAME and FIRSTNAME, we get the following tkprof output:

call	count	cpu	elapsed	disk	query	current	rows
Parse	1	0.00	0.08	0	0	0	0
Execute	1	0.00	0.00	0	0	0	0
Fetch	1	0.00	0.07	0	2	0	3
total	3	0.00	0.15	0	2	0	**3**

```
Rows    Execution Plan
-------  --------------------------------------------------
     0  SELECT STATEMENT   HINT: CHOOSE
     4    INDEX (RANGE SCAN) OF 'CUSTOMER_FOO_INDEX' (NON-UNIQUE)
```

Now the number of rows processed by the index more closely matches the number of rows retrieved by the query. We can therefore conclude that the index is efficient.

Use the row count column of tkprof output to highlight indexes that are inefficient. A higher than expected value in the row count column may indicate that not all columns in a concatenated index are being used.

THE FAST FULL-INDEX SCAN

We've seen a number of examples in which an index alone has been used to re-solve a query. Provided that all the columns needed to resolve the query are in the index, there is no reason why Oracle can't use the index alone to generate the result set.

In the past (prior to Oracle 7.3.3), using indexes to resolve queries that re-turned large portions of the table was possible but not usually efficient. To im-prove the efficiency of queries that can be resolved by reading an entire index, Oracle introduced the fast full-index scan in version 7.3.3.

While it's always been possible to resolve certain queries using an index alone, and while Oracle has defined a full-index scan path since version 7.2, the full fast scan offers some significant advantages:

❑ In an index range scan or full-index scan, index blocks are read in key order, one at a time. In a full fast scan, blocks will be read in the order in which they appear on disk and Oracle will be able to read multiple blocks in a sin-gle I/O, depending on the value of the server parameter DB_FILE_MULTI-BLOCK_READ_COUNT (multiblock reads are discussed further later in this chapter).

❑ The fast full-index scan can be performed in parallel, while an index range scan or full-index scan can only be processed serially. That is, Oracle can al-locate multiple processes to perform a fast full-index scan but can only use a single process for traditional index scans.

Although a full-table scan can use parallelism and multiblock read tech-niques, the number of blocks in a table will typically be many times the number of blocks in an index. The fast full-index scan will therefore usually outperform an equivalent full-table scan.

You can consider a fast full-index scan in the following circumstances:

❑ All the columns required to satisfy the query are included in the index.
❑ At least one of the columns in the index is defined as NOT NULL.
❑ The query will return more than 10 to 20% of the rows in the index.

The cost-based optimizer can use the fast full scan as it sees fit unless you have FAST_FULL_SCAN_ENABLED=FALSE or V733_PLANS_ENABLED= FALSE (depending on your version of Oracle).

To invoke the fast full scan manually, you use the INDEX_FFS hint:

```
SQL> SELECT /*+ index_ffs(c,pk_customers) */
  2         COUNT (*)
  3    FROM customers c;
```

```
Execution Plan
----------------------------------------------------
0       SELECT STATEMENT (Cost=56 Card=1)
1    0    SORT (AGGREGATE)
2    1      INDEX (FAST FULL SCAN) OF 'PK_CUSTOMERS'
             (UNIQUE) (Cost=56 Card=100000)
```

The index fast full scan can take advantage of optimizations normally only available to table scans, such as multiblock read (see later in this chapter for details of multiblock read) and parallel query. You can use the PARALLEL_INDEX hint to cause the fast full scan to be executed in parallel.

Counting the number of rows in a table is a perfect application for the fast full scan because there will almost always be an index on a NOT NULL column that could be used to resolve the query.

Figure 8.7 compares fast full-index scan with other techniques for counting the number of rows in a table. A parallelized fast full index scan was clearly the fastest way to resolve this query. Note also that other techniques that utilized only the index actually performed worse than the full-table scan. This is primarily because the full-table scan can take advantage of multiblock read (each I/O operation reads in more than one block of data) whereas traditional index scans read one block at a time.

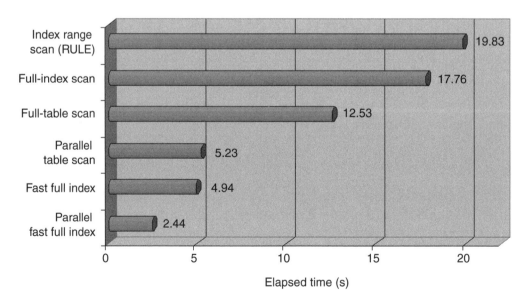

FIGURE 8.7 Comparing fast full-index scan to other means of counting the rows in a table.

Take advantage of the fast full-index scan for queries that can be resolved by reading all the rows in an index. Counting the number of rows in the table is a perfect example.

OPTIMIZING BITMAP INDEX ACCESS

If you are using bitmap indexes, there are a few configuration parameters you can tweak to enhance the performance of your bitmap indexes:

❑ Set an appropriate value for BITMAP_MERGE_AREA_SIZE.
❑ Exploit the MINIMIZE RECORDS_PER_BLOCK clause.

CONFIGURING BITMAP_MERGE_AREA_SIZE

BITMAP_MERGE_AREA_SIZE determines the amount of memory that is available to Oracle for performing merges of multiple bitmaps. The default value is one megabyte. You should ensure that this value is sufficient to hold all the bitmaps that will be merged as well as the resulting merged bitmap. If in doubt, you can increase this value provided that your operating system has enough physical memory to support a larger value.

Figure 8.8 illustrates the performance degradation that can occur if BITMAP_MERGE_AREA_SIZE is inadequately configured. This example was based on a four-way bitmap merge on a 1-million-row table.

The default one megabyte BITMAP_MERGE_AREA_SIZE is sufficient for merging four bitmaps with 1 million entries each. However, for tables much larger than this, an increase in BITMAP_MERGE_AREA_SIZE would be indicated.

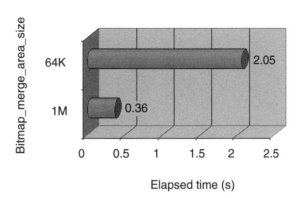

FIGURE 8.8 Effect of BITMAP_MERGE_AREA_SIZE parameter on a four-way bitmap merge query.

MINIMIZE RECORDS_PER_BLOCK

Oracle8i introduced a new clause to the ALTER TABLE statement that can improve the configuration of bitmap indexes created against that table. The MINIMIZE RECORDS_PER_BLOCK clause causes the maximum allowed number of rows that can be stored in a data block to be set to the maximum number of rows currently stored. In other words, once you apply MINIMIZE RECORDS_PER_BLOCK, no block will ever contain more rows than the currently most heavily populated block.

When Oracle knows the maximum number of rows that can ever be stored in a block, it is able to create more compact bitmap indexes. Smaller bit-maps means fewer I/Os to read the bitmap and can consequently improve performance.

However, setting MINIMIZE RECORDS_PER_BLOCK could have a negative effect on full-table scans. If the average row length reduces in the future, then Oracle may leave more empty space in the block than would otherwise be the case. This could cause the number of blocks to be allocated to increase and thereby harm full-table scan performance. However, if your row size is relatively constant, then the option is probably safe to use.

Figure 8.9 shows the reductions in block reads that resulted when bitmap indexes were rebuilt after the MINIMIZE RECORDS_PER_BLOCK setting was applied. The query was the same four-way bitmap index merge against the million-row table that was used earlier to measure the effect of the BITMAP_MERGE_AREA_SIZE setting.

The performance of bitmap indexes can sometimes be improved by increasing BITMAP_MERGE_AREA_SIZE or by applying the MINIMIZE RECORDS_PER_BLOCK clause to the underlying table.

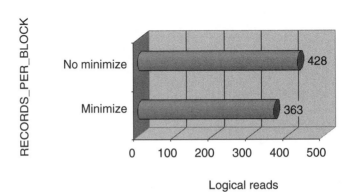

FIGURE 8.9   Effect of the MINIMIZE RECORDS_PER_BLOCK clause on bitmap performance.

OPTIMIZING HASH CLUSTERS

We first encountered hash clusters in Chapter 6. In a hash cluster, the value of the cluster key is transformed mathematically to a hash key that can be used to determine the physical location of rows matching the key value, thereby avoiding the I/O overhead of traversing an index structure.

In Chapter 6 we saw that hash clusters could be subject to a number of problems:

❏ If the amount of space reserved for individual hash keys is insufficient, then blocks may become chained, resulting in additional I/O overhead for retrieving the row.

❏ At the other extreme, if too much space is allocated to the hash cluster, then the hash cluster will be sparsely populated and full-table scans will be degraded.

Two clauses of the create cluster statement are of critical significance to the performance of a hash cluster:

❏ HASHKEYS, which specifies the expected number of hash values
❏ SIZE, which specifies the amount of storage required to store all rows associated with a hash value

Figures 8.10 and 8.11 illustrate the I/O requirements for key lookups and full-table scans for an indexed table and for two differently configured hash clusters based on the same table. The hash cluster can offer better performance for a key lookup, but only if the hash cluster is appropriately configured. Table scans

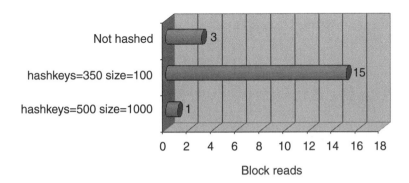

FIGURE 8.10 Number of blocks required to fetch a single key value for an unclustered (but indexed) table and for two differently configured hash clusters. The hash cluster can provide better performance, but only if properly configured.

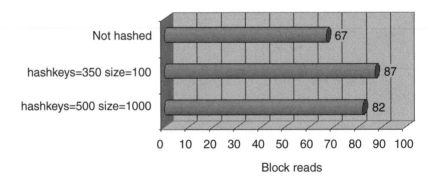

FIGURE 8.11   Blocks required for full-table scans of the tables/hash clusters shown in Figure 8.10. Hash clusters tend to require more reads for a full-table scan, although this depends on how well the hash cluster storage is configured.

of the hash clusters tended to require some additional I/O, but again this can depend on the configuration of the hash cluster.

The major consideration in optimizing the hash cluster is to determine accurately the SIZE and HASHKEYS settings. There are three pieces of information you need before you can calculate accurate values for these parameters:

❑   The number of rows in the hash cluster
❑   The number of distinct hash keys (for a unique index, equal to the number of rows in the cluster)
❑   The average length of a row in the hash cluster

Once this information is obtained, you can calculate the values of HASHKEYS and SIZE as follows:

$$\text{HASHKEYS} = number \_of \_distinct \_hash \_keys \_values$$

$$\text{SIZE} = \frac{total \_rows}{\text{HASHKEYS}} \times average \_row \_length \times 1.1$$

In the case of a unique key, set HASHKEYS to the number of rows in the table and SIZE to the average row length plus 10% to allow for variation in row sizes (this is the "1.1" ratio in the preceding formula).

If the data to be included in the hash table is already in a nonclustered table and the table has been analyzed, you can get an estimate of the average row length and the number of rows in the table with a query like this one:

```
SQL> select avg_row_len, num_rows
  2     from user_tables
```

```
  3   where table_name='CUSTOMERS'
  4   /

AVG_ROW_LEN  NUM_ROWS
-----------  ---------
         90      5150
```

You can get the number of distinct values for a column with a query such as this:

```
SQL> select num_distinct
  2     from user_tab_columns
  3     where table_name='CUSTOMERS'
  4       and column_name='CONTACT_SURNAME'
  5   /

NUM_DISTINCT
------------
         670
```

So, if we wanted to move the CUSTOMERS table into a hash cluster with CONTACT_SURNAME as the hash key (not that this would necessarily be a good choice for a cluster key), we could set hash keys to a value of about 670 (the number of distinct key values) and use the formula above to estimate SIZE:

$$\text{SIZE} = \frac{5150}{670} \times 50 \times 1.1 = 423$$

If the number of rows in the table increases, then the calculations will cease to be valid and the hash cluster may become deoptimized. Oracle will run out of space in the hash cluster for new rows and blocks will need to be chained. Rows in these chained blocks will require extra I/Os to retrieve and hence the hash cluster will lose its advantage over a B*-tree index. Figure 8.10 shows the effect on I/O when this occurs.

On the other hand, if we over configure the SIZE parameter, we risk wasting database space and degrading the performance of full-table scans (as shown Figure 8.11).

Ensure that you only use hash clusters for static tables, or be prepared to rebuild the hash cluster periodically. When deciding on a hash cluster, ensure that the SIZE and HASHKEYS parameters are correctly configured.

The aforementioned approach to sizing a hash cluster assumes that hash keys will be distributed evenly throughout the hash cluster. This assumption is usually a safe one, since Oracle's internal hashing algorithm has been designed to distribute values evenly across a wide range of data types and distributions. However, if you know that Oracle's hash function will lead to unevenly distributed hash keys, you can use the HASH IS syntax of the CREATE CLUSTER command to specify the hash function. There are two ways to do this.

❏ If you know that your cluster key will be evenly distributed, then you can specify the cluster key. This only works if the cluster key is an integer.
❏ Specify your own hash function, written in PL/SQL.

OPTIMIZING INDEX ORGANIZED TABLES

Earlier in this chapter, we discussed the circumstances under which you could consider storing your data in an index organized table (IOT). If you do implement an index organized table, there are a couple of basic principles you should consider to minimize the cost/benefit ratio:

❏ Determine an optional configuration for the overflow segment.
❏ Perform periodic rebuilds of the index organized table or otherwise ensure that the IOT structure remains efficient.
❏ Take advantage of index fast full scans.

CONFIGURING THE OVERFLOW SEGMENT

The INCLUDING clause determines which columns are stored in the B*-tree section of the index organized table and which are stored in a separate overflow segment.

It's not essential to have an overflow segment, but it's almost always desirable unless the number of columns in the table is very small (for instance, if the primary key of the table contains all of the columns in the table).

If many columns are stored in the leaf block, then the number of rows that can be stored in each block will be reduced. This will increase the number of entries that must be stored in each branch block, which in turn may require that another level of the B*-tree be provided. By creating an overflow segment, we increase the probability that the height of the B*-tree will not increase, but we make it more expensive to access the columns in the overflow segment.

The following CREATE TABLE statement creates an index organized customers table. The B*-tree is created using the CUSTOMER_ID primary key, and all columns up to and including ZIPCODE are stored in the index leaf blocks, while the remaining columns, including the blob column PICTURE, are stored in the overflow tablespace.

```
CREATE TABLE customers_iot
 (
  customer_id                 NUMBER NOT NULL
                              PRIMARY KEY,
  customer_name               VARCHAR2(40) NOT NULL,
  contact_surname             VARCHAR2(40) NOT NULL,
  contact_firstname           VARCHAR2(40) NOT NULL,
  phoneno                     VARCHAR2(12) NOT NULL,
  address1                    VARCHAR2(40) NOT NULL,
  address2                    VARCHAR2(40) NOT NULL,
  zipcode                     VARCHAR2(6) NOT NULL,
  date_of_birth               DATE NOT NULL,
  sales_rep_id                NUMBER NOT NULL,
  comment_id                  NUMBER,
  contact_gender              CHAR(1),
  process_flag                CHAR(1),
  picture                     BLOB
 )
ORGANIZATION INDEX INCLUDING zipcode
OVERFLOW TABLESPACE lob_ts;
```

Figure 8.12 shows the structure of an index organized table that includes an overflow segment. If we had created the table without an overflow segment, then all the columns—including any BLOBs under 4K[1]—would be stored in the leaf blocks. This might have meant that only one or two rows could have been stored in each leaf block. As a result, it may have been necessary to add an additional level to the B*-tree, as illustrated in Figure 8.13.

Clearly, the decision as to which columns are included in the B*-tree and which are placed in the overflow segment has a tremendous effect on the efficiency of the B*-tree and on the performance of various queries. Here are the basic considerations:

❏ If too many columns are included in the index segment, then the height of the B*-tree may increase. This will typically cause every access via the primary key to require an additional I/O.

❏ If you retrieve a column by the primary key and that column is in the overflow segment, you will experience an additional I/O anyway.

---

[1] If we had wanted to store BLOBs less than 4K out of the B*-tree, we could have used the DISABLE STORAGE IN ROW option. This is described in more detail in Chapter 16.

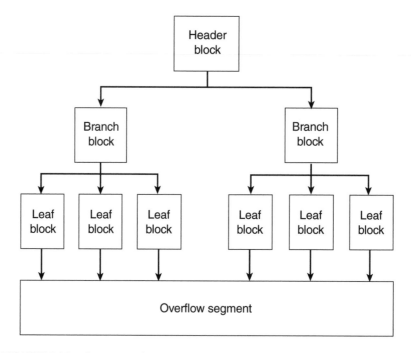

FIGURE 8.12   Structure of an index organized table with an overflow segment.

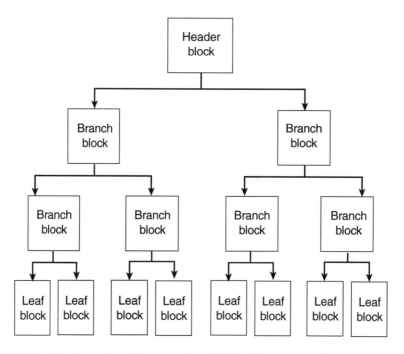

FIGURE 8.13   Structure of an index organized table without an overflow segment. If too many columns are stored in the leaf blocks, then the depth of the index may need to increase.

❏ If you access data that is in the B*-tree segment only via a full-table scan, then the overhead of reading rows from the overflow segment will be avoided.

❏ If you access data that is in the overflow segment, then you will have to scan both the B*-tree segment and the overflow segment. This will take longer than a full-table scan of a traditionally structured table.

Figure 8.14 compares the performance when performing full-table scans on the index only table and on an equivalent table with a heap structure (that is, a normal Oracle table). When the scan involves only columns that are stored in the leaf blocks, performance is improved dramatically due to the index's smaller size. However, when the scan must involve columns in the overflow block, performance degrades dramatically because Oracle must alternately scan leaf and overflow blocks.

> Think carefully about how to split your index organized table. Data in the index segment will be quicker to access while data in the overflow segment may take much longer to access. However, if you place too much data in the index segment, you risk adding another level to the B*-tree and losing the advantages of index organized tables.

PERIODIC REBUILD

Indexes tend to become sparse more quickly than tables when rows are deleted because it's not always possible to reuse empty index entries unless a suitable key value occurs. Since in the index organized table the index is the table, this

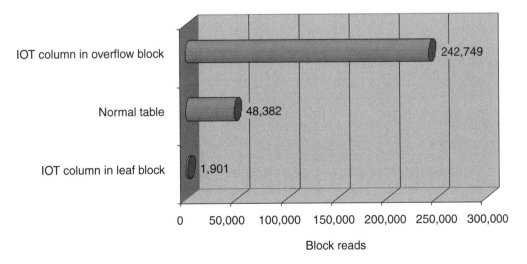

FIGURE 8.14   Index organized table scan performance comparison.

degradation will also affect scan performance in a way that doesn't occur in traditional tables. To counter this effect, you may need to rebuild an index organized table more frequently than a traditional table.

FAST FULL SCANS

If you need to scan your index organized table, it is essential that you take advantage of the fast full-index scan facility described earlier in this chapter. Without the fast full-index scan, you will be unable to use multiblock reads or exploit parallel query capabilities.

Fast full scan will normally be turned on by default, but it is possible to disable it in Oracle by setting FAST_FULL_SCAN_ENABLED to FALSE. Make sure that you don't inadvertently try to scan index organized tables with fast full scans disabled.

OPTIMIZING FULL TABLE SCANS

If a full-table scan is the only practical way of retrieving the required data, there are still options for improving the performance of your query:

❏ Reduce the number of block reads required for the scan by making the table smaller.

❏ Reduce the number of block reads required for the scan by making database I/O more efficient.

❏ Avoid the full-table scan by caching or sampling.

❏ Assign more resources to the scan by using the parallel query option.

IMPROVING THE SCAN BY MAKING THE TABLE SMALLER

The amount of work required to complete a full-table scan is essentially defined by the number of blocks to be scanned. There are a number of ways to reduce this number:

❏ Lower the high-water mark by rebuilding the table.

❏ Squeeze more rows into each block by reducing PCTFREE and increasing PCTUSED.

❏ Move large, infrequently accessed columns to a separate subtable.

❏ Encourage Oracle to keep table scanned blocks in memory within the buffer cache in the SGA by using the CACHE hint or by using named buffer pools.

Lowering the High-water Mark Oracle does not have to scan every block that is allocated to the table. For instance, when we first create a table with a large storage allocation, Oracle knows that none of the blocks contain data and so a full-table scan will be almost instantaneous, no matter how many blocks have been allocated to the table.

When a full-table scan is required, Oracle reads every block from the first block allocated to the highest block that has ever contained data. This highest block is called the high-water mark. For instance, if we insert enough rows into a table to cause 100 blocks to be populated, then a full-table scan will perform approximately 100 block reads. Even if we delete every row in the table, the high-water mark will still be at 100 blocks and the table scan will still need to read about 100 blocks.

It should therefore be apparent that if a table is subject to a large number of deletes, then the high-water mark will be higher than it would otherwise be. The average number of rows per block will decrease, and the I/O cost to retrieve each row will increase.

Unfortunately, Oracle doesn't provide a way to reset the high-water mark other than to truncate the table, which deletes all the data. To actually reset the high-water mark to its true value—without losing data—we have to rebuild the table. Exporting the table data, truncating the table, and then reimporting the data can achieve this. Another fast way to rebuild a table is to use a parallel, unrecoverable CREATE TABLE AS SELECT (see Chapter 9).

Tables that contain substantially fewer rows than they did in the past may require a rebuild in order to reset the high-water mark. This will reduce the number of blocks required for a full-table scan.

Optimizing PCTFREE and PCTUSED If you do decide to recreate a table in order to improve scan performance, you should carefully consider the storage characteristics of the table. Aim to configure the table to maximize the average number of rows stored in each block. The two relevant parameters are as follows:

❏ PCTFREE, which controls the amount of space reserved in the block for updates that increase the row length. When there is only PCTFREE% free space in the block, no more rows will be inserted.

❏ PCTUSED, which determines the point where a block that has reached PCTFREE will become reeligible for inserts when DELETEs reduce the number of rows in the block. When the block is only PCTUSED% full, new rows can once more be inserted into the block.

If a table is subject to both INSERTs and DELETEs, then the amount of space actually used up by data in a block is going to oscillate between PCTUSED and 100-PCTFREE. We might suspect that, on average, the block would be:[2]

$$PCTUSED + \frac{(100 - PCTFREE) - PCTUSED}{2} \text{ full}$$

The default values for PCTFREE and PCTUSED are 10 and 40, respectively. This means that we might expect that, on average, each block will be about 65% full:

$$40 + \frac{(100 - 10) - 40}{2} = 65\%$$

This means that the number of blocks required for a full-table scan defaults to about 150% of that required if the rows were fully packed into the blocks. While achieving a 100% block fill is not practical, it is often possible to get a better fill than that provided by the defaults. In particular, if a table is subject to inserts and deletes but never updates, or if the updates never increase the row length, then you can set PCTFREE to near 0. You can also increase PCTUSED. For instance, if we set PCTFREE to 0 and PCTUSED to 70, then blocks would be 85% full on average. This could result in a reduction in full-table scan I/O of more than 20%.

Although amending PCTFREE and PCTUSED can increase the number of rows per block—and hence improve full-table scan performance—you should use care when adjusting these settings.

❑ If PCTFREE is set too low and the table is subject to heavy update activity, then row fragmentation (or row chaining) can occur. This happens when an update causes a row to increase in length. If this increase cannot be accommodated by free space within the block, then the row will be relocated to a new block and a pointer to the new block will remain in the original block. Index entries will still contain the address of the original row. This means that an index lookup of the row will incur an additional I/O as Oracle accesses the original row, only to find that it must jump to the new row location. Excessive row fragmentation is generally a result of setting PCTFREE too low. Detection of these chained rows is discussed in Chapter 16.

❑ If you set PCTFREE very low, consider increasing the value of the INITRANS setting in the CREATE TABLE statement. This parameter controls the initial number of transaction slots within an Oracle data block and defaults to only one. When additional transaction slots are required, they are allocated from free space within the block. If PCTFREE is 0, it's possible that

---

[2] Actually, it might be less, since some blocks will not yet have reached 100-PCTFREE.

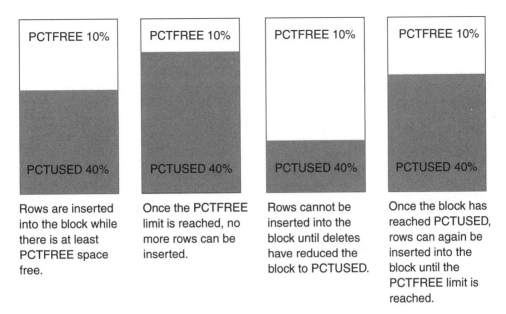

FIGURE 8.15   Effect of PCTFREE and PCTUSED.

the block will become completely full before an additional transaction slot is required. If this occurs, then multiple sessions will be unable to update the block concurrently and row-level locking will effectively break down to block-level locking.

❏   Setting PCTUSED too high can degrade performance of DML operations. If PCTUSED is high, then blocks that become eligible for inserts will contain a smaller amount of free space. This means that blocks will move on and off the list of free blocks (the freelist) more rapidly. This might increase the contention for free blocks.

❏   If the difference between PCTUSED and PCTFREE is less that the size of an average row, then blocks may be placed on the free list even though there is insufficient space for a new row. This will severely degrade insert performance.

If a table is subject to frequent table scans, ensure that PCTFREE is no higher than necessary, especially if the table is not updated. Also consider increasing PCTUSED, especially if there are not high rates of concurrent inserts.

Reducing the Row Length   If a table is often subjected to a full-table scan and contains large, infrequently accessed columns, you may be able to reduce the number of blocks to be scanned by moving these columns to another table. A good example of this technique is moving LONG columns to a subtable or using the DISABLE STORAGE IN ROW setting for BLOBs and CLOBs (discussed in more detail in Chapter 16).

For instance, let's imagine that we stored a bitmap image of every customer in the CUSTOMERS table but that we only accessed these bitmaps when we performed an index lookup of a single row (perhaps from a "customer details" screen). The average row length of the CUSTOMERS table is 86 bytes and it uses 264 2K blocks. If each bitmap consumed 20K on average, then we would require at least a further 96,000 blocks and a full-table scan would take several hundred times longer.

The solution to this problem is to move these long columns to a separate table with the same primary key. If you wish to retrieve the bitmap together with customer details, you will have to perform a join; this might slow the retrieval somewhat, but the small cost when viewing the bitmap will probably be justified by the large improvement in table scan performance.

In Oracle8 you would probably use BLOBS or CLOBS instead of LONGs. In this case you can move the long object to separate storage simply by using the DISABLE STORAGE IN ROW option of the LOB clause. For instance,

```
CREATE TABLE outofline_lob_table
(   id              number     NOT NULL PRIMARY KEY,
    control_data    char(200)  NOT NULL,
    lob_data        blob
)   LOB(lob_data) STORE AS (DISABLE STORAGE IN ROW )
```

Note that LOBs greater than 4K in length will be automatically stored in a separate segment anyway. Performance considerations of LOBs are discussed in detail in Chapter 16.

Putting LONG or LOB columns in a separate table is almost always a good idea if full-table scans are common, because these columns will often have a greater length than the rest of all the columns combined. You can also consider this technique for tables with infrequently accessed VARCHAR2 or CHAR columns. However, when you do need to access these columns, you will have to perform an otherwise unnecessary join. Consequently, it's not a good idea to move columns that are accessed frequently.

For index organized tables, the PCTTHRESHOLD and INCLUDING clauses define which columns are included in the B*-tree and which are specified in the overflow segment. We discussed these considerations earlier in this chapter.

> For tables in which full-table scan performance is critical, consider locating long, infrequently accessed columns in a separate table. For LOBs and CLOBs, consider the DISABLE STORAGE IN ROW clause.

MAKING DATABASE I/O MORE EFFICIENT

There are two database configuration items that can have a dramatic effect on table scan performance:

- ❑ DB_FILE_MULTIBLOCK_READ_COUNT, which defines the number of blocks that can be read in a single operating system I/O
- ❑ DB_BLOCK_SIZE which defines the size of each block

Multiblock Read   During a full-table scan, Oracle can read multiple contiguous database blocks in a single operating system I/O operation. This is commonly referred to as a multiblock read. The maximum number of blocks that can be read in a single operating system I/O is dependent on the following factors:

- ❑ On Windows NT/Windows 2000, the maximum number of blocks that can be read cannot exceed 128K (for 32-bit versions).
- ❑ On most versions of UNIX when the I/O is through a filesystem (e.g., not on raw devices), no more than 8K can be read in one physical I/O.
- ❑ On UNIX when the datafiles are located on a raw device, the maximum I/O rate varies from 64K (earlier versions of Solaris) to 1MB (latest version of HP-UX).

So, for instance, if you are on NT and your database block size is 8K, then setting the multiblock read to 16 will allow Oracle to read 128K in each I/O operation.

The parameter DB_FILE_MULTIBLOCK_READ_COUNT sets the number of blocks that can be read in a single operation. You can set it in the parameter file ('init.ora') or in ALTER SYSTEM or ALTER SESSION. You might issue the following command to set the multiblock read prior to a full-table scan:

```
ALTER SESSION SET db_file_multiblock_read_count=16
```

Figure 8.16 shows the performance improvements that can be gained by adjusting db_file_multiblock_read_count.

Block Size   The size of the Oracle block can have an influence on the efficiency of full-table scans. Larger block sizes can often improve scan performance. Every table in the database will have the same block size, which is set when the

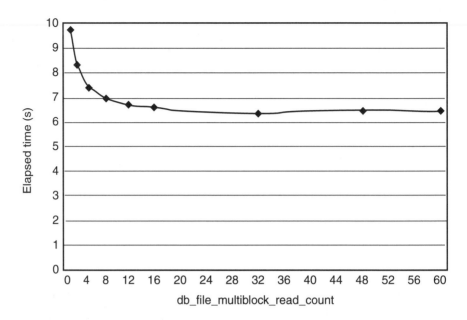

FIGURE 8.16 Effect of increasing db_file_multiblock_read_count on table scan performance (Windows NT).

database is created. A further discussion on determining an appropriate block size is contained in Chapter 19.

IMPROVING THE HIT RATE IN THE BUFFER CACHE

The *buffer cache* within the Oracle shared memory area (the *SGA*) exists to reduce the overhead of database accesses by caching frequently accessed blocks and thereby decreases the amount of I/O that is required. Full-table scans generally benefit less from buffer caching, because blocks retrieved from full scans are—by default—flushed out of the buffer cache almost immediately so that they don't monopolize blocks in the buffer cache that might be used more profitably to cache blocks retrieved by index scan.

Oracle's policy of favoring blocks retrieved from indexed retrieval in the buffer cache usually works well, since caching all the blocks from a full-table scan is impractical and would flush out blocks that have a higher probability of being accessed again in the near future. However, if you know that your full-table scan will be repeated in the near future, you can encourage Oracle to keep the blocks in the buffer cache by using one of the following methods:

❏ The CACHE setting of the CREATE TABLE or ALTER TABLE statements can be used to specify that blocks retrieved by full table scans should be kept in the buffer cache for a while rather than being flushed out immediately.

❏ The CACHE hint (defined in Chapter 5) performs the same function as the CACHE clause described previously, but affects only the current SQL statement.

❏ The buffer cache can be partitioned into three "pools": DEFAULT, KEEP, and RECYCLE. The KEEP pool can be used to create a separate buffer for tables that are accessed by full scan but that will benefit from caching. The RECYCLE pool is used for tables whose blocks should be recycled immediately, and DEFAULT is used for everything else. Carefully sizing these pools and allocating segments to them by using the BUFFER_POOL option of the STORAGE clause can fine-tune the hit rate for tables that are accessed frequently by full-table scan.

Table scans do not usually experience good hit rates in Oracle's buffer cache. If you need better hit rates for table scans, you may be able to improve the hit rate by using the CACHE clause, the CACHE hint, or by exploiting multiple buffer caches.

USING THE SAMPLE OPTION

Often when we perform full-table scans, we are seeking approximate answers to common business questions rather than seeking precise results for quantitative analysis. For instance, questions such as "What are our biggest-selling products?" or "What is the average height in America?" probably don't require that we look at every single row in our largest tables. Instead, we might be satisfied with an approximate answer based on a random sample of rows.

The Oracle8i SAMPLE clause allows us to perform such a random sample. Consider the following SQL, which lists products in order of their total sales values:

```
SELECT product_id,SUM(sale_value)
  FROM sales
 GROUP BY product_id
 ORDER BY 2 DESC;
```

If we were more interested in which product sold the most but weren't so interested in the exact amount sold, we might use the SAMPLE clause to extract a 5% sample, as follows:

```
SELECT product_id,SUM(sale_value)*20
  FROM sales SAMPLE(5)
 GROUP BY product_id
 ORDER BY 2 DESC;
```

A variation of the SAMPLE clause allows us to sample a random selection of blocks rather than a random selection or rows:

```
SELECT product_id,SUM(sale_value)*20
  FROM sales SAMPLE BLOCK(5)
 GROUP BY product_id
 ORDER BY 2 DESC;
```

Using the BLOCK option reduces the number of I/O operations that have to be performed to retrieve the sample but can reduce the accuracy of the sample, especially if your data is not evenly distributed throughout your table.

As you might expect, using the SAMPLE clause provides substantial reductions in query times. Figure 8.17 shows the reductions in elapsed times achieved for the preceding three sample SQL statements.

How accurate are the results for the SAMPLE clause? Each of our sample queries correctly identified the top-selling product, and each query came within 5% of the total sales for that product, so the results were not too bad. However, if your data is not distributed uniformly throughout the segment, or if the sample size is very low, then you can expect the accuracy to diminish.

The sample SAMPLE clause can be used to get approximate answers to aggregate queries that would normally require a full-table scan.

PARALLEL QUERY

One way to improve significantly the performance of any statement that involves a full-table scan is to take advantage of the parallel query option. Because of the importance and complexity of this topic, it is addressed in detail in Chapter 13.

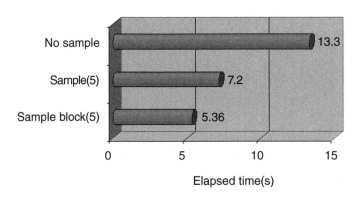

FIGURE 8.17 Performance improvements gained by the use of the SAMPLE clause.

To summarize, you can get significant improvements in full-table scan performance if any or all of the following are true:

❑ There are multiple CPUs on your host computer.
❑ There is spare CPU capacity.
❑ The data in your table is spread across multiple disk drives.

If these conditions are met, you can expect to get moderate to large improvements in the performance of full-table scans through parallel query technology. Refer to Chapter 13 for more details.

ARRAY FETCH

Oracle can retrieve rows either from the database one at a time or can retrieve rows in batches or arrays. *Array fetch* refers to the mechanism by which Oracle can retrieve multiple rows in a single fetch operation. Fetching rows in batches reduces the number of calls issued to the database server and can also reduce network traffic.

In some tools, it's necessary to explicitly define the arrays to receive the data. In other tools, the array processing is performed transparently and the size of the array is established by a configuration parameter. Guidelines for implementing array processing in popular client tools are contained in Appendix C.

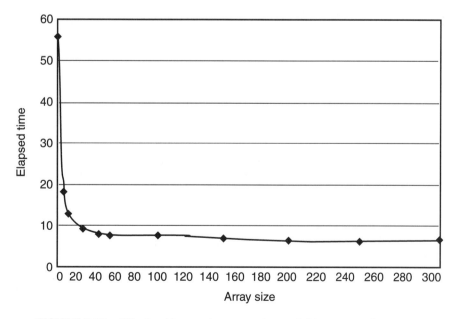

FIGURE 8.18 Effects of increasing array size on table scan performance.

Figure 8.18 shows the relationship between the size of the fetch array and the response time for a 10,000-row query. We can see that even relatively small array sizes (less than 20 rows per fetch) can result in very significant reductions in processing time. There are diminishing returns as the array size is increased.

Use array fetches to retrieve batches of rows from the database in a single call. This will reduce both database and network overhead. In general, array fetch can provide an about an order of magnitude (10 times) improvement in bulk queries.

OPTIMIZING FOR THE FIRST ROW

Often the time taken to retrieve the first row—or first few rows—is critical to the performance of on-line systems. For instance, consider one of the Web-based search engines, such as Alta Vista, that are used hundreds of thousands of times every day. If we enter a search key that will find matches in millions of pages, it is essential that we do not make the user wait for every hit to be returned before returning the first page of information. Since almost no one ever scrolls to the last pages of a Web search results page, the time taken to retrieve all the results (e.g., the last row) is far less important.

Optimizing for the retrieval of the first row is sometimes referred to as *optimizing for response time*, while optimizing for the retrieval of the final row is often termed *optimizing for throughput*.

You can instruct the Oracle optimizer to attempt to minimize the time taken to retrieve the first row by using the FIRST_ROWS hint or optimizer mode, as described in Chapter 5. However, there are a number of ways in which you can unintentionally prevent a first rows optimization path:

❑ The FOR UPDATE clause requires that all the rows that match the search criteria be locked before any rows can be returned. This means both that all rows must be identified and locked before the first row can be returned. Although the FOR UPDATE clause is useful when implementing a pessimistic locking strategy (described in detail in Chapter 18), it should never be used if you are optimizing for response time when large numbers of rows might match the search criteria.

❑ An ORDER BY clause might require that all rows be retrieved and sorted before the first row can be returned. The only way to avoid the full retrieval and sort is if there is an index on the ORDER BY columns that allows the rows to be returned in order. If you don't avoid the sort, then the first row can only be displayed after all rows have been extracted from the database and sorted. This topic is discussed in more detail in Chapter 10.

When you need to optimize for response time rather than throughput, be cautious of the FOR UPDATE and ORDER BY clauses—these can make optimization for the first row difficult or impossible.

SUMMARY

In this chapter, we examined ways of optimizing retrieval of data from a single table—a fundamental technique that underlies the construction of more complex SQL queries.

One of the principal decisions to be made when retrieving data from a table is whether to use a full-table scan or some form of indexed lookup. In extreme conditions, such as accessing a single row or accessing every row in the table, the decision is easy. Single-row lookups work best with indexed methods, while accessing the entire table is best done through a full-table scan. However, between these two extremes there is no "magic number" that defines the point at which an indexed retrieval becomes less efficient than a full-table scan. Depending on the distribution and nature of your data and the configuration of your Oracle instance, the break-even point can be anywhere from between 2 and 60% of table rows.

The cost-based optimizer will attempt to decide between full-table scans and index-based retrieval based on estimates of the number of rows to be returned by the query. These estimates can be very inaccurate if the data is unevenly distributed. You can improve the cost-based optimizer's decisions by creating histograms on columns to be searched. But remember that histograms cannot be used in conjunction with bind variables and are therefore usually not used in an OLTP environment.

The fast full-index scan can provide a powerful alternative to the full-table scan when the query references only columns in the index.

If an index-based access is required, Oracle's default B*-tree indexes provide good performance for a wide variety of query types. Under certain circumstances bitmap indexes, hash clusters, or index organized tables may provide a more suitable solution. However, each of these alternative indexing strategies carry a greater risk than the B*-tree solution and so should be used with care.

Bitmap indexes can offer good performance even when there are large numbers of distinct values, but storage requirements rise rapidly with the number of distinct values. Bitmap indexes are not suitable when multiple sessions perform concurrent modifications on the table because locking mechanisms on bitmap indexes are much more restrictive than on B*-tree indexes.

Certain types of query operations cannot take advantage of indexes. These operations can lead to unintentional table scans and are a common cause of poor application performance. Some of the things to look out for are as follows:

❏ Searching for NULL values in an indexed column

❏ Performing a NOT EQUALS (!=) operation on an indexed column when only a small proportion of rows satisfy the NOT EQUALS operation

❏ Using a function on an indexed column where there is no associated *functional* index

When using indexes, make sure that the indexes are selective. For instance, don't index a column that has only a few distinct values unless some of the values are very rare (and then use hints or histograms to encourage the use of the index).

Take advantage of concatenated indexes, which are indexes created against more than one column. A query will perform best if all the columns in the WHERE clause appear in the concatenated index. Remember that the leading columns in the concatenated index can be used to resolve queries that don't refer to all the concatenated index columns, but trailing columns cannot. Try to create concatenated indexes that can be used in a wide range of queries. Where possible, place the column with the most unique values first in the concatenated index.

The cost-based optimizer won't always be able to calculate the best execution plan, so be prepared to use hints when necessary to ensure that the best plan is chosen. Some of the circumstances in which hints are particularly useful are as follows:

❏ Columns do not have histograms or the use of bind variables prevents histograms from being used.

❏ Data values are unevenly distributed in the table.

❏ Range scans are being performed.

❏ The query contains OR conditions.

Hash clusters are an alternative to the use of traditional B*-tree indexes for exact value lookups, and a primary key may be a particularly suitable cluster key. However, if not configured correctly, hash clusters can result in either degraded full-table scans or hash key lookup performance. Tables that are subject to constant growth or are subject to frequent table scans are probably poor candidates for hash clusters.

Index organized tables can improve performance of certain queries and offer an easy way of splitting a table into two segments so that infrequently accessed columns are located in an overflow segment. Deciding how to split an index organized table is critical to the performance of the table.

If it is impractical to avoid a full-table scan, you can optimize table scan performance by

❏ Increasing the number of rows stored in each data block by reducing PCT-FREE and increasing PCTUSED, but not so far as to cause row chaining or degrade DML performance.

❏ Resetting the high-water mark by rebuilding the table after bulk deletes.

❏ Moving large, infrequently queried columns—especially LONG or VAR-CHAR2 columns—to a subtable. Using the DISABLE STORAGE IN ROW clause for LOBs can help achieve this result.

❏ Keeping moderate to small tables that are frequently scanned in memory with the CACHE hint or table parameter or using multiple buffer pools to preserve these tables in memory.

❏ Using the parallel query option. The parallel query option has the greatest potential for speeding up full-table scans, but your host computer must be suitably configured and you need to assess the impact on other concurrent operations.

❏ Using array fetch to increase the number of rows returned with each fetch operation.

TUNING JOINS AND SUBQUERIES

INTRODUCTION

In this chapter, we discuss ways of improving performance when two or more tables are joined. Most nontrivial SQL statements contain joins, and ensuring that the tables involved are joined in the most effective manner is an important factor when tuning Oracle SQL.

The Oracle optimizer will, of course, do its best to ensure that the types of joins and the order in which tables are joined is the best possible. Sometimes the optimizer will be unable to determine the best join plan because of limitations in its algorithms and its understanding of your data. It's then up to you to enforce the optimal join approach through hints or other means.

Subqueries are close relatives to joins. Subqueries allow a SQL query to be embedded in an SQL statement and can often perform similar operations to joins but possibly with greater or lesser efficiency. Subqueries can also be used to express the reverse of a join by retrieving rows from one table that have no match in a second table.

Subqueries can be used to formulate complex queries, and the more complex the query, the greater the likelihood that the optimizer will fail to reach the best solution. In this chapter, we discuss when to use subqueries, which sort of subquery to use, and ways of improving the performance of subqueries. The topics covered are as follows:

❏ Choosing between the various join methods—nested loops, sort merge, and hash join

❑ Choosing the optimum join order
❑ Clustering tables to improve join performance
❑ Improving the performance of special joins, such as outer joins, star joins, and hierarchical self-joins
❑ Using and optimizing subqueries
❑ Optimizing semijoins
❑ Optimizing antijoins

CHOOSING THE BEST JOIN METHOD

As we saw in Chapter 4, Oracle can perform joins using one of the following methods:

❑ In a nested loops join, Oracle performs a search of the inner table for each row found in the outer table. This type of access is most often seen when there is an index on the inner table; otherwise multiple nested table scans may result.
❑ When performing a sort-merge join, Oracle must sort each table (or result set) by the value of the join columns. Once sorted, the two sets of data are merged, much as you might merge two sorted piles of numbered pages.
❑ When performing a hash join, Oracle builds a hash table for the smaller of the two tables. This hash table is then used to find matching rows in a somewhat similar fashion to the way an index is used in a nested loops join.

SORT MERGE/HASH VERSUS NESTED LOOPS

In a sense, the sort-merge join and the hash join can be considered as the same family of joins—they provide good performance under similar conditions. On the other hand, the nested loops join suits a very different category of queries. So when determining the optimal join type, you might first decide if a nested loops join is appropriate.

The choice between the sort-merge/hash and nested loops approach should be based on

❑ The need for throughput versus the need for response time. Nested loops usually offer better response time, but sort merge can often offer better throughput.
❑ The proportion of the tables that are being joined. The larger the subset of rows being processed, the more likely that a sort merge or hash join will be faster.

❏ Indexes available to support the join. A nested loops approach is usually only effective when an index can be used to join the tables.

❏ Memory and CPU available for sorting. Large sorts can consume significant resources and can slow execution. Sort merge involves two sorts, while nested loops usually involve no sorting. Hash joins also require memory to build the hash table.

❏ Sort merge and hash joins may derive greater benefit from parallel execution, although nested loop joins can also be parallelized.

Table 9.1 provides general guidelines for deciding between the two join techniques. In borderline cases, you need to try both methods and use SQL_TRACE to determine which is superior.

TABLE 9.1 Determining the optimal join method

WHEN JOINING A TO B (IN THAT ORDER)	CONSIDER SORT MERGE OR HASH JOIN?	CONSIDER NESTED LOOPS USING AN INDEX ON B?
Both A and B are small.	Yes.	Maybe, depending how small the tables are.
Only selecting a small subset of rows from B (and B has an index).	No. Performing a table scan of B will be cost-inefficient.	Yes. The index will reduce the number of I/Os on B.
Want the first row as quickly as possible.	No. The first row won't be returned until both A and B are scanned, sorted, and merged or until the hash table has been built.	Yes. Rows can be returned as soon as they are fetched using the index.
Want to get all rows as quickly as possible.	Maybe.	Maybe. Nested loops may still get all rows before sort merge if other conditions apply.
Doing a full-table scan of A, and want to use parallel query.	Yes.	Yes. Nested loops can be resolved in parallel if the outer (first) table in the join is retrieved via a full-table scan.
Getting rows from A by an index lookup and want to use parallel query.	Yes. Sort merge and hash joins can proceed in parallel, even if one result set was retrieved by an index lookup.	No. Nested loops cannot be resolved in parallel unless the outer (first) table in the join was retrieved via a full-table scan.
Memory is limited and SORT_ AREA_SIZE or HASH_AREA_ SIZE is low.	Maybe not. Large sorts can be a significant overhead, especially if memory for sorts is limited. Hash joins can also require more memory than nested loops.	Yes. The nested loops join avoids sorting and is therefore less affected by memory limitations.

> The nested loops join method suits joins involving subsets of table data and where the join is supported by an index.

SORT MERGE VERSES HASH JOINS

Although there are a number of factors that bear on the decision to use the nested loops join in favor of other join methods, deciding between the sort-merge and hash-join methods is not difficult. Since the hash-join was introduced in Oracle 7.3, most experience suggests that the hash join method is superior to the sort-merge join in virtually all circumstances.

Oracle documentation and white papers acknowledge that the hash-join is superior. It is therefore surprising to find that the cost-based optimizer often prefers the sort merge. For instance, the following statement joins all rows in CUSTOMERS with SALES:

```
SQL> SELECT customer_name, sale_value
  2     FROM sales s, customers c
  3   WHERE s.customer_id = c.customer_id
```

By default, the optimizer chooses the sort-merge join, as shown in the following explain plan:

```
Execution Plan
----------------------------------------------------------
   0      SELECT STATEMENT
   1    0    MERGE JOIN
   2    1      SORT (JOIN)
   3    2        TABLE ACCESS (FULL) OF 'CUSTOMERS'
   4    1      SORT (JOIN)
   5    4        TABLE ACCESS (FULL) OF 'SALES'
```

To get a hash-join plan, we can use the USE_HASH hint, as follows:

```
  1   SELECT /*+ ORDERED USE_HASH(C) */
  2          customer_name, sale_value
  3     FROM sales s, customers c
  4*  WHERE s.customer_id = c.customer_id
SQL> /
```

```
Execution Plan
----------------------------------------------------------
    0        SELECT STATEMENT
    1    0   HASH JOIN
    2    1      TABLE ACCESS (FULL) OF 'SALES'
    3    1      TABLE ACCESS (FULL) OF 'CUSTOMERS'
```

Figure 9.1 compares the performance of the hash join with the sort merge for the preceding example.

> The hash-join algorithm almost always outperforms the sort-merge algorithm. However, the cost-based optimizer often favors the sort-merge join, so you may need to use the USE_HASH to take advantage of the faster hash join.

HOW THE OPTIMIZER MODE AFFECTS THE JOIN TYPE

We've seen that the sort-merge join is most efficient when all rows are being returned and that nested loops is best when a small number of rows are being returned. In a similar way, sort merge is favored when throughput is the goal and nested loops is favored when response time is the goal. As a result, the cost-based optimizer is strongly biased toward sort-merge and hash-join techniques when the optimizer goal is set to ALL_ROWS (the default) and biased toward nested loops when the goal is set to FIRST_ROWS.

The rule-based optimizer will almost always prefer an index-based nested loops join to a sort-merge join and is unable to perform a hash join. When users first shift from rule-based optimization to cost-based optimization, they often notice reduced response time. Upon examination, they discover that SQL statements previously resolved using nested loops are now being resolved by the cost-based optimizer using sort merge. The problem is that the default goal of the

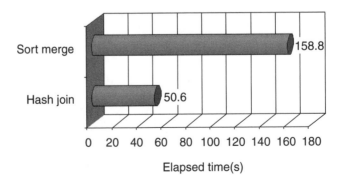

FIGURE 9.1   Hash-join and sort-merge performance.

TABLE 9.2   How optimizer mode affects join preference

MODE	BEHAVIOR
RULE	Favors nested-loops if an index is available to support it, sort merge otherwise.
FIRST_ROWS	Usually favors nested-loops if an index is available to support it, sort merge otherwise.
ALL_ROWS	Usually favors a sort merge or hash join.
CHOOSE	Same as CHOOSE if statistics exist on any of the tables, same as RULE otherwise.

cost-based optimizer is throughput (ALL_ROWS), and this default setting results in an increase in sort-merge joins. It's especially important when optimizing joins that the optimizer goal be set appropriately. If your aim is response time, make sure that your optimizer goal is set to FIRST_ROWS.

The setting of the initialization parameter OPTIMIZER_MODE or ALTER SESSION setting OPTIMIZER_GOAL has a significant effect on the join method-ologies that Oracle favors. The RULE setting invokes the rule-based optimizer, which favors index-based, nested loops joins whenever possible. FIRST_ROWS tends to favor nested loops if an index is present and sort merge otherwise. ALL_ROWS favors sort merge or hash joins and CHOOSE uses the RULE setting if no statistics are available and ALL_ROWS otherwise.

Table 9.2 summaries how optimizer mode affects join preference.

The cost-based optimizer will favor sort-merge joins when your optimizer goal is set to CHOOSE or ALL_ROWS. If you are primarily concerned with response time, set your optimizer goal to FIRST_ROWS. The cost-based optimizer will then favor the nested loops join.

OPTIMIZING THE JOIN

There are a few things you can do to optimize the join of your choice:

❑ For a nested loops join, ensure that the index used for the join contains as many columns as possible from the WHERE clause. If the index can also contain the columns in the SELECT list (if there are not too many), so much the better.

❑ For sort merge, optimize your database sort parameters (see Appendix D for details). Make sure that you eliminate any rows not needed in the result set before you perform the sort (perhaps an index will help here). If performing full-table scans, see Chapter 8 for guidelines for optimizing these scans.

❑ If performing hash joins, the configuration of your database is also important. See the section titled "Advanced Optimization of Hash Joins" on configuring HASH_AREA_SIZE and other configuration parameters that affect
   hash joins.

JOIN ORDER

Determining the best possible join order can be complex. There is often a large
number of potential access methods, join methods, and join orders. For the mathematically inclined, the number of possible join orders is the factorial of the number of tables in the FROM clause. For instance, if there are five tables in the FROM
clause, then the number of possible join orders is

$$5! = 5 \times 4 \times 3 \times 2 \times 1 = 120$$

The cost-based optimizer tries to work out the cost of a range of join orders
and methods. It has to make a lot of assumptions (for instance, the cost of sorting,
the number of rows to retrieve from an index lookup, and so on). The rule-based
optimizer uses a simpler set of rules of thumb to guess the best approach. Both
optimizers make mistakes, so it's up to you to try various join approaches.

It's not possible to predict which join approach will be the best for your
query, but the following are a good set of principles for your first try:

❑ The driving table—the first table in the join order—should be the one that
   has the most selective and efficient WHERE clause condition. That is, eliminate any rows from the result sets as early in the join order as possible. This
   will reduce the number of rows returned in each step.
❑ If you are joining small subsets of the tables involved, try to use nested
   loops for each subsequent join provided that there is a supporting index.
   Otherwise, use hash join in preference to sort merge.
❑ Make sure the indexes supporting the nested loops join contain all of the
   columns in the WHERE clause for the table being joined.

HOW JOIN METHOD AFFECTS JOIN ORDER

Each of the three join types have different performance profiles for specific join
orders.

Consider the case in which you are joining every row between two tables of
uneven size (perhaps CUSTOMERS [10,000 rows] and SALES [1,000,000 rows]):

❑ If joining using the sort-merge method, the join order is irrelevant. Each
   table must be fully read, sorted, and merged. The order in which the tables
   appear in the FROM clause or which table is referenced in the USE_MERGE
   hint is irrelevant.

❏ If joining using index-based nested loops, the inner (second) table should be the smaller of the two. This is because the overhead of performing N index lookups is higher than the overhead of full-table scanning N rows.

❏ If joining using the hash-join method, the inner (second) table should also be the smaller of the two. The hash-join algorithm works best when the hash table fits into memory and is on the smaller of the two tables. However, if the second table is very small, then this advice can be misleading, since the table might be too small to get any benefit from being hashed.

Putting this into practice, let's compare the performance of this nested loops query (joining SALES to CUSTOMERS with an index on CUSTOMERS):

```
SELECT /*+ ORDERED USE_NL(C) */
       customer_name, SUM (sale_value)
  FROM sales s, customers c
 WHERE s.customer_id = c.customer_id
 GROUP BY customer_name
```

With the performance of this query (joining CUSTOMERS to SALES via an index on SALES),

```
SELECT /*+ ORDERED USE_NL(S) */
       customer_name, SUM (sale_value)
  FROM  customers c,sales s
 WHERE s.customer_id = c.customer_id
 GROUP BY customer_name
```

As we can see from Figure 9.2, joining the larger table to the smaller table is much more efficient. Don't forget that the primary decision for a nested loops join

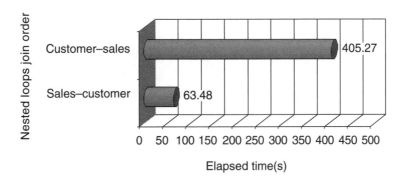

FIGURE 9.2 Effect of join order on nested loops join.

is which table has supporting indexes. If they both have equally good supporting indexes, then join the larger table to the smaller table.

To compare the effect of join order on the hash join, consider the following example, in which the CUSTOMERS table is hash joined to the SALES table (the hash table gets created on the SALES table):

```
SELECT /*+ ORDERED USE_HASH(S) */
       customer_name, SUM (sale_value)
  FROM customers c, sales s
 WHERE s.customer_id = c.customer_id
 GROUP BY customer_name
```

With the performance of this query, in which the hash table is created on the CUSTOMERS table,

```
SELECT /*+ ORDERED USE_HASH(C) */
       customer_name, SUM (sale_value)
  FROM sales s, customers c
 WHERE s.customer_id = c.customer_id
 GROUP BY customer_name
```

We can see from Figure 9.3 that joining the larger table to the smaller table offers significant performance improvements. However, when joining a very big table to a tiny table, you may find that having the massive table second in the join order is the better option because you don't get much benefit from hashing a tiny table.

Although it's worth remembering that both the nested loops and hash joins work best if the join order is from the larger table to the smaller table, it's much more important to eliminate the maximum number of rows in the first join because this reduces the number of rows that have to be joined at each succeeding

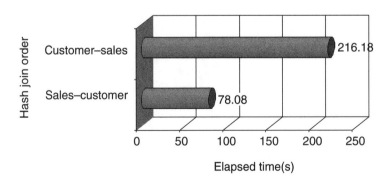

FIGURE 9.3 Effect of join order on hash join.

step. The optimizations we've seen involved joins of entire tables; in many circumstances you may join a small table to a larger table because you can eliminate rows from the smaller table using a WHERE clause condition.

The most important consideration in determining the join order is to eliminate unwanted rows as early as possible. Beyond this, both hash join and nested loops work best when joining a larger table to a smaller table. The sort-merge join is not affected by the order in which a larger and smaller table are joined.

USING HINTS TO CONTROL THE JOIN

If you feel that the optimizer has decided on a join order which is less than perfect—and you have an alternative in mind—you can use the following hints to influence the optimizer:

❏ The ORDERED hint instructs the optimizer to join the tables in the exact order in which they appear in the FROM clause.

❏ You can use the hints that determine access paths—such as FULL, INDEX, and HASH—to force the access required on the driving table.

❏ The hints USE_NL, USE_MERGE, and USE_HASH can force a particular join method.

When using USE_NL or USE_MERGE, it's important to remember that the table specified in the hint is the second (or inner) table in the join. For instance, if the join order is A, B, C, then the hint USE_NL(B) results in a nested loops join between A and B; USE_NL(C) results in a nested loops of B and C, and USE_NL(A) is meaningless, since A is the driving table.

The following example illustrates the use of these hints. ORDERED ensures that the tables are joined in the same order in which they appear in the FROM clause. The INDEX hint ensures we use an index to get the relevant product entry. USE_NL ensures that SALES is joined to PRODUCTS using the nested loops method, and USE_MERGE ensures that CUSTOMERS is joined with that result set using a sort merge.

```
SELECT   /*+ ORDERED INDEX(P PK_PRODUCTS) USE_NL(S)
            USE_MERGE(C) */
      p.product_description, s.sale_date,
      c.customer_name
  FROM products p, sales s, customers c
 WHERE p.product_id = s.product_id
   AND s.customer_id = c.customer_id
```

```
    AND c.customer_name = 'SMITH and sons'
    AND p.product_id = 1
Execution Plan:
MERGE JOIN   -> From the USE_MERGE hint
    SORT JOIN
      NESTED LOOPS->From the USE_NL hint
        TABLE ACCESS BY ROWID PRODUCTS
          INDEX UNIQUE SCAN PK_PRODUCTS -> INDEX hint
        TABLE ACCESS FULL SALES
    SORT JOIN
      TABLE ACCESS FULL CUSTOMERS
```

ADVANCED OPTIMIZATION OF HASH JOINS

Two database parameters—HASH_AREA_SIZE and HASH_MULTIBLOCK_IO_ COUNT—can be used to optimize the performance of hash joins. These parameters can be set in the Oracle configuration ("INIT.ORA") file and can also be set using the ALTER SESSION SET command.

HASH_AREA_SIZE   The configuration parameter HASH_AREA_SIZE limits the amount of memory that is available to the hash join for the creation and storage of the hash table. Increasing HASH_AREA_SIZE will improve the performance of a hash join up until the point at which the entire hash table fits into memory. After this point is reached, no further improvements will be achieved by increasing HASH_AREA_SIZE.

Figure 9.4 shows how increasing HASH_AREA_SIZE improved the performance of a hash join between our sample CUSTOMERS and SALES table (about 10,000 and 1,000,000 rows, respectively). Once Oracle was able to fit the hash table for CUSTOMERS into memory (at about 100K), increasing HASH_AREA_SIZE did not improve performance.

HASH_MULTIBLOCK_IO_COUNT   The other key hash join parameter is HASH_MULTIBLOCK_IO_COUNT. This parameter determines the number of blocks that will be written to, or read from, hash join partitions in a single IO. Increasing HASH_MULTIBLOCK_IO_COUNT will normally improve hash join performance until the point at which DB_BLOCK_SIZE*HASH_MULTIBLOCK_ IO_COUNT reaches an operating system–specific limit. Beyond this point, no further improvements will be expected. The limits are as follows:

❏ For 32-bit Windows NT and Windows 2000, 64K
❏ For UNIX when the datafiles are on filesystems, 8K
❏ For UNIX when the datafiles are on raw devices, somewhere between 64K and 1M, depending on the operating system version

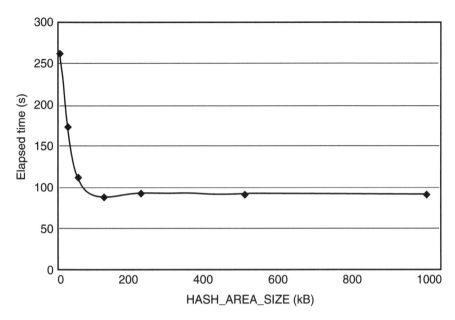

FIGURE 9.4 Effect of increase HASH_AREA_SIZE on a hash join. Performance improves until the entire hash table fits into memory; then no further improvements are gained.

Figure 9.5 shows the effect of varying HASH_MULTIBLOCK_IO_COUNT for a Windows NT system with an 8K block size. Performance improvements were not achieved after setting the parameter to 8, which corresponds to a 64K I/O size.

Increasing the HASH_MULTIBLOCK_IO_COUNT setting can improve the performance of hash joins if there is an I/O bottleneck, and usually high values are better. However, the setting of HASH_IO_MULTIBLOCK_IO_COUNT also affects the number of hash "buckets" that are created during hash joins of large tables. Higher values can decrease the number of buckets. For very large tables, it may be better to reduce HASH_IO_MULTIBLOCK_IO_COUNT to increase the number of hash buckets created.

Increases in the value of HASH_AREA_SIZE will improve the performance of hash joins up to the point at which the hash table fits into memory. Improving HASH_IO_MULTIBLOCK_IO_COUNT may improve the performance I/O-bound hash joins up to an operating system–dependent limit, although very large hash joins may perform better with a medium value.

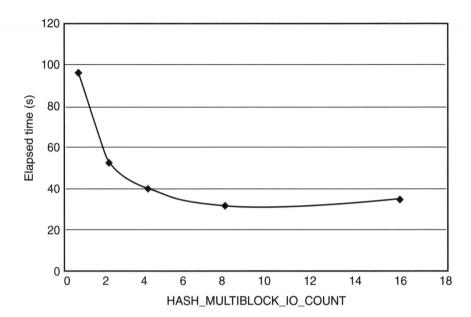

FIGURE 9.5   Effect of HASH_MULTIBLOCK_IO_COUNT on hash join performance (8K block size).

USING INDEX CLUSTERS

Index clusters, introduced in Chapter 3, allow rows from two or more tables that share a common key value to be stored within the same data blocks. In a sense, the index cluster is a way of "prejoining" two or more tables. Not surprisingly, clusters do improve the performance of joins. For instance, to improve the performance of the following query, we could create an index cluster for EMPLOYEES and CUSTOMERS based on the sales_rep_id/employee_id column.

```
select e.surname,c.contact_surname
  from employee_clus e,
       customer_clus c
 where e.employee_id=c.sales_rep_id
   and e.employee_id=20

Rows     Execution Plan
-------  --------------------------------------------------
      0  SELECT STATEMENT    HINT: CHOOSE
   3333   NESTED LOOPS
      1    TABLE ACCESS (BY ROWID) OF 'EMPLOYEE_CLUS'
      1     INDEX (UNIQUE SCAN) OF 'EMPLOYEE_CLUS_I0'
   3333    TABLE ACCESS (CLUSTER) OF 'CUSTOMER_CLUS'
```

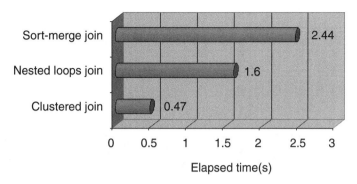

FIGURE 9.6   Relative performance of joining tables in an index cluster.

Figure 9.6 shows the improvement gained by clustering the two tables involved. Clustering the tables significantly improves join performance.

Despite the improvement to join performance provided by clustering, index clusters are rarely used in real-world applications and have a poor reputation in the Oracle community. While the use of index clusters can improve joins, other operations show a severe performance degradation. As with hash clusters, a poor setting for the SIZE parameter can negate the benefits of clustering. Further, when scanning individual tables in the cluster, all blocks in the cluster will need to be accessed (Figure 9.7).

Because of the drawbacks of clustering tables, most Oracle specialists choose not to cluster tables unless the tables are always accessed as joined. Even if these conditions are met, denormalizing the tables (see Chapter 14) may be a wiser alternative.

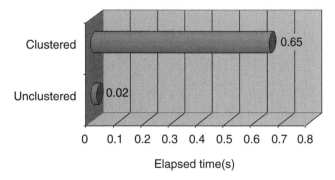

FIGURE 9.7   Elapsed time for the full-table scan of EMPLOYEES when clustered with EMPLOYEES and when unclustered.

Clustering tables can improve performance when the tables are joined but can degrade the performance of many other operations on the tables. Only consider clustering tables if they are almost always accessed together. Even then, consider alternatives such as denormalization.

SPECIAL JOINS

OUTER JOINS

You may recall from Chapter 2 that an outer join is one in which a row is returned from the outer table, even if there is no matching row in the inner table. The performance of an outer join is usually equivalent to that of the corresponding inner join, and all join methods are available. However, an outer join does impose a particular join order. If we perform an outer join of A to B (returning rows in B even if there are no matches in A), then the join order must be A, B; it cannot be B, A.

For instance, the following query joins departments to employees using an index and nested loops join:

```
  1   select d.department_name,e.surname
  2     from departments d,employees e
  3*  where d.department_id=e.department_id
SQL> /


Execution Plan
----------------------------------------------------------
  0      SELECT STATEMENT Optimizer=CHOOSE
  1    0    NESTED LOOPS
  2    1      TABLE ACCESS (FULL) OF 'EMPLOYEES'
  3    1      TABLE ACCESS (BY INDEX ROWID) OF
                                    'DEPARTMENTS'
  4    3        INDEX (UNIQUE SCAN) OF 'PK_DEPARTMENTS'
```

If we transform this query to an outer join so that departments without employees are included, we get the following result:

```
  1   select
  2   d.department_name,e.surname
  3     from departments d,employees e
  4*  where d.department_id=e.department_id(+)
SQL> /
```

```
Execution Plan
-------------------------------------------------------
    0       SELECT STATEMENT Optimizer=CHOOSE
    1    0    MERGE JOIN (OUTER)
    2    1      SORT (JOIN)
    3    2        TABLE ACCESS (FULL) OF 'DEPARTMENTS'
    4    1      SORT (JOIN)
    5    4        TABLE ACCESS (FULL) OF 'EMPLOYEES'
```

We can see that as a result of the outer join, not only has the join order changed, but the join method has also changed. We can use a nested loops join when employees are joined to departments because there is an index on DEPARTMENT_ID in the DEPARTMENTS table. When we change this join into an outer join, we must join in the opposite order—from departments to employees. There is no index on DEPARTMENT_ID in EMPLOYEES, so the only option is to use a sort merge or hash join.

You may encounter queries that specify the outer join operator incorrectly. For instance, in the following query the outer join is meaningless because the outer join might return rows where surname is NULL. Since we've specified that surname must be equal to 'SMITH,' these rows will be eliminated anyway:

```
SELECT d.department_name, e.surname
  FROM departments d, employees e
 WHERE d.department_id = e.department_id (+)
   AND surname = 'SMITH'
```

The query will return the same rows as the equivalent inner join, but because the outer join is specified, the join order must be DEPARTMENTS ➟ EMPLOYEES and cannot be EMPLOYEES ➟ DEPARTMENTS. This could limit the range of join and access methods and consequently degrade the query. Oracle (starting with version 7.3) can sometimes recognize such meaningless outer joins and eliminate them.

The outer join operation limits the join orders that the optimizer can consider. Don't perform outer joins needlessly.

STAR JOINS

The STAR schema is a way of organizing relational data that is very popular in data warehouses. In a STAR schema, business data are stored in one or more tables, referred to as fact tables. These tables can be joined to multiple dimension tables that contain the more static details. For instance, Figure 9.8 displays a simple STAR schema.

Note that there is no relationship between the dimension tables themselves, only between dimension tables and the fact table. Also, data in the fact table are not meaningful unless joined with data in the dimension tables.

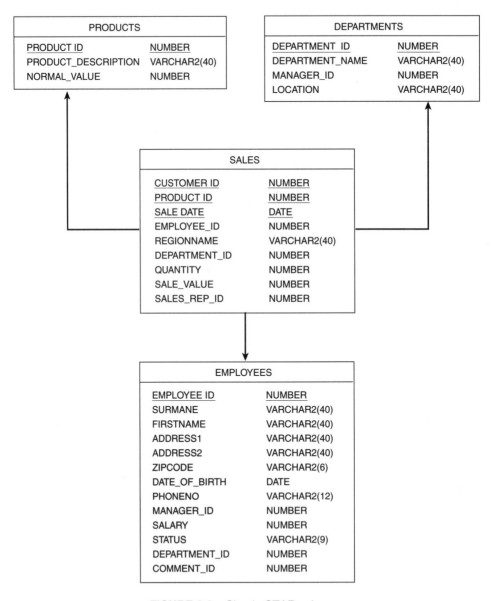

FIGURE 9.8   Simple STAR schema.

STAR queries have typically been poorly resolved in earlier versions of Oracle and cannot be efficiently optimized by the rule-based optimizer. For instance, the rule-based optimizer resolves the following query with a full-table scan of the relatively large sales table followed by a series of joins to the dimension tables:

```
select /*+RULE */ sum(sale_value)
  from departments d,
       employees e,
       products p,
       sales s                                       _ Fact table
 where p.product_description='Oracle Tune Tool mk 2'
   and e.surname='MCLOUGHLIN'
   and e.firstname='FREDERICK'
   and d.department_name='Database Products'
   and p.product_id=s.product_id
   and e.employee_id=s.sales_rep_id
   and d.department_id=s.department_id
```

```
Rows      Execution Plan
-------   -------------------------------------------------------
      0   SELECT STATEMENT    GOAL: HINT: RULE
      8    SORT (AGGREGATE)
      8     NESTED LOOPS
      9      NESTED LOOPS
   1212       NESTED LOOPS
 200000        TABLE ACCESS (FULL) OF 'SALES'
 200000        TABLE ACCESS (BY ROWID) OF 'PRODUCTS'
 200000         INDEX (UNIQUE SCAN) OF 'PK_PRODUCTS'
   1212       TABLE ACCESS (BY ROWID) OF 'EMPLOYEES'
   1212        INDEX (UNIQUE SCAN) OF 'PK_EMPLOYEES'
      9     TABLE ACCESS (BY ROWID) OF 'DEPARTMENTS'
      9      INDEX (UNIQUE SCAN) OF 'PK_DEPARTMENTS'
```

The Oracle cost-based optimizer can recognize STAR queries and will employ a special method to resolve them. Oracle's approach to implementing STAR queries is as follows:

❑ Identify the table with the most rows: This must be the fact table.
❑ Get result sets for all the dimension tables (usually, they will be subject to selection criteria in the WHERE clause, as in our previous example).
❑ Create a Cartesian product of the dimension result sets. A Cartesian product is the result of joining every row in one table with every row in another

table. Usually our dimension tables are small and perhaps only a few values satisfy the WHERE clause, so these Cartesian joins are not too expensive.

❏ Use a concatenated index to retrieve rows from the fact table for each row in the Cartesian product.

The rationale for this approach is based on the assumption that Cartesian joins, although inefficient in principle, allow us to delay querying the huge fact table until the last possible moment and allow us to use a concatenated index on the fact table matching the keys of the dimension tables.

The cost-based optimizer will sometimes recognize the STAR schema and perform this optimization automatically. Oracle also provides a special hint to force Oracle to use the STAR join method. This hint is called (not surprisingly) STAR. The STAR hint forces Oracle to consider a STAR join methodology in preference to other techniques. Using the STAR hint, we see that the dimension tables are subject to a Cartesian join and the fact table is accessed via the concatenated index:

```
Rows     Execution Plan
-------  ---------------------------------------------
      0  SELECT STATEMENT    GOAL: CHOOSE
      8   SORT (AGGREGATE)
      8    NESTED LOOPS
      1     MERGE JOIN (CARTESIAN)
      1      MERGE JOIN (CARTESIAN)
      1       TABLE ACCESS (BY ROWID) OF 'EMPLOYEES'
      2        INDEX (RANGE SCAN) OF 'EMPLOYEES_SURNAME'
      1       SORT (JOIN)
     50        TABLE ACCESS (FULL) OF 'DEPARTMENTS'
      1      SORT (JOIN)
    180       TABLE ACCESS (FULL) OF 'PRODUCTS'
      8     TABLE ACCESS (BY ROWID) OF 'SALES'
      9      INDEX   (RANGE SCAN) OF
                'SALES_REP_DEPT_PRODUCT_IDX' (NON-UNIQUE)
```

Figure 9.9 compares the performance of the rule-based optimizer, the cost-based optimizer, and the STAR hint. We can see that the STAR hint can lead to great improvements for suitable queries. The improvements will be even more marked for very large fact tables (since the bigger the table, the greater the incentive to avoid a full-table scan).

Consider using Oracle's STAR query optimization when joining a very large fact table to smaller, unrelated dimension tables. You will need a concatenated index on the fact table and may need to specify the STAR hint.

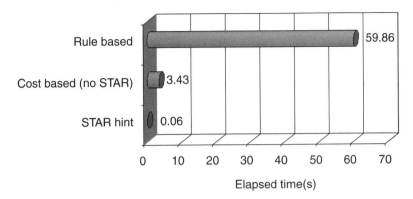

FIGURE 9.9 Performance of a STAR join under rule-based and cost-based optimizers and with the STAR hint.

STAR TRANSFORMATION

The approach to STAR queries outlined in the preceding section may fail for more complex schemas. For instance,

❏ If the number of rows called from the dimension tables is large, then the Cartesian products may become huge.
❏ Concatenated indexes that support all possible combinations of dimension keys will be required; this might not be practical.

To address these concerns, Oracle version 8 introduced the star transformation optimization. The star transformation uses bitmap indexes on the fact table to produce a superior execution plan for queries where the number of dimension tables is large or where it is not practical to provide concatenated indexes for all possible queries.

In a star transformation, the cost-based optimizer will transform the query from a join into a query against the fact table that contains subqueries against each of the dimension tables. For instance, consider the following star query:

```
SELECT /*+STAR*/ SUM (sale_quantity),
       SUM (total_price), COUNT (*)
  FROM sales_fact ss,
       sales_rep_dimension srf,
       period_dimension pf,
       department_dimension df,
       product_dimension prf
 WHERE ss.product_id = prf.product_id
   AND ss.department_id = df.department_id
```

```
      AND ss.sales_rep_id = srf.sales_rep_id
      AND ss.period_id = pf.period_id
      AND prf.description = 'SQL*Navigator'
      AND df.description = 'Melbourne'
      AND srf.surname = 'Harrison'
      AND srf.firstname = 'Guy'
      AND pf.year = 1998
      AND pf.quarter = 2
```

The star transformation would result in a statement that looks like this:

```
SELECT SUM (sale_quantity), SUM (total_price), COUNT (*)
  FROM sales_fact ss
 WHERE ss.product_id IN
       (SELECT product_id
          FROM product_dimension prf
         WHERE prf.description = 'SQL*Navigator')
   AND ss.department_id IN
       (SELECT department_id
          FROM department_dimension df
         WHERE df.description = 'Melbourne')
   AND ss.sales_rep_id IN
       (SELECT sales_rep_id
          FROM sales_rep_dimension srf
         WHERE srf.surname = 'Harrison'
           AND srf.firstname = 'Guy')
   AND ss.period_id IN
       (SELECT period_id
          FROM period_dimension pf
         WHERE pf.year = 1998
           AND pf.quarter = 2)
```

The transformed statement allows bitmap indexes on PRODUCT_ID, DEPART-MENT_ID, SALES_REP_ID, and PERIOD_ID to be used to resolve the query.

In general, we would not expect a merge of multiple bitmap indexes to out-perform a concatenated index containing all columns. However, it is often im-practical to create concatenated indexes for all possible combination of columns whereas because bitmap indexes may be used in any combination a single bitmap index on each column will be sufficient to support all query combinations.

For instance, our original query will perform well if there is a concatenated index on PRODUCT_ID, DEPARTMENT_ID, SALES_REP_ID, and PERIOD_ID. If the query is changed so that the product is no longer specified, then this con-catenated index can no longer be used effectively and query performance will degrade unless we create another suitable concatenated index. As the number of dimensions increases, the number of concatenated indexes required to support all possible query combinations rapidly becomes impractical. However, because bitmap indexes can be used in any combination, a single bitmap index on each column will support all possible queries.

However, bear in mind the restrictions on bitmap indexes:

❑ The index may become inefficient if the number of distinct values in a column is high (although, as we saw in Chapter 7, bitmap indexes remain efficient even with several hundred thousand values).

❑ Bitmap indexes are not suitable for tables with high concurrent transaction rates.

To allow for the star transformation, you should do the following:

❑ Make sure that the server parameter STAR_TRANSFORMATION_ENABLED is set to TRUE in your server intialization parameter file ("init.ora") or is set to TRUE by an ALTER SESSION statement.

❑ Have bitmap indexes where appropriate on fact table columns.

❑ Use the STAR_TRANSFORMATION hint if necessary to force the transformation, if the cost-based optimizer fails to perform the transformation.

Figure 9.10 illustrates performance characteristics of the star transformation. When a suitable concatenated index exists, the star transformation is somewhat slower than a traditional star execution plan. However, if a suitable concatenated index is not present, the star transformation results in a dramatic performance improvement.

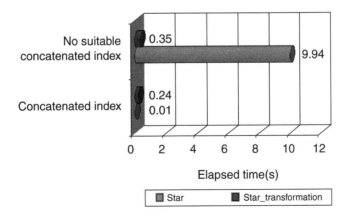

FIGURE 9.10 STAR transformation compared with standard STAR optimization.

HIERARCHICAL QUERIES

We introduced the hierarchical query using Oracle's CONNECT BY operator in Chapter 3. A hierarchical query, sometimes referred to as an explosion of parts, is a special case of self-join. In the hierarchical query, a column in the table points to the primary key of another row in the same table. This row, in turn, points to a further row and so on until the head of the hierarchy is reached. In our sample database, the MANAGER_ID and EMPLOYEE_ID columns of the employee table form such a hierarchy. The MANAGER_ID column points to the EMPLOYEE_ID of the rows manager. If we want to print the full organizational hierarchy, we can use the following query:

```
SELECT RPAD (' ', LEVEL * 3) || surname employee
  FROM employees
 START WITH manager_id = 0
 CONNECT BY PRIOR employee_id = manager_id;
```

For a hierarchical query of a large table to be efficient, you need an index to support the START WITH and CONNECT BY clauses. In the case of the preceding query, this means an index on MANAGER_ID. The index on MANAGER_ID is required to position at MANAGER_ID=0 initially and to find employees with a particular MANAGER_ID. Without the index on MANAGER_ID, we get the following execution plan for the preceding hierarchical query:

```
Rows        Execution Plan
-------     ------------------------------------------------
      0     SELECT STATEMENT    HINT: CHOOSE
    800      CONNECT BY
    800       TABLE ACCESS    (FULL) OF 'EMPLOYEES'
      1       TABLE ACCESS    (BY ROWID) OF 'EMPLOYEES'
 640000       TABLE ACCESS    (FULL) OF 'EMPLOYEES'
```

Note the 640,000 rows processed in the second full-table scan of EMPLOYEES. Since EMPLOYEES is an 800-row table, how can we process 640,000 rows? The figure 640,000 just happens to be the square of 800 ($800 \times 800 = 640,000$). For every row in the EMPLOYEES table, we have to perform a further scan of EMPLOYEES to find the matching MANAGER_IDs. Therefore, for each of 800 rows, we perform a table scan of 800 rows; hence $800 \times 800 = 640,000$—a classic nested table scans solution and a real performance problem.

Creating an index on MANAGER_ID leads to the following more palatable execution plan:

```
Rows        Execution Plan
-------     ------------------------------------------------
      0     SELECT STATEMENT    HINT: CHOOSE
```

```
 800   CONNECT BY
   2      INDEX (RANGE SCAN) OF 'EMPLOYEES_MANAGER_IDX'
   1      TABLE ACCESS   (BY ROWID) OF 'EMPLOYEES'
 799      TABLE ACCESS   (BY ROWID) OF 'EMPLOYEES'
1599       INDEX (RANGE SCAN) OF
                       'EMPLOYEES_MANAGER_IDX'
```

Figure 9.11 shows the improvement in performance obtained by creating the index on MANAGER_ID.

> When performing a hierarchical query using the CONNECT BY operator, ensure that both the START WITH and CONNECT BY clauses can be resolved using an index.

We may often wish to retrieve a subset of a hierarchy. For instance, to print the employee hierarchy only for a specific department, we might add a WHERE condition:

```
SELECT RPAD (' ', LEVEL * 3) || surname employee
  FROM employees
 WHERE department_id = (SELECT department_id
                          FROM departments
                         WHERE department_name =
                               'Compiler products')
 START WITH manager_id = 0
 CONNECT BY PRIOR employee_id = manager_id
```

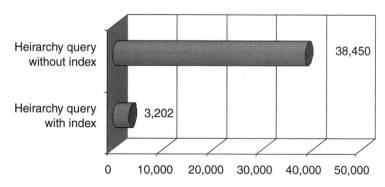

FIGURE 9.11 Improvements gained by supporting index on the CONNECT BY and START WITH clauses.

Unfortunately, Oracle builds the hierarchy before eliminating rows using the WHERE clause. In other words, the START WITH and CONNECT BY clauses are processed before the WHERE clause.

Provided that employees don't manage people outside their own department, we can get the same results, at a much reduced cost, by changing the START WITH clause so that we begin our join with the manager of the appropriate department:

```
SELECT RPAD (' ', LEVEL * 3) || surname employee
  FROM employees
 START WITH manager_id = (SELECT manager_id
                            FROM departments
                           WHERE department_name =
                                 'Compiler products')
CONNECT BY PRIOR employee_id = manager_id
```

The WHERE clause eliminates rows only after the entire hierarchy has been built and is less efficient than the START WITH clause. Figure 9.12 shows the performance improvements gained for our sample query.

If selecting only part of a hierarchy, eliminate rows using the START WITH clause rather than the WHERE clause. The WHERE clause will be processed only after the entire hierarchy has been built.

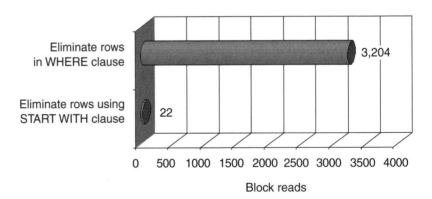

FIGURE 9.12 Improving the performance of a hierarchical query by moving the selection criteria from the WHERE clause to the START WITH clause.

Although the tuning of a simple hierarchical query is relatively straightforward, hierarchical queries have certain limitations that can affect the performance of any complex queries involving a hierarchical query.

A SELECT statement that includes a hierarchical query cannot include a join, nor can it include a subquery. As a result, if you try to include a hierarchical query within a more complex query, your options for tuning such a query become limited. You should therefore avoid placing hierarchical queries within subqueries and remember that they cannot themselves include subqueries or joins.

PARTITIONWISE JOINS

A partitionwise join can occur when two tables that share the same partitioning method are joined. Effectively, the partitionwise join allows the join to be processed as the aggregate of joins between individual partitions. This approach enhances the parallel processing of joins between very large tables. Partitionwise joins are discussed in more detail in Chapter 11.

SUBQUERIES

As described in Chapter 3, a subquery is a SELECT statement contained within another SQL statement. The other SQL statement, sometimes called the outer or parent statement, can be another SELECT statement, a DML statement (DELETE, INSERT or UPDATE), or a DDL statement (such as CREATE TABLE).

SIMPLE SUBQUERIES

A simple subquery is one that makes no reference to the parent query. In the case of a simple subquery, both the parent and child query are complete in themselves and could actually be executed independently. For instance, the following query returns the number of employees who share the honor of having the lowest salary in the firm:

```
SELECT COUNT (*)
  FROM employees
 WHERE salary = (SELECT MIN (salary)
                   FROM employees)
```

Such a query could easily be executed using the parent and the subquery separately:

```
SELECT MIN (salary)
  INTO :minsal
  FROM employees;
SELECT COUNT (*)
  FROM employees
 WHERE salary = :minsal;
```

It follows that since each subquery is executed independently, each can be optimized independently. For example, we would optimize the join query by first optimizing the query to find the minimum salary, and then optimize the query to find the count of a given salary. The obvious way to optimize each would be to create an index on the salary column. The optimization of simple subqueries is therefore relatively straightforward—optimize parent and child statements separately.

Although subqueries are often the best or only way of formulating a specific operation within a single SQL statement, they often require more resources than are absolutely necessary. For instance, our example subquery results in the following execution plan:

```
Rows        Execution Plan
-------     ------------------------------------------------
      0     SELECT STATEMENT    HINT: CHOOSE
      0      SORT (AGGREGATE) --Count the employees
    800       FILTER   --Find employees with that salary
    800        TABLE ACCESS (FULL) OF 'EMPLOYEES'
    800        SORT (AGGREGATE)   --Get the lowest salary
    800         TABLE ACCESS (FULL) OF 'EMPLOYEES'
```

As we might expect, two full-table scans of the EMPLOYEES table are required: one to find the maximum salary and another to get those employees with that salary. Without adding an index, it's hard to avoid these full-table scans using a single SQL statement. However, using PL/SQL, we can query the table only once:

```
DECLARE
   -- Query to retrieve employees in order of salary
   CURSOR emp_csr
   IS
      SELECT employee_id, surname, firstname,
             date_of_birth, salary
        FROM employees
       ORDER BY salary;
```

```
        last_salary   employees.salary%TYPE;
              -- Keep track of previous salary
        counter       NUMBER := 0;
              -- Count the number of rows
    BEGIN
      FOR emp_row IN emp_csr
      LOOP
        --
        -- Exit the loop if the salary is greater
        -- than the previous salary
        --
        EXIT WHEN counter > 0
              AND emp_row.salary > last_salary;
        -- Update the counter
        counter := counter + 1;
        -- save the salary
        last_salary := emp_row.salary;
      END LOOP;
      :min_salary_count := counter;
      -- Count of the lowest paid employees
    END;
```

With this approach, we scan the EMPLOYEES table only once. Furthermore, we stop fetching rows once we hit an employee on more than the minimum wage. This further reduces I/O and network traffic. Figure 9.13 shows the substantial improvement gained by using the PL/SQL approach.

Although the PL/SQL approach is a substantial improvement, the best results can be obtained if we create an index on salary. This changes the execution plan to two relatively inexpensive index lookups:

```
Rows      Execution Plan
-------   -------------------------------------------
    0     SELECT STATEMENT    HINT: CHOOSE
    0      SORT (AGGREGATE)
    2       INDEX (RANGE SCAN) OF 'EMPLOYEE_SAL_IDX'
    1        SORT (AGGREGATE)
    1         INDEX (RANGE SCAN) OF 'EMPLOYEE_SAL_IDX'
```

Using an index on salary also improves the performance of the PL/SQL approach. As Figure 9.13 shows, the PL/SQL approach requires only three I/Os, while the indexed SQL query requires four I/Os.

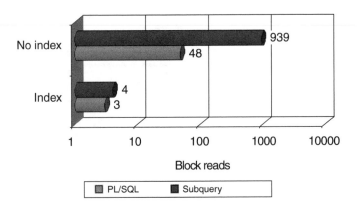

FIGURE 9.13 Performance of a correlated subquery and a PL/SQL alternative, with and without an index. (Note logarithmic scale: Each axis mark is 10 times the previous mark.)

SUBQUERIES WITH THE IN OPERATOR

Subqueries involving the IN operator are very common. They allow a result set to be returned from the child query and joined to the parent query. For instance, the following query returns the count of all customers who appear to be employees:

```
SELECT COUNT (*)
  FROM customers
 WHERE (contact_surname, contact_firstname,
        date_of_birth)
    IN (SELECT surname, firstname, date_of_birth
          FROM employees)
```

Most subqueries using the IN clause can be reformulated as a join. For instance, the following join will return the same rows as the previous example:

```
SELECT COUNT (*)
  FROM customers c, employees e
 WHERE c.contact_surname = e.surname
   AND c.contact_firstname = e.firstname
   AND c.date_of_birth = e.date_of_birth
```

Oracle will sometimes automatically transform a subquery containing the IN clause to the corresponding join statement, particularly if the join columns correspond to a unique or primary key.

If an IN subquery is not transformed to a join, Oracle will execute the subquery and create a temporary table based on the subquery. This temporary table will then be joined to the parent query, probably using a sort-merge join. For instance, our preceding subquery example resulted in the following execution plan:

```
Execution Plan
-----------------------------------------------------------
0        SELECT STATEMENT Optimizer=CHOOSE
1     0    SORT (AGGREGATE)
2     1      NESTED LOOPS
3     2        VIEW <- temporary table created
4     3          SORT (UNIQUE)
5     4            TABLE ACCESS (FULL) OF 'EMPLOYEES'
6     2          INDEX (RANGE SCAN) OF
                   'SURNAME_FIRSTNAME_DOB'
```

If you recode the same query as a join—or if Oracle transforms it into a join—then it is possible to use indexes that may exist on the table referenced in the subquery. Remember that in the subquery approach, a temporary table is created and this temporary table will have no indexes. As a join, we also have access to the more efficient hash-join algorithm.

When our query was reformulated as a join, we had the following execution plan:

```
Execution Plan
-----------------------------------------------------------
0        SELECT STATEMENT Optimizer=CHOOSE
1     0    SORT (AGGREGATE)
2     1      NESTED LOOPS
3     2        TABLE ACCESS (FULL) OF 'EMPLOYEES'
4     2        INDEX (RANGE SCAN) OF
                 'SURNAME_FIRSTNAME_DOB'
```

It's also possible for IN subqueries to be resolved using the semijoin algorithm. This depends on the settings for ALWAYS_SEMI_JOIN and on hints you can embed in the subquery. Semijoins are discussed in detail later in this chapter.

CORRELATED SUBQUERIES

A correlated subquery is one in which the child query is executed once for every row returned by the parent query. For instance, the following subquery finds employees with the highest salary within each department. To do this, it executes the subquery (get highest salary for a department) for every row in the parent query:

```
SELECT department_id, employee_id, surname, firstname
  FROM employees e1   -- Note "e1" alias
 WHERE salary =
      (SELECT  -- subquery executed once per employee
                  MAX (salary)
                FROM employees
          WHERE department_id = e1.department_id)
```

Because the subquery must be executed many times, it is essential that it be able to execute efficiently. This almost always means creating an appropriate index to support the subquery. With the default indexes on the EMPLOYEES table, we get the following execution plan:

```
Rows        Execution Plan
-------     ----------------------------------------------
      0     SELECT STATEMENT    HINT: CHOOSE
    800      FILTER
    800       TABLE ACCESS (FULL) OF 'EMPLOYEES'
  97789       SORT (AGGREGATE)
 497600        TABLE ACCESS (FULL) OF 'EMPLOYEES'
```

We can see that the execution plan is very expensive. We process almost 500,000 employee rows, although the table only contains approximately 800 rows. The high row count is because we are executing the subquery 800 times, performing a full-table scan of the table each time.

Clearly, we need to try and avoid the full-table scan within the subquery. If we create an index on DEPARTMENT_ID, we get the following execution plan:

```
Rows        Execution Plan
-------     ----------------------------------------------
      0     SELECT STATEMENT    HINT: CHOOSE
    800      FILTER
    800       TABLE ACCESS (FULL) OF 'EMPLOYEES'
  97789       SORT (AGGREGATE)
  97789        TABLE ACCESS (BY ROWID) OF 'EMPLOYEES'
  98410         INDEX (RANGE SCAN) OF 'DEPARTMENT_IDX'
```

We now use an index to retrieve employees for the appropriate department but still have to read each matching table row to retrieve the maximum salary. As a result, we've actually made matters worse (see Figure 9.14). However, if we create an index on DEPARTMENT_ID and salary, we get the following execution plan:

```
Rows        Execution Plan
-------     ----------------------------------------------
      0     SELECT STATEMENT    HINT: CHOOSE
```

```
   800   FILTER
   800    TABLE ACCESS (FULL) OF 'EMPLOYEES'
 97789    SORT (AGGREGATE)
 98410     INDEX (RANGE SCAN) OF 'DEPARTMENT_SAL_IDX'
```

We can now satisfy the subquery by index alone. Figure 9.14 shows the substantial improvement in I/O obtained.

For a correlated subquery, ensure that the subquery is completely optimized. If possible, allow the subquery to be resolved by a direct index lookup without a table access.

Using PL/SQL in place of correlated subqueries   We probably can't improve this query further using a single SQL statement, but it is possible to retrieve these rows even faster using PL/SQL. The approach is similar to that used for the simple subquery that found the employees with the minimum salary:

```
DECLARE
    -- Cursor to retrieve employees in department and
    -- descending salary order
    CURSOR emp_csr
    IS
        SELECT department_id, surname
          FROM employees
         ORDER BY department_id, salary desc;
```

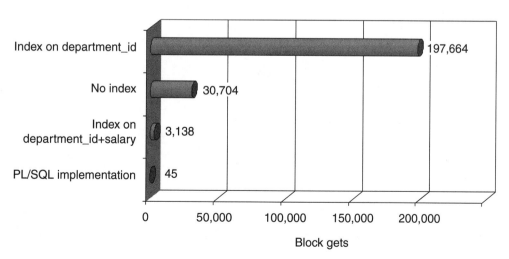

FIGURE 9.14   The effect of various indexes on a correlated subquery and a PL/SQL alternative.

```
        last_department_id
                employees.department_id%TYPE;
    counter                          NUMBER := 0;
BEGIN
    FOR emp_row IN emp_csr
    LOOP
        IF counter = 0 OR
            emp_row.department_id != last_department_id
        THEN
            -- The department id has changed, so output
            -- the employee name
            -- This will be the highest paid employee in
            -- the department
            dbms_output.put_line (TO_CHAR
                (emp_row.department_id) || ' ' ||
                emp_row.surname);
        END IF;

        -- Remember the last department_id
        last_department_id := emp_row.department_id;
        counter := counter + 1;
    END LOOP;
END;
```

Using this approach, we simply move once through the employees table in department and descending salary order. The first row for any department will be the employee with the highest salary for that department. Note that this PL/SQL doesn't cope with the case when two employees in a department both have the highest salary, but it could easily be amended to do so.

Using this approach, our I/O is down to its theoretical minimum—and we didn't need to use the index! Figure 9.14 compares the performance of this approach with subquery-based solutions.

The tkprof output now looks like this:

```
Rows       Execution Plan
-------    -------------------------------------------
      0    SELECT STATEMENT    HINT: CHOOSE
    800      SORT (ORDER BY)
    800        TABLE ACCESS (FULL) OF 'EMPLOYEES'
```

Correlated subqueries can often be more efficiently executed using a procedural approach, perhaps by using PL/SQL.

Correlated subqueries using EXISTS EXISTS is a special operator used only in subqueries and almost always in correlated subqueries. The EXISTS operator returns TRUE if the subquery returns one or more rows and FALSE otherwise. For instance, the following query uses the EXISTS operator to return department details only for departments with employees:

```
SELECT *
  FROM departments
 WHERE EXISTS
       (SELECT *
          FROM employees
         WHERE department_id = departments.department_id)
```

The principles for optimizing an SQL statement containing an EXISTS subquery are fundamentally the same as that for any correlated subquery: Optimize the execution of the subquery's SQL. As with previous examples, this optimization usually involves creating an appropriate index on the columns referenced in the subquery.

If you have an EXISTS subquery that cannot be optimized to use an index, you should ensure that it uses the semijoin optimization introduced in Oracle8. This is discussed in the section titled "Semijoins" later in this chapter.

Without an index on EMPLOYEES.DEPARTMENT_ID (and if semijoins are disabled), we get the following execution plan (note the 15,700 employee rows):

```
Rows      Execution Plan
-------   -----------------------------------------------
      0   SELECT STATEMENT    HINT: CHOOSE
     51    FILTER
     51     TABLE ACCESS (FULL) OF 'DEPARTMENTS'
  15700     TABLE ACCESS (FULL) OF 'EMPLOYEES'
```

If an index on employees.department_id is created, the execution plan changes (note only 51 rows accessed from our new index):

```
Rows      Execution Plan
-------   -----------------------------------------------
      0   SELECT STATEMENT    HINT: CHOOSE
     51    FILTER
     51     TABLE ACCESS (FULL) OF 'DEPARTMENTS'
     51     INDEX (RANGE SCAN) OF 'EMPLOYEE_DEPT_IDX'
```

When to use EXISTS Sometimes using the EXISTS operator is the only way to express a complex query. However, most other queries using EXISTS can

When using EXISTS, either ensure that the subquery can be executed efficiently (or use a semijoin optimization). Ideally, the subquery should be able to be satisfied using an index lookup only.

be reformulated as either a subquery using IN or a join. For instance, the following two statements are equivalent to our previous EXISTS example:

```
SELECT *
  FROM departments
 WHERE department_id
     IN (SELECT DISTINCT department_id
            FROM employees);

SELECT DISTINCT d.*
  FROM departments d, employees e
 WHERE d.department_id = e.department_id;
```

When deciding between basing your query on an EXISTS subquery or an IN subquery, consider the fundamental differences between the two approaches:

❏ An IN subquery is only executed once, while an EXISTS subquery is executed once per row of parent query.

❏ An IN subquery might not be able to take advantage of indexes on the subquery table, while EXISTS can.

❏ An EXISTS subquery can't take advantage of indexes in the parent query, while IN can.

❏ The optimizer will sometimes automatically translate IN-based subqueries into joins.

❏ The semijoin optimization (described in detail later in this chapter) can be used to provide an EXISTS-based subquery that cannot use an index with the performance of an equivalent IN-based subquery.

Table 9.3 compares the costs and benefits of the EXISTS and IN approaches for some typical scenarios.

Our example query is a good candidate for using EXISTS. The full-table scan of DEPARTMENTS is acceptable and unavoidable, and the DEPARTMENT_ID lookup in employees is supported by an index. The EXISTS formulation outperforms our alternative IN and join solutions, as shown in Figure 9.15. However, many queries that work well with the IN operator will suffer drastic performance degradation if recoded with EXISTS, so use EXISTS with caution.

TABLE 9.3   Deciding between IN and EXISTS subqueries

SITUATION	USE EXISTS?	USE IN?
There is an index available to support the execution of the subquery.	Yes.	Yes.
There is no index available to support the subquery.	No. Each execution of the subquery will require a table scan. Use a semijoin optimization if necessary.	Yes. The subquery is only executed once, so a scan may be acceptable.
The subquery returns a large number of rows.	Possibly not. EXISTS will retrieve these rows once for every row in the parent query. Use a semijoin optimization if necessary.	Yes. The subquery is only executed once, so retrieving large numbers of rows may be acceptable.
The subquery returns only one or a few rows.	Yes. The smaller the result set and subquery overhead, the more suitable EXISTS will be.	Yes, if indicated by other factors.
Most of the parent rows are eliminated by the subquery.	Possibly not. Since EXISTS will execute for every row in the parent query, the overhead will be high if only a minority of rows are eventually returned.	Yes. Since the subquery is executed only once, the parent rows will be eliminated efficiently.
There is an index in the parent column(s) that matches the subquery column(s).	Possibly not. EXISTS won't be able to take advantage of the index.	Yes. The IN subquery can use the index.

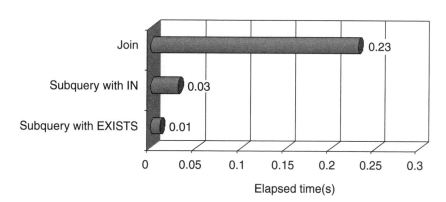

FIGURE 9.15   Performance of an EXISTS subquery versus an equivalent IN subquery and a join.

SEMIJOINS

Semijoins allow Oracle to optimize efficiently queries that include an EXISTS sub-query but that don't have an index to support efficient execution of the subquery. As we saw in the preceding section, these types of queries can perform badly if there is no supporting index because the EXISTS clause causes the subquery to be executed once for each row returned by the parent query. If the subquery involves a table scan or inefficient index scan, then performance will be poor. Without the semijoin optimization, the solution is either to create a supporting index or recode the statement as a join or as a subquery using the IN operator.

The semijoin method allows Oracle to transparently convert the EXISTS subquery into a join. The join is called a semijoin because unlike a regular join, only a single row will be returned from the driving table even if there are multiple matching rows in the join table.

Consider the following query, which attempts to select only those customers who are also employees:

```
SELECT contact_surname,contact_firstname,date_of_birth
  FROM customers c
 WHERE EXISTS
       (SELECT 1 from employees e
          WHERE e.surname=c.contact_surname
            AND e.firstname=c.contact_firstname
            AND e.date_of_birth=c.date_of_birth)
```

If there is no (surname, firstname, data_of_birth) index on employees, then Oracle will (by default) resolve the query as follows:

❑ Perform a full-table scan on customers.
❑ For each row retrieved from customers, perform a full-table scan on employees to search for a matching person. If a match is found, place the customers row in the result set.

As we saw in the preceding section, this algorithm can have disastrous performance implications if there is no supporting index. If there are 100,000 customers, then 100,000 scans of the employees table will result. As we can see from the following tkprof output, the unindexed EXISTS resulted in the processing of 80,000,000 employee rows (100,000 customers × 800 employees):

```
Rows      Execution Plan
-------   --------------------------------------------
      0   SELECT STATEMENT
 100000     FILTER
```

```
   100000    TABLE ACCESS    (FULL)  OF  'CUSTOMERS'
 80100000    TABLE ACCESS    (FULL)  OF  'EMPLOYEES`
```

We can persuade Oracle to use the semijoin algorithm by adding a MERGE_SJ hint to the query:

```
SELECT contact_surname,contact_firstname,date_of_birth
  FROM customers c
 WHERE EXISTS
        (SELECT /*+merge_sj*/ 1 FROM employees e
          WHERE e.surname||''=c.contact_surname
            AND e.firstname=c.contact_firstname
            AND e.date_of_birth=c.date_of_birth)
```

The tkprof explain plan now shows that each table is subject to only a single table scan. Note that the "MERGE JOIN (SEMI)" operation is shown in the explain plan:

```
Rows        Execution Plan
-------     ------------------------------------------------
      0     SELECT STATEMENT    GOAL: CHOOSE
      0     MERGE JOIN (SEMI)
  99928       SORT (JOIN)
  99928         TABLE ACCESS  (FULL) OF 'CUSTOMERS'
    800       SORT (UNIQUE)
    800         TABLE ACCESS  (FULL) OF 'EMPLOYEES'
```

Figure 9.16 shows the performance improvements gained by using the semijoin hint. Also shown is the performance of an EXISTS query, which had a supporting index, and of an equivalent statement using the IN operator. Note the logarithmic scale of Figure 9.16—each X-axis point is 10 times the previous mark.

Figure 9.16 shows that the semijoin hint can result in a dramatic improvement over an unindexed semijoin (down from 22 minutes to 7 seconds) and a substantial improvement over an EXISTS query that is supported by an appropriate index. The performance of the semijoin is equivalent to that of the corresponding IN-based subquery.

You can invoke a semijoin by adding the HASH_SJ (hash-join-based semijoin) or MERGE_SJ (sort-merge-based semijoin) to the EXISTS subquery. Alternately, you can set the configuration ("init.ora") parameter ALWAYS_SEMI_JOIN to HASH or MERGE. But be aware that if you set ALWAYS_SEMI_JOIN, it will change the execution plan both of EXISTS subqueries that don't have supporting indexes and also of subqueries that do have supporting indexes. There is a chance that the performance of the already optimized (e.g., supported by an index) subqueries will suffer slightly if ALWAYS_SEMI_JOIN is set. Setting

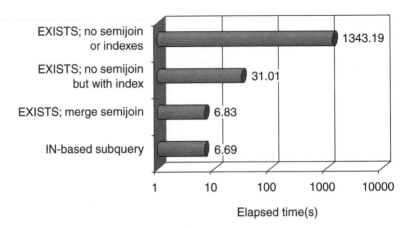

FIGURE 9.16 Semijoin performance improvements (note logarithmic scale).

ALWAYS_SEMI_JOIN can also cause IN-based subqueries to use the semijoin method.

In general, the cost of a badly formed EXISTS query is much greater than the slight degradation that may or may not occur to optimized EXISTS queries if they employ the semijoin algorithm. For this reason, it is usually safer to set ALWAYS_SEMI_JOIN to HASH or MERGE unless you are sure that all your EXISTS subqueries are fully optimized.

If you have an exists subquery without a supporting index, use the HASH_SJ or MERGE_SJ hints to resolve the query as a semijoin. You can also use the ALWAYS_ SEMI_JOIN configuration parameter, but this could have a slight negative effect for some indexed EXISTS subqueries.

ANTIJOINS

An antijoin is a query that returns rows in one table that do not match some set of rows from another table. Since this is effectively the opposite of normal join behavior, the term antijoin has been used to describe this operation. Antijoins are usually expressed using a subquery, although there are alternative formulations, as we will see.

ANTIJOIN WITH NOT IN

Perhaps the most natural and commonly used method for expressing the antijoin is to use the IN operator together with the NOT operator. For instance, the following query returns all employees who are not customers:

```
SELECT surname, firstname, date_of_birth
  FROM employees
 WHERE (surname, firstname, date_of_birth)
       NOT IN (SELECT contact_surname,
                      contact_firstname,
                      date_of_birth
                 FROM customers)
```

Although it is natural to express the antijoin using NOT IN, this type of query is executed inefficiently by the rule-based optimizer. In our example, the rule-based optimizer will undertake a full-table scan of customers for each row in employees. If a matching row is not found, then the employee row is returned. The rule-based optimizer doesn't use any indexes on CUSTOMERS because there is no WHERE clause in the subquery. The execution plan looks like this:

```
Rows        Execution Plan
-------     -------------------------------------------
       0    SELECT STATEMENT    GOAL: HINT: RULE
     800     FILTER
     800      TABLE ACCESS   (FULL) OF 'EMPLOYEES'
80000000      TABLE ACCESS   (FULL) OF 'CUSTOMERS'
```

Since there are 800 rows in employees and over 100,000 rows in customers, we end up processing 80 million (800 × 100,000) customer rows.

Luckily, the cost-based optimizer is clever enough to take advantage of indexes on the CUSTOMERS table and can avoid the unacceptable nested table scans. The cost-based optimizer's execution of the above query looks like this:

```
Rows        Execution Plan
-------     -------------------------------------------
       0    SELECT STATEMENT    GOAL: CHOOSE
     800     FILTER
     800      TABLE ACCESS   (FULL) OF 'EMPLOYEES'
     800      INDEX (RANGE SCAN) OF SURNAME_FIRSTNAME_DOB'
```

This is much more efficient. The rule-based optimizer requires almost 1 million block reads to resolve our example, whereas the cost-based optimizer only requires 6430 block reads. The rule-based optimizer does not handle NOT IN subqueries efficiently. If using rule-based optimization, use another antijoin method, such as NOT EXISTS, which we discuss next.

ANTIJOIN WITH NOT EXISTS

Our query to return all employees who are not customers could be formulated using NOT EXISTS rather than NOT IN:

```
SELECT surname, firstname, date_of_birth
  FROM employees
 WHERE NOT EXISTS
       (SELECT *
          FROM customers
         WHERE contact_surname = employees.surname
           AND contact_firstname = employees.firstname
           AND date_of_birth = employees.date_of_birth)
```

Using this style of query, we tell the optimizer to search for a matching row in customers for each row in employees. Since there is a WHERE clause in the subquery, even the rule-based optimizer can use available indexes. Both optimizers choose a plan like the following (although the rule-based optimizer may choose a different index if more than one is available):

```
Rows      Execution Plan
-------   --------------------------------------------------
      0   SELECT STATEMENT   GOAL: CHOOSE
    800    FILTER
    800     TABLE ACCESS(FULL) OF 'EMPLOYEES'
    800     INDEX (RANGE SCAN) OF 'SURNAME_FIRSTNAME_DOB'
```

We can see that this plan is virtually identical to the cost-based optimizer's plan for the NOT IN method. The cost-based optimizer treats NOT IN and NOT EXISTS equivalently. However, the rule-based optimizer will usually perform NOT EXISTS queries more efficiently than NOT IN queries.

If using rule-based optimization, avoid using NOT IN to perform an antijoin. Use NOT EXISTS instead.

ANTIJOIN USING MINUS

Another less common method of performing an antijoin is to use the MINUS operator. The MINUS operator returns all rows from one result set except those found in another result set. At first glance, MINUS would seem to be tailormade for the antijoin. However, there is a limitation: Each of the result sets must be identical with regard to the number and type of columns in each result set.

In the case of our antijoin example, a MINUS operation will work. For instance, the following query returns the same rows as our NOT IN and NOT EXISTS subqueries:

```
SELECT surname, firstname, date_of_birth
  FROM employees
MINUS
    SELECT contact_surname, contact_firstname,
           date_of_birth
      FROM customers
```

```
Rows      Execution Plan
-------   ------------------------------------------------
      0   SELECT STATEMENT    GOAL: CHOOSE
 100795   MINUS
    800     SORT (UNIQUE)
    800      TABLE ACCESS (FULL) OF 'EMPLOYEES'
 100000     SORT (UNIQUE)
 100000      TABLE ACCESS (FULL) OF 'CUSTOMERS'
```

Although the MINUS operation does not use an index, it actually gives us the best result of all the examples we have considered so far (see Figure 9.17). Of course, the optimal approach depends on the nature of the query and of the data, but the MINUS approach is worth considering if the number and types of columns are suitable. Remember, we could not use the MINUS method to retrieve employee_id because the number and types of columns in each query would not match:

```
SELECT surname, firstname, date_of_birth, employee_id
  FROM employees
MINUS
    SELECT contact_surname, contact_firstname,
           date_of_birth
      FROM customers
```

```
ORA-01789: query block has incorrect number of result
columns
```

The MINUS operator can be used to perform an antijoin efficiently. However, there are restrictions on the columns that can be returned in the query.

ANTIJOIN USING THE OUTER JOIN

Yet another way of implementing the antijoin operation is as an outer join. An outer join includes NULL for rows in the inner table that have no match in the outer table. We can use this feature to include only rows that have no match in the inner table. We could express our antijoin as an outer join as follows:

```
SELECT e.surname, e.firstname, e.date_of_birth
  FROM employees e, customers c
 WHERE c.contact_surname (+) = e.surname
   AND c.contact_firstname (+) = e.firstname
   AND c.date_of_birth (+) = e.date_of_birth
   AND c.contact_surname IS NULL
```

This approach leads to an execution profile very similar to that of the MINUS method and slightly more efficient than the NOT EXISTS and NOT IN methods.

```
Rows      Execution Plan
-------   ------------------------------------------------
      0   SELECT STATEMENT    GOAL: CHOOSE
    800    FILTER
      0     NESTED LOOPS (OUTER)
    800      TABLE ACCESS (FULL) OF 'EMPLOYEES'
    800      INDEX (RANGE SCAN) OF
                  'SURNAME_FIRSTNAME_DOB' (NON-UNIQUE)
```

USING THE ANTIJOIN HINTS

Because antijoins were frequently causes of poor performance, and because there was such a bewildering number of alternative measures for optimizing the antijoin, Oracle introduced specific hints for the antijoin in Oracle 7.3. These hints allow an antijoin using the NOT IN format to be performed using either sort-merge or hash-join techniques. The hints involved are HASH_AJ or MERGE_AJ and they must appear in a NOT IN subquery. For instance, the following query will use a hash-join-based antijoin:

```
SELECT surname,
       firstname,
       date_of_birth
  FROM employees
 WHERE (surname, firstname, date_of_birth) NOT IN
          (SELECT   /*+ HASH_AJ */contact_surname,
                    contact_firstname, date_of_birth
             FROM customers)
```

The HASH_AJ hint resulted in the following execution plan:

```
Rows         Execution Plan
-------      -----------------------------------------------
      0      SELECT STATEMENT    GOAL: CHOOSE
  28009       HASH JOIN (ANTI)
    800        TABLE ACCESS (FULL) OF 'EMPLOYEES'
 100000        VIEW
 100000         TABLE ACCESS (FULL) OF 'CUSTOMERS'
```

Performance from the hash antijoin was dramatically better than that for any other method we have tried. On the other hand, the MERGE_AJ hint resulted in performance that was only slightly better than the cost-based optimizer's default behavior. Figure 9.17 compares all the techniques.

To take advantage of Oracle's antijoin optimizations, the following must be true:

❑ Cost-based optimization must be enabled.
❑ The antijoin columns used must not be NULL. This either means that they are not NULL in the table definition or an IS NOT NULL clause appears in the query for all the relevant columns.
❑ The subquery is not correlated.
❑ The parent query does not contain an OR clause.
❑ The database parameter ALWAYS_ANTI_JOIN is set to either MERGE or HASH or a MERGE_AJ or HASH_AJ hint appears within the subquery.

COMPARISON OF ANTIJOIN TECHNIQUES

Figure 9.17 compares the performance of the antijoin methods we have discussed. Note that the scale of the chart is logarithmic, which means that each mark on the X-axis is 10 times the value of the previous mark.

The clear winner—at least for our example—is the hash antijoin. The clear loser is the NOT IN antijoin using rule-based optimization.

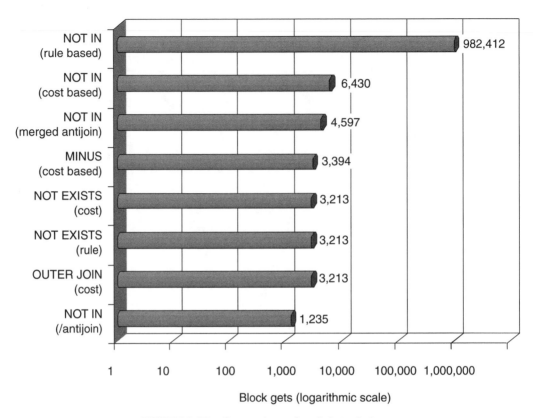

Block gets (logarithmic scale)

FIGURE 9.17   Comparison of antijoin techniques.

When you want to retrieve all rows in a table except those not found in another table (an antijoin), try to take advantage of Oracle's antijoin hints. Otherwise (if using rule-based optimization), use NOT EXISTS subqueries in preference to NOT IN subqueries.

SUMMARY

Joins are a fundamental operation that must be efficient if your SQL is to perform to requirements. Oracle provides three types of join operations:

❑   The nested loops join, which is suitable for joins of small subsets of tables where there is a supporting index. The cost-based optimizer will tend to favor this join when the optimizer goal is "FIRST_ROWS."

❏ The merge join, which sorts and merges result sets and is suitable when larger subsets of a table's data are being joined. The cost-based optimizer will tend to favor this join when the optimizer goal is "ALL_ROWS."

❏ The hash join, which requires the cost-based optimizer and Oracle 7.3 or higher. This join is suitable in most circumstances where a sort-merge join can be used and is particularly efficient for large tables where one table is larger than the other. However, you will often have to use a USE_HASH hint to get this join method.

The optimal join order can be difficult to determine when many tables are involved, but some fundamental considerations are as follows:

❏ Pick the table with the most selective WHERE condition, as the first or driving table.

❏ If there are no selective conditions in the WHERE clause, note that both nested loops and hash joins work best when joining a larger table to a smaller table.

❏ Ensure that all subsequent joins are efficient. This may mean creating an index to support a nested loops operation or forcing a hash join with the USE_HASH hint.

You can use the hints USE_MERGE, USE_NL, USE_HASH, and ORDERED to force the optimizer to use a particular join approach.

Hash joins can respond favorably to adjustments to the HASH_AREA_SIZE and HASH_MULTIBLOCK_IO_COUNT parameters. These parameters can be adjusted with an ALTER SESSION statement.

Index clusters allow more rows from two or more tables to be stored together based on a common key. Such tables can be thought of as prejoined. Using clusters does improve join performance, but other operations, such as full-table scans, can be severely degraded.

Outer joins, when used inappropriately, can restrict possible join order and sometimes degrade join performance. Only use the outer join if you are sure it is necessary.

Hierarchical self-joins using the CONNECT BY operator may perform poorly unless there are indexes to support the CONNECT BY and START WITH clauses. If you wish to extract only a subset of the hierarchy, try to do this by placing a condition in the START WITH rather than the WHERE clause.

STAR queries are common in data warehouses and involve a large central fact table joined to a number of unrelated dimension tables. The rule-based optimizer will generally perform STAR queries poorly. Although the cost-based optimizer does a better job, using the STAR hint can improve the performance of these types of queries remarkably. If you have (or can have) bitmap indexes on your fact table and have to support a large number of possible join combinations, the STAR_TRANSFORMATION method is worth considering.

Subqueries are related to joins in that they too can relate rows from multiple tables. Simple, uncorrelated subqueries can be enhanced by optimizing each of the component queries independently.

Subqueries using the IN and EXISTS operators provide similar functionality to the join operation. Some queries can be expressed using an IN subquery, an EXISTS subquery, or a join. Specific categories of queries and data distributions may benefit from different approaches. You may need to try each approach for individual queries.

Subqueries that are correlated to the parent query tend to be executed many times during statement execution. It is therefore important that these subqueries be able to execute quickly, preferably through a direct index lookup with no table access. If you have an EXISTS subquery that cannot be supported by an index, consider the semijoin hints (HASH_SJ and MERGE_SJ) or the ALWAYS_SEMI_ JOIN init.ora parameter.

A subquery combined with the NOT operator can perform the reverse logic of a join, returning only those rows from the parent query without a match in the subquery. Such antijoins are a definite problem for the rule-based optimizer if the IN operator is used. If using the rule-based optimizer, ensure that you create anti-joins with the EXISTS operator. Introduced in Oracle 7.3, the MERGE_AJ and HASH_AJ hints can be used to enhance antijoin performance. Using these hints can substantially improve antijoin performance.

SORTS, AGGREGATES, AND SET OPERATIONS

In this chapter, we look at improving the performance of SQL operations that require Oracle to order or group data.

Oracle may need to sort data as a result of an explicit request to return data in order (for instance, ORDER BY) or as a result of an internal intermediate operation that requires the data to be in sorted order (for instance, the INTERSECT operation). Sorts can consume significant computer resources and have a substantial effect on query performance. Knowing when Oracle performs sorts, ways of avoiding sorts, and how to optimize sorts is therefore useful when tuning SQL.

The GROUP BY operator aggregates rows with common values and returns a summary row for each group. Aggregate operations almost always involve sorting and have specific tuning requirements.

The set operations, UNION, INTERSECT, and MINUS, combine two or more result sets with the same number and types of columns into a single result set. Set operators usually involve sorts and are also discussed in this chapter.

The topics covered in this chapter are as follows:

- ❑ How and when Oracle performs sorts
- ❑ Performance problems that can be caused by sorts
- ❑ Avoiding accidental or unnecessary sorts

❑ Using and optimizing the GROUP BY clause and group function to aggregate data

❑ Using the set operators to combine or compare two result sets

❑ Alternatives to the MINUS and INTERSECT operators

SORT OPERATIONS

Sorting is one of the most fundamental operations undertaken by computers, especially in the field of data retrieval, and Oracle is no exception. The operations that may require Oracle to sort data are as follows:

❑ Creating an index

❑ Grouping or aggregating data via the GROUP BY or DISTINCT keywords

❑ Returning data in sorted order as a result of the ORDER BY clause

❑ Joining tables or result sets using the sort-merge method

❑ Using the set operators UNION, INTERSECT, or MINUS

❑ Performing certain subqueries

Sorting can require significant resources:

❑ CPU will always be consumed. The amount of CPU required is proportional to the size of the result set to be sorted.

❑ Oracle allocates an area of memory for the sort (primarily determined by the SORT_AREA_SIZE configuration parameter).

❑ If the area of memory is not sufficient for the sort to complete, Oracle allocates a temporary segment within a temporary tablespace. This is known as a disk sort. If a disk sort is required, there is the additional overhead of allocating space in the temporary segment and I/O to write and read back blocks from the temporary tablespace.

THE EFFECT OF SORT_AREA_SIZE

Disk sorts are much more expensive than in-memory sorts. The amount of memory allocated to sorts is controlled by the configuration parameter SORT_AREA_SIZE. This parameter can be adjusted for all sessions by changing the parameter in the configuration ("init.ora") file and can also be changed by an ALTER SESSION statement.

It is a common misconception that increasing SORT_AREA_SIZE will not improve sort performance unless the allocation is sufficient to avoid a disk sort. In fact, increasing sort area size will usually improve sort performance in two bursts.

Firstly, when SORT_AREA_SIZE is very low, increasing it will reduce the number of merge runs that will be required. Once SORT_AREA_SIZE reaches some threshold value, only a single merge run will be required and sort performance will hit a plateau. As SORT_AREA_SIZE increases, it will eventually reach a point at which the whole sort will fit into memory. A sudden increase in performance will be experienced, but after that improvement no further improvements will be observed.

Figure 10.1 shows the relationship between SORT_AREA_SIZE and response time for a sorted query of an 80,000-row, 6.5-MB table. Sort performance improved as SORT_AREA_SIZE increased from 32K to 128K. After that, no increases where experienced until the SORT_AREA_SIZE approached 5MB, after which no further improvements were experienced.

Increasing SORT_AREA_SIZE can reduce the chances that a disk sort will occur and—within certain ranges of values—can improve the performance of memory sorts.

THE SORT_AREA_RETAINED_SIZE PARAMETER

The SORT_AREA_RETAINED_SIZE parameter controls the amount of sort memory that is retained after the sort completes. You would be forgiven for thinking that this means that the memory goes back to the operating system, where it can

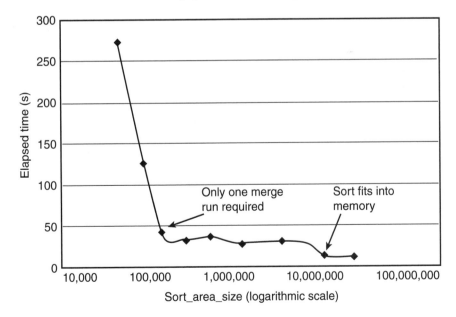

FIGURE 10.1 Effect of SORT_AREA_SIZE on sort performance.

be allocated to another user, but in fact it remains attached to your server process, where it can be used for other sorts or for other purposes. It will only truly be returned to the operating system when the session ends.[1] However, if you use multithreaded servers (MTS), then the memory can be used by other sessions that use the same server process.

In short, memory allocated for sorts never returns to the operating system until the session or multithreaded server terminates. Therefore, you need to be very careful about the setting of SORT_AREA_SIZE. If it is set too high, then you could cause a memory shortage on your system and cause heavy paging and swapping activity.

Setting a lower SORT_AREA_RETAINED_SIZE parameter does not cause sort memory to be released to the operating system. Make sure your setting for SORT_AREA_SIZE does not exceed the memory capacity of your system.

CONTENTION FOR DISK SORTS

When a disk sort occurs, Oracle must allocate storage in the temporary tablespace and perform physical disk I/Os to read and write to this tablespace. As well as slowing down the sort because of the relatively slower speeds of disk I/O when compared to memory operations, disk sorts can cause contention between sessions that access the temporary tablespace. There are a number of causes of this sort of contention:

❑ If your temporary tablespace is not truly temporary (that is, if it was not created with the TEMPORARY keyword) then sessions may contend for the space transaction lock, which is required whenever new extents are added to temporary segments. The solution is to apply the ALTER TABLESPACE tablespace_name TEMPORARY statement to the tablespace, which results in more efficient temporary segment allocation.

❑ Prior to Oracle 8i, the SORT_DIRECT_WRITES parameter allowed reads and writes from the temporary tablespace to bypass the buffer cache. If this facility was not enabled, contention for space in the buffer cache could cause free buffer waits, which could severely throttle sort throughput. Sort direct writes are always enabled in Oracle 8i.

❑ If the temporary tablepace is located on only a single disk device, it may cause that disk to become a bottleneck. Striping the temporary tablespace

---

[1]Oracle may actually free the excess memory, but because of the way operating systems work, the memory remains attached to the process and can only be made available to other processes if paged out by the operating system.

across multiple devices could be advisable (but don't use RAID 5 on heavily updated temporary tablespaces, because RAID 5 doubles write overhead).

These configuration issues will be revisited in Chapters 19 and 20.

If disk sorts are occurring, the configuration of the temporary tablespace and the database can be critical to ensure that contention for disk sort areas does not occur.

OPTIMIZER MODE AND SORTS

Because sort operations consume significant memory and CPU resources as well as database I/O, the cost-based optimizer has to make certain assumptions about the relative cost of these resources. For instance, the optimizer may have to perform a trade-off between I/O consumption and CPU consumption. The assumptions made by the cost-based optimizer may not be appropriate for your system and you will therefore sometimes need to override the cost-based optimizer's decisions.

If a sort is required to satisfy an ORDER BY clause, then all the rows must be accessed and sorted before the first row can be returned. Consequently, sort operations tend to result in poor response time, even if they deliver good throughput. For instance, imagine you want to return all the rows from a 100,000-row table in sorted order. For a batch report, you might be pleased if the rows were sorted in 10 seconds. However, if you are sitting in front of a customer inquiry screen, 10 seconds to return a single screen of data would be totally unacceptable! For these reasons, the cost-based optimizer tries to avoid sorts when the optimizer goal is set to FIRST_ROWS but favors sorts when the optimizer goal is set to ALL_ROWS. In other words, if there is an alternative to performing a sort (we'll consider some alternatives shortly) and the optimizer goal is FIRST_ROWS, Oracle is likely to choose the alternative path.

The cost-based optimizer will try to avoid sorting if the optimizer_mode=FIRST_ROWS.

UNNECESSARY SORTS

It's possible inadvertently to cause Oracle to perform a sort that you don't really require. This can happen for these reasons:

❑ Unnecessary use of the DISTINCT clause. The DISTINCT clause will almost always require a sort to eliminate duplicate rows. Some programmers like the DISTINCT clause so much that they use it in every select. Sadly, many client/server tools will also throw in a DISTINCT for good measure. Sometimes the DISTINCT clause is necessary and unavoidable, but bear in mind that it does have a sort overhead so use it only when necessary.

❏ Using UNION instead of UNION ALL. The UNION operator sorts the result set to eliminate any rows that are duplicated within the subqueries. UNION ALL includes duplicate rows and, as such, does not require a sort. Unless you require that these duplicate rows be eliminated, use UNION ALL.

❏ Performing sort-merge joins. As we saw in the previous chapter, the hash join is almost always a better choice than the sort-merge join and does not require a sort.

Don't use the DISTINCT operator unless you are sure that you need it. DISTINCT will usually perform a sort. Use UNION ALL in preference to UNION unless you really need to eliminate duplicates.

AVOIDING A SORT WITH AN INDEX

If an index exists with some or all of the columns in the ORDER BY clause, Oracle may use the index to fetch the rows in the required order and hence eliminate the sort operation. This can happen when:

❏ There is no WHERE clause that results in the use of a conflicting index.

❏ The columns to be sorted are not nullable (since NULL values won't appear in the index).

Oracle can read the rows in sorted order directly from the index provided that the index is on the same columns that appear in the ORDER BY clause. However, reading rows in key order requires a block-by-block full scan of the index, which is incompatible with the fast full scan described in Chapter 7. Although the fast full scan is much more efficient than the normal full-index scan, the fast full scan does not return rows in index order.

Although the use of an index may eliminate the need to perform a sort, the overhead of reading all the index blocks and all the table blocks may be greater than the overhead of performing the sort. However, using the index should result in a quicker retrieval of the first row since as soon as the row is retrieved it may be returned, whereas the sort approach will require that all rows be retrieved before the first row is returned. As a result, the cost-based optimizer will tend to use the index if the optimizer goal is FIRST_ROWS but will choose a full-table scan if the goal is ALL_ROWS.

A way of avoiding both sort and table lookup overhead is to create an index that contains all the columns in the select list as well as the columns in the ORDER BY clause. Oracle can then resolve the query via an index lookup alone. For instance, the following query will be optimized if there is an index on contact_surname, contact_firstname, date_of_birth and phoneno.

```
SELECT contact_surname, contact_firstname,
       date_of_birth, phoneno
  FROM customers c1
 ORDER BY contact_surname, contact_firstname,
          date_of_birth
```

Performance of the various methods is compared in Figure 10.2. Using an index to avoid a sort leads to vastly superior *response time* (time to retrieve the first row) but much poorer *throughput* (time to retrieve the last row).

Using an index to avoid a sort will generally lead to better response time (time to retrieve the first row) when retrieving rows in order. But such a plan will usually lead to much worse throughput (time to retrieve all rows).

EXPLOITING PARALLELISM

If rows have been retrieved from a full-table scan, Oracle can use the parallel query option to improve sort performance. Using the parallel query option effectively requires that certain conditions be met and that your database configuration

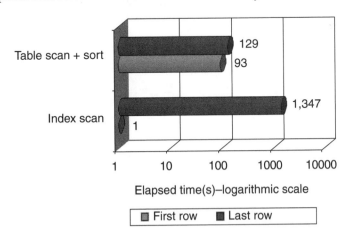

FIGURE10.2 Optimum sort plan can depend on whether you optimize for the first or last row.

is appropriate. We'll discuss these requirements and the parallel query option in detail in Chapter 12.

An operation that requires a sort may benefit from the parallel query option if

❑ The host has multiple CPUs.
❑ There is spare CPU capacity on the host.
❑ Data files are located on multiple physical disk devices (otherwise, the query may become I/O bound).

We'll discuss configuration and optimization of the parallel query option in Chapter 12. For now, bear in mind the following when contemplating paralleliz-ing a sort operation:

❑ Each sort process can allocate its own SORT_AREA_SIZE. This means that a query that normally requires a disk sort may avoid a disk sort when performed in parallel. There may, however, be an increase in memory requirements.
❑ If a disk sort is required, each sort process will allocate its own temporary segment in the temporary tablespace. This could result in contention, espe-cially in early versions of Oracle 7 (prior to 7.3).
❑ When using parallel query, there is a higher risk of degrading the perform-ance of the entire system with a single statement since a single statement may now use a greater proportion of CPU resources. Implement parallel query with care. Adjust the number of parallel query servers so that parallel operations are optimized without degrading the performance of the rest of the system.

When performing a sort based on a full-table scan, consider using the parallel query option to improve scan and sort performance, but watch for increased system overhead.

AGGREGATE OPERATIONS

Aggregate operations are those that use the GROUP BY clause or the group func-tions. Examples of the group functions are MAX, MIN, SUM, AVG, and COUNT. Each row returned by an aggregate operation summarizes data from multiple rows in the source data.

COUNTING THE ROWS IN A TABLE

One of the most common uses of an aggregate operation is the use of the COUNT function to count all the rows in a table. It's also subject to much rumor and misconception. Here are a few of the claims regarding row counting:

❑ When counting the number of rows in a table, use an index on a unique column. This will be faster since you can count the rows of the (usually) smaller index.

❑ When counting the number of rows in a table, use count(*). Oracle has some special optimizations for count(*).

❑ When counting the number of rows in a table, use count(0). By using a constant, you avoid having to read all the columns in the table.

Which is correct? It turns out that both the first and second suggestions have merit. If the size of a unique index is substantially smaller than the size of the table, then it can be quicker to count the rows using the index. In addition, Oracle does perform an optimization if the "count(*)" expression is encountered.

Consider counting all rows in the customers table using "COUNT(0)"; tkprof shows the following execution plan:

```
Rows      Execution Plan
-------   ---------------------------------------------
      0   SELECT STATEMENT    HINT: CHOOSE
   5151     SORT (AGGREGATE)       <-Note sort
   5151     TABLE ACCESS    HINT: ANALYZED (FULL) OF
'CUSTOMERS'
```

When using count(customer_id) and using the primary key index, we get the following execution plan:

```
Rows      Execution Plan
-------   ---------------------------------------------
      0   SELECT STATEMENT    HINT: CHOOSE
   5151     SORT (AGGREGATE)       <-Note sort
   5152     INDEX   (RANGE SCAN) OF 'PK_CUSTOMERS'
```

When we use "COUNT(*)" and a full-table scan, we get the following plan:

```
Rows      Execution Plan
-------   ---------------------------------------------
      0   SELECT STATEMENT    HINT: CHOOSE
      0     SORT (AGGREGATE)       <-No rows sorted!
   5151     TABLE ACCESS    (FULL) OF 'CUSTOMERS'
```

Note that although each execution plan shows a SORT (AGGREGATE) step, no rows are actually processed by the SORT associated with the count(*) method. This is the "special optimization"—Oracle will avoid a sort when you specify count(*).

Using an index to count the rows in a table has some merit: The index will be smaller than the table and most tables will have at least one index on a non-null column. However, reading all the rows in an index uses a less efficient mechanism than the full-table scan unless the fast full index scan is employed. We looked at the fast full scan in detail in Chapter 7, it is almost always the fastest way to count the rows in a table.

FINDING THE MAXIMUM OR MINIMUM VALUE

If you have an index on the column for which you are trying to locate the maximum or minimum value, then you can use that index to rapidly locate the value. In Oracle 8.0 and earlier, the execution plan may lead you to believe that a full scan of the index is taking place. For instance, the following execution plan was generated under Oracle 8.0.6:

```
SELECT MAX (salary)
  FROM employees


Rows    Execution Plan
------- -----------------------------------------------
      0  SELECT STATEMENT   GOAL: CHOOSE
      1   SORT (AGGREGATE)
      1    INDEX   (FULL SCAN) OF 'EMPLOYEE_SALARY_IDX'
```

A full-index scan might or might not be better than a full-table scan (remembering that a full-table scan can read multiple blocks in each I/O) but hardly seems the best course of action. Why can't Oracle simply go directly to the first or last leaf block to identify the highest or lowest value?

In fact, Oracle is indeed going directly to the maximum value in the preceding case. Note the row count of "1"—although the plan suggests that all the index entries are being read, in fact only the maximum value in the first leaf block is accessed.

The Oracle8i execution plan makes this clear:

```
Rows    Execution Plan
------- -----------------------------------------------
      0  SELECT STATEMENT    GOAL: CHOOSE
      1   SORT (AGGREGATE)
      1    INDEX (FULL SCAN (MIN/MAX)) OF
                'EMPLOYEE_SAL_IDX'
```

The full scan (min/max) step indicates that Oracle is going direct to the maximum or minimum value. This is vastly more efficient than performing a full-index or full-table scan.

> The fastest way to get the maximum or minimum value for a column is to have a B*-tree index on that column.

FINDING THE TOP 10

On Oracle newsgroups, common questions include "How do I get the top 10 rows in a table?" and "How do I find the second highest salary?" The solutions vary. Some are wrong, like this common mistake:

```
SELECT salary, employee_id
  FROM employees e
 WHERE ROWNUM <= 10
 ORDER BY salary desc
```

Because the WHERE clause is processed before the ORDER BY clause, this solution returns any 10 rows from the EMPLOYEE table sorted by SALARY. If—and only if—Oracle chooses to use an index on salary to retrieve the rows will the rows be in order.

Here's a more sophisticated solution:

```
SELECT employee_id, -salary salary
  FROM (SELECT DISTINCT -salary salary,employee_id
          FROM employees)
 WHERE rownum < 11
```

This works because DISTINCT performs a sort on -salary. The problem is that it's not guaranteed to work. There is no ORDER BY, and in some future release of Oracle, or under some circumstances we haven't tested, the query should return rows in any order. Therefore, it is bad practice to implement such a solution.

Prior to 8.1.6, the best solution was simply to stop fetching rows after the first 10 are selected. You can easily do this in PL/SQL or another procedural language:

```
DECLARE
   CURSOR c1
   IS
      --Cursor to retrieve employees
      -- in descending order of salary
```

```
      SELECT employee_id, salary
        FROM employees
       ORDER BY salary desc;

  r1    c1%ROWTYPE;
  i     NUMBER := 1;
BEGIN
   OPEN c1;
   i := 1;
   WHILE i <= 10   -- Only fetch the top ten.
   LOOP
      FETCH c1 INTO r1;
      dbms_output.put_line (r1.employee_id || ': ' ||
r1.salary);
      i := i + 1;
   END LOOP;
   CLOSE c1;
END;
```

8.1.6 ANALYTIC FUNCTIONS

The analytical functions introduced in 8.1.6 extend the ability of SQL to deal with
common data mining questions, such as "Who are the top 10 paid employees?"
This can now be done in a single SQL statement by taking advantage of the
RANK() operator:

```
SELECT *
  FROM (SELECT employee_id, salary,
           RANK() OVER (ORDER BY salary DESC) salary_rank
           FROM employees)
 WHERE salary_rank <= 10
```

In this case the RANK() function ranks the rows in employees in order of descending salary. Previously, it wasn't possible to retrieve the top 10 rows in a
table without resorting to potentially unreliable tricks.

However, the RANK() solution still requires a full-table scan in order for the
ranks of every row to be determined. It cannot use the descending index method
employed by our PL/SQL solution in the preceding section and so is still less efficient than procedural solution.

However, analytic functions can result in improved performance in other
circumstances. For instance, analytic functions allow us to implement cumulative
totals, moving average, and other sophisticated queries. As a simple example,
consider the case in which we wish to provide a report of each user's salary as a

percentage of the total salary budget. The following query does it but requires two full-table scans of the EMPLOYEE table:

```
SELECT employee_id, salary,
       salary * 100 / t.total_salary
  FROM employees, (SELECT SUM (salary) total_salary
                     FROM employees) t
 ORDER BY salary desc
```

```
Rows      Execution Plan
-------   -------------------------------------------
      0   SELECT STATEMENT    GOAL: CHOOSE
    800    SORT (ORDER BY)
    800     MERGE JOIN (CARTESIAN)
      2      VIEW
      2       SORT (AGGREGATE)
    800        TABLE ACCESS (FULL) OF 'EMPLOYEES'
    800     TABLE ACCESS   (FULL) OF 'EMPLOYEES'
```

Using an analytic function, we can do this with only one table scan:

```
SELECT employee_id, salary,
       salary * 100 / SUM (salary) OVER()
  FROM employees
 ORDER BY salary desc
```

```
Rows      Execution Plan
-------   -------------------------------------------
      0   SELECT STATEMENT    GOAL: CHOOSE
    800    WINDOW (SORT)
    800     TABLE ACCESS (FULL) OF 'EMPLOYEES'
```

Oracle 8.1.6 analytic functions can help avoid procedural or expensive self-join solutions to many common business and analytic queries.

GROUPING

The GROUP BY clause can be used to return aggregate values for each value in the columns in the GROUP BY clause. For instance, the following statement returns the amount of sales recorded against each customer:

```
SELECT customer_id, SUM (sale_value)
  FROM sales
 GROUP BY customer_id
```

Unless an index exists on CUSTOMER_ID and SALE_VALUE, this query can only be resolved by a full-table scan. Our optimization options would be limited to techniques such as increasing SORT_AREA_SIZE, using parallelism, and optimizing scan performance, as discussed in Chapter 7.

If we do have an index on CUSTOMER_ID and SALE_VALUE, Oracle will usually take advantage of it to avoid a sort. The execution plan would show an INDEX (FULL SCAN) and a GROUP BY NOSORT.

```
SQL> SELECT customer_id, SUM (sale_value)
  2    FROM sales
  3   GROUP BY customer_id
  4  /

Execution Plan
-----------------------------------------------------
0      SELECT STATEMENT Optimizer=CHOOSE
1    0    SORT (GROUP BY NOSORT)
2    1      INDEX (FULL SCAN) OF 'SALES_CUST_VALUE_IDX'
```

The "NOSORT" form of the GROUP BY operation occurs when the data are already returned in sorted order. This execution plan eliminates the need to do a sort and, since the index is smaller than the table, may reduce I/O, but remember that index full scans are not as efficient as full-table scans because they can only read a single block per I/O.

Because rows are returned in correct order by the index, Oracle can return the first grouping as soon as all rows for that group have been returned. In other words, this query optimizes very well for response time (time to retrieve the first row).

Another way to use the index to optimize the group by is to employ a fast full-index scan. As we saw in Chapter 7, the fast full-index scan can read a complete index quickly, although the rows in the index will not be returned in order. Using the INDEX_FF hint results in the following plan:

```
SQL> SELECT /*+ index_ffs(s,sales_cust_value_idx) */
            customer_id, SUM (sale_value)
  2    FROM sales s
  3   GROUP BY customer_id
  4  /
```

```
Execution Plan
-----------------------------------------------------
0         SELECT STATEMENT
1     0   SORT (GROUP BY)
2     1     INDEX (FAST FULL SCAN) OF
                  'SALES_CUST_VALUE_IDX'
```

This form of the query does require a sort, but the retrieval of rows through the fast full scan will be much more efficient than the index full scan.

Figure 10.3 compares the execution times for the table scan solution and for the two index-based queries. Both index-based queries are more efficient than the full-table scan. However, the fast full-index scan solution is superior to the index full scan in terms of throughput (time to retrieve the last row), while the index full scan—because it avoids a sort—offers superior response time (time to retrieve the first row).

> If using an index to optimize a GROUP BY, a fast full-index scan solution will probably result in better throughput, while an index full scan solution will probably result in better response time.

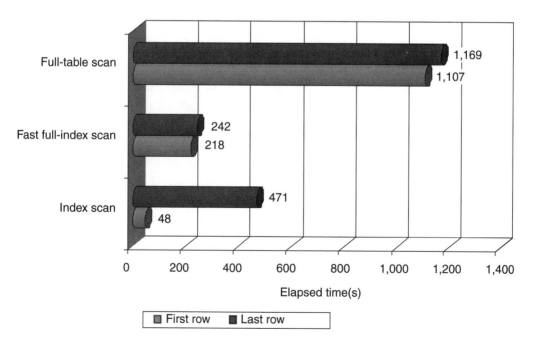

FIGURE 10.3 Using an index to optimize a GROUP BY.

THE HAVING CLAUSE

The HAVING clause can be used to eliminate rows from a GROUP BY after they have been aggregated. For instance, the following query eliminates departments with less than five employees:

```
SELECT department_id, COUNT (*), MIN (salary), AVG (salary),
MAX (salary)
  FROM employees
 GROUP BY department_id
HAVING COUNT (*) > 4
```

This is a valid use of HAVING and merely adds a filter condition after the aggregation. However, you should never use HAVING in place of WHERE. If rows can be eliminated by WHERE, then they will be eliminated *before* the aggregation, whereas HAVING eliminates rows *after* the aggregation. The fewer rows to be aggregated the better, and WHERE is therefore preferable to HAVING.

For instance, the following generates salary statistics only for departments in Hobart using the HAVING clause:

```
SELECT d.department_name, d.location, MAX (e.salary)
  FROM departments d, employees e
 WHERE d.department_id = e.department_id
 GROUP BY department_name, d.location
HAVING d.location = 'HOBART'
```

```
Rows     Execution Plan
-------  ----------------------------------------------------
      0  SELECT STATEMENT    HINT: CHOOSE
     50   FILTER   <-Remove non-Hobart departments
    799    SORT (GROUP BY)
    799     MERGE JOIN
    801      INDEX (RANGE SCAN) OF
                  'EMPLOYEE_DEPT_SAL_IDX' (NON-UNIQUE)
     51      SORT (JOIN)
     51       TABLE ACCESS (FULL) OF 'DEPARTMENTS'
```

We can see from the execution plan that all rows from EMPLOYEES must be merged and sorted before the FILTER step removes all non-Hobart locations.

On the other hand, using WHERE resulted in this plan:

```
SELECT d.department_name, d.location, MAX (e.salary)
  FROM departments d, employees e
 WHERE d.department_id = e.department_id
```

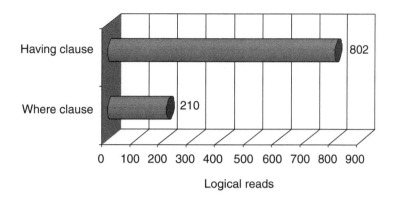

FIGURE 10.4   Eliminating rows with WHERE or HAVING clauses.

```
      AND d.location = 'HOBART'
   GROUP BY department_name, d.location

   Rows      Execution Plan
   -------   ---------------------------------------------
         0   SELECT STATEMENT    HINT: CHOOSE
       100    SORT (GROUP BY) <- Less rows to sort
       100     NESTED LOOPS
        51      TABLE ACCESS (FULL) OF 'DEPARTMENTS'
                -- Non-Hobart rows removed here
       100      TABLE ACCESS   (BY ROWID) OF 'EMPLOYEES'
       102       INDEX (RANGE SCAN) OF 'EMPLOYEE_DEPT_IDX'
```

Using WHERE allowed non-Hobart departments to be eliminated in the first execution step. As a result, fewer rows needed to be joined and to be sorted. Figure 10.4 shows the performance improvement obtained.

Where possible, use the WHERE clause in place of the HAVING clause to eliminate rows before they are grouped. Use the HAVING clause with group functions only.

SET OPERATIONS

The set operators, UNION, MINUS, and INTERSECT allow multiple result sets with the same number and type of columns to be combined into a single result set.

Oracle usually resolves a set operation as follows:

❏ The query defined by each component query is executed.
❏ The results of the combined queries are sorted by the entire select list.
❏ Depending on the type of set operation, the results are either combined, intersected, or subtracted.

An exception is the UNION ALL operation, which does not require that the component result sets be sorted.

The general procedure for optimizing a set operation is as follows:

❏ Optimize each component query, using principles already discussed.
❏ Optimize your database for sort operations—in particular, make sure SORT_AREA_SIZE is adequate.
❏ Consider an index on the columns in the select list. Such an index will be cheaper to scan than the table and will already be in sorted order. You can use this index either to avoid the sort (using the index full-scan method) or to improve throughput by using the fast full-index scans.

As well as following these general principles, you can often improve performance by employing alternatives to set operations.

UNION AND UNION ALL

The UNION operator is undoubtedly the most commonly used set operation. UNION differs from UNION ALL in that UNION will eliminate any duplicate rows across the two results sets, whereas UNION ALL returns all rows, even if duplicated. For instance, the following query returns all customers and all employees, but if a customer and employee have the same name and date of birth, they are only reported once (perhaps they are the same person and we don't want them reported twice):

```
SELECT contact_surname, contact_firstname, date_of_birth
  FROM customers
UNION
     SELECT surname, firstname, date_of_birth
       FROM employees

Rows     Execution Plan
------   -----------------------------------------
     0   SELECT STATEMENT    GOAL: CHOOSE
100800    SORT (UNIQUE)   <- eliminate duplicates
100800     UNION-ALL
```

```
100000      TABLE ACCESS (FULL) OF 'CUSTOMERS'
   800      TABLE ACCESS (FULL) OF 'EMPLOYEES'
```

The corresponding UNION ALL query returns the same result set, but if a matching row exists in both CUSTOMERS and EMPLOYEES, it will be reported twice:

```
SELECT contact_surname, contact_firstname, date_of_birth
  FROM customers
UNION ALL
        SELECT surname, firstname, date_of_birth
          FROM employees


Rows      Execution Plan
-------   --------------------------------------------
      0   SELECT STATEMENT    GOAL: CHOOSE
 100800    UNION-ALL
 100000     TABLE ACCESS (FULL) OF 'CUSTOMERS'
    800     TABLE ACCESS (FULL) OF 'EMPLOYEES'
```

You may notice that the execution plan for the UNION statement is almost exactly identical to that of the UNION ALL statement, except that the SORT(UNIQUE) step is absent in the UNION ALL version. Removing the sort from a large UNION can substantially speed up the query. In the case of the preceding example, UNION ALL took only 11.08 seconds, while UNION took 22.32 seconds (see Figure 10.5).

If you don't need to eliminate duplicate rows in a UNION operation, use UNION ALL instead of UNION. This will avoid a potentially expensive sort.

INTERSECT

The INTERSECT operation returns rows that are common to both tables or result sets. For instance, the following INTERSECT statement returns all customers who are also employees (or who at least have the same name and date of birth):

```
SELECT contact_surname, contact_firstname, date_of_birth
  FROM customers
INTERSECT
        SELECT surname, firstname, date_of_birth
          FROM employees
```

```
Rows       Execution Plan
-------    ------------------------------------------------
      0    SELECT STATEMENT   GOAL: CHOOSE
      0     INTERSECTION
  99995      SORT (UNIQUE)
 100000       TABLE ACCESS (FULL) OF 'CUSTOMERS'
    800      SORT (UNIQUE)
    800       TABLE ACCESS (FULL) OF 'EMPLOYEES'
```

You can alternately express an INTERSECT query as a join. If a sort-merge join is performed, you can expect the performance to be very similar to that of the IN-TERSECT since Oracle has to perform a sort and merge for both methods. However, using a join allows you to employ the nested loops or hash-join methods. Depending on the data being intersected, this can lead to substantial performance improvements. If one result set is a small subset of an entire table and the other result set has an index on join columns, then the nested loops join might be more effective than the INTERSECT. On the other hand, if the tables are large and/or we are scanning all rows of the tables, then a hash join is a viable alternative. For instance, our previous INTERSECT example is recoded as follows:

```
SELECT /*+ ORDERED USE_HASH(C) */
       c.contact_surname, c.contact_firstname,
       c.date_of_birth
  FROM employees e,customers c
 WHERE e.surname = c.contact_surname
   AND e.firstname = c.contact_firstname
   AND e.date_of_birth = c.date_of_birth
```

```
Rows       Execution Plan
-------    ------------------------------------------------
      0    SELECT STATEMENT   GOAL: CHOOSE
      0     HASH JOIN
    800      TABLE ACCESS (FULL) OF 'EMPLOYEES'
 100000      TABLE ACCESS (FULL) OF 'CUSTOMERS'
```

The elapsed time reduces from 17.28 to 3.81 seconds (see Figure 10.5).

When performing an intersect, consider recoding the statement to a join using either a nested loops or hash-join method.

MINUS

We saw in Chapter 8 how the MINUS operator can be used in place of an antijoin (for instance, a subquery using NOT IN). MINUS outperformed the antijoin, except in the case where a hash antijoin was performed. For instance, a MINUS statement like this

```
SELECT contact_surname, contact_firstname, date_of_birth
  FROM customers
MINUS
    SELECT surname, firstname, date_of_birth
      FROM employees
```

```
Rows        Execution Plan
-------     ----------------------------------------------
      0     SELECT STATEMENT     GOAL: CHOOSE
  99995      MINUS
  99995       SORT (UNIQUE)
 100000        TABLE ACCESS (FULL) OF 'CUSTOMERS'
    800       SORT (UNIQUE)
    800        TABLE ACCESS (FULL) OF 'EMPLOYEES'
```

can be expressed as a hash antijoin like this:

```
SELECT contact_surname,
       contact_firstname,
       date_of_birth
  FROM customers
 WHERE (contact_surname, contact_firstname,
        date_of_birth) NOT IN
       (SELECT /*+HASH_AJ */
               surname, firstname, date_of_birth
          FROM employees)
```

```
Rows        Row Source Operation
-------     ----------------------------------------------
  99995     HASH JOIN ANTI
 100000      TABLE ACCESS FULL CUSTOMERS
    800      VIEW
    800       TABLE ACCESS FULL EMPLOYEES
```

If conditions are right, the hash antijoin can significantly outperform the MINUS operation. In our example, elapsed time reduced from 19.71 to 7.93.

When performing a MINUS operation, consider recoding the statement into an ANTI-JOIN using the HASH_AJ hint.

SET OPERATIONS AND THEIR ALTERNATIVES

Figure 10.5 shows elapsed times for the set operations and alternatives for our examples. Keep the following points in mind:

❑ The alternatives do not always return exactly the same result set. Set operations (aside from UNION ALL) return distinct rows only and return rows in sorted order. If eliminating duplicates or returning rows in order is essential, you could modify the alternatives with the DISTINCT or ORDER BY clause, or you may wish to stick with the set operators.

❑ In the examples, CUSTOMERS is much bigger than EMPLOYEES. This is the ideal situation for the hash join and, consequently, hash-join alternatives did very well in our examples. Different data might give different results.

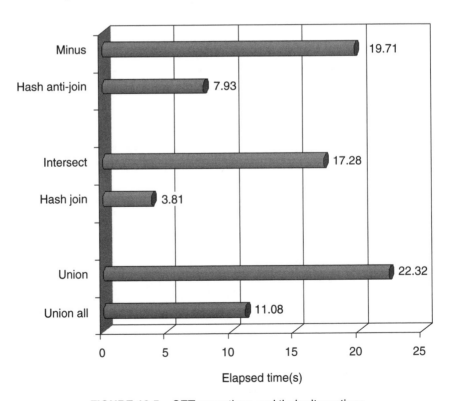

FIGURE 10.5   SET operations and their alternatives.

As always, it's up to you to try the alternatives and choose the solution most appropriate for your application.

❏ In these tests both SORT_AREA_SIZE and HASH_AREA_SIZE were set to 1 megabyte. Different settings for these parameters—or other configuration settings—might favor hash joins or sorts.

SUMMARY

Many Oracle procedures require sort operations. Sorts can be expensive, and avoiding sorting can result in significant improvements to query performance. The most common cause of Oracle sorts are as follows:

❏ Using the ORDER BY clause to return rows in sorted order
❏ Using the GROUP BY clause to return aggregated information
❏ Table joins using the sort-merge method
❏ Set operations such as UNION, MINUS, and INTERSECT

It's not uncommon inadvertently to cause Oracle to perform unnecessary sorts. This often occurs through unnecessary use of the DISTINCT keyword or the use of UNION in preference to UNION ALL.

An index can be used to perform an ORDER BY without a sort. This will be effective if you are optimizing for response time, rather than throughput, or when the query can be resolved entirely from the index. Oracle may use indexes to avoid sorts if the optimizer goal is FIRST_ROWS. Using the fast full-index scan can optimize both response time and throughput.

Database configuration can have a significant effect on sort performance. In particular, the magnitude of SORT_AREA_SIZE will have a direct impact on sort performance. Configuration of the temporary tablespace is also very important.

The GROUP BY clause returns one row for each unique combination of columns specified. The group functions can report on maximums, minimums, counts, averages, and other statistics for each group. Some ways of optimizing group operations are as follows:

❏ Operations that group data can show strong improvements when an index-only solution is possible. This will be possible if an index exists on all of the columns in both the GROUP BY and SELECT clauses. An index on the GROUP BY columns alone will not be helpful.
❏ Counting the number of rows in a table can be enhanced by counting the rows in an indexed column that is not nullable using the fast full-scan methodology. Alternately, use "count(*)" in preference to counting a constant or column because Oracle transparently avoids a sort in this circumstance.

- Finding a maximum or minimum value can often be performed more effectively by a PL/SQL block, especially if an index on the column in question exists.
- The analytical functions introduced in 8.1.6 can sometimes avoid costly self-joins when performing complex aggregate queries.
- Use the WHERE clause in preference to the HAVING clause whenever possible. WHERE eliminates rows before aggregation while HAVING eliminates the rows only after the aggregation has been performed.

The set operators UNION, INTERSECT, and MINUS allow multiple result sets to be combined or compared.

- The frequently used UNION operator is less efficient than UNION ALL, since UNION ALL doesn't require a sort to eliminate duplicates. Use UNION ALL in preference to UNION unless you need these duplicates eliminated.
- The set operators INTERSECT and MINUS can often be expressed more efficiently as a join or a hash antijoin.

Parallel SQL

In this chapter, we consider the use of Oracle's parallel SQL capabilities to improve the performance of your SQL statements.

In a serial (non-parallel) execution environment, a single process or thread[1] undertakes the operations required to process your SQL statement and each action must complete before the succeeding action can commence. The single Oracle process may only leverage the power of a single CPU and read from a single disk at any given instant. Because most modern hardware platforms include more than a single CPU and because Oracle data is often spread across multiple disks, serial SQL execution is unable to take advantage of all of the available processing power.

Parallel processing allows SQL execution to be broken down into multiple tasks, each of which can be undertaken by a different process. Each of these processes can use a different CPU or read from a different disk and so can make more effective use of computer resources.

Parallel processing can improve the performance of suitable SQL statements to a degree that is often not possible by any other method. However, not all SQL

---

[1]A process is a unit of execution with its own memory. A thread is also a unit of execution but shares memory with other threads within a process. On UNIX, Oracle server tasks are implemented as processes and on Windows as threads.

statements can use parallel processing and not all application environments are suitable.

In this chapter, we see how parallel SQL works, the circumstances under which parallel SQL can or should be used, and ways of getting the greatest benefit from this powerful facility. The topics covered include

- How parallel SQL works
- The performance improvements that can be achieved
- When to use parallel SQL
- How to use parallel SQL
- Explaining and optimizing parallel SQL
- Examples of parallel queries
- Using parallel DML and parallel DDL

UNDERSTANDING PARALLEL SQL

Parallel processing allows SQL execution to be divided into a number of separate tasks. Each of these tasks can be executed at the same time—in parallel—allowing full use of multiple CPUs available on midrange and high-end computers. For example, consider the following statement:

```
SELECT contact_surname, contact_firstname,
       date_of_birth, phoneno
  FROM customers c1
 ORDER BY contact_surname, contact_firstname,
          date_of_birth
```

If executing without the parallel query option, a single process would be responsible for fetching all the rows in the CUSTOMERS table. The same process would be responsible for sorting the rows to satisfy the ORDER BY clause. (See Figure 11.1).

We can request that Oracle execute this statement in parallel, for instance by using the PARALLEL hint:

```
SELECT /*+ PARALLEL(C1,2)   */
       contact_surname, contact_firstname,
       date_of_birth, phoneno
  FROM customers c1
 ORDER BY contact_surname, contact_firstname,
          date_of_birth
```

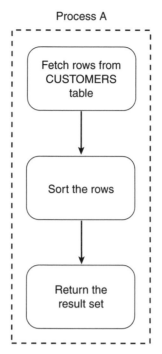

FIGURE 11.1 Serial execution of an SQL statement.

If parallel processing is available, the statement will be executed by two streams in parallel. Further, the scanning stage and the sorting stage will be executed by separate processes. A total of five processes will now be involved in the query, as shown in Figure 11.2.

WHAT SORT OF STATEMENTS CAN BE PARALLELIZED?

Parallel processing is only available to SQL statements that process an entire table or partition or that perform local index scans on partitioned tables. This includes

- ❏ SQL queries that contain at least one full-table scan
- ❏ Building or rebuilding an index
- ❏ Creating a table from a SELECT statement, provided that the SELECT statement performs a full-table scan
- ❏ An UPDATE or DELETE statement that is based on a full-table scan of a partitioned table (in Oracle8 or Oracle8i)
- ❏ A query on a partitioned table that uses a "local" index
- ❏ An INSERT based on a parallel subquery (in Oracle8 and Oracle8i)

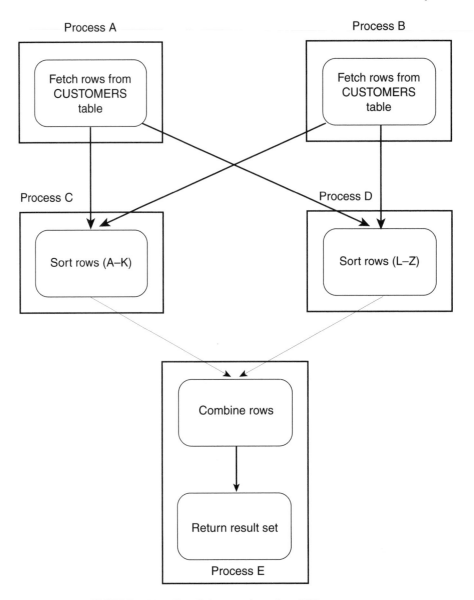

FIGURE 11.2   Parallel execution of an SQL statement.

In this chapter, we focus on parallel queries based on full-table scans. Other forms of parallel processing are discussed in subsequent chapters (see the section titled "Other Parallel Operations" later in this chapter).

WHAT SORT OF PERFORMANCE GAINS CAN BE ACHIEVED?

The performance improvements that you can expect to obtain from parallel SQL depend on the suitability of your host computer, Oracle configuration, and SQL statement. If all the conditions for parallel processing are met, you can expect to get performance improvements in line with the degree of parallelism (the number of concurrent streams of processing). For instance, if your degree of parallelism is three and all preconditions for parallel processing are met, then you could expect that your SQL statement might run up to three times faster. On the other hand, if your configuration is not suitable for parallelism, or if you try to achieve more parallelism than is practical for your situation, you might actually harm performance.

Figure 11.3 shows the improvement gains obtained by increasing the degree of parallelism for a SQL statement that performed a full-table scan and a sort against three differently configured hardware platforms. The first hardware platform had 8 CPUs and a high-performance RAID 0 (striped) disk array. The second computer had two CPUs and conventional disks. The third computer had a single CPU and single disk. As we can see, significant gains were achieved on the eight-way machine and minor gains on the two-way machine. Performance actually degraded substantially when we tried to use parallel processing on the single CPU/disk configuration

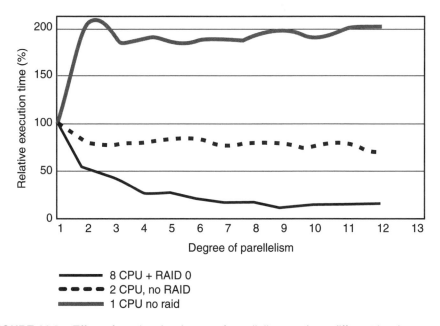

FIGURE 11.3 Effect of varying the degree of parallelism on three different hardware platforms.

Parallel processing can only help when your machine configuration is suitable. In-creasing parallelism beyond the capabilities of your hardware can actually harm performance.

WHEN IS PARALLEL ADVISABLE?

Here are some of the circumstances under which you can effectively use parallel SQL:

Your server computer has multiple CPUs   Parallel processing will usually be most effective if the computer that hosts your Oracle database has multiple CPUs. This is because most operations performed by the Oracle server (accessing the Oracle shared memory, performing sorts, disk accesses) require CPU. If the host computer has only one CPU, then the parallel processes may contend for this CPU and performance might actually decrease.

The data to be accessed is on multiple disk drives   Many SQL statements can be resolved with few or no disk accesses due to Oracle's buffer cache in the SGA shared memory area. However, full-table scans of larger tables—a typical operation to be parallelized—will tend to require significant physical disk reads. If the data to be accessed resides on a single disk, then the parallel processes will tend to line up for this disk and the advantages of parallel processing might not be realized.

It's usually up to your DBA to ensure that the data files that comprise your database are located across multiple devices, either by operating system striping or by manual creation of files across the devices. Guidelines for striping are contained in Chapter 19. Striping data files across multiple devices will also generally improve the performance of serial SQL in a multiuser environment since it will reduce the likelihood of a disk bottleneck.

The SQL to be parallelized is long running or resource intensive   Parallel SQL suits long-running or resource-intensive statements. This is because

❑   Parallel SQL must be based on a table scan.
❑   A single process can probably do scans of smaller tables efficiently.
❑   There can be an overhead in activating and coordinating the multiple parallel query processes.

Parallel processing is typically used for

❑   Long-running reports
❑   Bulk updates of large tables
❑   Building or rebuilding indexes on large tables

❑ Creating temporary tables for analytical processing

❑ Rebuilding a table to improve performance or to purge unwanted rows

Parallel processing is not usually suitable for transaction processing environments. In these environments, large numbers of users process transactions at a high rate. Full use of available CPUs is already achieved because each concurrent transaction can use a different CPU. Implementing parallel processing might actually degrade overall performance by allowing a single user to monopolize multiple CPUs. In these environments, parallel processing would usually be limited to MIS reporting, bulk loads, and index or table rebuilds, which would occur at off-peak periods.

The SQL performs at least one full-table or partition scan   Parallel processing is mostly enabled when an entire table or partition is being processed. For parallel queries, this implies a full-table scan, although not every table in the query needs to be accessed via a table scan. For instance, a nested loops join that uses an index to join two tables can be fully parallelized provided that the driving table is accessed by a table scan.

There is one exception to the full-scan rule. If a query against a partitioned table is based on a local partitioned index, then each index scan can be performed in parallel against each partition. This is discussed in more detail in Chapter 13.

There is spare capacity on your host   You are not likely to realize the full gains of parallel processing if your server is at full capacity. Parallel processing works well for a single job on an underutilized, multi-CPU machine. If all CPUs on the machine are busy, then your parallel processes will bottleneck on the CPU and performance will be degraded.

THE DEGREE OF PARALLELISM

The degree of parallelism defines the number of streams of execution that will be performed in parallel. In the simplest case, this translates to the number of parallel slave processes enlisted to support your SQL's execution. However, the number of parallel processes is more often twice the degree of parallelism for a multistage operation.

Figure 11.4 shows how parallel slaves are allocated for a degree of parallelism of two. For very simple statements, the degree of parallelism controls how many parallel slave processes are allocated. Most statements will consist of more than simply a full-table scan, and for these statements, Oracle will allocate a second set of parallel processes. For instance, if the statement includes an ORDER BY and a GROUP BY, then three sets of parallel processes are required, but because Oracle reuses the first set of parallel processes to perform the order by sort, only four parallel processes in total are utilized. Because Oracle reuses the parallel slaves within a statement, the number of parallel slaves allocated should never be more than twice the degree of parallelism.

SELECT /*+ PARALLEL(C, 2)*/* FROM CUSTOMERS

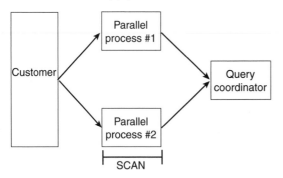

SELECT /*+ PARALLEL(S, 2)*/* FROM SALES S
   ORDER BY CUSTOMER_ID

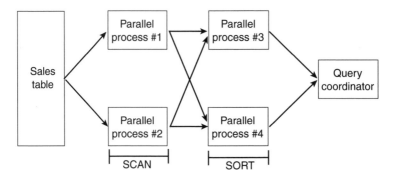

SELECT /*+ PARALLEL(S, 2)*/CUSTOMER_ID, SUM (SALE_VALUE)
   FROM SALES S
   GROUP BY CUSTOMER_ID
   ORDER BY 2

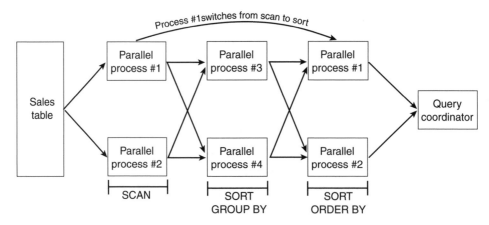

FIGURE 11.4 How processes are allocated for for a degree of parallelism of 2. Note that the number of processes is never more than twice the degree of parallelism (plus the query coordinator).

The default degree of parallelism, which is used if no explicit degree of parallelism is specified in the PARALLEL hint or table clause, is determined by the value of PARALLEL_THREADS_PER_CPU. So, for instance, if PARALLEL_THREADS_PER_CPU is set to 2 and there are four CPUs, then the default degree of parallelism will be 8. In previous versions of Oracle the default degree of parallelism was set to the number of CPUs available or the number of disk devices upon which the table was stored, whichever was smaller.

The Adaptive Multiuser protocol and automatic tuning settings   If the configuration parameter PARALLEL_ADAPTIVE_MULTI_USER is set to TRUE (the default is FALSE), then Oracle can adjust the degree of parallelism depending on the number of other sessions that are using parallel slaves. This algorithm can reduce the chance of a single user monopolizing the majority of parallel slave processes.

If the parameter PARALLEL_AUTOMATIC_TUNING is set to TRUE (the default is FALSE), Oracle will automatically configure a number of configuration parameters that affect parallel tuning. These include the maximum number of server processes (PARALLEL_MAX_SERVERS) and the PARALLEL_ADAPTIVE_MULTI_USER setting.

THE QUERY COORDINATOR

A query coordinator process is required whenever any SQL statement—including statements other than queries—is to be processed in parallel. The query coordinator invokes the parallel slaves and is the ultimate recipient of the output of parallel operations. In most environments, the query coordinator is simply the Oracle process that executed the SQL, sometimes called the *server* or *shadow* process. As a result, it is not usually necessary for Oracle to create an additional process to serve as the query coordinator.

PARALLEL SLAVE POOL

The Oracle server maintains a pool of parallel slave processes available for parallel operations. Database configuration parameters determine the initial and maximum size of the pool. If insufficient slaves are currently active but the pool has not reached its maximum value, then Oracle will create more slaves. After a configurable period of inactivity, slave processes will shut down until the pool is again at its minimum size. The configuration parameters controlling the size of the pool are listed in Appendix D.

If there are insufficient query processes to satisfy the degree of parallelism required by your statement, one of the following outcomes will result:

❏ If there are some parallel query slaves available but less than requested by your SQL statement, your statement may run at a reduced degree of parallelism.

❏ If there are no parallel query slaves available, your statement will run serially.

❏ Under specific circumstances, you may get an error. This will only occur if the database parameter PARALLEL_MIN_PERCENT has been set to a value that is higher than the percentage of required slaves that are available. For instance, if your query required 8 and only 5 were available (5/8 = 62%), then your query would execute in parallel if PARALLEL_MIN_PER-CENT was below 62. If PARALLEL_MIN_PERCENT was above 62, your statement would terminate with an error.

PARTITIONING OF DATA FOR PARALLEL PROCESSES

For all parallel operations, Oracle must split a table or result set into multiple sets of data in order to parallelize each step of a parallel operation.

In the case of a full-table scan, Oracle will allocate contiguous sets of blocks to each slave process.

In the case of sort operations, contiguous blocks of sort keys will be allocated to each slave process. For instance, one slave may be assigned to all rows with sort keys starting between A and L, the other slave allocated the sort keys between M and Z.

Table statistics are an important input to this partitioning process. If Oracle's assumptions about the spread of data are incorrect, then a particular parallel slave might have to process more than its fair share of data and the benefits of parallelism will be diminished.

USING PARALLEL QUERY

The parallel query option is the most frequently used of Oracle's parallel facilities. The parallel query option allows a SELECT statement that includes a full-table scan to be executed in parallel.

Because the parallel query option is so central to Oracle's parallel strategy, we examine parallel query in particular detail. Many parallel query principles also apply to other parallel facilities, such as parallel DML, parallel DDL, and parallel operations on partitions.

ENABLING PARALLEL QUERY

The parallel query option is invoked if the SQL statement includes a PARALLEL hint or if the PARALLEL clause has been associated with the table definition. In addition, the table to which the PARALLEL clause has been applied must be accessed via a full-table scan or must be a partitioned table accessed via a local index.

PARALLEL table clause   The PARALLEL clause of the CREATE or ALTER TABLE statement specifies the default degree of parallelism for the table. The default is NOPARALLEL, which means that the parallel query option will not be invoked unless a PARALLEL hint is used. For example,

```
ALTER TABLE SALES PARALLEL(DEFAULT)
```

specifies that full-table scans of SALES should use the parallel query option with the default degree of parallelism.

```
ALTER TABLE SALES PARALLEL(DEGREE 4)
```

specifies that full-table scans of SALES should use the parallel option with four degrees of parallelism.

```
ALTER TABLE SALES NOPARALLEL
```

specifies that full-table scans of SALES should not use the parallel query option unless instructed to do so with the PARALLEL hint. This is the default setting.

PARALLEL hint   The PARALLEL hint instructs the optimizer to use the parallel query option for the nominated table. It takes the form

```
/*+ PARALLEL(table_or_alias [,degree_of_parallelism])*/
```

The hint specifies the table to be processed in parallel and the degree of parallelism to be applied. If no degree of parallelism is specified, then the default degree of parallelism will be applied. Remember that, as with all hints, if the SQL statement refers to an alias, then it should refer to the same alias in the PARALLEL hint.

Note that although the PARALLEL hint specifies that a table access should be parallel, using it does not guarantee that other operations (such as joins) will be parallelized. Also remember that the PARALLEL hint will be ignored if the table is being processed using an access method other than a full-table scan. In some cases, you may wish to force a full-table scan using the FULL hint so that parallel execution can occur.

EXPLAINING AND TRACING PARALLEL SQL

When a parallel SQL statement is EXPLAINED, the OTHER_TAG column of the PLAN_TABLE can be used to determine which of the steps is executed in parallel. Table 11.1 shows the values of the OTHER_TAG column that applies to parallel queries.

TABLE 11.1 Values for the OTHER_TAG Column

VALUE FOR OTHER_TAG	MEANING
SERIAL (or blank)	The step was executed serially without any parallel processing.
PARALLEL_TO_PARALLEL	This tag denotes parallel processing that passes results to a second set of parallel processes. For instance, a parallel table scan may have passed results to a parallel sort.
PARALLEL_TO_SERIAL	This is the top level of a parallel query. The results were fed in parallel to the query coordinator.
PARALLEL_COMBINED_WITH_PARENT PARALLEL_COMBINED_WITH_CHILD	The step was executed in parallel. Either the parent step or the child step was also executed in parallel by the same process. For instance, in a parallel nested loops join, the parallel query process scanned the driving table and also issued index lookups on the joined table.
PARALLEL_FROM_SERIAL	A serial operation that passed results to a set of parallel processes. The presence of this tag may indicate a serial bottleneck within a parallel statement, since it suggested that parallel processing might wait on serial processing.

The OTHER_TAG column only became available in Oracle7.3. Traditional EXPLAIN queries and many tools that execute EXPLAIN PLANS (including tkprof) do not always make good use of this column. The Xplain tool available from this book's website can produce explain plan output that includes the OTHER_TAG column. You could also issue the following statement against the plan table manually:

```
SELECT RTRIM (LPAD ('+', 2 * LEVEL)) || ' ' ||
       operation || ' ' || options || ' ' ||
       object_name, other_tag, object_node
  FROM plan_table
 CONNECT BY PRIOR id = parent_id
 START WITH id = 0
```

Use the OTHER_TAG column of the PLAN_TABLE to determine the parallelism of each step in your SQL. Explain your SQL using a tool that makes good use of this column. Beware of the PARALLEL_FROM_SERIAL tag, which may point to a serial bottleneck.

The OTHER column of the PLAN_TABLE contains the SQL executed by the parallel slave. For the full-table scan step, this SQL will show the breakup of the table into parallel partitions. For instance, the following tkprof sample uses the OTHER column to show the CUSTOMER table being partitioned by ROWID ranges:

```
TABLE ACCESS (FULL) OF 'CUSTOMERS' [:Q33000]
    SELECT /*+ ROWID(A1)*/
            A1."CONTACT_SURNAME" C0,
            A1."CONTACT_FIRSTNAME" C1,
            A1."DATE_OF_BIRTH" C2,
            A1."PHONENO" C3
    FROM "CUSTOMERS" A1
    WHERE ROWID BETWEEN :1 AND :2
```

For a parallel query, the OBJECT_NODE column contains a tag for the result sets that are output by the parallel query. For instance, in the preceding tkprof sample, the value of the OBJECT_NODE column was :Q33000. The next step of the EXPLAIN PLAN shows the output from that scan step being sorted in parallel:

```
SORT (ORDER BY) [:Q33001]
    SELECT A1.C0 C0,A1.C1 C1,A1.C2 C2,A1.C3 C3
        FROM :Q33000 A1
    ORDER BY A1.C0,A1.C1,A1.C2
```

The contents of the OTHER column can be useful when trying to understand how parallel query works in general but are of limited use when trying to tune specific queries. The OBJECT_NODE column is more useful because it can reveal which steps are being executed by the same set of parallel query processes. For instance, in the next execution plan, we can see from the OBJECT_NODE that the sort and sort merge operations are executed by the same set of processes:

```
SELECT STATEMENT
    SORT ORDER BY (PARALLEL_TO_SERIAL) :Q193003
        MERGE JOIN (PARALLEL_TO_PARALLEL) :Q193002
            SORT JOIN (PARALLEL_COMBINED_WITH_PARENT)
                                            :Q193002
                TABLE ACCESS FULL SALES (PARALLEL_TO_PARALLEL)
                                            :Q193000
            SORT JOIN (PARALLEL_COMBINED_WITH_PARENT)
                                            :Q193002
                TABLE ACCESS FULL CUSTOMERS
                        (PARALLEL_TO_PARALLEL) :Q193001
```

USING THE V$PQ_TQSTAT VIEW

The V$PQ_TQSTAT view allows you to examine in detail the actual processing patterns of parallel execution. For instance, consider this simple parallel query:

```
SELECT /*+ PARALLEL(e,2) */ * FROM employees e
```

After we have executed this query, we can issue the following query against V$PQ_TQSTAT to show the execution patterns for the most recent parallel query (the query with the highest DFO_NUMBER):

```
SELECT tq_id, server_type, process, num_rows
  FROM v$pq_tqstat
 WHERE dfo_number = (SELECT MAX (dfo_number)
                           FROM v$pq_tqstat)
 ORDER BY tq_id, DECODE (SUBSTR (server_type, 1, 4),
               'Prod', 0, 'Cons', 1, 3);
```

TQ_ID	SERVER_TYP	PROCESS	NUM_ROWS
0	Producer	P001	408
0	Producer	P000	392
0	Consumer	QC	800

The output from this query shows that two parallel query slaves (P001 and P002) were employed to process the parallel query. They each read approximately half the table (408 rows and 392 rows respectively) and passed these on to the Query Coordinator (QC) process (the server process that initiated the query).

If there was a large discrepancy between the numbers of rows processed by each parallel slave, we might be concerned that we were not getting good parallelism and might look at reanalyzing the table or modifying the degree of parallelism.

Each value of TQ_ID represents a separate parallel execution step. In our example there was only one parallel step and only two parallel slaves. As the number of query slaves gets large and the number of execution steps increases, the amount of output generated by the V$PQ_TQSTAT query gets unmanageable. So, for instance, the query

```
SELECT   /*+ parallel(e,4) */department_id, SUM (salary)
  FROM employees e
 GROUP BY department_id
 ORDER BY 2 desc
```

would generate 22 lines of output. In this case, an aggregate query like the following probably gives a better overview of processing:

```
SELECT tq_id,
       server_type || DECODE (SUBSTR (process, 1, 2),
                      'QC', ' (QC)', '') server_type,
       COUNT (distinct process) no_of_processes,
       SUM (num_rows) total_rows,
       AVG (num_rows) average_rows,
       MAX (num_rows) maximum_rows,
       MIN (num_rows) minimum_rows
  FROM v$pq_tqstat
 WHERE dfo_number = (SELECT MAX (dfo_number)
                       FROM v$pq_tqstat)
 GROUP BY tq_id, server_type,
          DECODE (SUBSTR (process, 1, 2),
                  'QC', ' (QC)', '')
 ORDER BY tq_id, DECODE (SUBSTR (server_type, 1, 4),
                 'Prod', 0, 'Cons', 1, 3);
```

This admittedly complex query gives us a good summary of the parallel processing that has occurred:

TQ_ID	Category		Procs	Rows	Avg	Max	Min
0	Producer		4	741	185	219	156
0	Consumer		4	741	185	250	101
1	Producer		4	21	5	7	3
1	Consumer		4	21	5	6	5
1	Ranger	(QC)	1	21	21	21	21
2	Producer		4	21	5	6	5
2	Consumer	(QC)	1	21	21	21	21

This output—together with an examination of the explain plan—tells the following story:

❑ Four parallel slaves shared a scan of the table. They each processed about one-fourth of the table, although the heaviest loaded slave had 219 rows to process, while the lightest loaded had only 156 rows.

❑ The output from the scan was passed to the second set of slaves, which performed a sort-aggregate operation. The balance of this stage was not that good, with the heaviest loaded slave processing 250 rows, while the lightest loaded processed 101.

❑ The output from this step was 21 rows, one row for each DEPARTMENT_ ID. These rows were handed to a set of four slaves (these will be the same slave processes used in the first step) to be sorted to support the ORDER BY clause.

There are two reasons why you should use V$PQ_TQSTAT when tuning your parallel queries:

❑ The explain plan may show you that parallel query is expected, but it cannot tell you if it actually occurred or what the actual degree of parallelism is. Depending on the number of parallel slaves available, your query might run at reduced parallelism or even in serial. V$PQ_TQSTAT will reveal that this has happened.
❑ Effective parallelism depends on the even distribution of processing across the parallel slave processes. V$PQ_TQSTAT allows you to evaluate the efficiency of the load balancing across the parallel slaves.

You can query the V$PQ_TQSTAT table to determine the actual degree of parallelism used in your last parallel query and to ensure that there was a good load balance across parallel query slaves.

TUNING PARALLEL QUERY

Obtaining the best results often requires careful tuning of SQL statements and database server configuration and the appropriate use of parallelism. To ensure that your parallel SQL is fully tuned, you should

❑ Tune the Oracle server for parallel SQL.
❑ Use parallel query only when appropriate.
❑ Set an appropriate degree of parallelism.
❑ Analyze your tables.
❑ Ensure that all steps in a complex query are being executed in parallel.
❑ Use query techniques that favor parallelism, such as hash joins.
❑ Optimize your tables for parallel operations.

TUNING YOUR ORACLE SERVER FOR PARALLEL QUERY

As we noted earlier, you can't get full benefit from parallel query unless your computer is suitably configured. The fundamental hardware prerequisites for effective parallel query are as follows:

❏ Multiple CPUs to support multiple concurrent threads of execution.

❏ Multiple disk devices to support Oracle data files. It is equally important to ensure that the data is distributed evenly across these devices using striping (RAID0) or RAID5 (but watch out for the RAID5 write penalty). These issues are developed further in Chapter 18. You should ideally spread your data over as many disk devices as there are CPUs.

❏ Sufficient memory to support the memory allocations for multiple concurrent parallel processes. This includes memory for sort and hash areas.

Unlike most of the tuning techniques outlined previously, the parallel query option can be completely ineffective unless your Oracle server is appropriately configured. Follow the guidelines for configuring the server contained in Chapter 18 and Appendix D. In particular, the settings for the following parameters (each of which is described in Appendix D) are important:

❏ PARALLEL_THREADS_PER_CPU

❏ PARALLEL_ADAPTIVE_MULTI_USER

❏ PARALLEL_MAX_SERVERS

❏ OPTIMIZER_PERCENT_PARALLEL

❏ PARALLEL_MIN_PERCENT

If PARALLEL_AUTOMATIC_TUNING is set to TRUE, many of the parameters will be automatically adjusted by Oracle based on your machine configuration.

Configure your database for parallel query. Ensure that your data is spread across multiple disk devices, there is sufficient CPUs and memory, and parallel configuration parameters are set appropriately.

USE PQO APPROPRIATELY

The parallel query execution can consume many times the resources of serial query execution. If using the parallel query option doesn't result in a proportionate performance gain, then you may have consumed resources needlessly, resources that may have been required by other users. Avoid using the parallel query option if any of the following are true:

❏ The host computer has only a single CPU or the data to be accessed is not spread over multiple disk devices. You probably won't get a performance gain in these circumstances.

❏ The computer is near full capacity and there are other users competing for resources. If you use parallel query in these circumstances, you may improve your performance marginally, but substantially degrade performance for other users.

Don't use parallel query if your host computer is not suitably configured or if you are liable to severely degrade the performance of other users.

SET AN APPROPRIATE DEGREE OF PARALLELISM

The degree of parallelism determines the resources that will be assigned to your query and thus has a predominant effect on parallel query performance.

In Oracle 7.3, Oracle automatically set the degree of parallelism to either the number of CPUs available on the host computer or the number of disks used to store the table, whichever is smaller. This approach is a good starting point if the query is to be the only significant statement executing within the database. In Oracle8i, Oracle uses the setting of PARALLEL_THREADS_PER_CPU to set the default degree of parallelism. Because this approach ignores the number of disks, it may result in a less than optimal degree of parallelism if your data is spread over more disks than you have CPUs.

You may with to change the degree of parallelism if

❑ You have more disks than CPUs and don't believe that the operation will become CPU bound. In this case, you may wish to set the degree of parallelism to the number of disks.

❑ You want to limit the resources used by your query. If other SQL statements are executing concurrently on your server, it may be considerate to avoid using 100% of CPU resources. In this case, you might want to set the degree of parallelism to less than the number of CPUs or you may wish to set the PARALLEL_ADAPTIVE_MULTI_USER parameter to TRUE.

Set a degree of parallelism for your query that will maximize your throughput without having an unacceptable impact on other users.

ANALYZE YOUR TABLES

As with most operations that require the cost-based optimizer, parallel query execution is sensitive to table and index statistics generated by the ANALYZE command. The parallel query option is especially sensitive because it will use table statistics when partitioning blocks for the slave processes involved in full-table scans.

Use the ANALYZE command regularly on tables involved in parallel query.

ENSURE THAT ALL STEPS IN A COMPLEX QUERY ARE BEING EXECUTED IN PARALLEL

In a complex parallel SQL statement, it's important to ensure that all significant steps in the query execution are implemented in parallel. If one of the steps in a complex query is performed in serial, then the other parallel steps may have to wait for the serial step to complete and the advantages of parallelism will be lost. The OTHER_TAG column of the PLAN_TABLE will indicate such a step with the PARALLEL_FROM_SERIAL tag.

For instance, in the following query, the CUSTOMERS and PRODUCTS tables are accessed in parallel but the SALES table is accessed in serial. The serial full scan of SALES might ruin the overall performance of the query. This problem was caused because SALES used the NOPARALLEL setting, while CUSTOMERS and PRODUCTS had a default parallelism of 4.

```
SELECT customer_name, product_description,
       SUM (sale_value)
  FROM sales s, customers c, products p
 WHERE s.customer_id = c.customer_id
   AND s.product_id = p.product_id
 GROUP BY c.customer_name, p.product_description

Explain Plan:

SELECT STATEMENT
    SORT GROUP BY (PARALLEL_TO_SERIAL)
       SORT GROUP BY (PARALLEL_TO_PARALLEL)
          HASH JOIN (PARALLEL_COMBINED_WITH_PARENT)
             TABLE ACCESS FULL PRODUCTS
                               (PARALLEL_TO_PARALLEL)
             HASH JOIN (PARALLEL_TO_PARALLEL)
                TABLE ACCESS FULL CUSTOMERS
                                  (PARALLEL_TO_PARALLEL)
                TABLE ACCESS FULL SALES
                               (PARALLEL_FROM_SERIAL)
```

In complex queries, try to parallelize all query execution steps. Use the OTHER_TAG column of the plan table to highlight execution steps that are processed serially. Watch out for tables that are set to NOPARALLEL but are joined to tables that are parallel by default.

EXAMPLES OF PARALLEL QUERIES

In the following examples, we will see how to make effective use of parallel queries for a range of query types. We'll see how to use hints to invoke parallel query, how to avoid serial bottlenecks in our query and how to indicate which operations can be parallelized. In the examples, the tables have been created with the default option of NOPARALLEL. The default degree of parallelism is used throughout.

PARALLEL NESTED LOOPS JOIN

Because a nested loops join usually involves an index, it may at first seem surprising that it can be executed in parallel. However, provided that the driving table is based on a parallel full-table scan, the index lookups will be performed in parallel by the same processes that perform the full-table scan.

The following statement and EXPLAIN PLAN shows a parallel nested loops join between SALES and CUSTOMERS:

```
SELECT /*+ ordered use_nl(c) parallel(s)*/
       c.customer_name, s.sale_date, s.sale_value
  FROM sales s, customers c
 WHERE c.customer_id = s.customer_id
   AND s.sale_date > SYSDATE--365
 ORDER BY c.customer_name, s.sale_date

Explain Plan:

SELECT STATEMENT
    SORT ORDER BY (PARALLEL_TO_SERIAL)
      NESTED LOOPS (PARALLEL_TO_PARALLEL)
        TABLE ACCESS FULL SALES
                    (PARALLEL_COMBINED_WITH_PARENT)
        TABLE ACCESS BY INDEX ROWID CUSTOMERS
                    (PARALLEL_COMBINED_WITH_PARENT)
          INDEX UNIQUE SCAN PK_CUSTOMERS
                    (PARALLEL_COMBINED_WITH_PARENT)
```

The EXPLAIN PLAN shows us that the nested loops step was executed in parallel. The SALES table was scanned in parallel and the processes that scanned SALES also performed index lookups on CUSTOMERS. We can tell that the same processes were involved because of the PARALLEL_COMBINED_WITH_PARENT tag.

A second set of parallel processes sorted the joined rows in order to satisfy the ORDER BY clause.

HASH JOIN

The hash join is well suited to parallel execution. Provided both tables in the hash join are accessed via a parallel full-table scan, then parallelism through the entire join is achieved:

```
SELECT /*+parallel(s) parallel(c)*/
       c.customer_name, s.sale_date, s.sale_value
  FROM customers c, sales s
 WHERE c.customer_id = s.customer_id
   AND s.sale_date > SYSDATE--365
 ORDER BY c.customer_name, s.sale_date
```

Explain Plan:

```
SELECT STATEMENT
    SORT ORDER BY(PARALLEL_TO_SERIAL)
       HASH JOIN(PARALLEL_TO_PARALLEL)
          TABLE ACCESS FULL SALES(PARALLEL_TO_PARALLEL)
          TABLE ACCESS FULL CUSTOMERS
                              (PARALLEL_TO_PARALLEL)
```

However, if only one of the tables is scanned in parallel, then the PARALLEL_FROM_SERIAL tag indicates a potential bottleneck:

```
SELECT    /*+parallel(s)*/c.customer_name, s.sale_date,
s.sale_value
  FROM customers c, sales s
 WHERE c.customer_id = s.customer_id
   AND s.sale_date > SYSDATE--365
 ORDER BY c.customer_name, s.sale_date
```

Explain Plan:

```
SELECT STATEMENT
    SORT ORDER BY(PARALLEL_TO_SERIAL)
       HASH JOIN(PARALLEL_TO_PARALLEL)
          TABLE ACCESS FULL SALES(PARALLEL_TO_PARALLEL)
          TABLE ACCESS FULL CUSTOMERS
                              (**PARALLEL_FROM_SERIAL**)
```

ANTIJOIN

If we add a NOT IN condition to our query (and ALWAYS_ANTI_JOIN is not set), we can see that the parallel execution breaks down after the join of CUSTOMERS and SALES:

```
SELECT /*+ ordered use_nl(c) parallel(s)*/
       c.customer_name, s.sale_date, s.sale_value
  FROM sales s, customers c
 WHERE c.customer_id = s.customer_id
   AND s.sale_date > SYSDATE--365
   AND c.customer_id NOT IN (SELECT customer_id
                               FROM bad_customers)
 ORDER BY c.customer_name, s.sale_date
```

Explain Plan:

```
SELECT STATEMENT
    SORT ORDER BY   <- Serial
      FILTER        <- Serial
        NESTED LOOPS(PARALLEL_TO_SERIAL)
          TABLE ACCESS FULL SALES
                  (PARALLEL_COMBINED_WITH_PARENT)
          TABLE ACCESS BY ROWID CUSTOMERS
                  (PARALLEL_COMBINED_WITH_PARENT)
            INDEX RANGE SCAN PK_CUSTOMERS
                  (PARALLEL_COMBINED_WITH_PARENT)
          TABLE ACCESS FULL BAD_CUSTOMERS   <- Serial
```

As we saw in Chapter 7, Oracle's antijoin hint improves performance of serial antijoins. Additionally, it also allows a NOT IN operation to be executed in parallel. We can use this hint to improve parallelism by scanning the BAD_CUSTOMERS table in parallel:

```
SELECT /*+ ordered use_nl(c) parallel(s)*/
       c.customer_name, s.sale_date, s.sale_value
  FROM sales s, customers c
 WHERE c.customer_id = s.customer_id
   AND s.sale_date > SYSDATE--365
   AND c.customer_id NOT IN
       (SELECT /*+hash_aj parallel(bad_customers)*/
               customer_id
          FROM bad_customers)
 ORDER BY c.customer_name, s.sale_date
```

Explain Plan:

```
SELECT STATEMENT
    SORT ORDER BY (PARALLEL_TO_SERIAL)
      HASH JOIN ANTI (PARALLEL_TO_PARALLEL)
        NESTED LOOPS (PARALLEL_TO_PARALLEL)
          TABLE ACCESS FULL SALES
```

```
                (PARALLEL_COMBINED_WITH_PARENT)
    TABLE ACCESS BY INDEX ROWID CUSTOMERS
                (PARALLEL_COMBINED_WITH_PARENT)
        INDEX UNIQUE SCAN PK_CUSTOMERS
                (PARALLEL_COMBINED_WITH_PARENT)
    VIEW   VW_NSO_1 (PARALLEL_TO_PARALLEL)
        TABLE ACCESS FULL BAD_CUSTOMERS
                (PARALLEL_COMBINED_WITH_PARENT)
```

UNION AND SET OPERATORS

The UNION operation can be resolved in parallel provided that all tables in the union are accessed via parallel full-table scans:

```
SELECT /*+ parallel(c) full(c)*/
      contact_surname, contact_firstname
  FROM customers c
UNION
    SELECT /*+parallel(e) full(e)*/ surname, firstname
      FROM employees e
```

Explain Plan:

```
SELECT STATEMENT
    SORT UNIQUE (PARALLEL_TO_SERIAL)
      UNION-ALL (PARALLEL_TO_PARALLEL)
        TABLE ACCESS FULL CUSTOMERS
              (PARALLEL_COMBINED_WITH_PARENT)
        TABLE ACCESS FULL EMPLOYEES
              (PARALLEL_COMBINED_WITH_PARENT)
```

However, INTERSECT and MINUS operations are not resolved in parallel, even if the tables are scanned in parallel:

```
SELECT /*+ parallel(c) full(c) */
      contact_surname, contact_firstname
  FROM customers c
MINUS
    SELECT /*+parallel(e) full(e)*/surname, firstname
      FROM employees e
```

Explain Plan:

```
SELECT STATEMENT
    MINUS    <- Serial!
      SORT UNIQUE (PARALLEL_TO_SERIAL)
```

```
TABLE ACCESS FULL CUSTOMERS
            (PARALLEL_TO_PARALLEL)
SORT UNIQUE (PARALLEL_TO_SERIAL) \
TABLE ACCESS FULL EMPLOYEES
            (PARALLEL_TO_PARALLEL)
```

You may recall from Chapter 9 that a MINUS statement can be reformulated using NOT IN and that an INTERSECT can be reworded as a join. We saw that these join and antijoin alternatives could outperform the INTERSECT and MINUS operations. By using these alternatives to MINUS and INTERSECT, we can also take advantage of the parallel query option, since parallel query can be used for all types of joins and for antijoins using an antijoin hint.

> INTERSECT and MINUS operations do not parallelize. Use equivalent join and antijoin alternatives if you wish to parallelize these operations.

AGGREGATE OPERATIONS

Aggregate and sort operations will automatically parallelize if the preceding operations are performed in parallel. For instance, the following example shows ORDER and GROUP BY operations proceeding in parallel:

```
SELECT   /*+parallel(s) parallel(c)*/
      customer_name, SUM (sale_value) sale_total
  FROM sales s, customers c
 WHERE s.customer_id = c.customer_id
 GROUP BY c.customer_name
 ORDER BY 2 desc

Explain Plan:

SELECT STATEMENT
    SORT ORDER BY (PARALLEL_TO_SERIAL)
      SORT GROUP BY (PARALLEL_TO_PARALLEL)
        SORT GROUP BY (PARALLEL_TO_PARALLEL)
          HASH JOIN (PARALLEL_COMBINED_WITH_PARENT)
            TABLE ACCESS FULL CUSTOMERS
                    (PARALLEL_TO_PARALLEL)
            TABLE ACCESS FULL SALES
                    (PARALLEL_TO_PARALLEL)
```

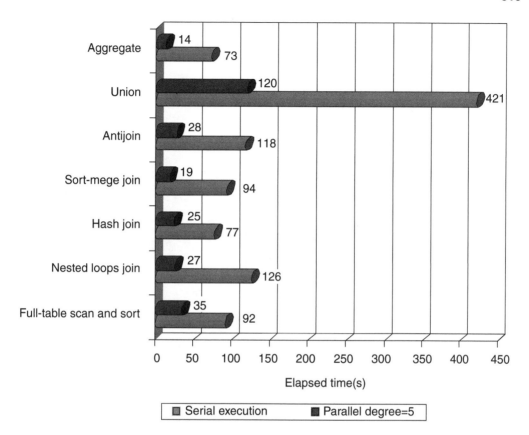

FIGURE 11.5   Performance of parallel query examples and their serial alternatives.

PARALLEL QUERY EXAMPLE PERFORMANCE

Figure 11.5 shows the performance improvements obtained from implementing the parallel query option for the query types used in our examples. We can see that each category of query responded well to parallel execution, with an average reduction in elapsed time of 75%. Your results will vary depending on your server configuration and the characteristics of your query and data.

OTHER PARALLEL OPERATIONS

Parallel query is probably the most powerful and widely used of Oracle's parallel offerings. However, there are many other operations that can proceed in parallel and that are discussed in depth in other chapters:

❑ DML operations can be processed in parallel on partitioned tables. INSERT operations can be processed in parallel on nonpartitioned tables. These topics are discussed in Chapter 12.

❑ Partitions offer parallel DML capabilities as outlined previously, and allow for parallel index scans and parallel partitionwise joins. These topics are discussed in Chapter 13.

❑ Many DDL operations can be processed in parallel. In particular, CREATE TABLE AS SELECT, CREATE INDEX, and ALTER INDEX REBUILD can all benefit extensively from parallel processing. These topics are discussed in the optimizing DDL section of Chapter 17.

SUMMARY

In this chapter, we've examined Oracle's parallel SQL capabilities. Using parallel SQL is one of the most effective ways of improving the performance of SQL that relies on full-table scans.

Parallel SQL works by allocating multiple processes, called parallel slaves, to the execution of the SQL statement. The execution of the SQL statement is partitioned into multiple segments and allocated to multiple slave processes. The degree of parallelism determines the number of parallel threads of SQL execution. You can set the degree of parallelism yourself or allow Oracle to use a default value. For most nontrivial SQL statements, Oracle will allocate twice as many parallel slaves as the degree of parallelism.

Parallel SQL is only effective under suitable conditions:

❑ The host computer has multiple CPUs and/or the database is spread across multiple disk devices.

❑ The SQL statement is based on at least one full-table scan of a large table.

❑ There is spare CPU and I/O capacity on the host computer.

Parallel SQL can be used for

❑ Queries based on a full-table scan (parallel query option)

❑ Index builds

❑ CREATE TABLE statements based on a query

❑ UPDATEs and DELETEs on partitioned tables

❑ Inserts based on a parallelized select statement

❑ Index lookups on a partitioned table

To optimize parallel SQL,

❏ Use EXPLAIN PLAN (or a tool that generates parallel execution plans) to examine the execution plans for your parallel SQL. Use the OTHER_TAG column to establish the parallelism of each step. Steps with an OTHER_TAG of PARALLEL_FROM_SERIAL may indicate a serial bottleneck to parallel execution.

❏ Ensure that your server is tuned for parallel SQL. It should have sufficient parallel slaves and data files striped across multiple disk devices.

❏ Set a suitable degree of parallelism.

❏ Analyze your tables.

❏ Use approaches that favor parallelism, such as hash joins, bitmap indexes, antijoins, and partition views or tables.

❏ Take advantage of the V$PQ_TQSTAT view, which can reveal the true degree of parallelism and the effectiveness of load balancing between parallel processes.

Optimizing DML

In this chapter, we look at issues relating to the performance of Data Manipulation Language (DML) statements. These statements (INSERT, UPDATE, and DELETE) alter the information contained within your Oracle database.

Even in transaction processing environments, most database activity is related to data retrieval. This is primarily because UPDATEs and DELETEs must retrieve the rows before they can be processed. Because DML operations usually have a query component, you can often tune DML statements using query optimization techniques.

One of the key features of relational databases is the ability to group multiple DML statements into a group of statements that must succeed or fail as a unit. These groups of statements are known as transactions. Transactions have distinct performance problems and tuning opportunities.

The topics covered in this chapter are as follows:

❑ Optimizing individual DML statements through the optimization of the WHERE clause and subqueries
❑ Alternatives to the DELETE statement (TRUNCATE and DROP PARTITION)
❑ Using TRUNCATE to delete all rows in a table
❑ Managing the effect of indexes on DML performance
❑ The effect of referential integrity constraints and triggers

❏ Optimizing INSERTS by using array processing and direct load inserts and
   by reducing freelist contention
❏ Optimizing transactions
❏ Using parallel DML

GENERAL OPTIMIZATIONS

OPTIMIZE THE WHERE CLAUSE FIRST

Much of the overhead involved in UPDATE and DELETE rows is incurred when
locating the rows to be processed. DELETE and UPDATE statements usually contain a WHERE clause that defines the rows to be deleted or updated. INSERT and
UPDATE statements can contain subqueries, which define either the data to be
inserted or the updated row values. The obvious first step in optimizing the performance of these statements is to optimize the WHERE clauses or subqueries.

These subqueries and WHERE clauses can be optimized using the same
principles discussed in previous chapters, such as

❏ Creating indexes on columns in the WHERE clause
❏ Using antijoin hints to improve performance of NOT IN subqueries
❏ Ensuring that correlated subqueries are efficient

If a DML statement contains a WHERE clause or a subquery, ensure that the subquery or WHERE clause is optimized using the standard query optimization principles.

INDEX OVERHEAD

In previous chapters, we have made extensive use of indexes to improve the
performance of queries. Usually, when we have been able to improve query performance by adding an index, we have done so. Although indexes can considerably improve query performance, they do reduce the performance of DML. All of
a table's indexes must be updated when a row is inserted or deleted and an index
must also be amended when an update changes any column that appears in the
index.

It is therefore important that all our indexes contribute to query performance[1] since these indexes will otherwise needlessly degrade DML performance.

---

[1]An exception can be made for foreign key indexes, which reduce lock contention, and for
unique constraint indexes. We may wish to keep these even if they don't contribute to
query performance.

In particular, you should be especially careful when creating indexes on frequently updated columns. A row can only be inserted or deleted once but may be updated many times. Indexes on heavily updated columns or on tables that have a very high insert/delete rate will therefore exact a particularly high cost.

Indexes always add to the overhead of INSERT and DELETE statements and may add to the overhead of UPDATE statements. Avoid overindexing, especially on columns that are frequently updated.

B*-tree Indexes versus Bitmap Indexes   The effort of maintaining a single bitmap is less than the overhead of maintaining a B*-tree structure. However, as the number of distinct values in the column increases, the number of bitmaps that must be maintained also increases. For this reason, unless your indexed column has only a few values, a bitmap index will have a stronger negative effect on DML statements than a B*-tree index.

Even more significantly, bitmap indexes break Oracle's row-level locking mechanism. When a bitmap index is updated, locks are applied to all the rows that have an entry in the bitmap segment. The bitmap segment can be up to half a database block in size and can store a lot of bitmap entries. For this reason, you are strongly advised not to implement bitmap indexes on tables that are subject to concurrent update activity in an OLTP environment.

Interestingly, it may appear that the row in question is not locked if you use the FOR UPDATE clause of the SELECT statement. This means that an application that checks for locked rows using FOR UPDATE NOWAIT may go ahead and issue an UPDATE statement on a row that is locked by a bitmap index.

Bitmap indexes usually have more maintenance overhead than B*-tree indexes, especially if there are a lot of distinct values for the column. Bitmap indexes also add a much greater lock overhead when there is concurrent DML activity.

Dropping and Rebuilding Indexes   INSERTs and DELETEs will be significantly slower for tables with a large number of indexes. If you are regularly inserting large numbers of rows into such a table during a batch window that has no associated query activity, then it may be worth dropping the indexes before the data load and re-creating them later. This will be especially effective if you use the UNRECOVERABLE clause (see Chapter 17) and parallel index creation option (see Chapter 17).

To reduce the overhead of deleting from heavily indexed tables, you should consider logically deleting the rows using a status column. Queries against the table would have a WHERE clause condition that eliminated the logically deleted rows. During a regular batch window the rows could either be deleted or the table could be rebuilt without the unwanted rows. You can rebuild a large table surprisingly quickly using CREATE TABLE AS SELECT with the UNRECOVERABLE and PARALLEL options. See Chapter 17 for details on the UNRECOVERABLE option and Chapter 11 for details of parallel table creation.

TRUNCATE VERSUS DELETE

The TRUNCATE TABLE command allows all rows to be removed from a table with minimal overhead. Emptying a table using the DELETE command results in a high overhead in rollback segment and redo log entries. Additionally, using TRUNCATE resets the table's high-water mark, which will improve subsequent full-table scans.

Strictly speaking, the TRUNCATE command is a Data Definition Language (DDL) statement rather than a DML statement. This means that it cannot be rolled back, and it issues an implicit COMMIT (so any preceding statements will be committed and also will become permanent).

Remember that TRUNCATE can only be used to remove all rows from a table.

When removing all rows from a table, use TRUNCATE in preference to DELETE.

DROP PARTITION VERSUS DELETE

One of the most powerful incentives for implementing partitions is the ability to purge unneeded rows from a table by dropping a partition instead of through DELETE statements.

Imagine that the SALES table is partitioned on SALE_DATE so that sales for each quarter are stored in a separate partition. Over time, old SALE details are aggregated and rows removed from the SALES table. By simply dropping the partition, we can remove all these rows almost immediately. Alternately, issuing a DELETE statement requires a large amount of I/O, both to identify and remove the rows and to identify and remove the index entries.

We expand on these issues in Chapter 13.

If deleting stale rows from large tables is a significant overhead, consider creating a table that is range partitioned on the date column that identifies the rows to be purged. You can then remove these rows by dropping the partition in question.

CORRELATED UPDATES

Updates often contain a subquery in the WHERE or the SET clause. When the same table is referenced in both the WHERE and in the SET clauses, duplicate processing and inefficient processing can occur. For example, the following update references the employee table in both the SET clause and the WHERE clause:

```
UPDATE customers c
   SET sales_rep_id =
       (SELECT manager_id
          FROM employee
         WHERE surname = c.contact_surname
           AND firstname = c.contact_firstname
           AND date_of_birth = c.date_of_birth)
  WHERE (contact_surname,
         contact_firstname,
         date_of_birth) IN
    (SELECT surname, firstname, date_of_birth
       FROM employees)
```

```
Rows     Execution Plan
-------  -------------------------------------------------
      0  UPDATE STATEMENT    GOAL: CHOOSE
  28009  HASH JOIN
    800   VIEW
    800    SORT (UNIQUE)
    800     TABLE ACCESS (FULL) OF 'EMPLOYEES'
                 -- Get manager_id
 100000   TABLE ACCESS (FULL) OF 'CUSTOMERS'
      0   TABLE ACCESS (FULL) OF 'EMPLOYEES'
                 -- From WHERE clause
```

Although the subquery in the WHERE clause can use an index to find rows to be processed, a second access of the EMPLOYEES table must be made to obtain the relevant manager_id column. At best, this will result in unnecessary index lookups; at worst, no index will be available and multiple table scans will be performed.

There is often no alternative to this format for the UPDATE statement, because there is simply no way to reference the employee rows to which the WHERE clause refers from the SET subquery.

Logically, we could perform the update more efficiently by using procedural logic, as in this PL/SQL block:

```
DECLARE
   CURSOR cust_csr is
           select c.rowid crowid,e.manager_id
             from customers c,
                  employees e
            where e.surname=c.contact_surname
              and e.firstname=c.contact_firstname
              and e.date_of_birth=c.date_of_birth;
BEGIN
   FOR cust_row in cust_csr LOOP
       update customers
          set sales_rep_id=cust_row.manager_id
        where rowid=cust_row.crowid;
   END LOOP;
END;
```

In the case where an index is not available to support the SET clause, the PL/SQL approach requires only a single scan of EMPLOYEES and reduces block gets from 8033 blocks to 1089 blocks.

REFERENTIAL INTEGRITY

Referential integrity constraints prevent a foreign key column from referring to nonexistent primary keys. For instance, the following constraint prevents the department_id column in SALES referring to a nonexistent customer:

```
ALTER TABLE sales
    ADD CONSTRAINT fk1_sales FOREIGN KEY (customer_id)
       REFERENCES customers (customer_id)
```

The presence of the foreign key constraint forces Oracle to check the CUSTOMER table for every row inserted into the SALES table. Not surprisingly, this slows down inserts into SALES (see Figure 12.1). Using referential integrity constraints helps ensure self-consistency within your database and is generally recommended. However, be aware of the impact during INSERTs (and UPDATEs of the foreign key).

Also remember that referential integrity constraints can result in Oracle locking the entire child table during an update to the parent table if a foreign key index does not exist. In our example, the SALES table might be subject to a full-table lock when rows are modified in the CUSTOMERS table unless there is an index on the CUSTOMER_ID column in the SALES table. These full-table locks could cause severe performance problems for sessions trying to perform DML against the SALES table.

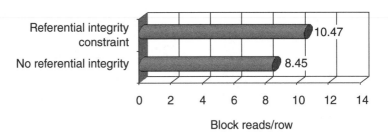

FIGURE 12.1   The effect of a foreign key constraint on inserts into the SALES table.

Use referential integrity constraints to maintain self-consistency in your data, but be aware of the performance impact for DML statements. Ensure that you have an index on the foreign key columns to avoid costly full-table locks.

TRIGGERS

Triggers are PL/SQL blocks that execute when specified DML operations occur. The overhead of executing the PL/SQL is going to depend on the contents of the trigger and the rate of DML on the table involved, but there will be an overhead. We will discuss the optimization of triggers in Chapter 14.

OPTIMIZING INSERTS

ARRAY INSERT

Array INSERT refers to the Oracle facility that allows more than one row to be inserted into a table in a single operation. This reduces communication traffic between your client program and the Oracle server. It also reduces the number of SQL calls executed. In many environments, array processing is provided transparently. Appendix C contains some guidelines for implementing array processing in commonly used development tools, and Chapters 14 and 15 describe how to implement array processing in PL/SQL and in Java.

   Array processing can have a dramatic effect on insert performance. Figure 12.2 shows the effect of varying the array size on the performance of a bulk insert.

Use the array INSERT facility whenever possible to improve bulk insert performance.

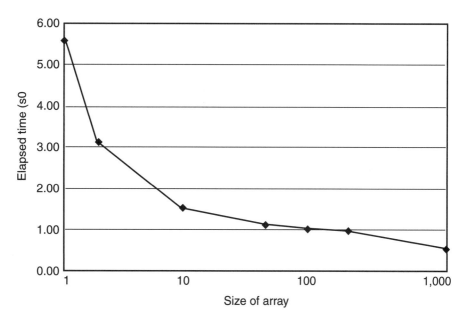

FIGURE 12.2 Effect of varying the array size on bulk insert performance.

DIRECT LOAD INSERTS

Users of SQL*LOADER will be familiar with its direct path mode. This mode allows data blocks to be constructed in memory and inserted directly into the database files, bypassing the Oracle buffer cache. Direct load insert uses a very similar model. Bypassing the buffer cache can reduce overhead and contention and can lead to substantial improvements in insert performance. To invoke the direct load insert, you should use the APPEND hint.

Because direct load insert creates only new blocks, free space in existing blocks cannot be used. If the table is partitioned, the blocks can be inserted into existing extents above the high-water mark (the highest block that ever contained data). If the table is unpartitioned, then new extents must be created. In either case, the high-water mark is increased. Because full-table scans always read every block up to the high-water mark, direct load inserts can increase full-table scan overhead more than conventional inserts.

There are other limitations of the direct load insert:

❏ After a direct load insert, you cannot modify or select from the table in question before issuing a commit or rollback.
❏ Direct load inserts cannot be performed on partitioned tables with global indexes.
❏ A direct load insert applies a full table DML lock to the table in question. No other concurrent insert, delete, or update operations are permitted.

❏ Direct load inserts do not support referential integrity constraints, triggers, replication, index organized tables, object tables, LOB columns, clustered tables, or distributed transactions.

An explain plan will denote the presence of a direct load operation with the "LOAD AS SELECT" operation:

```
Rows      Execution Plan
-------   -----------------------------------------------
     0    INSERT STATEMENT     GOAL: CHOOSE
     0    LOAD AS SELECT
     0      TABLE ACCESS (FULL) OF 'CUSTOMERS'
```

You might expect that the direct load insert algorithm would always be faster than a traditional insert. Surprisingly, the opposite is often true. During a normal insert operation, your server (or shadow) task need only insert into blocks held in memory within the SGA's *buffer cache*. These blocks are written out to disk asynchronously by the database writer process (DBWR). Provided that DBWR keeps up with your inserts, you will never have to wait for datafile write I/O (although you will usually need to wait for I/Os to the redo log when you issue a commit).

The situation is somewhat different during direct load inserts. Your shadow process is directly responsible for writing new blocks to the datafiles, and consequently you will now need to wait for this I/O to complete before your insert can finish. The result is that direct load insert statements often take longer to run than traditional inserts. Figure 12.3 compares the two insert algorithms.

If the direct load insert can actually take longer, why would anyone bother to use it? In fact, there are specific circumstances in which direct load insert can outperform traditional inserts:

❏ If there is a high level of contention for memory in the buffer cache, or there is a database writer bottleneck, then traditional inserts may have to wait for free buffers in the cache. In this circumstance, direct load insert might outperform a normal insert.

❏ Direct load insert can be performed in parallel (using the PARALLEL hint), whereas traditional inserts can only be performed in parallel on partitioned tables.

❏ By reducing the load on the database writer process and the buffer cache, direct load inserts may improve the performance of other operations that are executing concurrently.

❏ When the operating system supports asynchronous I/O, the direct mode insert can insert into multiple database files simultaneously, which will overcome the advantages of multiple database writers supporting the normal insert.

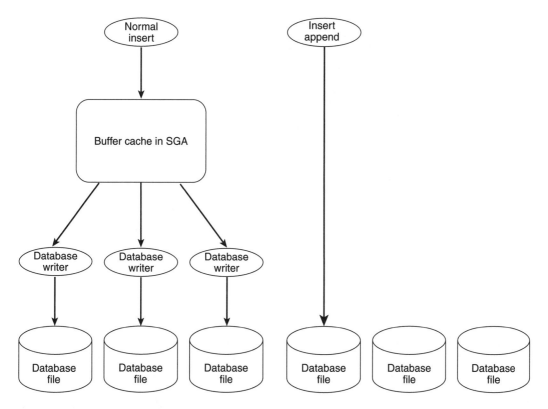

FIGURE 12.3   Insert append compared with Normal insert.

Figure 12.4 shows the performance for the following simple insert statement:

```
INSERT /*+append*/ INTO temp_table
SELECT * FROM customers
```

For a well-tuned database without contention for buffer cache blocks and well-configured database writers, the direct load insert actually took longer to complete than the traditional insert. However, for a poorly tuned database (small buffer cache, single database writer, asynchronous I/O disabled), the direct load insert performed substantially better than the traditional insert.

Consider direct mode insert (using the APPEND hint) when there is contention for blocks in the buffer cache or when you want to insert into an unpartitioned table in parallel.

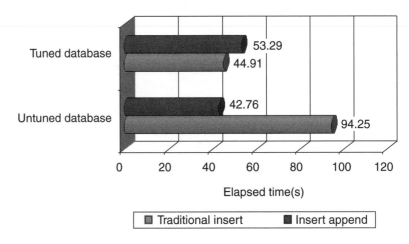

FIGURE 12.4   Direct load insert performance.

UNLOGGED OPERATIONS

In Oracle7 you can specify that a CREATE TABLE AS SELECT or a CREATE INDEX is "UNRECOVERABLE." This instructs Oracle not to generate redo log information for the operation and can result in significant reductions in build time, especially when used in conjunction with the PARALLEL clause. However, the objects thus created cannot be recovered from information contained in redo logs.

The NOLOGGING keyword replaces the UNRECOVERABLE keyword in Oracle8 (the UNRECOVERABLE keyword is retained for compatibility reasons). The NOLOGGING mode can be used for direct load inserts as well as for CREATE TABLE and CREATE INDEX. Because no redo log information is generated, the insert will be faster. But if there should be a disk failure before the next tablespace backup, all the information inserted will be lost.

You can specify the NOLOGGING keyword in CREATE TABLE, CREATE INDEX, ALTER TABLE, or ALTER INDEX statements, or you can specify it as the default for a tablespace. Once NOLOGGING is associated with a table, any direct mode inserts will automatically be performed without logging. Watch out for this if you have used the Oracle7 UNRECOVERABLE option to build tables: Under Oracle8 you'll need to issue an ALTER TABLE statement to turn the logging mode back on if you need to log subsequent direct load inserts.

Because the data inserted with the NOLOGGING mode can't be restored from redo logs, you're not likely to use this facility for your critical application data. You might use the nologging feature in the following circumstances:

❑ Loading a temporary table for intermediate processing in a long-running batch job
❑ Quickly building a dispensable summary or aggregate table

Also note that because redo log writes are performed asynchronously by the redo log writer, you might not obtain a noticeable performance improvement for many operations. However, you will see an improvement in commit times and may see a general systemwide performance improvement when redo log activity is a bottleneck.

You can use UNLOGGED to reduce the redo log overhead for INSERT operations. But make sure that you make special efforts to ensure that the objects involved can be recovered in the event that the database needs recovery.

FREELIST CONTENTION

When an Oracle session wants to INSERT a new row into a table, that session must find a block with enough free space available for the row to be INSERTed. A block will be eligible for INSERTs depending on the amount of free space in the block and the values of PCTFREE and PCTUSED, as explained in Chapter 7. Oracle maintains a list of blocks eligible for INSERTs that is called the *freelist*. If there is a large number of sessions concurrently inserting into a table, then there may be contention for these freelists.

We will see how to detect contention for freelists in Chapter 20. It's not easy to detect freelist contention or to determine which tables are experiencing freelist contention. If you suspect that many concurrent sessions will INSERT into one table, it may be wise to create this table with multiple freelists using the FREELISTS clause of the CREATE TABLE statement:

```
CREATE TABLE table_name
    (column specifications)
    STORAGE (FREELISTS number_of_freelists)
```

Prior to 8.1.6, you could not alter the number of freelists in a table without rebuilding the table. However, in 8.1.6 you can alter the number of freelists with the ALTER TABLE command:

```
ALTER TABLE customers STORAGE (FREELISTS 2);
```

Use the FREELISTS clause of the CREATE TABLE statement to create multiple freelists for tables that experience heavy concurrent insert activity.

OPTIMIZING TRANSACTIONS

A transaction is a set of DML statements that will succeed or fail as a unit. In Oracle (and in the ANSI standard), a transaction implicitly commences when a DML statement is issued, and completes with a COMMIT or ROLLBACK statement or when a program terminates.

DISCRETE TRANSACTIONS

Oracle includes a feature that is designed to speed up certain categories of transactions. This feature is known as *discrete transaction* and improves performance of transactions by eliminating some of the overhead of DML statements.

To understand how a discrete transaction works, let's review how Oracle processes DML statements in a normal transaction. For instance, consider the following statement:

```
UPDATE customer_account
   SET balance = balance - 20
 WHERE customer_id = 3
```

When this statement is issued, Oracle performs the following activities:

❏ The data block containing the relevant CUSTOMER_ACCOUNT row is retrieved. If the block is not in memory (in the SGA), then Oracle will retrieve the block from disk.

❏ An image of the row as it was before the update is copied to an Oracle rollback segment. This "before image" of the row can be used to revert the row to its original state in the event that a ROLLBACK is issued. The copy will also be used by other sessions that must access the old customer balance until a COMMIT is issued.

❏ The value of the BALANCE column is changed in the "current" version of the data block.

❏ An entry recording the changed values is written to the redo log. The redo log contains details of transaction information that can be used to reconstruct the transaction in the event of a system failure.

❏ If a COMMIT is issued, then the contents of the redo log are written to disk, making the changes permanent.

❏ If a ROLLBACK is issued, then the copy of the relevant blocks in the rollback segment is used to revert the block to its previous value.

In the case of a discrete transaction, changes to the data block and redo log are deferred until the last possible moment, when the transaction commits. No entries are made to the rollback segment because no changes are made until a COMMIT is issued; therefore, rollback information is not required.

As a result of this approach, discrete transactions have the following restrictions and consequences:

❏ If a discrete transaction queries a row that it has modified, it will see the unmodified value of the row, since the row is not truly changed until the commit is issued.

❏ Discrete transactions cannot be distributed transactions—that is, a discrete transaction cannot alter data in another database.

❏ Tables that contain referential integrity constraints may cause problems for discrete transactions. For instance, if we added a new department and then tried to add an employee to this department within the same discrete transaction, the operation may fail since the new department row has not yet really been added.

❏ Discrete transactions cannot change the same block twice.

❏ Discrete transactions can cause errors in queries that attempt to read the changed blocks while discrete transactions are in progress. For instance, suppose we attempt to issue a "sum(balance)" on customer accounts. If a discrete transaction alters a block after the query commences but before we encounter the block, we will encounter a problem when we come to read the changed block. Oracle will detect that the block has been changed since the query began and will attempt to find an older version of the row in the rollback segment. Since discrete transactions don't generate rollback segment information, we won't find a previous block and a "Snapshot too old" error will result.

These restrictions are fairly severe and violate ANSI standards and some commonsense expectations. Oracle received strong criticism when discrete transactions were introduced on the grounds that they were a "benchmark special": introduced to improve performance in standard industry benchmark tests but not useful in the real world. As a result, discrete transactions have a fairly poor reputation and are not used often in production systems.

However, if the circumstances favor discrete transactions, then significant performance improvements can be realized. For instance, on average, the following discrete transaction completed in 80% of the time of its nondiscrete equivalent (Figure 12.5):

```
CREATE PROCEDURE discrete_tran (
      p_customer_id NUMBER, p_product_id NUMBER,
      p_quantity NUMBER, p_value NUMBER)
IS
BEGIN
   dbms_transaction.begin_discrete_transaction;
```

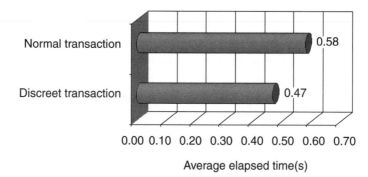

FIGURE 12.5   Relative performance of a discrete transaction.

```
INSERT INTO sales
        (customer_id, product_id, sale_date,
         quantity, sale_value)
      VALUES (p_customer_id, p_product_id,
                SYSDATE, p_quantity, p_value);

UPDATE customer_balance
   SET balance = balance--p_value
 WHERE customer_id = p_customer_id;

COMMIT;
END;
```

If you can tolerate the limitations of discrete transactions and need to improve the performance of some update-intensive operations, you may wish to consider using them. They suit small transactions in update-intensive environments where long-running queries do not occur.

Discrete transactions can improve the performance of certain small transactions in specific circumstances. However, they can prevent successful execution of long running queries.

OPTIONS OF THE SET TRANSACTION COMMAND

The SET TRANSACTION command allows you to control characteristics of your transaction. Some of these options have performance implications. Table 12.1 summarizes these commands and their implications.

Table 12.1   Options of the SET TRANSACTION Command

SET TRANSACTION OPTION	USAGE NOTES
USE ROLLBACK SEGMENT *segment_name*	This option allows you to specify the rollback segment to be used by your transaction. Oracle will usually assign a rollback segment to your transaction using load balancing algorithms, and it's generally not helpful to force the use of a particular segment. However, if you know that your transaction will affect a large number of rows (a bulk update, for instance) you may wish to explicitly choose a larger rollback segment. Performance will be improved, since dynamic growth of the rollback segment during your transaction will be avoided.
READ ONLY	This option prevents your transaction from seeing changes to rows that were made after your transaction began. This can be useful for reports comprising multiple SQL statements that need a consistent view of the data. However, enabling this option unnecessarily in a long-running set of queries may reduce the performance of your report. This is because additional visits to rollback segments will be required to obtain "before images" of rows. Accessing the rollback segments involves additional I/Os.

COMMIT FREQUENCY

A transaction is successfully terminated when a COMMIT statement is issued or when a COMMIT is issued implicitly, such as when a program successfully terminates. Committing a transaction causes the following events to occur:

❏   The transaction is marked as committed in the relevant rollback segment.
❏   The transaction is marked as complete in the redo log.
❏   The redo log entries are written to the redo log file on disk.

While the first two events occur in memory, the third event—writing to the redo log—always requires a write to disk. This is so your transaction is not lost if the system should crash and the information in memory is lost.

Since a COMMIT always requires some disk I/O, it follows that the more frequently a program commits, the more I/O overhead it will incur.

Usually, the determination of when to COMMIT a transaction is driven by application design or user requirements rather than by performance considerations. For instance, if users press a SAVE button in an on-line application, they have a reasonable expectation that the transaction is now saved, and this would require a COMMIT.

On the other hand, when coding bulk load or batch jobs, you may have some options as to how often to COMMIT. For instance, in the following PL/SQL code, we can adjust how often we COMMIT by altering the value of the *p_commitf* variable:

```
PROCEDURE p_update_status (p_commitf NUMBER := 1000)
IS
   counter_l                        NUMBER := 0;
   status_l                         VARCHAR2(10);
BEGIN
   FOR customer_row IN ( SELECT *
                            FROM customer_balance)
   LOOP
      counter_l := counter_l + 1;

      IF customer_row.balance < 0 THEN
         status_l := 'DEBIT';
      ELSE
         status_l := 'CREDIT';
      END IF;

      UPDATE customers
         SET status = status_l
       WHERE customer_id = customer_row.customer_id;

      IF counter_l > p_commitf THEN
         -- Commit every "p_commitf" rows
         COMMIT;
         counter_l := 0;
      END IF;
   END LOOP;
   COMMIT;
END;
```

Figure 12.6 shows elapsed times for various COMMIT frequencies. By reducing the COMMIT frequency, we reduced elapsed times for the job by more than 75%.

Since committing a transaction involves an I/O overhead, COMMIT infrequently during bulk updates.

LOCKING

Oracle applies a row-level lock to each row affected by a DML statement. This lock prevents other DML statements from affecting the row in question without hindering any queries on that row. The locks are released when a transaction terminates, usually as the result of a COMMIT or ROLLBACK statement.

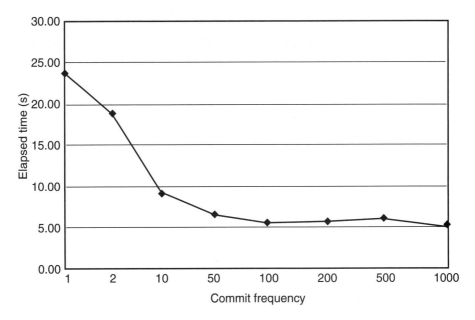

FIGURE 12.6   Performance impact of adjusting COMMIT frequency.

Contention for locks can severely impact the throughput of concurrent transactions. You can reduce the impact of locking on your application using the following guidelines:

❑ COMMIT transactions as soon as is logically possible in a transaction processing environment.

❑ Avoid holding locks during interaction with a user. Some applications allow a user to hold a lock pending the hit of an "OK" button. This can result in long delays for other users, especially if the user holding the lock goes to lunch!

❑ Carefully consider your locking strategy. An optimistic locking strategy, in which rows are locked at the last minute and an error is generated if another user changes the row, can result in less contention than the pessimistic locking strategy, in which the row is locked as it is fetched from the database. See Chapter 18 for a more detailed comparison of the two strategies.

❑ Ensure that columns with foreign key constraints are indexed if the parent table is subject to updates. Missing foreign key indexes can cause Oracle to lock the entire parent table against updates when a child table is updated.

Ensure that you minimize your locking contention by COMMITING transactions appropriately, avoiding user interaction while locks are held, and carefully considering your locking strategy.

PARALLEL DML

The ability to perform DML in parallel was introduced in Oracle8. INSERT statements can be processed in parallel on partitioned or unpartitioned tables, while UPDATE and DELETEs can be processed in parallel only on partitioned tables.

As with parallel query, the performance improvements gained by parallel processing of DML operations can result in greater gains than any other measure provided that the hardware is suitable for parallel processing.

PARALLEL INSERT

Unlike other forms of parallel DML, it's possible to perform an INSERT from a SELECT in parallel even if the table is not partitioned.

Parallel insert into nonpartitioned tables works in the direct insert (APPEND) mode discussed earlier. That is, blocks are created and formatted in session memory and inserted directly into the datafiles, bypassing the buffer cache. This also means that each parallel slave must insert into a separate extent or partition. For parallel insert into nonpartitioned tables, for each degree of parallelism at least one new extent will be created. As a result, parallel insert might result in a greater increase in storage allocation than a serial insert.

For a parallel insert into a partitioned table, each parallel slave is assigned a separate partition. The slaves may insert into an existing extent if space is available above the high-water mark. If no space is available, then new extents must be allocated.

PARALLEL UPDATE AND DELETE

UPDATEs and DELETEs on partitioned tables may be processed in parallel. Multiple parallel slaves processes will be allocated to the operation, although each partition will be allocated no more than a single process. For this reason, the degree of parallelism (number of parallel threads of execution) may be no more than the number of partitions in the table.

USING PARALLEL DML

To active parallel DML, you must first issue the ALTER SESSION ENABLE PARALLEL DML command.

As with parallel queries, parallel DML is initiated if there is a PARALLEL clause on the table or a PARALLEL hint within the SQL statement. For example, the following statement inserts all transactions older than one week into a TRANSACTION_ARCHIVE table. Note that the PARALLEL hint is used both in the INSERT statement and in the underlying SELECT. We also used the APPEND hint to invoke the direct insert mode.

```
INSERT  /*+parallel (t,5) append */
  INTO transaction_archive ta
SELECT /*+ parallel (t,5) */ *
  FROM transactions t
 WHERE transaction_date < sysdate -7
```

When using parallel DML, there are a couple of pitfalls you should try to avoid:

❏ For a parallel DML-based on a query, ensure that the query is also parallelized. For instance, it may not be effective to use a serial (perhaps index-based) SELECT to feed rows into a parallel INSERT.

❏ When using parallel DML on partitioned tables, you should make sure that the number of parallel slave processes can be evenly divided into the number of partitions. Otherwise, some of the parallel slaves will have more partitions to process than others and you won't get full benefit from your degree of parallelism.

Any Oracle user who has to deal with large tables can probably imagine a number of effective uses for parallel DML. Here are some of the more obvious:

❏ Parallel inserts into temporary tables (for instance, using parallel insert to populate a temporary report table)

❏ Bulk updates of tables for maintenance (for instance, giving every taxpayer a 10% reduction in their tax rate)

❏ Purging and archiving (for instance, using parallel insert to copy rows older than one year to an archive table and using parallel delete to remove the same rows from the source table)

RESTRICTIONS ON PARALLEL DML

There are a number of restrictions on parallel DML:

❏ As with direct load inserts, a parallel DML statement cannot appear as a transaction with other DML statements. The only statement that can follow a parallel DML statement is COMMIT or a ROLLBACK.

❏ You can't perform parallel DML on a partitioned table with a unique global index. For parallel insert, no global indexes are permitted.

❏ Tables that have triggers, or tables with self-referencing or delete cascade constraints, cannot be subject to parallel DML. The restriction on triggers is particularly significant since it means that any table that is replicated (for instance, the source table of a snapshot) cannot be subjected to parallel DML.

❏ Parallel DML statements cannot be used in distributed transactions.

❏ Parallel DML requires some additional resources. Each parallel slave requires its own transaction and rollback segment entry. There are also more freelist and enqueue resources required. A two-phase commit is necessary to complete the parallel DML

SUMMARY

In this chapter, we've discussed ways of improving the performance of DML statements—UPDATE, DELETE and INSERT—and of improving the performance of DML statements grouped in transactions.

The major principles for optimizing DML are as follows:

❏ Optimize the subqueries and WHERE clauses of the DML statements as you would optimize the performance of queries.

❏ Indexes slow down INSERTs, UPDATEs, and DELETEs. Ensure that all indexes "pay their way" in terms of improving query performance, and watch out for indexes on heavily updated columns.

❏ UPDATEs that contain subqueries within the SET clause may be executed more efficiently if recoded in PL/SQL.

❏ When deleting all rows in a table, TRUNCATE will be much faster than DELETE. Alternately, partitioning a table by a date column may allow you to drop a partition instead of issuing an expensive DELETE statement to remove "old" rows.

❏ An array INSERT can significantly improve performance when inserting many rows.

❏ Tables that must sustain high rates of INSERTs from multiple sessions may benefit from multiple freelists.

❏ Triggers and referential integrity may reduce the performance of DML statements. Referential integrity can incur a particularly high lock overhead if there is no index on the foreign key.

Oracle8 introduced some significant DML performance enhancements:

❏ Direct load inserts allow rows to be inserted above the high-water mark, bypassing Oracle's buffer cache. However, performance of direct load insert will sometimes be inferior to normal inserts unless there is contention for the buffer cache.

❏ Parallel DML allows DML operations to be performed in parallel, realizing dramatic improvements if the hardware platform supports parallel execution. Parallel insert can be performed on any table using the direct insert method, while parallel updates and deletes can only be performed on partitioned tables.

❏ The UNLOGGED option allows insert operations to be processed without generating significant redo log entries. These inserts will be lost, however, if a database failure occurs before the next tablespace backup.

Groups of DML statements that are combined in transactions can be subject to special optimizations:

❏ Discrete transactions can improve the performance of short transactions that meet specific guidelines.

❏ Although in many circumstances frequent COMMITS are required by application design, less frequent transactions can improve performance, especially for jobs that INSERT, UPDATE, or DELETE large quantities of data. On the other hand, committing frequently in a transaction processing environment can reduce lock contention. Choose the COMMIT frequency that best suits your application.

VLDB AND WAREHOUSING

INTRODUCTION

This chapter discusses SQL optimizations that are particularly applicable to very large databases (VLDBs or data warehouse environments).

Of course, databases are getting bigger all the time, and yesterday's VLDB would be nothing to boast about today. Consequently, these VLDB techniques are often applicable to OLTP and general-purpose databases as well.

This chapter discusses two major topics:

❑ The use of Oracle partitioning technologies
❑ Oracle8i materialized views and snapshots

PARTITIONING

As databases increase in size, maintaining and manipulating the data in very large tables can become problematic. Partitioning provides a "divide-and-conquer" solution to the problems associated with these very large tables. Oracle's approach to partitioning has evolved significantly in each recent release:

❑ Oracle 7.3 introduced the partition view feature. This is a simplistic form of partitioning in which every partition is actually a separate table. A view is constructed against the underlying table, which provides the illusion of a single large partitioned table.

❑ Oracle8 introduced a true partitioning scheme based on column ranges. For instance, a SALES table might be partitioned by year, so that sales for each year are stored in separate partitions. Each partition is a separate segment and can have distinct storage attributes and be stored in different table-spaces.

❑ Oracle8i introduced hash partitions, in which rows are allocated to partitions based on a hashing of some column value. Oracle8i also supports composite partitioning, in which the table is first partitioned by range and then further partitioned by hash within each range partition.

PARTITION VIEWS

A partition view allows you to split a logical table into multiple tables, each of which contains a specific range of data. A check constraint ensures that each table contains data only for the appropriate range. The partition view itself is a UNION ALL of each partition table.

A partition view can help performance when a large subset of a table is being accessed. If the proportion of the table being queried is too large to make practical an index-based retrieval, you may be able to use partition view to avoid a full-table scan.

In our sample database, we might be tempted to partition the SALES table in this way. For instance, we could partition the SALES table on calendar years using the following SQL:

```
CREATE TABLE sales1 as
      select * from sales
        where sale_date < '01-JAN-98';

ALTER TABLE sales1 ADD (CONSTRAINT s1_partition_chk
      CHECK (sale_date < '01-JAN-98'));

CREATE TABLE sales2 AS
      SELECT * FROM sales
        WHERE sale_date BETWEEN '01-JAN-98'
                            AND '31-DEC-98';

ALTER TABLE sales2 ADD (CONSTRAINT s2_partition_chk
      CHECK (sale_date BETWEEN '01-JAN-98'
                            AND '31-DEC-98'));

-- Create additional tables for other years
```

```
CREATE OR REPLACE VIEW partitioned_sales
AS
   SELECT *
     FROM sales1
   UNION ALL
           SELECT *
              FROM sales2
   UNION ALL
           SELECT *
              FROM sales3
   UNION ALL
           SELECT *
              FROM sales4
   UNION ALL
           SELECT *
              FROM sales5
```

The constraints allow the cost-based optimizer to work out which of the component tables need to be accessed to satisfy a query. Tkprof output for the following query shows that only the appropriate table is accessed:

```
select sum(sale_value)
  from partitioned_sales
 where sale_date between '01-JAN-96' and '31-JUL-96'

Rows       Execution Plan
-------    -------------------------------------------------
      0    SELECT STATEMENT    GOAL: CHOOSE
  23120      SORT (AGGREGATE)
  23120       VIEW OF 'PARTITIONED_SALES'
  23120        UNION-ALL (PARTITION)
  23120         TABLE ACCESS (FULL) OF 'SALES1'
      0         TABLE ACCESS (FULL) OF 'SALES2'
      0         TABLE ACCESS (FULL) OF 'SALES3'
      0         TABLE ACCESS (FULL) OF 'SALES4'
      0         TABLE ACCESS (FULL) OF 'SALES5'
```

Figure 13.1 compares I/O requirements for the preceding query for the SALES table and the partition view based on SALES. By avoiding the full-table scan, the query was able to complete in only a fraction of the time. When the proportion of the table to be accessed exceeds the break-even point for indexed retrieval but a full-table scan still requires more I/O than is acceptable, a partition view can be useful.

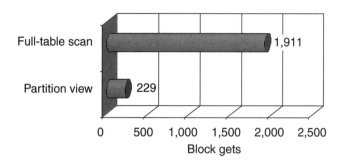

FIGURE 13.1 Comparison of I/O requirements for the SALES table and a partition view based on SALES.

Partition views can complicate application logic, however. In the case of our partitioned SALES table, we need to alter our INSERT statements to ensure that the rows are inserted into the appropriate partition. An UPDATE that would result in the row belonging in another partition would fail on a check constraint violation—we would have to delete the row and insert into a separate partition. You may be able to use synonyms to overcome some of these problems (for instance, creating a synonym CURRENT_SALES that points to the table containing this year's sales).

Partition views can be useful if the percentage of rows that you are retrieving is too high to allow an index to be helpful, but you are retrieving substantially less than the entire table. However, partition views can be difficult to administer. Oracle8 partitioned tables are usually a superior solution.

ORACLE8 RANGE PARTITIONS

Prior to Oracle8, every table was stored in one and only one database *segment*. Although these segments could be comprised of multiple database *extents*, you had little administrative control over these extents.

In Oracle 8.0 a table (and its indexes) may be range partitioned. A partitioned table is comprised of multiple segments. Each segment contains table rows that share the same range of values for a particular column.

The following SQL shows how such a partitioned table might be created:

```
CREATE TABLE sales_range_part
  (column definitions)
  PARTITION BY RANGE (sale_date)
  (PARTITION q198 VALUES LESS THAN
```

```
              (TO_DATE('1998-04-01', 'YYYY-MM-DD')) ,
PARTITION q298 VALUES LESS THAN
              (TO_DATE('1998-07-01', 'YYYY-MM-DD')) ,
PARTITION q398 VALUES LESS THAN
              (TO_DATE('1998-10-01', 'YYYY-MM-DD')) ,
PARTITION q498 VALUES LESS THAN
              (TO_DATE('1999-01-01', 'YYYY-MM-DD')) ,
PARTITION q199 VALUES LESS THAN
              (TO_DATE('1999-04-01', 'YYYY-MM-DD')) ,
PARTITION q299 VALUES LESS THAN
              (TO_DATE('1999-07-01', 'YYYY-MM-DD')) ,
PARTITION q399 VALUES LESS THAN
              (TO_DATE('1999-10-01', 'YYYY-MM-DD')) ,
PARTITION q499 VALUES LESS THAN
              (TO_DATE('2000-01-01', 'YYYY-MM-DD')) ,
PARTITION q100 VALUES LESS THAN
              (TO_DATE('2000-04-01', 'YYYY-MM-DD')) ,
PARTITION q200 VALUES LESS THAN
              (TO_DATE('2000-07-01', 'YYYY-MM-DD')) )
```

Each partition is a separate segment, and partitions can be stored in separate tablespaces and have individual storage definitions. Although partitions are implemented transparently to an application and need not be specified in SQL, SQL statements can specify a partition name. For instance, the following statement applies an update to an individual partition (S1) only:

```
UPDATE sales_part PARTITION(s1)
   SET purge_ind='Y'
 WHERE sale_value < 10000
```

Partition Indexes   Indexes may also be partitioned. While it's possible to create a partitioned index on an unpartitioned table, partitioned indexes will usually be created on a table that is itself partitioned.

If an index on a partitioned table is itself unpartitioned or is partitioned on different column range conditions from the source table, then the index is known as a *global index*.

Local indexes are partitioned in the same manner as their source table. If the leading columns of the index are also the columns upon which the index is partitioned, then the index is known as a *local prefixed index*.

Local indexes have some significant advantages over global indexes. If a partitioned table with a global index has a partition split, merge, or move, then the corresponding index partition will automatically have the same maintenance operation applied.

In general, local (partitioned) indexes help release the maximum benefits of partitioning. Avoid global indexes on partitioned tables.

Advantages of Range Partitions One of the advantages of Oracle8 partitions is the ability to perform administrative work on subsets of very large tables. In Oracle7, these very large tables pose special challenges. For instance, you may not be able to export very large tables within an acceptable time frame. With partitioned tables, you'll be able to reduce maintenance time by restricting maintenance to an individual partition or by performing operations on multiple partitions in parallel.

Partitioned tables can also improve the performance of table scans. If you issue a query based on the same columns by which a table is partitioned, the Oracle8 optimizer can restrict the scans to the relevant partitions. This is known as *partition elimination* or *partition pruning*. You can also manually restrict operations to a partition of interest by specifying the partition name after the table name.

As we saw in Chapter 12, partitioned tables can also be subject to parallel update and delete and parallel index scans.

Range partitioned tables also offer an excellent means of purging historical data. For instance, in our SALES partition we could quickly purge all data for a particular financial year simply by dropping the relevant partition. Provided that all indexes were local, this operation could be completed rapidly.

Three new columns in the plan table (the table that the EXPLAIN PLAN command populates) can be used to determine partition optimization. In particular, PARTITION_START and PARTITION_STOP indicate the partitions that will be used by a partition operation. New EXPLAIN PLAN access steps indicate that an operation will apply to a range of partitions or to a single partition. For instance, the following explain plan shows that a single partition is being accessed:

```
  1   SELECT SUM (sale_value)
  2     FROM sales_range_part
  3*  WHERE sale_date = SYSDATE
SQL> /

Execution Plan
-------------------------------------------------------
0       SELECT STATEMENT (Cost=40 Card=1 Bytes=22)
1    0    SORT (AGGREGATE)
2    1     PARTITION RANGE (SINGLE)
3    2       TABLE ACCESS (FULL) OF 'SALES_RANGE_PART'
```

The following execution plan shows that a range of partitions will be accessed:

```
SQL> SELECT SUM (sale_value)
  2    FROM sales_range_part
  3    WHERE sale_date > SYSDATE--90;

Execution Plan
-------------------------------------------------------
0       SELECT STATEMENT (Cost=400 Card=1 Bytes=22)
1    0  SORT (AGGREGATE)
2    1  PARTITION RANGE (ITERATOR)
3    2    TABLE ACCESS (FULL) OF
                  'SALES_RANGE_PART'
```

Restrictions on Range Partitioning   Although Oracle8 range partitioning is powerful and effective, there are some limitations:

❏ You can't create global bitmap indexes and you can't partition a bitmap index or a clustered table.

❏ Range partitions are not automatically balanced. That is, there is no guarantee that each partition will contain the same number of rows. If a single partition contains substantially more rows than the other partitions, then the advantages of partitioning will be diminished.

Figure 13.2 shows the row counts in the quarterly partitions of our sample partitioned SALES table. Sales have been uneven in our imaginary company, and consequently the balance between partitions is not good. The problem of unbalanced range partitions is addressed in Oracle8i with the introduction of *hash* and *composite* partitions.

Consider range partitioning when you want to take advantage of partition elimination for range queries or purge historical data by quickly dropping a partition.

HASH PARTITIONING

In an Oracle8i hash partition, rows are distributed to the various partitions based on the value of a specific column. However, in the case of hash partitions the column is subjected to a hashing algorithm to determine which partition the rows will be stored in. The hashing algorithm applies a mathematical function to the column value and assigns the row to its partition based on the return value of the function. This ensures that each partition has approximately the same number of rows. It also means that you can't reasonably anticipate which rows will end up

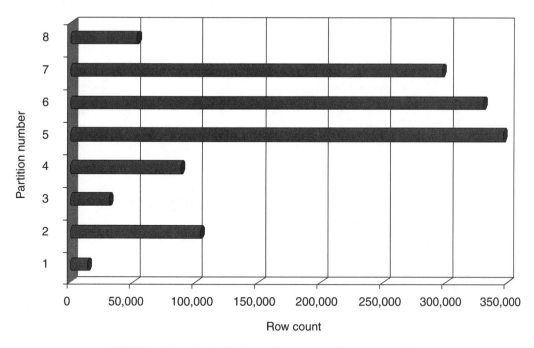

FIGURE 13.2 Lack of balance in our sample range partition.

in specific partitions. Rows that have adjacent column values will not necessarily end up in the same partition—in fact, they will probably be allocated to separate partitions.

The following statement creates a variant of the SALES table that is partitioned by the hash of SALE_DATE. Eight partitions are created with default storage attributes, though we could have explicitly named and supplied storage parameters for each partition:

```
CREATE TABLE  SALES_HASH_PART
(column definitions)
PARTITION BY HASH (sale_date) PARTITIONS 8
```

The big advantage of hash partitions is that they will usually be well balanced: Each partition will hold approximately the same number of rows. This improves the performance of many parallel operations on the partition. Figure 13.3 shows the balance of rows in a hash partition. Compare this with the lack of balance achieved during our range partitioning as shown in Figure 13.2. Note also that for a hash partition to be well balanced using the default hashing algorithm, the number of partitions must be a power of 2 (2, 4, 8, 16, 32, etc.).

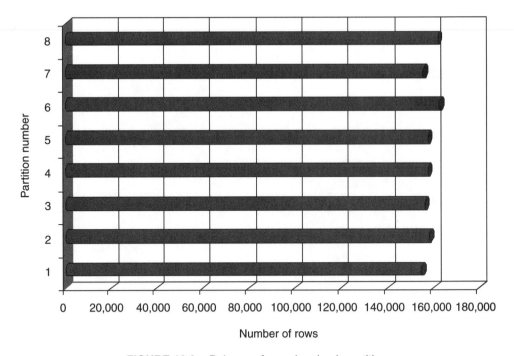

FIGURE 13.3   Balance of rows in a hash partition.

The big disadvantage of hash partitions is that you often won't get partition elimination for range-based queries such as "What were the total sales for quarter 4?" Furthermore, you can't purge old data using a hash partition. So, for instance, our range partition would have allowed us easily to remove all sales data for 1997. To do so for the hash partition will require all the overhead of locating and removing each individual row.

Consider hash partitioning when balance of rows between partitions is more important than the benefits of partition elimination or purging data by dropping a partition. Remember to make the number of partitions a power of 2.

COMPOSITE PARTITIONS

Composite partitioning is an attempt to combine the best features of range and hash partitioning. In a composite partition, the table is first partitioned by range value. Each range partition can be further subpartitioned by hash. This SQL statement creates such a composite partition that is range partitioned in the same manner as the range partition we created earlier but in which each range partition is composed of four hash subpartitions:

```
CREATE TABLE sales_comp_part
  (column definitions)
   PARTITION BY RANGE (sale_date)
   SUBPARTITION BY HASH (sale_date)
     (PARTITION Q198 VALUES LESS THAN
        (TO_DATE(' 1998-04-01', 'SYYYY-MM-DD'))
         SUBPARTITIONS 4,
      PARTITION Q298 VALUES LESS THAN
        (TO_DATE(' 1998-07-01', 'SYYYY-MM-DD'))
         SUBPARTITIONS 4,
      /* Definitions of other partitions */
      PARTITION Q200 VALUES LESS THAN
```

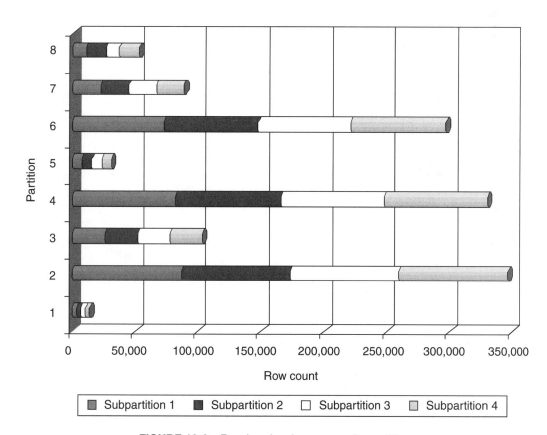

FIGURE 13.4 Row breakup in a composite partition.

```
(TO_DATE(' 2000-07-01', 'SYYYY-MM-DD'))
SUBPARTITIONS 4 )
```

Figure 13.4 shows the distribution of rows within a composite partition. The distribution of rows across the range partitions is as uneven as before. Within each partition, there are four hash subpartitions of equal size.

Because each range partition is of a different size, we still have a pretty uneven distribution of rows across subpartitions generally. We could get a better balance between subpartitions if we varied the number of subpartitions in each range partition. Figure 13.5 shows a better balanced composite partition. Depending on the size of the range partition, either one, two, or four subpartitions were created. The balance is still not perfect, but it is a big improvement on the layout shown in Figure 13.4.

If you need range partitioning but need good balance in the sizes of each partition, consider subpartitioning by hash (composite partitioning). You will probably need to adjust the number of subpartitions to achieve a good balance.

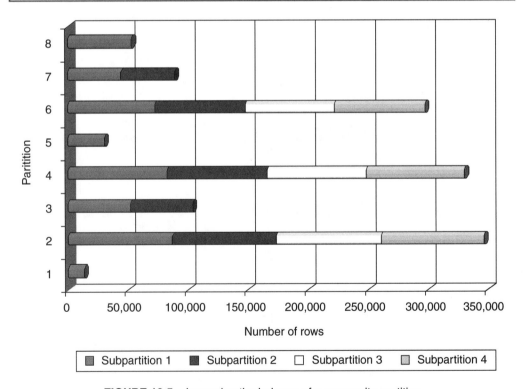

FIGURE 13.5   Improving the balance of a composite partition.

PARALLEL DML ON PARTITIONS

Only partitioned tables can be subjected to parallel UPDATE or DELETE operations. Parallel DML was discussed in detail in Chapter 12.

PARTITIONWISE JOINS

Oracle can sometimes improve the parallelism of a join if one or both of the tables concerned is partitioned. This can happen in one of two ways:

❑ If both tables are partitioned in the same manner (equipartitioned), then Oracle can join each partition separately and in parallel and then return the merged results.

❑ If only one of the tables is partitioned, then Oracle can partition the unpartitioned table on the fly into multiple result sets, which represent the partitioning scheme of the partitioned table, and then join these results sets to the table partitions in parallel.

You can perform partitionwise joins on tables that are partitioned by range, hash, or composite methods. However, the balance of rows across partitions is particularly significant in a partitionwise join to ensure than each parallel slave is given approximately the same amount of work. For this reason, partitionwise joins are most effective when both tables are equipartitioned by hash.

Partitionwise joins improve parallelism by streamlining the traffic between parallel query slaves. In a normal parallel join, Oracle has to direct rows read from the source table to the appropriate slave that is responsible for joining that range of rows. For instance, in a two-way sort-merge join, rows from A to K might be sent to one slave and rows from L to Z might be sent to another. In partitionwise join, rows read from a particular partition will be allocated to a single slave for joining.

Oracle will automatically perform a partitionwise join if it considers that the circumstances are favorable. For instance, in this example we have hash partitioned both the sales and customers table on the hash of CUSTOMER_ID. The "PARTITON HASH ALL" step indicates that the join was partitionwise:

```
select /*+ ordered use_hash(s) parallel(c,4)
parallel(s,4)   */
        c.customer_name,s.sale_date,s.sale_value
   from customers_hash_part c, sales_hash_cust s
  where c.customer_id=s.customer_id
```

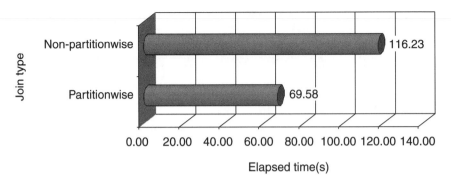

FIGURE 13.6 Partitionwise parallel join compared to standard parallel join.

```
Execution Plan
------------------------------------------------
SELECT STATEMENT    GOAL: CHOOSE
 PARTITION HASH (ALL) [:Q1584000]
   HASH JOIN [:Q1584000]
     TABLE ACCESS (FULL) OF 'CUSTOMERS_HASH_PART'
                   [:Q1584000]
     TABLE ACCESS  (FULL) OF 'SALES_HASH_CUST'
                   [:Q1584000]
```

For our example, the partitionwise hash join significantly outperformed a standard parallel hash join. Figure 13.6 shows the relative performance.

PARALLEL PARTITIONED INDEX SCANS

Prior to Oracle8, only queries that were based on full-table scans or fast full-index scans could be processed in parallel. In Oracle8 and Oracle8i, queries based on index range scans can be parallelized if the index is partitioned (e.g., a local index). The algorithm for this is similar to that of parallel DML for a partitioned table: Each slave process is allocated one of the index partitions and performs a scan on that partition only. Therefore, the degree of parallelism can be no greater than the number of partitions in the index.

   The PARALLEL_INDEX and NOPARALLEL_INDEX hints allow you to request or suppress parallel partitioned index scan. So the following statement uses four index scans in parallel to search for the biggest sale for product# 1:

```
SELECT   /*+ parallel_index(s)*/ MAX(sale_value)
  FROM sales_hash_part s
 WHERE product_id = 1
```

MATERIALIZED VIEWS AND SNAPSHOTS

SIMPLE SNAPSHOTS

Snapshots are a facility available in both Oracle7 and Oracle8. Views are sometimes referred to as stored queries. If so, then snapshots can be thought of as stored results. Like a view, a snapshot is based on a query. When a view is accessed, the underlying query is executed. In contrast, the query underlying a snapshot is executed at regular intervals—perhaps overnight or during some other off-peak period. As a result, snapshots can return results more quickly than a view or a query, but the results returned by a snapshot may not be totally current.

If it's not essential that a query return results that are completely up to date, then using a snapshot can result in performance improvements over an equivalent query or view. For instance, in our sample database we may frequently require a sum of sales totals for a particular customer. We might implement this by creating a view:

```
CREATE OR REPLACE VIEW sales_by_customer_v
AS
    SELECT s.customer_id, c.customer_name,
           SUM (s.sale_value) sale_value
      FROM sales s, customers c
     WHERE s.customer_id (+) = c.customer_id
     GROUP BY s.customer_id, c.customer_name
```

We could query against this view to find details for a particular customer:

```
SELECT *
  FROM sales_by_customer_v
 WHERE customer_id = 747
```

This approach is not particularly efficient since it requires a join of customer and sales tables whenever the query is issued. If we don't mind if our query returns results that are not absolutely current, we could create a snapshot based on the same query as the view. The snapshot could be refreshed nightly:

```
CREATE SNAPSHOT sales_by_customer_snp as
   SELECT s.customer_id, c.customer_name,
          SUM (s.sale_value) sale_value
     FROM sales s, customers c
    WHERE s.customer_id (+) = c.customer_id
    GROUP BY s.customer_id, c.customer_name
```

Not surprisingly, a query against the snapshot requires much less I/O than the query against the view. The I/O overhead of joining and finding the relevant rows occurred when the snapshot was last refreshed (probably during some off peak period) and so we don't have to experience that overhead when querying from the snapshot.

Figure 13.7 illustrates the performance characteristics of a snapshot compared to an equivalent explicit query. The snapshot substantially outperformed both the explicit query. If we weren't concerned that the results returned by the snapshot might not be totally current, then using the snapshot would be a good decision.

Consider using snapshots to facilitate complex queries on large tables where the results do not have to be entirely current.

SNAPSHOT LOGS

Snapshot logs can be used to optimize refreshing of snapshots based on simple queries. Once a snapshot log is created, any changes to the source table will be recorded in the log. When it is time to refresh the snapshot, this log can be examined to determine which rows in the snapshot need to be amended.

The use of a snapshot log can slow down DML operations on the source table, since each DML will result in an additional insert into the snapshot log. If there is heavy activity on the source table, contention for inserts into the snapshot log can result. In this case, it may be worthwhile creating the snapshot log with multiple freelists (see Chapter 20 for more information on freelists). Figure 13.8 illustrates the overhead of a snapshot log.

The enhanced performance of the snapshot refresh may justify the diminished update performance resulting the snapshot log. The key considerations are as follows:

❑ The higher the DML rate on the source table, the higher the overhead of maintaining the snapshot log.

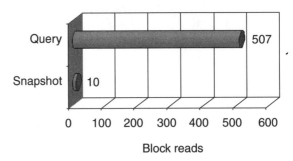

FIGURE 13.7   Obtaining summarized sales information for a customer via a view, an explicit query, and a snapshot.

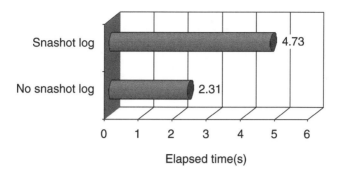

FIGURE 13.8 Effect of creating a snapshot log on update times (1000 updates).

❑ The larger the source table, the greater the incentive for maintaining the snapshot log, since the complete refresh will require a full-table scan. On the other hand, creating snapshot logs on small tables is usually not required, since the overhead of a complete refresh will be small.

❑ As the proportion of rows in the source table that need to be refreshed in the snapshot increases, the performance of complete and fast refreshes will converge. If a source table is subject to very high update activity, or refreshes are scheduled far apart, the performance of the fast refresh may be no better than that of the full refresh.

Figure 13.9 compares the performance of full and fast snapshot refreshes plotted against the percentage of rows changed in the parent table. In this example, the complete refresh was more efficient than the full refresh when more than 50% of the source table's rows were altered.

Use snapshot logs and the fast refresh mechanism when a minority of rows in the source table are changed. If a majority of rows are changed, avoid the overhead of the snapshot log and use complete refreshes, which will be faster than fast refreshes anyway.

If a source table for a simple snapshot is usually a good candidate for the fast refresh mechanism but is occasionally subject to bulk loads or complete rebuilds, you can use the following guidelines to avoid the overheads of the fast refresh:

❑ Drop the snapshot log before the bulk load. This will avoid the overhead of inserting rows into the snapshot log.

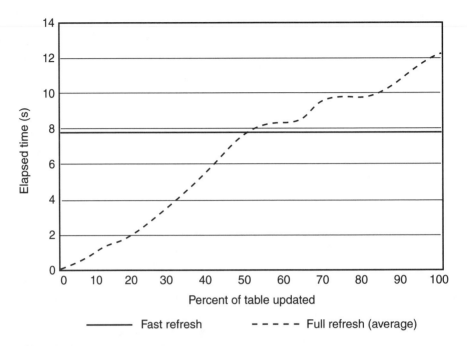

FIGURE 13.9   Performance of complete and fast snapshot refreshes plotted against the percent of the source table that has been updated.

❏ Consider dropping and re-creating the snapshot rather than executing a full refresh. A full refresh will often take longer than a snapshot rebuild because any indexes on the snapshot will have to be updated, which will be slower than rebuilding the indexes after the creation of the snapshot.

MATERIALIZED VIEWS

Materialized views evolved from snapshots and were introduced in Oracle8i. Like snapshots, they store the results of a query in a table and allow the results to be refreshed at scheduled intervals. However, materialized views differ from snapshots most significantly in the ability of the Oracle8i optimizer to rewrite queries transparently (Query rewrite) so that they use the materialized view instead of the table(s) listed in the FROM clause.

Query rewrite will occur only if the QUERY_REWRITE_ENABLED parameter is TRUE and if the user has the QUERY REWRITE privilege.

Materialized views also differ from traditional snapshots in that they support ON COMMIT refresh. If the REFRESH ON COMMIT clause is specified in the materialized view definition, then whenever a transaction commits against the base tables, an automatic refresh of the materialized view will occur.

There are a number of different ways to configure materialized views. In the following example we create a materialized view that represents sales totals by customer. We start by creating a materialized view log on the SALES table. Because we are going to use ON COMMIT refreshes, we use the INCLUDING NEW VALUES clause and specify the column values we want to store in the log.

```
CREATE MATERIALIZED VIEW LOG ON sales
  WITH ROWID, primary key (sale_value)
  INCLUDING NEW VALUES;
```

The following statement creates the materialized view:

```
CREATE MATERIALIZED VIEW sales_by_cust_mv
    USING INDEX
    REFRESH ON COMMIT
    ENABLE QUERY REWRITE
  AS SELECT customer_id,COUNT(*) as count_c_id,
            COUNT(sale_value) AS count_s_v,
            SUM(sale_value) AS sum_sale_value,
            COUNT(*) AS SALE_COUNT
        FROM sales
      GROUP BY customer_id;
```

Queries against the SALES table can now automatically be rewritten to use the materialized view:

```
SELECT SUM (sale_value)
  FROM sales
 WHERE customer_id = 3
```

```
Rows      Execution Plan
-------   -----------------------------------------------
      0   SELECT STATEMENT     GOAL: CHOOSE
      1     SORT (AGGREGATE)
      1       TABLE ACCESS (BY INDEX ROWID) OF
                  'SALES_BY_CUST_MV' <- Materialized view
      1         INDEX (RANGE SCAN) OF
                  'I_SNAP$_SALES_BY_CUST_MV'
```

We can avoid this automatic query rewrite by issuing an ALTER SESSION statement, which sets QUERY_REWRITE_ENABLED to FALSE, or by using the NOREWRITE parameter, as follows:

```
SELECT   /*+norewrite*/SUM (sale_value)
  FROM sales
 WHERE customer_id = 3

Rows     Execution Plan
-------  -------------------------------------------------
      0  SELECT STATEMENT    GOAL: CHOOSE
      1    SORT (AGGREGATE)
    258      TABLE ACCESS(BY INDEX ROWID) OF
                 'SALES'
    258        INDEX (RANGE SCAN) OF 'SALES_PK'
```

Figure 13.10 shows the performance improvement obtained by using query rewrite for this example. Of course, the performance improvements will depend on the nature of the stored query, but for aggregate queries the performance improvements can typically be as shown in this example. Note, too, that this performance improvement may come at the cost of accuracy (if the base table has changed since the last refresh) or DML performance on the base table (if the ON COMMIT option is used).

QUERY REWRITE INTEGRITY

Materialized views may be refreshed at regular intervals, on demand, or whenever a COMMIT is issued against one of the base tables that form the foundation for the view. Except in the latter case, it is possible that the materialized view data could be inconsistent with the source data.

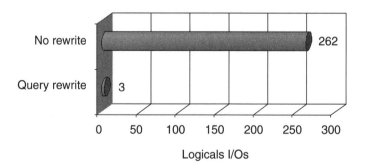

FIGURE 13.10 Example of query rewrite performance.

By default, Oracle will not perform query rewrite if it knows that the base table(s) have been modified since the query was last refreshed.

If you want query rewrite to occur even if the results might not be accurate, you can set the following command that instructs Oracle to consider query rewrite even if the materialized view in question contains "stale" data:

```
ALTER SESSION SET
            query_rewrite_integrity=stale_tolerated
```

OVERHEAD OF MATERIALIZED VIEW MAINTENANCE

Query rewrite can dramatically improve the performance of queries that access aggregate data, but there is always a cost:

- ❏ If a materialized view log is created, then modifications to the source table will be adversely affected.
- ❏ Refreshing the materialized view may require significant resources. If the materialized view is created with the REFRESH ON COMMIT attribute, then this overhead will be incurred whenever a transaction which updates the base table is committed.
- ❏ If the materialized view is not created with the ON COMMIT attribute, then queries that are rewritten might return different results from queries that were not rewritten. Since the query rewrite may occur without the user realizing it, this could result in the database apparently returning incorrect data.

Figure 13.11 shows the overhead of a materialized view with ON COMMIT refresh and materialized view log on a transaction that inserts 5000 rows into the SALES table. The materialized view and log were created with the statements listed earlier. We can see that the overhead of maintaining a materialized view can be severe. The situation could be even worse if there were concurrent inserts into the SALES table—sessions could contend for locks on the materialized view, further crippling performance.

There are therefore a couple of compelling reasons for caution when considering materialized view implementations:

- ❏ If you implement ON COMMIT refreshes, then you are liable to cause a dramatic increase in the overhead required to update the source table.
- ❏ If you don't implement ON COMMIT refreshes, then queries might be transparently rewritten to use "stale" materialized views and will return incorrect results.

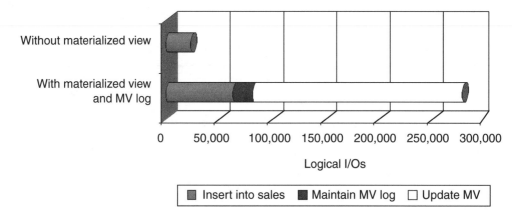

FIGURE 13.11   Overhead of materialized view logs and ON COMMIT refresh.

As a result of these limitations, materialized views only suit environments in which the source table is subjected to infrequent bulk loads (perhaps an overnight update into a data warehousing environment). In this case, the overhead of updating the materialized view and log will be limited. You might also be able to drop the materialized view log and set the materialized view to NEVER REFRESH while the data are being loaded. After the data load is complete, you could re-create the materialized view log and reset the materialized view to REFRESH ON COMMIT.

> Because of the overhead of materialized views and the risk of incorrect results if the ON COMMIT clause is not used, materialized views with query rewrite are only suitable to relatively static environments such as data warehouses.

USING DIMENSIONS

If you have a materialized view and have enabled query rewrite, you may create *dimensions* that define hierarchies within certain columns within the source table. For instance, the SALES table includes entries both for DEPARTMENT_ID and SALES_REP_ID. If it is true that a sales representative will always exist in only a single department, then we can use the CREATE DIMENSION command to create a dimension that represents this fact, as follows:

```
CREATE DIMENSION sales_rep_in_department
    LEVEL sales_rep IS sales.sales_rep_id
```

```
        LEVEL department IS sales.department_id
        HIERARCHY sales_rep_dept (
            sales_rep CHILD OF department)
```

Unless we set QUERY_REWRITE_INTEGRITY to TRUSTED, Oracle requires that we validate a dimension before we can use it (and, in fact, revalidate it whenever we add data to the base tables). To do this, we use the DBMS_SUMMARY.VALIDATE_DIMENSION procedure:

```
BEGIN
    dbms_summary.validate_dimension (
        dimension_name => 'SALES_REP_IN_DEPARTMENT',
        dimension_owner => 'SQLTUNE',
        incremental => FALSE,
        check_nulls => TRUE
    );
END;
```

If there are any rows that violate the dimension definition (for instance, a SALES_REP_ID entry that is associated with more than one DEPARTMENT_ID), then the details of the rows concerned will be written to the table MVIEW$_EXCEPTIONS.

Once the dimension has been validated, Oracle can take the dimension definition into account when performing query rewrite. The RECOMMEND_MV procedure can also use the dimensions to provide better advice on materialized view structure.

DBMS_SUMMARY PACKAGE

The DBMS_SUMMARY package (aliased as DBMS_OLAP) provides procedures that assist in the refresh of materialized views:

❏ REFRESH: Refresh a one or more materialized view.
❏ REFRESH_ALL: Refresh all materialized views.
❏ REFRESH_DEPENDENT: Refresh all materialized views that are dependent on a given base table.
❏ VALIDATE_DIMENSION ensures that a dimension is valid.
❏ RECOMMEND_MV generates recommendations regarding materialized views that may be advantageous based on the structure of your tables (foreign key constraints, dimensions, etc). A variant, RECOMMEND_MV_W, can also take into account workload statistics collected by Oracle Trace.

The DBMS_SUMMARY/DBMS_OLAP package is fully documented in the *Oracle8i supplied packages reference.*

SUMMARY

In this chapter, we have looked at two features of Oracle8 that can result in significant improvements to SQL performance for large database implementation such as data warehouses.

Oracle 7.3 introduced a primitive partitioning mechanism based on views. This was superceded in Oracle8 by true partitioned tables, which can be partitioned based on column value ranges. Oracle8i introduced hash partitioning, where partitions are based on the hash of a column value, and composite partitions, which are partitioned first by range and then within each range partition by hash.

Indexes can also be partitioned. To take advantage of partition maintenance facilities such as the ability to drop a partition quickly, you should normally create *local* indexes, which are partitioned in the same manner as their parent table.

Range partitions offer more potential for partition elimination and purging of old data than do hash partitions. On the other hand, hash partitions tend to be much better balanced—they tend to have a nearly equivalent number of rows in each partition. Remember that to get an even balance of rows in each hash partition you should set the number of partitions to a power of 2 (2, 4, 8, 16, etc.).

Composite partitions can be a useful "best of both worlds" solution. By subpartitioning by hash, we can even the distribution of rows in an unbalanced range partition. However, to do this, we may need to vary the number of subpartitions in each major partition.

Partitions offer the following major advantages:

❑ Queries that access too many rows for efficient index lookup might be able to be satisfied by one or only a few partitions. Since the alternative is a full-table scan, this can be a significant improvement.

❑ Partitions allow for parallel update and parallel delete and for parallel index scans.

❑ Partitionwise joins of partitioned tables can improve the performance of parallel joins.

Snapshots can be used to store the results of complex queries and allow rapid retrieval of results that may, however, be somewhat out of date. The performance of simple snapshot refreshes is improved by the creation of a snapshot log provided that only a small proportion of the source table has been changed.

Materialized views replace snapshots in Oracle8i and add two significant enhancements:

❑ Oracle can automatically rewrite queries to use the materialized view (if the database and user are suitably configured).

❑ The materialized view can be updated whenever a transaction against the source table is committed.

However, the overhead of materialized view maintenance can be very high, and you would normally only configure materialized views in static environments such as data warehouses.

USING AND TUNING PL/SQL

INTRODUCTION

PL/SQL implements a procedural language that is tightly integrated with Oracle SQL and that can be stored in the database as stored procedures, functions, and triggers. PL/SQL was described in Chapter 3.

PL/SQL offers a rich and productive environment in which to implement database-centric application logic. PL/SQL can often be used to enhance the performance of problem queries and can offer significant performance improvements for complex DML.

PL/SQL programs are highly tunable. Aside from generic code optimization strategies applicable to all procedural languages, PL/SQL has a number of features specifically designed to improve its performance. We'll look at each of these features and at the PL/SQL profiler, a powerful tool for identifying PL/SQL performance bottlenecks.

This chapter covers the following topics:

- ❏ Using PL/SQL in place of standard SQL
- ❏ Disadvantages of a PL/SQL approach
- ❏ Using PL/SQL to implement denormalization
- ❏ Using PL/SQL functions in standard SQL
- ❏ Principles of code optimization applied to PL/SQL

❑ Using array processing in PL/SQL
❑ Using and optimizing packages and procedures
❑ Optimizing PL/SQL cursors
❑ Using PL/SQL tables and Oracle temporary tables to cache frequently accessed values or to store intermediate results
❑ Using dynamic PL/SQL
❑ Using the PL/SQL profiler

PERFORMANCE CHARACTERISTICS OF PL/SQL

PL/SQL can often add to program functionality and programmer efficiency, and there are many cases where the use of a procedural language such as PL/SQL can do things that a nonprocedural language like SQL cannot. However, there are also a number of reasons why a PL/SQL approach may offer performance improvements over a traditional SQL approach.

PROCEDURAL APPROACH

You may recall from Chapter 3 that SQL is a nonprocedural language, which means that you don't have to specify how to retrieve data, only which data you want to retrieve. Although we can influence the retrieval strategy through hints and other methods, sometimes it can be almost impossible to get the cost-based optimizer to do our bidding even when we know exactly how the data should be retrieved.

When we think we know how the data should be retrieved but can't get the optimizer to play ball, we can sometimes use PL/SQL to force the desired approach.

REDUCTION IN CLIENT/SERVER TRAFFIC

In a traditional SQL-based application, SQL statements and data flow back and forth between the client and the server. This traffic can cause delays even when both client and server programs are on the same machine. If the client and server are on different machines, then the overhead is even higher. Using PL/SQL stored programs can eliminate much of this overhead. A succinct message is sent from the client to the server (the stored procedure execution request) and a minimal response is sent from the server to the client (perhaps only a return code). The reduction in network traffic can significantly enhance performance, especially in a client/server environment.

DIVIDE AND CONQUER COMPLEX STATEMENTS

The more complex a SQL statement is, the harder it is to optimize. This goes not only for human optimizers, but also for the optimization code in the Oracle kernel. You may have seen massive SQL statements that include multiple subqueries, set operations, and complex joins. It's not uncommon for these "monster" SQL statements to generate pages of explain plan output. Tuning these sorts of SQL statements can be next to impossible for either the human or software optimizer. It's often a winning strategy to break these massive SQL statements into smaller individual statements and optimize each individually. For instance, subqueries could be run outside of the SQL statement and the results forwarded to subsequent steps as query parameters or through temporary tables.

DRAWBACKS OF PL/SQL

Although there are certain circumstances in which a PL/SQL approach will yield large gains in performance, it is not always the best approach. Keep in mind the following drawbacks:

❏ The procedural nature of PL/SQL can exact a higher demand on the programmer than does straight SQL. The PL/SQL can be harder to code than the equivalent SQL statement.

❏ Although PL/SQL procedures and functions can return values, they cannot return result sets as such. A procedure can return a cursor variable and a package can include a globally accessible cursor definition, but these can't be used effectively in most development environments. When you need a set of data, a SELECT statement is usually still the most appropriate approach. However, the SELECT statement could access data in a temporary table populated by a PL/SQL routine.

❏ Although individual SQL statements within a PL/SQL program may be executed using the parallel query option (see Chapter 12 for more details of the parallel query option), the logic within the PL/SQL block is usually executed in serial. This may defeat attempts to leverage Oracle's parallel capabilities.

USING PL/SQL IN PLACE OF STANDARD SQL

In previous chapters, we've seen examples of how PL/SQL can be used in place of standard SQL to improve performance. Although it's not possible to categorize all the situations in which PL/SQL can be used in place of standard SQL, it's possible that PL/SQL is a valid alternative when

❑ There is little or no requirement to return large quantities of data (for instance, UPDATE transactions or when retrieving only a single value or row).

❑ Standard SQL requires more resources than seems logically required and no combination of hints seems to work. This is particularly likely if there are some implicit characteristics of the data that the optimizer cannot understand or where the SQL is particularly complex.

❑ You have a clear idea of how the data should be retrieved and processed but can't implement your algorithm using standard SQL.

MAXIMUMS AND MINIMUMS

In previous chapters, we've seen examples of how PL/SQL can be used to enhance the retrieval of data based on maximum or minimum conditions. In Chapter 9, we examined a PL/SQL alternative to a correlated subquery (retrieving the highest paid employees in each department) that executed in under 2% of the time taken by the standard SQL approach. In Chapter 10, we saw how PL/SQL (with appropriate indexes) can retrieve a maximum or minimum value in a fraction of the time taken by standard SQL, a 99% reduction in I/O requirements. Both these examples used PL/SQL to move through a table in index order and retrieve only those rows that are of interest. Standard SQL is less efficient when processing these types of requests, because it insists on processing all the rows and it sorts the results. For example, consider the query "What is the second biggest sale we ever made?" In standard SQL, the following query might be required:

```
SELECT *
  FROM sales
 WHERE sale_value =
       (SELECT MAX (sale_value)
          FROM sales
         WHERE sale_value <>
               (SELECT MAX (sale_value)
                  FROM sales))
```

```
Rows      Execution Plan
-------   -------------------------------------------------
      0   SELECT STATEMENT    GOAL: CHOOSE
      3    TABLE ACCESS    (FULL) OF 'SALES'
      2     SORT (AGGREGATE)
 322337     FILTER
 322343      TABLE ACCESS    (FULL) OF 'SALES'
             (get highest)
```

```
    2        SORT (AGGREGATE)
322342       TABLE ACCESS (FULL) OF 'SALES'
             (get 2nd highest)
```

This approach is obviously inefficient: It requires three full-table scans. An alternative approach can be constructed in PL/SQL as follows:

```
CREATE OR REPLACE PROCEDURE second_highest
AS
    CURSOR sale_csr
    IS
      SELECT sale_value
        FROM sales s
        ORDER BY sale_value desc;
    second_high_sale              NUMBER := 0;
    prev_sale                     NUMBER := 0;
    i                             NUMBER := 0;
BEGIN
    FOR sale_row IN sale_csr
    LOOP
      i := i + 1;

      IF i > 1 THEN
         IF     sale_row.sale_value < prev_sale
            AND second_high_sale = 0 THEN
            -- Found second highest!
            second_high_sale := sale_row.sale_value;
            dbms_output.put_line (' 2nd highest sale is'
                    || TO_CHAR (sale_row.sale_value));
         ELSIF sale_row.sale_value = second_high_sale
            THEN
            -- Another person earning second highest!
            dbms_output.put_line ('tied second highest:'
              || ' ' || TO_CHAR (sale_row.sale_value));
         ELSIF    sale_row.sale_value < prev_sale
               AND second_high_sale > 0 THEN
            -- Gone below second highest,  so exit;
            EXIT;
         END IF;
      END IF;

      prev_sale := sale_row.sale_value;
    END LOOP;
END;
```

The PL/SQL block requires only one scan of the SALES table and 6917 logical I/Os to complete, whereas the standard SQL consumes 18,843 blocks and requires three scans of the SALES table (Figure 14.1). In this example, creating an index on SALE_VALUE or using *8.1.6 analytic* functions could also improve performance. Nevertheless, a PL/SQL solution will still usually outperform a standard SQL statement in these circumstances.

IMPLEMENTING DENORMALIZATION

You can use database triggers to maintain denormalized data in your tables. For instance, a trigger could be used to maintain a copy of the department_name in the EMPLOYEES table. In the infrequent event that the department name changed, the trigger would update all matching rows in the EMPLOYEES table. This might avoid the most common reason for joining employees to customers. The following SQL implements this sort of denormalization:

```
CREATE OR REPLACE TRIGGER cutomer_insupd1
    BEFORE INSERT OR UPDATE OF department_id
    ON employees
    FOR EACH ROW
DECLARE
    CURSOR dept_csr (cp_dept_id NUMBER)
    IS
        SELECT department_name
          FROM departments
         WHERE department_id = cp_dept_id;
BEGIN
    OPEN dept_csr (:new.department_id);
    FETCH dept_csr INTO :new.department_name;
    CLOSE dept_csr;
END;
```

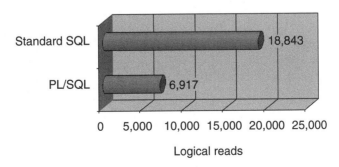

FIGURE 14.1 Finding the second highest sale using PL/SQL.

```
CREATE OR REPLACE TRIGGER department_insupd1
    BEFORE INSERT OR UPDATE OF department_name
    ON departments
    FOR EACH ROW
BEGIN
    UPDATE employees
        SET department_name = :new.department_name
      WHERE department_id = :new.department_id;
END; .
```

Implementing this sort of denormalization can lead to tremendous improvements if a join is avoided as a result. For example, for a query that returns all employees and the name of their departments, I/O requirements are reduced from 2414 block reads to just 67 block reads (Figure 14.2). Note, however, that an overhead is incurred whenever the trigger is made to fire.

Denormalizing a table is not something that should be done thoughtlessly, and we discuss the pros and cons of denormalizing your tables in Chapter 18. However, by using PL/SQL triggers, you can automate the maintenance of the denormalized data and reduce the application overhead of denormalization.

Consider using PL/SQL triggers to denormalize your tables. PL/SQL triggers can auto-mate and improve the efficiency of denormalization.

OPTIMIZING DML

We saw in Chapter 9 how PL/SQL could be used in place of a correlated update with great effect (I/O reduced to 13%). Correlated updates can perform poorly, especially when the same table is referenced in the SET and WHERE clauses or when there is not an index to support the subqueries.

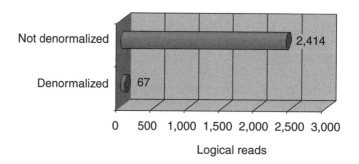

FIGURE 14.2   The effect of denormalizing the department name column into the EM-PLOYEES table on a query that returns department and employee names.

DML (UPDATE, INSERT, or DELETE) statements are often good candidates for conversion to PL/SQL:

❏ DML statements do not return result sets that PL/SQL would find difficult to display or pass back to the calling program.

❏ It's often tricky to formulate a DML operation that is based on a join query. DML statements do not support a FROM clause (except in a subquery). Using PL/SQL allows you to move through a join query issuing DML statements where appropriate.

❏ For DML statements that affect a large number of rows, PL/SQL can allow you to COMMIT at regular intervals, reducing the rollback segment overhead.

PL/SQL can offer substantial improvements to UPDATE and DELETE transactions, particularly in the case of a correlated UPDATE or an UPDATE based on a join query.

OPTIMIZING PL/SQL

CODE OPTIMIZATION

Usually, we think of PL/SQL as a database access language and concentrate on optimizing the SQL within the PL/SQL program. But as a procedural language, PL/SQL is subject to many of the same principles of optimization as other languages. There are circumstances in which PL/SQL itself—without any database accesses—can consume CPU resources at an excessive rate. Some of the basic principles for optimizing PL/SQL code (and indeed for other languages) are as follows:

❏ Optimize or minimize loop processing.
❏ Optimize conditional statements (such as IF).
❏ Avoid recursion.

Loop Processing   The LOOP–END LOOP clauses are used to execute the statements within the loop repeatedly. A badly constructed loop can have a drastic effect on performance. Two important principles in the optimization of loops are as follows:

❏ Try to minimize the number of iterations in the loop. Each iteration will consume CPU, so if you are finished in the loop, use the EXIT statement to move out of the loop.

❑ Make sure that there are no statements inside the loop that could be located outside of the loop. If a statement doesn't reference a loop variable, it's possible that it could execute outside the loop and perhaps execute only once, rather than many times.

The following code fragment illustrates a poorly designed loop:

```
FOR counter1 IN 1 .. 2000
   LOOP
      FOR counter2 IN 1 .. 2000
      LOOP
         modcounter1 := MOD (counter1, 10);
         modcounter2 := MOD (counter2, 10);

         sqrt1 := SQRT (counter1);
         sqrt2 := SQRT (counter2);

         IF modcounter1 = 0 THEN
            IF modcounter2 = 0 THEN
               sum1:=sum1+sqrt1+sqrt2;
            END IF;
         END IF;
      END LOOP;

   END LOOP;
```

There are some serious inefficiencies in this loop:

❑ Although we only want to process numbers divisible by 10 (the MOD function specifies that only multiples of 10 get processed), we are actually looping though every value from 1 to 2000. The FOR statement in PL/SQL doesn't allow you to iterate in multiples of 10, so it's easy to make this mistake. However, by using FOR, we've actually executed the statements inside each loop 10 times more often than necessary.
❑ The SQRT and MOD functions for counter1 are included within the second (inner) loop. This means that they are executed once for every iteration of the inner loop, even though the value of counter1 does not change. This means that counter1 must be executed 200 times more often than necessary.

The following code fragment implements the same logic as the previous example, but with optimized loop processing:

```
counter1 := 10;
WHILE counter1 <= 2000
```

```
LOOP
    sqrt1 := SQRT (counter1);
    counter2 := 10;
    WHILE counter2 <= 2000
    LOOP
        sqrt2 := SQRT (counter2);

        sum1:=sum1+sqrt1+sqrt2;

        counter2 := counter2 + 10;
    END LOOP;
    counter1 := counter1 + 10;
END LOOP;
```

In this example, we use the WHILE clause and manually increment the loop counter by 10. Consequently, we execute the inner loop only 2000 times rather than 4,000,000. The modulus calculations (MOD functions) are no longer necessary and the square root calculation on counter1 (SQRT function) has been moved out of the inner loop to the outer loop. This reduces the number of executions of this SQRT from 4,000,000 executions in the first example to only 2000 executions in this example. Figure 14.3 shows the performance improvements obtained.

The second example greatly outperforms the first example. The first example took 128 seconds to execute—over two minutes. The second example takes only 0.54 seconds to execute—almost instantaneous. So we can see that optimizing loop processing can lead to large improvements.

When possible, reduce the number of iterations of a PL/SQL loop. Each loop consumes CPU, so EXIT the loop if there is no need to continue. Also reduce processing within the loop by moving loop invariant statements outside of the loop if possible.

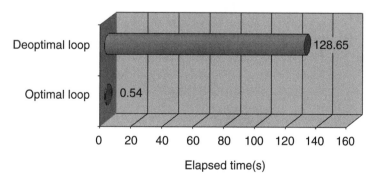

FIGURE 14.3 Improvement gained by optimizing loop processing.

IF Statements   When processing an IF statement with multiple conditions, PL/SQL will consider each condition specified in turn until a match is found. Once the match is found, PL/SQL doesn't have to evaluate any of the subsequent conditions. It therefore follows that if the most likely condition comes first in the IF block, then the average amount of processing that PL/SQL will have to do is reduced.

The following code fragment illustrates a deoptimized IF statement. The first condition will be true only 9 times out of 10,000 loops. The final ELSE condition will be true for 9910 of the 10,000 loops, but the preceding nine comparisons will be needlessly evaluated for each of these iterations.

```
FOR counter1 IN 1 .. 1000000
   LOOP
      IF counter1 < 10 THEN
         -- Do some processing;
      ELSIF counter1 < 20 THEN
         -- Do some processing;
      ELSIF counter1 < 30 THEN
         -- Do some processing;
      ELSIF counter1 < 40 THEN
         -- Do some processing;
      ELSIF counter1 < 50 THEN
         -- Do some processing;
      ELSIF counter1 < 60 THEN
         -- Do some processing;
      ELSIF counter1 < 70 THEN
         -- Do some processing;
      ELSIF counter1 < 80 THEN
         -- Do some processing;
         NULL;
      ELSIF counter1 < 90 THEN
      -- Do some processing;
      ELSE    -- counter above 91
         -- Do some processing;
      END IF;
   END LOOP;
```

The next example shows the IF block optimized. Now the most commonly satisfied expression is first in the IF structure. For most iterations, this first evaluation is the only one that needs to be performed:

```
FOR counter1 IN 1 .. 1000000
   LOOP
      IF counter1 >= 90 THEN
         -- Do some processing;
```

```
    ELSIF counter1 < 10 THEN
        -- Do some processing;
    ELSIF counter1 < 20 THEN
        -- Do some processing;
    ELSIF counter1 < 30 THEN
        -- Do some processing;
    ELSIF counter1 < 40 THEN
        -- Do some processing;
    ELSIF counter1 < 50 THEN
        -- Do some processing;
    ELSIF counter1 < 60 THEN
        -- Do some processing;
    ELSIF counter1 < 70 THEN
        -- Do some processing;
    ELSIF counter1 < 80 THEN
        -- Do some processing;
    ELSIF counter1 < 90 THEN
        -- Do some processing;
    END IF;
END LOOP;
```

Optimizing the IF statement reduced execution time from 4.86 seconds to 1.31 seconds. Figure 14.4 shows the improvement in performance.

If an IF statement is to be executed repeatedly, placing the most commonly satisfied condition earlier in the IF structure may optimize performance.

Recursion   A recursive routine is one that invokes itself. Recursive routines often offer elegant solutions to complex programming problems but tend to consume large amounts of memory and tend to be less efficient than an iterative alternative.

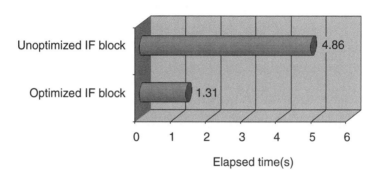

FIGURE 14.4   Performance of optimized and unoptimized IF structures.

Many recursive algorithms can be reformulated using nonrecursive techniques involving iteration. Where possible, you should give preference to the more efficient iterative. For example, the following procedure recursively generates the Fibonacci sequence, in which each element in the sequence is the sum of the previous two numbers.

```
PROCEDURE rec_fib (p_limit NUMBER)
IS
BEGIN
   IF p_limit > 1 THEN
      rec_fib (p_limit--1);
   END IF;

   dbms_output.put_line (p_limit || ' '
      || TO_CHAR (p_limit + p_limit--1));
END;    -- Procedure REC_FIB
```

The next example generates the same sequence without recursion:

```
PROCEDURE nonrec_fib (p_limit NUMBER)
IS
BEGIN
   FOR i IN 1 .. p_limit
   LOOP
      dbms_output.put_line (i || ' '
                || TO_CHAR (i + i--1));
   END LOOP;
END;    -- Procedure NONREC_FIB
```

Figure 14.5 shows the relative performance of the two approaches when calculating the Fibonacci sequence to 50,000. The recursive solution took more than 35 times as long to run as the nonrecursive solution.

Avoid recursive programming. Iterative solutions will almost always outperform recursive solutions.

ARRAY PROCESSING IN PL/SQL

We saw in Chapter 8 how array processing improves query performance and in Chapter 12 how array processing improves bulk inserts. Array processing is equally desirable in PL/SQL but prior to Oracle8i could only be implemented by using dynamic SQL and the DBMS_SQL package.

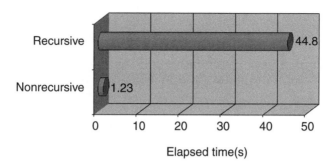

FIGURE 14.5 Relative performance for recursive and nonrecursive implementations of the Fibonacci sequence.

In Oracle8i, bulk processing is directly supported. The following code fragment shows an array query:

```
SELECT department_id, sale_value
    BULK COLLECT INTO l_department_id, l_sale_val
    FROM sales;

FOR i IN 1 .. l_department_id.COUNT
LOOP
    j := j + 1;
    /* Do something with the rows here */
END LOOP;
```

The following code fragment illustrates an array insert of 30,000 rows:

```
FORALL i IN 1 .. 30000
    INSERT INTO insert_test (x, y)
    VALUES (l_numbers (i), l_varchars (i));
COMMIT;
```

Array processing in PL/SQL leads to the same sorts of performance improvements as in other environments. Figure 14.6 illustrates the relative performance of the preceding two examples of array processing in PL/SQL as compared to their more traditional nonarray equivalents. As with array processing in other environments, you can expect significant performance improvements up to an order of magnitude (e.g., 10 times).

When processing or querying large number of rows, take advantage of Oracle8i array processing using the FORALL and BULK COLLECT clauses.

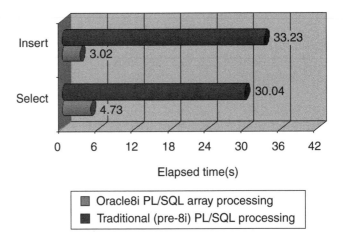

FIGURE 14.6   Relative performance of array processing in PL/SQL.

PARALLEL PL/SQL FUNCTIONS IN SQL

Using PL/SQL functions in SQL statements can be a powerful programming technique. One performance advantage of PL/SQL functions in SQL is the ability to run the PL/SQL routines in parallel. Currently, it's not possible to write a PL/SQL program that executes multiple threads of execution.[1]

Consider the following code fragment. It performs a parallel query on the JUNE_SALES table to collect all the sales amounts for that month. For each sale value it calculates the BIGCALC function, which implements some sort of computationally expensive business logic.

```
SELECT /*+  full(s) parallel(s,4) cache(s)*/ sale_value
     BULK COLLECT INTO t_num_tab
     FROM june_sales s;

FOR i IN 1..t_num_tab.COUNT LOOP
   result:=bigcalc(t_num_tab(i));
   -- Do something with the data
END LOOP;
```

Although the data are retrieved using four parallel streams of execution, the BIGCALC calculations can only be processed by a single process—the session running the PL/SQL program. However, if we recode our example to embed

---

[1]At time of this writing, Oracle 8i did not support parallel or multithreaded execution of PL/SQL. However, this facility is expected to be included in Oracle 9i.

BIGCALC into the SQL statement, we can arrange for BIGCALC to be processed in parallel by the parallel query slaves:

```
SELECT /*+  full(s) parallel(s,4) cache(s)*/
            bigcalc(sale_value)
    BULK COLLECT INTO t_num_tab
    FROM june_sales s;

FOR i IN 1..t_num_tab.COUNT LOOP
   result:=t_num_tab(i);
    -- Do something with the data
END LOOP;
```

Figure 14.7 compares the performance of the two examples when executed on a dual CPU Pentium Windows server. The sort of results you can expect to get from parallelizing PL/SQL functions depends most significantly on how CPU intensive the function is and on the number of CPUs available to you.

There are some limitations on the sort of PL/SQL functions that can be used as functions in SQL. Most important, such a function cannot modify any database tables or (in the case of functions in DML) read any database tables. PL/SQL functions that are to be parallelized are also forbidden to read or modify package public variables.

If your PL/SQL function is standalone (e.g., created with the CREATE FUNCTION statement), then Oracle can determine whether it is pure enough to run in parallel. However, if the function is within a PL/SQL package, then you should tell Oracle that the function is safe to execute in parallel using the PARALLEL_ENABLE clause and/or RESTRICT_REFERENCES pragma. For instance, this declaration in the package header asserts that BIGCALC does not read or write from database tables or package variables and that it is safe to run the function in parallel:

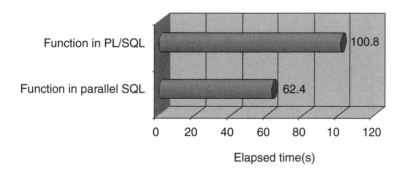

FIGURE 14.7   Processing PL/SQL functions in parallel.

```
FUNCTION bigcalc_parallel(p_input NUMBER)
        RETURN NUMBER PARALLEL_ENABLE;
PRAGMA restrict_references
        (bigcalc,wnds,wnds,rnps,wnps);
```

It is sometimes possible to achieve parallel execution of PL/SQL functions by embedding them in a parallel SQL statement.

WHERE CURRENT OF

It may happen that you find yourself opening a cursor against a table, performing some complex processing upon the data retrieved, and then updating the table row in question. For instance, the following fragment illustrates such a processing loop:

```
CURSOR sales_csr
IS SELECT *
     FROM sales
     WHERE sale_date > '01-DEC-99';

BEGIN
   FOR sale_row IN sales_csr
   LOOP
      IF sale_row.sale_value > 4000 THEN
         l_gstflag:=complex_function(sale_row.sale_value);
         UPDATE sales
            SET gst_flag=l_gstflag
          WHERE customer_id=sale_row.customer_id
            AND product_id=sale_row.product_id
            AND sale_date=sale_row.sale_date;
         l_sales_tot:=l_sales_tot+sale_row.sale_value;
      END IF;
   END LOOP;
```

The UPDATE statement within the loop uses the primary key of the table and is therefore a reasonably efficient index lookup. However, since we just fetched the row in question, why should we need to perform an index lookup? Shouldn't we already know where the row is?

In fact, the second index lookup is unnecessary. PL/SQL (and some other programming languages) can refer to the current row selected by the cursor using the clause WHERE CURRENT OF *cursor_name*. Using this notation, PL/SQL can use the row address (ROWID) stored in the cursor structure to locate the row without an index lookup. Using this method, our example now looks like this:

```
CURSOR sales_csr
    IS SELECT *
          FROM sales
         WHERE sale_date > '01-DEC-99'
           FOR UPDATE;     -- Need FOR UPDATE since using
                           -- WHERE CURRENT OF

BEGIN
    FOR sale_row IN sales_csr
    LOOP
        IF sale_row.sale_value > 4000 THEN
            l_gstflag:=complex_function(sale_row.sale_value);
            UPDATE sales
               SET gst_flag=l_gstflag
             WHERE CURRENT OF sales_csr;
            l_sales_tot:=l_sales_tot+sale_row.sale_value;
        END IF;
    END LOOP;
```

The WHERE CURRENT OF clause eliminates the I/Os involved with an index lookup and does improve the performance of the UPDATE statement. However, to use the WHERE CURRENT OF notation, you must first lock the rows involved using the FOR UPDATE clause in the cursor's SELECT statement. The FOR UPDATE clause also has the following side effects:

❑ All rows selected by the query must be locked before the first row can be returned. If you only intend to process a subset of rows, or if response time for the first row is your primary concern, then you probably don't want to use FOR UPDATE.

❑ Locking the rows requires a transaction entry to be made in every block to be updated. This involves a considerable I/O overhead and is another reason why you may not want to use the FOR UPDATE clause.

If you want to optimize the UPDATE statement by avoiding the unnecessary index read but don't wish to endure the locking overhead of the FOR UPDATE clause, you can keep track of the ROWID yourself and use it in subsequent updates. The following PL/SQL fragment illustrates this technique:

```
CURSOR sales_csr
IS SELECT sales.rowid sale_rowid,sales.*
```

```
        FROM sales
      WHERE sale_date > '01-DEC-99';

BEGIN
   FOR sale_row IN sales_csr
   LOOP
     IF sale_row.sale_value > 4000 THEN
        l_gstflag:=complex_function(sale_row.sale_value);
        UPDATE sales
           SET gst_flag=l_gstflag
         WHERE rowid=sale_row.sale_rowid;

        l_sales_tot:=l_sales_tot+sale_row.sale_value;
     END IF;
   END LOOP;
```

By using this technique, we avoid both the overhead of locking rows and the overhead of the needless index lookup.

A word of caution: Although the FOR UPDATE clause imposes a processing overhead, it does prevent another user from updating the row between the time you open the cursor and the time you issue your update. If there is any chance that such an event may render your update invalid or that you will overwrite another session's update, you should do one of the following:

❏ Use the FOR UPDATE clause and accept the performance consequences. This is referred to as the pessimistic locking strategy.

❏ Check that the row has not changed by including a check in the WHERE clause of the UPDATE statement. For instance, adding the condition "SAL=EMP_ROW.SAL" to the UPDATE statement might be sufficient. This is the optimistic locking strategy.

❏ If you are processing all or most of the rows in the table, you might consider issuing a LOCK TABLE statement to lock the entire table. This has less overhead than locking each row individually but will prevent any concurrent updates, even of rows not being accessed by our procedure

Figure 14.8 compares the execution times for the three approaches. Using the WHERE CURRENT OF cursor technique reduces the I/Os required for the UPDATE statement but imposes an additional I/O requirement because rows had to be locked by the FOR UPDATE clause. Fetching the row's ROWID and specifying this in the WHERE clause give a "best of both worlds" solution, at least from a performance perspective.

A more detailed comparison of the pessimistic and optimistic locking strategies are contained in Chapter 18.

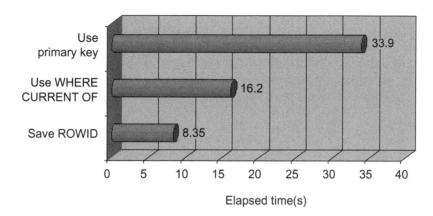

FIGURE 14.8 Comparison of techniques for updating a row you have just FETCHed.

Use the WHERE CURRENT OF clause, or store and use the ROWID when you want to modify a row you have just retrieved within a cursor.

USING THE RETURNING INTO CLAUSE

The RETURNING … INTO clause was introduced in Oracle8i. It lets you get information about the rows that have been processed by a DML statement such as UPDATE, INSERT, or DELETE. The RETURNING INTO clause can also be used in other procedural languages such as JDBC or PRO*C.

Suppose we have a routine that has to remove sales data for a particular product and report on how many dollars of sales where deleted. Prior to Oracle 8.1, we might have used the following logic:

```
CURSOR sales_csr IS
SELECT s.ROWID sales_rowid, s.sale_value
  FROM sales s
 WHERE product_id = p_product_id
   FOR UPDATE;

BEGIN

   FOR sales_row IN sales_csr LOOP
       l_sale_total:=l_sale_total+sales_row.sale_value;
       DELETE FROM sales
        WHERE CURRENT OF sales_csr;
   END LOOP;
```

In 8.1, we can enhance the logic to take advantage of bulk binds, but we still have to perform a SELECT and a separate DELETE:

```
SELECT s.ROWID sales_rowid, s.sale_value
  BULK COLLECT INTO t_rowids, t_sale_value
  FROM sales s
 WHERE product_id = p_product_id
   FOR UPDATE;

 FOR i IN 1 .. t_sale_value.COUNT
 LOOP
    l_sale_total := l_sale_total + t_sale_value (i);
 END LOOP;

 FORALL i IN 1 .. t_rowids.COUNT
    DELETE
      FROM sales
     WHERE ROWID = t_rowids (i);
```

The RETURNING clause allows us to retrieve information about the rows that were affected by the DML. Therefore, a better solution in 8.1 is to eliminate the SELECT statement and get the DELETE to pass back the information about the deleted rows (note that we can use BULK COLLECT within the RETURNING clause):

```
DELETE FROM sales
 WHERE product_id=p_product_id
 RETURNING sale_value BULK COLLECT INTO t_sale_value;

 FOR i IN 1..t_sale_value.COUNT LOOP
    l_sale_total:=l_sale_total+t_sale_value(i);
 END LOOP;
```

Figure 14.9 shows the results of the three preceding examples. Using RETURNING significantly improved performance.

Use the RETURNING INTO clause when you need to report on rows processed by a DML statement.

NOCOPY

The NOCOPY clause was introduced to the PL/SQL language in Oracle 8.1. NO-COPY helps the performance of subroutines that take potentially large PL/SQL tables as arguments. Without the NOCOPY argument, the PL/SQL tables in

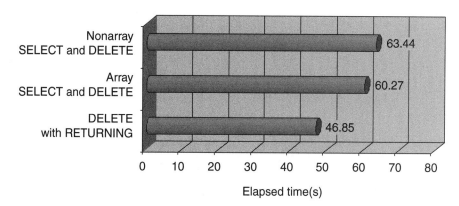

FIGURE 14.9   Using RETURNING to improve performance for PL/SQL that needs to report data processed by DML.

question will be copied and the copy passed to the subroutine. If the table is passed to an IN OUT parameter, it must be copied back to the original table when the subroutine completes. If the PL/SQL table is massive or the subroutine frequently executed, then these copies can consume significant resources.

In Oracle8i the NOCOPY argument can be used to indicate that rather than creating a copy of the PL/SQL table, the subroutine should work directly on the PL/SQL table itself. In other programming languages, this is sometimes referred to as passing an argument by reference rather than by value. This radically reduces the overhead of passing PL/SQL table arguments, especially if the PL/SQL table is large.

Consider the following function. It is used to create a virtual two-dimensional array in a PL/SQL table. You pass in the input table, a row number, and a column number, and you are returned the value within the table that corresponds to the row and column specified.

```
FUNCTION get_avalue
        (p_input_table IN OUT number_tab_type,
         p_row NUMBER, p_col NUMBER, p_num_cols NUMBER)
   RETURN NUMBER
IS
   l_index                      NUMBER;
BEGIN
   l_index := ((p_row--1) * p_num_cols) + p_col;
   RETURN (p_input_table (l_index));
END;
```

Such a routine could be called thousands of times during the execution of its parent program, and each time the PL/SQL table would be copied in and out of the subroutine. Such a function is a definite candidate for the NOCOPY clause.

To use the NOCOPY mode, we simply add the NOCOPY keyword to the parameter declaration:

```
FUNCTION get_avalue
    (p_input_table IN OUT NOCOPY number_tab_type,
```

Figure 14.10 shows the dramatic performance gains achieved by using the NOCOPY clause on the execution time for 1000 accesses of a 200,000-row input table (which corresponds to a 10,000-row, 20-column two-dimensional table).

Always consider Oracle8.1's NOCOPY clause when passing large PL/SQL tables as arguments to functions or procedures.

TAKE ADVANTAGE OF STORED PROGRAMS

Although PL/SQL can be submitted directly to the database as an anonymous block, its real power comes from the ability to store the program in the database.

Use Stored Programs Rather Than Anonymous Blocks   When you submit an anonymous PL/SQL block, you incur some overhead while Oracle parses the PL/SQL and validates the SQL. This means that an anonymous block will always run a bit slower than a stored object that implements the same logic. Therefore, implement your PL/SQL as stored programs (packages, procedures, functions) whenever possible.

Use Packages Rather Than Procedures   A PL/SQL package allows re-lated procedures, functions, cursor, and variable definitions to be stored together. Packages are useful from a programming point of view, since they allow related

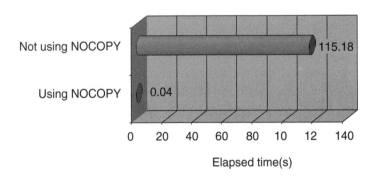

FIGURE 14.10   Performance improvements gained from using the NOCOPY keyword.

program units to be grouped and allow encapsulation of local variables and sub-routines. In an application that contains a complex set of interrelated procedures, using packages can also reduce *dynamic recompilation*.

Dynamic recompilation occurs when a PL/SQL program refers to another PL/SQL program that has changed. Oracle keeps track of dependencies between PL/SQL programs and other objects and will automatically mark dependent objects as needing recompilation when a PL/SQL program changes. PL/SQL packages consist of a package header and a body. Provided that the package header remains constant, the package body can be changed without requiring recompilation of dependent programs.

Pin Frequently Used Packages in the Shared Pool PL/SQL stored programs are stored within the Oracle shared memory area known as the shared pool. The shared pool contains a number of other objects, including standard SQL statements, object definitions, and sometimes private session objects. When the shared pool memory is exhausted, objects are "aged out" of the pool using a least recently used (LRU) algorithm. In some circumstances, the aging out of stored packages and procedures may result in a performance degradation when the package is next executed. You can prevent PL/SQL programs from being aged out of the shared pool by using the DBMS_SHARED_POOL package. For instance, the following command (from SQL*PLUS) keeps the COMPLEX_FUNCTION pinned in the shared pool:

```
SQL> exec sys.dbms_shared_pool.keep('COMPLEX_FUNCTION','P')
```

Your DBA will need to install the dbms_shared_pool package (using the dbmspool.sql script). If you want to use the package as a non-DBA, your DBA will need to grant execute permission on the package.

Take advantage of PL/SQL packages to reduce dynamic recompilation of sorted sub-programs. Consider pinning large or performance critical packages in the shared pool.

OPTIMIZING TRIGGERS

Using the UPDATE OF and WHEN Clauses The UPDATE OF clause of the CREATE TRIGGER statement allows a FOR UPDATE trigger to fire only when the nominated columns are updated. In a similar fashion, the WHEN clause can be used to prevent the execution of the trigger unless a logical condition is met. These clauses help to prevent the trigger from executing unnecessarily and can improve performance of DML operations on the table on which the trigger is based.

For example, the following trigger fires whenever any column in the EMPLOYEES table is updated:

```
CREATE OR REPLACE TRIGGER employee_upd
   BEFORE UPDATE OR INSERT
   ON employees
   FOR EACH ROW
DECLARE
   l_new_sal NUMBER;
BEGIN
   l_new_sal:=complex_function (:new.salary);l,
   IF :new.salary > 100000 THEN
      :new.adjusted_salary := l_new_sal;
   END IF;
END;
```

The following trigger is more efficient because it only fires when the SALARY column is updated, and only when the new value of SALARY is greater than $100,000:

```
CREATE OR REPLACE TRIGGER employee_upd
   BEFORE UPDATE OF salary OR INSERT
   ON employees
   FOR EACH ROW
   WHEN (new.salary > 100000)
DECLARE
   l_new_sal NUMBER;
BEGIN
   l_new_sal:=complex_function (:new.salary);
   IF :new.salary > 100000 THEN
      :new.adjusted_salary := l_new_sal;
   END IF;
END;
```

The optimized trigger only fires when the salary column is updated. This will improve the performance of updates that don't update the salary clause. The optimized trigger in the preceding example only fires if the new salary is above 100,000 so it probably won't fire for most employees. Figure 14.11 shows that for our example, the WHEN and UPDATE OF clauses significantly improved performance.

Make use of the OF COLUMNS and WHEN clauses of the CREATE TRIGGER statement to ensure that your trigger only fires when necessary.

Before and After Row Triggers Sometimes you may be able to implement a trigger so that it fires either BEFORE or AFTER the row is updated. Unless you have a specific reason to use the BEFORE trigger, use the AFTER

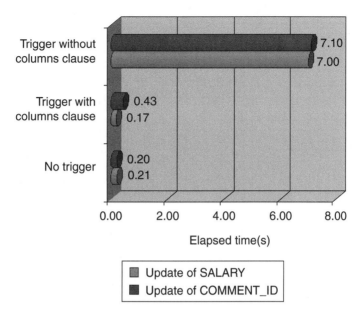

FIGURE 14.11 Using the WHEN and UDATE OF trigger clauses to reduce trigger overhead.

trigger in preference. The reason for this recommendation is that the BEFORE trigger locks the row in question before the trigger is executed. If the trigger then decides not to change the row in question, then this locking will have unnecessarily consumed database resources.

Similarly, avoid FOR EACH ROW triggers if possible. FOR EACH ROW causes the trigger to be executed for each affected row. Unless you need to process each row individually, this option should not be used.

> Don't use FOR EACH ROW triggers unnecessarily. If using FOR EACH ROW triggers, use AFTER triggers in preference to BEFORE triggers.

USE EXPLICIT CURSORS

PL/SQL allows an SQL statement to be included in a block without being explicitly associated with a cursor. For instance, the following is a commonplace expression in PL/SQL:

```
BEGIN
    SELECT customer_id
      INTO g_customer_id
```

```
      FROM customers c
   WHERE contact_surname = g_surname
     AND contact_firstname = g_firstname;
```

Although no cursor is declared in the PL/SQL, a cursor is in fact associated with such a statement and is created automatically by PL/SQL. Such a cursor is referred to as an *implicit* cursor.

Although implicit cursors can be convenient when programming, they can impose some execution overhead. Implicit cursors must return only a single row and Oracle must check to make sure that only one row is returned by performing a second implicit fetch statement after the first row is returned.

If the retrieval is based on an index, then the overhead will usually be negligible. However, if the retrieval is based on a table scan, then Oracle continues scanning until it finds an eligible row or reaches the end of the table. On average, this will result in twice as many block reads. Therefore, it is sometimes more efficient to use an explicit cursor as shown in the following code fragment:

```
   CURSOR customer_csr
   IS
       SELECT customer_id
         FROM customers c
        WHERE contact_surname = g_surname
          AND contact_firstname = g_firstname;
BEGIN
   OPEN customer_csr;
   FETCH customer_csr INTO g_customer_id;
   CLOSE customer_csr;
```

Figure 14.12 compares the I/O requirements of implicit and explicit cursors for table scans and for index lookups. In this example we were relatively lucky in that the required row was toward the "front" of the table. On average, we would expect the implicit cursor to require twice the number of block gets when compared with the implicit cursor.

Use explicit cursors in preference to implicit cursors created by SELECT statements embedded in PL/SQL, especially if the query might involve a full-table scan.

CACHING WITH PL/SQL TABLES

PL/SQL tables are analogous to arrays in other languages. Like arrays, PL/SQL tables can be used to remember, or to cache, frequently accessed codes or values. Using this technique, we can minimize our database accesses.

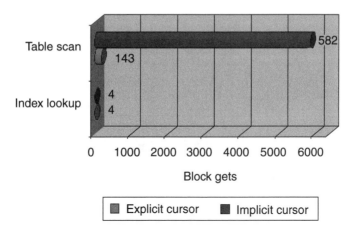

FIGURE 14.12 Performance of implicit and explicit cursors for table scans and index lookups.

The following example illustrates the technique. A PL/SQL table is used to hold the normal value for a product with a given product id. Only if the normal value is not found in the table will it be necessary to query the PRODUCTS table.

```
CURSOR product_csr (cp_product_id NUMBER)
IS
    SELECT normal_value
      FROM products
     WHERE product_id = cp_product_id;

l_product_normal_value
         products.normal_value%TYPE;
BEGIN
    -- Look in the PL/SQL table for the product_id
    BEGIN
        l_product_normal_value :=
            product_val_table (p_product_id);
    EXCEPTION
        WHEN NO_DATA_FOUND THEN
            -- Not found in the PL/SQL table so get from
            -- the database and add to the table
            OPEN product_csr (p_product_id);
            FETCH product_csr INTO l_product_normal_value;
            CLOSE product_csr;
            product_val_table (p_product_id) :=
                    l_product_normal_value;
    END;
```

```
INSERT INTO sales (customer_id, product_id,
        sale_date, quantity, sale_value)
VALUES (p_customer_id, p_product_id, SYSDATE,
        p_quantity,
        p_quantity*l_product_normal_value);
COMMIT;
END;
```

Caching is a powerful performance enhancer in any language. Figure 14.13 shows the improvement gained for executing our example 500 times across 10 product types, a reduction in execution time by about 50%.

The PL/SQL cache table is especially effective when the same PL/SQL function will be executed many times within a session. Because the cache table is destroyed when you disconnect from Oracle, you won't see much improvement if you execute the function only a couple of times in each session.

Using PL/SQL tables to cache frequently accessed values can improve performance markedly.

USING TEMPORARY TABLES

Because PL/SQL does not allow you to return a result set, it's common to create a table into which a PL/SQL program inserts report data. The calling program then queries the report table, prints the results, and deletes the data from the report table. For example, the following code fragment shows us populating a report table with the output of a complex calculation:

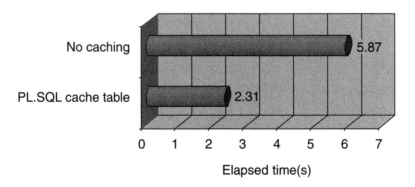

FIGURE 14.13   Improvement gained by implementing a PL/SQL cache table.

```
FOR sale_row IN ( SELECT * FROM sales t )
LOOP
    l_sale_adjustment := complex_calculations
                (sale_row.sale_value,
                sale_row.customer_id);
    INSERT INTO sales_report_p
            (customer_id, product_id, sale_date,
            adjusted_sale_value)
    VALUES (sale_row.customer_id, sale_row.product_id,
            sale_row.sale_date, l_sale_adjustment);
END LOOP;
```

Later, the calling program retrieves the rows from the report table and deletes them:

```
SELECT *
  FROM sales_report_p;
DELETE
  FROM sales_report_p;
```

Of course, the resources consumed by inserting and deleting from the report table are pure overhead—they have nothing to do with the job at hand but are simply necessary to work around limitation of the PL/SQL language. We can reduce the overhead of the DML on the report table if we set the NOLOGGING attribute (described in Chapter 12), but our PL/SQL routine is still going to spend too much time performing DML on the peripheral report table.

Oracle8i temporary tables are designed to reduce overhead when you need to store temporary information in a table structure. Temporary tables are identical in virtually every respect to permanent tables, but the data in the table are always visible only to the local session and will persist only for the duration of the session or transaction. The data in a temporary table are not logged and are not stored in rollback segments. The overhead of inserting and deleting from the temporary table is consequently much less than that for a permanent table.

Figure 14.14 shows the reduced overhead of using a temporary table for the preceding PL/SQL fragment. Using a temporary table radically reduced insert overhead and, because the data in the temporary table are deallocated after the session committed (the table was created with the ON COMMIT DELETE ROWS clause), eliminated the need to delete the rows.

Temporary tables are useful in a number of other circumstances:

❏ Copying rows from a remote table to local storage for more efficient execution
❏ Using temporary tables for intermediate storage, which allows you to break down complex SQL statements into multiple stages

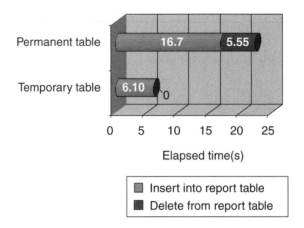

FIGURE 14.14 Temporary and permanent tables.

Take advantage of temporary tables when your PL/SQL needs to store data that does not need to persist beyond the session or the transaction

DYNAMIC SQL AND PL/SQL

Dynamic SQL are SQL statements that are constructed at run time rather than at design time. Such a program might even accept an SQL statement typed in at a terminal, process it, and return the results to the user.

Prior to Oracle version 8.1, dynamic SQL was supported mainly through the DBMS_SQL package. This package emulated the Oracle7 OCI interface, and its implementation required a lot of programmer effort.

In Oracle 8i the EXECUTE IMMEDIATE statement was introduced. This statement allowed for any statement—except those that returned multiple-row results sets—to be processed dynamically.

EXECUTE IMMEDIATE improves programmer productivity. However, DBMS_SQL offers some performance advantages in terms of array processing and cursor and control. In either case, care is needed to ensure good use of bind variables and optimal performance.

DBMS_SQL

DBMS_SQL allows for almost any sort of dynamic SQL statement or PL/SQL block to be executed. However, for any nontrivial statements DBMS_SQL may require many function calls. Figure 14.15 shows the basic sequence of calls in a DBMS_SQL package.

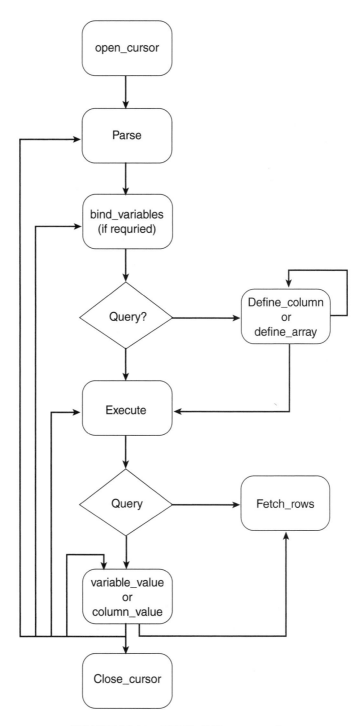

FIGURE 14.15 DBMS_SQL program flow.

As with all programming environments that support SQL execution, three major considerations are critical when optimizing the performance of DBMS_SQL:

❑ Making good use of bind variables
❑ Using array processing when appropriate
❑ Reusing cursors effectively

Bind Variables in DBMS_SQL Bind variables in PL/SQL are implemented using the BIND_VARIABLE and related functions.

The following fragment illustrates some DBMS_SQL that does not use bind variables. Elements from the tables `t_sales_rep_id` and `t_cust_ids` are concatenated to a string that is then parsed and executed. Each execution is in effect a unique SQL statement and the statement must be parsed with every execution. It's unlikely that this SQL will find matching shared SQL in the shared pool, so each parse call will be expensive:

```
FOR i IN 1 .. t_cust_ids.COUNT
LOOP
   l_cursor := dbms_sql.open_cursor;
   dbms_sql.parse (
           l_cursor,
           'UPDATE /*dynamic array*/' ||
                       l_tab_name ||
           '   SET sales_rep_id=' ||
                       t_sales_rep_id (i) ||
           ' WHERE customer_id=' ||
                       t_cust_ids (i),
           dbms_sql.native
        );
   rc := dbms_sql.execute (l_cursor);
   dbms_sql.close_cursor (l_cursor);
END LOOP;
```

Here is the same example implemented with bind variables. Note that as well as using the BIND_VARIABLE calls, only a single PARSE call is required despite the multiple EXECUTE calls. Using bind variables allows you to eliminate unnecessary parse overhead.

```
l_cursor := dbms_sql.open_cursor;
dbms_sql.parse (
           l_cursor,
           'UPDATE /*dynamic array*/' ||
               l_tab_name ||
```

```
            '    SET sales_rep_id=:sales_rep ' ||
            ' WHERE customer_id=:cust_id ',
            dbms_sql.native              );

FOR i IN 1 .. t_cust_ids.COUNT
LOOP
    dbms_sql.bind_variable (l_cursor, 'sales_rep',
                            t_sales_rep_id (i));
    dbms_sql.bind_variable (l_cursor, 'cust_id',
                            t_cust_ids (i));
    rc := dbms_sql.execute (l_cursor);
END LOOP;
dbms_sql.close_cursor (l_cursor);
```

Array Processing in DBMS_SQL   DBMS_SQL does allow for array processing. If we further amend our example to use the BIND_ARRAY call, we can execute all our updates in a single SQL call:

```
l_cursor := dbms_sql.open_cursor;
dbms_sql.parse (
        l_cursor,
        'UPDATE ' ||l_tab_name ||
        '    SET sales_rep_id=:sales_rep ' ||
        ' WHERE customer_id=:cust_id ',
        dbms_sql.native
      );
dbms_sql.bind_array (l_cursor, 'sales_rep',
                    t_sales_rep_id);
dbms_sql.bind_array (l_cursor, 'cust_id',
                    t_cust_ids);
rc := dbms_sql.execute (l_cursor);
dbms_sql.close_cursor (l_cursor);
```

Figure 14.16 shows the performance characteristics of the preceding DBMS_SQL examples for a 10,000-row input table. Implementing bind variables reduced execution time by 75%. Implementing array binds reduced that execution time by a further 45%.

If you go to the effort of using DBMS_SQL, make sure you exploit bind variables and array processing.

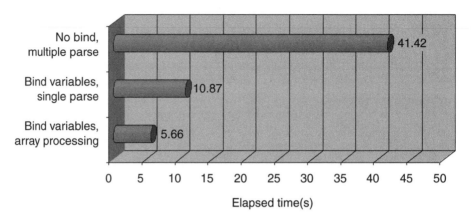

FIGURE 14.16   Optimization of DBMS_SQL with bind variables and array processing.

EXECUTE IMMEDIATE

The EXECUTE IMMEDIATE statement, introduced in Oracle 8i, allows for dynamic DML, DDL, and queries that return only a single row. EXECUTE IMMEDIATE is easy to use. The following example implements the same logic as was presented in our previous DBMS_SQL examples:

```
FOR i IN 1 .. t_cust_ids.COUNT
LOOP
    EXECUTE IMMEDIATE 'UPDATE /*simple n-dynamic*/' ||
                        l_tab_name ||
                        '   SET sales_rep_id=' ||
                        t_sales_rep_id (i) ||
                        ' WHERE customer_id=' ||
                        t_cust_ids (i);
END LOOP;
```

The preceding example does not use bind variables. Instead the values for sales_rep_id and customer_id are concatenated into the statement, and therefore we might expect it to perform poorly. To use bind variables with EXECUTE IMMEDIATE, you must employ the USING clause:

```
FOR i IN 1 .. t_cust_ids.COUNT
LOOP
    EXECUTE IMMEDIATE 'UPDATE /*n-dynamic with bind*/'
                        ||l_tab_name ||
                        '   SET sales_rep_id=:1 ' ||
                        ' WHERE customer_id=:2 '
            USING t_sales_rep_id (i), t_cust_ids (i);
END LOOP;
```

Using bind variables gives us a significant performance improvement, down from 39.9 seconds execution time to 13.8 seconds. However, the performance still lags behind the performance of DBMS_SQL with bind variables. This is because every execution of EXECUTE IMMEDIATE issues a new parse call even if the SQL is unchanged. In DBMS_SQL we were able to parse the statement once and then reexecute the statement multiple times without reparsing.[2]

Where possible, make sure you implement bind variables with the USING clause in EXECUTE IMMEDIATE.

Another feature of DBMS_SQL that is not supported in EXECUTE IMMEDIATE is array processing. As we have found, array processing offers significant performance improvements for statements that return large result sets or that insert or update large numbers of rows.

EXECUTE IMMEDIATE OR DBMS_SQL?

EXECUTE IMMEDIATE offers a tremendous reduction in complexity for PL/SQL programmers who want to implement dynamic SQL, and you can bet that it will be used a lot more frequently than DBMS_SQL. However, when performance really counts you may be better off using DBMS_SQL. DBMS_SQL offers the following advantages:

❑ You can implement array binds that will usually have the execution time of queries and DML that process many rows.
❑ You can reexecute cursors in DBMS_SQL without reparsing.

Figure 14.17 illustrates the relative performance of EXECUTE IMMEDIATE with DBMS_SQL for our example. Even without bind variables, DBMS_SQL is significantly faster because it didn't need to submit a parse call with each execution. When array processing is utilized in DBMS_SQL, execution time is halved.

You won't always need or be able to take advantage of the performance advantages offered by DBMS_SQL. Nevertheless, if writing dynamic SQL that is performance sensitive, consider DBMS_SQL.

Although it is more complex to implement, dynamic SQL using DBMS_SQL can often outperform dynamic SQL implemented using EXECUTE IMMEDIATE. This is particularly true when array processing or parse overhead is important.

---

[2]You can partially mitigate this problem by using the SESSION_CACHED_CURSORS parameter (see Chapter 4). However, saving cursors with DBMS_SQL still offers better performance.

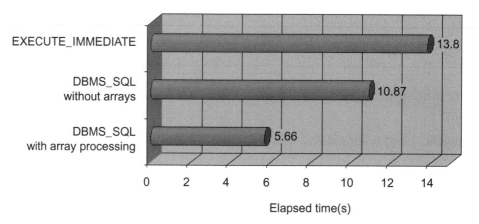

FIGURE 14.17 EXECUTE_IMMEDIATE versus DBMS_SQL.

USING THE PL/SQL PROFILER

One of the most important steps in code optimization is targeting the most time-consuming segments of a program for tuning. In PL/SQL prior to Oracle8i, this would usually involve instrumenting PL/SQL with queries that used the V$TIMER dynamic performance view to report on elapsed times for various code segments in 1/100ths of a second. This technique was cumbersome and only minimally useful, but it represented the only viable technique for determining the execution time of PL/SQL subroutines prior to Oracle8i.

The situation has improved immensely with the release of Oracle8i, because now we have the DBMS_PROFILER package, which can report execution times on a line-by-line basis and can report on code coverage (identifying lines of code that have not been executed).

A profiling session is initiated with the START_PROFILER call and terminated with STOP_PROFILER. For instance, the following block creates profiling data for the stored procedure "run_test":

```
DECLARE
    l_run_id NUMBER;
BEGIN
    l_run_id:=sys.dbms_profiler.start_profiler('Demo Run1');
    qra.run_test;
    l_run_id:=sys.dbms_profiler.stop_profiler;
END;
```

The DBMS_PROFILER package stores profile data into the tables PLSQL_PROFILER_RUNS, PLSQL_PROFILER_UNITS, and PLSQL_PROFILER_DATA (which you need to create from the file *proftab.sql)*. The following query reports on total execution time in ms for each line executed:[3]

```
SELECT u.unit_owner||'.'||u.unit_name,line#,
       round(d.total_time/1e8) total_ms,d.total_occur,
       s.text
  FROM plsql_profiler_runs r,
       plsql_profiler_units u,
       plsql_profiler_data d,
       all_source s
 WHERE r.run_comment='Demo Run1'
   AND r.runid=u.runid
   AND d.runid=u.runid
   AND u.unit_number=d.unit_number
   AND s.owner=u.unit_owner
   AND s.type=u.unit_type
   AND s.name=u.unit_name
   AND s.line=d.line#
 ORDER BY d.total_time desc
```

The query produces output like this:

PROGRAM UNIT	LINE	TIME (MS)	COUNT	TEXT
SYS.DBMS_SYS_SQL	781	169304	697	a0 2c 6a :2 a0 7e 51 b4 2e
SYS.DBMS_SYS_SQL	786	79290	662	8f a0 b0 3d 8f a0 b0 3d
EXPERT.QUEST_IX_CBO_RULE_PAK	217	64182	5	FOR r1 IN get_stale_tables LOOP
EXPERT.QUEST_IX_IO_EFFIC_RULE_PAK	854	28038	9	FOR r1 IN get_ts_io_times LOOP
EXPERT.QUEST_IX_RUN_ADMIN	896	23844	3	qre.evaluate_all_rules(l_run_id);
EXPERT.QUEST_IX_RULE_ENGINE	157	8894	356	FOR r1 IN c_html LOOP — For each html line
EXPERT.QUEST_IX_SEQUENCE_RULE_PAK	234	7519	96	FOR r1 IN get_seq_rates LOOP
SYS.DBMS_SYS_SQL	487	7377	59	3d 8f a0 b0 3d b4 55 6a
EXPERT.QUEST_IX_RUN_ADMIN	746	6726	1567	INSERT INTO quest_ix_run_metrics
EXPERT.QUEST_IX_RUN_ADMIN	21	6426	270	INSERT INTO uest_ix_run_log (run_qid,timestamp,log_entry_id,log_entry)

---

[3]Note that the profiler package would often give inaccurate execution times in 8.1.5. In 8.1.5 you should only take notice of the *relative* execution times. Although the absolute execution times are sometimes bogus, the absolute times will still help you identify hot spots in your code.

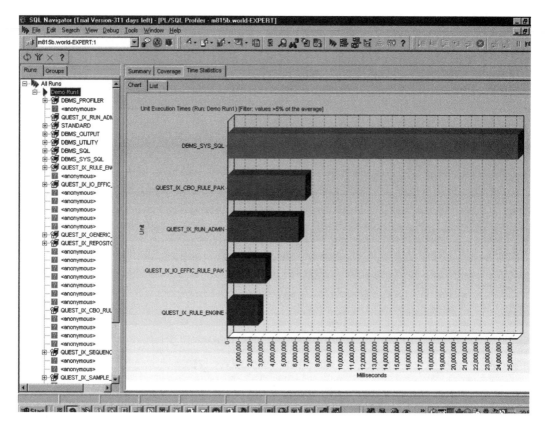

FIGURE 14.18 DBMS_PROFILER support in SQL*Navigator.

Take advantage of the DBMS_PROFILER package to identify hot spots in your PL/SQL code.

Using the profiler in this way can help you to identify individual lines of code that contribute most heavily to execution time. These lines should be amenable to some of the tuning techniques we've discussed in this chapter. Identifying the slowest parts of your code is an essential first step toward effective tuning. Therefore, any PL/SQL programmer who cares about execution time should be familiar with the profiler.

Of course, the profiler becomes more useful when integrated into a powerful integrated development environment. It's also clear that it would be useful to aggregate execution time by subroutines and allow the user to drill down from there into execution times for individual lines.

Quest software offers support for DBMS_PROFILER within its TOAD and SQL*Navigator products. Figure 14.18 shows execution times summarized by package in SQL*Navigator. The SQL*Navigator interface allows you to drill down into module names and individual lines of code. You can also view code coverage and jump to source code lines.

SUMMARY

In this chapter, we've seen how PL/SQL can be used in place of standard SQL to improve performance of certain operations. PL/SQL has the following advantages over ANSI SQL:

❏ It operates completely within the server environment, eliminating or reducing client/server traffic.
❏ It allows the programmer to specify the processing logic and to implement data access paths that might not be possible using standard SQL.
❏ It can provide a divide-and-conquer strategy for complex SQL statements.

PL/SQL is often more efficient than standard SQL for

❏ Operations that return limited amounts of data to the calling program
❏ Operations that seek maximum or minimum values via an index
❏ Correlated updates

PL/SQL can also be used in triggers to maintain denormalized or preprocessed data to assist in query performance.

There are a number of measures we can take to improve the performance of PL/SQL code. In particular,

❏ Use traditional code optimization techniques. In particular, avoid unnecessary loops and recursion and place the more frequently satisfied conditions first in IF clauses.
❏ Use the array processing facilities introduced in Oracle8i.
❏ Use the NOCOPY clause when passing large tables as arguments to PL/SQL routines.
❏ Use RETURNING . . . INTO when you need to report on the data affected by a DML statement.
❏ Use explicit cursors in PL/SQL. An implicit cursor will often perform additional fetches.

❏ Use the WHERE CURRENT OF CURSOR clause to access a row currently open in a cursor. Alternately, fetch and use the ROWID column if you want to avoid the overhead of the FOR UPDATE statement.

❏ Cache frequently accessed data values in PL/SQL tables.

When using EXECUTE IMMEDIATE, always use the USING clause to take advantage of shared SQL. If you have performance-critical SQL, consider using DBMS_SQL, which offers superior parsing and array processing.

Get to know the PL/SQL profiler (DBMS_PROFILER). It can pinpoint inefficiencies or tuning opportunities within your code.

USING AND TUNING ORACLE JAVA

The integration of a Java Virtual Machine (JVM) into the Oracle8i database server is easily one of the most significant technical innovations introduced by Oracle Corporation in recent years. The integrated JVM, called the *Aurora* JVM, leverages the Oracle multithreaded server architecture to deliver (so Oracle benchmarks suggest) a far more scalable platform for deployment of Java middle-tier programs. Furthermore, Oracle Corporation has integrated support for CORBA, Enterprise Java Beans (EJB), Java Message Service (JMS), JDBC and other Java-based middleware technologies. The result is that Oracle Corporation can now provide not just database services but also complete Java-based middleware solution.

As SQL developers we may or may not be interested in Java technologies. But because Oracle has integrated Java into the database engine itself, we have the opportunity to use Java as an alternative to SQL statements or to enhance the performance of SQL statements. We can use Java in exactly the same way as we can use PL/SQL. For instance, we can now write Java stored procedures to provide procedural alternative to complex, hard-to-optimize SQL or implement Java functions and call them from our SQL statements.

Oracle offers two SQL-aware Java interfaces:

❑ JDBC is a standards-based, low-level API that is similar in some respects to ODBC.

❑ SQLJ is a precompiler that converts high-level statements into low-level JDBC. In theory, it offers a greater degree of programmer productivity than SQLJ.

Many SQL developers will feel more comfortable with PL/SQL, and PL/SQL does provide a more productive environment for interacting with the Oracle database. As we have seen in previous chapters, in the right circumstances a PL/SQL solution can provide a significant performance gain over straight SQL. Why, then would we want to use Java instead of PL/SQL ?
There are a few reasons why Java might be a better choice than PL/SQL:

❑ As we will soon see, Java offers significant performance advantages for computationally expensive procedures.
❑ In theory (though probably not often in practice) Java stored procedures and functions could be more easily converted to run against other databases such as SQL*Server or DB2.
❑ Java procedures could be deployed at any tier in a complex application. For instance, a Java routine might run in a Java application sitting on the client, on an application server in the middle tier, or in the database server (e.g., Oracle8i) itself.

In this chapter, we cover the following topics:

❑ A brief comparison of Java performance compared with PL/SQL
❑ Techniques for optimizing JDBC
❑ Techniques for optimizing SQLJ

JAVA AS AN ALTERNATIVE TO PL/SQL

Which is the better choice on performance grounds: Java or PL/SQL? As usual, it depends on what you want to do. In this section we compare performance for procedures that perform CPU-intensive operations without database access and procedures that are database-centric.

COMPUTATIONALLY INTENSIVE ROUTINES

Consider a routine that calculates the number of prime numbers less than a given number. We could implement such a function easily enough in PL/SQL:

```
CREATE OR REPLACE
FUNCTION          NPRIMES ( p_in NUMBER) RETURN  NUMBER
```

```
IS
    nprimes NUMBER:=0;
BEGIN
    FOR i IN 2..p_in-1 LOOP
        IF MOD(p_in,i)=0 THEN
            nprimes:=nprimes+1;
        END IF;
    END LOOP;
    RETURN(nprimes);

END; — Function NPRIMES
```

We could also implement it in Java:

```
CREATE OR REPLACE AND RESOLVE JAVA SOURCE NAMED "cprime"
AS
import java.sql.*;
import oracle.jdbc.driver.*;
import java.math.*;

public class cprime {

  static public int nprimes(int in_num) {
    int i,j;
    int nprimes=0;
    for (i=2;i<in_num;i++)
      {
        if (in_num%i==0)
        {
          nprimes++;
        }
      }
    return(nprimes);
  }
}
.
.
/
CREATE OR REPLACE FUNCTION j_nprimes (p_in NUMBER)
   RETURN NUMBER
AS
   LANGUAGE JAVA
      NAME 'cprime.nprimes(int) return int';
.
/
```

Each procedure is a virtually line-for-line identical implementation. We might expect that Java would show a significant but modest performance improvement over PL/SQL; in fact, the Java routine is more than 10 times faster than the PL/SQL routine (measured over 1000 executions on Oracle 8.1.6 for NT4).

Here is another example that returns the sum of the square roots of each number from 1 to a number provided as a parameter:

```java
static public double calc(int in_num) {
    int i,j;
    double sumsqrt=0;
    for (i=2;i<=in_num;i++)
      {
        sumsqrt+=java.lang.Math.pow(i,.5);
      }
      return(sumsqrt);
    }
```

Here is the equivalent PL/SQL implementation:

```
CREATE OR REPLACE FUNCTION p_sumsqrt (in_num NUMBER)
    RETURN NUMBER
IS
    i                            BINARY_INTEGER;
    sumsqrt                      FLOAT := 0;
BEGIN
    FOR i IN 1 .. in_num
    LOOP
        sumsqrt := sumsqrt + POWER (i, .5);
    END LOOP;
    RETURN (sumsqrt);
END;
```

Again, the Java routine radically outperformed the PL/SQL implementation. In this case, the difference in performance was even more remarkable: The PL/SQL routine took over 100 times longer than the Java routine!

The previous two examples implemented both integer and floating point arithmetic and were heavily dependent on the efficiency of the mathematics libraries available to each language—in particular the implementations of power and modulus functions were critical to overall performance. This third example uses simple integer arithmetic involving addition, subtraction, multiplication, and division only:

```java
static public double basicmath(int in_num) {
    int i,j;
```

```
   double result=0;
   for (i=2;i<=in_num;i++)
     {
        result+=((4*i+5*i)/i+9*i-6*i);
     }
     return(result);
}
```

Here is the PL/SQL implementation:

```
CREATE OR REPLACE FUNCTION p_basicmath
    (in_num BINARY_INTEGER) RETURN NUMBER IS
    i BINARY_INTEGER;
    result BINARY_INTEGER:=0;
BEGIN
    FOR i IN 2..in_num LOOP
        result:=result+((4*i+5*i)/i+9*i-6*i);
    END LOOP;
      return(result);
END;
```

For this simple integer arithmetic example that involved no math library functions, the Java implementation was "only" five times faster than the PL/SQL implementation.

Figure 15.1 shows the results from our computationally expensive examples. In each case Java massively outperformed PL/SQL. These three cases suggest that PL/SQL is particularly inferior to Java when there is substantial floating point arithmetic or when the routines are heavily dependent on the performance of the underlying math libraries.

Use Java stored procedures in preference to PL/SQL stored procedures for computationally expensive tasks, particularly those involving floating point arithmetic.

DATABASE-INTENSIVE ROUTINES

PL/SQL is tightly integrated with the Oracle database server. PL/SQL datatypes are equivalent to Oracle native datatypes, so there is no datatype conversion required. On the other hand, JDBC interposes a generic layer between the Java code and SQL. For these reasons, we might expect Java to be less efficient for database-intensive operations.

Our first test case compared the performance of a simple transaction processing simulation implemented in Java and in JDBC. The implementation is a bit

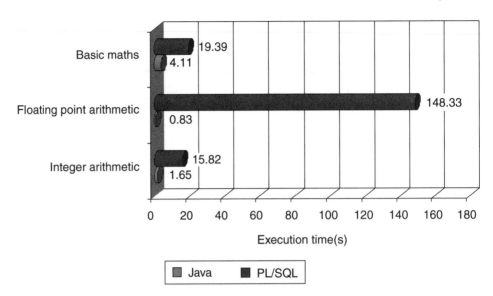

FIGURE 15.1   Java versus PL/SQL for compute-intensive tasks.

too lengthy to reproduce here but is available from the book's web site. Fragments of the JDBC transaction are introduced later in this chapter in the discussion of JDBC tuning. Both the JDBC and PL/SQL implementations accepted a customer ID, a product ID, and a quantity. The transaction involved querying the CUSTOMERS and PRODUCTS table, inserting a row into SALES, and then committing. Each test involved processing 10,000 transactions. Both implementations were run as stored procedures. For this transaction, the Java implementation was approximately 50% slower than the PL/SQL implementation. The results are illustrated in Figure 15.2.

A second test compared the performance of JDBC with PL/SQL for a routine that performed bulk processing. In this example, 100,000 rows were fetched from SALES and inserted into a temporary table. Each fetch and insert involved 50 rows. In this case, the JDBC implementation took more than twice as long as the PL/SQL implementation. These results are also shown in Figure 15.2.

Both routines used the performance-maximizing practices outlined in the previous chapter and later in this chapter. In each case, equivalent -sized arrays were used together with good cursor handling and bind variables. Analysis of tkprof and internal Oracle statistics indicated that JDBC simply used more CPU than the PL/SQL equivalents. This CPU overhead is probably the result of having to work with a longer code path and converting Oracle datatypes to native Java datatypes.

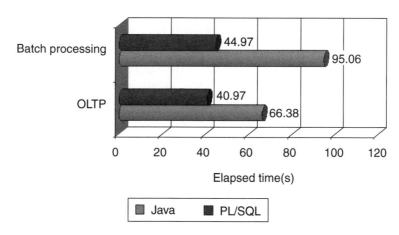

FIGURE 15.2   Comparison of JDBC and PL/SQL for database-intensive operations.

PL/SQL stored procedures will typically outperform JDBC stored procedures for database-intensive routines.

JAVA OR PL/SQL?

The preceding discussion has shown that neither JDBC nor PL/SQL is totally superior in performance terms. Java stored procedures are clearly preferable when computationally intensive operations must be performed. Similarly, PL/SQL stored procedures will outperform Java for database-intensive tasks. Luckily, it's not necessary for us to choose one language or the other; we can easily mix Java and PL/SQL routines in the one language to get a "best of both worlds" solution.

If performance is the only consideration, use Java stored procedures for computationally intensive routines and PL/SQL for database-intensive routines.

It's worth remembering that both Java and PL/SQL are undergoing rapid technological change. Java is a new Oracle technology, and it will improve in performance with each release. At the same time, the PL/SQL team has been challenged by Java and will introduce advanced features such as a PL/SQL compiler and multithreading in PL/SQL programs. In subsequent releases of Oracle, we might expect to see better compute-intensive performance from PL/SQL and better database performance from JDBC.

OPTIMIZING JDBC

In this section we briefly review the options for improving SQL statement execution in JDBC programs. As with most procedural languages that access Oracle data, the key measures for improving performance are as follows:

❑ Using bind variables
❑ Avoiding excessive parse calls
❑ Exploiting array processing

USING BIND VARIABLES IN JDBC

It is easy to use bind variables in JDBC. Unfortunately, it's slightly easier and more natural to omit bind variables, and consequently many beginner JDBC programmers fail to exploit them.

Here is a simple example program that doesn't use bind variables:

```
Statement msql=DefaultConnection.createStatement();

for(i=1;i<100;i++)
{
    msql.executeUpdate(
        "UPDATE employees SET salary=salary*1.1 "+
        " WHERE employee_id="+i);
}
```

Every time the executeUpdate method is called in the loop, a new SQL statement is generated that must be parsed. Even if a matching SQL statement is found in the shared pool, there is still a significant overhead. If a matching SQL statement is not found, then the optimizer must validate the statement, determine an execution plan, and store the SQL in the shared pool.

By using prepared JDBC statements, we can avoid this overhead:

```
PreparedStatement msql2=
    DefaultConnection.prepareStatement(
        "UPDATE employees SET salary=salary*1.1 "+
        " WHERE employee_id=:empid");

    for(i=1;i<100;i++)
    {
        msql2.setInt(1,i);
        rows=msql2.executeUpdate();

    }
```

The overhead of parsing every statement depends a lot on how I/O intensive the statement is and on the hit rate in the shared pool for similar statements. You can also use the CURSOR_SHARING facility of 8.1.6 discussed in Chapter 4 to force bind variables into statements that use literals as in our previous example. For our example, using preparedStatements reduced first execution time by more than half and shaved one-quarter off subsequent executions. Figure 15.3 illustrates these results.

Always use PreparedStatements with bind variables for statements that are executed repeatedly.

CURSOR HANDLING

An optimally configured JDBC program will never request that a statement that has been parsed once be parsed a second time. The most important consideration here is to implement PreparedStatements using bind variables. But once you have implemented PreparedStatements, it is important to ensure that Prepared-Statements that need to be reexecuted are not closed.

When you issue the close() method against a PreparedStatement, you release all resources allocated to the statement, including the Oracle cursor structure. This means that if you reexecute the statement you will need to reissue the prepareStatement() method and cause Oracle to reparse the statement. If you have used bind variables, the odds are that the statement will be found in the shared pool and only a soft parse will be required.

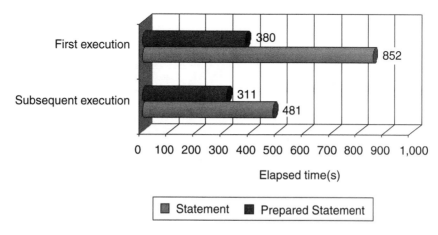

FIGURE 15.3 Comparison of JDBC performance for Statement objects and Prepared-Statement objects.

These soft parses are nowhere near as expensive as a hard parse, but they can still contribute substantially to execution time. It's easy to fall into this trap if you create your PreparedStatement object within a transaction method. If the PreparedStatement object can't scope beyond the method call, then you'll have to re-create it whenever the method is called. It's better to declare the PreparedStatement object as public and initialize it once during your programs initiation phase.

For a test in which a PreparedStatement was executed 100 times with changing bind variables, declaring the PreparedStatement once only reduced execution time by almost one-third. (Figure 15.4).

If you know you are going to reexecute a PreparedStatement many times, declare it as a public object and don't issue the close() method until after the last execution.

AVOID AUTOCOMMIT

The JDBC Connection class supports an autocommit property. If autocommit is TRUE, then the JDBC driver generates a COMMIT statement after every statement. As we saw in Chapter 12, reducing COMMIT frequency is one of the most important ways of increasing throughput of batched DML statements, so in general we would not want the autocommit property to be active.

By default, autocommit is enabled in the JDBC drivers for programs that are running outside of the database. For JDBC programs that run as stored procedures, autocommit is disabled.

You can check to see if autocommit is set—and disable it if it is—with the following statements:

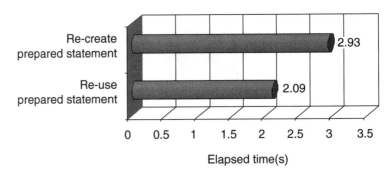

FIGURE 15.4   Reusing PreparedStatements reduces execution time.

```
if (DefaultConnection.getAutoCommit() == true )
    {
            System.out.println("Autocommit is on ");
            DefaultConnection.setAutoCommit(false);

    }
```

For JDBC programs that are running outside of a stored procedure, disable the auto-commit behavior with the setAutoCommit method.

USING ARRAY PROCESSING (JDBC 1.0)

In JDBC version 1.x, array processing is not supported explicitly. Oracle JDBC drivers prior to release 8.1.6 are based on the JDBC 1.x specification. Luckily, Oracle has added extensions to its JDBC 1.0 drivers to allow array processing to be enabled explicitly.

To include the JDBC 1.0 extensions in your program, you need to import the Oracle extensions:

```
import oracle.jdbc.driver.*;
```

To perform array fetch, you can cast your Connection object to the OracleConnection class and use the setDefaultRowPrefetch method to control the number of rows that will be fetched from the database in each fetch operation:

```
((OracleConnection)myconnect).setDefaultRowPrefetch(50);
```

The rest of your code remains unchanged. The array fetching occurs behind the scenes as you move through your result set.

To perform array insert or other array DML, you need to cast a PreparedStatement object to an OraclePreparedStatement and apply the setExecuteBatch method:

```
((OraclePreparedStatement)mypstmt).setExecuteBatch(50);
```

As with row prefetch, the rest of your code is unaltered. The Oracle driver transparently batches your bind variables as you apply them to your PreparedStatement and submits them when the batching threshold has been reached.

Using the Oracle extensions—or their JDBC 2.0 equivalents—is essential if you want to get the best JDBC performance. For the batch-processing example introduced earlier, setting setDefaultRowPrefetch and setExecuteBatch to 50 reduced execution time by 65% (see Figure 15.5).

Always use the Oracle array extensions setDefaultRowPrefetch and setExecteBatch when fetching or modifying multiple rows.

USING ARRAY PROCESSING (JDBC 2)

The JDBC 2 specification provides methods for implementing array processing without relying on the Oracle extensions discussed in the previous section. These JDBC 2 facilities are only available in Oracle JDBC drivers from release 8.1.6 onwards.

JDBC 2 statements support a setFetchSize method that works very similarly to setDefaultRowPrefetch extension except that it is applied to Statements, not Connections. For example, the following code fragment will implement array fetches of 20 rows each:

```
Statement stmt = DefaultConnection.createStatement();
stmt.setFetchSize(20);

ResultSet rset = stmt.executeQuery
            ("SELECT * " +
            "    FROM sales ");
rset.next () ;
while( rset.next () )
   { /*process the rows…*/ }
```

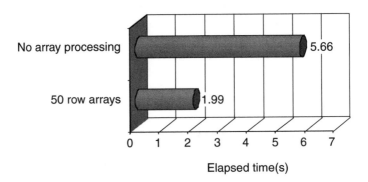

FIGURE 15.5   Using Oracle extensions to implement array processing.

Implementing array DML in JDBC 2 is a bit more complicated. A Statement object supports addBatch and executeBatch methods, which allow the program to construct and submit a batch of rows. It's up to the program to keep track of the number of rows in each batch and to call executeBatch when the desired numbers of rows have been added. The following example illustrates the technique:

```
InsertStmt=DefaultConnection.prepareStatement(
    "INSERT INTO sales " +
    " (customer_id, product_id, quantity, sale_value)"+
    "  VALUES (?,?,?,?)") ;
while( rset.next () )
  {
    InsertStmt.setInt(1, rset.getInt("customer_id"));
    InsertStmt.setInt(2, rset.getInt("product_id"));
    InsertStmt.addBatch();
    if (i++==batchsize) {
        i=0;
        InsertStmt.executeBatch();}
  }
  InsertStmt.executeBatch();
```

Both the JDBC 2 and Oracle JDBC 1 extensions are perfectly capable of delivering efficient array processing. The Oracle extensions are somewhat easier to use when implementing array DML. On the other hand, JDBC 2 techniques will be portable to any databases that support JDBC 2.

USING ORACLE DATATYPES

The Oracle extensions to JDBC allow you to define Java types that map directly to the underlying Oracle datatypes. Using these types allows you to avoid the overhead that occurs when JDBC converts Oracle datatypes to a corresponding Java class.

Unfortunately, the Oracle types do not support the full range of methods that are provided with the native Java types. For instance, the Java String class provides methods for concatenation and formatting of strings, and the Java Int type supports mathematical operations. These methods are not provided in the Oracle classes, so if you want to perform these operations you will need to cast the Oracle types to Java types; so if you do need to use the Java methods, it might be better to retrieve them as Java classes in the first case. However, if you are retrieving the data only to insert it into another table, then the Oracle datatypes will offer superior performance.

Here's an example query that uses Oracle types:

```
oracle.sql.NUMBER ocid;
oracle.sql.CHAR ocname;

stmt=(OracleStatement)
          DefaultConnection.createStatement();
OracleResultSet rset = (OracleResultSet)
          stmt.executeQuery
               ("SELECT customer_id, customer_name " +
               "   FROM customers " );
rset.next () ;


while( rset.next () )
{
   ocid=rset.getNUMBER("customer_id");
   ocname=rset.getCHAR("customer_name");
}
```

For the preceding example, using Oracle types reduced average execution time by about 4%.

If we use the OracleStatement and OracleResultSet classes, then we have the option to use the defineColumnType method of the OracleStatement class. This method allows us to declare the datatypes of the columns to be returned by the query, which reduces parse overhead because otherwise JDBC issues a call to the database to retrieve this information. The following example shows the usage of defineColumnType:

```
OracleStatement stmt3=(OracleStatement)
               DefaultConnection.createStatement();

stmt3.defineColumnType(1,Types.INTEGER);
stmt3.defineColumnType(2,Types.VARCHAR);

OracleResultSet rset3 = (OracleResultSet)
               stmt.executeQuery
                 ("SELECT customer_id, customer_name " +
                 "   FROM customers " );
```

The use of defineColumnType only improves performance when the Statement or PreparedStatement is being parsed. If you are following good practice and using PreparedStatements, then you probably won't notice significant improvements. However, if your program is for some reason required to perform frequent parses or cannot use PreparedStatements, then you may experience a more noticeable improvement. Testing with the preceding example showed that using defineColumnType reduced the overhead of creating a JDBC Statement by about 20%. However, if your parse overhead is only 10%—and we wouldn't really want to see it any higher—then this improvement might give you only a 2% overall benefit (e.g., 20% of 10% is 2%).

Using the Oracle JDBC extensions—including Oracle datatype classes and the defineColumnType methods—can result in small but significant performance improvements.

OPTIMIZING SQL

SQLJ is easier to write than JDBC. Unfortunately, in versions of SQLJ prior to 8.1.6 it was hard to implement array processing or efficient reuse of statements.

As with most programming languages that interact with Oracle, the three most important tuning principles (at least as far as interaction with the database is concerned) are as follows:

- ❑ Implementing bind variables
- ❑ Minimizing parse calls by ensuring efficient use of cursors
- ❑ Implementing array fetch and bind

BIND VARIABLES

Bind variables are easy to use in SQLJ. Any Java variable can serve as a bind variable, as shown in the following example:

```
int product_id=3;
int quantity=10;
int sale_value=1000;
int department_id=1;

#sql {INSERT INTO sales
      (customer_id,product_id, sale_date, quantity,
       sale_value, department_id)
      VALUES(:customer_id, :product_id, SYSDATE,
             :quantity,:sale_value,:department_id)};
```

CURSOR MANAGEMENT

In releases of SQLJ prior to 8.1.6, every execution of an SQL statement resulted in a new parse operation. Since SQLJ supports—even encourages—bind variables, these were soft parses that would usually find a matching statement in the shared pool. Nevertheless, these parse calls would generate significant overhead. Setting the option SESSION_CACHED_CURSORS to a sufficiently high value can help alleviate the overhead of these soft parses. To set session_cached_cursors in a SQLJ program, add the following statement:

```
#sql{ALTER SESSION SET session_cached_cursors=30};
```

In 8.1.6, Oracle introduced a statement caching facility that eliminates the need to set session_cached_cursors and that offers improved performance. The session cache works by creating JDBC PreparedStatements for SQL statements. A cache of these PreparedStatements is kept open, and if the SQL statement is reexecuted while the PreparedStatement is still in the cache, then the SQL can be reexecuted without requiring a reparse.

By default, there are five statements in the cache, but you can vary this by using the following syntax on the sqlj command line:

```
sqlj -P-Cstmtcache=20 yourfile.sqlj
```

Unfortunately, as of 8.1.6 it is not possible to apply this option to SQLJ programs that had been translated using the internal translator. This is, it is necessary to use the command line sqlj program and the loadjava program rather than using the CREATE JAVA SOURCE. Furthermore, it is necessary to load not just the resulting .java file, but also any .ser files created. So for the previous example, our loadjava statement might look like this:

```
loadjava -v -r -f -u uname/pass@db myfile.java
myfile_SJProfile0.ser
```

Make sure you size the SQLJ statement cache to a value that is appropriate for your application.

ARRAY PROCESSING

Array fetch can be enabled by using the JDBC setDefaultRowPrefetch method. You can apply the setDefaultRowPrefetch method to the connection underlying the SQLJ context. The following example does this for the default SQLJ context:

```
Connection con;
con= DefaultContext.getDefaultContext().getConnection();
OracleConnection ocon=(OracleConnection)con;
ocon.setDefaultRowPrefetch(30);
```

Array processing for DML statements is supported in SQLJ from 8.1.6 only. In this release, you can enable batching by using new methods that are associated with the execution context. setBatching enables batch processing; setBatchLimit determines the multiple size of a batch. ExecuteBatch processes the current batch, even if it has not reached the limit set by setBatchLimit. The following example uses these new methods:

```
ExecutionContext defaultectx ;
defaultectx=DefaultContext.getDefaultContext()
                .getExecutionContext();

defaultectx.setBatching (true);
defaultectx.setBatchLimit(20);

//… DML statements would go here

//Post any remaining elements in the batch before
//exiting
int[] updateCounts = defaultectx.executeBatch();

#sql{commit};
```

Make sure you use SQLJ batching to improve the performance of bulk inserts or other DML. This facility is only available in 8.1.6.

JDBC OR SQJ OR PL/SQL?

Having reviewed the performance characteristics of JDBC, SQLJ, and PL/SQL, we are in a good position to assess the relative merits of each language from a performance point of view. Remember that the decision to use a particular language should also be influenced by nonperformance considerations such as programmer productivity, available expertise, and portability. However, in this discussion we restrict ourselves to performance matters. Also remember that our interest here is in using Java to complement SQL performance by either using a procedural approach instead of a complex SQL query or by using stored functions inside SQL statements. That having been said we can conclude that:

❏ Java stored procedures outperform PL/SQL routines for computationally expensive routines.

❏ PL/SQL stored procedures outperform JDBC stored procedures for database-intensive procedures.

❏ Prior to 8.1.6, SQLJ was unable to provide efficient statement reuse or native array insert/DML and would generally show inferior performance to JDBC.

The consequence of these findings is clear: We should use Java stored procedures for computationally intensive routines and PL/SQL routines for database-intensive operations. If we are in an 8.1.6 or later environment, SQLJ and JDBC will offer similar performance profiles. However, prior to 8.1.6 we would prefer JDBC on performance grounds.

LOOKING INTO THE FUTURE

At the time this chapter was written, Oracle 8.1.6 was the latest release of Oracle available. The pace of development in the Java arena is so fast that you can almost guarantee that significant developments will have occurred since this chapter was written. Here are some of the developments that Oracle has foreshadowed in release 8.1.7 and beyond:

❏ Native Java compilation, which allows Java stored procedures to be compiled to native machine language and which was originally scheduled for 8.1.5, is now expected to be released in 8.1.7. This development will probably improve further computationally expensive Java stored procedures and may also improve the performance of database-intensive Java.

❏ JDBC Statement caching, in which the JDBC driver "remembers" the most recently executed SQL statements, will improve performance for programs that do not implement good cursor management.

❏ A new JDBC driver, currently referred to as the "HyperDriver", will be offered. This driver will be thinner than the current thin driver and will use an RPC (Remote Procedure Call) protocol called "Jolt" rather than the SQL*Net protocol.

SUMMARY

The existence of the Aurora JVM within the Oracle8i RDBMS gives us the option to use Java to supplement or replace SQL or PL/SQL code.

Java stored procedures provide superior performance to PL/SQL for computationally intensive routines, while PL/SQL still outperforms Java when the procedure is database intensive. Consequently, best performance will be achieved if we mix Java, PL/SQL, and SQL in our application.

JDBC is the low-level Java API that provides access to Oracle data from within Java. Like most procedural languages that access Oracle, it is important to manage cursors, implement bind variables, and exploit array processing. This is done in JDBC by

- ❏ Using PreparedStatements rather than Statement objects for SQL statements that are executed more than once
- ❏ Using bind variables within SQL statements and associating them with variable values with methods such as setInt
- ❏ Using the Oracle extensions to enable transparent array prefetch and update batching

In addition, the JDBC autocommit feature is enabled by default for external programs (those not running as stored procedures). This feature can cause a substantial overhead for programs that perform bulk updates.

Releases of SQLJ prior to 8.1.6 would be likely to run slower than equivalent JDBC programs because good cursor management because array processing was not directly supported. In release 8.1.6 these limitations were removed with the introduction of a configurable statement cache and batch processing extensions.

Java is a fast moving area of Oracle technology, and the findings presented in this chapter may become out of date quickly. Ensure that you are up to date with the latest Java technology offerings and with developments in PL/SQL.

ORACLE OBJECT TYPES

INTRODUCTION

The introduction of Object types in Oracle8 was arguably the most revolutionary change to the Oracle architecture since the introduction of PL/SQL[1]. Like PL/SQL. Oracle8 object types add a new dimension to the Oracle8 RDBMS that is outside the traditional relational database paradigm and in advance of clear industry standards or directions.

However, it seems that—unlike PL/SQL—the new Oracle8 object types are not destined to play a pivotal role in mainstream Oracle applications. Currently, Oracle8 objects types have a number of disadvantages:

❏ They add a layer of complexity to design and implementation.
❏ Support for objects in existing development and administration tools is sparse.
❏ They fall outside familiar relational database principles and introduce a steep learning curve for database practitioners.
❏ They often reduce the flexibility or ease of data retrieval.
❏ They do not yet support standard object-oriented features such as inheritance.

---

[1]Since then, the introduction of the Aurora JVM has proved even more revolutionary.

On the other hand, proponents of Object databases claim that object orientation offers better mapping of database objects to real-world objects and is in closer alignment with widely accepted object-oriented programming practices. Therefore, there may be situations in which an object-relational design will be dictated by the functional requirements of a system.

All systems have explicit or implicit performance requirements that are often as important as their functional requirements. There may be situations in which the object-relational design is indicated or contraindicated by these performance requirements. New object-relational features present a number of alternatives to traditional relational implementations. Few of these alternatives are performance neutral.

In this chapter we look at the performance characteristics of some object-relational alternatives to standard relational master-detail tables. We also consider the use of new BLOB types as opposed to the traditional LONG datatype.

OBJECT TYPE ALTERNATIVES TO MASTER-DETAIL TABLES

One of the most commonplace structures in a relational database is the master-detail or one-to-many relationship. This is easily represented in a relational database using PRIMARY KEY and FOREIGN KEY constraints. Figure 16.1 shows an example relational implementation. The table SUBJECTS holds personal details for 500 subjects who participated in a marketing survey. The table SCORES holds the results of 100 test questions answered by each subject.

THE VARRAY ALTERNATIVE

A varying array (VARRAY) is an Oracle8 collection datatype that is roughly equivalent to a repeating group in prerelational systems. A column defined as a VARRAY may store a fixed number of elements of a primitive datatype. VARRAYs are suitable when there is a fixed or limited number of elements. Luckily, our implementation involves exactly 100 detail scores so a VARRAY implementation is suitable. Figure 16.2 shows a simplified representation of the VARRAY design.

In our VARRAY implementation, all the score elements are stored in a single column located within the SUBJECT row. The order of the elements is significant. It represents the value of the columns SCORE_NO in the relational SCORES table. The following code shows DDL used to create a VARRAY table.

```
CREATE OR REPLACE TYPE score_array_t
        AS VARRAY(100) OF NUMBER;

CREATE TABLE subjects_v
```

SUBJECT_ID	Surname	First name	DOB
1	Smith	John	1/06/60
2	Jones	Mary	3/08/56
3	Hocks	Peter	4/09/65
4	Maher	Fred	5/09/65
5	Slater	Jenni	6/10/65
6	Thompson	Joan	12/09/62

Subject_id	Score_no	Score_value
1	1	87
1	2	67
1	3	58
1	4	98
1	5	87
1	6	67
1	7	87
1	8	67
1	9	58
1	10	98
1	11	87
1	12	67
. . .	. . .	. . .
500	100	87

FIGURE 16.1 Relational implementation of a master-detail relationship.

SUBJECT_ID	Surname	First name	DOB	Score(1)	Score(3)	Score(4)	Score (5)	Score(6)	.....	Score(100)
1	Smith	John	1/06/60	87	98	96	98	98	....	87
2	Jones	Mary	3/08/56	67	87	87	87	87	....	67
3	Hocks	Peter	4/09/65	58	67	67	67	67	....	58
4	Maher	Fred	5/09/65	96	87	87	87	87	....	98
5	Slater	Jenni	6/10/65	87	67	67	67	67	....	87
6	Thompson	Joan	12/09/62	67	67	67	67	67	....	67

FIGURE 16.2 VARRAY implementation.

```
(
    subject_id      NUMBER          NOT NULL PRIMARY KEY,
    surname         VARCHAR2(60)    NOT NULL,
    firstname       VARCHAR2(60)    NOT NULL,
    dob             DATE            NOT NULL,
    comments        varchar2(2000)  not null,
    score           score_array_t                    );
```

From Oracle8i onward, it is possible to specify out-of-line storage for VAR-RAYs. If this is done, the VARRAY data is stored in a separate LOB segment (we discuss LOBs in detail later in this chapter). For instance, this declaration specifies that the VARRAY should be stored in a LOB segment called SCORES_LOB and that the data should be cached in the buffer cache:

```
CREATE TABLE subjects_v_outofline
  (
    subject_id                  NUMBER NOT NULL,
    surname                     VARCHAR2(60) NOT NULL,
    firstname                   VARCHAR2(60) NOT NULL,
    dob                         DATE NOT NULL,
    comments                    VARCHAR2(2000) NOT NULL,
    score_a                     score_array_type
  )
  VARRAY score_a STORE AS LOB
        scores_lob( DISABLE STORAGE IN ROW CACHE);
```

Storing the VARRAY in a separate segment reduces the overhead when scanning the table for data not held in the VARRAY but increases the overhead when VARRAY data must be accessed.

NESTED TABLE IMPLEMENTATION

A nested table is an object type that has the characteristics of a relational table. A column may be defined that is of a datatype corresponding to the nested table. The values of the nested table are logically nested within the column (see Figure 16.3).

The following code shows the DDL used to create a nested table:

```
CREATE OR REPLACE TYPE score_ot as OBJECT
(
    item_number  NUMBER ,
    score        NUMBER );

CREATE OR REPLACE TYPE scores_nt AS TABLE OF score_ot;
```

Score_no	Score_value
1	87
2	67
3	58
4	98
5	87
6	67
....	....
100	98

SUBJECT_ID	Surname	First name	DOB	Test_Score
1	Smith	John	1/06/60	Nested table
2	Jones	Mary	3/08/56	Nested table
3	Hocks	Peter	4/09/65	Nested table
4	Maher	Fred	5/09/65	Nested table
5	Slater	Jenni	6/10/65	Nested table
6	Thompson	Joan	12/09/62	Nested table

Score_no	Score_value
1	87
2	67
3	58
4	98
5	87
6	67
....	....
100	98

FIGURE 16.3 Nested table implementation.

```
CREATE TABLE subjects_nt_scores
(
    subject_id              NUMBER          ,
    surname                 VARCHAR2(60)    ,
    firstname               VARCHAR2(60)    ,
    dob                     DATE            ,
    comments                VARCHAR2(2000)  ,
```

```
test_score                          scores_nt )
NESTED TABLE test_score STORE AS test_score_nt;
```

OBJECT TABLE IMPLEMENTATION

Object tables are tables whose attributes are defined as being of an Oracle object type. Every row in an object table has an object identifier (OID) that uniquely identifies the object row. Object identifiers can be used to locate a specific row in the corresponding object table. A column in another table can be defined as being of type "REF *object_type*", meaning that the column contains a reference to an OID for an *object_type* instance. Object type refs can thus be used to implement pointers to rows in other tables. These pointers can be used as an alternative to foreign keys for navigation between master-detail tables[2]

Columns with OID REFs can provide pointers from detail to master records, but it's more complicated to navigate from the master to the detail, since more than one OID REF will be required to find all details. We could implement a VARRAY of OID REFs, but it is probably more sensible to construct the detail table using a collection type (e.g., VARRAY or NESTED TABLE) and have a single OID REF in each table that points to the master or detail record. Figure 16.4 illustrates such an implementation.

SUBJECT_ID	Surname	First name	DOB	Score Oid
1	Smith	John	1/06/60	ref scores_type_o
2	Jones	Mary	3/08/56	ref scores_type_o
3	Hocks	Peter	4/09/65	ref scores_type_o
4	Maher	Fred	5/09/65	ref scores_type_o
5	Slater	Jenni	6/10/65	ref scores_type_o
6	Thompson	Joan	12/09/62	ref scores_type_o

Subject_oid	Score(1)	Score(3)	Score(4)	Score (5)	Score(6)	.....	Score(100)
ref subj_type_o	87	98	96	98	98	....	87
ref subj_type_o	67	87	87	87	87	....	67
ref subj_type_o	58	67	67	67	67	....	58
ref subj_type_o	96	87	87	87	87	....	98
ref subj_type_o	87	67	67	67	67	....	87
ref subj_type_o	67	67	67	67	67	....	67

FIGURE 16.4   Object table implementation.

---

[2]Note that a ref column may refer to objects in more than one table. The scope is qualifier can be used to limit the reference to specific tables.

The following code shows how these object table relationships can be established:

```
CREATE TYPE scores_type_o;

CREATE OR REPLACE TYPE subj_type_o AS OBJECT
(   subject_id              NUMBER           ,
    surname                 VARCHAR2(60)    ,
    firstname               VARCHAR2(60)    ,
    dob                     DATE             ,
    comments                VARCHAR2(2000),
    scores_oid              ref scores_type_o );

CREATE TABLE subjects_o OF subj_type_o;

CREATE OR REPLACE TYPE score_VARRAY_type_o
       AS VARRAY(100) OF NUMBER;

CREATE OR REPLACE TYPE scores_type_o AS OBJECT
(
    subject_oid     ref subj_type_o,
    scores          score_VARRAY_type_o );

CREATE TABLE scores_o OF scores_type_o;
```

PERFORMANCE COMPARISONS FOR OBJECT TYPES

In this section, we compare the performance of some typical queries for the implementations described in the previous section.

Performing a full-table scan of the master table is a common operation. For our example tables, we might wish to create a list of all subjects or compute the distribution of ages. Figure 16.5 shows the performance—in terms of logical block reads—of a full scan of each of the subject table implementations.

We can make the following conclusions from these results:

❑ VARRAY implementations can be costly when scanning the master rows, because the contents of the VARRAY are stored inside the master row itself. This increases the row length substantially and degrades full-scan performance. In Oracle 8.0 this effect is much more pronounced because VARRAYs are allocated fixed length storage.

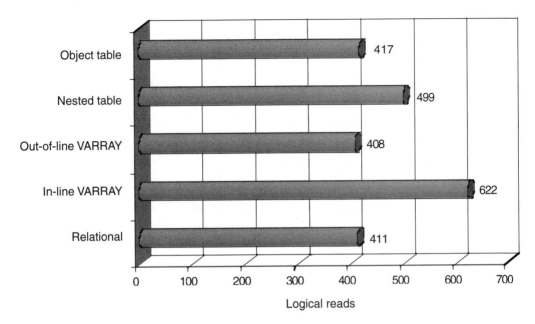

FIGURE 16.5 Full-table scan of the master table.

- ❏ Nested table performance is slightly worse than relational table performance. Each row in SUBJECTS_NT_SCORES contains a hidden column that contains a OID for that row. This corresponds to the hidden column NESTED_TABLE_ID in the nested table TEST_SCORE_NT. These hidden columns require 16 bytes of storage, which slightly increases the row length and degrades full-table scan performance.
- ❏ The performance of the object table solution is slightly worse than the relational solutions. The SUBJECTS_O table contains a REF column to the corresponding SCORES_O row and – being an object table itself—also includes a hidden column (SYS_NC_OID$) containing its own OID. A REF column requires 36 bytes of storage (42 bytes if THE WITH ROWID clause is specified) and an OID itself requires 16 bytes. The SUBJECTS_O table therefore requires an additional 52 bytes of storage in every row, which degrades full-table scan performance.

> In-line VARRAYs significantly increase row length and degrade full scans. If full-scan performance is critical, then store the VARRAY out of line. Other object solutions (nested tables, object tables) also slightly increase row length and degrade scan performance.

GETTING A SINGLE MASTER ROW

Performance for an indexed lookup against the master table is unremarkable. Each implementation allowed retrieval via a unique index and required the same number of logical reads. Figure 16.6 records these observations.

GETTING ALL DETAIL ROWS FOR A SINGLE MASTER ROW

Now we consider the case in which we retrieve all detail rows for a specific master record. In our example application, this might occur when collating an overall score for a single subject.

New Oracle8 syntax is required to implement this query for the object table type. The DEREF clause is used to retrieve the details for the object matching the OID REFerence stored in the table:

```
SELECT s.*, DEREF (scores_oid)
  FROM subjects_o s
 WHERE subject_id = 250;
```

Figure 16.7 shows the results.

The most notable result is the disappointing performance of a default nested table for this type of query. You'd be forgiven for assuming that since a nested table is logically nested inside the column of the master table, that there would be a built-in fast access mechanism to retrieve the data contained in the nested table for a specific row. In fact, no such default mechanism exists, and

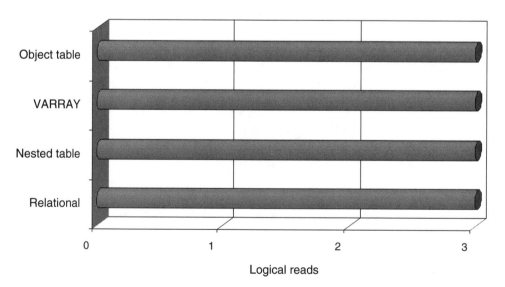

FIGURE 16.6   Retrieving a single master record via an index.

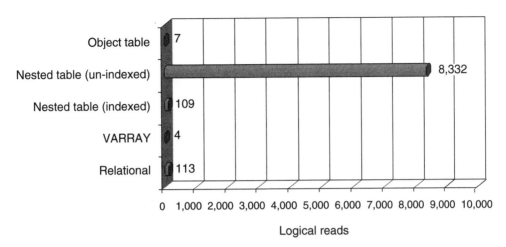

FIGURE 16.7   Retrieving all detail rows for a single master row.

access to a single row's nested table data requires that you scan the nested table data for all the rows.

To allow efficient access to nested table data, you need to create an index on the built-in column NESTED_TABLE_ID, which exists within the nested table as defined in the NESTED TABLE … STORE AS clause of the CREATE TABLE statement ("TEST_SCORE_NT" in our example). The following statement creates such an index. Note that we added ITEM_NUMBER to the index to optimize queries that might seek a specific row within the nested table.

```
CREATE INDEX test_score_nt_i1 ON
        test_score_nt(nested_table_id,item_number)
```

Once this index is created, the performance of the nested table query radically improved. This is probably the most important recommendation we can make when using nested tables: Always consider creating an index on the NESTED_TABLE_ID. For all tables of nontrivial size, nested table performance will degrade rapidly without such an index. You can add additional columns in the nested table to the index to optimize specific queries or to enforce uniqueness.

> When using nested tables of nontrivial size, strongly consider creating an index on (at least) the NESTED_TABLE_ID column of the nested table segment.

VARRAY and object table implementations significantly outperform the relational solution. This is to be expected since

❑ The VARRAY implementation does not require any join to or DEREF from another table—all data is held in line.

❑ The object table implementation also uses a VARRAY, so only one DEREF operation is required.

GETTING ONE DETAIL ROW FOR A SINGLE MASTER ROW

Suppose we only want to reference a single detail item for a specific master record. For instance, perhaps we are interested in the result of a single test question for a single subject. Issuing such a query in SQL requires some minor elaboration to our data model. You cannot reference a specific element of a VARRAY from within a SQL statement. However, we can remedy this deficiency by creating a new type, based on a VARRAY, that includes a method to return a specific element:[3]

```
CREATE OR REPLACE TYPE score_array_t1
      AS VARRAY(100) OF NUMBER;

CREATE OR REPLACE TYPE score_array_t AS OBJECT
(
   score score_array_t1,
   MEMBER FUNCTION score_val
         (p_item_number NUMBER) RETURN NUMBER,
   PRAGMA RESTRICT_REFERENCES
         (score_val,wnds,rnds,wnps,rnps)
);

CREATE OR REPLACE TYPE BODY score_array_t AS
   MEMBER FUNCTION score_val
          (p_item_number NUMBER) RETURN NUMBER IS
   BEGIN
      RETURN(SELF.score(p_item_number));
   END;
END;
```

With this new type in place, we can get the value for a specific element within the VARRAY as follows:

```
SELECT s.score.score_val(65)
  FROM subjects_v s
 WHERE subject_id=230;
```

---

[3]Note that once you do this, it might not be possible to store the VARRAY out of line, since the VARRAY clause will not recognize your object type as VARRAY.

For the object table, we use our new SCORE_VAL method together with the REF function to obtain the required score value:

```
SELECT s.scores.score_val(65)
  FROM scores_o s
WHERE REF(s)=(SELECT scores_oid
                FROM subjects_o
               WHERE subject_id=230);
```

We can retrieve a specific value from the nested table by using the TABLE operator (or, in Oracle 8.0, the "THE" operator) to return the nested table for a specific row:

```
SELECT sns.score
  FROM TABLE (SELECT test_score
                FROM subjects_nt_scores
               WHERE subject_id=230) sns
 WHERE sns.item_number=65;
```

Figure 16.8 shows the results.

VARRAY and relational solutions outperform the object table and nested table solutions, since the former include both SUBJECT_ID and SCORE_ID in the same table—so no join is required. Note that if the nested table was without the

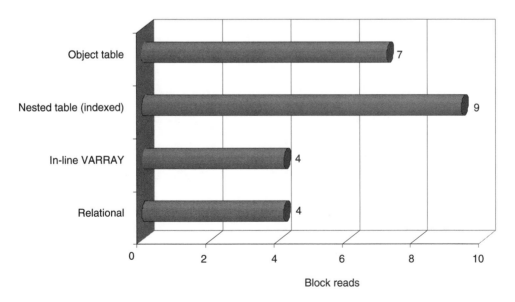

FIGURE 16.8   Retrieving a single detail row for a single master row.

index we created in the previous section, then nested table performance would have again been abysmal.

GETTING A SINGLE DETAIL ROW FOR ALL MASTER ROWS

In this test we evaluate the performance of queries that must select a single detail row for every master row. In our example, such a query might be required to answer the question "What was the average value for question 66?"

We can compose our query in a fairly straightforward way for VARRAY and object tables, using the SCORE_VAL method discussed in a previous step:

```
SELECT sum(s.score.score_val(66)) FROM subjects_v s;

SELECT sum(s.scores.score_val(66)) FROM scores_o s;
```

However, the nested table implementation makes this query difficult. There is no documented method for accessing a nested table outside of its parent table. Consequently, if we want to retrieve all rows for a specific score, we are forced to iterate through the subject rows involved, as shown in this PL/SQL procedure:

```
PROCEDURE p_nt_avg_score (p_item_number NUMBER)
IS
   CURSOR score_csr (cp_subject_id NUMBER)
   IS
      SELECT sns.score
        FROM TABLE (SELECT test_score
                      FROM subjects_nt_scores
                     WHERE subject_id = cp_subject_id) sns
       WHERE sns.item_number = p_item_number;

   score_row                      score_csr%ROWTYPE;
   total_score                    NUMBER := 0;
BEGIN
   FOR r1 IN ( SELECT subject_id
                 FROM subjects_nt_scores)
   LOOP
      OPEN score_csr (r1.subject_id);
      FETCH score_csr INTO score_row;
      CLOSE score_csr;
      total_score := total_score + score_row.score;
   END LOOP;
   dbms_output.put_line ('Total score: ' ||
                total_score);
END;
```

In this trial, object solutions fared weakly in comparison with the relational baseline. In the case of the VARRAY and object table, which incorporated a VAR-RAY, accessing an individual item required accessing the entire structure, which in practice involved a full-table scan of the relevant tables. In the case of the nested table, the inability to access the nested table details without also accessing the master row necessitated accessing all rows in both structures. Figure 16.9 shows the results.

> Nested tables make accessing the nested data across parent rows very inefficient. VARRAYs have a similar drawback when trying to access individual elements across multiple rows.

OPTIONS FOR IMPROVING OBJECT TABLE PERFORMANCE

The overhead of DEREFerencing an OID REFerence can be reduced by adding the WITH ROWID clause to the REF definition. This causes the ROWID of the target row to be stored "inside" the object REF. This allows the DEREF operation to locate rapidly the object instance (row) to be DEREFerenced.

If the WITH ROWID clause is not specified, Oracle will use a system index to locate the object instance specified. This index is created for each object table on the hidden column SYS_NC_OID$, which contains the value of the object identifier for the row. You can specify the name and storage for this index with the OIDINDEX clause to the CREATE TABLE statement.

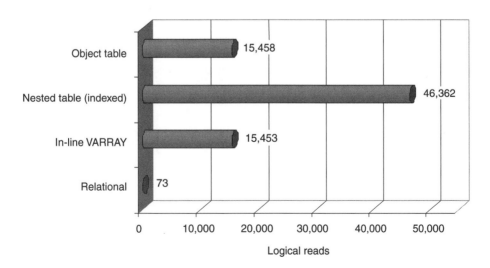

FIGURE 16.9   Fetching a single detail item for every master row.

If WITH ROWID is not specified, DEREFerencing a OID will require the normal two to four logical I/Os required by B*-tree index navigation together with the single logical I/O involved in accessing the REFerenced table. If WITH ROWID is set, then only a single logical I/O will be required. The effect of WITH ROWID is therefore to reduce the overhead of DEREFerencing by 50 to 75%.

Our example object tables used default settings for REF columns and so did not take advantage of the WITH ROWID optimization. However, separate timings confirmed a two-thirds reduction in logical I/O when the WITH ROWID clause was specified.

> If you require efficient navigation from REF columns to the referenced object row, consider using the WITH ROWID clause to store the column's ROWID in the REF column.

STORING A NESTED TABLE AS AN INDEX ORGANIZED TABLE

In Oracle 8.1, we are able to store a nested table in index organized table segment. This results in significant storage and performance improvements:

❏ As an index organized table, we provide an index structure into the nested_table_id column and the unique identifier of the nested table. As we saw earlier, such an index is essential for efficient nested table access

❏ In a normal (organization heap) nested table, the value of the NESTED_ TABLE_ID must be repeated for each row. However, in a compressed index organized table the value is not repeated, which saves storage. Furthermore, in a HEAP nested table we have to provide storage for both the nested table segment and the index on NESTED_TABLE_ID. In the index organized nested table we provide storage only for the nested table.

The following create table statement creates a index organized nested table:

```
CREATE TABLE subjects_nt_scores_iot
(
    subject_id              NUMBER          ,
    surname                 VARCHAR2(60)    ,
    firstname               VARCHAR2(60)    ,
    dob                     DATE            ,
    comments                VARCHAR2(2000)  ,
    test_score              scores_nt
)
    NESTED TABLE test_score STORE AS test_score_nt_iot (
            (PRIMARY KEY(nested_table_id, item_number))
            ORGANIZATION INDEX COMPRESS)
```

In Oracle 8.1, it is almost always best to create a nested table in an index organized table segment. This improves both performance and storage.

OBJECT TYPE OPERATIONS AND EXPLAIN PLAN

The previous discussion showed how a DEREFerenced object reference is obtained either by direct ROWID access or by navigation of the hidden index on the referenced table's OID. You might expect that EXPLAIN PLAN would reveal the exact access path used. Unfortunately, explain plan appears to be totally oblivious to DEREF operations. For a DEREF operation, explain plan indicates neither the object table(s) DEREFerenced nor the access method used. For instance, consider the following explain plan generated by tkprof:

```
SELECT s.*, DEREF(scores_oid)
 FROM subjects_o s
 WHERE subject_id=250


Rows      Execution Plan
-------   ------------------------------------------
     0    SELECT STATEMENT   GOAL: CHOOSE
     1     TABLE ACCESS (BY INDEX ROWID) OF 'SUBJECTS_O'
     1       INDEX (UNIQUE SCAN) OF 'SUBJECTS_O_I1'
```

The explain plan shows no indication that the SCORES_O table is accessed, let alone the access method (which would be a lookup of the hidden index). It's somewhat understandable that EXPLAIN PLAN does not show the access of SCORES_O, since the DEREF operation could actually access any object table that was of a compatible object type (unless the SCOPE IS clause had been specified). However, it would be nice if explain plan could at least acknowledge that a DEREFerence operation was performed.

EXPLAIN PLAN can also generate inadequate information for nested table accesses. For instance, the following nested table query uses the index TEST_SCORE_NT_I1—which we created—to join the table SUBJECTS_NT_SCORES to its nested table TEST_SCORE_NT. However, the execution plan makes no reference to these accesses:

```
SELECT * from subjects_nt_scores
 where subject_id=250


Rows      Execution Plan
-------   ------------------------------------------
     0    SELECT STATEMENT   GOAL: CHOOSE
```

```
1     TABLE ACCESS (BY INDEX ROWID) OF
         'SUBJECTS_NT_SCORES'
1       INDEX (UNIQUE SCAN) OF
         'SUBJECTS_NT_SCORES_I1'
```

EXPLAIN PLAN is the most fundamental tool for tuning SQL statements. However, be aware that it can provide incomplete information about object and nested table accesses.

ORACLE8 ALTERNATIVES TO THE ORACLE7 LONG TYPE

Oracle8 introduced a number of important enhancements for storing long and unstructured data. Previously, this data would typically be stored in a LONG datatype. Although Oracle7 longs can store large amounts of data, there were severe limitations. For instance,

❑ Only one long column was permitted per table.
❑ Long data was always stored in line with other table data, increasing the overall table size and degrading full-scan access.
❑ No random access to the data within the long was possible—all of the long needed to be retrieved in order to access any part of the long.

Oracle8 LOBS overcome many of these restrictions. There are a number of possible LOB configurations:

❑ Internal LOBS are stored within the database. They can store binary (BLOB) or character (CLOB) data.
❑ External LOBS (BFILEs) are stored outside of the database in operating system files.

Access to LOBs is made available through the DBMS_LOB package in PL/SQL or through new OCI functions. You cannot directly access the contents of a LOB through SQL.

A number of options are available for tuning LOB storage. We evaluate the following:

❑ CACHE/NOCACHE, which controls whether LOBs will be cached in memory.
❑ ENABLE I DISABLE STORAGE IN ROW. If set to ENABLE, LOBs less than 4 KB will be stored in line with the rest of the column data. If set to DISABLE, or if the LOB is greater than 4 KB, then the LOB will be stored in a separate segment.

PERFORMANCE COMPARISONS

For our performance comparisons, we look at six tables, each of which contains a different style of LOB. The variations are as follows:

- ❏ LONG column
- ❏ BLOB stored in line (ENABLE STORAGE IN ROW) with NOCACHE
- ❏ BLOB stored in line with CACHE option
- ❏ BLOB stored out of line (DISABLE STORAGE IN ROW) with NOCACHE
- ❏ BLOB stored out of line with CACHE options
- ❏ BFILE stored in operating system files

Each table comprises a short row containing identifying information and a LOB in one of the above styles between 1 and 32 KB in size.

Full-table Scan Performance Let's look first at the performance of a full-table scan against each table type. The query employed does not access any of the LOB or LONG columns. Figure 16.10 shows the timing for such a table scan.

All of the new object types radically outperformed the table containing the LONG datatype. This is simply because the long data is always stored in line with other table data. The LONGs increase the number of blocks allocated to the table and hence the number of blocks that must be read by the full-table scan.

The in-line LOB table (enable storage in row) performed somewhat worse than the BFILE and out-of-line LOB tables. This is simply because the in-line table

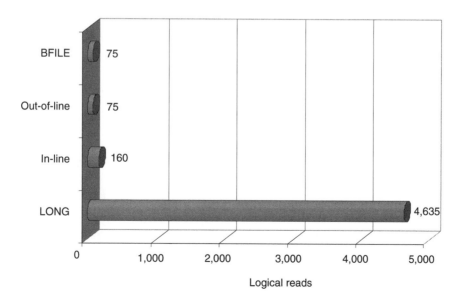

FIGURE 16.10   Performance of full scan (LOB not accessed).

stores all LOBs less than 4K in length in the main table. This increases the table length and hence the table scan overhead.

Because LOBs can be stored in a separate segment, they will have little or no effect on full-table scan performance.

Fetching the Entire LOB or LONG   In the next trial, we will look at the time taken to retrieve an entire LONG or LOB for a specific row. Figure 16.11 shows the average results for 100,000 queries of randomly selected rows. The results are plotted against the size of the LOB involved.

We can reach the following conclusions from these results:

❏   Access to BFILE data was significantly slower than access to internal LOB data. This result may, of course, vary depending on the qualities of the filesystem used to store BFILE and database files. In this case, BFILEs and database files were stored on filesystems with similar properties, although datafiles were spread (but not striped) on a number of physical disks while BFILEs were all stored on the same disk. An examination of wait events, as shown in V$SESSION_WAITS, showed that over 50% of wait events for BFILES were consumed by overheads such as finding, opening, and closing

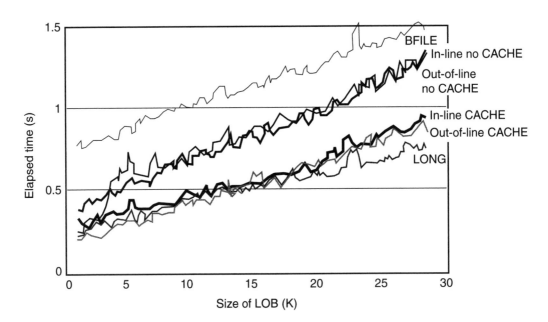

FIGURE 16.11   Performance retrieving LOBs of various sizes.

the file. These filesystem overheads may also contribute to the poor performance of the BFILE type.

❑ The CACHE setting resulted in significantly better performance than NOCACHE except for LOBs less than 4K in size and stored in line. In-line LOBs less than 4K are stored within the main segment and so benefit from standard Oracle buffer caching.

❑ Retrieval of long data was as good as—if not slightly better than—cached in line or out-of-line LOBs. LONGs are always stored in line and are always cached.

Using the CACHE setting improves LOB retrieval time, although possibly at the expense of other data stored in the cache.

Random Access to the LOB   While access to any part of a long always requires that the entire long be read, BFILEs and LOBs can be accessed randomly. Figure 16.12 shows the performance characteristics of this random access for access to the 10 first and 10 last bytes in LOB and BFILEs. Access times for a LONG are shown for comparison purposes.

We can see from Figure 16.12 that random access appears to work well—retrieval time for the bytes at the beginning or the end of the LOB or BFILE stay

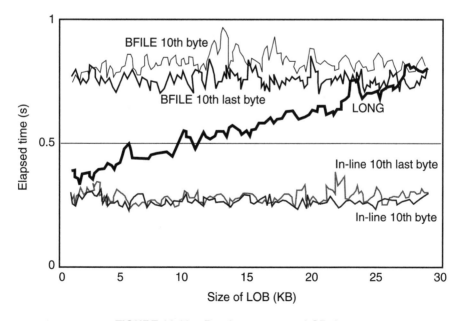

FIGURE 16.12   Random access to LOB data.

constant regardless of the size of the object. For objects that require random access, internal LOBs are clearly the datatypes of choice.

LOB types (CLOB, BLOB, BFILE) allow efficient random access to any part of the data, whereas with the LONG datatype, the entire structure must always be read.

SUMMARY

In this chapter we've looked at the performance aspects of Oracle8 object types and large objects (LOBs).

In general, the decision to use object types is more likely to be driven by functional requirements than by performance considerations. Indeed, there are probably more opportunities for harming performance in the object types than there are for performance gains. In addition, implementing Oracle object types can involve a quantum leap in complexity, which probably outweighs the performance advantages that can be achieved.

However, in some cases Oracle object types can offer performance advantages:

❏ VARRAYs can be used in some circumstances to denormalize detail records into a repeating group within the master record. This will result in improved performance when retrieving these details for a single master row. However, table scan performance for the master row will be degraded due to the longer row length. It may also be difficult to examine individual elements of the VARRAY across multiple master rows. VARRAYs can't be used where the number of detail elements is unlimited or unknown.

❏ Object identifiers (OIDs) can be used as alternatives to foreign keys. Navigating a REF to an OID can require less I/O than using a B*-tree index, specifically if the WITH ROWID option is exploited. However, the application is responsible for maintaining the integrity of these OID REFs.

❏ Nested tables seem to have the least to offer. Their internal implementation is virtually identical to the master-detail table and there are severe restrictions on the operations can be performed. If a nested table is implemented, it is almost always advisable to create an index on the hidden column NESTED_ TABLE_ID, which is contained in the table specified by the NESTED TABLE ... STORE AS ... clause. Alternately, creating the nested table as an index organized table will automatically create the required index and is also more storage efficient.

Oracle LOB types—the BLOB, CLOB, and BFILE—offer superior performance in a number of ways to the older LONG datatype. In particular,

❏ LOBs can—and any LOB greater than 4K will—be stored in a separate segment from the main table. The reduces or eliminates the severe table-scan penalties traditionally associated with LONG columns.

❏ LOBs need not take up space in the buffer cache. Although CACHEing longs may lead to better retrieval times for the LOB, flooding the buffer cache with LOB data may negatively affect the performance of other users or other SQL.

❏ LOBs offer true random access—it is possible to access any part of the LOB without having to read it all. In contrast, accessing LONG data is an all-or-nothing process.

Although LOBS offer all these advantages, there is one significant disadvantage: LOB data cannot be accessed from normal SQL. It is necessary to use PL/SQL, Java, OCI, PRO*C, or some other LOB-enabled development tool.

MISCELLANEOUS TOPICS

INTRODUCTION

This chapter considers various miscellaneous topics—those that don't fit neatly into any of the categories we have already considered. The topics include

- ❑ Optimizing statements involving views
- ❑ Optimizing distributed SQL
- ❑ Optimizing sequences
- ❑ Taking advantage of the DECODE statement
- ❑ Optimizing Data Definition Language statements
- ❑ Optimizing statements involving the dynamic performance views ("V$" views)

OPTIMIZING VIEWS

A view can be thought of as a virtual table or as a stored query. A view's definition consists of a standard SQL query. When a view is accessed, the view's query is retrieved and any additional WHERE conditions are merged into the final query. For instance, suppose we create a view like this:

```
CREATE VIEW department_summ_view
AS
   SELECT d.department_name,
          COUNT (e.salary) employee_count,
          SUM (e.salary) total_salary
     FROM departments d, employees e
    WHERE e.department_id = d.department_id
    GROUP BY d.department_name
```

We can get summary information for a department by issuing the following query:

```
SELECT *
  FROM department_summ_view
 WHERE department_name = 'Database development'
```

Oracle will push the WHERE clause from this query into the view definition so that the query that is finally executed will be equivalent to this:

```
SELECT d.department_name, COUNT (e.salary) employee_count,
SUM (e.salary) total_salary
  FROM departments d, employees e
 WHERE e.department_id = d.department_id
   AND d.department_name = 'Database development'
 GROUP BY d.department_name
```

When optimizing views, it's most important to optimize the query upon which the view is based. In the case of our example view, we would need to ensure that the join between departments and employees was optimized. In the case of the join in the view, a sort merge or hash join would be appropriate, since all rows in each table participate in the join.

However, when we issue a query against the view that includes some additional selection criteria, the optimal plan for the view changes. For instance, once we query against a particular department using the DEPARTMENT_SUMM_VIEW, the join of choice becomes nested loops and an index on EMPLOYEES. DEPARTMENT_ID becomes desirable.

When optimizing a view, consider not only optimizing the query that defines the view but also queries that result from merging of additional selection criteria into the view. Create indexes or histograms or take other means to optimize the queries that are likely to be generated when resolving queries on the view.

HINTS IN VIEWS

Hints can be embedded into a view definition. This can be useful when optimizing the execution of the view and can be useful to influence the performance of SQL over which you have little or no control.

For instance, some client/server development or ad hoc query tools may generate SQL that is generated dynamically and that can't be amended by the user. We can hope that the cost-based optimizer generates effective plans in these cases, but we may find that the SQL generated is performing badly and we don't have the option to use hints. In these circumstances, we could create a view that contains the hint we wish to use and ensure that this view is referenced by the client tool.

Embed hints in views to influence SQL generated by third-party query or development tools that generate SQL over which you have no control.

DISTRIBUTED SQL

A distributed SQL statement is one that accesses tables that reside in more than one Oracle database. Distributed SQL is made possible by Oracle's SQL*NET product, which allows tables located in separate instances of Oracle, possibly on different server computers, to be accessed as if they were local.

You can formulate a distributed query by including a database link referencing a foreign database in the WHERE clause:

```
SELECT e.surname, e.employee_id, e.firstname
  FROM employees@node2 e --"node2" is remote DB
 WHERE e.surname = 'SMITH'
   AND e.firstname = 'DAVID'
```

HOW ORACLE PROCESSES DISTRIBUTED SQL

Oracle resolves a distributed query as follows:

❏ If all of the tables exist within the same remote database, then the entire statement is sent to that database for execution

❏ If the tables referenced in the distributed SQL exist within multiple databases, then the optimizer will determine an execution plan in much the same way as it would for nondistributed SQL. The optimizer will take into account the available indexes and the cost-based optimizer will obtain table statistics for remote tables. The cost based optimizer will also try to estimate the additional network costs involved in a distributed table access, although these estimates may be little better than guesses (the cost-based optimizer won't know how fast or how busy network connections to other databases may be)

For each table involved in a multiple database distributed SQL, Oracle will issue SQL to the remote database to retrieve the data. Sorts, joins, and other operations will be performed at the site executing the query (the driving site).

The execution plan shows that Oracle resolves a simple remote query such as our previous example by sending the entire query to the remote database. The query is optimized by the remote database's optimizer, and a result set is passed back to the calling database:

```
SELECT e.surname, e.employee_id, e.firstname
  FROM employees@node2 e
 WHERE e.surname = 'SMITH'
   AND e.firstname = 'DAVID'


Rows      Execution Plan
-------   ------------------------------------------------
      0   SELECT STATEMENT (REMOTE)
Preceding line indicates entire statement is remote
      0   TABLE ACCESS (BY ROWID) OF 'EMPLOYEES'
              [NODE2.WORLD]
      0     INDEX  (RANGE SCAN) OF 'EMPLOYEES_SURNAME'
                (NON-UNIQUE) [NODE2.WORLD]
```

EXPLAINING DISTRIBUTED SQL

When a distributed SQL statement is explained, the plan table will contain some special information as shown in Table 17.1.

These columns aren't always reported by traditional queries against the plan table, and it's difficult to produce a well-formatted plan using the OTHER

TABLE 17.1 Explain plan columns for distributed queries

COLUMN NAME	DESCRIPTION
OPERATION	If "REMOTE", then this step will be executed at the remote node.
OBJECT_NODE	Contains the identifier of the remote node.
OTHER_TAG	Will contain the tag (SERIAL_FROM_REMOTE) if the OTHER column contains the text of an SQL statement being executed at a re mote node.
OTHER	Contains the text of the SQL text executed at the remote site.

column because of the restrictions on LONG columns. Tkprof will produce well-formatted distributed Explain plans automatically as well the SQL*PLUS autotrace facility. The Xplain tool will also produce suitably formatted output.

PROBLEMS WITH DISTRIBUTED SQL

Distributed SQL presents unique problems for the Oracle optimizer and the SQL programmer. Distributed SQL statements often perform poorly and can be difficult to optimize. Some of the reasons are as follows:

❑ The databases involved in the distributed SQL may have very different performance characteristics. For instance, the version of Oracle or the host configuration (number of CPUs, memory, and operating system) may differ. The optimizer may not be able to take all of these factors into account.

❑ Although the cost-based optimizer will factor in some network overhead when formulating a distributed execution plan, it has no knowledge of the capacity or utilization of the network between two databases.

❑ Oracle's approach of generating a separate SQL statement for each table participating in a distributed join sometimes results in tables that reside on the same database being joined across the network.

❑ It's harder for the SQL programmer to tune distributed SQL since EXPLAIN PLAN and tkprof output will only show the SQL sent to the remote node, not the execution plan at the remote node. In complex cases, it may be necessary to obtain execution plans from the remote node using EXPLAIN PLAN.

DISTRIBUTED JOINS

One of the more common distributed SQL operations is the distributed join. The following example illustrates a three-way join involving two remote databases:

```
SELECT dp.department_name, e.surname, c.customer_name
  FROM employees@node2 e,
       departments@node1 dp,
       customers@node2 c
 WHERE dp.department_id = e.department_id
   AND c.sales_rep_id = e.employee_id
   AND dp.department_name = 'Database Products'

Rows      Execution Plan
-------   -------------------------------------------------
      0   SELECT STATEMENT   HINT: CHOOSE
   6646     MERGE JOIN
```

```
   66    SORT (JOIN)
   66     NESTED LOOPS
    1       REMOTE [NODE1.WORLD]
                SELECT "DEPARTMENT_ID","DEPARTMENT_NAME"
                  FROM "DEPARTMENTS" DP
                  WHERE "DEPARTMENT_NAME"=
                     'Database Products'
   66       REMOTE [NODE2.WORLD]
                SELECT
"EMPLOYEE_ID","SURNAME","DEPARTMENT_ID" FROM
                  "EMPLOYEES" E WHERE :1="DEPARTMENT_ID"
100000     SORT (JOIN)
100000       REMOTE [NODE2.WORLD]
                SELECT "CUSTOMER_NAME","SALES_REP_ID"
                  FROM "CUSTOMERS" C
```

We can interpret this execution plan as follows:

1. Oracle starts by issuing an SQL statement to node1 which will retrieve the department ID for the department "Database Products."
2. For each row returned (only one in this case), Oracle issues an SQL statement to NODE2 to get the employee details for all employees in matching departments using the nested loops join method.
3. Oracle then issues a query to NODE2 to retrieve all customers. The customers are then sort merged with the result set from step 2.

This execution plan is the same as the plan that would be generated if the tables were all local. Oracle accesses table statistics and index details at the remote node and determines that appropriate indexes exist to support a nested loop join.

A potential problem with this approach is Oracle's strategy of performing each table access with a separate SQL statement, even when multiple tables reside on the same node. This strategy can increase the number of requests to the remote node and can lead to tables being joined across the network.

IMPROVING DISTRIBUTED JOINS WITH VIEWS

If you determine that a distributed query is locally joining two tables from the same remote database and you suspect that the join would be more efficient if performed at the remote site, you can create a view at the remote site that pre-joins the tables involved.

For instance, in the previous example, we joined EMPLOYEES and CUSTOMERS locally, even though they were both located on the same remote node. If we create a view that joins the two tables on node2,

```
CREATE VIEW employees_and_customers
AS
    SELECT e.surname, e.employee_id,
           e.firstname, e.department_id, c.customer_name
      FROM employees e, customers c
     WHERE c.sales_rep_id = e.employee_id
```

We can now issue a query that refers to the remote view. This results in the two tables being joined at the remote node:

```
SELECT d.department_name, e.surname, e.customer_name
  FROM employees_and_customers@node2 e, departments@node1 d
 WHERE d.department_id = e.department_id
   AND d.department_name = 'Database Products'
```

```
Rows      Execution Plan
-------   ---------------------------------------------

      0   SELECT STATEMENT    HINT: CHOOSE
   6646    NESTED LOOPS
      1     REMOTE [NODE1.WORLD]
               SELECT "DEPARTMENT_ID","DEPARTMENT_NAME"
                 FROM "DEPARTMENTS" D
                WHERE "DEPARTMENT_NAME"=
                      'Database Products'
   6646     REMOTE [NODE2.WORLD] -- Entire view is remote
               SELECT "SURNAME", "DEPARTMENT_ID",
                      "CUSTOMER_NAME"
                 FROM "EMPLOYEES_AND_CUSTOMERS" E
                WHERE :1="DEPARTMENT_ID"
```

For this example, performing the join at the remote node results in a substantial performance gain, since otherwise we would have to retrieve all the customer details across the network. In this example, the remote node was also on a more powerful computer, so the SORT operation could be performed more efficiently.

Note that you cannot use an in-line view to obtain this effect. The in-line view will evaluated locally, not at the remote node.

Creating a view of a table join at a remote node can cause the join to be executed at the remote node rather than at the driving site. This may improve performance if conditions are suitable.

CHOOSING THE BEST DRIVING SITE

The driving site is the site at which the SQL is optimized and at which nonremote operations such as joins and sorts are performed. The driving site will usually be the site at which the SQL is executed, unless one of the following conditions is true:

❑ If all the tables referenced in the SQL exist on the same remote node, then Oracle will send the entire SQL to the remote node and the remote node will be the driving site. For instance,

```
SELECT dp.department_name, e.surname
  FROM employees@node3 e, departments@node3 dp
 WHERE dp.department_id = e.department_id

Execution Plan:

SELECT STATEMENT REMOTE -- Entire statement remote
    NESTED LOOPS
       TABLE ACCESS FULL DEPARTMENTS
       TABLE ACCESS BY ROWID EMPLOYEES
           INDEX RANGE SCAN EMPLOYEE_DEPT_ID
```

❑ If you INSERT, UPDATE or DELETE from a remote table, the optimizer may send the query to the remote site for execution. For instance, the following INSERT will be executed from NODE1, the REMOTE(!) steps indicate that the SQL statements were sent back to the originating node for processing:

```
INSERT INTO junk@node1
    SELECT e.surname, d.department_name
      FROM employees e, departments d
     WHERE e.department_id = d.department_id

Execution Plan:

  INSERT STATEMENT REMOTE   --Executed at node1
    MERGE JOIN
      SORT JOIN
        REMOTE(!): SELECT "DEPARTMENT_ID",
                            "DEPARTMENT_NAME"
                    FROM "DEPARTMENTS"
      SORT JOIN
        REMOTE(!): SELECT "SURNAME","DEPARTMENT_ID"
                      FROM "EMPLOYEES" A3
```

❏ The hint "DRIVING_SITE(*table_alias*)" will cause the driving site to be the node at which the nominated table is located. The following example shows the effect of the DRIVING_SITE hint:

```
SELECT    /*+ driving_site(E) execute the query
            at node1*/
        dp.department_name, e.surname,
        c.customer_name
  FROM employees@node1 e,
        departments@node1 dp,
        customers c
  WHERE dp.department_id = e.department_id
    AND e.surname = 'SMITH'
    AND e.firstname = 'DAVID'
    AND c.sales_rep_id = e.employee_id

Execution plan:

  SELECT STATEMENT REMOTE    -- Remote Statement
    NESTED LOOPS
      NESTED LOOPS
        TABLE ACCESS BY ROWID EMPLOYEES
              INDEX RANGE SCAN EMPLOYEES_SURNAME
        TABLE ACCESS BY ROWID DEPARTMENTS
              INDEX UNIQUE SCAN PK_DEPARTMENTS
      REMOTE (!)   --Send back to originating node
        SELECT "CUSTOMER_NAME","SALES_REP_ID"
          FROM "CUSTOMERS" A1
          WHERE "SALES_REP_ID"=:1
```

The choice of the driving site for a distributed query can have a tremendous effect on the performance of distributed SQL. Consider the following when deciding on a driving site:

❏ The driving site is usually the site that performs CPU-intensive operations such as joins and sorts. Therefore, the driving site will ideally be on the most powerful computer involved in the distributed SQL

❏ Network overhead is a major factor in the performance of distributed SQL. Therefore, the site with the most local data is a good candidate for the driving site

❏ Since the driving site performs the query optimization and joins, using the site with the most recent version of Oracle installed may improve performance. For instance, in a distributed join between databases running Oracle 8i, 7.2, and 7.1, the Oracle8i site would be a good candidate for the driving site since it would have superior optimization facilities and would be able to take advantage of hash joins and other features

---

Choose the driving site for your distributed SQL carefully. The ideal driving site is the site with the most powerful processing capabilities, the most local data, and the most recent version of Oracle.

IMPROVING DISTRIBUTED QUERIES WITH SNAPSHOTS

In Chapter 13, we discussed the use of snapshots to improve the performance of complex queries that aren't required to produce information that is totally current. While this is a useful and valid utilization of snapshots, snapshots were primarily designed to replicate data across the network and thus affect the performance of distributed queries.

If we query against a locally maintained snapshot that is based on a remote table, we are avoiding the overhead of network operations and may also get the advantage of reduced join or sort overheads (if using complex snapshots).

Of course, snapshots are only as current as their most recent refresh. Only use snapshots when obtaining potentially out-of-date information is acceptable.

Using snapshots as an alternative to distributed queries can reduce your query time remarkably. But remember that data returned from snapshot queries may be out of date.

COMPARISON OF DISTRIBUTED JOIN PERFORMANCE

Figure 17.1 compares the elapsed time for a distributed join, a distributed join using a remote view, and a local join using snapshots. For our example, using a remote view almost halved execution time; but remember that your results may vary—make sure you try alternate approaches. Using local snapshots reduced execution time by 90%. You will almost always realize improvements on distributed joins if you use snapshots, but remember that the improvement may be at the expense of accuracy.

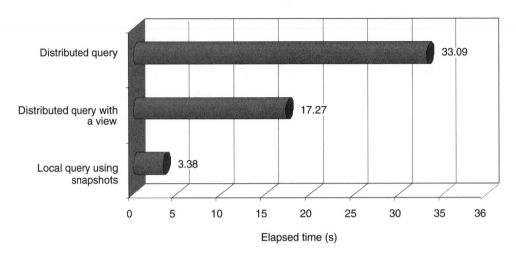

FIGURE 17.1   Comparison of distributed join, distributed join with remote view, and local join using snapshot of remote data.

SEQUENCES

Sequences (or sequence number generators) efficiently generate unique sequential numbers. Sequences are primarily intended to speed up the process of acquiring a unique primary key value. Obtaining a unique primary key value without a sequence would usually involve selecting the next key value from a sequence number table. The following PL/SQL procedure illustrates the sequence table technique:

```
CREATE OR REPLACE PROCEDURE get_seq_table (nbr NUMBER)
AS
   CURSOR get_seq_csr
   IS
      SELECT last_sequence + 1
        FROM sequence_table
         FOR UPDATE;

   i                                   NUMBER;
   new_sequence                        NUMBER;
BEGIN
   FOR i IN 1 .. nbr
   LOOP
      OPEN get_seq_csr;
```

```
            FETCH get_seq_csr INTO new_sequence;
            CLOSE get_seq_csr;
            -- Do something with the sequence
            UPDATE sequence_table
               SET last_sequence = new_sequence;
            -- Commit to release locks
            COMMIT;
      END LOOP;
END;
```

Obtaining a unique key value in this way has the following problems:

❑ The FOR UPDATE clause locks the sequence number table to ensure that no two users get the same sequence number. This can lead to lock contention

❑ I/O is required to fetch the sequence number, lock the row, UPDATE the row and COMMIT the change. This can become a substantial overhead in a transaction processing environment

Using a sequence generator avoids most of these overheads. In particular, sequences involve no locks and there is no contention between sessions that are obtaining sequence numbers. However, sequence numbers can only be accessed from within an SQL statement, and you may sometimes SELECT a sequence number from the DUAL table, as in the following example:

```
CREATE OR REPLACE PROCEDURE get_seq_1 (nbr NUMBER)
AS
   i                                   NUMBER;
   new_sequence                        NUMBER;

   CURSOR get_seq_csr
   IS
      SELECT seq_1.nextval
        FROM dual;
BEGIN
   FOR i IN 1 .. nbr
   LOOP
      OPEN get_seq_csr;
      FETCH get_seq_csr INTO new_sequence;
      CLOSE get_seq_csr;
   -- Do something with the sequence number

   END LOOP;
END;
```

Although the accesses of the DUAL table are not in themselves resource intensive, they can add up in a transaction processing environment. You can reduce the impact of these lookups by specifying that the sequence increment by some higher number. For instance, we can define a sequence with increments of 500:

```
CREATE SEQUENCE seq_500 INCREMENT BY 500
```

We are now effectively fetching the sequence number in batches of 500, and we can alter our program to fetch a new batch only every 500th number:

```
CREATE OR REPLACE PROCEDURE get_seq_500 (nbr NUMBER)
AS
   i                                  NUMBER;
   new_sequence                       NUMBER;

   CURSOR get_seq_csr
   IS
      SELECT seq_500.nextval
        FROM dual;
BEGIN
   FOR i IN 1 .. nbr
   LOOP
      -- every 500 iterations, get a new sequence number
      IF    MOD (i, 500) = 0
         OR i = 1 THEN
         OPEN get_seq_csr;
         FETCH get_seq_csr INTO new_sequence;
         CLOSE get_seq_csr;
      ELSE
         new_sequence := new_sequence + 1;
      END IF;

   -- Do something with the sequence number

   END LOOP;
END;
```

Figure 17.2 compares the performance of the sequence number table, a default sequence generator, and fetching sequences in batches of 500. The sequence generator outperforms the sequence table, and fetching sequences in batches of 500 further enhances performance.

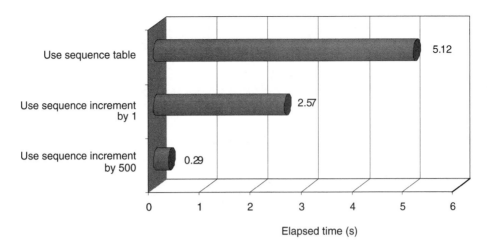

FIGURE 17.2 Time taken to generate 2000 unique keys using a sequence table, a default sequence generator, and a sequence generator, with a 500 increment.

CACHING SEQUENCE NUMBERS

One of the reasons sequence numbers are efficient is that the numbers are cached in Oracle's shared memory area—the SGA. By default, 20 sequence numbers are cached. Once the 20 numbers are allocated, Oracle must fetch a further 20 from the database. If sequence numbers are being allocated at a very high rate, you can improve the performance by increasing the cache size when you create the sequence:

```
CREATE SEQUENCE seq_cached CACHE 100
```

The CREATE SEQUENCE command also includes an ORDER clause, which, if used, guarantees that sequence numbers will be generated in sequential order. This option is intended for use with the Oracle Parallel Server (OPS) option. In a non-OPS system, sequence numbers are always generated in sequential order. Users sometimes specify the ORDER option in the mistaken belief that doing so is necessary to avoid generating sequence numbers in a random order. Specifying ORDER in the CREATE SEQUENCE command can have dire consequences for sequence performance as it effectively disables the sequence cache mechanism and requires a data dictionary transaction every time a sequence number is issued. You should not specify the ORDER clause unless you are in a parallel server environment and, even then, only if you absolutely require that sequence numbers be generated in sequential order.

Figure 17.3 illustrates the effect of changing the CACHE setting and of using the ORDER clause.

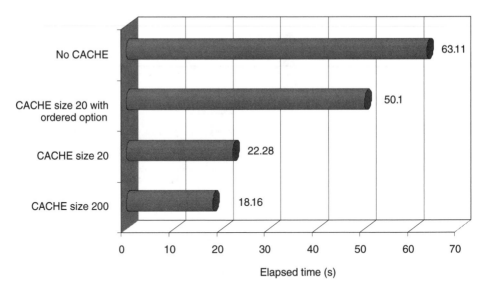

FIGURE 17.3   Effect of CACHE and ORDER clauses on sequence performance.

> When creating sequences, specify a cache value that reflects the frequency with which the sequence will be accessed. Do not specify the ORDER option unless you are in a parallel server environment.

"MISSING" SEQUENCE NUMBERS

Although sequences are an efficient way of allocating unique key values, they have one feature that is sometimes regarded as undesirable: Sequence numbers can be skipped. Sequence numbers can be skipped in the following circumstances:

❏ A transaction obtains a sequence number, but for some reason the transaction fails and a ROLLBACK is issued. The sequence number issued will not be reallocated

❏ If the Oracle server fails, then all numbers in the sequence cache will be lost

❏ If the amount of space reserved for sequence numbers in the SGA is insufficient for the sequences in use, the sequence numbers in the cache may be discarded

Normally the skipping of sequence numbers is inconsequential. After all, the numbers by themselves mean nothing. However, there is sometimes an application requirement that primary key values not be skipped. In this case, if a transaction INSERTing a new row is ROLLBACKed, then the sequence number should be made available to the next transaction. If such a requirement exists, then the use of a sequence generator is not appropriate, and you may be forced to use a sequence table.

Before implementing a sequence table in preference to a sequence generator, try to ensure that the requirement for contiguous number ranges is unavoidable. Using a sequence table will not only increase the I/O overhead of obtaining a sequence number but could also lead to lock contention for the sequence table in a transaction processing environment. If you must use a sequence table lookup, try to defer locking the sequence table until the last possible stage in your transaction. This will reduce the duration of any locks.

Use sequence generators in preference to sequence tables unless there is a definite requirement that no unique key values be skipped. When using a sequence generator, ensure that the CACHE value is appropriate and consider fetching sequence numbers in batches in busy transaction processing environments.

USING DECODE

The DECODE operator is a powerful but underutilized extension to ANSI standard SQL. DECODE allows an expression to be replaced (or decoded) with an alternate value. In some respects, it's similar to an embedded IF statement.

Decodes are useful when aggregating data based on some complex condition that can't be expressed using standard SQL. Without DECODE, these queries can often only be resolved through multiple table scans.

For example, suppose we wanted to count the number of customers in the under 25, 25–40, and over 40 age groups. Using standard SQL, we would probably issue a query similar to this ("f_age" is a user PL/SQL function that simply returns age in years):

```
SELECT '< 25 ' age, COUNT (*)
  FROM customers
 WHERE f_age (date_of_birth) < 25
UNION
     SELECT '25-40' age, COUNT (*)
       FROM customers
      WHERE f_age (date_of_birth) BETWEEN 25 AND 40
UNION
     SELECT '> 40' age, COUNT (*)
       FROM customers
      WHERE f_age (date_of_birth) > 40
```

This example returns the required rows but requires three table scans to do so. If we increase the number of categories, we will require more scans and performance will degrade further.

Using the DECODE and SIGN operators, we can retrieve the same results with a single scan of the CUSTOMERS table:

```
SELECT SUM(DECODE(sign(f_age(date_of_birth)-25),
           -1,1,0)) under_25,
       SUM(DECODE(SIGN(f_age(date_of_birth)-25),
                          -1,0,
           DECODE(SIGN(f_age(date_of_birth)-40),
           -1,1,0))) "25_to_40",
       SUM(DECODE(SIGN(f_age(date_of_birth)-40),
           1,1,0)) over_40
  FROM customers
```

The SQL is somewhat more complex. Let's consider each nesting of functions in the first expression (the under 25 expression):

❏ The f_age variable returns the age of the customer in years. By subtracting 25 from that age, we return a negative number if the customer is under 25

❏ The SIGN function returns "–1" if its argument is less than "0" and "1" if the argument is greater than "0"

❏ The DECODE function returns "1" if the SIGN returns "–1" and "0" otherwise. In other words, the DECODE function returns "1" if the customer is under 25 and "0" otherwise

❏ The sum function adds the results of the decode function. Since the decode returned "1" only if the customer is under 25, the sum function returns the number of customers under 25

A similar technique was employed to count customers between 25 and 40. Two decodes were used: one to test if the customer was under 25 and one to test if the customer was over 40. If neither test succeeded, then a "1" was returned by the DECODE.

Not surprisingly, using the DECODE required only a third of the block reads required by the UNION solution. If the number of categories was increased, the difference would have been even more marked. Figure 17.4 shows the timings.

Consider using DECODE to compile aggregate statistics for expressions that are too complex for a GROUP BY clause. You can aggregate ranges by using the SIGN function.

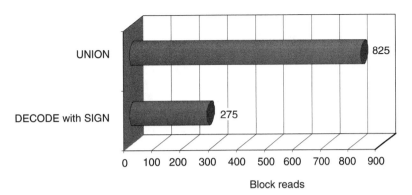

FIGURE 17.4   Aggregating CUSTOMERS using a UNION query compared with the use of DECODE and SIGN.

OPTIMIZING DATA DEFINITION LANGUAGE

Data Definition Language (DDL) is the component of SQL that allows schema objects (tables, views, indexes, etc.) to be CREATEd, ALTERed, or DROPed. Generally, we create schema objects once only and don't need to be too concerned about execution time. In any case, schema objects that are created as empty objects usually don't take too long to generate.

However, there are times when the performance of DDL can be very important:

❑   When creating a table as a query, perhaps for temporary processing or in order to rebuild the table to improve table scan performance

❑   When creating a new index

❑   When rebuilding an index to optimize storage or to improve index scan performance

The options for improving the performance of these operations are as follows:

❑   Using ORACLE parallel processing capabilities

❑   Reducing redo log overhead by using the UNRECOVERABLE or NOLOGGING options

❑   Rebuilding indexes in place with the REBUILD clause of the ALTER INDEX statement

BUILDING TABLES WITH NOLOGGING

The CREATE TABLE statement allows a table to be created from a query. This can be used to create a temporary table as a subset of the source table, to create a new permanent table for some purpose, or to rebuild the source table to improve scan performance or change storage characteristics.

The query used to create the new table should be tuned using the principles outlined earlier That is, optimization of table accesses, joins, sorts, and other mechanisms.

The NOLOGGING or UNRECOVERABLE[1] clauses of CREATE TABLE instructs ORACLE not to create redo log entries for the new table. This can significantly improve the performance of the table creation. The table is created using the same approach as unlogged inserts described in Chapter 12.

If you create a table using the NOLOGGED option, none of the data inserted into the table during its creation will be written to the redo logs. In the event of a database roll-forward recovery, the data in the table will not be restored unless a tablespace backup has occurred since the table is created. Furthermore, any subsequent data inserted to the table will also be unlogged and hence unrecoverable. If you want to revert to logging after creating the table, you should use the ALTER TABLE statement to set the LOGGING option.

You can also use the UNRECOVERABLE or NOLOGGING option when creating an index.

Consider using the NOLOGGING option when creating temporary tables or indexes. Be aware that objects created with the NOLOGGING option will not be restorable until they are included in a backup.

THE INDEX REBUILD OPTION

The REBUILD clause of the ALTER INDEX statement allows an index to be rebuilt using the index itself as the source of data. This is substantially faster than using the table as the source of data since the index will typically be smaller than the source table.

ONLINE INDEX REBUILD

Oracle8i offers the "ONLINE" option, which can be used in conjunction with the REBUILD option. Prior to Oracle8i, index rebuilds always applied a table lock to the underlying table that prevented any concurrent DML activity. The ONLINE option prevents this restrictive locking.

Note that using the ONLINE option won't improve the performance of the index build. In fact, the build may take longer if concurrent DML activity occurs.

---

[1]In Oracle 7.3, the UNRECOVERABLE clause only provided this functionality. In Oracle8, NOLOGGING replaces the UNRECOVERABLE keyword that is still supported for compatibility reasons.

PARALLEL OPTIONS

Indexes and tables created with subqueries can take advantage of Oracles's parallel processing capabilities. Using parallel DDL can result in tremendous performance improvements if the prerequisites are met. Using the unlogged and parallel options together can result in even faster index of table builds. Parallel DDL is discussed in detail in Chapter 11.

Using parallel and unlogged options in conjunction is the fastest way to create tables from subqueries and indexes.

TUNING ACCESS TO THE V$ TABLES

The Oracle RDBMS makes available an extensive collection of metrics that can be used for database monitoring and performance tuning. The Dynamic Performance Views—sometimes referred to as "V$" objects—provide the most convenient access to these metrics. These views provide windows into many aspects of Oracle's internal operations and are the basis for most performance monitoring tools and scripts. Using these views, it is possible to display details of connected sessions, I/O rates, cached SQL statements, and a wealth of other information.

Writing queries against the V$ views presents special challenges for the SQL programmer. Because these tables are not really tables at all—rather externalizations of internal Oracle memory structures—they are not subject to the usual rules of query optimization. Additionally, there are a number of special features and caveats that must be taken into consideration to ensure efficient access to these structures.

IMPLEMENTATION OF DYNAMIC PERFORMANCE VIEWS

Although it may be correct in a limited sense to describe the V$ objects as views they are not in the same category of objects as views created by database users. For instance, although you may find definitions of "V_$SYSTAT" in ALL_VIEWS, the definition merely points to an object "V$SYSTAT" that is not defined in the data dictionary.[2] Oracle sometimes refer to this underlying object as a fixed table—"fixed" presumably in the sense that rows may not be inserted, deleted, or updated via SQL.

---

[2]There are, however, a small number of v$ views that are defined in the same way as regular views.

X$ OBJECTS

Underlying the V$ objects are the X$ tables. These X$ tables are representations of selected structures within the Oracle kernel. Usually these X$ objects map to specific regions within the Oracle SGA. The names of the X$ tables and their columns are derived from the names of internal structures and fields and are usually difficult to decipher.

X$ objects are visible only from the SYS account, although they can be made available to other users by creating a view against them and granting access to this view to the required users.

V$ VIEWS

While X$ objects may be obscurely named, subject to change, and essentially undocumented, V$ objects are documented, maintain some compatibility between versions, and have meaningful table and column names. While Oracle's original intent in providing the dynamic performance views may have been for internal use only, it is now recognized that the Oracle community has come to depend on these views for monitoring, troubleshooting, and tuning.

V$ views are derived from underlying X$ objects through a SQL definition; although as noted earlier, this SQL definition is not stored within the data dictionary table DBA_VIEWS. The V$ table V$FIXED_VIEW_DEFINITION provides the SQL statement that describes how V$ objects are created from X$ objects. Note that this table appears to have some inaccuracies. For instance, it describes V$SQL as being based on X$KGLCURSOR, whereas EXPLAIN PLAN suggests that V$SQL is actually based on X$KGLOB.

GV$ VIEWS

When examining V$FIXED_VIEW_DEFINITION, you may discover that many V$ objects are based on "GV$" objects of the same name. These GV$ objects are required in OPS environments to query statistics for a particular parallel server instance. In a non-OPS environment the V$ and GV$ views are essentially identical.

FIXED VIEW INDEXES

Prior to Oracle 7.2, accesses to the dynamic performance views always required a full scan of the underlying memory structure. In general, these full scans were not overly expensive, since usually no I/O was involved. However, for monitoring tools performing frequent polling or requiring responsive drill-down capabilities, the overhead could be excessive. As databases increased in size, the problem magnified since SGA memory structures also became larger.

In Oracle 7.2, indexes on the X$ tables were introduced. These indexes are not normal Oracle indexes, and you will not find their definitions in DBA_IN-DEXES. They are presumed to be externalizations of hash access methods used within the Oracle code for efficient location of specific data items. As we shall see, these indexes can be effective in optimizing queries against the fixed tables but behave differently from traditional Oracle indexes.

QUERIES TO EXTRACT VIEW INFORMATION

Three queries can be used to obtain information about the dynamic performance views.

This first query lists all the V$ and X$ tables:

```
select name
  FROM v$fixed_table;
```

This query lists the V$ tables and their definitions:

```
SELECT view_name,view_definition
  FROM v$fixed_view_definition
 ORDER by view_name;
```

This query shows the indexes available on the X$ tables:

```
SELECT table_name,index_number,column_name
     FROM v$indexed_fixed_column
      ORDER BY table_name,index_number
```

Using the output from these queries it is possible—although time consuming and frustrating—to map the columns in a V$ table to its X$ source and from there to determine if a column is indexed. We can go further and write a report that performs some of these correlations. However, there is no simple SQL query that can determine if a given V$ column is indexed.

LISTING OF V$ AND X$ TABLES

To optimize queries against V$ tables, it is important to understand the relationship between the V$ tables and the underlying X$ views.

Table 17.2 lists some of the more commonly used V$ tables.

Table 17.3 Lists the X$ tables that comprise some of the more common V$ objects, and lists the indexes that exist on the V$ tables.

TABLE 17.2 Summary of Essential V$ Table

CATEGORY	NAME	DESCRIPTION
SESSION statistics	V$ACCESS	Objects accessed by the session
	V$OPEN_CURSOR	Details of each open cursor
	V$SESS_IO	I/O rates for a session
	V$SESSION	Session details
	V$SESSION_EVENT	Summary of the number and time spent waiting on events
	V$SESSION_WAIT	Details of any current wait for a session
	V$SESSTAT	Statistics for a session
	V$LOCK	Locks held and requested
SGA statistics	V$DB_OBJECT_CACHE	Objects cached in the shared pool
	V$SGA	Summary of SGA memory allocations
	V$SGASTAT	Details of SGA memory allocations
	V$SQL	SQL statements in the shared pool including children
	V$SQLAREA	SQL statements in the shared pool grouped by statement
	V$SQLTEXT	Text of SQL statements in the shared pool
System configuration	V$BGPROCESS	Background processes
	V$BUFFER_POOL	Size and activity of each buffer pool in the buffer cache
	V$CONTROLFILE	Control file details
	V$DATABASE	Database definitions
	V$DBFILE	Database files
	V$INSTANCE	Configuration details for the instance
	V$LOG	Redo log file details
	V$LOGFILE	Redo log file details
	V$PROCESS	Details of each process or thread attached to the instance
System performance	V$FILESTAT	I/O statistics for each database file
	V$LATCH	Latch get/miss statistics (parents & children)
	V$LIBRARYCACHE	Get miss/rates for each library cache area
	V$PQ_SYSSTAT	Statistics for parallel query slaves
	V$QUEUE	Activity in the MTS queues
	V$ROLLSTAT	Rollback segment statistics
	V$SHARED_SERVER	Shared server statistics
	V$SORT_SEGMENT	Utilization of sort segments in temporary table-spaces
	V$SYSSTAT	System performance statistics
	V$SYSTEM_EVENT	Summary of systemwide wait events
	V$TRANSACTION	Details of each active transaction
	V$WAITSTAT	Breakdown of buffer busy waits by buffer type

TABLE 17.3 V$ object source tables and indexes

V$ OBJECT	X$ OBJECTS	INDEXED COLUMNS
V$ACCESS	X$KGLOB, X$KGLDP, X$KGLLK	
V$BH	XBH, XLE	
V$DATABASE	X$KCCDI	
V$DATAFILE	X$KCCFE, X$KCCFN, X$KCVFH	FILE#
V$FILESTAT	X$KCCFE, X$KCFIO	
V$LATCH	X$KSLLD, X$KSLLT	
V$LOCK	X$KSQRS, X$KTCXB, X$KSQEQ, X$KTADM, X$KDNSSF, X$KSUSE	
V$OPEN_CURSOR	X$KGLLK	HASH_VALUE
V$PROCESS	X$KSUPR	ADDR, PID
V$SESSION	X$KSUSE	SID
V$SESSION_EVENT	X$KSLES, X$KSLED	
V$SESSION_WAIT	X$KSUSECST, X$KSLED	SID
V$SESSTAT	X$KSUSESTA, X$KSUSD	SID
V$SESS_IO	X$KSUSIO	SID
V$SGA	X$KSMSD	
V$SQL	X$KGLOB	HASH_VALUE
V$SQLAREA	X$KGLOB	
V$SQLTEXT	X$KGLNA	HASH_VALUE
V$SQL_BIND_DATA	X$KXSBD	
V$SQL_SHARED_MEMORY	X$KGLOB, X$KSMHP	HASH_VALUE
V$SYSSTAT	X$KSUSGSTA	STATISTIC#
V$SYSTEM_EVENT	X$KSLEI, X$KSLED	
V$SYSTEM_PARAMETER	X$KSPPI, X$KSPPSV	
V$TRANSACTION	X$KTCXB	
V$LOCK	X$KTCXB, X$KSQEQ, X$KTADM, X$KDNSSF	LADDR?
V$OBJECT_DEPENDENCY	X$KGLOB , X$KGLDP	

PERFORMANCE-CRITICAL VIEWS

Many of the dynamic performance views are either small or statically sized. For instance, regardless of the size of the database, V$SYSSTAT will always have a fixed number of rows (about 200). While you can get an individual statistic using the index on STATISTIC#, retrieving all statistics will usually have an acceptable performance cost that will remain constant as your database grows.

However, many other tables can become very large and grow in proportion with the size of the database. For instance, V$SESSTAT will have about 200 rows for each connected session. As the number of sessions grows, the size of the structure—and the time taken to scan the structure—will increase. Retrieving 200,000 rows from the structure in order to determine a single statistic for a single user in a 1000 session database will probably be unacceptable (1000 users times 200 statistics equals 200,000 rows).

Another table that may cause performance problems is V$SQL or V$SQL-TEXT. In large databases, the size of the SQL area within the shared pool will often be quite large—80MB is not uncommon. It would be unacceptable to have to scan this structure whenever you drilled down into a user's SQL statement or to scan the SQL area frequently to determine the "top 10" SQL statements.

Queries against these large structures must be well tuned. However, tuning guidelines for V$ tables are different from those that apply to traditional tables. In the next section we will develop a set of guidelines for writing efficient V$ queries.

PERFORMANCE TUNING V$ QUERIES

The objectives in tuning V$ queries are similar to those we've developed for tuning normal SQL statements. Some of the main objectives are to ensure that:

❏ An appropriate index is used to retrieve a row.
❏ The join order and method is optimal.
❏ Unnecessary database accesses are minimized.

USING THE INDEXES TO LOCATE A ROW

Where an index exists on a V$ table, it will normally be used whenever the column is used for an exact lookup. EXPLAIN PLAN reveals that this is so through the special access path "FIXED TABLE FIXED INDEX". For instance, the following query uses the SID index on V$SESSION:

```
select *
  from v$session where sid=171

  Rows    Plan
  ------  -------------------------------------------
     1    FIXED TABLE FIXED INDEX #1 X$KSUSE

cpu=1 elapsed=1 logical=0 physical=0
```

Remembering that the index is not really an Oracle B*-tree index and in fact has more in common with a hash cluster, it's not surprising to see that the index is disabled if a range scan is attempted:

```
select *
  from v$session where sid<8

Rows    Plan
------  --------------------------------------------
   700    FIXED TABLE FULL X$KSUSE

cpu=19 elapsed=19 logical=0 physical=0
```

However, there are other restrictions that aren't so easy to explain. For instance, the index is disabled if a function is applied to a bind variable:

```
select *
  from v$session where sid=round(:sid)

  Rows    Plan
  ------  --------------------------------------------
    700    FIXED TABLE FULL X$KSUSE

cpu=19 elapsed=19 logical=0 physical=0
```

Using functions can also disable the V$ indexes for columns in join conditions.
By default, the index won't be applied if there is an OR or IN condition:

```
select *
  from v$session s
 where sid in (171,262)

  Rows    Plan
  ------  --------------------------------------------
    700    FIXED TABLE FULL X$KSUSE

cpu=20 elapsed=21 logical=0 physical=0
```

However, the USE_CONCAT hint can be used to encourage the use of the index:

```
SELECT /*+USE_CONCAT(S)*/ *
  FROM v$session s
 WHERE sid in (171,262)

  Rows    Plan
  ------  --------------------------------------------
     0    CONCATENATION
     1      FIXED TABLE FIXED INDEX #1 X$KSUSE
     1      FIXED TABLE FIXED INDEX #1 X$KSUSE
```

```
cpu=0 elapsed=0 logical=0 physical=0
```

Bind Variables   If you EXPLAIN a V$ query that uses a bind variable, you may find that the execution plan shows that the index is not used. For instance, in SQL*PLUS,

```
SQL> SELECT * FROM v$session WHERE sid=:b1;

Execution Plan
-----------------------------------------------------------
0        SELECT STATEMENT Optimizer=CHOOSE
1    0   FIXED TABLE (FULL) OF 'X$KSUSE'
```

Surprisingly, in this instance EXPLAIN PLAN is actually generating an incorrect plan. If we examine the output of a trace file generated as a result of ALTER SESSION SET SQL_TRACE TRUE, we find the following indication that the index was used:

```
STAT #1 id=1 cnt=1 pid=0 pos=0 obj=0 op='FIXED TABLE
FIXED INDEX #1 X$KSUSE '
```

It is a relief to determine that bind variables did not suppress the V$ indexes. Bind variables are an important measure in reducing parse overhead for any SQL query, and for queries that perform no I/O (such as V$ queries), parse overhead can be a significant component of the overall execution time. You should use bind variables wherever possible in your V$ queries. However, as we noted earlier, indexes are disabled if a function is applied to the bind variable.

Indexes on the V$ tables can only be used for exact lookups and will be disabled if a function is applied to either side of the equality condition.

OPTIMIZING V$ JOINS

As with traditional SQL statement tuning, optimizing the join order and method is one of the most important steps towards optimizing the entire statement. However, V$ statements pose special problems because

❑ Neither the cost-based optimizer (CBO) nor the rule-based optimizer (RBO) recognizes the presence of V$ indexes when determining join order or method.
❑ There are never any optimizer statistics held against the V$ or X$ tables, and consequently the CBO has no information to use to determine the best join order.

As a consequence, join order for a V$ query will be entirely determined by the order of tables in the from clause. If the optimizer mode is CHOOSE, then the RBO will be used since there are no statistics against any of the tables. Therefore, join order will be right to left if OPTIMIZER_MODE is CHOOSE or RULE and left to right if OPTIMIZER_MODE is FIRST_ROWS or ALL_ROWS.

Here's an example. The optimizer used V$PROCESS as the driving table, although the index on V$SESSION.SID would have made it the more logical starting point:

```
select *
  from v$session s, v$process p
 where sid=171
   and s.paddr=p.addr

  Rows    Plan
  ------  ---------------------------------------------
      1   MERGE JOIN
     16     FIXED TABLE FULL X$KSUPR
      1     SORT JOIN
      1       FIXED TABLE FIXED INDEX #1 X$KSUSE
```

The ORDERED Hint The most important hint for optimizing join order is the ORDERED hint. Using the ORDERED hint, you can specify tables in the FROM clause in the order in which you believe they should be joined. The optimizer will then use any available V$ indexes to optimize the join. In the case of our last example, using ORDERED resulted in the expected join operation:

```
SELECT /*+ORDERED */ *
  FROM v$session s,v$process p
 WHERE sid=171
   AND s.paddr=p.addr

  Rows    Plan
  ------  ---------------------------------------------
      1   NESTED LOOPS
      1     FIXED TABLE FIXED INDEX #1 X$KSUSE
      1     FIXED TABLE FIXED INDEX #1 X$KSUPR
```

Outer Joins Note that unlike joins on regular tables, the outer join operator prevents an index-based nested loops resolution for a V$ query:

```
SELECT  /*+ORDERED */ *
  FROM v$session s,v$process p
 WHERE sid=:sid
   AND s.paddr=p.addr(+)
```

```
Rows    Plan
------  -------------------------------------------------
    1   NESTED LOOPS OUTER
    1     FIXED TABLE FIXED INDEX #1 X$KSUSE
   21     VIEW V$PROCESS
  300       FIXED TABLE FULL X$KSUPR
```

Choosing the Join Method   The indexed join method is not always the best method for joining V$ tables. When joining two large regular tables it is better to use sort-merge or hash-join techniques if large proportions of the tables are being joined. Likewise, is also better to suppress the index join if you are joining all or most of a v$ table.

If you do not wish to have an index used to join your V$ tables, use the USE_HASH or (less preferably) USE_MERGE hints to specify an explicit join method.

If you can't optimize a join to your satisfaction—for instance, you want an indexed outer join—consider breaking your statement into a number of separate statements and passing query parameters between them. You can do this in PL/SQL or other procedural language.

Because there are no statistics on V$ tables, the optimizer is unable to determine a proper join order or method. You need to use hints to force an optimal join order.

SUMMARY

In this chapter, we've looked at some miscellaneous techniques for improving SQL performance.

❑ Optimizing the performance of views involves optimizing the SQL statement upon which the view is based and also the SQL that is likely to result when selection criteria are "pushed up" into the view

❑ Creating views that contain hints can be a useful technique for optimizing ad hoc queries and SQL generated by query tools

❑ Distributed SQL can require careful optimization. The choice of the driving site can have a big influence on overall performance. Views can be useful to encourage tables at remote sites to be joined on their home host rather than at the driving site. Snapshots can reduce the overhead of SQL dramatically for static tables

❑ Oracle sequences are an efficient mechanism of generating primary key values and should be used in preference to sequence tables or other mechanisms. The performance of sequences can be improved by setting an appropriate cache value and by fetching sequences in batches

❑ The DECODE operator can be used to perform complex aggregations that might otherwise need to be performed via multiple queries

❑ Oracle provides special facilities to enhance the creation of tables and indexes. The UNRECOVERABLE or NOLOGGING options can be used to suppress the logging of the CREATE INDEX and CREATE TABLE AS SELECT operations. Parallel processing can also be employed for these statement types. Existing indexes can be rebuilt efficiently using the REBUILD option

❑ The V$ views—also called the dynamic performance tables—contain information that is invaluable for Oracle performance tuning. However, because these tables are not really tables at all, but rather representations of Oracle internal memory, normal rules for tuning SQL do not always apply. Using the indexes on these views (again, not real indexes) is essential to get the best performance.

Part IV: Beyond SQL Tuning

Chapter 18

APPLICATION DESIGN ISSUES

In previous chapters, we've looked at writing SQL statements that will perform well against an existing data model. Although we've felt free to create indexes when appropriate—and in a few cases, to de-normalize or replicate data—in general, we have assumed that the data model is fundamentally fixed. This assumption is realistic, because in real life changing the data model of a production (or even pre-production) application is prohibitive—it requires rebuilds of affected tables and reworking of multiple program modules.

The data model can have an overwhelming impact on the performance of SQL statements. It's common at the end of a tuning exercise to conclude that an SQL statement cannot be made efficient without a change to the data model—and that such a change is impractical. It follows that the ultimate success of our SQL tuning endeavors is dependent on the quality of our data model, and that the time to tune the data model is before implementation.

Beyond the logical structure of the data model, there are issues relating to the physical implementation of the model that can have a big impact on your performance. This includes the mapping of logical entities to physical tables, indexing choices, and denormalization.

The design of an application can also have a big impact. A well-designed application will reduce unnecessary statement parsing, redundant requests for data, and lock contention.

In this chapter, we develop some basic principles for constructing a data model that can support efficient SQL and high-performance applications. Data modeling itself is a complex topic that can (and does) fill many books. We can't hope to cover the entire topic here and will instead focus on the transition from a logical model, which models the data in a way independent of performance and implementation, to a physical model, which describes the actual tables, indexes, and other structures that will exist in the actual database.

We then look at some application design decisions that can affect SQL performance.

BUILDING TUNING INTO THE DESIGN PROCESS

Guidelines such as those contained in this chapter can be useful in avoiding common performance pitfalls in database and application design. However, given the wide variety of application architectures and performance requirements, it is not possible to provide guidelines that will suit every situation. It's therefore important to build performance tuning into the design process itself.

DEFINE YOUR PERFORMANCE REQUIREMENTS EARLY

Many applications are developed under extreme schedule pressure, and these applications often fail to consider or define performance requirements until after the system is delivered. This failure to consider performance can be disastrous for a performance-critical application.

The performance requirements for an application are as real and often as important as its functional requirements. The performance requirements for the system and for specific modules or transactions should be defined early in the system's development life cycle, usually during requirements analysis.

By defining the performance requirements early, we ensure that the requirements are available to those involved in modeling, designing, and constructing the system. As part of a formal systems requirement, performance becomes something that must be considered in system and acceptance testing phases.

If performance requirements are not defined early, then there may be no effort to provide an acceptable level of performance and the ultimate performance of the system will be disappointing.

IDENTIFY CRITICAL TRANSACTIONS

Most applications have a number of critical modules or transactions that can make or break the system. For instance, in a banking system, deposit and withdrawal transactions might comprise 99% of all transactions. Identify these critical transactions and ensure that all features of the design support their effective implementation.

MEASURE PERFORMANCE AS EARLY AS POSSIBLE

During the build phase, measure the performance of the system regularly. This might require obtaining realistic test data volumes and may not be a trivial task. However, by measuring the performance of the system at an early phase you allow performance problems to be identified and corrected as they occur. The traditional approach of ignoring performance until a volume or stress test is conducted right before implementation increases the risk of delivering a poorly performing system.

CONSIDER PROTOTYPING CRITICAL PORTIONS OF THE APPLICATION

If the performance requirements of your system are critical, it may be worth prototyping critical transactions before commencing a full-blown construction phase. Doing this allows you to prove that the data model and system design can deliver the required performance. If the prototype indicates that the required performance cannot be achieved, there will at least be time to modify the design before too much of the system has been constructed.

Prototyping with SQL can be practical since you may only need to code a few critical pieces of SQL rather than writing many lines of procedural code. However, you will need to assemble realistic test volumes, and this may present difficulties.

Build performance tuning into your data modeling and application design process. Define performance requirements in the system requirements specification and measure performance during the build phase, or even earlier, by using prototype transactions.

ESTABLISHING AN EFFICIENT PHYSICAL MODEL

A well-designed data model can serve as a solid foundation for building a robust and efficient database application. In contrast, a poorly constructed data model can lead to persistent difficulties in meeting performance targets and can shorten considerably the life of your application.

As in most aspects of software development, the cost of correcting deficiencies in the data model multiplies as the development life cycle progresses. When the data model exists only in a CASE repository or on paper, it may take a few minutes or hours to remodel some performance-critical aspect. When the data model is implemented in a mission-critical production system, reworking the same aspect may require reworking and retesting dozens of software programs, conceivably incorporating hundreds of SQL statements. The conversion from the old to the new model in a very large database may also require significant downtime.

This is why it is important to incorporate performance requirements in the data model as early as possible, and why the extra effort spent in tuning the data model will be repaid many times in reduced tuning effort following system implementation.

LOGICAL AND PHYSICAL DATA MODELING

Application data models are commonly created in two phases. The logical data model results from a process of identifying the data items that must be stored and processed by the application. For relational database implementations, this usually involves constructing a normalized entity-relationship model, although other representations—such as an object-oriented model—are emerging. The purpose of the logical model is to ensure that the information requirements of the proposed system are correctly defined and to serve as the basis for further design.

The logical data model is then mapped to the physical data model. For a relational database, the physical data model describes the tables, indexes, views, keys, and other characteristics of the database. In traditional methodologies, performance requirements are ignored during the logical modeling process and are first considered during the physical modeling process.

An alternative to the purist's approach—in which performance requirements are ignored during logical design—might be termed the pragmatist's approach. The pragmatic logical data modeler will be aware of performance requirements and will attempt to produce a logical model that supports these without compromising business requirements. When the physical model is constructed, any divergence from the logical model for performance reasons will be minimized, which will improve maintainability of both models and enhance the performance of the physical system.

OBJECT-ORIENTED MODELING

In the past few years, an overwhelming enthusiasm for the Unified Modeling Language (UML) and for object oriented modeling has developed. How does this affect the physical and logical modeling of Oracle databases?

The general topic of object-oriented database design is way beyond the scope of this book. However, it is useful to make the following observations:

❑ Although UML does not implement a diagram type for relational databases, the UML class diagram in many respects represents a "superset" of the information shown in a entity-relationship diagram.

❏ While Oracle8 object extensions cannot be properly modeled in entity-relationship diagrams, they can be modeled in UML.

❏ Modeling in UML results in a more integrated model of data and behavior than more traditional modeling, where program structure and database design were modeled independently.

❏ UML modeling does not naturally lend itself to a sharp distinction between logical and physical modeling.

Unless you make heavy use of Oracle8 object types—which is not advisable for most applications—the use of UML or logical modeling in general should not substantially affect the final database design. If you start with an ERD (entity-relationship diagram) you will need to map this into a physical representation that Oracle and your application can deal with efficiently. If you start with a UML description of an application, you will need to perform a similar task.

CONVERTING THE MODEL FROM LOGICAL TO PHYSICAL

Since most methodologies regard the physical modeling phase as the most appropriate stage for introducing performance considerations, this phase is critical to the ultimate performance of our application.

Unfortunately, the professionals who are concerned with data modeling usually specialize in logical modeling and have little expertise in SQL tuning. Conversely, those charged with developing and managing the application usually have little input into the data modeling process. The sad result is that many physical models are exact replicas of the source logical model. Performing a one-to-one mapping of a logical model to a physical model is usually simple to achieve (perhaps requiring only a single click in a CASE tool). However, such a translation rarely results in a physical design that will support a high performance application. Invest time in the physical modeling process—the dividend will be a physical model that can support your performance requirements.

Don't create a physical model that is a one-to-one representation of the logical model. Take the time to build a physical model that allows your application to reach its full performance potential. Remember that time spent during physical modeling is likely to be repaid many times during production tuning.

MAPPING ENTITIES OR CLASSES TO TABLES

An entity in a logical model, or a class in a UML class diagram, often translates to a table in the physical model. In entity-relationship diagrams, this transformation is usually straightforward except when the entity contains subtypes.

Subtypes are used to categorize or partition a logical entity and help to classify the types of information that is within the entity. A subtype will usually have a set of attributes that are held in common with the parent entity (the supertype) and other attributes that are not shared with the supertype or other subtypes.

Figure 18.1 shows how a PEOPLE entity could be split into subtypes of CUSTOMER and EMPLOYEE.

When translating entity subtypes into tables, we have the following options:

❑ Create a table for the supertype and for each subtype. The supertype table contains only columns that are common to both subtypes.

❑ Create a table for the supertype only. Attributes from all subtypes become columns in this super-table. Typically, columns from subtype attributes will be nullable, and a category column indicates the subtype in which a row belongs.

❑ Create separate tables for each subtype without creating a table for the supertype. Attributes from the supertype are duplicated in each table.

Figure 18.2 illustrates three options for translating the entities in Figure 18.1 from a logical to physical model. The three solutions will result in very different performance outcomes. In particular, creating tables for the supertype and each subtype is likely to reduce performance in most circumstances, except where only the supertype is subject to a full-table scan. Table 18.1 compares the performance of each of the three solutions for common database operations.

When implementing tables derived from subtypes, avoid implementing both supertype and subtype tables. Instead, implement a single table for all subtypes, or multiple sub-tables without a supertype table.

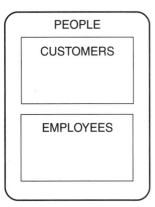

FIGURE 18.1 Representation of subtypes in an entity-relationship diagram.

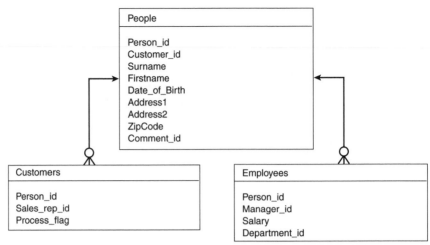

Option 1: Implement subtypes as a master table with detail tables for each subtype

Option 2: Implement subtypes in a single table

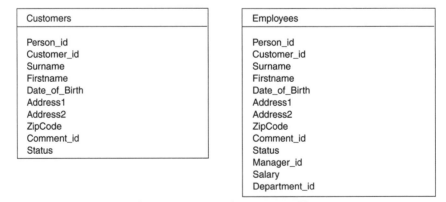

Option 3: Implement subtypes as two tables

FIGURE 18.2 Options for physically modeling logical subtypes.

TABLE 18.1 Performance of various sub-type/super-type implementations

OPERATION	SINGLE TABLE	SEPARATE SUBTYPE AND SUPERTYPE TABLES	SEPARATE SUBTYPE TABLES ONLY—NO SUPERTYPE TABLE
Inserting a new row	Single insert only.	Two inserts will be required.	Single insert only.
Updating a row	Single update only.	Usually a single update. If you need to update super-type and sub-type columns, then two updates will be required.	Single update only.
Fetching a single row via an index	Single table access.	If you need rows from both subtype and supertype, then a join will be required.	Single table access.
Full-table scan super-type columns only	Slowest, since row length may be increased by columns from both subtypes.	Fastest, since super-table row length will be short.	OK. Row length will be greater than for a supertype/subtype split but shorter than for the single-table solution.
Full-table scan sub-type and supertype columns	Good.	Poor, since a join to one or more subtype tables will be required.	Best. No joins are required and no irrelevant columns need be scanned.

USING ARTIFICIAL PRIMARY KEYS

A *natural key* is constructed from unique attributes that occur normally within the entity. An *artificial key* contains no meaningful column information and exists only to identify the row uniquely. There is a continual debate within the database community regarding the merits of artificial primary keys versus the natural keys.

Natural keys may consist of multiple columns and may be composed of any datatype. In contrast, artificial keys are usually sequential numbers. For instance, the natural key for a CUSTOMER table might be a combination of the "government allocated corporation number" together with department or address (if we anticipate multiple "customers" within a single large corporation). An artificial key could be comprised of a single numeric column populated by an Oracle sequence.

Without entering into the wider debate of the merits of natural keys from a data modeling and design perspective, it is worth considering the merits of artificial keys from a performance perspective. There is little doubt that artificial keys generally result in superior performance:

❑   An artificial key will usually consist of a single numeric column. If a natural key consists of non-numeric or concatenated columns, then the key length will be longer and joins and index lookups will be less efficient.

❑   Since an artificial key contains no meaningful information, it should never need to be updated. If a natural primary key is updated, then updates to any referencing foreign keys will be required—which may significantly increase I/O overhead and lock contention.

❑   Artificial keys result in smaller indexes and may result in a shallower index tree. This will help optimize index lookups.

Clearly there will often be a requirement for the natural key columns to exist within the table and for these columns to be accessible via an index lookup. To allow for this, you can simply create an index or unique constraint on these columns.

> Where possible, use numeric artificial keys, populated by sequences, in preference to natural keys comprising concatenated or nonnumeric columns.

CHOOSING BETWEEN VARCHAR2 AND CHAR DATATYPES

Oracle provides two datatypes for character columns—VARCHAR2 and CHAR.[1]

The CHAR datatype stores fixed-length character data. If a string value shorter than the length of the CHAR column is inserted, it is blank padded to the length of the CHAR column. For instance, if the value "Fred" is inserted into a CHAR(12) column, it will be stored as "Fred . . .". Thus a CHAR(12) column always requires 12 bytes of storage.

As the name implies, the VARCHAR2 datatype stores variable-length character strings. VARCHAR2 columns are never implicitly blank padded and require storage only for the length of the data value inserted.

VARCHAR2s and CHARs behave differently in some comparison operations and it is generally regarded as unwise to mix them arbitrarily within a data model.

Because VARCHAR2 columns tend to require less storage, rows that are comprised of VARCHAR2s tend to be shorter than rows based on CHAR columns; and hence tables that are constructed with VARCHAR2s will also be smaller. Smaller tables will be less expensive to scan, and indexes on VARCHAR2s will be smaller and somewhat more efficient.

---

[1]Oracle also supports a VARCHAR datatype, which is identical in operation to the VARCHAR2. However, the ANSI standard has yet to finalize the definition of the VARCHAR datatype and hence its definition in Oracle may change in the future. Therefore, it is recommended that you use the VARCHAR2 datatype, for which upward compatibility is assured.

CHAR datatypes do have at least one performance advantage over VAR-CHAR2s. When a CHAR column is updated so that it becomes longer, free space within the row for the update is guaranteed. On the other hand, if a VARCHAR2 column is updated, it is possible that there will not be sufficient free space to support the update. This may result in the row being chained to a separate block, degrading index lookups on this row.

> Use VARCHAR2s in preference to CHARs in order to reduce row length and optimize table scans unless the risk of row chaining is excessive.

USING LONGS AND LOBS

Prior to Oracle8, the LONG datatype was the only option for simply storing large amounts of unstructured data. From Oracle8 onward, the LOB and BFILE datatypes provide more sophisticated functionality.

We looked at LONGs and LOBs in great detail in chapter Chapter 16 and briefly recap here. Where there is a need to store a large amount of freeform data, the following options exist:

❏ Store it in a LONG column.
❏ Store it in a LOB.
❏ Store it as multiple VARCHAR2 strings in a detail table (this might not be possible for all types of data but is an option for large amounts of text).

As we saw in Chapter 16, the following considerations will determine the optimal solution:

❏ Data in a LONG column are always stored with other table data, increasing the row length and degrading full-table scans. In constrast, most LOB data are stored in a separate segment.
❏ At least part of the data is a LONG column is accessible directly from SQL. LOB data can only be obtained by using programmatic interfaces that are implemented in PL/SQL, Java, OCI and other languages.
❏ It is possible to access randomly parts of LOB data. However, LONG data can only be read sequentially, incurring a large overhead when only accessing particular portions of the data.
❏ LOB data can be stored in operating system files (BFILEs).

In general, the use of either LONG or LOB data is a choice that should not be made lightly. If it is possible to represent the structure using VARCHAR2 datatypes, then you should consider doing so. For instance, a documentation system could represent each line of text as a VARCHAR2 rather than representing the whole document as a LOB.

If you do need to store large amounts of data, Oracle8 LOBs are superior to Oracle7 LONGs in almost all respects. The only significant drawback of LOBs is that you will be unable to access their data directly from SQL—you will have to write a program.

BFILEs allow you to store and manage your LOB data in operating system files. For some applications this will be a critical advantage. However, remember that this data will be read only, will not be subject to database backups, and may be less performance efficient than LOBs within the database.

Don't use LONG or LOB datatypes in your design unless you have fully considered the benefits and limitations and have considered alternative storage options. LOBs should generally be used in preference to LONG data.

OPTIONAL ATTRIBUTES AND NULL VALUES

Standard modeling guidelines suggest that optional attributes should become NULL columns. However, as we have seen in earlier chapters, NULL values can have a significant effect on performance of your SQL. The following performance factors can influence the decision to allow NULL values:

❑ NULL values cannot be indexed, and it will usually require a full-table scan to find NULL values with the IS NULL clause.

❑ The use of NULL values can reduce average row lengths, thus improving full-table scan performance.

❑ If most column values are NULL and queries seek only values that are not NULL, then an index on the column will be compact and efficient.

Therefore, when determining the nullability of a column, consider whether it will ever be required to search for a row where the column is NULL. If the answer is yes, then don't make the column NULL. Instead, define the column as NOT NULL and apply a default value.

Don't define a column as nullable if it is expected that queries will be constructed that will search for the NULL values. Instead, define the column as NOT NULL with a default.

In the case of character data, the default value will usually be a string such as "UNKNOWN." In the case of numeric data, it can be more difficult to determine an appropriate default value. For instance, consider a statistical database that contains the column AGE. Index-based scans on age are common, as are queries to find rows where the age is unknown. If we create a default value for such a column, we will distort attempts to retrieve average, maximum, or minimum ages in the database. In cases such as this, it may be necessary to use NULLs and either accept the consequent difficulty in quickly identifying unknown ages or use denormalization to create an indexed indicator column (AGE_KNOWN=N) that flags rows where the age is unknown.

INDEXING ISSUES

Making correct indexing decisions is critical to database performance. This topic is the subject of Chapter 6, so we briefly recap here:

❑ For most applications, specifying a minimum but complete set of indexes to support anticipated critical queries is the primary consideration.
❑ Creating a suitable set of concatenated indexes is critical. Indexing individual columns only is a common mistake.
❑ The B*-tree index type is flexible and suitable for most applications.
❑ Bitmap indexes are suitable for large, static tables where the number of query column combinations exceeds the practical limit of concatenated indexes.
❑ Hash clusters may be suitable for relatively static tables where fast primary key lookup is an overriding concern.

DENORMALIZATION

Normalization is the process of eliminating redundancy and repeating groups from the data model and ensuring that key attributes are correctly defined. A normalized data model is the usual output from the logical modeling stage.

Denormalization is the process of reintroducing redundant, repeating or otherwise nonnormalized structures into the physical model, almost always with the intention of improving performance.

Normalized data models tend to be inherently reasonably efficient and they are certainly easier to maintain. Denormalization, although sometimes desirable, entails certain risks:

❑ Denormalizing may improve the performance of certain key transactions or queries but may inadvertently make other operations awkward, inefficient, or impossible. For instance, repeating groups often seem to be a useful denormalization because they avoid a join to a detail table. However, producing statistical information—such as averages—from repeating groups may be difficult.
❑ Denormalization will almost always lead to higher insert and update overhead.

❏ Because denormalization introduces redundant information, it can also allow for inconsistent information. This can occur if the application code that is maintaining the denormalized data develops software faults or if the use of an ad hoc tool avoids the denormalization routines. These inconsistencies may be difficult to detect and correct. The cost of the inconsistencies may be huge (for instance, if the denormalized aggregate invoice total was inaccurate).

❏ A software development and maintenance cost is associated with maintaining the denormalized data. Database triggers and snapshots reduce this cost since the code to maintain any replicated or redundant data can be stored within the database and need not be embedded in the application code. Database triggers also help to avoid inconsistencies arising if data are manipulated from outside of the application (from SQL*PLUS, for instance).

Denormalization is not, therefore, something that should be undertaken lightly. Make sure you have fully compared the costs and benefits of each proposed de-normalization. Ideally, you should test the performance gains (and costs) of the denormalization within your performance-tuning environment.

Replicating Column Values to Avoid Joins   One common denormalization is the replication of a column in a related table so as to avoid a join. We saw an example of this kind of denormalization in Chapter 14 when we replicated the DEPARTMENT_NAME column into the EMPLOYEES table. This is a common form of denormalization and can be very effective since joins can multiply the cost of a query considerably.

Consider replicating columns to avoid excessive joins in critical queries. This can be very effective when the denormalized data are stored on static lookup tables.

"Roll Up" Aggregation   Queries that generate totals or aggregations can be expensive and are often too resource intensive to be run in prime time. One solution is to maintain a "totals" table that allows ready access to this information. Such a summary table can be maintained in the following ways:

❏ If real-time summary data are required, the summary data can be updated whenever the source data is changed. This can be done manually, perhaps using a database trigger or by using Oracle8i materialized views with ON COMMIT update defined. While this approach will allow real-time totals to be accessed without the overhead of on-line aggregation, it will have a negative impact on sales transaction processing—as we saw in Chapter 13 when looking at materialized views. There is also a danger that the heavy update activity on the summary table may lead to unacceptable lock contention.

❏ If real-time summary information is not essential, then the summary table can be populated by regularly scheduled jobs, possibly during off-peak processing periods. Oracle's snapshot/materialized view mechanism provides a convenient means of implementing such an approach. The approach has the advantage of eliminating any overhead during peak transaction processing periods but does provide a less up-to-date view of the summary information.

Queries that perform aggregate operations can be resource intensive. Consider maintaining denormalized aggregate information, possibly by using materialized views.

Indexing Calculated Columns or Functions   Another common denormalization technique involves replicating an amended version of a column within the source table. This has often been used to maintain case-insensitive representations of surnames to allow for a case-insensitive index search. In Oracle8i, this can often be achieved through the use of functional indexes, described in Chapter 6.

Maintain redundant columns with derived data if you are required to perform indexed searches on derived values. In Oracle8i, ensure that a functional index is not a more efficient approach.

Creating Artificial Subtypes   We discussed earlier the issues involving the translation of logical subtypes into physical tables. In general, we found that implementation of subtypes as detail tables generally diminished the performance of commonplace SQL operations.

However, if a large table is to be subjected to frequent table scans, but only a small portion of columns are usually queried, then it can be worthwhile to split the table in two, especially if the infrequently accessed columns are very long.

We considered a good example of this technique in Chapter 8. If the EMPLOYEE table contained a long column with a high-resolution image of each employee, then we would expect full-table scan performance to be poor. However, we wouldn't normally require that the image be accessed when performing a full-table scan—it might only be accessed when accessing all details for a specific employee via an on-line query. In this case, we could improve the performance of full-table scans and improve buffer cache efficiency by moving the long columns to a subtable.

Oracle8 and Oracle8i will sometimes allow you to split a table into multiple segments while still retaining a single logical table. For instance,

- ❏ LOB data can be stored in a separate segment.
- ❏ In an index organized table, some rows will be stored in an overflow segment.

If a large table is expected to be subject to frequent table scans, consider moving long, infrequently accessed columns to a separate subtable to reduce row length and improve table scan performance.

Implementing Denormalization   Prior to the introduction of Oracle version 7, implementing redundant or derived columns required extensive changes to all application code to ensure that the redundant information was kept current. Even if this code was implemented successfully, there was a danger that an update might be issued from an ad hoc tool (SQL*PLUS, for instance) and fail to update the redundant or derived columns.

Database triggers provide an easier, safer, and often more efficient means of maintaining denormalized information. A database trigger will fire regardless of the tool used to update the source data, so the risk of inconsistent data is reduced. By using triggers, application logic can be kept simpler and independent of changes to the database schema.

Use database triggers to maintain denormalized data in preference to application code. Database triggers reduce the risk of inconsistent denormalized data, simplify application code, and will often perform more efficiently.

STAR SCHEMAS

Star schemas, in which a single massive fact table is associated with multiple small dimension tables, is a flexible design for efficiently storing large quantities of historical data. We looked at Oracle's optimizations for Star joins in Chapter 9. When considering the implementation of Star schemas, there are two significant considerations:

- ❏ Oracle's optimizations for star schema joins is only available when the cost-based optimizer is enabled. If your star schema is going to be implemented in an environment in which the rule-based optimizer is enabled, you will need to take special care to optimize queries manually.

❏ Bitmap indexes can be particularly effective when combined with a star schema.

See Chapter 9 for a more detailed discussion on star schema processing

PARTITIONING

We examined partitioning in detail in Chapter 13.

When considering the physical implementation of very large databases, selecting a partitioning strategy can be a significant decision. Partitioning large tables and indexes can ease maintenance headaches and improve the performance of parallel queries and DML. The following guidelines summarize some of the issues considered in Chapter 13:

❏ For tables that store large amounts of time-based data, consider implementing a time-based range-partitioning scheme. This will allow you to purge old data quickly by dropping the relevant partition.

❏ For large tables subject to massive bulk update, consider implementing a partitioning scheme so that parallel DML is available. Evenly balanced partitions are important for parallel operations, so consider hash-based or composite partitioning for these tables.

❏ Global indexes on partitioned tables involve some restrictions and should be avoided where possible.

See Chapter 13 for more advice on partitioning

CONSIDERING ORACLE OBJECT TYPES

Oracle8 object types—VARRAY, object tables, nested tables—were a revolutionary change to the Oracle RDBMS. We examined the performance of Oracle Objects in Chapter 16.

Should we consider Oracle object types in the design of new applications? At this time the answer would seem to be no. My personal reservations regarding Oracle objects stem from the following observations:

❏ Oracle object types do not implement key features of true objects, such as inheritance.

❏ Traditional relational structures usually perform as well as or better than the object alternatives.

❏ Accessing data in Oracle objects often requires awkward SQL or—in many cases—must be accessed from within PL/SQL or another programming languages.

❏   Oracle Corporation seems to have shifted its focus from supporting object types as schema objects and is now focusing on integrating Java and CORBA—both with their own object models—into the RDBMS.

A more detailed discussion on the pros and cons of Oracle objects is contained in Chapter 16.

APPLICATION DESIGN

Application design won't have the same direct and fundamental effect on a SQL statement's performance as the data model. However, there are some application design considerations that affect your ability to tune your SQL or to get the maximum benefit from well-tuned SQL.

INTEGRATING SQL_TRACE

We've made extensive use of SQL_TRACE/tkprof trace output throughout this book. It is convenient to be able to enable SQL_TRACE when required.

Although Oracle provides facilities for enabling SQL_TRACE for an entire database or for a specific session, it is most convenient if SQL_TRACE is enabled by the application itself. Within the application, you might enable SQL_TRACE

❏   By a command line switch
❏   By the presence of an environment variable
❏   From a menu option in an interactive application

After SQL_TRACE has been enabled, it is handy to issue a dummy SQL statement to "tag" the trace file. For instance,

```
select 'Tracing Program117' from dual;
```

The SQL statement will be written to the trace file and so trace files for "Program117" will be easy to locate.

> Build the ability to enable SQL_TRACE into your application. "Tag" the trace files by issuing a dummy SQL statement.

PROFILING

Generating SQL traces will be invaluable when performance-tuning your application. However, SQL tracing only provides one part of the puzzle. To get the complete picture, your application should be able to generate performance data such as

❑ Critical transactions per second

❑ Elapsed time for a critical transaction

❑ Elapsed time spent in various critical sections

❑ Number of times key modules were visited

This information can help you locate the hot spots within your application that will be most suitable for tuning. This may not always relate to SQL tuning but will often point to the need for related measures, such as caching or array processing.

Some tools and environments allow profiling information, such as function call counts and elapsed times, to be generated automatically. In other tools, you may need to write your own code to collect this information. In PL/SQL, you can use the DBMS_PROFILER package (described in Chapter 14) to collect profile data.

Build into your application the ability to report on critical performance indicators. Consider the use of profiling tools to determine the time spent in various subroutines.

LOCKING STRATEGY

Oracle locks database rows either when they are modified or when they are selected with the FOR UPDATE clause. If another session wishes to lock or update an already locked row, it will normally wait until competing locks have been released. Extended waiting for database locks can have a ruinous effect on both throughput and response time. The designers of a high-performance application must adopt a locking policy that minimizes lock waits.

The Pessimistic Locking Strategy The pessimistic locking strategy is based on the assumption that a row may be updated by another user between the time you fetch it and the time you update it. To avoid any contention, the pessimistic locking strategy requires that you lock the rows as they are retrieved. The application is therefore assured that no changes will be made to the row between the time the row is retrieved and the time it is updated.

The Optimistic Locking Strategy The optimistic locking strategy is based on the assumption that it is unlikely that an update will be applied to a row between the time it is retrieved and the time it is modified. Based on this assumption, the optimistic locking strategy does not require that the row be locked when fetched. However, to avoid the possibility that the row will be updated between retrieval and modification, it will be necessary to check that the row has not been changed by another session when being modified or locked. This can be done by checking a timestamp value or by checking that the original selection criteria still apply. If the row has been modified, then it will be necessary either to retry the transaction or return an error to the user.

The optimistic and pessimistic locking strategies are diagrammed in Figure 18.3. Each strategy has its strengths and weaknesses, and the choice of strategy can affect the performance of your application. Consider the following points when deciding upon an appropriate locking strategy:

❑ The optimistic locking strategy tends to hold locks for shorter periods of time, thus reducing the potential for lock contention.

❑ In an interactive application, the pessimistic locking strategy can allow locks to be held indefinitely. This is a common phenomenon in an interactive application that fetches and locks data pending and waits for the user to hit the "OK" button. It's possible for the row to remain locked for hours if the user "goes to lunch," not realizing that a lock has been placed on the row displayed.

❑ If the optimism in the optimistic locking strategy is misplaced—if it is reasonably common for rows to be updated by other sessions between retrieval and update—then the optimistic locking strategy can lead to poor batch performance or user frustration as a high proportion of updates are rejected with a "try again" message.

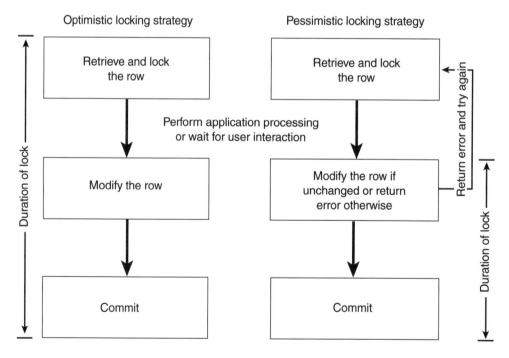

FIGURE 18.3 Optimistic and Pessimistic locking compared.

> Choose a locking strategy that is right for your application. When possible, implement the optimistic locking strategy, which tends to reduce the duration that locks are held.

REDUCING PARSING

We examined the process by which Oracle parses (prepares for execution) SQL statements in Chapter 4. Reducing parse overhead is relatively easy when writing an application but can be very difficult once the application is complete. Minimizing parse overhead requires that your application

- ❑ Always uses bind variables instead of literals.
- ❑ Does not discard cursors (SQL statement handles) for statements that are likely to be re-executed.

More information on this topic is contained in Chapter 4 and in Appendix C.

CACHING

No matter how well you tune your SQL, each SQL query will involve a substantial overhead. Control must be passed from your application to the Oracle server (often across a network), which must undertake complex processing. Any steps that reduce the number of SQL statement executions will usually be effective in improving the performance of your application.

One of the most effective ways of reducing SQL calls is to cache frequently accessed data within your application. This involves allocating an area of local memory—usually an array variable or PL/SQL table—and storing data items retrieved from the database in this memory. When a new data item is required, the program will first scan the cache to see if it has already been read. If the data are found in the cache, then a database access is avoided. If not found, then the data item can be retrieved from the database and stored in the cache. We saw an example of caching in Chapter 14.

Caching particularly suits small, frequently accessed tables that contain static lookup values (for instance, a table of product codes, status codes, etc).

Here are some considerations to keep in mind when implementing caching:

- ❑ Caches consume memory on the client program. In many environments, memory is abundant and is of little consequence. However, for large tables and memory-constrained environments, the implementation of a caching strategy could actually degrade performance by inducing paging or swapping (see Chapter 20 for a discussion on paging and swapping).
- ❑ When caches are relatively small, sequential scanning (i.e., examining each entry in the cache from the first entry to the last) will probably result in

adequate performance. However, if the cache is larger, the sequential scan may start to degrade performance. To maintain good performance, it may be necessary to implement advanced search techniques such as hashing or binary chop.

❏ If the table being cached is updated during program execution, then the changes may not be reflected in your cache unless you implement some sophisticated synchronization mechanism. For this reason, local caching is best performed on static tables.

Caching frequently accessed data from small or medium-sized static tables can be effective in improving program performance. However, beware of memory utilization and program complexity issues.

CLIENT/SERVER PARTITIONING

Oracle's ability to store and execute PL/SQL programs within the database server provides you with the capability to locate application logic either within the client environment or within the server environment. If client and server are located on computers with different processing capacities (for example, PC clients and a high-end UNIX server), client/server partitioning configurations may substantially affect performance.

Guidelines from the early days of client/server environments suggested moving as much processing logic as possible to the server, since the processing capacities of the server would typically be several times greater than the capabilities of the client platform. With the increasing processing capabilities of client machines in recent years and the increased use of lower-end hardware as database servers, the differential is not so great and each case must now be judged on its merits.

Transactions that perform substantial database manipulation but that have minimal input and output requirements are good candidates for server side processing, since a server side implementation will reduce network traffic.

Alternatively, operations that require user interaction or are required to return sets of data are difficult to implement in Oracle stored programs and may not perform efficiently. These operations may be best implemented in client code.

If the sum of processing power in the client machines outstrips the processing power available in the server (for instance, Pentium-based client workstations interacting with a relatively small NT server), then implementing substantial application logic on the server may result in a server bottleneck and poor performance.

If the processing power of the server hardware is much greater than that available on the client side (for instance, a high-end UNIX SMP server and low-end Pentium clients), then it may be advantageous to reduce the processing requirements of the clients by moving application logic to the server.

Carefully consider the break-up of application processing between client-based processing and server-based PL/SQL stored programs. Keep in mind the level of user interaction and database processing required by each transaction and the relative power of client and server hardware.

Three-tier Applications While client/server application developments are still common, the direction for many future developments is based on a three-tier, Internet-enabled application. The applications generally involve a very thin Web client, a middle tier that implements business logic, and a database tier.

The middle tier in such an application might be the Web server running Java servlets that communicate with the database via JDBC or CGI callouts, or it might be a dedicated application server.

In these cases, there is a strong incentive to isolate database logic to the server layer and processing logic to the middle tier. The upper tier will normally be concerned only with presentation logic.

MESSAGING WITH ADVANCED QUEUING

Messaging-oriented middleware (MOM) is a term that describes a mechanism by which components of an application can communicate asynchronously. In a messaging model, an application component might place an order onto a queue. Another component might be responsible for processing these orders when time permits.

Messaging middleware provides the services that allow these components, which could be located on a remote host, to queue and dequeue messages. Messaging products offer certain facilities such as priorities, reliability, persistence, security, and so on.

In Oracle8, a messaging system known as Oracle Advanced Queuing was introduced to the Oracle RDBMS. Advanced Queuing is implemented over the top of Oracle tables and so inherits the security, backup, and SQL access features of Oracle.

In Oracle 8.1.6, Oracle implemented a JMS (Java Messaging Service) interface to Advanced Queuing. JMS is a Java standard that defines a common Java interface to any messaging product.

The existence of a reliable messaging interface integrated with the Oracle RDBMS provides options for application design that were previously less practical. The decision to use messaging middleware will usually be driven by the requirements of the application, but performance implications could also drive the decision.

Messaging middleware can help break the conflict between response time–driven and throughput-driven performance requirements. In a messaging system, it is possible to provide a response before all of the work is done—you trust that the remaining work will be done since it has been placed on the necessary queue. This sort of technique works particularly well for e-commerce. After placing an order and getting immediate on-line confirmation, your order is placed on a queue for processing. At some later stage, you receive e-mail confirmation that the order is being processed.

CONCURRENCY AND PARALLELISM

We noted in Chapter 11 that the full power of computers with multiple CPUs often will not be realized unless some degree of parallel processing can be implemented. Oracle has implemented parallel processing capabilities for a wide range of SQL statements, but it is still not possible to use Oracle's parallel capabilities in all circumstances. Even if database operations can be parallelized, this might be of no avail if all application processing occurs serially.

When writing long-running, database-intensive programs, it is important to ensure that multiple instances of the same job can be run in parallel. For example, consider a monthly billing program written in C, Java, or some other procedural language. The job might run through the SALES table and generate invoices for outstanding sales. We could, of course, use the parallel query option to scan the SALES table in parallel, but because only one instance of the billing program would be running, it is unlikely that we would be able to exercise all of the host's CPU capacity since the billing program itself would only be able to utilize a single CPU.

The obvious solution—to run multiple billing programs concurrently—may not be as simple to implement as it might seem. If each instance of the billing program were to perform a full-table scan of SALES, then an I/O bottleneck would be likely. Further, how do we prevent multiple instances of the program from issuing invoices to the same client?

One solution would be partitioning the invoices to be issued by the customer and executing background billing jobs for each customer. The master program would need to ensure that the required number of jobs were kept active concurrently. Simplified pseudocode for the job might look like this:

```
FOR each customer
    SUBMIT billing job for customer
    INCREMENT jobs_running BY 1
    WHILE jobs_running >= number_of_jobs_to_run DO
        WAIT for a job to finish
        DECREMENT jobs_running BY 1
    END WHILE
NEXT customer
```

More complex logic may be required in many circumstances; and job schedulers available on some platforms may remove the need to control the number of jobs running.

In general, when requiring to run multiple jobs in parallel,

❑ Implement a mechanism of partitioning work to each job.

❑ Implement a means of keeping a specified number of jobs active at any given time.

❑ Eliminate any contention for resources between jobs such as database locks, output files, etc.

Ensure that long-running batch jobs can make use of available processing power by running in parallel.

SUMMARY

Although SQL tuning can lead to impressive improvements in application performance, the data model and the application design often provide the ultimate constraints on the performance that can be achieved. It is common to find that SQL performance cannot be improved without substantial and costly changes to the underlying database architecture.

In this chapter, we've developed some guidelines for developing high-performance data models and application designs.

Of fundamental importance in effective high-performance design is to incorporate tuning into the design process. Identify the performance requirements of the system early and build measurement and testing of these requirements into the project plan.

When developing the physical data model, keep these basic principles in mind:

❑ Avoid implementing separate tables for each subtype entity because of the probable join overhead.

❑ Make use of sequences to create artificial primary keys. These will often be more efficient in joins and lookups than natural keys, which might be non-numeric or concatenated.

❑ Use the VARCHAR2 datatype in preference to the CHAR attribute because it reduces row length and improves the efficiency of full-table scans.

❑ Avoid LONG columns if possible—consider implementing the LONG as a VARCHAR2 or as a subtable of VARCHAR2s.

❑   Be careful when creating columns that can be NULL. If a query will search for these NULL values, an indexed retrieval will not be possible. Consider using NOT NULL together with the DEFAULT option.

Denormalization is the process of introducing redundant or derived information into the data model in order to improve performance. Denormalizing the data model has a number of risks on maintainability and performance grounds and should not be undertaken lightly. However, if properly implemented, denormalization can greatly improve query performance. Some of the denormalizations that you might wish to consider are as follows:

❑   Replicating columns to avoid joins
❑   Maintaining derived values to reduce aggregate operations or to allow indexed lookup of derived values
❑   Moving long, infrequently accessed columns to a detail table
❑   Maintaining real-time or regularly updated summary data tables

Where possible, implement denormalization using Oracle triggers and snapshot technology. This reduces the risk of inconsistencies, simplifies application logic, and is often the most efficient mechanism.

Partitioning large tables can improve queries that need to access only some of the table's partitions and can allow for easier table maintenance. True partition tables are only available in Oracle8, but you can achieve some of the benefits in Oracle7 by using partition views.

Effective application design will allow you to get the most out of your SQL by avoiding processing bottlenecks and building tuning facilities into the application.

❑   Ensure that your application supports some mechanism for invoking the SQL_TRACE facility and for reporting performance metrics.
❑   Adopt an appropriate locking model for your application. The optimistic locking model reduces the duration of locks and will usually provide good performance, providing that there is little contention for the same rows. If contention for rows is high, use the pessimistic model. Never allow locks to be held indefinitely at a user's discretion.
❑   Where possible, use caching in your application to reduce the number of requests made to the database. If possible (and this usually depends on the size of the tables), never ask the database for the same data twice.
❑   In a client/server environment, ensure that the split of processing between the client and the server is optimal. Using stored procedures and triggers moves much of the processing load from the client to the server and reduces parse overhead. If you have "big" servers and "little" clients, moving the bulk of the processing load to the server is probably a wise move.

❑ Make sure that your application design doesn't prevent concurrent processing. For instance, exclusive locks on a file or on a single row in the database may allow only a single thread of execution to proceed concurrently. This will lead to poor performance in interactive applications and failure to leverage the power of all CPUs in a batch environment.

Chapter 19

ORACLE SERVER DESIGN

The term *database server* can refer to an Oracle database instance or may be used to refer to both the Oracle instance and the host computer on which it resides. In this chapter, we provide an introduction to sizing and configuring a database server that will support your application and allow your SQL to perform to its peak potential.

Although the database server can have a significant effect on the performance of SQL, you cannot usually compensate for untuned SQL by improving your database server. When SQL is untuned, its resource requirements might be magnified tens or hundreds of times. In this case, improving the configuration of your database server is likely to have a marginal effect at best on your SQL's performance. On the other hand, once your SQL is tuned, it's possible that the database server configuration can become the limiting factor. A well-sized and -configured database server allows your SQL to reach its peak performance potential.

In this chapter, we provide a brief overview of server configuration issues, including the following:

❏ Establishing a realistic configuration for your computer hardware in terms of memory, disk devices, network and CPU
❏ Using RAID devices

❏ Designing the Oracle instance, including redo log placement and backup strategy
❏ Creating tablespace layouts to suit your application
❏ Configuring the Oracle shared memory area (SGA)
❏ Using optional features such as multithreaded servers and parallel query
❏ Advanced Oracle configuration issues

A REVIEW OF THE ORACLE ARCHITECTURE

Before we can begin configuring our high-performance server, we need to ensure that we have a firm grasp on basic Oracle database components. A detailed examination of the Oracle architecture is beyond the scope of this book, refer to Oracle documentation or other texts (see Appendix E) for more detailed coverage.

Figure 19.1 illustrates some of the basic components of an Oracle server at the memory, database, and disk layers.

At the physical file level, we have the following components:

❏ Database files are disk files that contain the data that comprise an Oracle database.
❏ A tablespace is a logical structure that contains and groups the segments (mainly tables and indexes) that comprise a database. A tablespace may consist of more than one database file, but any given database file may belong to only one tablespace.
❏ Database segments include user objects such as tables, indexes, rollback segments and temporary segments. A segment can belong to only one tablespace. However, a table or index can be comprised of more than one segment and can therefore be contained within more than one tablespace. Tables and indexes can consist of multiple segments when they are partitioned, have a LOB segment, or have an index organized overflow segment.
❏ Rollback segments are used to store original (or "before image") copies of database blocks that have been changed but not committed. Rollback segments contain the information that must be restored if a ROLLBACK command is issued.
❏ Temporary segments are used to store data needed for large sorts or for large intermediate temporary tables created during SQL statement execution.
❏ Redo logs contain details of transactions that may not be written to the database files. The primary purpose of redo logs is to allow for the recovery of the database in the event of a system or database failure.

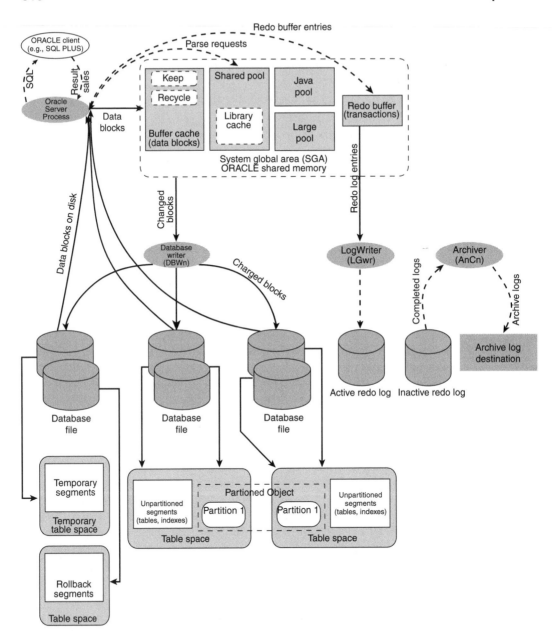

FIGURE 19.1   Basic database components.

At the memory level, we have the following constructs:

❏ The Oracle System Global Area is an area of shared memory that is used to store information that can be shared by multiple sessions.

❏ The buffer cache is an area in the SGA that contains copies of blocks from database files. The buffer cache exists primarily to reduce disk I/O by allowing sessions to access frequently or recently accessed data in memory. The buffer cache can be subdivided into three pools: the default pool, the recycle pool, and the keep pool.

❏ The shared pool contains cached SQL and PL/SQL statements, data dictionary information, and sometimes private session information (if multithreaded servers are enabled).

❏ The large pool contains session-specific information for sessions that are connected through multithreaded servers or through the Oracle XA (TP monitor) interface, or for certain internal operations.

❏ The Java pool contains Java objects shared across processes.

❏ The redo buffer contains redo log entries that have not yet been written to the redo logs. The redo buffer is flushed periodically and is always flushed when a COMMIT occurs.

The following processes (or threads on Windows platforms) exist for every Oracle instance:

❏ Server processes perform SQL processing on behalf of an Oracle session. A server process can either perform processing for a single session only (a dedicated server) or for multiple sessions (a multithreaded server). In some operating systems (VMS, for instance), the server process and the user process can be combined. In other operating systems and in client/server configurations, the user process and the server process are separate.

❏ Background processes perform specialized tasks on behalf of the all sessions. For instance, the database writer (DBWR) is responsible for writing changed blocks from the buffer cache to the database files. The log writer (LGWR) is responsible for writing blocks from the redo buffer to the redo logs. The archiver (ARCH) processes copies completed redo logs to backup storage. Other processes (SMON, PMON) perform housekeeping functions, and some processes may be running only if certain Oracle options are enabled.

SIZING THE HOST COMPUTER

Determining the optimum hardware configuration for an application is a complex procedure that cannot always be reduced to a simple set of guidelines. The four main resources to size are as follows:

Memory,   which is required by each database process and user process and by Oracle's shared memory areas

Disks,   which must be sufficient in size to store the data required by the database and sufficient in number to support the I/O requirements of the database

CPU,   which must support the processing requirements of Oracle and user processes

Network,   which must support communication between processes on multiple machines in a client/server configuration.

DETERMINING MEMORY REQUIREMENTS

Ensuring that there is sufficient free memory on your host computer is essential to maintain reasonable performance levels. In most operating systems, memory requirements can be calculated using the following formula:

memory = system + (#user × user_overhead) + SGA + (#servers server_size)

The terms in the formula are as follows:

System: The system memory overhead. This includes memory required for the system kernel, buffers, and other purposes. The value is operating system dependent. On a midrange UNIX server, the value may be between 100 and 200 MB.

#user: The number of user processes that are resident on the server. In a client/server configuration, there may be no clients on the server; whereas in a batch system, the "users" are batch programs that are resident on the server machine.

*User_*   The memory required by each user program. This is applica-
overhead: tion specific, and you would generally have to measure the memory utilization of your program using an operating system utility to determine its value.

SGA   The size of the System Global Area. The optimal size of the SGA depends on your application, and adjusting the size of the SGA is a common tuning measure. On a midrange UNIX server, most SGAs use between 50 and 150 MB of memory, although very large SGAs are often implemented. If you use multithreaded servers, you will need to allocate additional storage for session information within the SGA and, ideally, configure the large pool so that it is large enough to contain this memory. If you use Java stored procedures, CORBA objects, or Enterprise Java Beans, you will need to configure the Java pool with at least 50 to 100 MB of memory.

#servers: The is the number of database server processes implemented on your system. If you implement dedicated servers, then the value will be equivalent to the number of users on your system plus the number of background processes. If you use multithreaded servers, then the number can be much smaller—perhaps one server per 10 users—plus the number of background processes. There will be a minimum of four background processes on your system, but a more common minimum is six. Additional background processes may be created for parallel query servers, for distributed database operations, and for archiving of redo logs.

*Server_* *size:* The is the amount of memory required for each Oracle server process and can be dependent on the version of Oracle and the operating system. In UNIX, the value is almost always 1.5 to 2 MB.

Let's suppose we are sizing a UNIX database server. We know that the number of concurrent users will be about 500 and that a client/server configuration will be used. A large, high-end UNIX machine is required, so let's assume that the system overhead is about 150 MB. We plan to use dedicated database servers and to enable the parallel query option with a maximum of 50 query processes. We can't be totally sure what the size of the SGA will be, but because we're not using MTS or Oracle Java, it's unlikely to be more than 200 MB.

We know that the number of background processes will be 6 + 50 (minimum + parallel query processes). The number of user server (shadow) processes will be 500 (one per user). Assuming 1.5 MB of memory per process, the total requirement for server processes is $(500 + 6 + 50) \cdot 1.5$ MB = 834 MB. Adding our system requirement and SGA requirement gives a total of 834 MB+200MB + 150 MB=1184 MB.

It's wise to add some additional memory to allow for errors or unanticipated load.

Some 32-bit architectures support a maximum of 2 GB (or 4 GB) of memory. If your memory requirements exceed the maximum memory requirements for the hardware, you could try implementing multithreaded servers, a transaction monitoring software, or a three-tier architecture to reduce memory requirements. Most UNIX systems now have 64-bit variants that can exceed the 2 GB limitation.

The architecture of Oracle in a Windows[1] environment is somewhat different. Oracle under Windows takes advantage of Window's strong support for

---

[1]By "Windows" I mean Windows NT 4.0 and Windows 2000, but not Windows 98 or Windows 95. Although Oracle can run under Windows 98 and 95, they are not suitable operating systems for database servers.

threads. On Windows, the Oracle instance is implemented as a single NT process. Because each thread shares the same memory space, there is no need to implement the SGA in shared memory as such. Instead, the SGA is implemented within the instance's process memory and is available to all threads within the process.

In NT version 4.0, a process may address up to 4 GB of virtual memory. However, 2 GB of this memory is reserved for system overhead, allowing only 2 GB for Oracle. This 2 GB might sound like a generous memory allocation for an Oracle instance, but remember that this area of memory must be sufficient to store the SGA and data segments for all Oracle sessions. Also, the 2 GB is a virtual memory limit—it's possible that 2 GB of virtual memory will be expended when physical memory utilization is far less.

There are a number of ways in which you can exceed the 2 GB limit. In Windows NT server Enterprise edition, the system component of process memory can be reduced to 1 GB, allowing up to 3 GB of memory for the Oracle instance.

Oracle8i can address more than 4 GB of physical memory on Windows NT and Windows 2000 on suitable hardware that has been correctly configured. The document "Oracle8i Support for Very Large Memory Configurations" explains how to do this. You can get the document http://technet.oracle.com/doc/oracle8i_816/vlm/A83669_01.pdf from the Oracle technical network (http://technet.oracle.com) .

CONFIGURING DISK DEVICES

A major aim of configuring an Oracle server is to ensure that disk I/O does not become a bottleneck. While there may be some differences in the performance of disk devices from various vendors—especially if the devices are in some sort of RAID configuration (discussed in detail later)—the major restraining factor on disk I/O is the number of disks acquired and the spread of I/O between these devices.

If possible, estimate the physical I/O that will be generated by your database, and use this figure to determine the number of devices that would be required to support the configuration.

How Many Disks are Required for Database Files?   For a simplistic example, consider a transaction processing system in which 99% of the transactions were simply GET ROW, UPDATE ROW, and COMMIT. The peak transaction rate has been specified at 50 transactions per second.

We know that we will be using an index lookup to retrieve the row and that this lookup will require three or four index block lookups (index head block, one or two branch blocks, and one leaf block) and one table block lookup. Therefore,

$$\text{I/Os required to fetch row} = 4.5$$

We will use the FOR UPDATE clause to lock the row as it is retrieved. This will require a further I/O to update the transaction list in the block itself and an I/O to update the rollback segment.

$$I/Os \text{ required to lock row} = 2$$

Updating the row using the ROWID or CURRENT OF CURSOR clause will require an I/O to update the block and the rollback segment.

$$I/Os \text{ required to update the row} = 2$$

Committing the row will involve an I/O to the redo log, but because the redo log should be on a dedicated device, we can overlook that I/O while we calculate the datafile's I/O. The total number of datafile I/Os for our transaction would appear to be about 8.5 (4.5 + 2 + 2). To be safe, let's double that estimate to account for overheads and special circumstances (data dictionary reads, chained rows, etc.) and allow 17 I/Os per transaction.

We expect Oracle's buffer cache to allow many of our I/Os to be satisfied in memory without requiring a disk I/O. Eighty percent is at the low end of hit rates in the buffer cache, so let's assume that disk I/Os will be about 20% of "logical" I/Os. Remember that our peak transaction rate is about 50/second, so we can conservatively estimate that datafile I/O will be

$$\text{Disk I/Os per second} = 17 \times 20\% \times 50 = 170$$

Disk capacities vary, but disks in common usage can perform 20 random I/Os per second comfortably and as much as 50/second in bursts. Using the figure of 20 I/Os per second, we expect to require as many as 170/20 = 8.5 disk devices and to spread our data evenly over these devices in order to satisfy database file I/O.

There are a number of factors that bear on the accuracy of this estimate:

❑ We assumed a hit rate in the buffer cache of about 80%. However, hit rates of 90 to 95%—or even higher—are not uncommon, so our estimate is conservative (that is, our estimate errs on the side of caution).

❑ Disk capacities can vary, and the implementation of disk caches, solid-state disk, or RAID technology can have a big influence on the performance of your disk devices. Your disk vendor may be able to provide accurate random I/O rates. Make sure that your vendor does not try to persuade you to accept the sequential I/O rate when estimating index read throughput.

❑ We've assumed an efficiently implemented transaction: efficient index lookup, using the ROWID to update the rows, and so on. If the transaction turns out to be implemented less efficiently, then our disk requirement estimate may be inadequate.

Disks for Redo Devices When the transaction is committed, the redo log entry in the redo log buffer must be written to disk. The characteristics of the redo log writes are very different from those of the data file I/O. First, they are sequential I/Os, which means that each access follows the previous access on the disk. The disk drive does not have to "seek" the disk block to access, and so sequential I/Os are much faster than random I/Os. Most disk devices can perform about one hundred sequential I/Os per second. Second, the I/Os are write-only and will attempt to write through any disk cache. These factors combine to suggest that transaction processing will be optimized if a redo log is on a dedicated disk device. Of course, if your database is primarily read-only, then redo log I/O is unlikely to be an issue and the redo logs can be placed in virtually any convenient location.

The number of disk devices available to your database determines the maximum I/O rate that can be achieved. Try and calculate the likely I/O rates and use these rates to estimate the number of disk devices required by your application. Redo logs should be on a dedicated device if there is significant update activity.

Disk Sizes From the preceding discussion, it might be apparent that small capacity disk devices will result in a potentially greater I/O rate than large disk devices for a database of a known size. Unfortunately, disks are getting bigger, and the best per-megabyte cost ratio is obtained with larger disks. Consequently, there is a temptation to buy bigger disks. Try to resist this temptation. Remember that in most cases, an 8-GB disk has half the I/O capacity of two 4-GB disks.

RAID RAID (Redundant Array of Independent Disks) arrays are an increasingly popular way of delivering fault-tolerant, high-performance disk configurations. There are a number of levels of RAID and a number of factors to take into consideration when deciding upon a RAID configuration and the level of RAID to implement.

Three levels of RAID are commonly provided by storage vendors:

❑ RAID 0 is sometimes referred to as striping disks. In this configuration, a logical disk is constructed from multiple physical disks. The data contained on the logical disk is spread evenly across the physical disk, and hence random I/Os are also likely to be spread evenly. There is no redundancy built into this configuration, so if a disk fails, it will have to be recovered from a backup.

❑ RAID 1 is referred to as disk mirroring. In this configuration, a logical disk is comprised of two physical disks. In the event that one physical disk fails, processing can continue using the other physical disk. Each disk contains identical data and writes are processed in parallel, so there should be no negative effects on write performance. Two disks are available for reads, so there can be an improvement in read performance.

❑ In RAID 5, a logical disk is comprised of multiple physical disks. Data is arranged across the physical devices in a similar way to disk striping (RAID 0). However, a certain proportion of the data on the physical devices is parity data. This parity data contains enough information to derive data on other disks should a single physical device fail.

It's common to combine RAID 0 and RAID 1. Such striped and mirrored configurations offer protection against hardware failure together with spread of I/O load.

Figure 19.2 illustrates various RAID configurations.

Performance Implications of RAID   Both RAID 0 and RAID 5 improve the performance of concurrent random reads by spreading the load across multiple devices. However, RAID 5 tends to degrade write I/O, since both the source block and the parity block must be read and then updated. The degradation becomes extreme if a disk fails, since all disks must be accessed in order to rebuild a logical view of the failed disk.

Neither RAID 0 nor RAID 5 offers any performance advantages over single disk configurations when sequential reads or writes are being undertaken.

The performance of RAID 0 + RAID 1 for database files, and RAID 1 for redo logs, is generally superior to any other configuration and offers full protection from media failure. However, RAID 5 requires less disk space than a RAID 0 + 1 configuration and may provide acceptable performance in many circumstances.

Battery-backed Caches in RAID Devices   The write penalty associated with RAID devices—and with disk systems in general—can be reduced by the use of a nonvolatile cache. The non-volatile cache is a memory store with a battery backup, which ensures that the data in the cache is not lost in the event of a power failure. Because the data in the cache is protected against loss, the disk device can report that the data has been written to disk as soon as it is stored in the cache. The data can be written down to the physical disk at a later point.

Battery-backed caches can improve the performance of writes immensely, especially when the application requests confirmation that the data written has actually been committed to disk, which Oracle always does. Such caches are common in RAID devices, mainly because they help to alleviate the overhead of disk writes in a RAID 5 configuration. With a large enough cache, the RAID writes overhead can be practically eliminated for some applications. However, if the

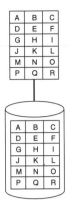
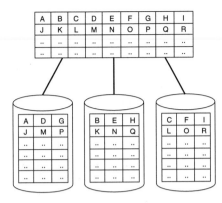

1. A normal disk without any RAID level

2. RAID level 0, or striping. Data are evenly distributed across multiple disks, but there is no redunancy.

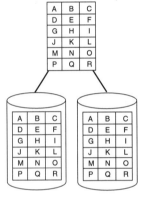
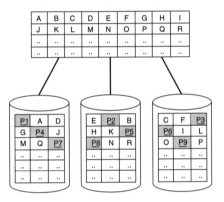

3. RAID 1. Data are replicated on two disks but there is no spread of data.

4. RAID 5. Data are spread across multiple devices. Parity information (P1, P2, etc.) can be used to reconstruct data if any single disk fails.

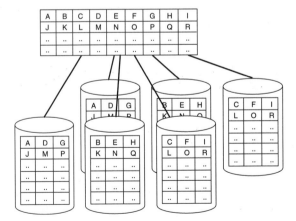

5. RAID 0 + 1 can be combined to provide both spreading of data and redundancy.

FIGURE 19.2   RAID configurations.

cache fills with modified data, disk performance will reduce to that of the underlying disks and a substantial and sudden drop in performance may occur.

If considering a RAID 5-based solution, give preference to RAID arrays which are configured with a non-volatile cache. Such a cache can reduce the write I/O overhead associated with RAID5.

Even if you're not using a RAID 5 configuration, a nonvolatile cached disk array is worth considering if you can afford it and your I/O requirements are high. When such systems are combined with best-practice disk configurations such as those discussed later in this chapter, truly amazing performance improvements can be obtained. In particular, redo log sync writes can effectively occur asynchronously in such a configuration, eliminating the only I/O wait that will always affect user processes in traditional implementations.

The most commonly cited example of a nonvolatile cached disk array is the EMC Symmetrix line. EMC devices are highly reliable, and this reliability extends beyond the RAID configurations into individual disk components and software architecture. EMC devices also provide for remote replication and fail-over and have extensive experience working with Oracle databases. Unfortunately, this sort of configuration can be extremely pricey and is usually only cost-justified for performance critical applications.

CONFIGURING CPU

While we can estimate disk and memory requirements fairly accurately before a system is built, it is far more difficult to estimate accurately an application's CPU requirements.

The CPU requirements for an Oracle database server will be determined by

❏ Operating system type
❏ Hardware type
❏ Database I/O rates
❏ Frequency and types of transactions

Since CPU requirements are so hard to estimate, you could use some of the following methods to arrive at a suitable CPU configuration:

❏ Consider the CPU requirements of similar systems. A similar system is one with a similar transaction type (e.g., OLTP or OLAP), transaction rate, network model (e.g., client/server or batch), data volumes, and application characteristics.

❑ Measure the CPU requirements of your application before acquiring hardware. It may be possible to defer hardware acquisition until after volume testing. In this case, you may be able to measure the CPU requirements of the system in a test environment and extrapolate those requirements to a production configuration.

❑ Benchmark test your system on multiple hardware configurations. If your system is likely to require a substantial hardware investment, or if your organization is a significant client, vendors will often be willing to make hardware available for benchmark testing. You'll need to develop a simulation of your application, and this may not be trivial. However, the vendor will often provide access to performance tuning experts, and at the conclusion of the benchmark test you should have a good idea of your application's CPU requirements.

❑ Acquire a configuration with room for growth. The majority of large-scale Oracle applications are currently implemented on Symmetric Multi-Processor (SMP) UNIX minicomputers with the capacity for multiple CPUs. Windows based servers are also available that allow for multiple CPUs. By acquiring a machine with the capability to add more CPU capacity, you insure against the possibility that the initial configuration may have insufficient CPU capability. You may have to buy more CPUs, but you will not have to replace the entire host computer.

Improvement Gained by Adding More CPUs   As more CPUs are added to an SMP machine, the overhead of coordination between the multiple CPUs increases. This means that a diminishing return is obtained as more CPUs are added. Moving from a single CPU to two CPUs may result in an almost doubling of processing capacity. However, moving from four to eight CPUs might result in only a 50% improvement (see Figure 19.3).

Because of the scalability deficiencies of multi-CPU systems, it is better to have a smaller number of more powerful CPUs than to have a large number of less powerful CPUs. Don't assume that doubling the number of CPUs will double the processing capacity.

THE NETWORK

For many application architectures, particularly distributed database designs and client/server systems, the configuration of the network can have a major influence on overall application performance. The emerging significance of the internet as a universal wide area network can also sometimes affect performance.[2]

---

[2]It is becoming unusual for SQL to traverse the Internet. A few years ago, it was envisaged that JDBC-enabled Java applets would reside on the browser and retrieve data directly from the database. This paradigm has almost completely given way to a three-tier architecture in which a middle tier (application server or servlettes within the Web server) communicates with the database and renders the resulting information in HTML or XML.

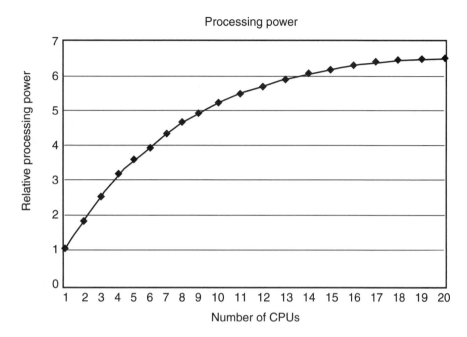

FIGURE 19.3 Scalability provided by multiple CPUs.

The network can affect application performance in one of two ways:

❑ The time taken for a single network packet to be transmitted between two hosts (latency) strongly affects response time.
❑ The amount of data that can be transmitted between two hosts in a given unit of time (bandwidth).

As with CPU requirements, it is can be difficult to calculate network requirements before a system has been built and measured, and a detailed examination of network issues is beyond the scope of this book. Therefore, a similar approach to CPU sizing is recommended:

❑ Determine the network requirements of your system. When client and server programs share a single host, the network component will be minimal. Client/server applications may generate a moderate network component. Distributed databases and applications that transfer large quantities of data in bulk will have a high network component.
❑ Model your network requirements. A single SQL*NET packet is usually 2K in size. If you can determine how many packets are going to be transferred between two hosts, then you are in a good position to present bandwidth requirements to networking experts.

❑ Consider the requirements of similar systems.

❑ Talk to vendors and networking experts.

❑ Benchmark test or trial your application.

❑ Configure a solution with room for growth.

ESSENTIAL CONSIDERATIONS FOR DATABASE CONFIGURATION

Having ensured that the host computer is suitably configured to support the resource demands of your application, you are now in a position to design a high-performance Oracle database. Before you build your database, there are certain key configuration decisions that you need to consider.

DETERMINING PROCESSING CHARACTERISTICS

First, ensure that you have a clear understanding of the processing characteristics of the applications that are to run on your high performance database. For instance,

❑ Is the database being used for on-line transaction processing or is the database more suited to long-running queries?

❑ Will there be overnight batch loads?

❑ How many on-line users will be required?

❑ Will there be large sorts?

❑ What are your backup requirements?

Most of the recommendations in this chapter are based on the assumption that the database will be subject to long-running queries, on-line transactions, and bulk loads. In other words, the recommendations are for a database that is ready for anything.

AVAILABILITY REQUIREMENTS

High availability is becoming the norm for many computer systems, and Oracle databases are no exception. You need to have a clear understanding of the uptime requirements for your database. If even short downtimes are unacceptable, you'll probably want to consider fault-tolerant disk devices and consider Oracle fail-over offerings or even Oracle Parallel Server (OPS).

From a performance point of view, the higher the level of availability, the more essential it becomes to determine correctly your configuration since it may be difficult or impossible to change these without an outage. In particular,

❏ Storage clauses for schema objects need to be optimal, since it may be impossible to rebuild these objects with changed configurations later.

❏ Instance parameters that require a database restart need to be set correctly.

❏ Decisions regarding filesystem types and disk configurations might be impossible to change after the database is in production.

BACKUP STRATEGY

The backup mechanism selected for your database has a significant influence on its optimal configuration. Oracle allows database backups to occur when the database is on line and allows a database to be restored to any point in time. To enable the on-line backup and point-in-time recovery, the database must be running in archivelog mode.

Archivelog mode requires that redo logs be copied to a separate location (the archivelog destination) as they are filled. This involves additional I/O on redo log devices and on the archivelog destination. If a redo log file needs to be reused before it has been archived, then the database operations will suspend until the archive completes. It's therefore essential that archive logging is optimized and that bottlenecks and processing interruptions are avoided.

Before designing the high-performance database, it's wise to determine the backup requirements of the database. If in doubt, assume that archivelog mode will be enabled.

DATABASE BLOCK SIZE

The database block is the smallest unit of Oracle storage. Datafiles, buffer cache entries, tables, and almost all Oracle structures are composed of database blocks. The size of the database blocks is set when the database is created and cannot be changed thereafter unless the database is re-created.

Oracle recommends that the database block size be set to a multiple of your operating system block size. However, the default value is often substantially less than the block size used by the operating system.

For a high-performance database system, ensure that the database block size is at least the size of the operating system block size. Because operating system I/O on partial blocks can be very inefficient, it might be slower to process a 2K block than an 8K block if the filesystem block size is 8K. On many UNIX operating systems, the operating system block size is 8K. On Windows, the block size is 4K.

Ensure that your database block size is at least as large as your operating system block size.

Increasing the block size beyond the operating system block size will be most beneficial for applications that frequently perform full-table scans, since the number of I/Os required to scan the table may be reduced. For OLTP applications, smaller block sizes (but not usually below the operating system block size) are recommended, since most table accesses will be via an index that will only be retrieving a single row. For very large databases, increasing the block size will reduce the height of the B*-tree index, giving potential improvements to both table scans and index lookups.

OPTIMIZING DATABASE I/O

OPTIMIZING DATA FILE I/O

Oracle server processes read from database files when a requested data item cannot be found within the Oracle buffer cache. Waiting for data from disk is one of the most common reasons for delays experienced by server processes, and so any reduction in these delays will help improve performance.

Writes to the database files are made on behalf of the user by one or more database writer (DBWR) processes. These I/Os are random in nature. Although user processes do not wait for DBWR to complete its writes on their behalf, if DBWR falls behind sufficiently the Oracle buffer cache will fill up with "dirty" blocks and waits will occur when user processes try to introduce new blocks into the cache.

Optimizing datafile I/O can be achieved by

❑ Getting a good hit rate in the buffer cache
❑ Striping datafiles across a sufficient number of disk.
❑ Optimizing database writer performance

Buffer Cache Hit Rate   If a data block requested for read is already in the buffer cache, then a disk read will be avoided. Avoiding disk reads in this manner is one of the most significant optimizations that can be made to an Oracle database. In the next chapter, we'll see how to monitor database hit rates. If the hit rate is low or the absolute number of disk reads too high, then increasing the size of the buffer cache can significantly improve disk performance.

We speak more on sizing the buffer cache later in this chapter and on monitoring buffer cache performance in Chapter 20.

Reduce your disk read overhead by adequately sizing your buffer cache.

REDO LOG CONFIGURATION

When a transaction is committed, a physical write to the redo log file must occur. The write must complete before the commit call returns control to the user; and hence, redo log writes can provide a limit to throughput of update intensive applications.

Redo log I/O will be optimized if the log is on a dedicated device and there is no contention for the device. If this is achieved, then the disk head will already be in the correct position when the commit is issued and write time will be minimized (the disk won't need to "seek").

Since the log writes are sequential and are performed by the logwriter processes only, there is little advantage in striping. Since LGWR is write-only to these devices, the performance degradation caused by RAID 5 is likely to be most significant, even if the volume is dedicated to redo logs (because of contention with the archiver process).

To insure against any loss of data in the event of a media failure, the redo logs must be mirrored. Oracle provides a software mirroring capability (redo log multiplexing), although hardware mirroring (RAID 1) is nearly always more efficient.

To maximize transaction processing performance, locate redo logs on a fast dedicated disk device.

Because switching between redo logs results in a database checkpoint, and because a log cannot be reused until that checkpoint is completed, large and numerous logs can result in better throughput. By increasing the number of logs, we reduce the possibility that a log will be required for reuse before its checkpoint is complete. By increasing the size of the logs, we reduce the number of checkpoints that must occur.

The optimal size for your redo logs will depend on your transaction rate. You will want to size the logs so that log switches do not occur too rapidly. Since you will usually allocate dedicated devices for redo logs, there is likely to be substantial disk capacity available for logs. It's often easiest to overconfigure the log size and number initially. Log sizes of 64MB to 256MB are not uncommon. Configuring up to 10 to 20 redo logs is also not unusual.

OPTIMIZING ARCHIVING

Archived logs are copies of on-line redo logs that can be used to recover a database to point of failure or another point in time after a backup has been restored. Archive logging is also required if on-line backups are desired.

Once a redo log file is filled and Oracle moves to the next log file, the archiver process (ARCH) copies the recently filled log to an alternate location. If the archiver reads from a log on the same physical device as the current log being written, then the sequential writes of the log writer will be disrupted. If the log writer falls sufficiently behind, then the database may stall since a log file cannot be reused until it has been archived.

It is therefore important to optimize the performance of the archiver. Alternating redo logs over two devices can minimize contention between the archiver and the log writer. The redo log writer can write to one device while the archiver is reading from the other device. Since the archiver must be capable of writing at least as fast as the log writer, the archive destination should either be a dedicated device or a dedicated set of disks in a RAID 0 + 1 (mirrored and striped) configuration.

If running in archivelog mode and in a high-update environment, allocate an additional dedicated device (for a total of two) for the redo logs and another dedicated device (or devices) for the archive destination.

STRIPING AND RAID

We saw at the beginning of this chapter how the ultimate limit on I/O performance is dictated by the number of devices and the spread of data across these devices. You should first ensure that there is a sufficient number of disks to support your projected I/O rates. You should also ensure that data are spread as evenly as possible across these disks and that there are no disk hot-spots.

There are three ways to spread data across devices:

❑ RAID 0 or striping
❑ RAID 5
❑ Oracle striping

We discussed RAID 5 earlier in this chapter. Remember that RAID 5 can decrease write performance unless the RAID array is associated with a battery-backed memory cache—and often even then.

Generally, RAID 0 is recommended on performance grounds. If RAID 0 is not available, you should manually stripe your tablespaces across multiple devices. Manual or Oracle striping is achieved by allocating many small files to each tablespace and spreading these files across multiple disks.

Because a table extent must be located within a single database file, tables consisting of a single extent will not be able to be manually striped. In this case, you will probably want to ensure that heavily utilized tables (and indexes) are composed of a large number of extents. You may wish to reduce the size of your datafiles to that of a single extent (plus a one-block overhead).

Use some form of striping for your database files, but avoid RAID 5 unless your write activity is very low or the disk array has a nonvolatile cache. Oracle striping can be used if RAID 0 striping is not available.

ASYNCHRONOUS I/O

Asynchronous I/O allows a process to write to multiple devices simultaneously. Without asynchronous I/O, a process must wait for each I/O to complete before requesting the next I/O. As we shall see a bit later in this chapter, asynchronous I/O is probably the single most significant factor affecting database writer performance.

Asynchronous I/O is always available on Windows NT or Windows 2000. However, as we shall see, asynchronous I/O on UNIX usually requires the use of raw devices.

On Oracle8, you enable asynchronous I/O (provided that the operating system is correctly configured) with the DISK_ASYNCH_I/O parameter.

RAW PARTITIONS

A raw partition (or raw device) is an area of disk that has not been formatted as a filesystem and is not under the control of any filesystem layer. Oracle can write directly to the raw partition, bypassing the filesystem buffer and filesystem code layers.

Using raw partitions entails a significant administrative overhead and complicates database backup and configuration. Some of these disadvantages are alleviated by the use of Logical Volume Management software. However, raw devices offer significant performance advantages, especially on UNIX:

- ❏ Better multiblock read under UNIX. Multiblock read allows Oracle to read multiple blocks in a single Operating system read request. However, under most UNIX filesystems, this will be limited to the filesystem block size (usually 8K), while on raw devices 64 K to 1 MB can be read (depending on the OS type).
- ❏ In UNIX, updates to datafiles on UNIX filesystems often need to update UNIX inodes (a sort of directory entry). Because inodes are often located in the first blocks of the filesystem, they can become a hot spot, even when the filesystem is striped across multiple disks.

❑ On UNIX, true asynchronous I/O is not usually available unless the data is on a raw partition.[3] As we will see, asynchronous I/O is critical to optimal database writer performance.

❑ Filesystems have a significant overhead in terms of memory requirements, code path, and CPU. Removing this overhead can result in a 10 to 50% improvement in database I/O. This improvement can be seen on both Windows and UNIX platforms.

The use of raw partitions is a controversial topic in the Oracle community, and there is no clear consensus on the appropriate use of raw partitions. However, the following positions seem fairly well accepted:

❑ Where there is no bottleneck in the I/O subsystem, no improvement in application performance will be gained by a switch to raw devices.

❑ For heavily loaded, I/O-bound applications, some improvement in performance will be realized by the move to raw devices.

My personal preference is to implement raw devices for any performance critical database, especially under UNIX.

Under the UNIX or NT operating systems, consider the use of raw devices for databases with high I/O requirements.

OPTIMIZING THE DATABASE WRITERS

The database writer process (DBWR) is the only process that writes modified database blocks from the buffer cache to the database files. The database writer writes asynchronously. This means that a user process never needs to wait for the database writer write to complete. However, if the DBWR falls behind sufficiently, then the buffer cache will fill up with "dirty" blocks and waits will occur while user processes try to introduce new blocks into the cache.

Keeping the database writer optimized is therefore critical to maintaining database throughput. The best way to optimize database writer throughput is to spread I/O across multiple disk devices and allow the database writer to write to these disk devices in parallel.

The most effective way of parallelizing database writer activity is to enable asynchronous I/O, as described previously.

---

[3]It's true that on some operating systems, asynchronous I/O is offered even on filesystems. However, this is usually an emulation of asynchronous I/O using threads and is significantly inferior to the real thing.

If asynchronous I/O is not available, you can simulate it using the DBWR_ IO_SLAVES configuration parameter. This creates multiple slave processes that process I/O requests on behalf of the main database writer. This is bound to be less efficient than asynchronous I/O but will be better than a single database writer.

Even when asynchronous I/O is available, you can still configure multiple database writers using the DB_WRITER_PROCESSES parameter. This might be necessary on very high-throughput databases if you suspect that a single database writer is unable to fetch batches of dirty blocks from the SGA fast enough. This would probably only happen if the disk I/O subsystem was so fast (perhaps an EMC array with a large cache) that the DBWR bottleneck was shifted from disk I/O to SGA operations.

Optimize database writer performance by striping database files across multiple devices and enabling some form of parallel database write capability. Asynchronous or list I/O is preferred. If these facilities are not available, create multiple database writers with the DBWR_IO_SLAVES parameter.

ROLLBACK SEGMENT CONFIGURATION

The configuration of your rollback segments can have an important effect on the performance of your database, especially for transactions that modify data. Any operation that modifies data in the database must create entries in a rollback segment. Queries that read data that have been modified by uncommitted transactions will also need to access data within the rollback segments.

Poorly tuned rollback segments can have the following consequences:

❑ If there are too few rollback segments, transactions may need to wait for entries in the rollback segment.

❑ If rollback segments are too small, they may have grown dynamically during the transaction and later shrink back (if the rollback segment has an optimal size specified).

❑ Poorly tuned rollback segments can lead to transaction failure (failure to extend a rollback segment) or query failure ("snapshot too old").

The following guidelines may serve as a starting point for rollback segment configuration for a transaction processing environment:

❑ The number of rollback segments should be at least one-quarter of the maximum number of concurrently active transactions. In batch environments, this may mean allocating a rollback segment for each concurrent job.

❑ Set OPTIMAL or MINEXTENTS so that the rollback segment has at least eight extents. This minimizes waste and contention when a transaction tries to move into an already occupied extent.

❑ Make all extents the same size.

❑ Allow ample free space in the rollback segment tablespace for rollback segment expansion. Large, infrequent transactions can then extend a rollback segment when required. Use OPTIMAL to ensure that this space is reallocated when required.

It's difficult to determine the optimal setting for rollback segments by theory alone. Rollback segments should be carefully monitored and storage should be adjusted as required. We discuss ways of monitoring rollback segments in Chapter 20.

TEMPORARY TABLESPACES

As discussed in Chapter 10, a sort operation that cannot be completed in memory must allocate a temporary segment. Temporary segments may also be created to hold intermediate result sets that do not fit in memory. The location of these temporary segments will be determined by the TEMPORARY tablespace clause in the CREATE or ALTER USER command. You should always allocate at least one tablespace for temporary segments.

When creating a tablespace that holds these temporary segments, it is important to ensure that the TEMPORARY clause is applied. If temporary sort segments are created in a standard tablespace, then each sort will create a new temporary segment and, if the initial extent is not sufficient, allocate new extents as the sort proceeds. Allocating and extending these segments requires the session to obtain the space transaction (ST) lock, and it is not uncommon to see heavy contention for this lock when sort segments are not stored in TEMPORARY tablespaces.

The extent size in the temporary tablespace should be at least the same as the memory allocation provided by the SORT_AREA_SIZE parameter (plus one block for the segment header).

Make sure that the tablespace that holds temporary segments is created with the TEMPORARY clause of the CREATE TABLESPACE.

The temporary tablespace should be large enough to hold all concurrent temporary segments. If it is not, then errors may be returned to SQL statements that attempt to allocate additional space. It's not easy to predetermine how large disk sorts will be, so it may be necessary to refine your first estimates. You can measure the size of temporary segments using the V$SORT_SEGMENT view.

SIZING THE SGA

The size and configuration of the SGA can have a substantial effect on the performance of your database. This is not surprising, since the SGA exists primarily to improve performance by buffering disk reads and reducing the need for SQL statement parsing.

It's difficult to determine in advance exactly how large the various components of the SGA should be. In this section, we provide an overview of the components of the SGA and some general sizing considerations. In the next chapter, we'll see how we can monitor the usage of the SGA and amend its storage to improve performance.

BUFFER CACHE

As we saw earlier, the buffer cache area of the SGA holds copies of data blocks in memory to reduce the need for disk I/O. The following principles are relevant to the sizing of the buffer cache:

❑ You aim to size the buffer cache so that sessions rarely need to read data blocks from disk. In general, you should attempt to get a hit rate of 90% or better—this means that 90% of all read requests are satisfied from the cache without requiring a disk access.

❑ In general, the higher the rate of I/O activity, the greater your incentive to obtain a high hit rate. For instance, if your logical I/O rate is only 500 reads per second, then a hit rate of 90% translates into 50 reads/second, a rate that could be satisfied comfortably by two disk devices. However, if the logical I/O rate is 5000 reads/ second, then the physical I/O rate associated with a 90% hit rate will be 500 reads/second, which will probably overtax a disk configuration under 12 or more disks. In this case, you might need to aim for a hit rate of 95% or better.

❑ Applications that perform frequent full table scans of very large tables are unlikely to achieve a good hit rate in the buffer cache.

❑ Adjusting the size of the buffer cache is one of the most fundamental tuning options. You need to ensure that there is enough free memory on your system to allow for an increase if required.

Buffer cache sizes vary depending on application characteristics and I/O rates. Many applications get good performance from a buffer cache as small as 10 MB. High-performance applications may have buffer caches of 50 to 100 MB, and caches of over 200 MB are not rare.

KEEP AND RECYCLE POOLS

Oracle8 allows you to partition the buffer cache into three pools. Each pool has a separate allocation of memory and a separate set of LRU latches. Each segment in the database can be allocated to one of the three pools.

The multiple pools serve two important purposes:

❑ They help ensure that critical lookup table data remain in memory.
❑ They help ensure that blocks from large "one-off table" scans do not displace blocks that are more likely to be required in the future.

To understand the rationale for the multiple pools, it's necessary to understand the algorithms that Oracle employs in its attempt to keep the most frequently accessed blocks in the cache.

Oracle uses a modified LRU (least-recently used) algorithm to determine which blocks are retained in the cache. This algorithm has the following features:

❑ When a block is read from an index lookup, a small table scan (<5 blocks), or a table scan of a larger table that has the CACHE attribute set, the blocks are placed in the middle of the LRU list. If necessary, blocks that are on the LRU end of the list are flushed from the cache to make way for the new blocks.
❑ As blocks in the cache are accessed, they tend to move toward the MRU (most recently used) end of the list.
❑ Blocks read from table scans of large (>5 blocks) tables where the CACHE setting was not in effect are placed immediately on the LRU end of the list and are therefore subject to being flushed out almost immediately.

This algorithm attempts to retain in memory those blocks that are most likely to be reused. The KEEP pool allows you to nominate an area of memory for blocks that, although obtained through table scans or relatively infrequently accessed, should be kept in memory. The RECYCLE pool nominates an area reserved for blocks that will probably not be required again even though they may have been obtained by small table scan or index lookup.

By setting up KEEP and RECYCLE pools, you help ensure that the hit rate in the remaining pool —DEFAULT—is not affected by one-off scans and that certain data that you know will be required again will remain in memory.

The BUFFER_POOL_KEEP and BUFFER_POOL_RECYCLE parameters control the size and number of LRU latches for each pool. You can assign tables to the appropriate pool using the BUFFER_POOL option of the storage clause.

SHARED POOL

The shared pool is another large and performance-critical area of memory held in the SGA. The major components of the shared pool are as follows:

❑ The library cache, which stores parsed representations of SQL and PL/ SQL blocks. The purpose of the library cache is to reduce the overhead of parsing SQL and PL/SQL by the caching and sharing of parsed SQL statements.

❑ The dictionary cache (sometimes called the row cache) caches data dictionary information. The data dictionary contains information about the database objects, users and other information defining the database. Because the data dictionary is referenced so frequently, it is cached separately in this special area.

The size of the shared pool is determined by a single database configuration parameter (SHARED_POOL_SIZE) and the individual components of the shared pool cannot be separately sized. As with the buffer cache, it's not possible to determine the exact optimal size in advance. It's often necessary to monitor and adjust the shared pool until the optimal setting is found.

The following considerations are relevant when sizing the shared pool:

❑ The default value for the shared pool tends to be too small for many applications.

❑ If your application makes extensive use of large PL/SQL stored packages, your shared pool requirements will be higher.

It's not uncommon for shared pools of 100 MB or higher to be allocated, although smaller allocations may also be adequate.

THE LARGE POOL

The large pool is an area in memory used to store large memory allocations. It is primarily intended for session-specific information for sessions that are supported by multi-threaded servers (MTS) or through Oracle's XA interface for TP monitors.

You configure a large pool by setting a value for LARGE_POOL_SIZE. Memory larger than the value set by the parameter LARGE_POOL_MIN_ALLOC will be allocated within the large pool.

Using a large pool is recommended when you are using multithreaded servers to ensure that session memory does not push out SQL and PL/SQL statements from the shared pool.

JAVA POOL

The Java pool maintains memory used by the Java Virtual Machine (JVM) that is included within the Jserver option of Oracle8i. If you are not using Java stored procedures, enterprise Java Beans or any of the other features included in the

Jserver option, you can set JAVA_POOL_SIZE to 0.[4] If you are using Java, you will probably need to set it to at least 50 MB during installation of the Java option, after which 20 MB seems to be adequate for casual use.

REDO BUFFER

The redo buffer contains redo entries destined for the redo log. The redo log is flushed periodically or when a COMMIT occurs. Unlike the other areas in the shared pool, it is not wise to oversize the redo buffer. If the redo buffer is too large, the log writer process may have to work harder when a flush is required.

The log buffer is normally flushed when it reaches one-third of its capacity or when a COMMIT occurs. If the COMMIT occurs when the log buffer is almost one-third full, then the COMMIT will have to wait while I/O is performed to flush the buffer. Generally speaking, we want COMMITs to wait on only a single I/O, and therefore we would size the log buffer at about three times the maximum write I/O size for the operating system. So if the maximum write size on your system was 64K, then a log buffer of 192K would be optimal.[5]

MULTITHREADED SERVERS

Without multithreaded servers, each Oracle session will usually acquire a dedicated server process.[6] If MTS is enabled, processes can share servers. This reduces the overall number of server processes required. Figure 19.4 illustrates the architecture.

If implemented appropriately, MTS can reduce the overall memory requirements for an Oracle implementation. In some circumstances, implementing MTS may avoid Oracle internal bottlenecks by reducing the number of server processes competing for limited resources. However, if implemented inappropriately, MTS can have a negative effect on performance. If user processes must wait for a server or dispatcher process to become available, then performance will degrade substantially.

Before implementing MTS, you need to make two decisions:

---

[4]In 8.1.5, you cannot set it lower than 1 MB due to a bug.

[5]If you really must have a larger log buffer, you can set the undocumented parameter _LOG_IO_SIZE to specify the threshold that triggers a flush.

[6]VMS is the notable exception, where the system architecture allows client and server code to safely coexist in a single process.

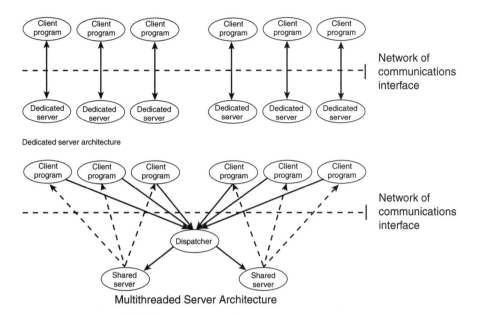

FIGURE 19.4 Multithreaded server architecture and dedicated server architecture.

❏ Is MTS appropriate for your application?
❏ What is the optimal user to server process ratio?

MTS is suitable for interactive applications, since an interactive application will involve a substantial amount of "think time" while the user assimilates data, decides upon a course of action, or is simply busy typing. With these applications, high user to server ratios will be possible, since server processes will usually be idle. On the other hand, applications that are continually busy, such as intensive batch processing or data loads, will tend to consume all the resources of a dedicated server and so will not benefit from shared servers.

If it's decided that MTS is appropriate, the user to server ratio will depend on the estimated proportion of time that user processes are idle, at least in terms of database activity. If you expect your processes to be idle 90% of the time, you might consider implementing one shared server per 10 users. The number of dispatchers will usually be less than the number of servers—a ratio of one dispatcher per 5 to 10 servers might be appropriate.

In the next chapter, we'll see how the server processes can be monitored and these ratios adjusted. In Appendix D, configuration parameters that affect MTS are defined.

PARALLEL QUERY PROCESSES

Another important consideration is the configuration of parallel query processes to support parallel SQL. As we saw in Chapter 11, parallel SQL can contribute substantially to performance of individual queries. However, many environments are totally unsuitable for the parallel query option. For instance, a transaction processing environment is unlikely to benefit from the parallel query option—the transactions are unlikely to use table scans and parallelism is usually achieved by multiple sessions executing concurrently. However, parallel SQL may still be used in overnight batch processing where a few sessions must perform a great deal of processing in a short time.

Review the guidelines in Chapter 11 carefully to determine if parallel SQL is appropriate for your application. Then configure the number of parallel slaves appropriately. Guidelines for configuring the database for parallel processing are given in Appendix D.

SUMMARY

In this chapter, we've briefly reviewed the principles of Oracle database design for high-performance systems. These guidelines should help you construct an Oracle database that will provide a sound foundation for high-performance SQL. However, remember that database server configuration is not a replacement for tuning of SQL statements.

Ensuring that your host computer is appropriately sized is an essential prerequisite for good database and SQL performance:

❑ Memory requirements can be estimated fairly accurately from the size of your user population.

❑ The performance that can be obtained from your disk subsystem is essentially dependent on the number of disks allocated to your system and the technique used to spread datafiles across these disks. When determining disk requirements, remember that it's the number of disks—not the size of disks—which limits the I/O capacity of your system.

❑ RAID 5 arrays are an increasingly popular means of spreading disk I/O and economically providing fault tolerance, but have definite drawbacks for write-intensive Oracle databases. Redo logs should almost never be located on a RAID 5 array, and datafiles should be located on RAID 5 only if the database is predominantly read-only.

❑ It is far more difficult to accurately estimate CPU and network requirements for a system. Experience, expert vendor advice, and comparison with similar systems can help when formulating an initial estimate. Benchmark testing or simulations of your system can be used to obtain more accurate estimates. Ensuring that your configuration is capable of growth is usually a wise decision.

When building a high-performance database, ensure that there is no inherent contention for resources and that all processing flows within the database architecture are free to proceed full speed.

❑ Understand the uses to which the database will be put. Know the transaction types, timings, and backup strategy.

❑ Setting the database block size is an important decision, and the block size cannot be changed easily after the database is created. Choose a block size that is at least as big as your operating system block size. Decision support databases or data warehouses may benefit from a larger block size while transaction processing databases may benefit from a smaller block size.

❑ Redo log throughput is a critical factor for databases with high update rates (for instance, bulk updates and OLTP). Redo logs should be on a fast device with low contention. Ideally, at least one disk should be allocated exclusively for redo logs. Redo logs should not be located on RAID 5 devices.

❑ If the database is in archivelog mode, then best performance will be achieved if redo logs are alternated between two dedicated devices. The archivelog destination should also be on a dedicated device.

❑ Database files should be striped across multiple disks. RAID 5 may be an acceptable way of doing this for read-intensive databases, although RAID 0 + 1 will usually give better performance. If no striping or RAID technology is available, tablespaces can be manually striped.

❑ There should be separate tablespaces for system objects, rollback segments, tables installed by tools, and temporary segments. In addition, application tables and indexes should be in separate tablespaces. One effective way of arranging objects in multiple tablespaces is to do so in such a way that all extents in a tablespace are the same size. This eliminates free space fragmentation and improves performance and maintainability.

❑ Rollback segments should be configured so that there are sufficient rollback segments for concurrent transactions, as well as no need for rollback segment expansion in the event of normal transactions, but sufficient free space for expansion if an unusually large transaction is encountered.

❑ Multiple buffer pools can be used to optimize the overall hit rate by isolating frequently buffered blocks from scanned segments from segments unlikely to be revisited and from blocks retrieved by index scans.

❑ Create a temporary tablespace large enough to contain all concurrent temporary segments. In Oracle 7.3 and above, use the TEMPORARY keyword to optimize extent allocation and make the extent size a multiple of the SORT_AREA_SIZE+1 block. Before Oracle 7.3, make the extent size large enough so that sorts do not normally have to allocate a second extent.

❏ Implementing multithreaded servers can conserve operating system memory. However, if the demand for multithreaded servers exceeds the number available, then contention for the servers will occur and performance will diminish.

❏ Ensure that database writer performance is optimal. This involves ensuring an effective spread of database files across multiple disks and allowing the database writer to perform writes to multiple disks in parallel. On some operating systems, a single database writer can write in parallel using asynchronous or list I/O. On other operating systems, it will be necessary to configure multiple database writers using the DB_WRITERS parameter.

❏ On either UNIX or NT operating systems, consider the use of raw disk partitions instead of operating system filesystems for your database files and redo logs. Raw partitions are complex to administer and do not suit all applications, but applications with high I/O rates may benefit.

ORACLE SERVER TUNING

INTRODUCTION

If your SQL is poorly tuned, it will usually provide poor performance no matter how well tuned the database server might be. However, after your SQL is perfectly tuned, you may still be disappointed with its performance. A common cause of this poor performance at this stage is a bottleneck or inefficiency in the database server. If you configured your server using the guidelines introduced in Chapter 19, you will have reduced the chances of such bottlenecks occurring. Even so, a database server may require fine-tuning to match specific application requirements. If the initial configuration of the server was not perfect, server tuning may be able to detect or compensate for deficiencies in that initial configuration.

This chapter provides an Overview of Oracle server performance diagnosis and treatment. The topics covered are as follows:

❑ Monitoring the operating system to detect and remedy contention or resource shortages in memory, CPU, or disk subsystems

❑ An overview of Oracle processing flows architecture and the bottlenecks and inefficiencies that can develop

❑ Methods of monitoring an Oracle server

❑ Key efficiency indicators, which reveal the effectiveness of the various Oracle processes and memory stores

❑ Using Oracle wait events to detect bottlenecks and contention for key resources

❑ Advanced tracing options

❑ Other common Oracle performance problems and tuning opportunities

EVALUATING OPERATING SYSTEM PERFORMANCE

A good place to start when diagnosing a poorly performing Oracle system is to examine the load on the operating system. The operating system provides key resources such as CPU, memory, and disk I/O. By monitoring the operating system, we will be able to detect any shortfall in system resources (for instance, insufficient memory) or contention for resources (such as a hot disk).

OPTIONS FOR MONITORING THE OPERATING SYSTEM

Oracle is available on a wide range of operating systems and hardware platforms, and it's not possible to provide detailed guidance for them all. However, all modern operating systems provide some form of monitoring that can reveal the usage of computer resources. You should consult your operating system documentation for detailed descriptions of these tools.

"Standard" UNIX contains only minimal monitoring tools. Most UNIX versions will include a version of the sar (System Activity Reporter) program. This program can collect system performance indicators such as CPU, memory, and disk utilization. It reports only in text mode. Other UNIX systems may not include sar but will provide a program called vmstat, which can provide similar, although less comprehensive, performance statistics.

Because sar and vmstat are difficult to use and provide no graphical display, most vendors implement alternative performance monitors. Additionally, a character-based program called top is available on most UNIX systems, and provides summary performance information and a "top processes" display.

Windows NT and Windows 2000 provide a graphical performance monitor program that you will find in the "Administrative Tools (common)" folder on Windows NT and in the control panel under Windows 2000. Pressing control-alt-delete on Windows also gives access to the task manager, which can show resource utilization by process and show basic CPU and memory utilization.

As well as the aforementioned standard tools, there are third-party tuning and monitoring tools available for most of the operating systems, especially for variants of the UNIX operating system.

MEMORY BOTTLENECKS

A shortage of available memory on a host computer will usually lead to severe performance degradation.

Most host operating systems (Netware is a notable exception) support *virtual memory*, which allows the memory accessed by processes to exceed the actual memory available on the system. The memory in excess of actual memory is stored on disk. Disk accesses are several orders of magnitude slower than memory accesses, and so applications that need to access virtual memory located on disk will typically experience significant performance degradation.

When a process needs to access virtual memory that is not in physical memory, a *page fault* occurs and the data is retrieved from disk (usually from a file known as the swapfile or from the program's executable file) and loaded into main memory. If free physical memory becomes very short, most operating systems will look for data in main memory that have not been accessed recently. The operating system will move the data from main memory to the swapfile until sufficient free memory is available. The movement of data between the swapfile and main memory is known as paging.

The *scan rate*, a standard metric under UNIX, reveals the rate at which the operating system searches for memory to page out of the system. Increases in the scan rate can indicate increasing pressure on available memory.

If free physical memory becomes very short, the operating system may move an entire process out of main memory. This is known as swapping. Any level of swapping is usually a sign that a memory shortage has reached the crisis point. However, note that in many modern variants of UNIX and Windows, a more efficient algorithm, which involves deactivating the process and allowing the standard algorithms to move the data out of memory, has replaced the swapping algorithm.

Acceptable levels of swapping, paging, and free memory vary between operating systems. However, the following principles apply to most operating systems:

- ❑ There should be no swapping.
- ❑ Paging activity should be low and regular. Sudden peaks of paging activity may indicate a shortage of memory.
- ❑ There should be sufficient free physical memory for all database processes and the Oracle SGA. Although virtual memory allows the computer to continue operation when all physical memory has been exhausted, the cost in performance terms is usually too high.

Options for Treating Memory Shortages   If monitoring of the operating system leads to the conclusion that memory resources are inadequate, two remedies are available:

❑   Acquire additional memory.
❑   Reduce memory consumption.

If acquiring additional memory is not an option, we can attempt to reduce Oracle's memory consumption, as follows:

❑   Reduce parameters that control the size of the Oracle server processes. The two main options are SORT_AREA_SIZE and HASH_AREA_SIZE. These parameters control the amount of memory allocated for sorts and hash joins. If they are set unnecessarily high, memory may be wasted.
❑   Reduce the size of the SGA. It's possible that the buffer cache or shared pool is oversized and wasting memory. If you aren't using Java, make sure that JAVA_POOL_SIZE is set to 0 or (8.1.5 only) 1 MB.
❑   Reduce the number of server processes. This can be achieved by implementing shared server processes (multithreaded servers, discussed in Chapter 19). This may be an effective way of reducing memory requirements but may backfire if performance degrades because of contention for the shared servers.

If you observe a shortage of free memory, swapping, or excessive paging, you probably have a memory bottleneck. Acquire more memory or take action to reduce memory requirements.

I/O BOTTLENECKS

Disk I/O bottlenecks are also a common cause of poor database performance. Disk I/O bottlenecks occur whenever the disk subsystem cannot keep up with read or write requests. This may be recognized from a number of performance metrics:

❑   Disk % busy. If a disk is perpetually more than 50% busy, then it is likely that I/O requests to that disk are being delayed.
❑   Disk queue length. This is a measure of the number of requests queued against the disk and should not average more than one or two. If the queue is long but the disk is not busy, then the bottleneck may reside in the disk controller rather than the disk itself.

If you perceive that a particular disk is forming a bottleneck, the action depends on the types of files stored on the disk.

❑   If the disk contains Oracle database files, you should attempt to spread the files across multiple disk devices. The options for spreading I/O were discussed in Chapter 19 and include using RAID, operating system striping, or Oracle striping.

❑ If the disk contains redo logs, ensure that no other active files exist on the same device. If you're in archivelog mode, alternate redo logs across multiple devices to eliminate contention with the archiver process.

❑ If the disk contains archived redo logs, ensure that there is no process competing with the archive process for the device. It's common for this device to become very busy in bursts because when a log is archived, the archiver will copy the log to the archive destination in one operation.

Don't forget that if your SQL is poorly tuned, it may be generating excessive I/O requirements. Make sure that SQL is well tuned before shifting disks around.

Ensure that no disk devices are forming a bottleneck for your system. Spread data files across multiple devices and ensure that the redo logs are on fast dedicated devices.

CPU BOTTLENECKS

In a well-tuned Oracle database, memory and disk resources do not form a bottleneck. As load on such a database increases, the CPU becomes the critical resource and eventually no further increases in throughput are possible due to CPU limitations.

In one sense, such CPU bottlenecks are healthy, since they indicate that other subsystems are not constraining performance and that all available CPU can be used. However, excessive CPU utilization can also indicate that the application or Oracle is performing inefficiently. Possible causes of excessive CPU requirements in Oracle are as follows:

❑ **Inefficient SQL.** SQL that has excessive I/O requirements will not only tax the I/O subsystem but may also heavily load the CPU. This is because most of the overhead of Oracle logical I/O occurs in memory, and the manipulation of Oracle shared memory is a CPU-intensive operation.

❑ **Excessive sorting.** Sorts can be very CPU intensive. If your application performs very frequent in-memory sorts, then it may result in a CPU bottleneck. It may be possible to reduce this overhead by eliminating accidental sorts or using indexes to retrieve rows in the desired order. These issues are discussed in Chapter 9.

❑ **Excessive parsing.** We discussed the overheads of SQL statement parsing in Chapter 4. Applications which discard SQL cursors or that force reparsing by using literals instead of bind variables which cause Oracle to perform

CPU-intensive parse operations more frequently. Later in this chapter, we will see how to measure the degree and cost of the parse overhead. Guidelines for implementing cursor reuse and bind variables for various development tools are given in Appendix C.

If your application is CPU bound, you have the option of either increasing the amount of available CPU or reducing the demand for CPU. You may be able to add CPUs to your system or upgrade your CPU to a faster model. Keep in mind that the improvement gains realized by adding CPUs diminish as more CPUs are installed. It is usually better to have faster CPUs rather than more CPUs.

To reduce the CPU requirements of your application, tune the application's SQL and minimize unnecessary reparsing by using bind variables and performing efficient cursor management (Appendix C).

If your application is CPU bound, consider reducing CPU load by tuning SQL or eliminating unnecessary parsing. If adding CPU, remember that the benefit of additional CPUs diminishes as the number of CPUs added increases.

If your database server has multiple CPUs, it's possible that individual processes can become CPU bound even if the system as a whole is not. Since a single process can only make use of a single CPU, a single process blocked on a CPU will only consume 25% of the CPU resources of a four-CPU machine. If you detect or suspect that a process is blocked in this manner, you could try and parallelize the operation, either by using parallel SQL (Chapter 11) or by parallelizing the application (Chapter 18).

RECOGNIZING ORACLE DATABASE BOTTLENECKS

ORACLE PROCESS FLOWS

Effective operation of the Oracle database depends on an efficient and unconstricted flow of SQL and/or data between user processes, Oracle processes, Oracle shared memory, and disk structures. Figure 20.1 illustrates some of these process flows.

In Chapter 19 we briefly defined the components of the Oracle architecture, such as database files, redo logs, and the SGA. Refer to that chapter if you are unsure of the definition of any of those items.

In the following discussion, we make frequent references to "latches." These are Oracle internal locks that prevent processes from concurrently updating the

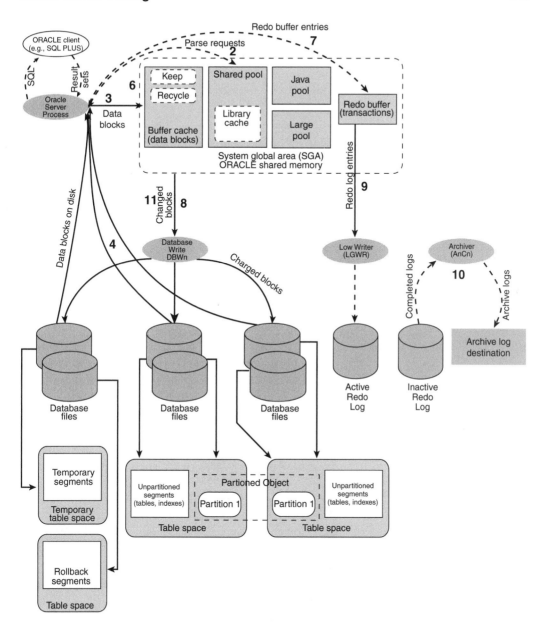

FIGURE 20.1 Oracle process flows.

same area within the SGA. We will elaborate on the use of latches and latch contention later in this chapter.

To understand the process flows within an Oracle instance, consider the following short SQL transaction:

```
select * from employees
 where employee_id=:1
   for update of salary;

update employees
   set salary=:2
 where employee_id=:1;

commit;
```

The numbered labels in Figure 20.1 correspond to the following activities:

1. The client program (SQL*PLUS, Visual Basic, Java program, or some other tool) sends the SELECT statement to the server process.
2. The server process looks in the shared pool for a matching SQL statement. If none is found, the server process will parse the SQL and insert the SQL statement into the shared pool. Parsing the SQL statement requires CPU, and inserting a new statement into the shared pool requires a latch.
3. The server process looks in the buffer cache for the data blocks required. If found, the data block must be moved on to the most recently used end of the least recently used (LRU) list. This, too, requires a latch.
4. If the block cannot be found in the buffer cache, then the server process must fetch it from the disk file. This will require a disk I/O. A latch must be acquired before the new block can be moved into the buffer cache.
5. The server process returns the rows retrieved to the client process. This may involve some network or communications delay.
6. When the client issues the UPDATE statement, the process of parsing the SQL and retrieving the rows to be updated must occur. The UPDATE statement then changes the relevant blocks in shared memory and updates entries in the rollback segment buffers.
7. The UPDATE statement will also make an entry in the redo log buffer, which records the transaction details.
8. The database writer background process copies modified blocks from the buffer cache to the database files. The Oracle session performing the update does not have to wait for this to occur.
9. When the COMMIT statement is issued, the log writer process must copy the contents of the redo log buffer to the redo log file. The COMMIT

statement will not return control to the Oracle session issuing the commit until this write has completed.

10. If running in archivelog mode, the archiver process will copy full redo logs to the archive destination. A redo log will not be eligible for reuse until it has been archived.

11. At regular intervals, or when a redo log switch occurs, Oracle performs a checkpoint. A checkpoint requires that all modified blocks in the buffer cache be written to disk. A redo log file cannot be reused until the checkpoint completes.

Our aim in tuning and monitoring the Oracle instance is to ensure that data and instructions flow smoothly through and between the various processes and that none of these flows becomes a bottleneck for the system as a whole. Monitoring scripts and tools can be used to detect any blockages or inefficiencies in each of the aforementioned processing steps.

COLLECTING PERFORMANCE DATA

To diagnose and remedy server bottlenecks, we need tools that can help us measure the load and efficiency of the various process flows:

❑ Monitoring tools, which are provided with the Oracle software
❑ Third-party commercial tools
❑ Home-grown and public domain tools

The V$ Tables   The ultimate source of Oracle instance performance information is the dynamic performance table (or V$ table). These are not true tables, but are instead representations of Oracle internal memory structures that can be queried using SQL. These tables contain a wealth of information from which we can derive significant performance information. However, using the V$ views directly requires some experience.

Further information about the V$ tables is contained in Chapter 17.

Oracle-supplied Tools   The Oracle distribution includes a pair of SQL scripts that can be used to collect useful SQL statistics for a time interval. The script utlbstat.sql is run at the commencement of the period of interest and the utlestat.sql is run at the end of the period. The utlestat script produces a report on changes in the values of significant columns in the V$ tables. While this information can be highly significant, the report provides little interpretation and reports mainly raw data.

The statspack—provided in Oracle 8.1.7 and also available from http://technet.oracle.com—works under the same principles as the utlbstat/utlestat scripts but has some powerful advantages. Most notably, it can automatically collect statistics at regular interval and calculates some useful performance ratios.

To use the statspack, run the script *statscre.sql*. Once this is done, you can collect a snapshot by running the *statspack.snap* PL/SQL routine. You can schedule regular collections by running the *statsauto.sql* script. To generate output from the statistical collections, run the *statsrep.sql* script.

Commercial Tools   There is a fairly active marketplace for Oracle server performance tuning tools. Oracle itself offers tuning and diagnostic packs that plug into Oracle Enterprise Manager and can collect and display performance statistics. Many other Oracle performance-tuning and monitoring products are available from companies such as Savant and BMC.

Since the first edition of this book was published, I have been working at Quest Software, where I designed and helped develop the Spotlight on Oracle product shown in Figure 20.2. This product shows a diagrammatic representation of the Oracle architecture and graphically represents any bottlenecks it represents. Behind the main screen, there is a wealth of diagnostic screens showing

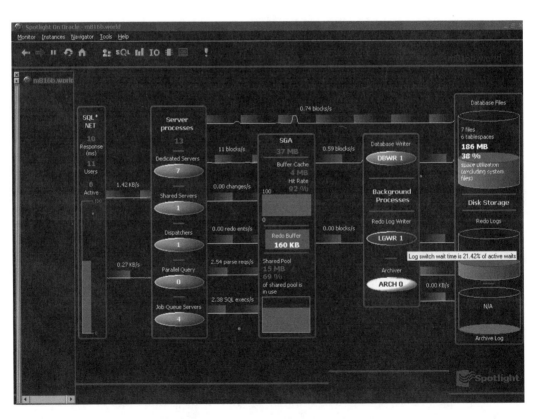

FIGURE 20.2   The Spotlight on Oracle product.

details of connected sessions, I/O, SGA utilitization, and resource-intensive SQL. Although as the architect of this product I am bound to be biased toward it, I can tell you that this product implements all of the monitoring principles outlined in this chapter. You can find out more about Spotlight at http://www.quest.com.

The Authors Tuning Scripts   Because the tools provided with a default Oracle instance are inadequate for detailed performance analysis, and because sophisticated third-party tool sets often are not available, many professionals develop their own tool kit for monitoring Oracle performance. This book's Web site includes my own tuning scripts developed for this purpose. With the advent of the Oracle statspack, it may be that these scripts will eventually be unnecessary. However, at the moment I prefer to use the scripts I have developed because they include reports not yet available in statspack.

The tuning scripts report against the contents of the V$ tables either overall or for a specific period. These scripts bear some similarity to the utlbstat and utlestat scripts provided by Oracle but also report significant performance ratios directly and attempt to flag significant or problem results. Two versions of each script are provided. Scripts ending in "stA" calculate statistics for the period since the database was last started. Scripts ending in "stS" calculate statistics for a sample time period, which you define using the samp_srt and samp_end scripts.

MONITORING LOAD

The performance of an SQL statement is often related to the overall load placed on an Oracle database. It is therefore important to have some idea of the average loads to which your Oracle instance is subjected. Some of the more frequently used measures of load are as follows:

- ❏ Logical I/Os per second. This is a measure of the number of requests for Oracle data blocks made by Oracle sessions.
- ❏ SQL executions per second. This statistic reflects the number of SQL statements submitted to the database each second. A related measure is the number of parse requests per second, which is the number of times a session requests an SQL statement be parsed.
- ❏ Transactions per second. This measure indicates the number of COMMIT or ROLLBACK statements issued each second.

Sudden changes in these load indicators may result if unusually resource-intensive ad hoc SQL is issued or if application usage patterns suddenly change. The degree to which these load indicators change after SQL tuning can also help you judge the effectiveness of your tuning. You can measure these rates through third-party monitoring tools, Oracle's statspack, or db_stA.sql /db_stS.sql scripts in my tuning scripts.

KEY EFFICIENCY RATIOS

Certain key ratios can be used to determine the efficiency with which the Oracle database is being used. For instance, the buffer cache hit ratio indicates the frequency with which required blocks are not found in the buffer cache and must be fetched from disk. A low value indicates an inefficient use of the SGA and potential for performance improvements.

The db_stA.sql or db_stS.sql scripts can report on these ratios. Figure 20.3 shows sample output from this script.

Buffer Cache Hit Rate This ratio describes the percentage of time a required data block was found in the buffer cache. For most applications, a value in excess of 90%—and often much higher—is desirable.

The buffer cache hit ratio is one of the most significant tuning ratios. Untuned values can lead to unnecessarily high disk I/O rates and contention for internal resources (latches).

To improve the buffer cache hit ratio, increase the size of the buffer cache by increasing the size of the DB_BLOCK_BUFFERS configuration parameter (see Appendix D).

Applications that perform frequent table scans of large tables may see little benefit from increasing the buffer cache. For these applications, low buffer cache hit ratios may be unavoidable.

To improve the buffer cache hit ratio, increase the number of buffer cache blocks with the DB_BLOCK_BUFFERS configuration parameter.

Using multiple buffer caches is also an effective way to improve the hit rate. As outlined in Chapter 19, multiple buffer caches allow you to provide separate areas of memory blocks retrieved from ad hoc and essentially nonrepeatable queries and for blocks retrieved from tables that, although accessed by table scan, are likely to be accessed again.

You can get an indication of the usage of each cache by examining the following report, which is shown at the end of the db_stA report:

```
Buffer pool analysis: M816B  22/05/00:21:24

sampled since database startup at 20/05:23:20

                      Logical   Physical    miss
Buffer      Blocks      Reads      Reads     rate
-------   ---------  ---------  ---------  -------
KEEP          100      31396      31183    99.32
RECYCLE       100       1995         16      .80
DEFAULT       350     583714     131485    22.53
```

```
Database efficiency indicators: MLBDB     22/05/00:19:51

      sampled since database startup at 28/04:10:46

NAME                                             Value
-------------------------------------    ------------
buffer cache hit ratio:                        98.4052
buffer hit ratio (index):                      99.9267
buffer hit ratio (scan):                       51.4728
dictionary cache hit rate:                     99.2303
library cache get hit ratio:                   96.8253
library cache pin hit ratio:                   99.2417

Immediate latch get rate:                      99.9806
Willing to wait latch get rate:                99.9911

buffer busy wait ratio:                         0.0001

chained fetch ratio:                            0.1208

CPU parse overhead:                             0.0004
parse/execute:                                 20.3094

redo space wait ratio:                          0.1528

disk sort ratio:                                0.5126

rows from idx/total rows:                      18.3777
short/total table scan ratio:                  91.5997
table scan phys IO/tot phys IO:                36.7161

DBWR Avg scan depth:                          728.3969
DBWR LRU free buffers:                        589.8731
DBWR summed scan/buffer scan:                   1.1998

sample time (h):                             1462.6931

SQL executions/sec:                             4.3503
checkpoint start/hour:                          0.3412
logical reads/sec:                            181.2436
physical reads/sec:                             2.8905
redo KB/sec:                                    0.9098
transactions/sec:                               0.0157

blk changes per transctn:                     370.1986
calls per transctn:                           153.6923
commits/(commits+rollbacks):                   99.8436
logical reads/exec:                            41.6627
rows per sort:                                112.1498
```

FIGURE 20.3 Output provided by the db_stA.sql and db_stS.sql scripts.

If you have correctly sized and assigned segments to each buffer pool, you would expect an excellent hit rate in the KEEP pool, a lower—but still high—hit rate in the DEFAULT pool, and possibly a low hit rate in the RECYCLE pool.

Index Buffer Cache Hit Rate   It's possible to determine a separate hit rate for indexed and table-scan based queries. This is shown in the db_stA report as follows:

```
NAME                                                Value
----------------------------------------    -------------
buffer cache hit ratio:                           98.4052
buffer hit ratio (index):                         99.9267
buffer hit ratio (scan):                          51.4728
```

The calculation for indexed and scan hit rates relies on comparing statistics held in separate V$ tables, some of which are updated at different times. This can render the calculations slightly inaccurate, especially if the sampling period is short. However, when accurate, the indexed hit rate can be a better indicator than the combined hit rate. This is because increasing the buffer cache is more effective at improving the performance of indexed lookups. You may be unable to improve the overall hit rate markedly when increasing the buffer cache size, but you might see significant improvements in the indexed query hit rate.

Library Cache Get Hit Rate   The library cache get hit ratio describes the frequency with which a matching SQL statement is found in the shared pool when an SQL parse request is issued by a session. If a matching SQL statement is not found in the library cache, then the SQL statement must be parsed and loaded into the library cache. Low hit rates will therefore result in high CPU consumption (from parsing) and possible contention for library cache latches (when the new SQL is loaded into the library cache). An acceptable rate for the library cache get hit rate is 90 to 95% or higher.

The most frequent cause of high miss rates in the library cache is the use of literals rather than bind variables in SQL statements. Bind variables reduce parse overhead by allowing otherwise identical SQL statements with different query parameters to be matched in the shared pool. However, bind variables preclude the use of column histograms and are not suitable in all circumstances. The trade-off between bind variables and histograms was discussed in Chapter 4.

To increase the get hit rate in the library cache, ensure that bind variables rather than literals are used in your SQL statements. But beware of disabling column histograms.

Library Cache Pin Hit Rate   A library cache pin miss occurs when a session executes an SQL statement that it has already parsed but finds that the statement is no longer in the shared pool. This will happen if the statement has been "aged out" of the library cache to make way for new SQL statements. We expect a very high ratio for the pin hit ratio, since we would hope that once parsed, an SQL statement stays in the shared pool if we continue to execute it.

Low values (below 99%) for the library cache pin hit ratio usually imply that the shared pool is too small and that SQL statements are being aged out of the library cache prematurely.

Dictionary Cache Hit Rate   The dictionary cache contains information about the structure of objects within the database. This information is frequently accessed during SQL statement parsing and during storage allocation.

The dictionary cache is stored in the shared pool, and low hit rates (below 95%) probably indicate that the shared pool is too small.

Low hit rates for the library cache pin hit ratio (<99%) or for the dictionary cache hit ratio (<95%) probably indicate that the shared pool is too small. Increase the size of the shared pool with the SHARED_POOL configuration parameter.

Latch Get Rate   Latches are Oracle internal locks that protect memory structures in the SGA. The latch get rate reflects the proportion of times that requests for latches are satisfied without waiting. Latch hit rates should be high, usually over 99%. For a detailed discussion, see the section on latches later in this chapter.

Chained Fetch Ratio   This ratio represents the number of times sessions attempting to read a row had to perform an additional read because the row had been chained to another block. This will occur when an update to a row causes the row length to increase, but there is insufficient free space in the block for the expanded row.

The typical cause of chained rows is an inadequate value for PCTFREE, which is the amount of space within a block reserved for updates. PCTFREE is discussed in detail in Chapter 8. You can find tables that contain chained rows with the ANALYZE TABLE command, which will store a count of the chained rows in the USER_TABLES view. Tables with chained rows may need to be rebuilt using a higher value for PCTFREE.

A high value for the chained fetch ratio (>0.1%) suggests a need to rebuild tables with a higher value for PCTFREE.

Parse Ratio   The parse/execute ratio reflects the ratio of parse calls to execute calls. Because parsing is an expensive operation, we hope that statements will be parsed once and then executed many times. High parse ratios (>20%) may result from the following circumstances:

❑   If literals rather than bind variables are used as query parameters, then the SQL will need to be reparsed on every execution. You should use bind variables whenever possible, unless there is a pressing reason for using column histograms (see Chapter 8).

❑   Some development tools or techniques result in SQL cursors being discarded after execution. If a cursor is discarded, then the parse will be required before the statement can be reexecuted.

❑   If an application is discarding cursors, it may be possible to relieve some of the parse overhead by creating a session cursor cache. This can be done by using the SESSION_CACHED_CURSORS configuration parameter. This setting allows Oracle to maintain a cache of SQL statements in the session memory. If a session requests a parse of a statement that it has already parsed previously, then it might be found in the cache and reparsing avoided.

❑   The cached cursor efficiency ratio shows the efficiency of the session cursor cache. It reflects the proportion of times that a parse request was satisfied from an SQL statement in the session cursor cache. If the parse ratio is high but the cached cursor efficiency is low, then it is likely that the high parse rate is caused by a failure to use bind variables.

CPU Parse Overhead   The CPU parse overhead describes the proportion of CPU time consumed by server processes due to the parsing of SQL statements. If this ratio is low, then reducing the parse ratio will probably not result in a significant performance boost. The higher the ratio, the more incentive you have to reduce parsing. The CPU parse overhead can be low even if the parse ratio is high—if the SQL being generated is very I/O intensive. In these circumstances, it may not matter that the statement is parsed every time.

If both the parse/execute ratio and the CPU parse overhead are high, then you have a strong incentive to reduce the parse overhead of your application. Use bind variables, reuse SQL cursors, or try enabling a session cursor cache.

Disk Sort Ratio   This ratio records the proportion of Oracle sorts that were too large to be completed in memory and that consequently involved sorting using a temporary segment. Disk sorts are probably unavoidable if your application performs sort merge joins, aggregation, or ordering of large tables. However, if your application performs only small sort operations, you can attempt to reduce the disk sort ratio by increasing SORT_AREA_SIZE. Only do this if you have spare memory capacity on your server computer.

> Consider increasing the value of SORT_AREA_SIZE if you have a high disk sort ratio.

Index Fetch Ratio This ratio describes the proportion of rows that were obtained via a ROWID lookup (almost always from an index scan) versus those retrieved from a full-table scan. The appropriate value for this statistic depends on your application. You should bear in mind that a single large scan can retrieve a large number of rows and hence disturb this ratio. However, in transaction processing environments, you will probably want the index fetch ratio to be high.

UNDERSTANDING ORACLE WAIT EVENTS

In a perfect Oracle implementation, the Oracle server process would be able to perform its tasks using its own resources without experiencing any delays. However, in reality, Oracle sessions often wait on system or database requests or for resources to become available.

Using our earlier example—where a session selected a row, updated it, and then committed—and using Figure 20.1, let's see where the server process might have to wait:

1. While the application is idle, the server process will be waiting for a message from the client.
2. When the server process parses a new SQL statement and the statement has not previously been executed, it will have to acquire a latch to add the new statement to the library cache. If the latch required is held by another session, then the server process may have to wait for the latch to become available.
3. The server process also has to acquire a latch when executing an SQL statement held in the shared pool and may have to wait on the latch if it is currently held by a different session.
4. When accessing a data block in the buffer cache, the server process will have to change the location of the block on the least recently used LRU list. This will require obtaining, and possibly waiting for, the appropriate latch.
5. If the block is not in the buffer cache, the session will have to issue and wait for an I/O request to obtain the block. Moving a new block into the buffer cache also requires a latch, which might be unavailable and cause a wait.
6. Changing the data block requires obtaining latches both to change the block itself and to make an entry in the redo log buffer. Additionally, if there is insufficient free space in the redo log buffer, the session will need to wait for the log writer process to make space available.
7. When a COMMIT is issued, the session will need to wait for the log writer process to write the blocks in question to the redo log file.

8. The log writer session itself may need to wait if the redo log is full and the next redo log has an outstanding checkpoint or archive operation.

We can see that there are many reasons why an Oracle session may need to wait. Some of these waits—such as waiting for I/O operations—are inevitable, although we can reduce them in many cases by tuning I/O, the buffer cache, or the SQL involved. Other operations, such as waiting for latches, can indicate inefficiencies in your configuration and opportunities for further tuning.

The wait_stA.sql and wait_stS.sql scripts report on the occurrences and duration of the various wait categories either for a sample period or since the database was last started. Figure 20.4 shows some sample output from this report. Waits that indicate idle sessions or no activity are excluded from the report. For the remaining waits, the report shows the number and duration (in 1/100ths of a second) for the waits both as an absolute value and as a percentage of total waits.

Db File Waits Wait conditions starting with the phrase "db file" (db file parallel write, db file scattered read, db file sequential read, or db file single write) all occur when an Oracle session issues an I/O request against an Oracle datafile. The session will use the operating system's read system call and wait while the I/O subsystem performs the I/O.

```
        Top ORACLE Wait events: MLBDB          23/05/00:19:59
           sampled since database startup at 28/04:10:46

                                              Time
                              No of  Pct of  Waited Pct of
Event name                    waits  Waits   (secs)  Time
---------------------------- ---------- ------ -------- ------
direct path write             3,801,138 16.31  111,905 78.29
db file parallel write           30,444   .13    8,038  5.62
db file sequential read         724,890  3.11    6,761  4.73
db file scattered read          413,969  1.78    6,284  4.40
control file sequential read    442,645  1.90    4,390  3.07
direct path read                235,039  1.01    1,623  1.14
refresh controlfile command      76,407   .33    1,564  1.09
log file parallel write         629,914  2.70      442   .31
SQL*Net more data to client   4,571,890 19.62      362   .25
log file switch completion          600   .00      343   .24
enqueue                           1,478   .01      275   .19
control file parallel write     718,813  3.09      250   .17
log file switch (checkpoint         359   .00      217   .15
incomplete)

log file sync                    42,920   .18       79   .06
```

FIGURE 20.4 Output from the wait_stA.sql script.

As noted earlier, database file writes are performed only by the database writer, and so db file write waits are never experienced by user sessions. User sessions do, however, read data from database files directly and will almost always experience db file read waits.

Unless your entire database is cached in memory, waiting for db file I/O is inevitable and the presence of db file waits does not indicate that anything is amiss within the database. In most healthy databases, db file waits can account for 80 to 90% of all nonidle wait times.

Db file waits can be reduced by

❑ Reducing the I/O requirements of SQL statements through SQL tuning
❑ Optimizing disk I/O and striping datafiles
❑ Reducing I/O requirements by increasing the size of the buffer cache

Log File Sync/Write Waits Just as Oracle sessions must inevitably wait for db file I/O, they must also wait for log file I/O. These waits occur when a COMMIT is issued. As revealed earlier, a COMMIT will cause the redo log writer session to flush the contents of the redo log to the redo file. The user session must wait for this write operation to complete before the COMMIT statement will return control.

The session issuing the COMMIT will wait on the *log file sync* event. When the log writer process issues the I/O request, it will wait on the *log file parallel write* event.

Both these wait events are inevitable and often account for 10 to 20% of total nonidle wait times in a healthy database.

The average wait time for a log file parallel write is an important measure. It indicates how quickly the log writer process can flush the redo buffer and is a good indicator of the efficiency of the redo log device. Values of 0.2 (hundredths of a second) are good, and values of up to 5 (hundredths of a second) are not unusual. Values above this range may indicate contention for the redo log device.

Log Buffer Space This wait occurs when a session needs to write a redo log entry but there is no space in the redo log buffer. You can reduce this wait by increasing the size of the log buffer (LOG_BUFFER parameter) or by optimizing the performance of the logwriter. Avoid making the log buffer too large, because the bigger the log buffer, the more I/Os will be required to clear it during a commit. Log buffers greater than 300K may cause degradation of COMMIT performance.

Log buffer space waits suggest that either the log buffer is too small or that the redo logfile layout is suboptimal.

Log File Switch Completion The event occurs when a session needs to write to the redo log but Oracle is in the process of switching the active log from one log file to another. If this wait is occurring frequently, then it probably means that your log files are too small and that log switches are therefore happening too often.

Log File Switch (Checkpoint Incomplete) This wait occurs when Oracle needs to switch to a new log, but the checkpoint that commenced when that log was filled has not completed. This usually means that your log files are too small or that there should be more of them.

Log File Switch (Archiving Needed) This wait occurs when Oracle needs to switch to a new log, but the log is still waiting for archiving. This might mean that your log files are too small or that there should be more of them. It might also indicate that the archiver process cannot archive as fast as the log writer can write logs, which implies that you should optimize archive logging as described in the previous chapter.

Log file switch waits for checkpoint, archiving, or completion can indicate that your redo log and archive log configuration needs improvement.

Buffer Busy Waits This event occurs when a session cannot access a needed block in the SGA because it is in use by another session. The two most common causes are insufficient free lists for a table or too few rollback segments.

You can distinguish between the two causes by considering the V$WAITSTAT table, displayed by the script busy_stA.sql/busy_stS.sql (see Figure 20.5). If the predominant waits are for data block or freelist, then it is likely that you need to create multiple FREELISTS (using the FREELIST clause of the CREATE or ALTER TABLE statement) for tables that are subject to heavy concurrent inserts. If the leading category is for either "undo header" or "undo block," then you may need to create additional rollback segments.

Since one of the classes in V$WAITSTAT is 'freelist', it's not surprising that many people have concluded that the freelist wait class—and only the freelist wait class—indicates that a table may require additional FREELISTS. In fact, freelist contention shows up as contention for 'data block'. Multiple sessions will obtain the same block from the single freelist and both will attempt to insert into that block. One of the sessions will then experience a 'buffer busy' wait on 'data block'.

Unless you have multiple freelist groups—typically only used in Oracle Parallel Server configurations—you will not experience any freelist buffer busy waits because freelists are housed in the segment header and not in a dedicated block.

"Buffer busy" waits usually indicate that heavily inserted tables should be recreated with multiple free lists or that there are insufficient rollback segments.

```
   ♀           Buffer busy statistics: MYDB      23/05/00:21:13
                 sampled since database startup at 15/05:11:14

                                                     Time
                                       Pct of      waited   Pct of
   Class                       Waits    waits         (s)     Time
   ------------------     ------------  -------  -----------  -------
   undo header                    45     8.36           2    58.79
   data block                    490    91.08           1    41.21
   sort block                      0     0.00           0     0.00
   save undo block                 0     0.00           0     0.00
   segment header                  2     0.37           0     0.00
   save undo header                0     0.00           0     0.00
   free list                       0     0.00           0     0.00
   undo block                      1     0.19           0     0.00
   extent map                      0     0.00           0     0.00
   bitmap block                    0     0.00           0     0.00
   bitmap index block              0     0.00           0     0.00
   unused                          0     0.00           0     0.00
   system undo header              0     0.00           0     0.00
   system undo block               0     0.00           0     0.00
```

FIGURE 20.5   Output from the busy_stA.sql script.

Free Buffer Waits   Free buffer waits occur when a session wishes to read a data block from a database file on disk into the buffer cache. If there are no un-modified ("clean") blocks in the buffer cache, then the session will have to wait for the database writer process to write modified ("dirty") blocks to disk in order for free buffers to be made available.

Normally, the database writer is constantly writing dirty buffers to disk, so this event should rarely occur. When it does occur, it is usually due to one of the following reasons:

❑   Untuned disk layout. If datafiles are not spread evenly across disk devices, then a single disk may form a bottleneck to both read and write perform-ance. In this circumstance, the database writer may not be able to clear dirty blocks from this device as rapidly as they are created.

❑   Untuned database writers. To write efficiently to multiple disk devices, you must either configure multiple database writers or implement asynchro-nous or list I/O, as discussed in Chapter 19. This will help the database writer keep up with changes to the buffer cache.

Write Complete Waits   This wait occurs when a session tries to modify a block that is currently being written to disk by the database writer process. This will, of course, happen occasionally; but if it is contributing significantly to overall waits, then it may indicate inefficiencies in the database writer. The treatment may involve optimizing datafile I/O and database writer configuration by spreading datafiles across multiple disks, using multiple database writers, or employing asynchronous or list I/O.

"Free buffer" and "write complete" waits often indicate inefficiencies in the database writer process or untuned disk I/O.

Enqueue Waits   Enqueue waits occur when a session waits to obtain a lock. In most cases, this will occur because of a lock on a table or row that the waiting session wishes to lock or modify. In some circumstances, the lock involved may be an Oracle internal lock. If the database is well tuned and the application design is sound, then enqueue waits should be negligible. Common causes of excessive enqueue waits are as follows:

❑   Contention for a specific row in the database. The application design may require that many processes update or lock the same row in the database. Once common example of this phenomenon is when primary keys are generated using a sequence table (see Chapter 11).

❑   Table locks caused by unindexed foreign keys. If an unindexed foreign key is updated, then the parent table will be subjected to a table lock until the transaction is complete. This was discussed in Chapter 9.

❑   "Old-style" temporary tablespaces. If the tablespace nominated as the temporary tablespace has not been identified with the TEMPORARY clause (introduced in Oracle 7.3), then sessions may contend for a space transaction lock.

❑   The space reserved for transactions within a data block is too small. By default, only one transaction slot for tables or two for indexes is allocated when the table or index is created. If additional transaction slots are required, they are created provided that there is free space in the block. However, if all transaction slots are in use and there is no free space in the block, then a session wishing to lock a row in the block will encounter an enqueue wait, even if the row in question is not actually updated or locked. This phenomenon can occur if both PCTFREE and INITRANS were set too low.

Enqueue waits occur when a process is waiting to obtain a lock. This may mean contention for specific rows in the database, table locks resulting from unindexed foreign keys, or contention for Oracle internal locks.

There is a widespread belief that setting a high value for ENQUEUE_RESOURCES can reduce waits for enqueues. However, this idea represents a fundamental misunderstanding of enqueues. An enqueue wait cannot complete until the party holding the required lock releases it. When the holding party releases the lock the waiting session will be notified immediately. The setting of ENQUEUE_RESOURCES therefore does not affect the duration of the wait.

If the setting for ENQUEUE_RESOURCES is very low, then a request for an enqueue may fail with an ORA-0052 "maximum number of enqueue resources exceeded" error.

Row Cache Lock Waits This wait event occurs when a session needs to update information in the data dictionary. The data dictionary contains information about the structure of the database, including tables, indexes, users, and storage allocation.

Row cache lock events should be negligible. They have been observed when sequences are created with the ORDER clause or NOCACHE clause. This causes each sequence access to write to the data dictionary and results in heavy loading on the row cache lock.

Latch Free Waits Latches are Oracle internal locking mechanisms that prevent multiple sessions from simultaneously updating the same item within Oracle shared memory (SGA). If a session needs to acquire a latch that is held by another session, then a latch free wait may occur.

The presence of latch free waits of any significant magnitude may indicate a bottleneck within the SGA. The specific action depends on the latch and is discussed in an upcoming section on latches.

Events That Are Safe to Ignore There are some events that occur when a session is idle or waiting for instructions and that are not significant from a performance point of view:

❑ NULL event
❑ SQL*NET message from client
❑ SQL*NET more data from client
❑ Parallel query dequeue wait
❑ Client message
❑ Smon timer
❑ Rdbms ipc message
❑ Pmon timer
❑ WMON goes to sleep
❑ Virtual circuit status
❑ Dispatcher timer
❑ Pipe get

LATCH WAITS

We saw in our example scenario that most operations that affect the contents of the SGA require that the process acquire a latch. A latch is similar to a lock, but instead of preventing two sessions from concurrently changing the same row, a latch prevents two sessions from altering the same area in shared memory at once.

Latches are usually held for a brief interval, and in a healthy database, there should be little or no contention for latches. Unfortunately, busy databases often suffer considerably from latch contention.

If a process requires a latch and cannot obtain it on the first attempt, a latch miss will result. The session will repeatedly attempt to obtain the latch up to the value of the configuration parameter spin_count. This technique is known as acquiring a spin lock. If the session still cannot obtain the latch, then the session will relinquish the CPU and a latch sleep will result. A latch sleep will be recorded as a latch free wait. When the session "wakes up," it will repeat the attempt to obtain the latch.

Problems obtaining latches will have already been revealed in the "latch get rate" section of the db_stA or db_stS report. This ratio records what proportion of latch requests could be satisfied on the first attempt.

Contention for latches is revealed by low overall latch get rates and by significant "latch free" waits. Both ratios should normally be less than 1%.

Latch problems will also be revealed by the wait_stA or wait_stS report. If latch free waits are significant—say, more than 1% of total waits—then there may be a latch contention problem.

If you observe indications of latch contention, run the latch_stA or the latch_stS report. This report will show the relative frequency of gets, misses, and sleeps for the various latches. Figure 20.6 shows some sample output from this report.

The latches that contribute to a high proportion of misses or sleeps deserve attention. Not surprisingly, the latches that are used most heavily and that therefore typically suffer the most contention are the latches associated with the three major areas of the SGA: the buffer cache latches, the library cache latches, and the redo buffer latches.

Buffer Cache Latches   Two main latches protect data blocks in the buffer cache. The *cache buffers lru chain* latch must be obtained in order to introduce a new block into the buffer cache and when writing a buffer back to disk. A *caches buffer chains* latch is acquired whenever a block in the buffer cache is accessed (pinned).

Contention for these latches usually typifies a database that has very high I/O rates. It may be possible to reduce contention for the *cache buffers lru chain* latch by increasing the size of the buffer cache, thereby reducing the rate at which new blocks are introduced into the buffer cache.

Reducing contention for the cache buffers chains latch will usually require reducing logical I/O rates by tuning and minimizing the I/O requirements of application SQL.

```
         ORACLE latch statistics:MYDB            23/05/00:21:42
                  sampled since database startup at 15/05:11:14


    Latch                            % of  % of  Sleep   Miss
    Name                     Gets    gets  Sleep rate%   rate%
    --------------------- ----------  ----- ----- ------  ------
    cache buffers chains     3.54E+08  68.1  59.3   0.00    0.03
    cache buffers lru chain  4.97E+07   9.6  31.7   0.01    0.35
    transaction allocation   5.72E+07  11.0   3.4   0.00    0.07
    library cache            9.51E+06   1.8   2.4   0.00    0.03
    Checkpoint queue latch   2.54E+07   4.9    .9   0.00    0.01
    cache buffer handles     7.10E+05    .1    .5   0.00    0.09
    messages                 4.20E+06    .8    .5   0.00    0.02
    shared pool              1.49E+06    .3    .4   0.00    0.02
    redo copy                5.89E+05    .1    .2   0.00    0.05
    redo allocation          9.01E+05    .2    .2   0.00    0.01
    row cache objects        7.16E+06   1.4    .2   0.00    0.01
    session allocation       1.41E+06    .3    .1   0.00    0.01
    virtual circuit buffers  6.41E+05    .1    .1   0.00    0.22
    session idle bit         2.26E+06    .4    .1   0.00    0.00
    redo writing             7.20E+05    .1    .0   0.00    0.01
    enqueues                 8.60E+05    .2    .0   0.00    0.00
    virtual circuit queues   5.30E+05    .1    .0   0.00    0.01
```

FIGURE 20.6   Latch statistics report from ltch_stA.sql.

You can create additional cache buffers lru chain latches by adjusting the configuration parameter DB_BLOCK_LRU_LATCHES.

Contention for the cache buffer lru chain and cache buffer chain latches can occur if a database sustains high physical or logical I/O rates. Reduce I/O rates by tuning SQL or increasing the size of the buffer cache. Increasing the values of DB_BLOCK_LRU_ LATCHES may help.

Library Cache Latches   Library cache latches protect the cached SQL statements and objects definitions held in the library cache within the shared pool.

The library cache latch must be obtained in order to add a new statement to the library cache. During a parse request, Oracle searches the library cache for a matching statement. If one is not found, then Oracle will parse the SQL statement, acquire the library cache latch, and insert the new SQL. Contention for the library cache latch can occur when an application generates very high quantities of unique, unsharable SQL—usually because literals have been used instead of bind variables. If the library cache latch is a bottleneck, try to improve the use of bind variables within your application. Misses on this latch may also be a sign that your application is parsing SQL at a high rate and may be suffering from excessive parse CPU overhead as well.

The library cache pin latch must be obtained when a statement in the library cache is re-executed. Misses on this latch occur when there are very high rates of SQL execution. There is little you can do to reduce the load on this latch, although using private rather than public synonyms (or even direct object references such as OWNER.TABLE) may help.

Contention for library cache and library cache pin latches can occur when there is heavy parsing or SQL execution rates. Misses on the library cache latch is usually a sign of excessive reparsing of nonsharable SQL.

Redo Buffer Latches Two latches control access to the redo buffer. The redo allocation latch must be acquired in order to allocate space within the buffer. The redo copy latch is then acquired in order to copy redo entries into the buffer.

Prior to Oracle8i, you can adjust the parameters LOG_SIMULTANEOUS_COPIES to control the number of redo allocation latches. In Oracle8i, this defaults to twice the number of CPUs on the system and should not be changed.

You may observe seemingly high contention for the redo copy latch but this is really an artifact of the way in which Oracle obtains this latch. Oracle tries each of the redo copy latches in turn without waiting for the latch. Only if all the latches are busy will Oracle spin on the latch or enter a *latch free wait* state. However, because a miss on each of the latches is still recorded, it is common to see a high miss rate on this particular latch.

High miss rates on the redo copy latch are normal and do not usually indicate serious latch contention.

Shared Pool Latch The shared pool latch is required when sessions need to allocate or deallocate space within the shared pool. Heavy contention for this latch can actually suggest that the shared pool is too big, because large shared pools may generate excessively long freelists that are scanned while holding the latch.

Spin Count and Latch Sleeps If a session "sleeps" because it cannot obtain a latch response, time will be significantly degraded. You can decrease the probability of the session sleeping by increasing the value of the configuration parameters _LATCH_SPIN_COUNT_SPIN_COUNT[1] or SPIN_COUNT. This parameter controls the number of attempts the session will make to obtain the latch before sleeping. "Spinning" on the latch consumes CPU, so if you increase this parameter, you may see an increase in your system's overall CPU utilization. If your computer is near 100% CPU utilization and your application is throughput driven rather than response time driven, you could consider decreasing SPIN_COUNT in order to conserve CPU.

Adjusting SPIN_COUNT is a trial-and-error process. In general, only increase SPIN_COUNT if there are enough free CPU resources available on your system; and decrease it only if there is no spare CPU capacity.

> If you encounter latch contention and have spare CPU capacity, consider increasing the value of SPIN_COUNT. If CPU resources are at full capacity, consider decreasing the value of SPIN_COUNT.

OTHER BOTTLENECKS

Bottlenecks in Server Processes   When you configure the Oracle multithreaded server or parallel query option, additional background processes are created:

❑ Dispatchers, which receive SQL requests from client processes and pass these requests to shared servers

❑ Shared server processes, which perform SQL operations on behalf of client processes

❑ Parallel slave processes, which are used for the parallel execution of SQL statements

The number of these processes will vary within high and low values determined by Oracle configuration parameters. These parameters are detailed in Appendix D.

The serv_stA.sql script or serv_stS scripts display statistics for multithreaded and parallel servers. Example output is shown in Figure 20.7.

If the dispatcher or shared servers show a high busy rate, it's possible that you may need to add more dispatcher or shared server processes. Note, however, that short term or sporadic high busy rates can severely impact response time during peak activity, even if the average busy rate seems acceptable.

If all parallel query slaves are busy, statements requesting parallel execution may run serially or at a reduced level of parallelism. This is shown by the statistic "% parallel operation is downgraded" in the serv_stA/serv_stS report. Ensure

---

[1]The format of the SPIN_COUNT parameter has changed in various Oracle versions. It may be represented in your system as SPIN_COUNT, LATCH_SPIN_COUNT or_SPIN_COUNT.

```
Shared and Parallel server statistics: M816B    24/05/00:21:13
          sampled since database startup at 23/05:19:56

Statistic                                                       Value
--------------------------------------------------- ------------
Dispatcher busy%                                                0.066
Shared Servers busy%                                            0.444
COMMON queue avg wait %                                         0.005
DISPATCHER queue avg wait %                                     0.735
Parallel Query Servers Highwater                               2.000
Total parallel operations                                      6.000
% parallel operations downgraded                              16.667
mts_servers                                                    1.000
mts_max_servers                                               20.000
mts_max_dispatchers                                            5.000
parallel_min_servers                                          0.000
parallel_max_servers                                          2.000
```

FIGURE 20.7   Parallel query and multithreaded server statistics reported by serv_stA or serv_stS scripts.

that there is an appropriate number of parallel servers to service the parallel processing demand. However, never configure more parallel servers than your system configuration can reasonably sustain. If you see parallel operations being downgraded but the number of servers already meets the capacity of your system, consider running your parallel queries at a reduced degree of parallelism. Chapter 11 contains more guidance on this topic.

Ensure that the number of dispatchers, parallel servers, and shared servers is properly configured. Too few servers can degrade the performance of sessions connecting via MTS or parallel servers. Too many servers may overload CPU, disk, or memory resources.

Rollback Segments   Any session that modifies a row must make an entry in a rollback segment. If there are too few or too small rollback segments, then delays may occur as sessions wait for a free extent within a rollback segment or entry in the rollback segment's transaction table. You may have seen evidence of these delays as buffer busy waits when using the wait_stS or busy_stS scripts.

The scripts rbs_stS or rbs_stA can display detailed statistics for all rollback segments. Example output is provided in Figure 20.8.

Ideally, Oracle sessions will not need to wait for rollback segments and rollback segments will extend or contract only occasionally.

```
                 Rollback segment statistics: MYDB
    18/10/96:07:22
                     Sampled since database startup

                  Current              High
    Rollback        Size   Optimal    Water  No. of Avg Shrink
    Segment         (KB)     (KB)     (KB)  Shrinks     (KB) Extents
    ------------   --------  --------  --------  -------  ----------  -------
    SYSTEM           552                552       0          0        7
    RS01           52912     5120     69432      40       3535      189
    RS02            9232     5120      9792       5       1120       33
    RS03           43952     5120     43952       0          0      157
    RS04            5312     5120     18472       3       5040       19
    RS05            5312     5120      8112       4       1330       19
    RS06            5312     5120     23512       5       4760       19
    RS07            5312     5120     88752       5      17416       19
    RS08            5312     5120     11192       3       2240       19
    RS09            5312     5120     88192       3      27720       19
    RS10            5312     5120     82872       3      26320       19
    RS11            5312     5120     89592      18      10624       19
    RS12            5312     5120     14272       3       3640       19

    Rollback
    Segment              Gets         Writes waits/writes % waits/gets %
    ------------   ----------  ------------  ---------------  ------------
    SYSTEM               454          6393           .0000         .0000
    RS01            3361391     458440991           .0032         .4365

    RS02             157243      50727517           .0003         .0808
    RS03              50264      24475613           .0001         .0318
    RS04             454204      71203482           .0003         .0493
    RS05             102979      43441644           .0001         .0418
    RS06             253273     116848368           .0000         .0197
    RS07            1160275     134877511           .0001         .0114
    RS08             452659      70006858           .0004         .0566
    RS09            1134542     131937362           .0014         .1666
    RS10             782929      99279203           .0001         .0068
    RS11            6550807     602308131           .0053         .4893
    RS12             162088      52741664           .0001         .0339
```

FIGURE 20.8 Output from the rbs_stA script.

The "waits/writes" and "waits/gets" columns in the rbs_st scripts indicate the proportion of read and write requests made to a rollback segment that needed to wait. If waits are significant (perhaps greater than 0.5%), then you may need to add more rollback segments.

The values for optimal, high water mark, and shrinks can be used to determine if our rollback segments are appropriately sized:

❑ If the average size of the rollback segment is less than the optimal setting, then OPTIMAL is probably too high.

❑ If there are large numbers of shrinks but the average size shrunk is small, the rollback segment is probably shrinking too often. Try increasing the value of OPTIMAL.

❑ If there are only a few shrinks but the average size of the shrinks is high, then the rollback segment is probably well configured and only expanding occasionally for very large transactions.

If sessions are waiting to make entries in the rollback segments, increase the number or size of rollback segments. Set the OPTIMAL size of the rollback segment so that dynamic extension and contraction occurs only rarely.

IDENTIFYING RESOURCE INTENSIVE SQL

It's not uncommon for an otherwise well-tuned database or application to be bought to its knees by a couple of untuned SQL statements (or even one). Luckily, Oracle keeps track of SQL statements that have been executed and maintains performance statistics for each. This information is stored in the database table V$SQL. You can query this table to isolate SQL statements that are consuming excessive resources.

For instance, the following query sorts SQL statements cached in the shared pool by the number of buffer gets (logical reads) to executions. In other words, it displays the most expensive statements first:

```
SQL> l
  1  select  executions,buffer_gets,disk_reads,rows_processed,
  2          buffer_gets/decode(executions,0,1,executions)
            gets_per_execute,
  3          sql_text
  4    from v$sql
  5*  order by buffer_gets/decode(executions,0,1,executions)  desc
```

```
SQL> /

...


EXECUTIONS BUFFER_GETS DISK_READS ROWS_PROCESSED GETS_PER_EXECUTE
---------- ----------- ---------- -------------- ----------------
SQL_TEXT
------------------------------------------------------------------
         1      141153        343              1           141153
select sum(sale_value)   from departments d,       employees e,
       products p,         sales s  where p.product_description='O
RACLE Tune Tool mk 2'    and e.surname='MCLOUGHLIN'     and e.firs
tname='FREDERICK'    and d.department_name='Database Products'
 and p.product_id=s.product_id     and e.employee_id=s.sales_rep_i
d    and d.department_id=s.department_id

         1      100416       2254              1           100416
begin   quest_ix_rule_engine.evaluate_all_rules(p_run_id => :p_ru
n_id); end;
```

A number of sophisticated third-party tools allow you to search for expensive SQL and then provide a tuning environment in which you can use EXPLAIN PLAN and other methods to tune the SQL. An example of such a product is Quest Software's SQLab product.

SUMMARY

In this chapter, we've explored methods of monitoring an Oracle database server and detecting bottlenecks and inefficiencies in Oracle process flows.

A good place to start in the diagnosis of Oracle server performance problems is with an examination of operating system performance indicators. The various operating systems differ in the details of performance tuning and in the performance monitoring tools available but share some fundamental principles:

❑ Shortages in available physical memory will almost always lead to dramatic performance degradation. Ensure that there is adequate physical memory available at all times. Shortages in memory often show up as high rates of paging and swapping. The most effective remedy for memory shortages is to add additional memory to the configuration, although Oracle's memory requirements can be reduced by downsizing the SGA or implementing multithreaded servers.

❑ I/O bottlenecks may occur if a particular disk or disks is continually busy. You can eliminate I/O bottlenecks by distributing database files evenly across physical devices or reducing I/O requirements by increasing the size of the buffer cache or tuning SQL.

❑ Oracle is designed so that the CPU will provide the ultimate limitation on performance. If CPU utilization is continually high, it may indicate a need to upgrade the server hardware. Reducing CPU requirements in Oracle may be possible by tuning SQL and reducing parsing.

The Oracle architecture implements a complex interaction between user and database processes, shared memory, and datafiles. If a bottleneck prevents an efficient flow of processing through this architecture, then your SQL may be unable to perform to its potential.

The default monitoring tools provided by Oracle are not very powerful, but there are many third-party tools that can assist in monitoring.

There are a number of critical efficiency indicators that can help you determine if Oracle is operating efficiently:

❑ The buffer cache hit ratio, which reflects the proportion of database I/Os that were satisfied by data blocks held in the buffer cache. For transaction processing systems, high ratios are recommended—greater than 90 to 95%. For applications that perform frequent scans of large tables, it may not be possible to achieve such a high hit rate.

❑ The library cache hit ratio reflects the number of parse requests that found a matching SQL statement in the library cache. Low ratios can occur when literals are used in place of bind variables and can result in excessive CPU overhead and latch contention.

❑ The library cache pin hit ratio and the dictionary cache hit ratio reflect the efficiency of the Oracle shared pool. Low hit ratios usually mean that the shared pool should be increased in size.

❑ The parse ratio represents the proportion of calls to the database that were requests to parse new SQL statements. High ratios may indicate that poor SQL statement handling in the application and may result in excessive CPU consumption.

❑ The redo space ratio reflects the proportion of redo log entries that had to wait for free space in the redo log buffer. High values may indicate that the redo log buffer should be increased in size.

❑ The disk sort ratio reports the percentage of sorts that could not be satisfied in memory and therefore had to allocate or use a temporary segment. Disk sorts may be unavoidable, but if your disk sort ratio is very high, you might consider allocating more memory to sorts via the configuration parameter SORT_AREA_SIZE.

❑ The index fetch ratio shows you the proportion of rows that were obtained via an index or ROWID lookup. In a transaction processing environment, low values may indicate excessive full-table scans.

Oracle sessions often have to cease SQL processing in order to wait for a resource to become available. Analyzing waits and eliminating unnecessary waits is an important step in curing server bottlenecks.

❑ Waits for database file reads are inevitable and usually account for the vast majority (80 to 90%) of waits in a well-tuned system.

❑ Waits for redo log writes are also inevitable and may account for 10 to 20% of waits.

❑ The presence of buffer busy waits can be an indication of freelist or rollback segment contention.

❑ Free buffer waits and write complete waits may indicate database writer inefficiencies or, in earlier versions of Oracle, heavy disk sort activity.

❑ Enqueue waits indicate contention for database locks.

❑ Latch waits indicate contention for structures within the SGA. Cache buffer latches indicate heavy activity in the buffer cache and may indicate excessive I/O rates. Library cache latches indicate contention for the SQL cache in the shared pool and possibly excessive unsharable SQL. Redo allocation and redo copy latches indicate contention for the log buffer.

Other areas of contention are as follows:

❑ If you are using multithreaded servers, sessions may be waiting for a server or dispatcher to become available. If you observe this, you should increase the number of available servers or dispatchers.

❑ Parallelized SQL statements may encounter dramatic reductions in performance if there are not sufficient parallel slave processes to allow execution to proceed in parallel.

❑ Sessions may wait for rollback segments if there are too few rollback segments or if the number of extents or size of segments is too small. Excessive dynamic extension and contraction of rollback segments can also lead to performance problems.

❑ A few resource-intensive SQL statements can degrade the performance of the entire system. Use shared pool browsers to identify these SQL statements.

REFERENCE

In this section, we summarize commands and options that you may need on a day-to-day basis when writing and tuning high-performance SQL. The concepts and facilities referred to here are covered in greater depth in the main sections of this book.

HINTS

The Optimizer is that part of Oracle which determines how the SQL will be executed. Among other things, the optimizer may decide in which order to join tables, whether to use an index, and so on. Hints are instructions which you can include in your SQL statement to instruct or "guide" the Oracle query optimizer. Using hints you can specify join orders, type of access paths, indexes to be used, the optimization goal and other directives.

An optimizer hint appears as a comment following the first word of the SQL statement (e.g. SELECT, INSERT, DELETE or UPDATE). A hint is differentiated from other comments by the presence of the plus sign ("+") following the opening comment delimiter ("/*"). For instance, the FULL hint in the following example tells the optimizer to perform a full table scan when resolving the query:

```
SELECT /*+ FULL(E) */ *
FROM employee e
WHERE salary > 1000000
```

HINT	DESCRIPTION
ALL_ROWS	**ALL_ROWS** Use the cost based optimizer and optimize for the retrieval of all rows
AND_EQUAL	**AND_EQUAL**(*table_name index_name index_name ....*) Retrieve rows from the specified table using each of the specified indexes and merge the results.
APPEND	**APPEND** Invokes a direct load insert. Only valid for INSERT ... SELECT FROM statements.
BITMAP	**BITMAP**(*table_name index_name*) Retrieve rows from the specified table using the specified bitmap index.
CACHE	**CACHE**(*table_name*) Encourages rows retrieved by a full table scan to remain in the buffer cache of the SGA.
CHOOSE	**CHOOSE** If statistics have been collected for any table involved in the SQL statement, use cost-based/all-rows optimization, otherwise use rule based optimization.
CLUSTER(*table_name*)	**CLUSTER**(*table_name*) Use a cluster scan to retrieve table rows.
DRIVING_SITE	**DRIVING_SITE**(*table_name*) For a distributed SQL statement, causes the site at which the specified table resides to be the driving site.
FIRST_ROWS	**FIRST_ROWS** Specifies that the cost based optimizer should optimize the statement to reduce the cost of retrieving the first row only.
FULL	**FULL**(*table_name*) Use a full table scan to retrieve rows from the specified table.
HASH	**HASH**(*table_name*) Use a hash scan to retrieve rows from the specified table. The table must be stored in a hash cluster.
HASH_AJ	**HASH_AJ** Perform a anti-join using hash join methodology. This hint must appear after the select statement of a NOT IN subquery.
HASH_SJ	**HASH_SJ** Appears within an EXISTS subquery. Invokes a hash semi-join.
INDEX	**INDEX**(table_name [index_name]) Use the specified index to retrieve rows from the table or, if no index specified, use any index.
INDEX_ASC	**INDEX_ASC**(table_name [index_name]) Specifies an ascending index range scan using the specified index or, if no index is specified, any suitable index.
INDEX_COMBINE	**INDEX_COMBINE**(table_name [index_name...]) **INDEX_COMBINE** instructs the optimizer to combine the specified bitmap indexes. If no bitmap indexes are specified, the optimizer will choose suitable bitmap indexes.

(continued)

HINT	DESCRIPTION
INDEX_DESC	INDEX_DESC(table_name [index_name]) pecifies an descending index range scan using the specified index or, if no index is specified, any suitable index.
INDEX_FFS	INDEX_FFS(table_name [index_name]) Invokes a fast full index scan using the specified index or, if no index is specified, any suitable index. A fast full scan reads all the index in block order using multi-block reads and possibly parallel query.
MERGE	MERGE Instructs the optimizer to perform complex view merging when resolving a query based on a view or which includes a subquery in the where clause.
MERGE_AJ	MERGE_AJ Perform a anti-join using sort-merge join method. This hint must appear after the select statement of a not in subquery
MERGE_SJ	MERGE_SJ Appears within an EXISTS subquery. Invokes a sort-merge semi-join.
NO_EXPAND	NO_EXPAND(table_name) Oracle will sometimes expand statements with OR conditions into multiple SQL statements combined by a union operation. This hint instructs the optimizer not to do this, even if it calculates that such a transformation would be beneficial.
NO_INDEX	NO_INDEX(table_name [index_name]) NO_INDEX suppresses the use of the named index or, if no indexes are specified, all indexes on the nominated table.
NO_MERGE	NO_MERGE Instructs the optimizer not to perform complex view merging when resolving a query based on a view or which includes a subquery in the where clause.
NO_PUSH_PRED	NO_PUSH_PRED Do not push join conditions from the where clause into a view or subquery.
NOAPPEND	NOAPPEND Suppresses direct load insert in an INSERT ... SELECT FROM statement.
NOCACHE	NOCACHE(table_name) Discourages ORACLE from keeping rows retrieved by a full table scan in the buffer cache of the SGA. Overrides the cache setting on the create or alter table statement.
NOPARALLEL	NOPARALLEL(table_name) Don't use parallel processing for the SQL statement. Overrides the parallel setting on the create or alter table statement
NOPARALLEL_INDEX	NOPARALLEL_INDEX(table_name index_name) NOPARALLEL_INDEX suppresses parallelism in fast full index scans or in partitioned index access.
NOREWRITE	NOREWRITE NOREWRITE prevents the sql statement from being "re-written" to take advantage of materialized views. It overrides the server parameter QUERY_REWRITE_ENABLED.

HINT	DESCRIPTION
ORDERED	**ORDERED** Instructs the optimizer to join the tables in exactly the left to right order specified in the from clause.
ORDERED_PREDICATES	**ORDERED_PREDICATES** Ordered predicates causes predicates in the WHERE clause to be evaluated in the order in which they appear in the WHERE clause.
PARALLEL(*table_name, degree_of_parallelism*)	**PARALLEL**(*table_name, degree_of_parallelism*) Instructs the optimizer to perform parallel scans on the nominated table. If no degree of parallelism is specified, the default will be used.
PARALLEL_INDEX	**PARALLEL_INDEX**(*table_name* [*index_name*]) Parallelises a fast full index scan or an index scan against a partitioned index.
PQ_DISTRIBUTE	**PQ_DISTRIBUTE**(*table_name outer_distribution inner_distribution*) This query determines how a parallel join using table_name will be executed. Valid options for *outer_distribution* and *inner_distribution* are (not all combinations are valid) HASH, BROADCAST, NONE, PARTITION.
PUSH_JOIN_PRED	**PUSH_JOIN_PRED** PUSH_JOIN_PRED pushes conditions from the WHERE clause into a view or subquery.
PUSH_SUBQ	**PUSH_SUBQ** This hint causes sub-queries to be processed earlier in the execution plan. Normally subqueries are processed last unless the SQL statement is transformed into join.
REWRITE	**REWRITE**(*view_name* [*view_name...*]) Restrict query rewrite to only those materialized views specified in the hint.
ROWID	**ROWID**(*table_name*) Perform a rowid access.
RULE	**RULE** Use rule based optimization.
STAR	**STAR** Consider the STAR join methodology in preference to other methods.
STAR_TRANSFORMATION	**STAR_TRANSFORMATION** Requests that the star transformation optimization be performed. This transforms a star query into a alternate form which can take advantage of bitmap indexes.
USE_CONCAT	**USE_CONCAT** ORACLE will sometimes expand statements with OR conditions into multiple SQL statements combined by union all. This hint instructs the optimizer to do this, even if it calculates that such a transformation would not be beneficial.
USE_HASH	**USE_HASH**(*table_name*) When joining to this table, use the hash join method.
USE_MERGE	**USE_MERGE**(*table_name*) When joining to this table, use the sort-merge join method.
USE_NL	**USE_NL**(*table_name*) When joining to this table, use the nested-loops join method.

EXPLAIN PLAN AND SQL TRACE

CREATING THE PLAN TABLE

To create the plan table, run the script utlxplan.sql from SQL*PLUS. The script can usually be found in the rdbms/admin subdirectory of the Oracle distribution.

RUNNING EXPLAIN PLAN

The syntax of the explain plan statement is:

```
EXPLAIN PLAN [SET STATEMENT_ID='text']
            [INTO table_name]
        FOR sql_statement
```

If "INTO table_name" is not specified then a plan table named PLAN_TABLE will be used.

The "SET STATEMENT_ID" option allows multiple plans to be stored in a single table.

FORMATTING EXPLAIN PLAN OUTPUT

The following query generates formatted output from the plan table:

```
SELECT LPAD(' ',2*(LEVEL-1))||operation||' '||options
           ||' '||object_name
           ||' '||DECODE(id, 0, 'Cost = '||position)
"Query Plan"
  FROM plan_table
 START WITH id = 0 AND statement_id = 'statement_id'
CONNECT BY PRIOR id = parent_id AND statement_id
='statement_id'
```

ENABLING SQL_TRACE

SQL trace can be initiated from within a session by the command:

```
ALTER SESSION SET SQL_TRACE TRUE;
```

"Advanced" tracing—which includes details of resource waits—can be enabled with the command:

```
ALTER SESSION SET EVENTS '10046 TRACE NAME CONTEXT FOREVER,
LEVEL 8';
```

FINDING THE TRACE FILE

Trace files generated by the SQL trace facility are written to the directory specified by the configuration parameter USER_DUMP_DEST. You can determine the location of this directory with the following query:

```
SELECT VALUE
  FROM v$parameter
 WHERE name = 'user_dump_dest'
```

RUNNING TKPROF

Basic usage for tkprof:

```
tkprof trace_file_name output_file_name
       table=name_of_alternate_plan_table.
       explain=username_and_password_to_use_with_explain
       sort=sort_options
```

Commonly used sort options are:

(prsela,exeela,fchela)	sort statements by elapsed time
(prscpu,execpu,fchcpu)	sort statements by CPU time
(exeqry,execu,fchqry,fchcu)	sort statements by logical I/O
(exedsk,fchdsk)	sort statements by physical I/O

A more complete list of options is included in Chapter 7.

SQL*PLUS AUTOTRACE OPTION

The AUTOTRACE option can be used in SQL*PLUS to display execution plans and statistics.

The AUTOTRACE command has the following usage:

```
SET AUTOTRACE {OFF|ON|TRACE[ONLY]}[EXPLAIN] [STATISTICS]
```

ON starts tracing, OFF inhibits it.

TRACEONLY suppresses query output and displays trace output only.

EXPLAIN causes EXPLAIN PLAN output to be printed for each statement executed.

STATISTICS causes SQL statement execution statistics to be printed for each statement executed.

ALTERING SESSION SETTINGS

You can alter the configuration of your session with the ALTER SESSION command. The general form of the alter session command is:

```
ALTER SESSION SET option = value
```

The following performance-related options can be set with alter session:

TABLE A.1 Options of the ALTER SESSION statement.

OPTION	EFFECT
SQL_TRACE	TRUE causes SQL trace information to be written to the trace file. FALSE stops tracing.
OPTIMIZER_GOAL	Sets the optimization strategy for the session. Valid values are: RULE, CHOOSE, FIRST_ROWS, ALL_ROWS
SESSION_CACHED_ CURSORS	Defines the number of cursors to be cached locally. High values improve the performance for programs that discard cursors for SQL statements that are eventually re-executed.
CLOSE_OPEN_ CACHED_CURSORS	If TRUE, cached cursors are closed when a commit is executed. A value of TRUE saves memory, but FALSE can reduce parse overhead.
HASH_JOIN_ ENABLED	If TRUE, hash joins will be performed if the optimizer determines that they are beneficial. A value of FALSE prevents hash joins in any circumstances.
HASH_AREA_SIZE	Amount of memory available for hash join operations. Larger values can improve performance of hash joins.
PARTITIONED_ VIEW_ENABLED	If TRUE, Oracle will perform partition view optimizations as described in Chapter 11.

COLLECTING TABLE STATISTICS

THE ANALYZE COMMAND

Prior to Oracle8i, the ANALYZE command was the only supported method for collecting table statistics. It has the following syntax:

```
ANALYZE {TABLE | INDEX | CLUSTER} segment_specification
     [{COMPUTE STATISTICS |
       ESTIMATE STATISTICS}
            [FOR {TABLE |
                 ALL [INDEXED] COLUMNS
                        [SIZE histogram_size] |
```

```
        column_list [SIZE histogram_size]   |
        ALL [LOCAL] INDEXES ] } ... ]
    SAMPLE sample_size [ROWS|PERCENT] ]
[DELETE STATISTICS]
[VALIDATE REF UPDATE [SET DANGLING TO NULL] ]
[VALIDATE STRUCTURE [CASCADE] [INTO table_spec] ]
[LIST CHAINED ROWS [INTO table_spec] ]
```

ANALYZE examines and/or validates the storage and data distribution of a table, index, partition or cluster. This information can be stored in the data dictionary and may be used by the Oracle optimizer to determine SQL execution plans. Alternately, inefficiencies or errors in object storage or structure may be revealed.

In Oracle 8i, the DBMS_STATS package can perform some of the functions of the ANALYZE command with greater efficiency.

Segment_specification specifies a table, index, cluster, partition or subpartition to be analyzed.

COMPUTE STATISTICS indicates that every block allocated to the segment should be examined to calculate statistics.

ESTIMATE STATISTICS indicates that a random sample of segment entries should be examined to calculate statistics. The SAMPLE clause specifies the percentage or absolute number of rows to examine.

The FOR clause determines if table indexes will be created and/or *column histograms* created. Multiple FOR clauses may be specified.

FOR TABLE indicates that the table should be analyzed.

FOR ALL COLUMNS indicates that histograms should be generated for each column in the table.

FOR ALL INDEXED COLUMNS indicates that histograms should be generated for each column in the table which is included in an index.

FOR *column_list* indicates that the specified list of columns should have histograms generated.

FOR ALL INDEXES indicates that all indexes associated with the table should be analyzed. The LOCAL clause, when used with a partitioned table restricts the analyze to *local indexes* only.

DELETE STATISTICS causes all statistics for the nominated object to be removed.

VALIDATE REF UPDATE checks the validity of *REF* datatypes. If the REF contains a *ROWID*, ANALYZE will check that the *ROWID* of the relevant object row to which the REF column refers is correct and will correct the ROWID if it is incorrect. If SET DANGLING TO NULL is specified then any REF which points to an object row which no longer exists will be set to NULL.

VALIDATE STRUCTURE validates the structure of the object. If CASCADE is specified, then any indexes belonging to the object will also be checked. If the INTO clause is specified, then ROWIDS for rows which are in an incorrect partition will be stored in the specified table. By default this table is called INVALID_ROWS and is created by the script *utlvalid.sql*.

LIST CHAINED ROWS finds any rows that have been migrated into chained blocks and stores them in the specified table. The default table name is CHAINED_ROWS and is created by the script *utlchain1.sql* which is included in the Oracle distribution.

THE DBMS_STATS PACKAGE

The DBMS_STATS package provides utilities for managing Optimizer statistics. It is available in Oracle8.1.5 and beyond.

This package provides the functionality of the ANALYZE command together with the ability to export and import optimizer statistics and collect statistics in parallel.

Optimizer statistics may be held in local tables identified by the *stattab* parameter in many of the DBMS_STATS procedures. If this parameter is null then the procedures work against the live data dictionary statistics tables. *Statid* allows multiple sets of statistics to be stored in a single *stattab*.

DBMS_STATS FUNCTION OR PROCEDURE	DESCRIPTION
CONVERT_RAW_VALUE	CONVERT_RAW_VALUE(*rawval, resval*) CONVERT_RAW_VALUE converts a raw maximum or minimum endpoint value for a histogram bucket into an "actual" value that is of the same datatype as the column to which the histogram belongs. *Rawval* is the raw representation of the endpoint. *Resval* is the actual value which should be of the datatype datatype NUMBER, VARCHAR2, DATE, BLOB, CLOB or BILE.
CONVERT_RAW_VALUE NVARCHAR	CONVERT_RAW_VALUE_NVARCHAR(*rawval, resval*) CONVERT_RAW_VALUE_NVARCHAR is the same as CONVERT_RAW_VALUE except that the *rawval* must be taken from an NVARCHAR column and *resval* must be of type NVARCHAR.
CONVERT_RAW_VALUE_ ROWID	CONVERT_RAW_VALUE_ROWID(*rawval, resval*) CONVERT_RAW_VALUE_ROWID is the same as CONVERT_RAW_VALUE except that the *rawval* must be taken from an rowid column and *resval* must be of type ROWID
CREATE_STAT_TABLE	CREATE_STAT_TABLE(*ownname, stattab, tblspace*) CREATE_STAT_TABLE creates a table which can be passed as a *stattab* argument to other procedures in this package. *Ownername* defines the account which owns the table. *Stattab* is the name of the table. *Tblspace* defines the tablespace in which *stattab* will be created.

DBMS_STATS FUNCTION OR PROCEDURE	DESCRIPTION
DELETE_COLUMN_STATS	DELETE_COLUMN_STATS(*ownname, tabname, colname, partname, stattab, statid, cascade_parts*)
	DELETE_COLUMN_STATS removes column statistics from a local statistics table or from the data dictionary.
	Ownername, *tabname* and *colname* define the column for which statistics will be deleted.
	Partname defines a partition for which statistics are to be deleted. if NULL then all partitions will be processed.
	Stattab defines a local statistics table created by CREATE_STAT_TABLE from which statistics will be deleted.
	if NULL, then statistics are deleted from the data dictionary.
	If *stattab* is not NULL then *statid* may be specified to identify a specific set of statistics within *stattab*.
	Cascade_parts, if TRUE, requires that statistics for all partitions or sub-partitions also be deleted.
DELETE_INDEX_STATS	DELETE_INDEX_STATS(*ownname, indname, partname, stattab, statid, cascade_parts*)
	DELETE_INDEX_STATS removes index statistics from a local statistics table or from the data dictionary.
	Ownername and *indname* define the index for which statistics will be deleted.
	Partname defines a partition for which statistics are to be deleted. If NULL then all partitions will be processed.
	Stattab defines a local statistics table created by CREATE_STAT_TABLE from which statistics will be deleted. If NULL, then statistics are deleted from the data dictionary. If *stattab* is not NULL then *statid* may be specified to identify a specific set of statistics within *stattab*.
	Cascade_parts, if TRUE, requires that statistics for all partitions or sub-partitions also be deleted.
DELETE_SCHEMA_STATS	DELETE_SCHEMA_STATS(*ownname, stattab, statid*)
	delete_schema_stats deletes all statistics for the current schema.
	Ownname defines the schema for which statistics will be deleted.
	Stattab defines a local statistics table created by CREATE_STAT_TABLE from which statistics will be deleted. If NULL, then statistics are deleted from the data dictionary. If *stattab* is not NULL then *statid* may be specified to identify a specific set of statistics within *stattab*.
DELETE_TABLE_STATS	DELETE_TABLE_STATS(*ownname, tabname, partname, stattab, statid, cascade_parts, cascade_columns, cascade_indexes*)
	DELETE_COLUMN_STATS removes table related statistics from a local statistics table or from the data dictionary.
	Ownername and *tabname* define the table for which statistics will be deleted.
	Partname defines a partition for which statistics are to be deleted. If NULL then all partitions will be processed.

(continued)

DBMS_STATS FUNCTION OR PROCEDURE	DESCRIPTION
	Stattab defines a local statistics table created by CREATE_STAT_TABLE from which statistics will be deleted. If NULL, then statistics are deleted from the data dictionary. If *stattab* is not NULL then *statid* may be specified to identify a specific set of statistics within *stattab*.
	Cascade_parts, if TRUE, requires that statistics for all partitions or sub-partitions also be deleted.
	Cascade_columns, if TRUE, requires that statistics for all columns of the table also be deleted.
	Cascade_indexes, if TRUE, requires that statistics for all indexes belonging to the table be deleted.
DROP_STAT_TABLE	DROP STAT_TABLE(*ownname, stattab*)
	DROP_STAT_TABLE drops a statistics table created by CREATE_STAT_TABLE. *Ownname* and *stattab* define the table to be dropped.
EXPORT_COLUMN_STATS	EXPORT_COLUMN_STATS(*ownname, tabname, colname, partname, stattab, statid*)
	EXPORT_COLUMN_STATS copies data dictionary statistics for the column defined by *ownname,tabname* and *colname* into the local statistics table *stattab*. *Statid* optionally identifies the identifier within the *stattab*.
	If *partname* is specified then only statistics for the specified partition are exported.
EXPORT_INDEX_STATS	EXPORT_INDEX_STATS(*ownname, indname, partname, stattab, statid*)
	EXPORT_INDEX_STATS copies data dictionary statistics for the index defined by *ownname* and *indname* into the local statistics table *stattab*. *Statid* optionally identifies the identifier within the *stattab*.
	If *partname* is specified then only statistics for the specified partition are exported.
EXPORT_SCHEMA_STATS	EXPORT_SCHEMA_STATS(*ownname, stattab, statid*)
	EXPORT_SCHEMA_STATS copies data dictionary statistics for the schema defined by *ownname* into the local statistics table *stattab*. *Statid* optionally identifies the identifier within the *stattab*.
EXPORT_TABLE_STATS	EXPORT_TABLE_STATS(*ownname, tabname, partname, stattab, statid, cascade*)
	EXPORT_TABLE_STATS copies data dictionary statistics for the table defined by *ownname* and *tabname* into the local statistics table *stattab*. *Statid* optionally identifies the identifier within the *stattab*.
	If *partname* is specified then only statistics for the specified partition are exported.
	Cascade, if TRUE, requires that column and index statistics for the table also be exported.
GATHER_DATABASE_STATS	GATHER_DATABASE_STATS(*estimate_percent, block_sample, method_opt, degree, granularity, cascade, stattab, statid, options, objlist*)
	GATHER_DATABASE_STATS collects optimizer statistics for all schemas in the database.

DBMS_STATS FUNCTION OR PROCEDURE	DESCRIPTION
	Estimate_percent specifies the percentage of rows to sample. If null, then statistics are computed on all rows.
	If *block_sample* is TRUE, then a random selection of blocks – rather than a random selection of rows – are sampled.
	Method_opt is a string of the form
	FOR ALL [{INDEXED | HIDDEN}]
	COLUMNS [SIZE *histogram_size*]
	See the ANALYZE command in the previous section for details of the *method_opt* clause.
	Degree indicates the degree of parallel execution for statistics gathering. If NULL, the default for the table is used.
	Granularity determines the level of statistics gathering for partitioned tables. It must be one of 'DEFAULT', 'PARTITION', 'SUBPARTITION', 'GLOBAL', or 'ALL'.
	Cascade, if TRUE, indicates that statistics for indexes should be collected for each table processed.
	Stattab defines a local statistics table created by CREATE_STAT_TABLE in which statistics will be stored. If NULL, then statistics are deleted from the data dictionary. If *stattab* is not NULL then *statid* may be specified to identify a specific set of statistics within *stattab*.
	Options defines the criteria for statistics collection. It is one of 'GATHER STALE', 'GATHER EMPTY','LIST STALE' or 'LIST EMPTY' or may be omitted.
	Objlist is a table of type DBMS_STAT.OBJECTTAB which itself is a record of type DBMS_STAT.OBJECTELEM. Objects which satisfy the 'LIST STALE' or 'LIST EMPTY' options are stored in this structure.
GATHER_INDEX_STATS	**GATHER_INDEX_STATS**(*ownname, indname, partname, estimate_percent, stattab, statid*)
	Gather_index_stats collects optimizer statistics for a specific index as defined by *ownname* and *indname*.
	If *partname* is specified then only statistics for the specified partition are collected.
	Estimate_percent specifies the percentage of rows to sample. If null, then statistics are computed on all rows.
	Stattab defines a local statistics table created by CREATE_STAT_TABLE in which statistics will be stored. If NULL, then statistics are deleted from the data dictionary. If *stattab* is not NULL then *statid* may be specified to identify a specific set of statistics within *stattab*
GATHER_SCHEMA_STATS	**GATHER_SCHEMA_STATS**(*ownname, estimate_percent, block_sample, method_opt, degree, granularity, cascade, options, objlist*)
	GATHER_SCHEMA_STATS collects optimizer statistics for all schemas in the database.

(continued)

DBMS_STATS FUNCTION OR PROCEDURE	DESCRIPTION
	Estimate_percent specifies the percentage of rows to sample. If null, then statistics are computed on all rows.
	If *block_sample* is TRUE, then a random selection of blocks — rather than a random selection of rows — are sampled.
	Method_opt is a string of the form
	FOR ALL [{INDEXED | HIDDEN}]
	COLUMNS [SIZE *histogram_size*]
	See the ANALYZE command in the previous section for details of the *method_opt* clause.
	Degree indicates the degree of parallel execution for statistics gathering. If NULL, the default for the table is used.
	Granularity determine the level of statistics gathering for partitioned tables. It must be one of 'DEFAULT', 'PARTITION', 'SUBPARTITION', 'GLOBAL', or 'ALL'.
	Cascade, if TRUE, indicates that statistics for indexes should be collected for each table processed.
	Stattab defines a local statistics table created by CREATE_STAT_TABLE in which statistics will be stored. If NULL, then statistics are deleted from the data dictionary. If *stattab* is not NULL then *statid* may be specified to identify a specific set of statistics within *stattab*.
	Options defines the criteria for statistics collection. It is one of 'GATHER STALE', 'GATHER EMPTY','LIST STALE' or 'LIST EMPTY' or may be omitted.
	Objlist is a table of type DBMS_STAT.OBJECTTAB which is itself a record of type DBMS_STAT.OBJECTELEM. Objects which satisfy the 'LIST STALE' or 'LIST EMPTY' options are stored in this structure.
GATHER_TABLE_STATS	GATHER_TABLE_STATS(*ownname, tabname, partname, estimate_percent, block_sample, method_opt, degree, granularity, cascade, stattab, statid*)
	GATHER_TABLE_STATS collects statistics for a single table.
	Ownname and *tabname* identify the table for which statistics are to be collected and *partname* optionally identifies a partition within that table.
	Estimate_percent specifies the percentage of rows to sample. If null, then statistics are computed on all rows.
	If *block_sample* is TRUE, then a random selection of blocks — rather than a random selection of rows — are sampled.
	Method_opt is a string of the form
	FOR ALL [{INDEXED | HIDDEN}]
	COLUMNS [SIZE *histogram_size*] [*column_list*]
	See the ANALYZE command in the previous section for details of the *method_opt* clause.
	Degree indicates the degree of parallel execution for statistics gathering. If NULL, the default for the table is used. Collection of statistics for indexes is not parallelized.

DBMS_STATS FUNCTION OR PROCEDURE	DESCRIPTION
	Granularity determine the level of statistics gathering for partitioned tables. It must be one of 'DEFAULT', 'PARTITION', 'SUBPARTITION', 'GLOBAL', or 'ALL'.
	Cascade, if TRUE, indicates that statistics for indexes should be collected for each table processed.
	Stattab defines a local statistics table created by CREATE_STAT_TABLE in which statistics will be stored. If NULL, then statistics are deleted from the data dictionary. If *stattab* is not NULL then *statid* may be specified to identify a specific set of statistics within *stattab*.
GENERATE_STATS	GENERATE_STATS(*ownname, objname, organized*)
	GENERATE_STATS is used to generate statistics for indexes (including bitmap indexes) using table statistics already collected as the data source.
	Ownname and *objname* identifies the object that contains the source statistics.
	Organized is a number from 0-10 indicating the degree to which consecutive entries in the index tend to reside in the same data block. 0 indicates high organization.
GET_COLUMN_STATS	GET_COLUMN_STATS(*ownname, tabname, colname, partname, stattab, statid, distcnt, density, nullcnt, srec, avgclen*)
	GET_COLUMN_STATS retrieves column level statistics.
	Ownname, tabname, colname and *partname* identify the column and (optionally) the partition from which statistics will be extracted.
	Stattab defines a local statistics table created by CREATE_STAT_TABLE from which statistics will be extracted. If NULL, then statistics are extracted from the data dictionary. If *stattab* is not NULL then *statid* may be specified to identify a specific set of statistics within *stattab*.
	The OUT parameters *distcnt, density, nullcnt* and *avgclen* receive the number of distinct values, column density, number of nulls and average length of the column.
	Srec is a variable of type DBMS_STATS.STATREC which is a record holding minimum, maximum, and histogram values for the column.
GET_INDEX_STATS	GET_INDEX_STATS(*ownname, indname, partname, stattab, statid, numrows, numlblks, numdist, avglblk, avgdblk, clstfct, indlevel*)
	GET_INDEX_STATS retrieves index statistics.
	Ownname, indname and *partname* identify the index and (optionally) the partition from which statistics will be extracted.
	Stattab defines a local statistics table created by CREATE_STAT_TABLE from which statistics will be extracted. If NULL, then statistics are extracted from the data dictionary. If *stattab* is not NULL then *statid* may be specified to identify a specific set of statistics within *stattab*.

(continued)

DBMS_STATS FUNCTION OR PROCEDURE	DESCRIPTION
	The OUT parameters *numrows, numlblks, numdist, avglblk, avgdblk, clstfct* and *indlevel* receive the number of leaf blocks, number of distinct keys, average number of leaf blocks for each distinct key, average number of table blocks each distinct key, clustering factor and height of the index or partition.
GET_TABLE_STATS	GET_TABLE_STATS(*ownname, tabname, partname, stattab, statid, numrows, numblks, avgrlen*)
	GET_TABLE_STATS retrieves table statistics.
	Ownname, tabname and *partname* identify the table and (optionally) the partition from which statistics will be extracted.
	Stattab defines a local statistics table created by CREATE_STAT_TABLE from which statistics will be extracted. If NULL, then statistics are extracted from the data dictionary. If *stattab* is not NULL then *statid* may be specified to identify a specific set of statistics within *stattab*.
	The OUT parameters *numrows, numblks* and *avgrlen* retrieve the number of rows, number of blocks and average row length for the table or partition.
IMPORT_COLUMN_STATS	IMPORT_COLUMN_STATS(*ownname, tabname, colname, partname, stattab, statid*)
	IMPORT_COLUMN_STATS transfers column statistics for the column identified by *ownname, tabname, colname* and optionally *partname* (partition) from the local statistics table *stattab*, and optionally from the statistics set identified by *statid*, into the data dictionary.
IMPORT_INDEX_STATS	IMPORT_INDEX_STATS(*ownname, indname, partname, stattab, statid*)
	IMPORT_INDEX_STATS transfers index statistics for the index identified by *ownname, indname* and optionally *partname* (partition) from the local statistics table *stattab*, and optionally from the statistics set identified by *statid*, into the data dictionary.
IMPORT_SCHEMA_STATS	IMPORT_SCHEMA_STATS(*ownname, stattab, statid*)
	IMPORT_SCHEMA_STATS transfers all statistics for the schema identified by *ownname* from the local statistics table *stattab*, and optionally from the statistics set identified by *statid*, into the data dictionary.
IMPORT_TABLE_STATS	IMPORT_TABLE_STATS(*ownname, tabname, partname, stattab, statid, cascade*)
	IMPORT_TABLE_STATS transfers table statistics for the table identified by *ownname, tabname* and optionally *partname* (partition) from the local statistics table *stattab*, and optionally from the statistics set identified by *statid*, into the data dictionary.
	Cascade, if TRUE, indicates that statistics for the tables indexes and columns should also be imported.
PREPARE_COLUMN_VALUES	PREPARE_COLUMN_VALUES(*srec, histogramt_array*)
	PREPARE_COLUMN_VALUES prepares column statistics which can be loaded by SET_COLUMN_STATS. *Input_array* contains the start and end values of a height-balanced histogram (or simply minimum and maximum values if there are only 2 entries).

DBMS_STATS FUNCTION OR PROCEDURE	DESCRIPTION
	Srec is a record of type DBMS_STATS.STATREC. *Srec.epc* should be set to the number of elements in the input array. Other fields in Srec contain the internal representation which can be fed to SET_COLUMN_STATS.
PREPARE_COLUMN_ VALUES_NVARCHAR	PREPARE_COLUMN_VALUES_NVARCHAR(*srec, nvmin, nvmax*) PREPARE_ COLUMN_VALUES_NVARCHAR is the same as PREPARE_COLUMN_VALUES but works on Nvarchar columns. Because such columns do not support histograms, *nvmin* and *nvmax* specify minimum and maximum values for the column instead of the *histogram_array* used in PREPARE_COLUMN_ VALUES.
PREPARE_COLUMN_ VALUES_ROWID	PREPARE_COLUMN_VALUES_ROWID(*srec, rwmin, rwmax*) PREPARE_COLUMN_VALUES_ROWID is the same as PREPARE_COLUMN_VALUES but works on ROWID columns. Because such columns do not support histograms, *rwmin* and *rwmax* specify minimum and maximum values for the column instead of the histogram_array used in prepare_column_ values.
SET_COLUMN_STATS	SET_COLUMN_STATS(*ownname, tabname, colname, partname, stattab, statid, distcnt, density, nullcnt, srec, avgclen, flags*) SET_COLUMN_STATS stored column-level statistics. *Ownname, tabname, colname* and *partname* identify the column and (optionally) the partition for which statistics will be stored. *Stattab* defines a local statistics table created by CREATE_STAT_TABLE in which statistics will be stored. If NULL, then statistics are stored in the data dictionary. If *stattab* is not NULL then *statid* may be specified to identify a specific set of statistics within *stattab*. The parameters *distcnt, density, nullcnt* and *avgclen* set the number of distinct values, column density, number of nulls and average length of the column. *Srec* is a variable of type DBMS_STATS.STATREC which is a record holding minimum, maximum, and histogram values for the column. *Flags* are currently unused and should be left NULL.
SET_INDEX_STATS	SET_INDEX_STATS(*ownname, indname, partname, stattab, statid, numrows, numlblks, numdist, avglblk, avgdblk, clstfct, indlevel, flags*) SET_INDEX_STATS stores index statistics. *Ownname, indname* and *partname* identify the index and (optionally) the partition for which statistics will be stored. *Stattab* defines a local statistics table created by CREATE_STAT_TABLE into which statistics will be stored. If NULL, then statistics are stored in the data dictionary. If *stattab* is not NULL then *statid* may be specified to identify a specific set of statistics within *stattab*. The parameters *numrows, numlblks, numdist, avglblk, avgdblk, clstfct* and *indlevel* set the number of leaf blocks, number of distinct keys, average number of leaf blocks for each distinct key,

(continued)

DBMS_STATS FUNCTION OR PROCEDURE	DESCRIPTION
	average number of table blocks each distinct key, clustering factor and height for the index or partition.
	Flags are currently unused and should be left null.
SET_TABLE_STATS	SET_TABLE_STATS(*ownname, tabname, partname, stattab, statid, numrows, numblks, avgrlen,* flags)
	SET_TABLE_STATS set table statistics.
	Ownname, tabname and partname identify the table and (optionally) the partition for which statistics will be stored.
	Stattab defines a local statistics table created by CREATE_STAT_TABLE into which statistics will be stored. If NULL, then statistics are stored in the data dictionary. If stattab is not NULL then statid may be specified to identify a specific set of statistics within stattab.
	The parameters numrows, numblks and avgrlen set the number of rows, number of blocks and average row length for the table or partition.

GLOSSARY

Aggregate operations   Aggregate operations are those which group related rows and return a single row for each group. For example, returning the total number of employees in each department. Aggregate operations are invoked by the GROUP BY operator.

Analyze   The analyze command collects table and index statistics which help the Oracle optimizer choose the best execution plan for a SQL statement.

Anti-Join   An anti-join returns all rows in one table which do not have a matching row in the other table. It is typically implemented using a NOT IN subquery.

ARCH process   See Archiver process

Archived log   A redo log which has been copied by the archiver process to an alternative location, usually as a backup measure or to maintain a standby database.

Archiver process   The archiver process is an Oracle process which is responsible for copying completed redo logs to an alternative destination if the database is running in ARCHIVELOG mode.

Array processing   Array processing allows a single SQL call to process multiple rows. For instance, a single execution of an insert statement could add multiple rows, or a single fetch from a select statement could return multiple rows.

In programming environments array variables are use to hold the rows fetched or inserted. In many development and enquiry tools, array processing is enabled transparently and automatically.

Artificial key   An artificial key is a unique which is contains no real-world information. Artificial keys are usually generated using Oracle sequences. Compare with natural key.

Asynchronous I/O   Asynchronous I/O allows a process to submit multiple IO requests without waiting for each to complete. In practice, this means a single process can utilize the bandwidth of multiple disks.

Aurora   The name of the Java Virtual Machine (JVM) incorporated into Oracle8i.

Autonomous transaction   An autonomous transaction runs within—but outside the scope of—another transaction. Commits and rollbacks issued within the autonomous transaction do not affect the parent transaction.

B-tree index   An index structure which takes the form of an hierarchy or inverted "tree." This is the default format for Oracle indexes.

Bfile   A BFILE is an external file which appears within the database as a LOB datatype. BFILES can be accessed only by the DBMS_LOB package.

Binary chop   A procedure for searching a sorted list of items. The list is successively divided into two sections and the section which must contain the desired item further sub-divided. Eventually the remaining portion is sufficiently small to enable a sequential scan. This technique is useful in programs which cache table data to avoid excessive database access.

Bind variables   Bind variables allow the variable portions of an SQL statement — such as the data values to be inserted or the search criteria — to be defined as "parameters" to the SQL statement.

The use of bind variables allows SQL statements to be re-executed without re-parsing the SQL statement. The alternative approach, where substitution variables are embedded as literals within the SQL statement requires that the SQL statement be re-parsed when the substitution variables change.

Bitmap indexes   A bitmap index contains a bitmap for each unique value of the indexed column. These bitmaps can be efficiently manipulated to process queries which are predicated on multiple columns each of which has only a few distinct values.

BLOB   Binary Large Object. In Oracle, a BLOB may store up to 4GB of unstructured binary data.

Block   The basic unit of storage in an ORACLE instance. Block sizes most commonly range between 2 and 8 KB.

Block cleanout   During modifications to data blocks, the System Change Number (SCN) for the change is not yet known because the transaction has not yet been committed. Block cleanout is the process of updating these SCN numbers. For most blocks, this will occur when the transaction is committed, but for some blocks it will occur when the block is next read.

Branch blocks   The middle level of blocks in a B-tree index. Each branch block contains a range of index key values and pointers to the appropriate leaf blocks.

Buffer cache   The area of the SGA which caches data blocks. If a session requires a data or index block from a database file it will first check the contents of the buffer cache. Data blocks are cleared from the buffer cache according to a Least Recently Used algorithm.

Cardinality   A measure of the number of unique values within a column or an index. The higher the cardinality of the index, the fewer the number of rows which will be returned by an exact lookup of a key value and hence the more useful the index will be.

Checkpoint   A checkpoint occurs when all database blocks which have been modified prior to a specific moment in time are written to disk. Checkpoints can be configured to occur at regular intervals and always occur when Oracle switches redo log files. Redo logs cannot be reused until the checkpoint completes, because only then does Oracle know that the information in the redo log is no longer required in the case of instance failure.

Checkpoint process The checkpoint process updates datafile headers during check-points.

CKPT process See Checkpoint process

CLOB Character Large OBject. A CLOB may store up to 4GB character data.

Clone database A copy of a database which is used to perform tablespace point in time recovery.

Cluster Clusters are a form of table storage in which the physical location of a row is dependent on the value of the row. An index clusters stores rows from one or more tables in the same segment. Rows with common cluster key values are stored together. In a hash cluster, the location of rows in a single table is dependent on the hashed value of the table's key.

Collection Collections are datatypes made up of more than one element. Two collection types are nested tables and VARRAYs.

Concatenated index An index which is comprised from more than one column.

Consistent read ORACLE queries return rows which are consistent with the time at which the query commenced. This consistent read may require access to rows which have changed since the query commenced - these rows are accessed from rollback segments.

Constraint Constraints provide restrictions on the data values which can be stored in Oracle tables. Primary key and Unique constraints prevent rows with duplicate values for the key columns being stored. Foreign key constraints allow only rows which match the primary key of another table to be stored. Check constraints provide some logical condition which must be satisfied for all rows.

CORBA Common Object Request Broker Architecture. CORBA is a standard which allows for distributed execution and management of program objects. Oracle8i includes a Java-based CORBA 2.0 Object Request Broker (ORB). The Oracle8i ORB can provide access to Java programs stored in the database.

Correlated subquery A correlated subquery is a subquery which references a value from the parent query in its where clause. Correlated subqueries may be executed once for each row returned by the parent query.

Cursor A session memory structure which contains an SQL statement or PL/SQL block. Otherwise referred to as a context area.

Dangling An object ref which contains an object identifier to a non-existent object.

Data dictionary The data dictionary comprises a set of Oracle tables which contain the definitions of all objects within the database. The data dictionary is stored in the SYS account.

Database writer process The database writer process is responsible for writing modified blocks from the buffer cache in the SGA to database files on disk. Depending on the configuration of the Oracle database, there may be more than one database writer process active.

DBWR process See Database writer process

DDL Data Definition Language. The Data Definition Language of SQL provides commands for creating and maintaining database objects

Dedicated server A dedicated server process performs database operations on behalf of a single client program. Compare with shared server.

Degree of parallelism The number of parallel threads of execution for parallel SQL. If there are no limits on the number of CPUs and disks available, doubling the degree of parallelism can be expected to double the throughput of the SQL statement.

Denormalization   The process of re-introducing redundant or derived information into a data model usually with the aim of improving performance.

Discrete transaction   A special transaction mode with fairly severe limitations but which when used appropriately can substantially improve transaction performance.

Dispatcher process   The dispatcher process is responsible for mediating multi-threaded server connections. When a client program requests a multi-threaded server connection, the listener allocates a dispatcher to the client. When the client submits an SQL request, the dispatcher allocates the SQL to an appropriate shared server process. Thus, the client may utilize multiple shared servers, but maintains a connection to only one dispatcher.

DML   Data Manipulation Language. The Data Manipulation Language of SQL provides commands for updating, deleting or inserting rows into database tables.

Domain index   A domain index is a user-defined index typically created on complex datatypes whose algorithms and optimizer characteristics are provided by the user. Domain indexes are created using the Oracle Data Cartridge Interface API.

Driving table   The driving table is the table which is accessed first in a table join. Choosing the best driving table is a key decision when optimizing join order.

Dynamic performance tables   A set of views which provide access to Oracle performance information. The information in the dynamic performance tables comes not from physical tables, but from externalization of Oracle memory structures.

EJB   See Enterprise Java bean

Enterprise Java beans   A Java bean is a reusable component written in Java—typically designed to run in a client or browser environment. The Enterprise Java Beans (EJB) standard defines extensions to the bean architecture to allow Java Beans to perform server-based and transactional processing. Oracle8i supports enterprise Java beans within the JServer environment.

Event   Oracle events set debugging flags within the Oracle instance. Events may be set by the EVENT initialization parameter or through the ALTER SESSION SET EVENTS statement. Oracle recommends that event codes only be set on advice from Oracle Worldwide support

Exception   In PL/SQL exceptions are raised either explicitly by the RAISE statement, or when an Oracle error occurs. Exception handlers can be declared which define actions that occur when specific exceptions are raised.

Extent   An extent is the fundamental unit of space allocation for a segment. Segments are comprised of one or more extents. As data is added to a segment, additional extents are automatically allocated as required, subject to storage allocation parameters specified in the segments STORAGE definition.

Foreign key   A column or columns within one table which relate to the primary key of a "master" or "parent" table. These matching foreign and primary key columns can be used to join the two tables.

Fragmentation   Oracle can experience fragmentation in one of the following ways:

Free space in datafiles may fragment so that even if there is sufficient free space overall there is insufficient contiguous free space to allocate an extent.

Segment storage may fragment when may extents are allocated. This is usually harmless.

Rows may fragment when a row expands beyond the storage available in the block. The row will then migrate leaving the original ROWID and pointer ROWID only in the original block.

Memory in the shared pool may fragment when many small allocations prevent sufficient contiguous space being available for large memory allocations.

Freelist A free list is a list of blocks which are eligible for insert. Each segment contains at least one freelist. Multiple freelists can be configured using the FREELISTS clause if the segment is subject to high concurrent insert rates.

Multiple freelist groups can be configured in an Oracle Parallel Server environment so that each instance inserts rows into specific blocks.

Functional index A functional index is one which is based on a function or expression rather than on a simple column or columns.

Hash cluster See Cluster

Hash join Hash join is one of the algorithms which Oracle can use to join two tables.

In a hash join a hash table, a sort of on-the-fly index, is constructed for the larger of the two tables. The smaller table is then scanned, and the hash table used to find matching rows in the larger table.

Hashing In general, hashing refers to the technique of mathematically transforming a key value into a relative address which can be used to rapidly locate a record. ORACLE uses hashing as a table access method (hash clusters) and to optimize certain join operations (hash join). Hashing is also used extensively within internal SGA operations.

Hierarchical query Hierarchical queries are a special case of a self-join in which each row recursively accesses child rows revealing a hierarchy of parent-child relationships. This is sometimes referred to as "explosion-of-parts."

High water mark The high water mark indicates the highest block in a segment which has ever contained data. The high water mark increases as rows are inserted into the segment. However, deleting rows will not reduce the high water mark.

Full table scans access all rows in the segment up to the high water mark.

Hint Hints are instructions which you can include in your SQL statement to instruct or "guide" the optimizer

An optimizer hint appears as a comment following the first word of the SQL statement (e.g., SELECT, INSERT, DELETE or UPDATE). A hint is differentiated from other comments by the presence of the plus sign ("+") following the opening comment delimiter ("/*").

IIOP Internet Inter-ORB Protocol. The protocol by which CORBA clients make requests across the internet for CORBA mediated services. Oracle8i supports IIOP requests.

Index cluster See Cluster.

Index-organized table An index-organized table appears to the user as a table but has the physical organization of a B-tree index. Leaf nodes in the B-tree contain primary key column values and selected columns. Other columns are stored in an overflow segment.

Instance An Oracle instance consists of an SGA and Oracle system ("detached") processes. An instance differs from a database in that a database may be associated with multiple instances in a parallel server environment.

Intersect INTERSECT is a set operator which returns the rows which are common to two result sets.

ITL Interested Transaction List. Each block contains an ITL which contains details of transactions which hold or which want row level locks within the block.

JDBC An API which allows Java programs to communicate with relational databases. Oracle8i includes built-in support for JDBC

Job queue process   The job queue processes are responsible for executing jobs submitted via the DBMS_JOB package. The number of job queue processes is controlled by the JOB_QUEUE_PROCESSES initialization parameter.

JServer   The Java Server platform provided by Oracle8i. Jserver includes the Aurora JVM, native JDBC and SQLJ support, the VisiBroker ORB and Enterprise JavaBeans support.

JVM   Java Virtual Machine. A JVM is a program which simulates a hardware platform which runs Java bytecode. Oracle8i includes a JVM—called Aurora—which allows it to support native Java.

Latch   Latches are internal Oracle locking mechanisms which generally protect memory structures in the SGA.

LCK0 process   See Lock process

Leaf blocks   The lowest level of blocks in a B-tree index. Each leaf block contains a range of index key values and pointers (ROWIDS) to appropriate blocks.

Lgwr   See Log writer process

Library cache   The library cache is a section of the shared pool which contains shared SQL and PL/SQL structures.

Listener process   The listener process establishes network connections to the Oracle instance. A client program requests a connection from the listener which either spawns a dedicated server process or assigns a dispatcher process for a shared server connection.

Lob   Large OBject. In Oracle, LOBs can be external—the BFILE datatype, or internal as CLOBs or BLOBs.

LOB locator   The LOB locator is stored within a table which includes a lob datatype and serves as a pointer to a LOBs location. LOBs are typically not stored within the segment itself, so the LOB locator could reference an external file (BFILE) or location of a CLOB or BLOB within a LOB segment.
      Obtaining a LOB locator is the first step in retrieving or manipulating a LOB.

Locally managed tablespace   Locally managed tablespaces maintain storage allocation information within a structure located within each datafile. Dictionary-managed tablespaces store this information within the data dictionary.

Lock process   An Oracle parallel server process which mediates inter-instance locking.

Log writer process   The log writer process (LGWR) is responsible for writing transaction entries from the log buffer in the SGA to the redo logs.

LRU   Least Recently Used. The Least Recently Used algorithm is used by Oracle to remove cached data blocks which have least recently been accessed. When a block is read from disk, it is placed on the Most Recently Used end of the LRU list, unless it has been read in from a table scan of a "large" table and the CACHE hint has not been specified. If it is not re-accessed it moves over time to the least recently used end of the list and eventually is flushed from the cache.

Materialized view   A materialized view is a table which contains the results of a query. Suitable queries may be transparently "rewritten" to use the materialized view if permitted and if the optimizer considers that the materialized view will offer superior performance.

Minus   A set operation which returns all rows in one results set which do not also appear in a second result set.

Mount   An intermediate stage during the startup of an Oracle instance. When the database is mounted, the SGA has been allocated, processes started and control files have been opened but the datafiles are not yet accessed. Certain maintenance operations require that the database be mounted but not open.

MTS   Multithreaded Server. MTS refers to the architecture which includes dispatchers, shared servers and listener processes.

Multiblock read   Multi-block reads occur when Oracle reads more than one database block in a single read operation. This most commonly occurs when Oracle is performing a full table scan or an index scan.

Multi-byte character set   Most western languages can be represented with each character stored in a single byte. Other languages—for instance Kanji—require multiple bytes per character.

National language support   National Language Support (NLS) allows Oracle to adapt to variations in languages and national conventions. NLS allows the language of error messages, the format of dates and currencies and the character set to be adjusted.

Natural key   A unique identifier for a table which is composed of naturally occurring columns in the table. Compare with artificial key.

Nested loops join   A join method in which each row of the outer table is read. For each row, a lookup of the inner table is undertaken. This best suits joins where the inner table is accessed via an index lookup.

Nested table   An Oracle8 collection type in which a column is defined as containing an embedded ("nested") table.

NLS   See National language support.

NULL values   NULL values indicate that a value is missing, unknown or inapplicable. The use of null values extends the normal two valued logic to a three-valued logic. Null values are important in SQL tuning because they are not generally stored in indexes and therefore present unique tuning problems.

Object identifier   An object identifier is a unique system generated number associated with every row of an object table.

Object type   Oracle object types are complex datatypes which include both attributes and methods.

Object view   An object view is a view which maps relational data to an Oracle object type.

OID   See Object identifier

OLAP   On-Line Analytical Processing. On-line analytical processing involves the real-time manipulation of large quantities of data generally for the purpose of facilitating business decisions. OLAP databases are typified by large data volumes and infrequent, long running queries.

OLTP   On-Line Transaction Processing. OLTP databases typically have a very high rate of update and query activity. OLTP is typified by high rates of index lookups, single-row modifications and frequent commits.

OPS   See Oracle Parallel Server

Optimistic locking strategy   A locking strategy based on the assumption that a row is unlikely to be changed by another session between the time the row is queried and the time it is modified. Optimistic locking minimizes the lock duration but requires that the transaction be aborted if the row is changed by another session.

Optimizer   See query optimizer

Oracle parallel server   Oracle Parallel Server (OPS) is an advanced Oracle configuration in which more than one instance open a single Oracle database. The advantages of OPS are possible scalability and fault tolerance.

ORB   Object Request Broker. A component of the CORBA architecture which coordinates requests for distributed objects. Oracle8i includes a Java-based CORBA 2.0 Object Request Broker (ORB).

Outer join   A join in which rows are returned from one of the tables, even if there is no matching row in the other table. This is achieved in Oracle using the "(+)" operator in the WHERE clause.

Outer table   The outer table is the first table processed in a join of two tables.

Overloading   Overloading refers to the practice of defining functions and procedure which have the same name, but which differ in the number or types of arguments. This allows for the development of routines which perform the same logical function on different datatypes.

Package   A package is a group of related functions, procedures and declarations. Packages allow the interface to be declared separately from the implementation, thus providing some degree of encapsulation of program code.

Parallel execution   The execution of an SQL operation using multiple processes or threads. This improves performance when there are multiple disk devices or CPUs available. In Oracle7, only queries and certain DDL operations can be executed in parallel. In Oracle8, DDL may also be executed in parallel under specific circumstances.

Parallel query   See Parallel Execution.

Parsing   The process of preparing a SQL statement for execution. This involves checking the statement for syntax errors, checking for a matching statement in the shared pool and determining the optimal execution plan. Parsing can contribute significantly the processing overhead, especially in OLTP like environments.

Partition   Partitioned objects are stored in multiple segments. This allows for objects to be spread across tablespaces and provides many maintenance and performance advantages for very large tables and indexes.

Pessimistic locking strategy   A locking strategy based on the assumption that a row might be changed between the time it is fetched and the time it is updated. Pessimistic locking involves locking the row when it is selected to prevent any concurrent updates.

PGA   Program Global Area. An area of memory in the server process which contains stack space and—depending on whether the server is shared or dedicated—session specific information.

PMON process   See Process monitor process

Primary key   The column or columns which uniquely identify a row in a table. Primary key constraints prevent duplicate values for primary keys, and allow referential integrity enforcement for table with corresponding foreign keys.

Process   A process is a unit of execution in a multi-processing environment. A process will typically execute a specific program and will have a unique and private allocation of memory. The operating system will determine the process's access to resources such as CPU, physical memory and disk.

Process monitor process   The process monitor (or PMON)

QMN process   See Queue monitor process

Query optimizer The optimizer is that part of the Oracle program which determines how the data required by a SQL statement will be retrieved. Among other things, the optimizer determines if any indexes will be used and the order in which tables will be joined.

Queue monitor process An Oracle process which monitors queues used by the Advanced Queuing facility.

RAID Redundant Array of Independent Disks. RAID is commonly used to describe configuration of multiple physicals disks into one or more logical disks. RAID 0 is commonly referred to a "striping" and RAID 1 as "mirroring". The other popular RAID configuration, RAID 5, stripes data across multiple drives while storing sufficient parity information on all drives to allow data to be recovered should any single drive fail.

Random I/O I/O in which a specific disk block are directly accessed. This is typical of the I/O which results from indexed lookups.

RDBMS Relational DataBase Management System.

RECO process See Recoverer process

Recoverer process An Oracle background process which performs resolution of failed distributed transactions.

Recursive SQL Recursive SQL is SQL which is generated by Oracle in order to retrieve data dictionary or other information which is required to parse or execute an SQL statement. Recursive SQL is only generated when the required information is not found in the row cache

Recursive Transaction A recursive transaction is a transaction which is generated by Oracle in order to process an SQL statement. Recursive transactions typically update the data dictionary.

Redo logs Oracle files that are used to record all changes made to objects with a database. When a COMMIT is issued, the changes made within the transaction are recorded in the redo log. The redo log can be used to restore the transaction in the event of a system failure.

REF A REF datatype stores a pointer to an object row. The REF datatype contains the object identifier and—optionally—the ROWID of the object row.

Referential integrity Referential integrity ensures that foreign keys correctly map to primary keys. A referential constraint will prevent the insert or update of foreign keys for which there are no matching primary keys and will either prevent the deletion of primary keys if foreign keys exist or delete these foreign key rows (delete cascade).

   Referential integrity can result in table-level locking if there are no indexes on the foreign keys.

Result sets The output from a SQL query is a result set. Results sets have the same tabular construction as tables. Results sets are also created during intermediate SQL operations. For instance in a multi-table join, each successive join create a result set. The final result set is the output of the query.

Rollback segments Rollback segments store the contents of a row before it is modified by a DML (update, insert delete) statement. This information is used in the event of a ROLLBACK, to provide a consistent view of the table for queries which commenced before the transaction was committed and to record the eventual success of a transaction.

Row cache A cache within the SGA which holds data dictionary information.

Row level locking   In general, ORACLE only ever locks a row which is modified by a DML statement. Page, block or table locks are not normally applied and read locks are never applied.

ROWID   The ROWID uniquely identifies a row by it's physical location. The ROWID of a row—if known—is the fastest way to access a row. An index will contain the ROWIDs for rows matching specific key values thus providing quick access to these rows.

Savepoint   A savepoint provides a point to which a transaction can be reverted without rolling back the entire transaction.

Schema   A schema is a collection of database objects which are logically related. In Oracle a schema is synonymous with a database account.

SCN   See System change number

Segment   A segment is an object within an Oracle database which consumes storage. Examples are tables, indexes, rollback segments, temporary segments and clusters.

Selectivity   A measure of the number of table entries for each index key. The less rows in the table which match specific index keys, the more selective is the index.

Semi-join   A semi-join is a join which returns rows from a table which have matching rows in a second table but which does not return multiple rows if there are multiple matches. This is usually expressed in oracle using a WHERE EXISTS subquery.

Sequence generator   An Oracle sequence generator returns unique number which are often used to populate primary keys. Oracle sequence generators are non-blocking and are independent of transactions.

Sequential I/O   I/O in which multiple disk or database blocks are read in sequence. This is typical of the I/O which results from full table scans.

Serial execution   The execution of an SQL statement using a single process or thread. This requires that each stage of the SQL operation be processed one after the other. Compare with parallel execution.

Server process   See Shadow process.

SGA   An area of Oracle shared memory which is available to all server processes. It contains cached data, shared SQL statements, message areas and other shared structures.

Shadow process   In many environments, the Oracle program runs in a separate process from the client program (for instance, SQL*PLUS). This "server" process is referred to as the shadow process.

Shared global area   See SGA

Shared pool   An area of the SGA which stores parsed SQL statements, data dictionary information and some session information. The shared pool reduces parse overhead by caching frequently executed SQL statements.

Shared server   A shared MTS (Multi-threaded server) process performs database operations on behalf of multiple client programs.

SMON process   See System monitor process

SMP   Symmetric multi-processing. A SMP machine contains multiple, equivalent CPUs. The SMP architecture dominates mid-range UNIX computers and is increasingly popular on Microsoft NT systems.

Snapshot   A snapshot is a table which is defined as the results of a query—typically one which replicates data from a remote site. Snapshots are often used as a means of replicating data but can also be used to store regularly refreshed aggregate or summary data. In Oracle8i, snapshots and materialized views are synonymous.

SNMP   Simple Network Management Protocol. A protocol which allows services on the network to be identified and to report status information. Oracle databases can be located and queried using the SNMP protocol.

SNP process   See Job queue process

Sort merge   Sort merge is one of the algorithms that Oracle can use to join two tables. When applying the sort merge algorithm, ORACLE sorts each table (or the result set from a previous operation) on the column values used to join the two tables. ORACLE then merges the two sorted result sets into one.

SQL_TRACE   The SQL_TRACE facility allows SQL statements and execution statistics to be recorded to a trace file for diagnostic or tuning purposes. The trace file may be formatted by the TKPROF utility.

SQLJ   SQLJ is a standard API which allows SQL statements to be embedded in Java programs. These SQL statements are translated to JDBC calls before execution by the SQLJ translator.

Standby database   Standby databases replicate a primary database and can provide a "fall-over" in the event that the primary database fails. Standby databases are implemented by forwarding redo logs to the standby database as they complete in the primary database. These logs are then applied to the standby database so the database remains one log file or more "behind" the primary database.

Star join   The STAR schema is a way of organizing relational data which is very popular in data warehouses. In a STAR schema, business data is stored in one or more large tables, referred to as "fact" tables. These tables can be joined to multiple smaller "dimension" tables which contain the more static details. A join of these tables is referred to as a star join.

Striping   A familiar term for RAID 0. Striping involves spreading data evenly across a number of disks, thus allowing higher data transfer rates than would otherwise be possible.

System change number   The System Change Number (SCN) is a global number which is updated whenever a transaction commits. The SCN is recorded in rollback segments and in data blocks and allows Oracle to determine if data has changed since a query commenced and to locate the appropriate rollback segment block to reconstruct the block as it was before the query commenced.

System global area   See SGA

System monitor   The system monitor process is responsible for performing instance recovery at startup, for cleaning up temporary segments and for coalescing free space within tablespaces.

Table scan   A full table scan involves reading every block allocated to a table up to the table's high water mark. This is the default access path for a query where there are no appropriate indexes on the table or when the cost based optimizer determines that index paths will be less efficient than a table scan.

Tablespace   A tablespace is a structure which houses database segments. A tablespace is comprised of one or more datafiles. Neither segments nor datafiles may span tablespaces, although partitioned objects (which are comprised of multiple segments) may be housed in multiple tablespaces.

Temporary segment   A temporary segment is a segment created within the tablespace assigned as TEMPORARY to the session which is used to support large sorts and intermediate result sets.

Thread A thread is a unit of execution which shares it's memory space with other threads. Threads can be implemented within processes on some systems or may be used in place of processes in others (for instance, in Windows NT).

Transaction A transaction is a set of DML (update, delete or insert) operations which succeed or fail as a unit. A transaction is successfully terminated by the commit statement or aborted with the rollback statement.

Trigger A trigger is a PL/SQL stored program which is executed when specified events occur. Prior to Oracle8i these event were always DML on database tables, but from Oracle8i onwards the events may also be DDL events or database wide events such as startup or shutdown.

Truncate Truncate involves rapidly removing all rows from a table. Rather than issue a transaction to delete the rows, Oracle simply marks all blocks as unused.

Two-phase commit Two-phase commit terminates a distributed transaction. In the first phase, all nodes prepare the commit. In the second phase, all nodes confirm that they are ready to commit and proceed to commit the transaction.

Two-task Oracle's two-task architecture provides separation between client programs and the database server programs. In the two-task architecture , Oracle client programs cannot access the SGA or datafiles directly. Instead they communicate with a server process or thread which performs these services on their behalf.

Union A set operation in which the results of two queries which return result sets with the same structure are concatenated.

VARRAY A type of collection. A varray is a fixed sized array of simple datatypes which can be stored in within a database column.

View Views are often referred to as "stored queries" or "virtual tables." A view presents to the user of a database as a table, but is defined as the result set of a specified query.

CONFIGURING DEVELOPMENT TOOLS

INTRODUCTION

This appendix provides a concise overview of some of the configuration considerations affecting SQL performance in some popular development tools.

The most significant performance improvements for SQL embedded in these development environments will be realized by following the guidelines contained in the main sections of this book. However, when the SQL is tuned, overheads resulting from untuned client tools can prevent the SQL from reaching its full potential.

The development tools we'll be considering are:

❑ Oracle Precompilers
❑ Oracle Forms
❑ Oracle Objects for OLE
❑ ODBC
❑ Oracle Call Interface (OCI)
❑ Java
❑ ADO

The configuration issues we'll consider are:

❑ Enabling array fetch to improve query performance. Using the array fetch facility reduces the number of calls to Oracle and network traffic—especially in the client server environment. The use of the array fetch was discussed in Chapter 6.

❑ Ensuring that SQL statement, or cursors, are re-used within the application. This reduces the number of parse calls to Oracle and thus reduces CPU overhead and database contention. SQL statement parsing was discussed in Chapter 3.

❑ Using bind variables to ensure that SQL is sharable across sessions. This reduces parse overhead by increasing the chance that if a matching SQL statement will be found in the shared pool. SQL statement parsing was discussed in Chapter 3.

ORACLE PRECOMPILERS

The Oracle precompilers are a set of pre-processors which allow SQL statements to be embedded in high level languages such as C, COBOL, FORTRAN, Pascal, Ada and PL/1.

ARRAY PROCESSING IN THE PRECOMPILERS

All of the Oracle precompilers fully support array processing. However, array processing must be explicitly specified within the program code: it is never transparently implemented.

When using array processing, bind variables are defined in the host language as single dimensional arrays. These arrays can be FETCHed into, used in the values clause of an INSERT statement or in a WHERE clause. The FOR clause of the EXEC SQL statement can be used to limit the number of elements processed. If the FOR clause is not specified, the entire array is used.

BIND VARIABLES IN THE PRECOMPILERS

The pre-compilers fully support bind variables. In versions 1.x of the precompilers bind variables should be declared within EXEC SQL BEGIN DECLARE SECTION and EXEC SQL END DECLARE SECTION statements. In version 2.x of the precompilers any variable may be used as a bind variable.

CURSOR RE-USE IN THE PRECOMPILERS

The Oracle pre-compilers implement a cursor cache to enable frequently executed cursors to be re-executed without re-parsing. This cursor cache is automatic and requires no special action to implement, but can be tuned using compile time options. These options are:

MAXOPENCURSORS	To specify the minimum size of the cursor cache.
HOLD_CURSOR	To specify that subsequent cursors should not be aged out of the cursor cache.

RELEASE_CURSOR   To specify that subsequent cursors should not
                              be stored in the cursor cache

During a pre-compiler session, Oracle will keep open as many cursors as necessary, even if this exceeds MAXOPENCURSORS. However, if a cursor is closed and then reopened, the precompiler program can avoid a re-parse if it finds the statement in the cursor cache. Therefore, it is usually worth increasing MAXOPENCURSORS from it's default of 10. The optimum value is the number of re-executable SQL statements in the program.

However, each cursor takes memory and in some circumstances you may need to set MAXOPENCURSORS lower than optimal. If this happens, you can determine which SQL statements get cached by using the HOLD_CURSOR and RELEASE_CURSOR options.

If RELEASE_CURSOR=YES is in effect, subsequent SQL statements will not be placed in a local cursor cache. This is useful for SQL statements which are not likely to be re-executed.

If HOLD_CURSOR=YES is in effect, subsequent SQL statements be added to the SQL cache permanently and will not be "aged out". This is useful for SQL statements which will be re-used frequently when MAXOPENCURSORS has a low value.

If neither RELEASE_CURSOR or HOLD_CURSOR is in effect then SQL statements will be placed in the cursor cache but may be "aged out" of the cache if a new SQL statement requires an entry in the cache.

RELEASE_CURSOR and HOLD_CURSOR options take effect at compile time, not at run time. This means that they effect all subsequent statements in the program file, regardless of module structure or run-time flow of execution. The usual way to control these options is to surround an SQL statement. For instance, in the following example, the fetch from dual is not added to the cursor cache:

```
EXEC Oracle OPTION(RELEASE_CURSOR=YES);
EXEC SQL SELECT USER
              INTO :USER
              FROM DUAL;
EXEC Oracle OPTION(RELEASE_CURSOR=NO);
```

ORACLE FORMS DEVELOPER

Oracle Forms is a development tool oriented towards developing data entry screens that work against Oracle databases.

ARRAY PROCESSING IN ORACLE FORMS

Oracle Forms transparently implements array processing for Form blocks. The size of the array is set to the number of rows displayed plus 3 additional rows, but can be adjusted using the "Records Buffered" property for the block.

You can disable array processing altogether by specifying array=NO on the command line. Doing this is not recommended.

BIND VARIABLES IN ORACLE FORMS

Bind variables are automatically and transparently implemented for SQL generated from Oracle Forms blocks. In procedure and trigger code, PL/SQL variables are translated by PL/SQL into bind variables.

CURSOR RE-USE

Oracle Forms assigns and re-uses individual cursors for each SQL statement contained in the form unless you specify the OptimizeTP=NO option on the command line, in which case only SELECT statements are allocated separate cursors. Setting OptimizeTP=NO may save memory, but is likely to increase parse overhead.

ORACLE OBJECTS FOR OLE

Oracle objects for OLE is an Oracle product which allows application environments which support OLE automation to access an Oracle database. It is most commonly used with Microsoft Visual Basic.

ARRAY PROCESSING WITH ORACLE OBJECTS FOR OLE

Array processing is implemented transparently in Oracle Objects for OLE. The size of the array is defined by the FetchLimit setting of the "[Fetch Parameters]" section of the ORAOLE.INI file. The default value is 20.

BIND VARIABLES IN ORACLE OBJECTS FOR OLE

Oracle Objects for OLE supports bind variables. They are represented by the Ora-Parameter object and the OraParamaters collection of an OraDatabase object. Within an SQL statement the parameters are referenced using the usual leading-colon convention.

To create a bind variable, you must use the Parameter.Add method of the database object. For example, the following code fragment creates an "employee_id" bind variable.

```
OraDatabase.Parameters.Add "employee_id", 0, 1
sql_text = "select * from employees
where employee_id=:employee_id"
Set EmployeeDyn = OraDatabase.DbCreateDynaset(sql_text, &H0&)
```

CURSOR RE-USE IN ORACLE OBJECTS FOR OLE

Cursors are represented as dynasets in Oracle objects for OLE. Providing that your dynasets are not deallocated, your cursors will be re-usable.

ORACLE CALL INTERFACE (OCI)

The Oracle Call Interface (OCI) is the fundamental programming interface to Oracle. All the Oracle development tools discussed in this appendix are constructed directly or indirectly on OCI. As the lowest level interface to Oracle, OCI includes all of the performance facilities present in higher-level environments. However, more work is often required to implement these features.

The OCI interface changed remarkably in Oracle8. The low level interface provided by the traditional interface—which we'll refer to as OCI7—was replaced by a more opaque interface—OCI8.

ARRAY PROCESSING IN OCI7

OCI7 fully supports array processing. To use array processing, you must use the appropriate OCI calls. To issue array DML, you must use the OEXN call instead of the OXEC call. To fetch an array of data you should use OFEN in place of OFETCH. You declare the input or output arrays using the standard techniques for your programming language.

ARRAY FETCH IN OCI8

The OCIDefineByPos() call allows you to define an array to receive output variables. The OCIStmtFetch() call allows you to provide an array size for each fetch operation.

BIND VARIABLES IN OCI7

Any host variable can become a bind variable in OCI. Bind variables are prefixed by colons in the SQL statement in the normal manner. If using the largely obsolete OBNDRN call to bind your variables then the bind variables are denoted by numbers (e.g., ":1",":2") in the SQL statement, otherwise the bind variables are defined as colon-prefixed names (e.g., ":SURNAME").

You bind each variable to the SQL statement with a separate call to the bind function. Three bind functions exist in OCI (OBNDRN, OBNDRV and OBNDRA). The OBNDRA call provides the most functionality and should be used in new applications.

BIND VARIABLES IN OCI8

Bind variables are represented as symbolic names prefixed by colons. The OCIBindByName() or OCIBIndByPos() calls allow you to associate these names with program variables.

CURSOR RE-USE IN OCI

Cursor re-use is completely under the control of the programmer in OCI.

In OCI, a cursor memory area is created with the OOPEN call and associated with an SQL statement (e.g., parsed) with the OPARSE call. Once the cursor is created, it can be bound to host variables (OBNDRA), executed (OEXN or OXEC), fetched from (OFEN) or closed (OCLOSE).

For SQL statements which are to be re-executed, allocate a distinct and dedicated cursor. Do not close the cursor (OCLOSE) after statement execution—this completely de-allocates the memory and the SQL statement. You can re-use the cursor simply by re-binding and re-executing the cursor. If a query cursor has not yet retrieved all rows, you can cancel the query using OCAN without destroying the cursor area.

For statements which are not re-used you can either destroy the cursor (OCLOSE) or parse a new statement into the existing memory area using OPARSE.

ODBC

ODBC (Open Database Connectivity) is a server independent API which allows client programs to issue SQL against virtually any back-end database. ODBC drivers are available for a very wide variety of back-end database servers, including Oracle. Client programs issue generic SQL requests which the ODBC driver translates into server-specific SQL.

The ODBC API fully supports bind variables, array processing and cursor re-use. However, the ODBC API is a very low-level implementation and is commonly accessed using middleware layers which allow a more high-level and productive programming environment.

The vendors who develop ODBC based middleware products must often compromise performance for portability. For instance, not all server databases support bind variables and as a result many ODBC products do not implement a bind variable capability. Array fetch and cursor re-use are more frequently, but not universally, implemented.

If contemplating an ODBC interface to an Oracle database evaluate ODBC middleware carefully and ensure that it implements bind variables, array processing and cursor re-use. In Visual Basic, you may wish to consider Oracle Objects for OLE as a high-performance alternative to ODBC.

Oracle releases it's own ODBC driver which fully supports array processing and efficient cursor handling.

ADO (ACTIVEX DATA OBJECT)

ADO is the most recent in a series of data access interfaces offered by Microsoft and primarily used within Visual Basic.

BIND VARIABLES IN ADO

Bind variables in SQL statements within ADO are represented by "?" characters. The Parameters collection of the Command object allows you to assign formal names to these parameters after which the parameters can be assigned new values directly, using the notation: Command("parameter")=value.

ARRAY HANDLING IN ADO

The GetRows method of the recordsetobject can retrieve multiple records into a two dimensional array in a single operation, thus allowing array fetch.

JAVA

We discussed the optimization of Java code in detail within chapter 15, so we will just briefly recap here.

BIND VARIABLES IN JDBC

To use bind variables in JDBC, it is firstly necessary to make use of the prepared-Statement object rather than the possibly easier Statement object. Bind variables within the prepared Statement can be represented by either a colon-prefixed variable name or a "?" placeholder. SetXXX methods – where XXX corresponds to a datatype such as "Int" – allow you to set the values of the bind variables.

BIND VARIABLES IN SQLJ

In SQLJ, any Java variable can serve as a bind variable. Bind variables are represented by colon-prefixed names that correspond to the Java variable names.

ARRAY PROCESSING IN JDBC

In JDBC 1.x, array fetch is not directly supported. You can, however, set a default pre-fetch size using the Oracle extensions to JDBC. The following statement sets the pre-fetch to 50:

```
((OracleConnection)myconnect).setDefaultRowPrefetch(50);
```

ARRAY PROCESSING IN SQLJ

Array fetch can be enabled by using the JDBC setDefaultRowPrefetch method. You can apply the setDefaultRowPrefetch method to the connection underlying the SQLJ context. This is described in detail in Chapter 15.

CURSOR HANDLING IN JDBC

In JDBC, the allocation and deallocation of cursors is explicitly controlled by the programmer. Prepared Statements represent open cursors and will continue to be maintained until explicitly closed with the close() method.

CURSOR HANDLING IN SQLJ

Prior to 8.1.6, SQLJ programs will automatically close all cursors when statement execution completes. From 8.1.6, SQLJ programs can be compiled with the -P-Cstmtcache=N directive, which causes the SQLJ precompiler to maintain a cache of N SQL statements and re-cycle them on a least-recently-used basis.

ORACLE SERVER CONFIGURATION

In this appendix we look at Oracle server configuration parameters that may affect the performance of your SQL. These parameters are contained in a configuration file, typically referred to as the init.ora file, although the actual name will usually include the Oracle instance identifier (Oracle_SID). DBA authority is required to alter these parameters.

You can determine the current values for these parameters with the following query (see your DBA if you don't have access to the V$PARAMETER view):

```
SELECT name, VALUE, description
  FROM v$parameter;
```

Configuration parameters which commence with an underscore ("_") are undocumented parameters. These are not included in Oracle documentation and are not included in the v$parameter view. You can list the names and values of these parameters with the following query (which must be run while connected as SYS or INTERNAL):

```
SELECT ksppinm name, ksppstvl, ksppdesc
  FROM x$ksppi x,
       x$ksppcv y
 WHERE x.indx = y.indx
   AND TRANSLATE (ksppinm,  '_',  '#') LIKE '#%'
```

You should change Oracle server parameters—especially undocumented parameters—with care. Always keep a backup copy of the init.ora file, preferably via version control software, so that you can revert to previous settings if you experience any problems.

Note also, that many parameters may be changed dynamically, either by issuing an ALTER SYSTEM or ALTER SESSION statement.

Oracle server configuration parameters change from release to release and some parameters are operating system specific. This appendix details only parameters which are performance related and specifically related to SQL statement performance. You should refer to Oracle documentation—specifically the Oracle server Reference Manual—for detailed documentation of all parameters.

PARAMETERS AFFECTING SQL TRACING

Adjusting these parameters are useful when using the SQL trace facility (discussed in some detail in Chapter 7).

_trace_files_public	This undocumented parameter causes Oracle to generate trace files which can be read by any user. If this parameter is not set, Oracle may generate trace files which are readable only to DBA accounts. Set this parameter to true if you want users to be able to analyze their own trace files and you are satisfied that no sensitive information is hard-coded into SQL statements
max_dump_file_size	The maximum size of a trace file in Oracle blocks. Setting this parameter to a low value can conserve disk space but you may lose valuable information in the trace file.
sql_trace	If set to TRUE, all Oracle sessions with generate SQL trace files. You should normally have this parameter set to FALSE, since a significant disk space and performance overhead will result if all sessions are being traced. However, there may be circumstances in which setting this parameter temporarily is the only way to obtain required trace output.
timed_statistics	If this parameter is set to TRUE, then Oracle sessions will maintain elapsed and cpu timings for internal operations. This will allow tkprof to report cpu and elapsed times for SQL statement execution and will allow a number of server per-

formance metrics to be accessed (for instance the TIME_WAITED column in V$SYSTEM_EVENT which records the time spent waiting for various system resources).

Because the overhead of setting TIMED_STA-TISTICS to TRUE is fairly low, and the information is provides is so useful, many DBAs leave TIMED_STATSITICS=TRUE always.

user_dump_dest This parameter specifies the directory to which user trace files initiated by the SQL trace facility will be written.

PARAMETERS AFFECTING SQL PROCESSING

These parameters affect the way in which Oracle processes your SQL and the resources available for certain SQL operations.

always_anti_join If set to TRUE, Oracle will use the anti-join optimizations automatically. If set to FALSE, Oracle will only perform an anti- join if the HASH_AJ or MERGE_AJ hints are used. See Chapter 9 for more information on anti-joins.

Since Oracle's anti-join methods usually improve performance, it is recommended that this parameter be set to TRUE.

always_semi_join This parameter determines the algorithm that will be used to perform a semi join based on an EXISTs subquery (see chapter 9). NESTED_ LOOPS—the default—results in the subquery being executed once for every row retrieved by the master query. HASH or MERGE cause the hash or sort merge join algorithm to be employed. HASH is usually the most efficient algorithm.

close_cached_open_ cursors If set to TRUE, cursor definitions are discarded in PL/SQL when a COMMIT is issued. This frees memory but increases the parse overhead, since SQL statements must be re-parsed in each transaction. The default value of FALSE allows cursor definitions to be retained across COMMITS and is recommended unless memory is very scarce.

cursor_space_for_time	Setting this parameter to true ensures that SQL statements are never aged out of the shared pool providing that there is at least one open cursor referencing the statement. A value of TRUE also causes cursor information which is not shared to be retained between executions.
	The default value of FALSE allows SQL statements to age out of the shared pool even if a cursor is open on the statement. However, this should rarely occur.
	Set this value to TRUE if you are sure that your shared pool is large enough to hold all concurrently opened SQL statements (you should probably increase it anyway if it is not) and there is ample free memory available for client processes.
discrete_transactions_enabled	If set to TRUE, discrete transactions (see Chapter 12) are permitted.
fast_full_scan_enabled	Enable or disable the fast full index scan query access path (chapter 8). Neccessary in version 7.3 and 8.0 only; The fast full index scan is available by default in 8.1.
hash_area_size	This parameter controls the amount of memory available (in bytes) to a session performing a hash join. Increasing this parameter will improve hash join performance up to the point at which the entire hash table fits in memory. After this point, increasing hash_area_size will have no effect.
hash_join_enabled	If set to FALSE, hash joins are not permitted. Since hash joins are very efficient there is usually no reason to change the default value of TRUE.
hash_multiblock_io_count	HASH_MULTIBLOCK_IO_COUNT specifies the number of blocks a hash join will read or write in a single I/O. May be modified by either ALTER SESSION or ALTER SYSTEM
optimizer_features_enable	Sets the compatibility version for the Oracle query optimizer, features introduced in later versions of the optimizer will not be used.
optimizer_index_cost_adj	OPTIMIZER_INDEX_COST_ADJ adjusts the cost of index-based plans. The default is 100. Lower

	values effectively discount the cost of index accesses
optimizer_max_ permutations	OPTIMIZER_MAX_PERMUTATIONS deter mines then number of join permutations which the optimizer will consider. The default is 80,000.
optimizer_mode	Sets the default optimization mode for the instance. Valid values are CHOOSE (the default), RULE, FIRST_ROWS, and LAST_ROWS. Chapter 3 discusses the optimizer_mode setting in some detail.
optimizer_percent_ parallel	Optimizer_percent_parallel determines the degree to which parallel query will be considered when calculating execution plans. 0 ignores parallelism, 100 uses maximum parallelism.
partition_view_ enabled	If FALSE, partition view processing is disabled. Partition view processing allows Oracle to skip unneeded tables in a view which contains multiple UNIONed tables.
	Set to TRUE if you wish to take advantage of partition views as described in Chapter 13.
session_cached_ cursors	This parameter controls the number of cursors cached in a session-specific cache. If the client program is re-using cursors efficiently, this cache will have little effect. However, if a program is discarding cursors which are later re-executed, increasing this parameter can have a significant effect on parse overhead.
star_transformation_ enabled	If TRUE, Oracle can take advantage of the star transformation plan, in which Star joins are rewritten to take advantage of bitmap indexes on the fact table.

PARAMETERS AFFECTING SORTING

sort_area_retained_ size	SORT_AREA_SIZE sets the maximum amount of session memory available for all concurrent sort while SORT_AREA_RETAINED_SIZE specifies the maximum amount of session memory available for any individual sort. A single query may need to perform more than one sort (a good example is a sort merge from a non-indexed

join), although it's unusual for more than two to be required concurrently. If each sort can fit into a SORT_AREA_RETAINED_SIZE and all sorts can fit into SORT_AREA_SIZE, then the sort can be performed in memory. SORT_AREA_RETAINED_SIZE defaults to SORT_AREA_SIZE and there is usually little incentive to change this default.

sort_area_size

The amount of memory available to an Oracle session for sorting. Increasing this value reduces the possibility that a large sort will have to write to temporary segments and will improve the performance of sorts.

Setting an appropriate value of SORT_AREA_SIZE is the most significant server-side optimization for sorting.

Since each session will allocate it's own SORT_AREA_SIZE and because this memory is never released back to the operating system, you should ensure that SORT_AREA_SIZE is increased only to the degree necessary to reduce disk sorts.

See Chapter 20 for information on monitoring sort activity.

sort_direct_writes

If set to TRUE or AUTO, the sorts which exceed SORT_AREA_SIZE will write directly to disk bypassing the buffer cache. This improves performance for the session performing the sort and also avoids filling the buffer cache with sort blocks.

SETTINGS AFFECTING PARALLEL PROCESSING

optimizer_percent_parallel

This parameter determines the amount of weight the optimizer gives to parallel processing in determining the optimal execution plan.

A value of 0 will cause the optimizer to ignore parallel processing when determining an execution plan, while a setting of 100 will cause the optimizer to fully "discount" the estimated cost of a parallel query based on the degree of parallelism selected. Intermediate settings result in a proportional reduction in parallel query costs.

	High values should only be used if your system and application are well suited to parallel query. Low values will encourage the use of indexes and other access methods which prevent parallelism.
parallel_adaptive_ multi_user	If true, Oracle dynamically adjusts query parallelism when multiple parallel queries run concurrently.
parallel_automatic_ tuning	If true, then Oracle will choose intelligent de faults for most parallel query tuning parameters.
parallel_default_ max_instances	Default degree of parallelism for parallel hints or table clauses which use the DEFAULT clause.
parallel_max_servers	The maximum number of parallel servers which can run concurrently. If this value is set too low, SQL which would otherwise be executed in parallel will either be executed serially or will return an error (depending on the value of PARALLEL_MIN_PCT). If set too high, your server may be overloaded by parallel processes.
parallel_min_percent	This parameter defines the minimum acceptable percentage of parallel slaves which must be available for the SQL to run. If less than the PARALLEL_MIN_PCT% slaves are available an error is returned.
	For instance, if your query required 8 and only 5 were available (5/8=62%) then your query would execute in parallel if PARALLEL_ MIN_PERCENT were below 62. If PARALLEL_ MIN_PERCENT were above 62 your statement would terminate with an error.
parallel_min_servers	This setting determines the minimum number of parallel servers allocated to your instance. These servers will be allocated when the instance is started and will never be removed. Idle servers can take up system memory whereas creating new server processes takes time. If you have sufficient memory, set this parameter to the value of PARALLEL_MAX_SERVERS to avoid any delay while starting servers.
parallel_server_ idle_time	This parameter defines the number of minutes that a server can be idle before being deactivated. Servers will never be deactivated unless

	the total number exceeds PARALLEL_MIN_SERVERS. Avoid setting this parameter too low, since constant activation and deactivation of parallel processes will waste system resources
parallel_threads_ per_cpu	PARALLEL_THREADS_PER_CPU sets the de fault number of parallel slaves which should be initiated per CPU.
query_rewrite_ enabled	if true, queries may be rewritten to take advantage of materialized views.
query_rewrite_ integrity	If STALE_TOLERATED, then rewrite can be per formed on materialized views that are stale. If ENFORCED, then rewrites can only be performed using materialized views that are up to date and using dimensions that have been validated. TRUSTED indicates that dimensions should be used even if they have not been validated.

PARAMETERS AFFECTING THE SGA

These parameters affect the size and composition of the System Global Area or SGA. This is an area of shared memory which exists primarily to improve performance and enable communication between Oracle sessions.

buffer_pool_keep	BUFFER_POOL_KEEP defines he number of block buffers and LRU latches in the "keep" buffer pool. Available in versions 8 and 8.1.
	Multiple buffer pools are discussed in Chapter 19.
	Format is ("BUFFERS:no_buffers, LRU_LATCHES:no_latches")
buffer_pool_recycle	BUFFER_POOL_RECYLE defines he number of block buffers and LRU latches in the "recycle" buffer pool.
	Multiple buffer pools are discussed in Chapter 19.
	Format is ("BUFFERS:no_buffers, LRU_LATCHES:no_latches")
db_block_buffers	The size of the buffer cache in database blocks. The buffer cache maintains database blocks in memory using a Least Recently Used (LRU) algorithm. If a required block can be found in the buffer cache then a disk read will be avoided and performance will be improved. This is pos-

	sibly the most significant performance-related parameter. You can increase the size of the buffer cache if you have sufficient free memory and you determine that the "hit rate" is too low. See Chapter 20 for details on monitoring the buffer cache hit rate.
db_block_size	The database block size in bytes. This cannot be changed once the database has been created. It should be at least as high as the operating system block size. See Chapter 19 for more information on setting this parameter.
large_pool_min_alloc	LARGE_POOL_MIN_ALLOC sets the minimum allocation size in bytes from the large pool.
large_pool_size	LARGE_POOL_SIZE sets the size in bytes of the large pool, which is an are of the shared pool which provides dedicated memory for MTS and XA configurations.
log_buffer	Size of the redo log buffer in bytes. When processes change a data block, they create an entry in this buffer. When a COMMIT occurs, or when the reaches a certain threshold, the buffer is flushed to disk. You should normally increase the size of the redo log buffer if you observe log space waits (see Chapter 19).
shared_pool_ reserved_min_allo	The shared pool may be partitioned into two partitions based on the size of the objects stored. This parameter defines the minimum size for objects to be stored in the "reserved" area of the shared pool. The purpose of the reserved area is to provide an area of memory unaffected by the fragmentation caused when small objects are moved in and out of the shared pool.
shared_pool_ reserved_size	Size in bytes of the reserved area of shared pool. Objects—typically PL/SQL objects—which are larger than SHARED_POOL_ RESERVED_MIN_ ALLOC will be stored in this area of the shared pool.
shared_pool_size	The size in bytes of the shared pool. The shared pool is a part of the SGA which stored data dictionary information, cached SQL statements and object definitions and some session information. There are a number of metrics which can indi-

cate if your shared pool is too small. See Chapter 20 for more details.

SERVER TUNING PARAMETERS

These parameters affect the overall performance of the Oracle server. Many of these parameters are described in Chapters 19 and 20.

checkpoint_process	Create a dedicated process to perform updates of file headers during checkpoints. Enabling this process increases process overhead (by one process) but reduces the overhead of checkpoints on the logwriter, especially for database with a large number of data files.
compatible	This parameter enables features of Oracle which are specific to particular releases of Oracle. Setting this value to the current version of Oracle will usually result in increased performance by enabling new features but may impede any attempt to downgrade the version of Oracle.
db_block_lru_latches	Number of LRU latches. A session must acquire an LRU chain latch whenever a block is read in from disk. You may need to increase this value if you encounter contention for the cache buffer lru chain latch.
db_file_multiblock_ read_count	Maximum number of blocks read in a single I/O during a sequential read. Higher values can significantly improve the performance of table scans. The amount read can not exceed 64K on many platforms. On at least some versions of UNIX, setting USE_READV to true can allow larger values.
db_writers	Number of database writer processes. If asynchronous or list I/O is available, then such I/O should normally be used in preference to multiple database writers. However, when asynchronous or list I/O is not available and datafiles are located on multiple disks, setting db_writers to the number of disk can result in a very significant performance improvement.
log_simultaneous_ copies	The number of redo buffer copy latches. Increase this value if you observe contention for the redo

	copy latch. Undocumented (eg, prefixed by "_" on recent versions of Oracle).
sequence_cache_ entries	The number of sequences which can be cached in memory. If this value is not as large as the number of sequences concurrently in use then processes which require a new sequence number may incur a disk I/ O and degraded performance.
spin_count (or _spin_ count)	Number of times to spin on a latch miss. Increasing the value of this parameter increases the probability that a latch can be obtained without a latch sleep, but will increase CPU utilization. Increase this parameter only if there is free CPU on the database server.

Undocumented (eg, prefixed by "_" on recent versions of Oracle). |
| **use_async_io** | On some operating systems, this parameter must be set to TRUE if asynchronous I/O is to be used. On other platforms it is sufficient to use raw devices and set db_writers=1. |

Bibliography and Resources

In this section, you will find pointers to resources which can provide Oracle information to enhance topics included in this book or to explore topics beyond the scope of this book.

INTERNET SITES

By far the newest and most exciting sources of Oracle information can be found on the internet. Here are some of the other useful resources:

NEWSGROUPS AND MAILING LISTS

Even before the advent of the World Wide Web, the internet was alive with Oracle-related news groups and mailing lists. These newsgroups are still one of the best ways to exchange Oracle information and keep abreast of new developments. Some of the groups you may wish to join are:

comp.databases.oracle.misc	Oracle related topics
comp.databases.oracle.marketplace	Oracle-related jobs, etc
comp.databases.oracle.server	Oracle database administration/server topics
comp.databases.oracle.tools	Oracle software tools/applications

| Oracle-L mailing list | General mailing list for Oracle-related information. To join, send email to LISTSERV@KBS.NET with "SUBSCRIBE ORACLE-L your_real_name" in the message body |

WEB SITES

Attempting to create a definitive list of web sites is a futile task. However, here are just a few of the sites which offer useful information:

The Oracle Technology Network http://technet.oracle.com/

This site contains perhaps the most extensive and authoritative technical information available on the web. It includes full cross-version and cross-platform Oracle documentation sets, technical bulletins, discussion papers, code samples, downloadable software and more.

You need to register to get access to member services, but the registration is free.

Oracle Support Services http://www.oracle.com/support/

If you have an Oracle support account, you can access the Oracle support metalink site which offers on-line documentation and bulletins, support forums and patch downloads

Ixora http://www.ixora.com.au/

Steve Adams, author of the O'Reilly book "Oracle internal services", is without doubt one of the most knowledgeable Oracle performance experts alive. He shares his knowledge at the Ixora site, which is the home site for his Oracle/Unix consulting firm.

Deja News Power Search http://www.dejanews.com/home_ps.shtml/

Chances are that if you have a problem or query, it has already been asked and answered on the Oracle Usenet newsgroups. DejaNews allows you to search a huge archive of newsgroups including the comp.databases.oracle.*.

The Database Domain http://www.dbdomain.com/

This site has Oracle articles, software downloads, web-based training and links. There are both member-only and free sections.

RevealNet Pipelines http://www.revealnet.com/pipeline.htm

RevealNet's pipelines offer hints and tips for DBAs and PL/SQL developers together with on-line discussion forums.

OraPub http://www.orapub.com

This site includes many useful articles on Oracle administration, performance tuning and capacity management.

International Oracle User Group http://www.ioug.org/

If you are a member of IOUG, you can get access to utilities, news and archives of the IOUG select magazine.

The Oracle Underground FAQ http://www.onwe.co.za/frank/faq.htm
As well as an extensive set of answers to Frequently Asked Questions, this site has probably the most extensive set of links to other web sites.

Oracle Magazine http://www.oramag.com/
This site has an archive of Oracle's own Oracle Magazine.

The Ultimate Software Consultants (TUSC) http://www.tusc.com/tusc/document.html
TUSC have a large collection of documents and presentations prepared by their Oracle consultants.

ORACLE TECHNICAL DOCUMENTATION

The Oracle documentation set is comprehensive, well-organized and accurate. All too often it seems that users of the Oracle system reach for the manuals only as a last resort. Always have a current set of Oracle documentation available and use them as a primary resource. Oracle now makes all documentation available on a single CD-ROM.

The following Oracle documents particularly useful when tuning SQL:

Oracle8i SQL Language Reference	This manual completely documents Oracle SQL including all options and facilities discussed in this book.
Oracle8i Designing and Tuning for Performance	This manual contains valuable guidance on the optimization of the Oracle server. Although the guidelines for tuning SQL are not extensive, good documentation of hints, explain plans and tkprof are included.
Oracle8i Concepts	Explains the architecture and operation of the Oracle server, including details of query optimization and SQL statement processing.
Oracle8i Reference	Documents the Oracle data dictionary, including dynamic performance views and documents server initialization parameters.

BOOKS

A number of books are available which cover Oracle server tuning and concepts. Here are the author's favorites:

Scaling Oracle8i™: Building Highly Scalable OLTP System Architectures by James Morle; Addison-Wesley Pub Co	Very strong coverage of Oracle internals, especially as they relate to performance and scalability
Oracle 24X7 Tips & Techniques by Venkat S. Devraj, Ravi Balwada; Computing McGraw-Hill (Oracle Press)	A lot of useful performance tuning and database administration advice.
Oracle8 & UNIX Performance Tuning Ahmed Alomari; Prentice Hall, October, 1998	Strong coverage of Oracle tuning on UNIX systems.
Oracle8 Advanced Tuning and Administration Aronoff, Loney, Sonawall ; Oracle Press, June, 1998	Very strong coverage of EXPLAIN PLAN, SQL and database tuning.
Oracle PL/SQL Programming Steven Feuerstein, Bill Pribyl; O'Reilly & Associates	The classic PL/SQL programming book. Some coverage of PL/SQL performance tuning.
Oracle PL/SQL Programming: Guide to Oracle8i Features by Steven Feuerstein; O'Reilly & Associates	Good coverage of the Oracle8i PL/SQL performance improvements.
Software Engineering With Oracle: Best Practices for Mission-Critical Systems by Elio Bonazzi; Prentice Hall, 1999	Describes best practices for Oracle Software design and implementation.
Oracle8i Internals Services for Waits, Latches, Locks, and Memory by Steve Adams; O'Reilly & Associates,1999	This book is short, but packed with information about Oracle's internal algorithms.
Oracle Performance Tuning Tips and Techniques Niemiec, Brown and Trezzo; Oracle Press, May 1999	A reasonably comprehensive survey of Oracle tuning techniques, aimed at beginner and intermediate administrators.
Oracle Performance Tuning, 2nd Edition Peter Corrigan and Mark Gurry; O'Reilly, 1996	A classic book that is dated in some areas, but still very relevant in terms of tuning and design practices.

Oracle8i Tips & Techniques by Douglas Scherer, William Gaynor, Arlene Valentinsen, Sue Mavris, Xerxes Cursetjee; McGraw-Hill Professional Publishing (Oracle Press) 1999

Very good coverage of new features in Oracle8i.

International Oracle Users Group   The International Oracle Users Group (IOUG) is an independent, nonprofit organization which exists to encourage and facilitate the use of Oracle software. Local chapters of the IOUG exist in most countries and municipalities.

By joining an Oracle user group, you get access to other users of Oracle software. Local user groups may hold special presentations or issue local newsletters. In addition to these local benefits, IOUG issues an international magazine "SELECT" and participates heavily in the various annual regional conferences.

Visit the IOUG web site at www.ioug.com for more information.

INDEX